What Is a Thesaurus?

"A Thesaurus is the opposite of a dictionary. You turn to it when you have the meaning already but don't yet have the word. It may be on the tip of your tongue, but what it is you don't yet know. It is like the missing piece of a puzzle. You know well enough that the other words you try out won't do. They say too much or too little. They haven't the punch or have too much. They are too flat or too showy, too kind or too cruel. But the word which just fills the bill won't come, so you reach for the Thesaurus."

—From the Introduction by I. A. RICHARDS

ROGET'S

Pocket Thesaurus

BASED ON
*ROGET'S International Thesaurus
of English Words and Phrases*

Edited by
C. O. SYLVESTER MAWSON

Assisted by
KATHARINE ALDRICH WHITING

PUBLISHED BY POCKET BOOKS NEW YORK

POCKET BOOKS, a division of Simon & Schuster, Inc.
1230 Avenue of the Americas, New York, N.Y. 10020

Copyright 1922, 1942 by Thomas Y. Crowell Company;
copyright 1946 by Simon & Schuster, Inc.

Published by arrangement with Thomas Y. Crowell Company,
publishers of *Roget's International Thesaurus*

ISBN: 0-671-50470-3

First Pocket Books printing September, 1946

125   124   123

POCKET and colophon are registered trademarks
of Simon & Schuster, Inc.

Printed in the U.S.A.

INTRODUCTION

A *Thesaurus*, says the dictionary, is "a treasury or storehouse; hence a repository, especially of words, as a dictionary." But, in a sense, this book is the opposite of a dictionary. You turn to a dictionary when you have a word but are not sure enough what it means—how it has been used and what it may be expected to do. You turn to the *Thesaurus* when you have your meaning already but don't yet have the word. It may be on the tip of your tongue, or in the back of your mind or the hollow of your thought, but what it is you don't yet know. It is like the missing piece of a puzzle. You know well enough that the other words you try out won't do. They are not the right shape. They say too much or too little. They haven't the punch or have too much. They are too flat or too showy, too kind or too cruel. But the word which just fills the bill won't come, so you reach for the *Thesaurus*.

Like the dictionary, it is a dangerous book in all sorts of ways. Sometimes you wake up—after half an hour—and realize that the problem of the missing word is still where it was. You have just been wandering happily about in the treasure house looking its riches over, forgetting what you came in for. It has worse dangers. Sometimes the words you find start new streams of thought which wash everything out.

Then not the word only but the idea too will be missing. In this "Lost Chord" situation, the best thing to conclude is that so evanescent an idea was hardly worth keeping. Sometimes, worse still, Temptation assails you. Instead of the right word—the word your thought was yearning for as its mysterious predestined mate—some brazen hussy or wastrel of a vocable, never met and never thought of before, seizes your regard.

> *O these encounterers*
> *That give a coasting welcome ere it comes*

Beware! As Confucius' pupil said, "For one word a man is often deemed to be wise and for one word he is often deemed to be foolish. We ought to be careful indeed what we say."

A big vocabulary is a grand thing when well understood and resourcefully used. But all grandeurs have their penalties. It is the business of a *Thesaurus* to take us into all verbal company—to introduce us to every sort and condition of word, with no guarantee, expressed or implied, as to what they may not do to us if we trust them without proper inquiry.

> *Who hath given man speech*
> *Or who hath set therein*
> *A thorn for peril and a snare for sin*

cries the Chorus in *Atalanta in Calydon.*

The great Railway strike in England turned upon the phrase "definitive terms." One side took it to mean "unchangeable"; the other explained too late that they only meant "full and detailed." Well does Peter Mark Roget observe, "A misapplied or misapprehended term is sufficient to give rise to fierce and interminable disputes; a misnomer has turned the tide of popular opinion; a verbal sophism has decided a party question; an artful watchword, thrown among combustible materials has kindled the flame of deadly warfare and changed the destiny of an empire."

That is the tragic side. The comic possibilities more concern us here. People who swagger about in borrowed words may, like Porthos in *The Three Musketeers*, impress the inexperienced. They bring the wrong sorts of smiles to the lips of the discerning.

To know the words without the things is perilous indeed. "How often," said the lecturer, "have I dallied by the shores of Lac Leman or strolled on the delightful slopes overlooking Lake Geneva." "Pardon me," said a member of the audience, "but are they not synonymous?" "You may think so, Sir," replied the speaker, "but for my part I consider Lac Leman by far the more synonymous of the two." Awful warnings of this sort abound. "I always tell my children to look it up in the dictionary or the encyclopedia," said the Sea Captain. "That is what they are there for. Always be exact . . . No, I don't wear my ribbons in public places. Seems to me they are a bit promiscuous."

But when is a word our own? What is a mastery of language? How in fact do we acquire a vocabulary worthy of the name?

The answer of course is: By experience with words, by living with great books and good talkers, by watching their words at work and at play—in brief, by becoming *familiar* with words. Mere acquaintanceship with them is not profitable here. An acquaintance is one whose name and face you know, without more than a rough idea of his being and business. A familiar is one about whom you know as much as possible. Words are astonishingly like people. They have characters, they almost have personalities—are honest, useful, obliging . . . or treacherous, vain, stubborn . . . They shift, as people do, their conduct with their company. They are an endless study in which we are studying nature and ourselves at that meeting point where our minds are trying to give form to or take it from the world.

Peter Mark Roget a century ago had high hopes of the help his arrangement of words might be to thought and to the construction of a common second language such as Basic English may become. There is nothing fantastic about such hopes. In drawing up his scheme of divisions his model was biological classification. He was a physician and Secretary of the Royal Society. But we need not take Roget's actual categories too seriously. To criticize them would be to bring up all the hardest problems there are. They serve their purpose—which is to remind us systematically of all that we know about words. "It is not sufficiently considered," said Dr. Johnson, "that men require more often to be reminded than to be informed." For information about words we go to the dictionary—the bigger it is the better. We go to the *Thesaurus* in the hope that something we really know already will come back to us in our need. How vast is the realm of our current oblivion. "I know," said Benjamin Paul Blood, "as having known, the secret of existence." Nothing will better make us realize how nearly true this is than an hour spent in the treasury. How incredibly much we understand if only we can mobilize our understanding. Roget's *Thesaurus* is one of the greatest of all *memoria technica*. It is an astonishing thought that we can carry it in the pocket.

I. A. RICHARDS

CONTENTS

POCKET THESAURUS AND WORD FINDER

CLASS I
WORDS EXPRESSING ABSTRACT RELATIONS

CLASS II
WORDS RELATING TO SPACE

CLASS III
WORDS RELATING TO MATTER

CLASS IV
WORDS RELATING TO THE INTELLECTUAL FACULTIES

CLASS V
WORDS RELATING TO THE VOLUNTARY POWERS

CLASS VI
WORDS RELATING TO THE SENTIENT & MORAL POWERS

ABBREVIATIONS USED IN THIS BOOK

abbr. abbreviated, abbreviation
adj. adjective, adjectival expression
adv. adverb, adverbial expression
Am. *or* Amer. America, American
Am. hist. American history
Am. Ind. American Indian
anat. anatomy
anon. anonymous
Ar. Arabic
arch. architecture
archæol. archæology
arith. arithmetic
astrol. astrology
astron. astronomy
Bib. Biblical
biol. biology
bot. botany
Brit. British
Can. Canada, Canadian
chem. chemistry
Chin. Chinese
class. classical
colloq. colloquial
com. commerce, commercial
conj. conjunction
Du. Dutch
Dan. Danish
dial. dialect, dialectal
dim. diminutive
E. East
eccl. ecclesiastical
Eng. English, England
erron. erroneous, -ly
esp. especially
exc. except
F. French
fem. feminine
fig. figurative, -ly
G. *or* Ger. German
Gr. Greek
Gr. Brit. Great Britain
her. heraldry
Hind. Hindustani
hist. history, historical
Icel. Icelandic
Ind. Indian
Ir. Irish, Ireland
int. interjection
It. Italian

Jap. Japanese
joc. jocular
L. Latin
l.c. lower case
masc. masculine
math. mathematics
mil. military
Moham. Mohammedan
myth. mythology
n. noun
naut. nautical
neut. neuter
Norw. Norwegian
obs. obsolete
opp. opposed
orig. original, -ly
parl. parliamentary
path. pathology
Pg. Portuguese
pharm. pharmacy
philos. philosophy
physiol. physiology
pl. plural
pol. *or* polit. political
pop. popular, -ly
prep. preposition
prov. proverb, provincial
psychol. psychology
R. C. Ch. Roman Catholic Church
relig. religion
rhet. rhetoric, rhetorical
Russ. Russian
S. Am. South American
Scand. Scandinavian
Scot. Scottish, Scotland
sing. singular
Skr. Sanskrit
Sp. Spanish
surg. surgery
Sw. Swedish
tech. technical
theat. theatrical
theol. theology
typog. typography
Univ. University
U. S. United States
v. verb
zool. zoology

x

HOW TO USE THE BOOK

I. To find a synonym or antonym for any given WORD:

Turn to the Index* and find the particular word or any term of kindred meaning; then refer to the category indicated (the numbers printed in bold face at the top outer corner of each page). There in its proper grouping, the indexed word will be found, together with a wide selection of related terms. Synonyms and antonyms are placed in adjoining positions. For example, suppose a synonym is wanted for the word "cold" in the sense of "indifferent." Turn to the Index, where the following references will be found:

> cold, *adj.*
> *frigid* **383**
> *insensible* **823**
> *indifferent* **866**

The italicized words give the general sense of the synonyms in the respective categories. The bold-faced figures denote that the indexed word is itself the heading or keyword of a distinct group. Thus, in this example, under **383** we find a list of adjectives grouped under the word "cold" in the literal sense of the term.

Turning to No. **866** (the sense required), we read through the varied list of synonyms ("indifferent, frigid, lukewarm," etc.) and select the most appropriate expression. To widen the selection, suggested references are given to allied lists; while in the adjoining category (No. **865**) are grouped the corresponding antonyms ("eager, keen, burning, ardent," etc.). The groups are arranged, not merely to supply synonyms for some special word, but also to suggest new lines of thought and to stimulate the imagination.

II. To find suitable words to express a given IDEA:

Find in the Index some word relating to the idea, and the categories referred to will supply the need.

For example, suppose a writer wishes to convey the idea of "rest." Turning to No. **265**, he will find *nouns* giving such associated senses as "quiet," "pause," "resting place," or *verbs* with the sense of "be still," "remain," "quell," or *adjectives* such as "quiescent," "still," "silent," and the like. The mere reading of the entire list will help to crystallize the idea and give it utterance.

III. To find appropriate words or new ideas on any given SUBJECT:

Turn up the subject or any branch of it. The Index itself will frequently suggest various lines of thought, while reference to the indicated groups will provide many words and phrases that should prove helpful.

Thus, suppose "poetry" is the theme, No. **597** will be found most suggestive. Or again, the subject may be "the drama" (**599**), "music" (**415**), "the vegetable kingdom" (**367**), "national legislatures" (**696**), "psychical research" (**992a**), or

*(page 311)

xi

"mythology" (979). The writer may perhaps be hazy about the titles of the ruling chiefs of India. Reference to 875 will prevent his applying a Hindu title to a Mohammedan prince. He may wish to know the term for a "plain" in different parts of the world; No. 344 will tell him exactly. The subject may be such an everyday one as "food" (298), "automobiles" (272), "aviation" (267 and 269a), or various kinds of "amusements" (840); whatever it is, the search will not prove altogether unprofitable.

N.B.—To grasp the underlying principle of the classification, study the *Tabular Synopsis of Categories* (pp. xiv-xxviii).

The guide numbers always refer to the *section* numbers in the text, and *not* to pages.

PLAN OF CLASSIFICATION

xiii

TABULAR SYNOPSIS OF CATEGORIES

Class I. ABSTRACT RELATIONS

I. EXISTENCE

II. RELATION

III. QUANTITY

IV. ORDER

66. Beginning   67. End
                 68. Middle
69. Continuity   70. Discontinuity
71. Term
72. Assemblage   73. Dispersion
74. Focus
75. Class
76. Inclusion   77. Exclusion (from a class)
78. Generality   79. Specialty
80. Rule   81. Multiformity
82. Conformity   83. Unconformity

V. NUMBER

84. Number
85. Numeration
86. List
87. Unity   88. Accompaniment
89. Duality
90. Duplication   91. Bisection
92. Triality
93. Triplication   94. Trisection
95. Quaternity
96. Quadruplication   97. Quadrisection
98. Five, etc.   99. Quinquesection, etc.
100. Plurality   100a. Fraction
                 101. Zero
102. Multitude   103. Fewness
104. Repetition
105. Infinity

VI. TIME

106. Time   107. Absence of Time
108. Period (definite)   109. Course (indefinite)
110. Durability   111. Transience
112. Perpetuity   113. Instantaneity
114. Chronometry   115. Anachronism
116. Priority   117. Posteriority
118. Present time   119. Different time
120. Simultaneousness
121. The Future   122. The Past
123. Newness   124. Oldness
125. Morning   126. Evening
127. Youth   128. Age
129. Infant   130. Veteran
              131. Adolescence
132. Earliness   133. Lateness
134. Timeliness   135. Untimeliness
136. Frequency   137. Infrequency
138. Periodicity   139. Irregularity

VII. CHANGE

VIII. CAUSATION

Class II. SPACE

I. SPACE IN GENERAL

II. DIMENSIONS

208. Depth
209. Shallowness
210. Summit
211. Base
212. Verticality
213. Horizontality
214. Pendency
215. Support
216. Parallelism
217. Obliquity
218. Inversion
219. Crossing
220. Exteriority
221. Interiority
222. Centrality
223. Covering
224. Lining
225. Clothing
226. Divestment
227. Environment
228. Interlocation
229. Circumscription
230. Outline
231. Edge
232. Inclosure
233. Limit
234. Front
235. Rear
236. Side
237. Opposite
238. Right
239. Left

III. FORM

240. Form
241. Absence of Form
242. Symmetry
243. Distortion
244. Angularity
245. Curvature
246. Straightness
247. Circularity
248. Convolution
249. Rotundity
250. Convexity
252. Concavity
251. Flatness
253. Sharpness
254. Bluntness
255. Smoothness
256. Roughness
257. Notch
258. Fold
259. Furrow
260. Opening
261. Closure
262. Perforator
263. Stopper

IV. MOTION

264. Motion
265. Rest
266. Journey
267. Navigation
268. Traveler
269. Mariner
269a. Aeronaut
270. Transference
271. Carrier
272. Vehicle
273. Ship
274. Velocity
275. Slowness
276. Impulse
277. Recoil
278. Direction
279. Deviation

CLASS III. MATTER

I. MATTER IN GENERAL

II. INORGANIC MATTER

(1) SOLIDS

(2) FLUIDS

(5) *Sound*

402. Sound	403. Silence
404. Loudness	405. Faintness
406. Snap	407. Roll
408. Resonance	408a. Nonresonance
	409. Sibilation
410. Stridency	
411. Cry	412. Ululation
413. Melody. Concord	414. Discord
415. Music	
416. Musician	
417. Musical Instruments	
418. Hearing	419. Deafness

(6) *Light*

420. Light	421. Darkness
	422. Dimness
423. Luminary	424. Shade
425. Transparency	426. Opacity
	427. Semitransparency
428. Color	429. Absence of Color
430. Whiteness	431. Blackness
432. Gray	433. Brown
434. Red	435. Green
436. Yellow	437. Purple
438. Blue	439. Orange
440. Variegation	
441. Vision	442. Blindness
	443. Dim-sightedness
444. Spectator	
445. Optical Instruments	
446. Visibility	447. Invisibility
448. Appearance	449. Disappearance

Class IV. INTELLECT
I. FORMATION OF IDEAS

450. Intellect	450a. Absence of Intellect
451. Thought	452. Absence of Thought
453. Idea	454. Topic
455. Curiosity	456. Incuriosity
457. Attention	458. Inattention
459. Care	460. Neglect
461. Inquiry	462. Answer
463. Experiment	
464. Comparison	
465. Discrimination	465a. Indiscrimination
466. Measurement	
467. Evidence	468. Counterevidence

CLASS V. VOLITION

I. INDIVIDUAL VOLITION

869. Satiety

870. Wonder

871. Expectance

872. Prodigy

873. Repute

874. Disrepute

875. Nobility

876. The People

877. Title

878. Pride

879. Humility

880. Vanity

881. Modesty

882. Ostentation

883. Celebration

884. Boasting

885. Insolence

886. Servility

887. Blusterer

III. SYMPATHETIC AFFECTIONS

888. Friendship

889. Enmity

890. Friend

891. Enemy

892. Sociality

893. Seclusion. Exclusion

894. Courtesy

895. Discourtesy

896. Congratulation

897. Love

898. Hate

899. Favorite

900. Resentment

901. Irascibility

901a. Sullenness

902. Endearment

903. Marriage

904. Celibacy

905. Divorce. Widowhood

906. Benevolence

907. Malevolence

908. Malediction

909. Threat

910. Philanthropy

911. Misanthropy

912. Benefactor

913. Evildoer

914. Pity

914a. Pitilessness

915. Condolence

916. Gratitude

917. Ingratitude

918. Forgiveness

919. Revenge

920. Jealousy

921. Envy

IV. MORAL AFFECTIONS

922. Right

923. Wrong

924. Authorization

925. Impropriety

926. Duty

927. Dereliction of Duty

927a. Exemption

928. Respect

929. Disrespect

930. Contempt

931. Approbation

932. Disapprobation

933. Flattery

934. Detraction

935. Flatterer
937. Vindication
939. Probity

942. Disinterestedness
944. Virtue
946. Innocence
948. Good Man. Good Woman
950. Penitence
952. Atonement
953. Temperance

955. Asceticism
956. Fasting
958. Sobriety
960. Purity

963. Legality
965. Jurisprudence
966. Tribunal
967. Judge
968. Lawyer
969. Lawsuit
970. Acquittal
973. Reward

936. Detractor
938. Accusation
940. Improbity
941. Knave
943. Selfishness
945. Vice
947. Guilt
949. Bad Man. Bad Woman
951. Impenitence

954. Intemperance
954a. Sensualist

957. Gluttony
959. Drunkenness
961. Impurity
962. Libertine
964. Illegality

971. Condemnation
972. Punishment
974. Penalty
975. Scourge

V. RELIGIOUS AFFECTIONS

976. Deity
977. Angel
979. Mythic and Pagan Deities
                980a. Specter
981. Heaven
983. Theology
983a. Orthodoxy
985. Revelation (Biblical)

987. Piety

990. Worship

978. Satan
980. Evil Spirits

982. Hell

984. Heterodoxy
986. Sacred Writings (Non-
     Biblical)
988. Impiety
989. Irreligion
991. Idolatry
992. Sorcery
992a. Psychical Research
993. Spell
994. Sorcerer

995. Churchdom
996. Clergy
998. Rite
999. Canonicals
1000. Temple

997. Laity

ROGET'S POCKET THESAURUS AND WORD FINDER

CLASS I

WORDS EXPRESSING ABSTRACT RELATIONS

I. EXISTENCE

1. EXISTENCE.—*N.* existence, being, entity, subsistence, presence, omnipresence, ubiquity.

reality, actuality, fact, matter of fact, truth, verity.

essence, inner reality, vital principle.

Science of existence: ontology.

V. exist, be, subsist, live, breathe; vegetate; happen, take place; occur, prevail.

consist in, lie in; be comprised in.

abide, continue, endure, last, remain.

Adj. existent, subsistent, extant; afloat, on foot, current, prevalent.

real, actual, positive, absolute; veritable, true; substantial, essential.

well founded, well grounded, authentic.

Adv. actually, in fact, in reality; indeed.

2. NONEXISTENCE.—*N.* nonexistence, inexistence; nonentity; nullity; nihilism; blank; absence, emptiness, void, vacuum; nothingness.

annihilation, extinction, destruction, abolition, extirpation, nirvana, obliteration.

V. not exist, be null and void; cease to exist; pass away, perish, be *or* become extinct; die out; disappear, vanish, fade, melt away, dissolve, be no more; die, etc., 360.

annihilate, nullify; abrogate, etc., 756; destroy, etc., 162; remove, displace, vacate; obliterate, extirpate.

Adj. inexistent, nonexistent; negative, blank; null, missing, absent, etc., 187.

unreal, baseless, unsubstantial, shadowy, spectral, visionary.

unborn, uncreated, unbegotten.

1

extinct, gone, lost, departed; defunct, etc. (*dead*), 360.
fabulous, ideal, etc. (*imaginary*), 515.

3. SUBSTANTIALITY.—*N.* substantiality; person, thing, object, article; something, a being, creature, body, substance, matter, etc., 316; groundwork, materiality.

Adj. substantial, essential; personal, bodily, corporeal, tangible, etc. (*material*), 316.

4. UNSUBSTANTIALITY.—*N.* unsubstantiality, nothingness, nihility; bubble, etc., 353.

nothing, naught, *nil* [L.], nullity, zero, cipher; blank, void, hollowness.

thing of naught, man of straw, lay figure; nonentity.

phantom, apparition, specter, shadow, dream, vision, will-o'-the-wisp, *ignis fatuus* [L.].

V. vanish, evaporate, fade, sink, fly, dissolve, melt away; die away, die out; disappear, etc., 449.

Adj. unsubstantial; baseless, groundless; ungrounded; without foundation.

visionary, imaginary, immaterial, spectral, etc., 980*a*; dreamy; shadowy; ethereal, airy, gaseous, imponderable, tenuous, vague, vaporous, dreamlike, illusory, unreal.

vacant, vacuous; empty, void, blank, hollow.

5. SUBJECTIVENESS.—*N.* subjectiveness, intrinsicality, inherence, immanence, indwelling; ego; essence, quintessence, elixir; gist, pith, core, kernel, marrow, backbone, heart, soul, life, substance.

principle, nature, constitution.

temper, temperament; spirit, humor, quality, disposition.

aspect, mood, feature, peculiarity, idiosyncrasy.

Adj. intrinsic, subjective; fundamental, implanted, inherent, essential, natural; innate, inborn, inbred, ingrained, indwelling, immanent, inwrought; radical, incarnate, hereditary, inherited, congenital, indigenous, native; in the grain, bred in the bone, instinctive; characteristic, ineradicable, fixed.

Adv. practically, virtually, substantially, in effect.

6. OBJECTIVENESS.—*N.* objectiveness, extraneousness, extrinsicality.

Adj. extrinsic, objective; extraneous, external, incidental, accidental, nonessential, unessential, accessory; contingent, fortuitous, casual.

implanted, ingrafted; inculcated, infused.

7. STATE.—*N.* state, condition, category; estate, lot, mood, temper.

dilemma, pass, predicament, quandary, corner, fix [*colloq.*], plight.

frame, fabric, stamp, mold; constitution.

form, shape; tone, tenor, trim, guise, fashion, mode, style, character.

8. CIRCUMSTANCE.—*N.* circumstance, situation, phase, position; footing, standing, status.

occasion, juncture, contingency.

predicament, emergency; exigency, crisis, pinch, pass, plight.

Adj. circumstantial, conditional, provisional; contingent, incidental; adventitious.

Adv. thus, in such wise; in *or* under the circumstances (*or* conditions).

accordingly, that being the case; since, seeing that.

conditionally, provided, if, in case; if so, unless, in the event of; provisionally.

II. RELATION

9. RELATION.—*N.* relation, bearing, relativity, reference, connection, concern; analogy; similarity; homogeneity, affinity, alliance, nearness, association; consanguinity, etc., 11; relationship, relevancy.

ratio, proportion; comparison.

link, tie, bond.

V. relate to, refer to; bear upon, regard, concern, touch, affect, pertain to, belong to; correlate.

associate, connect; link, bind.

Adj. relative, relating to, referable to; belonging to.

related, connected, associated, affiliated; allied, collateral, cognate, affinitive.

relevant, applicable, in the same category.

Adv. as regards, concerning, with relation to, with regard to; by the way, in the matter of.

10. [Want or absence of relation] IRRELATION.—*N.* irrelation, dissociation; inapplicability; disconnection, disjunction; inconsequence, disagreement, heterogeneity; irrelevancy.

V. have no relation to, have no bearing upon, have nothing to do with.

Adj. unrelated, irrespective, unallied, disconnected, unconnected, heterogeneous; isolated.

extraneous, strange, alien, foreign, outlandish, exotic.

irrelevant, inapplicable, not pertinent, unessential, inapposite, beside the mark.

remote, farfetched, out-of-the-way, forced, detached, apart. incidental, parenthetical, episodic.

Adv. parenthetically, by the way, by the by; incidentally, without regard to.

11. [Relations of kindred] CONSANGUINITY.—*N.* consanguinity, relationship, kindred, blood; parentage, paternity; lineage, connection, alliance; people [as, *my people*], family, ties of blood, blood relation.

kinsman, kinsfolk; kith and kin; relative, relation; connection; next of kin; near relation, distant relation.

family, fraternity; brotherhood, sisterhood.

race, stock, generation; clan, tribe; strain, breed.

V. be related to, claim kinship with.

Adj. related, akin, consanguineous, allied, affiliated; kindred.

12. [Double or reciprocal relation] CORRELATION.—*N.* correlation, interdependence, reciprocity, mutuality, correspondence, interchange, exchange, barter.

alternation, seesaw, to-and-fro.

V. reciprocate, alternate, interact; interchange, exchange; correlate.

Adj. reciprocal, mutual, correlative; correspondent, corresponding; alternate; interchangeable; equivalent, complementary.

13. IDENTITY.—*N.* identity, sameness, unity, convertibility; equality, etc., 27; homogeneity; self, oneself.

monotony, repetition, etc., 104.

facsimile, etc. (*copy*), 21; similarity, etc., 17; exactness, fidelity; same, selfsame, counterpart.

V. coincide, coalesce.

treat as identical (*or* the same), render identical; identify.

Adj. identical, self, selfsame, ditto.

coincident, coinciding, coalescent, indistinguishable; one; equivalent, convertible, equal.

14. CONTRARIETY.—*N.* contrariety, contrast, foil, antithesis, counterpart, complement; oppositeness; antagonism, opposition, clashing, repugnance, antipathy.

inversion, subversion, reversal, the opposite, the reverse, the inverse, the converse, antipodes.

V. be contrary, contrast with, oppose, differ from.

invert, reverse, turn topsy-turvy, turn upside down, transpose. contradict, contravene; antagonize, etc., 708.

Adj. contrary, opposite, counter, adverse, averse, converse, reverse; opposed, antithetical, contrasted, antipodean, diametrically opposite; antagonistic, conflicting, inconsistent, contradictory; hostile, inimical.

15. DIFFERENCE.—*N.* difference, dissimilarity, variance, variation, variety; diversity, divergence, heterogeneity, contrast, antithesis; disagreement, disparity, inequality, distinction, contradiction, contrariety.

nice (*or* fine, subtle) distinction, discrimination; modification.

V. differ, vary; mismatch, contrast; diverge from, depart from, deviate from; modify, change, alter.

discriminate, distinguish, etc., 465.

Adj. different, diverse, heterogeneous; varied, variant, divergent, incongruous, modified; diversified, various.

other, another, not the same; unequal, etc., 28; unmatched, widely apart.

distinctive, characteristic, discriminative, distinguishing; diagnostic.

16. UNIFORMITY.—*N.* uniformity; homogeneity, stability, continuity, permanence, consistency, accordance, conformity; agreement, etc., 23; consonance.

regularity, constancy, evenness, sameness, unity, even tenor, routine.

V. accord with, etc., 23; conform to; assimilate; level, smooth.

Adj. uniform, homogeneous, of a piece, consistent; even, equable, constant, level; invariable, regular, unvaried, undiversified, unvarying, singsong, dreary, monotonous.

Adv. always, ever, evermore, perpetually, forever, everlastingly, invariably.

16a. WANT OF UNIFORMITY.—*N.* diversity, irregularity, unevenness; uncomformity, dissimilarity, dissimilitude, divergence, heterogeneity.

Adj. diversified, varied, irregular, checkered, uneven; multifarious, of various kinds.

17. SIMILARITY.—*N.* similarity, resemblance, likeness, semblance, affinity, approximation, parallelism; agreement, etc., 23; analogy, correspondence; brotherhood, family likeness.

repetition, etc., 104; sameness, etc. (*identity*), 13; uniformity, etc., 16.

the like; match, fellow, companion, pair, mate, twin, double, counterpart, brother, sister; one's second self, *alter ego* [L.]; chip of the old block, birds of a feather.

simile, parallel, type, image, etc. (*representation*), 554.

V. resemble, look like, favor [*colloq.*], follow, echo, reproduce, bear resemblance; savor of, smack of; approximate; parallel, match, rhyme with; take after; imitate, etc., 19.

Adj. similar, resembling, like, alike; twin.

analogous, parallel, of a piece; such as.

akin to, etc. (*consanguineous*), 11; correlative, corresponding, cognate, allied to.

approximate, near, close, something like, near [as, *near* silk, *colloq.*], mock, pseudo, simulating, representing.

exact, etc. (*true*), 494; lifelike, faithful, true to life; the very image of, cast in the same mold.

Adv. as if, so to speak; as it were, as if it were; *quasi* [L.], just as.

18. DISSIMILARITY.—*N.* dissimilarity, dissimilitude; unlikeness, diversity, disparity, divergence, variation; difference, etc., 15; novelty, originality.

V. **vary**, etc. (*differ*), 15; differ from; diversify.

Adj. **dissimilar**, unlike, disparate; divergent, nonidentical, unique, new, novel, unprecedented, original; diversified, etc., 16*a*.

Adv. **otherwise**, alias.

19. IMITATION.—*N.* imitation, copying; repetition, duplication; quotation; reproduction.

mockery, aping, mimicry.

simulation, impersonation; parrotism, parrotry; representation, etc., 554; semblance, pretense; copy, etc., 21.

paraphrase; parody, etc., 21.

plagiarism; forgery, etc., 544.

imitator, echo, cuckoo, parrot, ape, monkey, mimic; copyist.

V. **imitate**, copy, mirror, reflect, reproduce, repeat; do like, echo, re-echo, catch; match, parallel; forge, counterfeit.

mimic, ape, simulate, impersonate, act, etc. (*drama*), 599; represent, etc., 554; parody, travesty, caricature, burlesque, take off, mock; borrow.

follow in the steps (*or* wake) of, take pattern by, follow suit [*colloq.*], follow the example of, walk in the shoes of, take after, model after; emulate.

Adj. **imitative**, modeled after; molded on, borrowed, counterfeit, imitation, false, pseudo, near [as, *near* silk, *colloq.*]; mock, mimic.

Adv. **literally**, verbatim, word for word, exactly, precisely.

20. NONIMITATION.—*N.* nonimitation, originality, creativeness.

Adj. **unimitated**, uncopied; unmatched, unparalleled; inimitable, etc., 33; unique, original, primordial, creative; exceptional, rare, uncommon, unexampled, out-of-the-way, unwonted.

20a. VARIATION.—*N.* variation, alteration, change, imitation; modification; discrepancy.

divergency, deviation, deflection; aberration; innovation.

V. **vary**, etc. (*change*), 140; deviate, etc., 279; diverge; alternate.

Adj. **varied,** modified; diversified, etc., 16*a*; dissimilar, etc., 18.

21. [Result of imitation] **COPY.**—*N.* copy, facsimile, counterpart, effigy, form, likeness, similitude, semblance, cast, tracing; imitation, etc., 19; model, representation, study; portrait, etc., 554; duplicate, transcript, transcription; reflection, shadow, echo; reprint, replica, transfer, reproduction, repetition.

servile copy, counterfeit, forgery.

parody, caricature, burlesque, travesty, paraphrase; cartoon.

Adj. **faithful,** lifelike, similar, close, exact.

22. [Thing copied] **PROTOTYPE.**—*N.* prototype, original, model, pattern, precedent, standard; type; archetype, exemplar, example.

copy, text, design; keynote.

die, mold; matrix, last, mint, seal, punch, stamp, intaglio, negative.

V. be an example, set an example.

23. AGREEMENT.—*N.* agreement, accord, accordance, unison, harmony, concord, union, unity, unanimity; understanding, *entente cordiale* [F.], concert [as, the *concert* of Europe].

conformity, uniformity, consistency; correspondence, parallelism, apposition.

fitness, aptness, relevancy; pertinence, aptitude, propriety, applicability, admissibility, compatibility.

adaptation, adjustment, accommodation; assimilation.

consent, etc. (*assent*), 488; concurrence, consensus; co-operation.

V. **agree,** accord, harmonize; correspond, tally, consent, etc. (*assent*), 488; suit, fit, befit; square with, dovetail, match, resemble, parallel.

adapt, accommodate, graduate; adjust, etc. (*render equal*), 27; regulate, reconcile.

Adj. **agreeing,** accordant, correspondent, congenial; coherent; harmonious, reconcilable, conformable; consistent, compatible; in accordance with, in harmony with, in keeping with.

apt, apposite, pertinent, pat; to the point; happy, felicitous, germane, applicable, relevant, admissible.

fit, adapted, appropriate, suitable; meet, etc. (*expedient*), 646.

24. DISAGREEMENT.—*N.* disagreement, discord, dissonance, disunion, discrepancy, unconformity, incongruity, dissension, conflict, opposition, antagonism, difference, misunderstanding.

disparity, disproportion; inequality, variance, divergence.

unfitness, inaptitude, impropriety, inapplicability, irrelevancy.

V. **disagree,** clash, conflict, dispute, quarrel, jar, interfere.

Adj. **disagreeing,** discordant, inharmonious; hostile, antagonistic, repugnant, clashing, jarring, factious, dissentient, incompatible, irreconcilable, inconsistent with; incongruous; repugnant to.

inapt, inept, inappropriate, improper, unsuited, unsuitable, inapplicable; unfit, unbefitting, unbecoming; ill-timed, unseasonable, ill-adapted, infelicitous, irrelevant.

uncongenial, unsympathetic, ill-assorted, mismatched.

Adv. in defiance of, in contempt of, in spite of.

III. QUANTITY

25. [Absolute quantity] QUANTITY.—*N.* quantity, magnitude; size, bulk, volume, mass, amount, measure, measurement, substance, strength.

[Science of quantity] mathematics.

[Definite quantity] armful, handful, mouthful, spoonful, stock, batch, lot, dose; quota, pittance, driblet.

Adj. quantitative, some, any, more or less.

26. [Relative quantity] DEGREE.—*N.* degree, grade, step, extent, measure, amount, ratio, standard, height, pitch; reach, mark, stage, rate, range, scope, caliber; gradation, shade; tenor, compass; sphere, station, rank, standing; interval, space [*music*]; intensity, strength.

V. graduate, calibrate, measure.

Adj. comparative, gradual, shading off.

Adv. by degrees, gradually, step by step, little by little, inch by inch, drop by drop; to some extent.

27. [Sameness of quantity or degree] EQUALITY.—*N.* equality, parity, symmetry, balance, poise; evenness, monotony, level; equivalence, equipoise, equilibrium; par, quits; distinction without a difference, identity, similarity.

tie, dead heat; drawn game, drawn battle; neck-and-neck race.

match, peer, compeer, equal, mate, fellow, brother; equivalent.

V. equal, match, keep pace with, run abreast; come up to; balance.

equalize, level, dress [*mil.*], balance, handicap, trim, adjust, poise; strike a balance; restore equilibrium.

Adj. equal, even, level, monotonous, symmetrical, co-ordinate; on a par with, on a level with, up to the mark.

equivalent, tantamount; quits; synonymous; convertible; all one, all the same; drawn [as, *a game*].

Adv. equally, to all intents and purposes.

28. [Difference of quantity or degree] INEQUALITY.—*N.* inequality, disparity, odds; difference, etc., 15; unevenness, shortcoming; superiority, etc., 33; inferiority, deficiency, inadequacy.

V. **be unequal,** have the advantage, turn the scale; overmatch, etc., 33; fall short of.

Adj. **unequal,** uneven, partial, inadequate, deficient; overbalanced, unbalanced, top-heavy, lopsided.

unequaled, unparalleled, unrivaled, unique, matchless, inimitable, peerless.

29. MEAN.—*N.* **mean,** medium, average, balance, rule, run, golden mean, middle; compromise, neutrality.

V. **average,** split the difference, strike a balance, pair off.

Adj. **mean,** intermediate; middle, etc., 68; average, normal, standard; neutral.

mediocre, middle class, bourgeois, commonplace.

Adv. **on an average,** in the long run; in round numbers.

30. COMPENSATION.—*N.* **compensation,** equation; indemnification; compromise, measure for measure, retaliation, equalization.

setoff, offset; makeweight, counterpoise, ballast; indemnity, equivalent, *quid pro quo* [L.]; amends, counterbalance, counterclaim.

pay, payment, reward, etc., 973.

V. **compensate,** indemnify; counterpoise, balance, counterbalance, offset, set off; square, make up for, equalize, etc., 27; recoup, redeem; pay, reward, etc., 973.

Adj. **compensating,** compensatory, equivalent, equal.

Adv. **notwithstanding,** but, however, yet, still, nevertheless, although, though; howbeit, albeit; at all events, in spite of, despite, on the other hand, at the same time.

31. GREATNESS.—*N.* **greatness,** vastness, magnitude; size, etc., 192; multitude; immensity, enormity, might, strength, intensity, fullness.

great quantity, quantity, deal [*colloq.*], volume, bulk, mass, heap; stock, store, load, shipload; abundance, sufficiency.

fame, distinction, grandeur, dignity; importance, etc., 642.

V. **be great,** soar, tower, loom, rise above, transcend; bulk, bulk large.

enlarge, etc. (*increase*), 35; wax, magnify, grow, expand, swell, dilate.

Adj. **great,** large, considerable, big, bulky, huge, etc., 192; titanic; voluminous, ample, abundant; many, etc., 102; full, intense; signal.

goodly, noble, precious, mighty; extraordinary; important, etc., 642; supreme, etc., 33; complete, etc., 52; arrant, downright; uttermost; profound, intense, consummate; rank, unmitigated, glaring, flagrant.

world-wide, widespread, far-famed, extensive.

august, grand, dignified, sublime, majestic.

vast, immense, enormous, extreme; inordinate, excessive, extravagant, monstrous, crass, gross; towering, stupendous, prodigious.

unlimited, etc. (*infinite*), 105; unutterable, indescribable, ineffable, unspeakable, inexpressible, fabulous.

absolute, positive, stark, decided, unequivocal, essential, perfect.

remarkable, notable, noticeable, noteworthy, renowned.

Adv. **in a great or high degree:** greatly, much, indeed, very, very much, most; pretty, enough, in a great measure, passing, richly; on a large scale; by wholesale; mightily, powerfully; extremely, exceedingly, intensely, indefinitely, immeasurably, incalculably, infinitely.

in a positive degree: truly, etc. (*truth*), 494; decidedly, unequivocally, absolutely, essentially, fundamentally, radically, downright, in all conscience.

in a complete degree: entirely, completely, wholly; abundantly, amply, fully, widely.

in a supreme degree: pre-eminently, superlatively, supremely, incomparably.

in a too great degree: immoderately, monstrously, preposterously, exorbitantly, excessively, enormously, out of all proportion.

in a marked degree: particularly, remarkably, singularly, curiously, uncommonly, unusually, peculiarly, notably, signally, strikingly, pointedly, chiefly; famously, egregiously, prominently, glaringly, emphatically, incredibly.

in a violent degree: furiously, violently, severely, desperately, tremendously, extravagantly.

in a painful degree: painfully, sadly, sorely, bitterly, piteously, grievously, miserably, cruelly, woefully, lamentably, shockingly, frightfully, dreadfully, fearfully, terribly, horribly, distressingly, balefully.

32. SMALLNESS.—*N.* smallness, littleness, paucity; fewness, sparseness, scarcity, insignificance, unimportance.

small quantity, modicum, minimum; atom, particle, trifle, electron, molecule, corpuscle, point, speck, dot, mote, jot, iota; minutiæ, details; tittle, spark; grain, scruple, minim; drop, sprinkling, dab, dash, tinge, dole, mite, bit, morsel, crumb, scrap, shred, tag, splinter, rag; snip, sliver, paring, shaving, hair; thimbleful, handful, capful, mouthful; fragment, fraction.

V. **be small,** lie in a nutshell.

diminish, etc. (*decrease*), 36; contract, shrink, dwindle, wane.

Adj. **small,** little, stunted; diminutive, etc. (*small in size*), 193; minute, miniature, inconsiderable, paltry, etc. (*unimportant*), 643; scanty, scant, limited, meager, sparing; few, etc., 103; moderate, modest.

inappreciable, infinitesimal, atomic, microscopic, molecular.

mere, simple, sheer, stark, bare.

Adv. in a small degree: to a small extent, on a small scale; a little, slightly, imperceptibly; miserably, wretchedly; insufficiently, imperfectly, faintly, feebly, passably.

in a certain or limited degree: partially, in part, in a certain degree, to a certain degree *or* extent; comparatively, rather, in some degree *or* measure; somewhat; simply, only, purely, merely; at least, at most, ever so little, thus far, after a fashion.

almost, nearly, well-nigh, not quite, all but, near upon, close upon, near the mark; within an ace (*or* inch) of, on the brink of; scarcely, hardly, barely, only just, no more than.

in an uncertain degree: about, thereabouts, somewhere about, nearly.

in no degree: noway, nowise, not at all, not in the least, not a bit, not a jot, in no wise, in no respect, by no means, on no account.

33. SUPERIORITY.—*N.* superiority, majority, plurality; advantage; preponderance, prevalence.

nobility, etc. (*rank*), 875; superman, overman.

supremacy, supremeness, primacy, pre-eminence, lead; maximum, record; crest, climax, culmination, summit, peak, transcendence; lion's share, excess, surplus, overweight, redundance.

V. exceed, excel, transcend, outdo, outbalance, overbalance, outweigh, outrank, outrival, out-Herod Herod; pass, surpass, overtop, overmatch; cap, culminate, beat, cut out [*colloq.*]; beat hollow [*colloq.*], outstrip, eclipse, throw into the shade; predominate, prevail; precede, take precedence, come first, bear the palm, break the record.

Adj. superior, greater, major, higher, exceeding; distinguished, ultra.

supreme, greatest, maximum, utmost, paramount, pre-eminent, foremost, crowning, excellent, peerless, matchless; unrivaled, unparalleled, unequaled, unapproached, unsurpassed; superlative, incomparable, transcendent.

Adv. beyond, more, over; over and above; at its height.

in a superior or supreme degree: eminently, pre-eminently, surpassing, superlatively, supremely, principally, especially, particularly, peculiarly.

34. INFERIORITY.—*N.* inferiority, shortcoming, deficiency; minimum; imperfection; meanness, poorness, baseness, shabbiness.

Personal inferiority: the people, etc., 876; subordination.

V. be inferior, fall short of, come short of, not come up to; become smaller, decrease, yield the palm, play second fiddle.

Adj. inferior, smaller; less, lesser, deficient, reduced, lower, subordinate, secondary, junior, minor, humble; second rate; unimportant, etc., 643.

Adv. less, short of, under.

35. INCREASE.—*N.* increase, augmentation, addition, enlargement, extension, expansion, growth, increment, accretion, development, accumulation, inflation, enhancement, aggravation, exaggeration.

gain, produce, product, profit, advantage, booty, plunder.

V. increase, augment, add to, enlarge, etc., 31; advance, rise, mount, ascend.

aggrandize, raise, exalt; deepen, heighten, lengthen, thicken; inflate, intensify, enhance, magnify, redouble, double; aggravate, exaggerate.

Adj. increasing, growing, crescent, multiplying, intensifying, intensive.

Adv. crescendo, increasingly.

36. DECREASE.—*N.* decrease, diminution, lessening, subtraction, reduction, abatement, declension; shrinkage, contraction, curtailment, abridgment.

subsidence, wane, ebb, decline; ebb tide, neap tide, ebbing.

V. decrease, diminish, lessen; abridge, shorten, shrink, contract; dwindle, fall away, waste, wear; wane, ebb, decline, subside, languish, decay, crumble.

discount, belittle, minimize, depreciate, extenuate, lower, weaken, attenuate; dwarf, reduce, shorten, subtract; mitigate, ease, moderate.

Adv. decrescendo, decreasingly.

37. ADDITION.—*N.* addition, annexation, accession, re-enforcement; increase, etc., 35; increment.

affix, codicil, tag, appendage, postscript, adjunct, supplement; accompaniment, insertion.

V. add, annex, affix, subjoin, tack to, append, tag, attach; interpose, introduce, insert.

compute, total, cast (*or* sum, count) up.

re-enforce, strengthen, augment.

Adj. additional, supplemental, supplementary; extra, spare, further, fresh, more, other, auxiliary, contributory, accessory.

Adv. in addition, more; and, also, likewise, too, furthermore, further; besides, to boot; over and above, moreover; as well as, together with, along with, in conjunction with.

38. DEDUCTION.—*N.* deduction, subtraction, retrenchment; abstraction, mutilation, amputation, curtailment, abbreviation.

rebate, etc. (*decrement*), 40*a*; minuend, subtrahend; decrease, etc., 36.

V. deduct, subtract, retrench; withdraw; take from, take away; detract, reduce, eliminate, diminish, curtail, shorten; deprive of, etc. (*take*), 789; weaken.

mutilate, amputate, cut off, cut away, excise.

pare, thin, prune, scrape, file.

Adv. less; short of; minus, without, except, excepting, with the exception of, save, exclusive of.

39. [Thing added] ADJUNCT.—*N.* adjunct, addition, affix, suffix, appendage, annex, augmentation, increment, re-enforcement, accessory, accompaniment, etc., 88; addendum (*pl.* addenda); complement, supplement, sequel.

rider, thin, offshoot, episode, side issue, corollary, codicil, etc. (*addition*), 37.

V. add, annex, etc., 37.

Adj. additional, etc., 37.

40. [Thing remaining] REMAINDER.—*N.* remainder, residue, remains, remnant, rest, relic; leavings, odds and ends, residuum, dregs, refuse, stubble, ruins, wreck, skeleton, fossil, stump, rump.

surplus, excess; balance [*commercial slang*], result; superfluity, redundance; survival.

V. remain, survive, be left; exceed.

Adj. remaining, left, residual, residuary; over, odd; surviving; net; superfluous, etc. (*redundant*), 641.

40a. [Thing deducted] DECREMENT.—*N.* decrement, discount, rebate, defect, loss, deduction; waste.

41. MIXTURE.—*N.* mixture, admixture, junction, etc., 43; amalgamation, combination, etc., 48; infusion, transfusion; infiltration; interlarding, interpolation, etc., 228; adulteration.

Thing mixed: tinge, tincture, touch, dash, smack, spice, seasoning, infusion.

Compounds: alloy, amalgam; brass, pewter; miscellany, medley, mess, hash, hodgepodge, patchwork, jumble; potpourri, mosaic.

half-blood, half-breed, half-caste, crossbreed; mulatto, quadroon, octoroon, Eurasian; mule, cross, hybrid, mongrel.

V. mix, join, etc., 43; combine, etc., 48; mingle, commingle, intermingle, interlard, interpolate, intertwine, interweave; associate with.

imbue, infuse, diffuse, suffuse, transfuse, instill, infiltrate, dash, tinge, tincture, season, blend, cross; alloy, amalgamate, compound, adulterate.

Adj. **mixed,** composite, half-and-half, hybrid, mongrel, heterogeneous; motley, variegated, miscellaneous, promiscuous, indiscriminate.

Adv. **among,** amid, with; in the midst of.

42. [Freedom from mixture] SIMPLENESS.—*N.* simpleness, purity, homogeneity.

elimination, sifting, purification, etc. (*cleanness*), 652.

V. **render simple,** simplify.

sift, winnow, bolt, eliminate; exclude, get rid of; clear, purify, etc. (*clean*), 652.

Adj. **simple,** uniform, homogeneous, single, pure, clear; elemental, elementary.

43. JUNCTION.—*N.* junction, joining, union; connection, conjunction, annexation, attachment; marriage, wedlock; confluence, communication, meeting, reunion; assemblage, etc., 72; coherence, etc., 46; combination, etc., 48.

joint, joining, juncture, pivot, hinge, articulation; seam, gore, gusset, link, bond.

contingency, emergency, predicament, crisis, concurrence.

V. **join,** unite, connect; associate; put together, piece together, embody.

attach, fix, fasten, bind, secure, tighten, clinch, tie, strap, sew, lace, stitch, knit, button, buckle, hitch, lash, splice, gird, tether, moor, picket, chain; fetter, hook, link, yoke, bracket; marry; bridge over, span.

pin, nail, screw, bolt, hasp, clasp, clamp, rivet; solder, cement, etc., 46.

entwine, interlace, intertwine, interweave; entangle.

Adj. **joined,** joint; corporate, compact.

firm, fast, close, tight, taut, secure, inseparable, indissoluble.

Adv. **jointly,** in conjunction with, etc. (*in addition to*), 37; fast, firmly.

44. DISJUNCTION.—*N.* disjunction, disconnection, disunion, disengagement, dissociation, discontinuity, etc., 70; isolation, insularity, insulation, separateness; dispersion.

separation, parting; detachment, segregation; divorce; cæsura, division, subdivision, break, fracture, rupture; dismemberment, dissection, disintegration, severance, disruption, cleavage.

fissure, breach, rent, rift, crack, slit, cut, incision.

V. **disjoin,** disconnect, disengage, disunite, dissociate, divorce, part, detach, unfasten, separate, disentangle, cut off, segregate; set apart, keep apart; insulate, isolate; cut adrift, loose, set free, liberate.

divide, sunder, subdivide, sever, dissever, cut, chop, saw, snip, nip, cleave, rive, rend, slit, rip, split, splinter, chip, crack, snap, break, tear, burst; wrench, rupture, hack, hew, slash, slice, carve, quarter, dissect, anatomize; partition, parcel.

disintegrate, dismember, disband; disperse, etc., 73; dislocate, break up.

part, part company; separate, leave; alienate, estrange.

Adj. **disjoined,** discontinuous, disjunctive; isolated, insular; separate, apart, asunder, loose, free, adrift.

Adv. **separately,** one by one, severally, apart, asunder.

45. [Connecting medium] VINCULUM.—*N.* vinculum, link; connective, connection; junction, etc., 43; hyphen; bracket; bridge, steppingstone; bond, cord; rope, line, cable, hawser, painter; chain; string, etc. (*filament*), 205.

fastening, tie; ligament, ligature; strap; tackle, rigging; yoke, band, headband, fillet, snood, brace, thong, girdle, noose, lariat, lasso, knot, girth, cinch.

cement, glue, gum, paste, size, solder, mortar, plaster, putty.

shackle, rein, etc. (*means of restraint*), 752.

V. **bridge over,** span; connect, etc., 43.

46. COHERENCE.—*N.* coherence, cohesion, cohesiveness, adherence, adhesion, adhesiveness; conglomeration, aggregation, consolidation, soldering, connection; relativity.

tenacity, toughness; stickiness; inseparability.

conglomerate, concrete, etc., 321.

V. **cohere,** adhere, coagulate, stick, cling, cleave, hold, close with, clasp, hug.

glue, agglutinate, cement, paste, gum; solder, weld; cake, consolidate, solidify, agglomerate.

Adj. **adhesive,** cohesive, adhering, tenacious, tough; sticky, etc., 352.

47. INCOHERENCE.—*N.* incoherence, nonadhesion; looseness, laxity, relaxation; loosening, disjunction, etc., 44.

V. **loosen,** make loose, slacken, relax; unglue, etc., 46; detach, etc., 44.

Adj. **nonadhesive,** noncohesive, incoherent, detached, loose, baggy, slack, lax, relaxed, segregated, unconsolidated; uncombined, etc., 48.

48. COMBINATION.—*N.* combination, mixture, etc., 41; junction, etc., 43; union, unification, synthesis, incorporation, amalgamation, coalescence, fusion, brew, blend, blending; centralization.

alloy, compound, amalgam, composition, resultant.

V. combine, unite, incorporate, alloy, intermix, interfuse, interlard, amalgamate, embody, absorb, blend, merge, fuse, consolidate, coalesce, solidify, impregnate, centralize.

league, federate, confederate, fraternize, club, associate, amalgamate, couple, pair, ally.

Adj. combined, conjoint; ingrained, imbued.

allied, amalgamated, federate, confederate, corporate, leagued.

49. DECOMPOSITION.—*N.* decomposition, analysis, dissection, dissolution, breakup; disjunction, etc., 44; disintegration.

decay, rot, putrefaction, putrescence, putridity, caries, corruption.

V. decompose, analyze, dissolve; resolve into its elements, dissect, disintegrate, disperse; crumble into dust.

rot, decay, consume, putrefy.

50. [Principal part] WHOLE.—*N.* whole, totality, integrity, entirety, completeness; integer, integral.

all, the whole, total, aggregate, sum, sum total.

bulk, mass, lump, tissue, staple, body, greater part, main part; lion's share.

V. form a whole, embody, amass; aggregate, assemble; amount to.

Adj. whole, total, gross, entire; complete, etc., 52; wholesale, sweeping; comprehensive.

indivisible, indissoluble, indissolvable.

Adv. wholly, altogether; as a whole, totally, completely, entirely, all, all in all, wholesale, in a body, collectively, in the aggregate, in the main, on the whole, bodily, substantially.

51. PART.—*N.* part, portion; item, particular; aught, any; division; sector, segment; fraction, fragment; detachment, subdivision.

section, chapter, verse; article, clause.

piece, lump, bit, cut, cutting; chip, chunk, slice, scrap, crumb, morsel, moiety, particle; installment, dividend; share.

member, limb, arm, wing, scion, branch, bough, joint, link, offshoot, ramification, twig, spray, spring; runner, tendril; leaf, leaflet; stump.

V. part, divide, disjoin, etc., 44; partition, etc. (*apportion*), 786.

Adj. fractional, fragmentary, sectional; incomplete, partial.

divided, broken, cut, cropped, shorn.

divisible, dissoluble, dissolvable.

Adv. partly, in part, partially; piecemeal, by installments, in detail.

52. COMPLETENESS.—*N.* completeness, intactness, completion, etc., 729; fill, saturation, entirety; totality, integrity; per-

fection, etc., 650; solidarity, unity, all, high tide, flood tide, spring tide.

V. **complete,** etc. (*accomplish*), 729; fill, charge, load, replenish; make up, eke out, supply deficiencies; fill up, fill in, satiate; saturate.

Adj. **complete,** entire, whole, intact, perfect, full, absolute, thorough; solid, undivided.

brimful, brimming, chock-full; saturated, crammed; replete, etc. (*redundant*), 641; fraught, laden.

exhaustive, radical, sweeping, thoroughgoing.

regular, unmitigated, sheer, unqualified, unconditional, free, abundant, etc. (*sufficient*), 639.

completing, supplemental, supplementary.

Adv. **completely,** altogether, outright, wholly, totally, utterly, quite; effectually, fully, in all respects, in every respect; out and out; throughout, from first to last, from head to foot, from top to toe, every whit, every inch.

53. INCOMPLETENESS.—*N.* **incompleteness,** deficiency, shortcoming, want, lack, insufficiency, imperfection, etc., 651; immaturity.

Part wanting: defect, deficit, omission; shortage; break, etc. (*discontinuity*), 70; missing link.

V. **be incomplete,** fall short of, lack, etc. (*be insufficient*), 640.

Adj. **incomplete,** uncompleted, imperfect, unfinished; defective, deficient, wanting, failing, in arrear, short, short of; perfunctory, sketchy, crude, immature.

mutilated, garbled, hashed, mangled, butchered, docked, truncated.

in progress, in hand; going on, proceeding.

54. COMPOSITION.—*N.* **composition,** constitution; make-up; combination, etc., 48; embodiment; formation.

authorship, compilation, composition, production, invention; writing.

painting, etching, design, etc. (*painting*), 556; relief, etc. (*sculpture*), 557.

typesetting, typography, etc., 591.

V. **be composed of,** consist of.

include, etc., 76; contain, hold, comprehend, admit, embrace, embody.

compose, constitute, form, make; fabricate, weave, construct; compile, scribble, draw, write.

55. EXCLUSION.—*N.* **exclusion,** omission, exception, rejection, repudiation; exile, seclusion, lockout, ostracism, prohibition.

separation, segregation, elimination, expulsion.

V. **exclude,** bar; leave out, shut out; reject, repudiate, black-ball, ostracize; lay aside, put aside, set apart; relegate, segregate; strike off, strike out; neglect, banish, etc. (*seclude*), 893; separate, etc. (*disjoin*), 44.

pass over, omit; eliminate, weed out.

Adj. **exclusive,** inadmissible, preclusive, preventive, prohibitive.

Adv. **except,** exclusive of, save.

56. COMPONENT.—*N.* **component,** integral part, element, constituent, ingredient, contents; feature; member, etc. (*part*), 51; personnel.

V. **enter into,** be *or* form part of, etc., 51; merge in, share in, participate; belong to, appertain to; combine, unite.

form, make, constitute, compose, fabricate, etc., 54.

Adj. **inherent,** intrinsic, essential.

inclusive, all-embracing, comprehensive.

57. EXTRANEOUSNESS.—*N.* **extraneousness,** extrinsicality; exclusion; alienism.

foreign body (substance *or* element).

alien, stranger, intruder, interloper, foreigner, newcomer; immigrant, emigrant; outsider, barbarian, tenderfoot [*slang*].

Adj. **extraneous,** foreign, alien, exterior, external; outlandish, barbaric, barbarian.

excluded, inadmissible; exceptional.

Adv. **abroad,** in foreign parts, in foreign lands; oversea, overseas.

IV. ORDER

58. ORDER.—*N.* **order,** regularity, uniformity, symmetry, harmony; course, routine; method, disposition, arrangement, array, system, economy, discipline, orderliness, subordination.

gradation, progression; series, etc. (*continuity*), 69.

rank, place, etc. (*term*), 71.

V. **adjust,** regulate, systematize, standardize; time.

Adj. **orderly,** regular; in order, in trim, neat, tidy, methodical, uniform, symmetrical, shipshape, businesslike, systematic, normal, habitual.

Adv. **in order,** methodically, in turn, in its turn; step by step; systematically, by clockwork.

59. DISORDER.—*N.* **disorder,** derangement; irregularity; untidiness; anomaly, etc. (*unconformity*), 83; anarchy, anarchism; disunion; discord.

confusion, disarray, jumble, botch, litter, farrago, mess, muddle, hodgepodge, imbroglio, chaos, clutter, medley.

   complexity, complication, entanglement, intricacy; perplexity; network, maze, labyrinth; wilderness, jungle; tangled skein.

   turmoil, ferment, etc. (*agitation*), 315; trouble, disturbance, convulsion, tumult, uproar, riot, rumpus [*colloq.*], fracas, pandemonium, Babel, saturnalia.

   V. **disorder,** botch, disturb, derange, etc., 61; entangle, ravel, ruffle, rumple.

   Adj. **disorderly,** out of order, out of place, irregular, desultory; anomalous, etc. (*unconformable*), 83; disorganized; straggling; unmethodical, unsystematic; untidy, slovenly, messy [*colloq.*], indiscriminate, chaotic, confused; deranged, etc., 61; topsy-turvy, disjointed, out of joint.

   complex, intricate, complicated, perplexed, involved, entangled, knotted, tangled, inextricable.

   troublous, tumultuous, turbulent; riotous, etc. (*violent*), 173.

   60. [Reduction to Order] ARRANGEMENT.—*N.* arrangement, plan, etc., 626; preparation, provision; disposal, disposition; distribution, sorting, assortment, allotment, apportionment, graduation, organization, groupings; analysis, classification, division, systematization, codification.

   Result of arrangement: orderliness, form, array, digest; synopsis, etc. (*compendium*), 596; table; register, etc. (*record*), 551; organism; stipulation, settlement.

   V. **arrange,** dispose, fix, place; form; set in order, set out; compose, space, range, graduate, marshal, array, rank, group, parcel out, allot, apportion, distribute, assign the parts; dispose of, assort, sort; tidy [*colloq.*].

   classify, class, file, list; register, etc. (*record*), 551; catalogue, tabulate, index, alphabetize, grade, codify.

   methodize, regulate, systematize, co-ordinate, organize; unravel, disentangle.

   Adj. **arranged,** embattled, in battle array; cut and dried; methodical, orderly, regular, systematic, on file; tabular.

   61. [Bringing into disorder] DERANGEMENT.—*N.* derangement, muss [*colloq.* U. S.], mess; disorder, etc., 59; discomposure, disturbance; disorganization, dislocation; inversion, etc., 218; insanity, etc., 503.

   V. **derange,** disarrange, discompose, displace, misplace; mislay, disorder; disorganize; embroil, convulse, unsettle, disturb, confuse, trouble, perturb, disconcert, jumble; muddle; unhinge, dislocate, put out of joint, throw out of gear.

   turn topsy-turvy, etc. (*invert*), 218; bedevil; complicate, involve, perplex, confound; tangle, entangle; tousle [*colloq.*], dishevel, ruffle; rumple, etc. (*fold*), 258; become insane, etc., 503.

litter, scatter; mix, etc., 41.

62. [Consecutive Order] PRECEDENCE.—*N.* precedence, the lead, superiority, etc., 33; importance, consequence; premise; antecedence, precursor, etc., 64; priority, preference.

prefix, affix; preamble; prelude, overture, voluntary.

V. precede, forerun, come before, come first; head, lead, lead the way; introduce, usher in; rank, outrank; take precedence.

prefix; premise, prelude, preface; affix.

Adj. preceding, precedent, antecedent; anterior; prior, etc., 116; before; former, foregoing, aforesaid, said; introductory, etc., 64.

Adv. before; in advance, etc. (*precession*), 280.

63. SEQUENCE.—*N.* sequence, train; following, succession; afterclap, afterglow, aftermath, afterpiece, aftertaste.

continuation, prolongation; order of succession.

V. succeed, come after, ensue, come next.

follow, tag [*colloq.*], heel, dog, shadow, hound, hunt; trace, retrace.

append, place after, subjoin.

Adj. succeeding, sequent; subsequent; proximate, next; consecutive, etc. (*continuity*), 69.

latter, posterior, etc., 117.

Adv. after, subsequently; behind, etc. (*rear*), 235.

64. PRECURSOR.—*N.* precursor, antecedent, precedent, predecessor; forerunner, pioneer; outrider; leader, bellwether; herald, harbinger.

prelude, preamble, preface, prologue, foreword, proem, exordium, introduction; heading, frontispiece, groundwork; preparation, etc., 673; overture, voluntary; premises.

prefigurement, etc., 511; omen, etc., 512.

Adj. introductory, preludial, prefatory, precursory, inaugural, preliminary.

65. SEQUEL.—*N.* sequel, suffix, tail, queue, train, wake, trail, rear; retinue, suite; appendix, postscript, postlude, conclusion, epilogue; peroration; codicil; continuation; appendage, tag, aftergrowth, afterpiece, afterthought, second thoughts; outgrowth.

follower, successor, pursuer, adherent, partisan, disciple, client; sycophant, parasite.

66. BEGINNING.—*N.* beginning, commencement, opening, outset, incipience, inception; introduction, etc. (*prelude*), 64; initial; inauguration, embarkation, rising of the curtain; curtain raiser, maiden speech; exordium; outbreak, onset, brunt; initiative, first move; start, starting point; dawn, etc. (*morning*), 125.

origin, etc. (*cause*), 153; source, rise; bud, germ, egg, embryo, rudiment; genesis, birth, nativity, cradle, infancy.

head, heading; title page; van, etc. (*front*), 234.

entrance, entry; inlet, orifice, mouth, porch, portal, portico, door; gate, gateway; postern, wicket, threshold, vestibule; border, frontier.

rudiments, elements, outlines, grammar, alphabet, ABC.

V. begin, commence; rise, arise; originate, initiate, open, start; dawn, set in, take its rise, enter upon; set out, etc. (*depart*), 293; embark in; make one's debut; institute; set about, set to work; make a start; break ground, cross the Rubicon; undertake, etc., 676.

usher in, lead the way, take the lead *or* initiative; inaugurate, head; lay the foundations, etc. (*prepare*), 673; found, etc. (*cause*), 153; set up, set on foot, launch, broach; open up, open the door to.

come into existence, take birth; burst forth, break out; spring up, crop up.

recommence; begin at the beginning, begin again, start afresh.

Adj. initial, prime, introductory, incipient; inaugural; embryonic, rudimentary; primal, primary, primeval, etc. (*old*), 124; aboriginal; natal.

first, maiden, foremost, front, head, leading.

Adv. first, in the first place, in the bud, in embryo, from the beginning, formerly.

67. END.—*N.* end, close, termination, conclusion, finish, completion, finis, finale, period, term, terminus, last, extreme, extremity; fag end, tip, nib, point, tail, tag, peroration, appendix, epilogue; consummation, denouement, fall of the curtain; goal, destination, terminal, limit, stoppage; expiration; dissolution, death, etc., 360; doomsday.

last stage, evening (*of life*); *coup de grâce* [F.], deathblow; knockout.

V. end, close, finish, terminate, conclude; expire, die, etc., 360; come to a close, perorate; run out, pass away.

bring to an end, put an end to, make an end of; achieve, etc. (*complete*), 729; stop, etc., 142.

Adj. final, terminal, conclusive; crowning, etc. (*completing*), 729; last, ultimate; hindermost; rear, etc., 235.

ended, settled, decided, over.

Adv. finally, in fine; at the last; once for all.

68. MIDDLE.—*N.* middle, midst, thick, midmost; mean, etc., 29; medium, middle term; center, core, kernel, nucleus, hub, heart, bull's-eye; mid-course, neutrality, compromise.

equidistance, bisection; equator, diaphragm, midriff.

Adj. **middle,** medial, mid, midmost; intermediate, equidistant, central, pivotal, mediterranean, equatorial.

Adv. **midway,** halfway, in the middle; amidships.

69. [Uninterrupted sequence] CONTINUITY.—continuity, continuousness, succession, round, suite, progression, series, train, chain; scale; gradation, course; perpetuity.

procession, cavalcade, parade; column; retinue, cortege, funeral, ovation.

pedigree, genealogy, lineage, history, family tree, race; ancestry, descent, family, house; line, line of ancestors; strain.

rank, file, line, row, range, tier.

V. **arrange in a series,** string together, file, list, thread, tabulate.

Adj. **continuous,** continued; consecutive, progressive, gradual, serial, successive; uninterrupted, unbroken, entire; linear; perennial, constant.

Adv. **continuously,** in a line, in succession, in turn; running, gradually, in file, in single file, in Indian file.

70. [Interrupted sequence] DISCONTINUITY.—*N.* discontinuity, disconnectedness; disconnection, etc., 44; interruption, break, fracture, flaw, fault, crack, cut; gap, etc. (*interval*), 198; intermission, alternation.

V. **alternate,** interchange, intermit.

discontinue, pause, interrupt, intervene; break, break off; interpose, etc., 228; disconnect, etc. (*disjoin*), 44; dissever.

Adj. **discontinuous,** disconnected, broken, interrupted, fitful, irregular, spasmodic, desultory; intermittent, alternate, recurrent, periodic.

Adv. **at intervals,** by snatches, by jerks, by fits and starts.

71. TERM.—*N.* term, rank, station, stage, step; degree, etc., 26; scale, grade, status, state, position, standing, footing, place, mark, period, range.

72. [Collective Order] ASSEMBLAGE.—*N.* assemblage, collection, levy, gathering, ingathering, mobilization, meet, forgathering, muster, team; concourse, conflux, congregation.

meeting, levee, reunion, drawing room, at home; social gathering, 892; assembly, congress, house, senate, legislature, etc., 696; convocation, caucus, convention.

company, platoon, faction, caravan, posse, watch, squad, corps, troop, troupe; army, regiment.

miscellany, miscellanea, compilation; symposium; library, etc. (*store*), 636.

crowd, throng; flood, rush, deluge; rabble, mob, host, etc. (*multitude*), 102; rout, press, crush, horde, body, tribe; crew, gang, knot, squad, force, band, party; bunch, drive, roundup.

clan, brotherhood, association, etc. (*party*), 712.

group, cluster, clump, set, batch, lot, pack; budget, assortment, bunch; parcel, packet, bundle, package, bale, fagot, wisp, truss, tuft, shock, clump; grove, thicket; rick, stack, sheaf, swath; volley, shower, storm, cloud.

accumulation, etc. (*store*), 636; heap, lump, pile, mass, pyramid; drift, snowball, snowdrift; amassment; conglomeration, aggregation, concentration, convergence, congestion, quantity, etc. (*greatness*), 31.

V. **be** *or* **come together,** assemble, collect, muster; meet, unite, join, rejoin; cluster, flock, swarm, surge, stream, herd, crowd, huddle, throng, associate; congregate, concentrate, resort, forgather.

bring together, assemble, muster, collect, gather; hold a meeting, convene, convoke; rake up, dredge, heap, mass, pile; pack, cram, lump together; compile, group, concentrate, unite, amass, accumulate, hoard, store.

Adj. **dense,** serried, teeming, swarming, populous.

73. DISPERSION.—*N.* dispersion, disjunct on, etc., 44; divergence, radiation, broadcast, spread, dissemination, diffusion, dissipation, distribution; apportionment, allotment.

V. **disperse,** scatter, sow, disseminate, sow broadcast, diffuse, radiate, broadcast, shed, spread, bestrew, dispense, disband, dismember, distribute; apportion, etc., 786; dispel, cast forth, draft off; strew, cast, sprinkle; issue, deal out, retail, utter.

Adj. **scattered,** disseminated, strown, strewn, dispersed, diffuse, diffusive, sparse, broadcast, sporadic, widespread; epidemic, etc. (*general*), 78; adrift, stray; disheveled.

74. [Place of meeting] FOCUS.—*N.* focus, center, gathering place, rendezvous, rallying point, headquarters, resort, haunt, retreat, club; tryst, trysting place, place of meeting.

V. **focus,** bring to a point, bring to a focus; rally, meet.

75. [Distributive Order] CLASS.—*N.* class, division, subdivision, category, head, order, section; department, province, domain, sphere.

kind, sort, type, estate, genus, species, variety, family, race, tribe, caste, clan, breed, kin; clique, coterie, set; sect, gender, sex.

description, denomination, persuasion, connection, designation, character, stamp; selection, specification.

76. INCLUSION.—*N.* inclusion, admission, incorporation, comprisal, reception.

composition, embodiment, formation.

V. **include,** comprise, comprehend, contain, admit, embrace, receive, inclose, etc. (*circumscribe*), 229; incorporate, cover, embody, encircle; reckon among, number among; refer to; place under, arrange under, take into account.

Adj. **inclusive,** included, including; comprehensive, sweeping, all-embracing.

77. EXCLUSION [from a class].—*N.* **exclusion,** rejection; *see* exclusion (*from a compound*), 55.

78. GENERALITY.—*N.* **generality,** universality, catholicity, miscellany, miscellaneousness; common run, prevalence, rifeness.

everyone, everybody, all hands [*colloq.*], all the world and his wife [*humorous*], anybody.

V. **be general,** prevail.

render general, spread, broaden, universalize, generalize.

Adj. **general,** generic, collective; current, wide, broad, comprehensive, sweeping; encyclopedic, panoramic; widespread, etc. (*dispersed*), 73; common, prevalent, prevailing, rife, epidemic.

universal, catholic, world-wide.

every, all, unspecified, miscellaneous, indefinite.

Adv. **generally,** always, in general, generally speaking; for the most part.

79. SPECIALTY.—*N.* **specialty,** speciality, individuality, peculiarity; personality, characteristic, mannerism, idiosyncrasy, singularity, originality; trait, distinctive feature.

particulars, details, items, counts; minutiæ.

V. **specify,** particularize; individualize, specialize; designate, determine; denote, indicate, point out, select, differentiate; itemize, enter into detail.

Adj. **special,** especial, particular, individual, specific, proper, personal, original, private, respective, definite, minute, certain, peculiar, marked, appropriate, characteristic, exclusive, restricted; singular, exceptional; typical, representative.

Adv. **each,** apiece, one by one, severally, respectively, in detail.

namely, that is to say, viz.; to wit.

80. RULE.—*N.* **regularity,** uniformity, constancy, clockwork precision; punctuality, etc. (*exactness*), 494; even tenor, rut; system; routine, custom; formula; canon, convention, maxim, rule, regulation; standard, model, precedent; conformity, etc., 82.

law, order of things; normality, normalcy, normal state, ordinary condition, standing order; hard and fast rule.

Adj. **regular,** uniform, symmetrical, constant, steady; according to rule, etc., 82; normal, habitual, customary, etc., 613; methodical, orderly, systematic.

81. MULTIFORMITY.—*N.* **multiformity,** variety, diversity.

Adj. **multiform,** multifold, multifarious, multiplex; manifold, many-sided; protean, heterogeneous, motley, mosaic.

indiscriminate, irregular, diversified, diverse; of every description.

82. CONFORMITY.—*N.* conformity, observance; conventionality, etc. (*custom*), 613; agreement, accord.

example, instance, exemplification, illustration, specimen, sample.

conventionalist, formalist, bromide [*slang*], Philistine.

V. **conform to,** adapt oneself to.

be regular, travel in a rut; obey rules; agree with, comply with, fall in with; be guided by, harmonize, conventionalize, follow the fashion; do at Rome as the Romans do; swim with the stream.

exemplify, illustrate, cite, quote.

Adj. **conformable to rule,** adaptable, consistent, agreeable, compliant; regular, etc., 80; according to rule, well regulated, orderly, uniform, symmetric.

conventional, etc. (*customary*), 613; ordinary, common, habitual, usual; strict, rigid, uncompromising.

typical, normal, formal; canonical, orthodox, exemplary, illustrative, in point.

Adv. **conformably,** by rule; in accordance with, in keeping with; according to; as usual, as a matter of course.

invariably, etc. (*uniformly*), 16.

83. UNCONFORMITY.—*N.* **nonconformity,** unconformity, nonobservance, unconventionality, informality; anomaly, anomalousness, exception, peculiarity; breach *or* violation of custom; eccentricity, oddity, rarity.

individuality, singularity, originality, idiosyncrasy, mannerism.

aberration, irregularity; singularity; exemption; qualification, proviso.

nonconformist, Bohemian, nondescript character, original, freak, prodigy, wonder, miracle, curiosity.

mongrel, half-caste, etc., 41.

outcast, outlaw, Ishmael, pariah.

V. **be uncomfortable,** leave the beaten path; break (*or* violate) a law *or* custom; stretch a point.

Adj. **uncomfortable,** exceptional, eccentric; abnormal, unnatural, anomalous, misplaced, out of order, irregular, arbitrary, lawless; informal, stray, eccentric, peculiar, exclusive, egregious.

unusual, unaccustomed, unwonted, uncommon; rare, singular, unique, curious, odd, extraordinary, strange, monstrous; wonderful, etc., 870; remarkable, noteworthy, queer, quaint, nondescript, original, unorthodox, unconventional, Bohemian, unprecedented, unparalleled, unexampled, unheard of; fantastic, newfangled, eccentric, grotesque, bizarre; unfamiliar, outlandish.

heterogeneous, amorphous, mongrel, hybrid; unsymmetric, etc., 243.

Adv. unconformably; except, unless, save.

V. NUMBER

84. NUMBER.—*N.* number, symbol, numeral, figure, cipher, digit, integer, round number; series.

sum, product, total, aggregate, difference.

ratio, proportion, percentage; progression; arithmetical progression.

power, root, exponent, index, logarithm.

85. NUMERATION.—*N.* numeration, numbering; tale, tally, enumeration, reckoning, computation, calculation, calculus; measurement, etc., 466; statistics.

arithmetic, algebra, differential calculus, calculus of differences.

muster, poll, census, roll call; account, etc. (*list*), 86.

Instruments: abacus, calculating machine, adding machine, cash register.

arithmetician, calculator, algebraist, geometrician, trigonometrician, mathematician, actuary, statistician.

V. **number,** count, enumerate; call over, run over; take an account of, call the roll, muster, poll; sum up, cast up; tell off, cipher, reckon, reckon up, estimate, compute, calculate.

check, prove, demonstrate, balance, audit, overhaul, take stock.

total, amount to, come to.

Adj. **numeral,** numerical; arithmetical, analytic, algebraic, statistical, computable, calculable, commensurable, commensurate.

86. LIST.—*N.* list, catalogue, card index; inventory, schedule; register, etc. (*record*), 551; account; bill, bill of costs; tally, file, index, table, contents; book, ledger; synopsis, syllabus; scroll, screed, invoice, manifest, bill of lading; prospectus, program; bill of fare, menu; score, bulletin, census, statistics, returns; directory, atlas, gazetteer; calendar, almanac.

dictionary, lexicon, glossary, vocabulary, wordbook, thesaurus.

roll; muster roll; roll of honor; roster, slate, poll, panel.

V. **list,** enroll, schedule, inventory, register, catalogue, invoice, bill, book, slate, post, docket; empanel, tally, file, index, tabulate, enter, census.

87. UNITY.—*N.* **unity,** oneness; individuality; unification, etc., 48; completeness, completion.

one, unit; individual.

V. isolate, insulate.

render one; unite, etc. (*join*), 43, (*combine*), 48.

Adj. one, sole, lone, single, solitary; individual, apart, alone; unaccompanied, unattended, singlehanded; singular, odd, unique, isolated; insular.

88. ACCOMPANIMENT.—*N.* accompaniment, adjunct, accessory; context; appendage, appurtenance; attribute.

company, association, partnership; companionship.

attendant, companion, associate, colleague, partner; consort, spouse; satellite, hanger-on, shadow; escort, suite, train, retinue, convoy, follower, etc., 65.

V. accompany, attend, convoy, chaperon; associate with, couple with.

Adj. accompanying, fellow, twin, joint; associated with, coupled with; accessory, attendant.

Adv. with, withal; together with, along with, in company with; therewith, herewith; and, etc. (*addition*), 37.

together, in a body, collectively, in conjunction.

89. DUALITY.—*N.* duality, dualism; duplicity; polarity.

two, deuce, couple, couplet, both, twain, brace, pair, twins, Castor and Pollux, gemini, fellows; yoke, span; distich.

V. pair, mate, couple, bracket, yoke.

Adj. two, twain, both; dual, twin; duplex, etc., 90; tête-à-tête.

90. DUPLICATION.—*N.* duplication, doubling, reduplication; iteration, etc. (*repetition*), 104; renewal.

duplicate, facsimile, copy, replica, counterpart, etc. (*copy*), 21.

V. double; redouble, reduplicate; repeat, etc., 104; renew, renovate.

Adj. double; doubled; twofold, two-sided, duplex; double-faced, double-headed; twin, duplicate, second; dual.

Adv. twice, once more; over again, etc. (*repeatedly*), 104.

91. [Division into two parts] **BISECTION.**—*N.* bisection, halving, bifurcation, forking, branching, ramification, dichotomy.

half, moiety.

V. bisect, halve, divide, separate, split, cut in two, cleave. fork, bifurcate, branch off *or* out, ramify.

Adj. bisected, cloven, cleft; bifurcated; semi-, demi-, hemi-.

92. TRIALITY.—*N.* triality [*rare*], trinity,[1] triunity.

three, triad, triplet, trio; triangle, trident, tripod, trireme, triumvirate.

third power, cube.

Adj. three; triform, tertiary.

93. TRIPLICATION.—*N.* triplication, triplicity; trilogy.

V. treble, triple; cube.

Adj. treble, triple; threefold; third.

[1]*Trinity* is hardly ever used except in a theological sense; *see* Deity, 976.

Adv. three times, thrice; in the third place, thirdly; threefold, triply, trebly.

94. [Division into three parts] TRISECTION.—*N.* trisection, tripartition, third, third part.

V. trisect, divide into three parts, third.

95. QUATERNITY.—*N.* quaternity [*rare*], four, quartet, quadruplet; square, quadrilateral; quadrangle.

V. square, biquadrate, reduce to a square.

Adj. four; quadratic; quadrangular, quadrilateral.

96. QUADRUPLICATION.—*N.* quadruplication.

V. quadruplicate, multiply by four.

Adj. fourfold, quadruple; fourth.

Adv. four times, in the fourth place, fourthly.

97. [Division into four parts] QUADRISECTION.—*N.* quadrisection, quadripartition; quartering; fourth; quart, quarter; farthing; quarto.

V. quarter, divide into four parts, quadrisect.

98. FIVE, ETC.—*N.* five, quintet, pentagon, pentameter.

six, half a dozen; hexagon, hexameter, sextet.

seven, heptagon, heptameter, heptarchy.

eight, octave, octagon, octameter, octavo, octet.

nine, nonagon.

ten, decade, decagon, decasyllable, decemvir, decemvirate, decennium.

twelve, dozen; thirteen, long dozen, baker's dozen; twenty, score; fifty, half a hundred; sixty, threescore; seventy, threescore and ten; eighty, fourscore; ninety, fourscore and ten.

hundred, centenary, century; bicentenary, tercentenary.

thousand, millennium; myriad.

V. quintuplicate, sextuple; centuplicate.

Adj. five, fifth, quintuple; pentangular, pentagonal. sixth, sextuple, hexagonal, hexangular. seventh, septuple, heptagonal, heptangular. eight, octuple, octagonal, octangular. tenth, tenfold, decimal, decagonal, decasyllabic. eleventh, undecennial, undecennary. twelfth, duodenary, duodenal. sixtieth, sexagesimal. seventieth, septuagesimal.

centuple, centuplicate, centennial, centenary; hundredth; thousandth, millenary, millennial, etc.

99. QUINQUESECTION, ETC.—*N.* quinquesection, division by five, etc., 98; decimation; tithe; fifth, etc.

Adj. decimal, tenth; duodecimal, twelfth; sexagesimal, sexagenary; hundredth, centesimal; millesimal, etc.

100. [More than one] PLURALITY.—*N.* plurality, one or two, two or three, etc.; a few, several; multitude, etc., 102; majority.

Adj. plural, more than one, upwards of, some, certain.

100a. [Less than one] FRACTION.—*N.* fraction, fractional part; part, portion, fragment, etc., 51.

Adj. fractional, fragmentary, inconsiderable, partial.

101. ZERO.—*N.* zero, nothing; naught, nought; cipher; none, nobody.

102. MULTITUDE.—*N.* multitude, multitudinousness, multiplicity; profusion, etc. (*plenty*), 639; legion, host, array, army, galaxy; numbers, scores; heap, power, sight, lot, lots [*all five colloq.*], swarm, bevy, cloud, flock, herd, drove, shoal, school, flight, covey, hive, brood, litter, farrow, fry, nest; mob, crowd, etc. (*assemblage*), 72.

V. be numerous, swarm with, teem with, be alive with, crowd, swarm, outnumber, multiply; people.

Adj. many, several, sundry, various, alive with; numerous; profuse, manifold, multitudinous, teeming, populous, outnumbering, crowded, thick, galore [*colloq.*]; thick-coming, endless, etc. (*infinite*), 105.

103. FEWNESS.—*N.* fewness, paucity, scarcity, sparseness, sparsity; handful; small quantity, etc., 32; rarity, infrequency; minority.

Diminution of number: reduction, weeding, elimination; decimation; eradication.

V. render few, reduce, diminish, weed out, eliminate, thin, decimate.

Adj. few, scant, scanty; thin, rare, scarce, sparse, few and far between; exiguous; infrequent.

104. REPETITION.—*N.* repetition, iteration, recapitulation, reiteration; monotone; duplication, reduplication, monotony, harping, recurrence; reappearance, reproduction; periodicity, etc., 138; succession, run; alliteration; rhythm, tautology; diffuseness, redundancy.

echo, encore, burden of a song, refrain, undersong.

cuckoo, etc. (*imitation*), 19; reverberation, vibration, resonance; drumming, etc. (*roll*), 407; renewal, etc. (*restoration*), 660.

V. repeat, iterate, reiterate, redouble, reproduce, echo, re-echo, drum, harp upon, hammer; rehearse; resume, return to, recapitulate.

recur, revert, return, reappear; renew, etc. (*restore*), 660.
duplicate, reduplicate.

Adj. repeated, repetitious, recurrent, recurring; frequent, incessant; redundant, tautological; another.

monotonous, harping, iterative, unvaried; habitual, etc., 613.
aforesaid, aforenamed: said.

Adv. **repeatedly,** often, again, anew, afresh, once more; ditto, encore, again and again; over and over, frequently, etc., 136.

105. INFINITY.—*N.* **infinity,** infinitude, infiniteness; perpetuity, immortality; inexhaustibility, immensity, boundlessness.

V. **be infinite,** have no limits (*or* bounds), go on forever.

Adj. **infinite,** immense; numberless, countless, measureless, innumerable, immeasurable, incalculable, illimitable, interminable, unfathomable; without limit, without end, limitless, endless, boundless; untold, unnumbered, unmeasured, unbounded, unlimited; perpetual, etc., 112.

VI. TIME

106. TIME.—*N.* **time,** duration; period, term, stage, space, span, spell, snap, season; course.

intermediate time, while, interim, interval; intermission, interregnum, interlude; respite.

era, epoch, eon, cycle, age, reign, dynasty, administration.

V. **continue,** last, endure, stay, go on, remain, persist, abide, stand, stick [*colloq.*], hold out; intervene; elapse, etc., 109.

pass time, spend *or* while away time, tide over; employ time; seize an opportunity; linger on, drag on; tarry, etc., 110; waste time, etc. (*be inactive*), 683; procrastinate, etc., 133.

Adj. **permanent,** etc. (*durable*), 110; timely, opportune, seasonable.

Adv. **while,** whilst, during; in the course of; in the time of, when; meantime, meanwhile, in the meantime, in the interim; from day to day; for a time, for a season; till, until, up to, yet; the whole time, all the time; throughout; for good, permanently, always.

then, hereupon, thereupon, whereupon.

107. Absence of time.—*N.* **no time.**

Adv. **never,** ne'er; at no time, at no period; on no occasion, nevermore.

108. [Definite duration or portion of time] PERIOD.—*N.* **period;** octave, semester, quarter, moon, year, decennial, decennium; decade, lifetime, generation; epoch, era, century, age, millennium.

109. [Indefinite duration] COURSE.—*N.* **corridors** (*or* sweep, vista, halls, progress, process, lapse, flow, tide, march, flight) of time; duration, etc., 106.

indefinite time: eon, age.

V. **elapse,** lapse, flow, run, proceed, advance, pass; fly, slip, slide, glide; crawl, drag; expire, go by, pass by, be past.

Adv. **in time,** in due time (*or* season, course); in course of time, in the fullness of time.

110. [Long duration] DURABILITY.—*N.* durability, durableness, permanence, continuance, persistence, lastingness, standing; immutability, stability; survival; longevity, etc. (*age*), 128; delay, etc. (*lateness*), 133; slowness.

an age, a long time, eon, century, an eternity; perpetuity, etc., 112.

V. **last,** endure, stand, remain, abide, continue, etc., 106.

tarry, etc., 133; drag on, protract, prolong; spin out, eke out, draw out; temporize, gain time.

outlast, outlive, survive.

Adj. **permanent,** durable, lasting; chronic, long-standing; persistent; lifelong, livelong; endless, fixed, long-lived, perennial; perpetual, etc., 112.

prolonged, protracted, spun out; lingering, long-winded; slow, etc., 275.

Adv. **long,** for a long time; long ago, etc. (*in a past time*), 122; all the day long, the livelong day; all the year round; permanently.

111. [Short duration] TRANSIENCE.—*N.* transience, transiency, evanescence, impermanence; changeableness, etc., 149; mortality; span; nine days' wonder, bubble; interregnum, interim.

velocity, etc., 274; suddenness, abruptness.

V. **be transient,** flit, pass away, fly, gallop, vanish, sink, melt, fade, evaporate.

Adj. **transient,** transitory, passing, evanescent, fleeting, fugitive; temporal, temporary, provisional, provisory; cursory; short-lived, ephemeral; deciduous; perishable, mortal; precarious; impermanent.

brief, quick, brisk, fleet; meteoric, volatile, summary; pressed for time, etc. (*haste*), 684; sudden, momentary, spasmodic, instantaneous.

Adv. **temporarily,** for the moment, for a time; awhile, soon, etc. (*early*), 132; briefly.

112. [Endless duration] PERPETUITY.—*N.* perpetuity, eternity, aye; immortality, perpetuation.

V. **eternalize,** immortalize, eternize, perpetuate.

Adj. **perpetual,** eternal, everlasting, continual, endless, unending; ceaseless, incessant, uninterrupted, unceasing; interminable; unfading, never-ending, deathless, immortal, undying, imperishable.

Adv. **perpetually,** always, ever, evermore, aye; forever, in all ages, without end, to the end of time; till doomsday; constantly, etc. (*very frequently*), 136.

113. [Point of time] INSTANTANEITY.—*N.* **instantaneity,** instantaneousness; suddenness, abruptness.

moment, instant, second, twinkling, flash, breath.

V. **be instantaneous;** flash.

Adj. **instantaneous,** momentary, extempore, sudden, abrupt.

Adv. **instantaneously,** in no time; presto, instanter, in a trice, in a jiffy [*colloq.*], suddenly, in the same breath; at once, plump; immediately, etc. (*early*), 132; extempore, on the spur of the moment; slapdash, etc. (*haste*), 684.

114. [Estimation, measurement, and record of time] CHRONOMETRY.—*N.* **chronometry,** chronology, horology.

almanac, calendar; register, registry; chronicle, annals, journal, diary.

timekeeper, clock, watch, repeater; chronometer, timepiece; dial, sundial, hourglass.

V. **register,** date, chronicle; measure time, beat time, mark time.

Adj. **chronologic** *or* **chronological,** temporal.

115. [False estimate of time] ANACHRONISM.—*N.* **anachronism,** error in time, error in chronology, misdate; anticipation; disregard (*or* neglect, oblivion) of time.

V. **misdate;** antedate, postdate, anticipate; take no note of time.

Adj. **misdated;** undated; overdue; out of date, anachronistic, behind time, ahead of time.

116. PRIORITY.—*N.* **priority,** predecessor, precedence, preexistence; precursor, antecedent, forerunner; the past, etc., 122.

V. **precede,** come before; pre-exist; forerun; go before, lead, head; presage, herald, usher in, introduce, announce.

be beforehand. etc. (*be early*), 132; anticipate, forestall.

Adj. **prior,** previous, preceding, anterior, antecedent; preexistent; former, aforementioned, foregoing, before-mentioned, aforesaid, said; introductory, etc. (*precursory*), 64.

Adv. **before,** prior to; earlier; previously, ere, already, yet, beforehand; on the eve of.

117. POSTERIORITY.—*N.* **posteriority;** succession, sequence; following, continuance, prolongation; futurity, future; successor; sequel, etc., 65; remainder.

V. **follow after,** pursue, come after, go after; succeed, supervene; ensue, result.

Adj. **subsequent,** posterior, following, after, later, succeeding, successive, ensuing, posthumous; future, etc., 121; after-dinner.

Adv. **subsequently,** after, afterward, since, later; next, close upon, thereafter, thereupon.

118. PRESENT TIME.—*N.* the present time, the present juncture *or* occasion; the times, time being; twentieth century.

Adj. present, actual, instant, current, latest, existing.

Adv. at this time, at this moment, etc., 113; now, at present; today, nowadays; already; even now, but now, just now; for the time being.

119. DIFFERENT TIME.—*N.* different time, other time.

Adv. then, at that time (*or* moment, instant); on that occasion. when; whenever, whensoever; whereupon, upon which; at various times.

once, formerly, once upon a time.

120. SIMULTANEOUSNESS.—*N.* simultaneousness, synchronism, coexistence, coincidence, concurrence.

contemporary, coeval.

V. coexist, concur, accompany, keep pace with; synchronize.

Adj. simultaneous, coexisting, coincident, synchronous, concomitant, concurrent; coeval; contemporary, contemporaneous.

Adv. simultaneously, together, in concert; in the same breath.

121. THE FUTURE.—*N.* future, futurity, hereafter, time to come; morrow, tomorrow, by and by, doomsday, day of judgment, crack of doom.

approach of time, advent; destiny, etc., 152.

heritage, heirs, posterity, descendants.

prospect, anticipation, expectation; foresight, etc., 510.

V. anticipate, expect, await, foresee; forestall, etc. (*be early*), 132.

approach, await, threaten; impend, etc. (*be destined*), 152; come on, draw near.

Adj. future, to come; coming, impending, overhanging, imminent; next, near, close at hand; eventual, ulterior; prospective, in prospect.

Adv. prospectively, hereafter, in future; in course of time, eventually, ultimately, sooner or later.

soon, early; on the eve of, on the point of, about to.

122. THE PAST.—*N.* the past, past time, days of yore, days of old, times past, former times, yesterday, the olden time; retrospection, memory, priority.

antiquity, antiqueness, time immemorial, history, remote time; remote past; paleontology, archeology, antiquarianism.

antiquary, antiquarian, archeologist.

ancestry, lineage, forefathers.

V. pass, lapse, blow over.

Adj. past, gone, gone by, over, passed away, bygone, elapsed,

lapsed, expired, extinct, exploded, forgotten, irrecoverable; obsolete, antiquated, outworn.

former, pristine, quondam, late; ancestral.

foregoing, last, latter; recent.

looking back, retrospective, retroactive; archeological.

Adv. formerly, of old, of yore, time was, ago; anciently, long ago; lately, latterly, of late; ere now, before now, hitherto, heretofore; already, yet, up to this time.

123. NEWNESS.—*N.* newness, novelty; youth, juvenility, immaturity.

innovation; renovation, restoration.

upstart, *nouveau riche* [F.], parvenu.

modernism, modernness, modernity; modernization; latest fashion.

V. renew, renovate; rejuvenate; modernize.

Adj. new, novel, recent, fresh, green; young, etc., 127; raw, immature; virgin, untried; modern, late; newborn, new-fashioned, newfangled, newfledged; just out [*colloq.*], unhandled; brand-new, up-to-date [*colloq.*], renovated, spick-and-span.

Adv. newly, afresh, anew, lately, just now, latterly, of late.

124. OLDNESS.—*N.* oldness, age, antiquity.

maturity, matureness, ripeness.

decline, decay; senility, superannuation, dotage.

archaism, antiquarianism; thing of the past, relic of the past.

tradition, custom, immemorial usage, common law; folklore.

V. be old, have had its day, have seen its day.

become old, age, fade.

Adj. old, ancient, antique; time-honored, venerable, hoary; elder, eldest; firstborn; senile, etc., 128.

primitive, prime, primeval, aboriginal; antediluvian, prehistoric, dateless, patriarchal, archaic, classic, medieval; ancestral.

immemorial, traditional, unwritten, inveterate, rooted.

antiquated, of other times, of the old school, old world; obsolete, out-of-date, out-of-fashion, gone by, stale, old-fashioned, exploded, extinct, timeworn, crumbling, secondhand.

125. MORNING. [Noon]—*N.* morning, morn, forenoon, antemeridian, A.M., prime, dawn, daybreak; dayspring, peep of day, break of day, aurora, sunrise, daylight, cockcrow.

noon, midday, noonday, noontide, meridian, prime; nooning, noontime.

spring, springtide, springtime, seedtime; vernal equinox.

summer, summertide, summertime, midsummer.

Adj. matin, matutinal.

noon, noonday, midday.

spring, vernal.

summer, estival.

126. EVENING. [Midnight]—*N.* evening, eve, decline of day, close of day, eventide, vespers, nightfall, curfew, dusk, gloaming, twilight, sunset, sundown, bedtime.

afternoon, post meridiem [L.], P.M.

midnight; dead of night, witching time.

autumn, fall; harvesttime; autumnal equinox; Indian summer.

winter.

Adj. vesper, nightly, nocturnal; autumnal.

wintry, winterly.

127. YOUTH.—*N.* youth; juvenility; infancy, babyhood; childhood; boyhood, girlhood; rising generation; minority, immaturity, teens, tender age, bloom.

cradle, nursery.

flower of life, springtide of life, seedtime of life, golden season of life; heyday of youth, school days.

Adj. young, youthful, juvenile, green, callow, sappy, beardless, underage, in one's teens; younger, junior; newfledged, unfledged, unripe.

128. AGE.—*N.* age; oldness, old age, advanced age, senility, years, gray hairs, declining years, decrepitude, superannuation, second childhood, dotage; vale of years, decline of life; green old age, ripe age; longevity.

seniority, eldership, primogeniture; elders, etc. (*veteran*), 130; dean, father.

V. age, grow old, decline, wane.

Adj. aged; old, etc., 124; elderly, senile; ripe, mellow, declining, waning, past one's prime; gray, gray-headed, hoar, hoary, venerable, patriarchal, timeworn, antiquated, effete, decrepit, superannuated; advanced in life (*or* years); stricken in years; doting, etc. (*imbecile*), 499.

older, elder, oldest, eldest; senior; firstborn.

129. INFANT.—*N.* infant, babe, baby; nursling, suckling.

child, tot, mite, chick, kid [*slang*], little one, brat, pickaninny [*colored child*], urchin, elf.

youth, boy, lad, laddie, slip, sprig, stripling, youngster, cub, whippersnapper [*colloq.*], schoolboy, hobbledehoy, young hopeful, cadet, minor.

girl, lass, lassie, wench, damsel; maid, maiden, virgin; nymph, colleen, flapper, minx, schoolgirl; hoyden, tomboy, romp.

Adj. infantile, infantine, puerile, boyish, girlish, childish, babyish, kittenish; boylike, girllike, newborn; young, etc., 127.

130. VETERAN.—*N.* veteran, old man, patriarch, graybeard;

grandfather, sexagenarian, octogenarian, nonagenarian, centenarian; Methuselah; elders, forefathers; dotard, etc., 501.

granny, crone, hag, beldam.

Adj. veteran; aged, etc., 128.

131. ADOLESCENCE.—*N.* adolescence, majority, adulthood, womanhood, manhood, virility; flower of age; full bloom; spring of life.

man, etc., 373; woman, etc., 374; adult.

middle age, maturity, full age, prime of life, meridian of life.

V. come of age, come to man's estate, come to years of discretion; attain majority; come out [*colloq.*].

Adj. adolescent, pubescent, of age, of full age, of ripe age; out of one's teens, grown up, full-grown, manly, manlike, virile, adult; womanly; marriageable.

middle-aged, mature, in one's prime; matronly.

132. EARLINESS.—*N.* earliness, punctuality, promptitude, readiness, expedition, quickness, haste, etc. (*velocity*), 274; suddenness.

prematurity, precocity, precipitation, anticipation.

V. be early, be beforehand.

anticipate, forestall, take time by the forelock, steal a march upon; bespeak, secure, engage, pre-engage.

accelerate, expedite, etc. (*quicken*), 274; make haste, etc. (*hurry*), 684.

Adj. early, timely, seasonable, punctual, forward; prompt, etc. (*active*), 682.

premature, precipitate, precocious, anticipatory.

sudden, instantaneous, immediate; unexpected, etc., 508.

imminent, impending, near.

Adv. early, soon, anon, betimes, ere long, before long; punctually, in time; on time, on the dot [*slang*].

beforehand; prematurely, too soon; precipitately, hastily; in anticipation; unexpectedly, unawares.

suddenly, etc. (*instantaneously*), 113; at short notice, extempore; on the spur of the moment, at once; on the spot, on the instant, at sight, offhand, straight, straightway; forthwith, immediately, quickly, speedily, apace; presently, by and by, directly.

133. LATENESS.—*N.* lateness; tardiness, etc. (*slowness*), 275.

delay, procrastination, postponement, adjournment, prorogation, retardation; protraction, prolongation; moratorium; aftertime; respite, truce, reprieve, stop, stay, suspension, remand.

V. be late, tarry, wait, stay, bide, take time; dawdle, etc. (*be inactive*), 683; linger, loiter, gain time; hang fire; stand over, lie over; hang.

put off, defer, delay, lay over, suspend; stave off; retard, postpone, adjourn, prorogue, procrastinate; dally, prolong, protract, spin out, draw out, table, lay on the table, shelve; reserve, temporize, filibuster, stall [*slang*].

be kept waiting, dance attendance; cool one's heels [*colloq.*]; await, expect, wait for.

Adj. **late**, tardy, dilatory; slow, leisurely, behindhand, backward, unpunctual; overdue, belated, delayed; posthumous.

Adv. **late**; backward, at the eleventh hour, at length, at last, ultimately; behind time; too late.

slowly, deliberately, at one's leisure.

134. TIMELINESS.—*N.* **timeliness**, opportunity, opening, occasion, show [*colloq.*]; suitable time *or* season, high time; nick of time; golden opportunity, clear stage, fair field; spare time, leisure.

crisis, turn, emergency, juncture, conjuncture; turning point.

V. **improve the occasion**; seize an opportunity; use (*or* profit by) an opportunity; give (*or* grant) an opportunity; suit the occasion, etc. (*be expedient*), 646; strike the iron while it is hot, make hay while the sun shines.

Adj. **timely**, well timed, opportune, seasonable; appropriate, suitable.

lucky, providential, fortunate, happy, favorable, propitious, auspicious.

occasional, accidental, extemporaneous, extemporary; contingent, provisional.

Adv. **opportunity**, in due time; for the nonce; in the nick of time, just in time; at the eleventh hour, now or never.

by the way, by the by; while on this subject, speaking of; extempore; on the spur of the moment.

135. UNTIMELINESS.—*N.* **untimeliness**, unseasonableness, unsuitable time, improper time; evil hour; intrusion; anachronism.

V. **be ill-timed**, mistime, intrude, come amiss, break in upon; be busy, be occupied, be engaged.

lose an opportunity; neglect an opportunity; allow *or* suffer the opportunity to pass (*or* slip, go by, escape); waste time; let slip through the fingers.

Adj. **ill-timed**, mistimed, ill-fated, ill-omened, ill-starred; untimely, unseasonable, out of season; inopportune, inconvenient, untoward, unlucky, inauspicious, unpropitious, unfortunate, unfavorable, unsuited; inexpedient.

unpunctual, etc. (*late*), 133; premature, etc. (*early*), 132.

136. FREQUENCY.—*N.* **frequency**, repetition, iteration, reiteration.

V. keep on; reiterate, repeat, recur, etc., 104; do nothing but.

Adj. frequent, not rare, thick-coming, incessant, perpetual, continual, constant, habitual, etc., 613.

Adv. often, oft, ofttimes, frequently; repeatedly, in quick succession; daily, every day; habitually, commonly.

perpetually, continually, constantly, incessantly, at all times.

sometimes, occasionally, at times, now and then, again and again.

137. INFREQUENCY.—*N.* infrequency, infrequence, rarity; uncommonness.

Adj. infrequent, uncommon, sporadic; rare, few, scant, scarce; unprecedented.

Adv. seldom, rarely, scarcely, hardly; not often, infrequently, uncommonly, sparsely, scarcely ever, hardly ever.

138. REGULARITY [of recurrence].—*N.* periodicity, intermittence; oscillation, vibration; beat, pulse, pulsation; rhythm, alternation; round, revolution, rotation, regularity, bout, turn; routine; cycle.

anniversary, biennial, triennial, quadrennial, quinquennial, sextennial, septennial, octennial, decennial; tricennial, jubilee, centennial, centenary, bicentennial, bicentenary, tercentenary; birthday, natal day, fete day, saint's day, feast, festival, fast, holiday.

Christmas, Yuletide, New Year's Day, Ash Wednesday, Maundy Thursday, Good Friday, Easter; Halloween, All Saints' Day; All Souls' Day; Candlemas; Memorial *or* Decoration Day, Independence Day, Labor Day, Thanksgiving, ground-hog day, woodchuck day, leap year, St. Swithin's Day, Midsummer Day; May Day.

V. return, revolve, recur, come round again; beat, pulsate; alternate; intermit.

Adj. periodic, periodical; serial, recurrent, cyclic, cyclical, rhythmic, recurring, intermittent; alternate, every other; every.

regular, steady, constant, methodical, punctual.

Adv. by turns, in turn, in rotation, alternately, off and on, round and round.

139. IRREGULARITY [of recurrence].—*N.* irregularity, uncertainty, unpunctuality; fitfulness, capriciousness.

Adj. irregular, uncertain, unpunctual, capricious, erratic, desultory, fitful, flickering; rambling, spasmodic; unmethodical, unsystematic, unequal, uneven, variable.

Adv. by fits and starts.

VII. CHANGE

140. CHANGE.—*N.* change, alteration, mutation, permutation, variation, modification, modulation, inflection, mood, qualification, innovation, deviation, shift, turn; diversion, variety, break.

conversion, etc. (*gradual change*), 144; revolution, etc., 146; inversion, reversal; displacement, transposition, removal, transference.

transformation, metamorphosis, transfiguration, transmutation; transubstantiation; transmigration, metempsychosis; avatar.

changeableness, etc., 149.

V. change, alter, vary, modulate, diversify, qualify, tamper with; turn, shift, veer, jibe, jib, tack, chop, warp, swerve, deviate, dodge; turn aside; take a turn, turn the corner.

modify, work a change, patch, piece, transform, transfigure, transmute, convert, revolutionize; metamorphose, ring the changes; innovate, introduce new blood, shuffle the cards; shift the scene, turn over a new leaf.

recast, remodel; reverse, etc., 218; convert into, etc., 144.

Adj. changed, newfangled; changeable, changeful, variable, devious, transitional.

141. PERMANENCE.—*N.* permanence, fixity, persistence, endurance; durability; standing, *status quo* [L.]; maintenance, preservation, conservation; conservatism; stability, constancy; quiescence, etc., 265; obstinacy, inflexibility.

V. endure, persist, remain, stay, tarry, rest, hold, last, bide, abide, dwell, maintain, keep; stand fast, subsist, live, outlive, survive; hold one's ground (*or* footing).

Adj. permanent, stable, fixed, settled, established, irremovable, durable; unchanged, intact, inviolate; persistent; conservative; unfailing, unfading.

Adv. for good, at a stand, at a standstill, as you were!

142. CESSATION.—*N.* cessation, discontinuance; intermission, remission; suspense, suspension; interruption; stop; hitch [*colloq.*]; stoppage, halt.

pause, rest, lull, respite, truce, armistice, stay; interregnum. **In debate:** closure, cloture.

deadlock, checkmate, dead center, dead stand, dead stop; end. punctuation: comma, semicolon, colon, period, full stop; cæsura.

V. cease, discontinue, desist, stay; break off, leave off; hold, stop, pull up, stop short; check, stick, hang fire; halt, pause, rest; come to a stand; arrive, etc., 292; go out, die away, wear away, pass away, lapse; be at an end.

have done with, give over; give up, etc. (*relinquish*), 624.

interrupt, suspend, intermit, remit; put an end to, bring to a stand (*or* standstill), stop, cut short, arrest.

143. CONTINUANCE [in action].—*N.* continuance, continuation; pursuance, maintenance, extension, perpetuation, prolongation; persistence, perseverance; repetition.

V. **continue,** persist, go on, keep on, hold on; abide, pursue; stick to; maintain its course; keep up, drag on, stick [*colloq.*], persevere, endure, carry on; keep the field, keep the ball rolling.

sustain, uphold, hold up, follow up, perpetuate, prolong, maintain; preserve.

Adj. **continuing,** uninterrupted, unvarying, persistent, unceasing, unvaried, sustained, chronic; undying, immortal, perpetual.

144. [Gradual change to something different] CONVERSION. —*N.* **conversion,** reduction, transmutation, assimilation; chemistry, alchemy; growth, progress; naturalization; transportation.

passage, transit, transition, transmigration; shifting, flux; phase.

convert, neophyte, proselyte; pervert, renegade, apostate, turncoat.

V. **be converted into;** become, turn to *or* into; turn out, lapse, shift; pass into, grow into, merge into; melt, grow, wax, mature, mellow.

convert into, resolve into; make, render; mold, form, remodel, reform, reorganize; bring to, reduce to.

145. REVERSION.—*N.* **reversion,** return; revulsion; turning point, turn of the tide; alternation, rotation; inversion, etc., 218; recoil, reaction; retrospection, retrogression; restoration, relapse, atavism, throwback.

V. **revert,** reverse, return, turn back; relapse; invert; recoil; retreat; restore; undo, unmake; turn the scale.

146. [Sudden or violent change] REVOLUTION.—*N.* **revolution,** revolt; breakup; destruction, etc., 162; clean sweep, debacle, overturn, overthrow, rebellion, rising, uprising, mutiny, counterrevolution, bolshevism.

spasm, convulsion, throe, revulsion; earthquake, eruption, upheaval, cataclysm, explosion.

V. **revolutionize,** revolt, rebel, rise; remodel, recast.

Adj. **revolutionary,** catastrophic, cataclysmic, cataclysmal, insurgent, Red, insurrectionary, mutinous, rebellious; bolshevistic *or* bolshevik.

147. [Change of one thing for another] SUBSTITUTION.—*N.* **substitution,** commutation, supplanting.

substitute, scapegoat; alternative; makeshift, temporary expedient, shift, apology, stopgap; alternate; dummy, double; changeling; representative, deputy.

price, purchase money, consideration, equivalent.

V. **substitute,** put in the place of, change for, give place to; take the place of, supplant, supersede, replace, cut out [*colloq.*]; commute, redeem, compound for.

Adj. substituted, vicarious.

Adv. instead; by proxy; in place of, in lieu of.

148. [Double or mutual change] INTERCHANGE.—*N.* interchange, exchange; commutation, permutation; transposition, shuffle; alternation, reciprocity; swap [*colloq.*], barter, exchange; retaliation, reprisal; retort, requital, cross fire.

V. interchange, exchange, bandy, barter, transpose, swap [*colloq.*], reciprocate, commute; give and take, retaliate; retort; requite.

Adj. reciprocal, mutual; interchangeable.

international, interstate, interurban, interdenominational; interscholastic, intercollegiate.

Adv. in exchange, vice versa, conversely, by turns, turn about.

149. CHANGEABLENESS.—*N.* changeableness, mutability, inconstancy; versatility, mobility; instability, vacillation, irresolution, indecision; fluctuation, vicissitude; alternation, oscillation.

Comparisons: moon, kaleidoscope, chameleon, quicksilver, shifting sands, weath‐ ercock, vane, weathervane, harlequin, turncoat; wheel of fortune.

restlessness, fidgets, disquiet; disquietude, unrest; agitation, etc., 315.

V. fluctuate, vary, waver, flicker, flutter, shift, shuffle, shake, totter, tremble, vacillate, shift to and fro; oscillate, pulsate, vibrate; alternate.

Adj. changeable, changeful; changing, mutable, variable, kaleidoscopic; protean, versatile, mobile.

inconstant, unsteady, unstable, unfixed, unsettled; fluctuating, wavering, vibratory, restless, tremulous; erratic, fickle; mercurial, irresolute, indecisive; capricious, fitful, spasmodic; vagrant, wayward; desultory, transient, etc., 111.

150. STABILITY.—*N.* stability, immutability, unchangeableness, constancy; immobility; soundness, vitality, stabilization; stiffness, solidity; permanence, etc., 141; obstinacy, obduracy.

fixture, establishment; leopard's spots.

standpatter [*politics*].

V. be firm, stick fast; stand firm, remain firm; stand pat [*colloq.*].

establish, settle, fix, set, stabilize; retain, keep hold; make good, make sure; fasten, etc. (*join*), 43; perpetuate.

settle down; strike root, take root.

Adj. unchangeable, immutable; unaltered, unalterable, constant; permanent, persistent, invariable, undeviating; stable, durable, perennial; irretrievable, irrevocable, indissoluble, indestructible, imperishable, indelible.

fixed, steadfast, firm, solid; deep-rooted, ineradicable; fast, steady, confirmed, inveterate; immovable, rooted; settled, stereotyped, established, vested; obstinate, etc., 606; incontrovertible, valid.

stuck fast, transfixed, aground, stranded.

151. PRESENT EVENTS.—*N.* eventuality, event, occurrence, incident, affair, transaction, proceeding, fact; phenomenon.

circumstance, particular; happening, adventure; crisis, pass, emergency, contingency; concern, business.

consequence, issue, result, termination, conclusion.

affairs, matters; the world, life, things, doings; the times.

V. happen, occur; take place, come to pass, take effect; present itself; fall out, turn out, befall, betide; turn up, crop up, arrive; ensue, result; arise, start; take its course, pass off.

experience; meet with; fall to the lot of; be one's lot; find, encounter; undergo, pass through, go through, endure, bear, suffer, abide, stand, brook.

Adj. eventful, stirring, full of incident; memorable, momentous, signal; current, on foot, at issue, in question; incidental.

Adv. eventually, ultimately, finally; in the event of, in case.

152. FUTURE EVENTS.—*N.* destiny, fatality, fate, lot, doom, fortune; future, future state; future existence, hereafter; next world, world to come; life to come; prospect.

V. impend, hang over, threaten, loom, await, approach; foreordain, preordain; destine, predestine, doom.

Adj. impending, destined; coming, in store, to come, instant, at hand, near, imminent; in the wind, in prospect.

Adv. in time, in the long run; all in good time; eventually.

VIII. CAUSATION

153. CAUSE.—*N.* cause, origin, source, principle, element; prime mover, ultimate cause; author, producer, creator, determinant; mainspring, agent; leaven; groundwork, foundation, support.

causality, causation; origination; production, etc., 161.

spring, fountain, well; fountainhead, reservoir, wellspring; genesis; derivation; remote cause; influence.

pivot, hinge, turning point; heart, hub, focus.

reason, reason why; ground, occasion; final cause; undercurrents.

rudiment, egg, germ, nucleus, seed.

nest, cradle, nursery, birthplace, hotbed.

V. cause, originate, give rise to, occasion, sow the seeds of; bring to pass, bring about; produce; create, develop; set on foot, entail; found, institute.

procure, induce, draw down, superinduce, evoke, elicit, provoke.
contribute, conduce to, have a hand in, influence; determine, decide, turn the scale.

Adj. **causal,** original; primary, originative, generative, productive, creative; formative; radical; in embryo, embryonic.

Adv. **from the beginning,** in the first place; because, etc., 155.

154. EFFECT.—*N.* **effect,** consequence; aftergrowth, afterclap, aftermath; derivative; derivation; result; resultant; upshot, issue, outcome, conclusion; catastrophe, end; development, outgrowth; fruit, crop, harvest, product.

production, work, handiwork, fabric, performance; creature, creation; offspring, offshoot; first fruits.

V. **be the effect of,** be due to, be owing to; originate in *or* from; rise from, spring from, emanate from, come from, issue from, flow from, result from; depend upon, hang upon, hinge upon, turn upon.

Adj. **owing to;** resulting from; due to; caused by; derived from, evolved from; derivative; hereditary.

Adv. **consequently,** it follows that, as a consequence, in consequence; necessarily, eventually.

155. [Assignment of cause] ATTRIBUTION —*N.* **attribution,** theory, assignment, reference to, accounting for; imputation; derivation.

explanation, interpretation, reason why.

V. **attribute to,** ascribe to, impute to, refer to, lay to, trace to; blame; saddle; account for, derive from; theorize.

Adj. **attributed;** attributable, referable; due to; owing to.

Adv. **hence,** thence, therefore, for, since, on account of, because, owing to; forasmuch as; whence.

why? wherefore? whence? how comes it? how is it? how so?

156. [Absence of assignable cause] CHANCE[1].—*N.* **chance,** accident, fortune, hazard, luck, fluke [*cant*], casualty, hit; fate, lottery, tossup [*colloq.*]; throw of the dice; heads or tails, wheel of fortune.

probability, possibility, contingency, odds, run of luck; main chance.

gamble, speculation, gaming, game of chance.

V. **chance,** turn up; fall to one's lot; be one's fate; stumble on, light upon; blunder upon, hit, hit upon.

Adj. **casual,** fortuitous, accidental, chance, haphazard, random, incidental, unintentional, unpremeditated.

---

[1]The word *chance* has two distinct meanings: the first, the absence of assignable *cause*, as above; and the second, the absence of *design*—for the latter see 621.

Adv. by chance, by accident; at random, casually; perchance, etc. (*possibly*), 470.

157. POWER.—*N.* power; potency, efficacy, puissance, might, energy, vigor, force; ascendancy, sway, almightiness, omnipotence; authority, weight, control; influence, predominance.

ability, competence, efficiency, efficacy; validity, cogency; vantage ground.

capability, capacity: faculty, quality, attribute, endowment, virtue, gift, property, qualification.

V. empower; give *or* confer power; invest, endue; endow, arm; strengthen, etc., 159.

electrify, magnetize, energize, galvanize.

Adj. powerful, puissant, potent, capable, able; cogent, valid, effective, effectual, efficient, efficacious, adequate, competent; predominant; mighty, omnipotent, almighty.

forcible, energetic; influential; productive.

electric, magnetic, galvanic, dynamic, potential.

Adv. by virtue of, by dint of.

158. IMPOTENCE.—*N.* impotence; inability, disability, incapacity, incapability; ineptitude; inefficiency, incompetence, disqualification; inefficacy, etc. (*inutility*), 645; failure, etc., 732.

helplessness, prostration, paralysis, collapse, exhaustion, senility, superannuation, decrepitude, imbecility, inanition.

mollycoddle, old woman, milksop, sissy [*colloq.*], mother's darling.

collapse, faint, swoon, drop; go by the board; end in smoke, etc. (*fail*), 732.

render powerless, disable, disarm, incapacitate, disqualify, unfit, invalidate, undermine, deaden, cramp, tie the hands; prostrate, paralyze, muzzle, cripple, maim, lame, throttle, strangle, silence, spike the guns; unhinge, unfit; put out of gear.

unman, unnerve, devitalize, attenuate, enervate.

shatter, exhaust; weaken, enfeeble.

Adj. powerless, impotent, helpless; incapable, incompetent, inefficient, ineffective, unfit, unfitted, unqualified, disqualified; crippled, disabled; senile, decrepit, superannuated; paralytic, paralyzed, nerveless, out of joint, out of gear; unnerved, unhinged; done up [*colloq.*], done for [*colloq.*], dead-beat [*colloq.*], exhausted, shattered, prostrate, demoralized, harmless; unarmed, weaponless, defenseless.

nugatory, null and void, inoperative, good for nothing, ineffectual, inadequate, inefficacious, etc. (*useless*), 645.

159. STRENGTH.—*N.* strength; power, etc., 157; energy, vigor, force; main (*or* physical, brute) force; spring, elasticity.

vitality, virility, lustihood, stamina, nerve, muscle, sinews, physique; grit.

athletics, athleticism; gymnastics, calisthenics.

athlete, gymnast, acrobat; Atlas, Hercules.

strengthening, invigoration, refreshment.

Science of forces: dynamics, statics.

V. strengthen, invigorate, brace, nerve, fortify, buttress, sustain, harden, steel; gird, set up, gird up one's loins; recruit, set on one's legs [*colloq.*]; vivify; refresh, reinforce, restore.

Adj. strong, mighty, vigorous, forcible; hard, stout, robust, sound, sturdy, husky [*colloq.*], hardy, powerful, potent, puissant.

resistless, irresistible, invincible, impregnable, unconquerable, indomitable, incontestable, valid; overpowering, overwhelming, all-powerful.

able-bodied; athletic, Herculean, muscular, brawny, wiry, well knit, sinewy, strapping, stalwart, lusty.

manly, manful; masculine, male, virile, in the prime of manhood.

Adv. strongly, by force, by main force.

160. WEAKNESS.—*N.* weakness, debility, relaxation, languor, enervation; impotence, etc., 158; infirmity, effeminacy; fragility; inactivity, etc., 683.

anemia, bloodlessness, deficiency of blood, poverty of blood.

loss of strength, delicacy; decrepitude; invalidism.

V. be weak; drop, crumble, give way; totter, dodder; tremble, shake; halt, limp; fade, languish, decline, flag, fail.

weaken, enfeeble, debilitate, shake, relax, sap, enervate, unnerve; cripple, unman; cramp, reduce, sprain, strain, dilute, impoverish.

Adj. weak, faint, feeble, infirm; impotent; relaxed, unnerved, unstrung, limp, strengthless, powerless; weakly, sickly, flaccid.

soft, effeminate, womanish.

frail, fragile; flimsy, sleazy, papery, unsubstantial, gimcrack, rickety, jerry-built; broken, decrepit, lame, shattered, shaken, crazy, shaky, tumbledown.

unsound, spent, effete; decayed, rotten, worn, seedy, languishing, wasted, laid low, the worse for wear; on its last legs.

161. [Power in operation] PRODUCTION.—*N.* production, creation, construction, formation, fabrication, manufacture; building, architecture, erection; organization; establishment; workmanship, performance; achievement; flowering, efflorescence, fruition; genesis, birth; evolution, development, growth; breeding; propagation.

publication; works, opus (*pl.* opera) [L.]; authorship.

structure, building, edifice, fabric, erection, pile.

V. **produce,** perform, operate, do, make, form, construct, fabricate, frame, contrive, manufacture; build, raise, rear, erect; establish, constitute, compose, evolve, coin, organize, institute; achieve, accomplish.

flower, blossom, bear fruit, bear, bring forth, give birth to, usher into the world; generate, propagate, engender, create; breed, develop, bring up.

induce, superinduce; cause, etc., 153.

Adj. **productive;** prolific, etc., 168; creative, formative, constructive; generative; teeming.

162. [Nonproduction] DESTRUCTION.—*N.* **destruction;** waste, dissolution, breaking up, disruption; disorganization; demolition, overthrow, subversion, suppression; abolition, etc., 756; sacrifice; ravage, devastation, incendiarism; revolution, etc., 146; road to ruin; sabotage.

fall, downfall, ruin, perdition; breakdown, breakup; cave-in [*colloq.*]; wreck, shipwreck, cataclysm.

extinction, extermination, annihilation; doom, crack of doom.

V. **perish,** fall, fall to the ground, tumble, topple; fall to pieces, break up, crumble, go to wrack and ruin; go by the board, be all over with, go to pieces, totter to its fall.

destroy, do (*or* make) away with, waste; nullify, annul, sacrifice, demolish, overturn, overthrow, overwhelm; upset, subvert, put an end to; do for [*colloq.*], undo, break down, cut down, pull down, dismantle, mow down, blow down; suppress, quash, put down, crush, blot out, efface, obliterate, cancel, erase, strike out, expunge, delete; dispel, dissipate, dissolve; consume.

smash, crash, quell, squash [*colloq.*], shatter, shiver, batter; tear (*or* pull, crush) to pieces; ruin, fell; sink, swamp, scuttle, wreck, shipwreck, engulf, submerged; lay in ruins, raze, level; deal destruction, lay waste, ravage, gut; devour, desolate, devastate, blast, exterminate, eradicate, annihilate.

Adj. **destructive,** subversive, cataclysmic, ruinous, incendiary, suicidal, deadly, all-destroying, all-devouring.

163. REPRODUCTION.—*N.* **reproduction,** renovation; restoration, etc., 660; renewal, revival, regeneration, revivification; apotheosis; resuscitation, reanimation, resurrection, reappearance.

V. **reproduce,** restore, etc., 660; revive, renovate, renew, repeat, regenerate, revivify, resuscitate, reanimate, refashion, multiply.

Adj. **reproductive,** resurgent, reappearing; renascent; Hydra-headed.

164. PRODUCER.—*N.* **producer,** originator, inventor, author,

47   CAUSATION   164–170

founder, generator, mover, architect, grower, raiser, introducer, creator; maker, etc. (*agent*), 690; prime mover.

165. DESTROYER.—*N.* destroyer, wrecker, annihilator; cankerworm, etc. (*bane*), 663; assassin, etc. (*killer*), 361; executioner, etc. (*punish*), 975; iconoclast, vandal, nihilist.

166. PATERNITY.—*N.* paternity, fathership, fatherhood; parentage.

parent, father, sire, dad [*colloq.*], papa, pater [*colloq.*], daddy [*colloq.*], paterfamilias; ancestor.

motherhood, maternity, mother, dam, mamma, mammy, mam [*colloq.*], matriarch, materfamilias.

stem, trunk, tree, stock, pedigree, house, lineage, line, family, race, tribe, clan; genealogy, family tree, descent, extraction, birth, ancestry; forefathers, forebears.

Adj. parental; paternal; maternal; ancestral, linear, patriarchal; racial.

167. POSTERITY.—*N.* posterity, progeny, breed, issue, offspring, brood, family, children, heirs; rising generation.

descendant, scion, offshoot, chip of the old block, heir, heiress, heir apparent, heir presumptive.

child, son, daughter, baby, kid [*colloq.*], imp, brat, cherub, tot, innocent, urchin, chit [*colloq.*]; infant, etc., 129.

lineage, line, straight descent, heredity, sonship, primogeniture.

Adj. hereditary, lineal.

filial, sonlike, daughterly, dutiful.

168. PRODUCTIVENESS.—*N.* productiveness, fecundity, fertility, luxuriance; multiplication, propagation, fructification.

V. fructify; generate, impregnate; teem, spawn, multiply; produce, etc., 161; conceive.

Adj. productive, prolific, copious; teeming, fertile, fruitful, plenteous, luxuriant; generative, life-giving; originative.

169. UNPRODUCTIVENESS.—*N.* unproductiveness, infertility, sterility, barrenness, unfruitfulness; unprofitableness, etc. (*inutility*), 645.

waste, desert, Sahara, wild, wilderness.

V. be unproductive; hang fire, flash in the pan, come to nothing.

Adj. unproductive, barren, unfertile, arid, sterile, unfruitful, fruitless, useless, fallow; unprofitable, etc. (*useless*), 645.

170. AGENCY.—*N.* agency, operation, force, function, office, maintenance, exercise, work, swing, play.

causation, impelling force; mediation, intervention, instrumentality; influence, etc., 175; action, etc. (*voluntary*), 680; method, procedure.

V. operate, work; act, perform, play, support, sustain, maintain, take effect, quicken, strike; have play, have free play; bring to bear upon.

Adj. operative, efficient, efficacious, practical, effectual; at work, on foot; acting, in operation, in force, in action.

171. ENERGY.—*N.* energy, force; intensity, vigor, strength, backbone [*colloq.*], vim [*colloq.*], mettle, pep [*slang*], fire, go [*colloq.*], high pressure; human dynamo.

activity, agitation, effervescence, ferment, fermentation, ebullition, stir, bustle; voluntary, energy, etc., 682; mental energy, etc., 604; resolution, stimulation; exertion, etc. (*effort*), 686.

V. give energy, energize, stimulate, strengthen, invigorate, kindle, excite, inflame, exert; sharpen, intensify.

Adj. energetic, strong, forcible, active, strenuous, brisk, forceful, mettlesome, enterprising, go-ahead [*colloq.*]; potent, etc. (*powerful*), 157; intense, keen, sharp, acute, incisive, trenchant.

poignant, virulent, caustic, corrosive, mordant; harsh, stringent, drastic.

172. INERTNESS.—*N.* inertness, inertia, inactivity, torpor, languor, quiescence, inaction, passivity, stagnation.

mental inertness; sloth; inexcitability, etc., 826; irresolution, indecision, vacillation; obstinacy, etc., 606.

V. be inert, hang fire, be inactive; smolder.

Adj. inert, inactive, passive; torpid, etc., 683; sluggish, logy, stagnant, dull, heavy, slack, tame, slow, lifeless, dead.

latent, dormant, smoldering, unexerted.

Adv. in suspense, in abeyance.

173. VIOLENCE.—*N.* violence, vehemence, might, impetuosity, boisterousness, disorder, effervescence, ebullition; turbulence, bluster; uproar, riot, row [*colloq.*], rumpus [*colloq.*].

ferocity, rage, fury, exasperation; malignity; severity, etc., 739; force, brute force; outrage.

fit, paroxysm, spasm, convulsion, throe; hysterics, passion, etc., 825.

outbreak, outburst, discharge, volley, explosion, blast, detonation, eruption, volcano, earthquake, thunderstorm.

fury, berserk, dragon, demon, tiger, wild beast; fire-eater [*colloq.*], etc. (*blusterer*), 887.

V. be violent; ferment, effervesce; rampage; run wild, run amuck, rage, roar, riot, storm; boil, boil over; fume, foam, ride roughshod, out-Herod Herod.

explode, go off, detonate, fulminate, let off, let fly, discharge, thunder, blow up, flash, flare, burst.

render violent; stir up, quicken, excite, incite, urge, lash, stimulate; irritate, inflame, kindle, foment, exasperate, convulse, infuriate, madden, lash into fury.

Adj. violent, vehement, acute, sharp; rough, tough [*colloq.*], rude, bluff, brusque, abrupt, boisterous, wild, impetuous, rampant; savage, fierce, ferocious.

turbulent, tumultuous; disorderly, raging, troublous, riotous, obstreperous, uproarious; frenzied, mad, insane; desperate, rash; infuriate, furious, frantic, outrageous; stormy, etc. (*wind*), 349.

fiery, flaming, scorching, hot, red-hot.

unbridled, unruly; headstrong, ungovernable, uncontrollable, irrepressible.

spasmodic, convulsive, explosive; detonating; volcanic, meteoric.

Adv. violently, amain; by storm, by force, by main force, with might and main, at one fell swoop; in desperation, with a vengeance.

174. MODERATION.—*N.* moderation; lenity, etc., 740; temperateness, temperance, gentleness, mildness, quiet, sobriety; mental calmness, composure, etc. (*inexcitability*), 826.

alleviation, assuagement, mitigation, relaxation, tranquilization, pacification.

moderator; sedative, lenitive, palliative; opiate, balm.

V. moderate, slacken, soften, mitigate, palliate, alleviate, allay, assuage, appease, temper, mollify, lull, soothe, compose, still, calm, cool, quiet, tranquilize, hush, quell, sober, pacify, smooth, deaden, smother; blunt, subdue, chasten; weaken, etc., 160; lessen, decrease; check, tame, curb, restrain.

Adj. moderate, gentle, mild; cool, sober, temperate, reasonable, lenient, measured; calm, unruffled, quiet, tranquil, still, halcyon; peaceful, peaceable, pacific.

Adv. in moderation, within bounds.

175. [Indirect Power] INFLUENCE.—*N.* influence; importance, etc., 642; weight, pressure, pull [*colloq. or slang*]; interest; preponderance, prevalence, sway; predominance, upper hand, ascendancy; dominance, reign; control, domination, hold; authority, power, potency, capability, spell, magic, magnetism.

footing; purchase, support; play, leverage, vantage ground, advantage.

patronage, protection, auspices; patron, etc. (*auxiliary*), 711; tower of strength.

V. be influential, carry weight, sway, bias, actuate, weight, tell; magnetize, work upon; take root, take hold; pervade, run through; be rife.

dominate, subject; predominate, outweigh; override, overbear; have *or* gain the upper hand, prevail.

lead, control, rule, manage, master, get control of, make one's influence felt; take the lead, pull the strings; turn the scale; set the fashion.

Adj. influential, effective, potent; important, etc., 642; weighty; prevalent, rife, rampant; dominant, predominant, authoritative, recognized.

Adv. with telling effect, with authority.

176. TENDENCY.—*N.* tendency, aptness, aptitude, proneness, proclivity, bent, turn, tone, bias, set, warp, leaning (*with* to *or* toward), predisposition, inclination, liability, propensity, susceptibility; quality, nature, temperament; idiosyncrasy; cast, vein, grain, humor, mood, trend, drift.

V. tend, contribute, conduce, lead, influence, dispose, incline, verge, bend to, warp, turn, work toward, gravitate toward, trend; affect; carry, redound to, bid fair to; promote, etc. (*aid*), 707.

Adj. tending; conducive, working toward, in a fair way to, likely to, calculated to; liable, etc., 177; subservient, instrumental, useful; subsidiary, accessory.

177. LIABILITY.—*N.* liability, susceptibility; possibility, contingency.

V. be liable, incur, lay oneself open to, be subjected to, run the chance, stand a chance; lie under, expose oneself to, open a door to.

Adj. liable, subject, in danger, open to, exposed to; answerable, responsible, accountable, amenable; apt to; dependent on.

contingent, incidental, possible, on the cards, within range of, at the mercy of.

178. CONCURRENCE.—*N.* concurrence, co-operation, collaboration; conformity, agreement, accord; alliance; complicity, collusion, partnership, union.

V. concur, conduce, conspire, contribute; agree, unite, harmonize, combine; hang *or* pull together, co-operate; keep pace with, run parallel.

Adj. concurrent, conformable, joint, co-operative, concordant, harmonious, in alliance with, of one mind, at one with.

179. COUNTERACTION.—*N.* counteraction, opposition; contrariety, contradiction; antagonism, polarity; clashing, collision, interference, resistance, friction; reaction, recoil; counterblast, neutralization, check, hindrance; repression, restraint.

V. counteract, clash, cross, interfere with, conflict with; contravene; jostle; militate against, stultify, antagonize, frustrate, oppose, overcome, overpower, withstand, resist, impede, hinder, repress, restrain; recoil, react.

neutralize, offset, undo, cancel; counterpoise, counterbalance.
Adj. antagonistic, conflicting, reactionary; contrary, etc., 14.
Adv. although, notwithstanding; in spite of; against.

CLASS II

WORDS RELATING TO SPACE

I. SPACE IN GENERAL

180. [Indefinite space] **SPACE.**—*N.* space, extension, extent, proportions, expanse, stretch; room, accommodation, capacity; scope, compass, range, latitude, field; sweep, play, swing; spread, expansion.

elbowroom, leeway, seaway, headway; margin; sphere, arena.

open space, free space, void, waste, desert, wild, wilderness; moor, down, downs, upland, moorland; prairie, steppe, llano, campagna.

unlimited space; heavens, ether, infinity; world, wide world.

Adj. spacious, roomy, extensive, extended, expansive, capacious, ample; widespread, vast, world-wide, wide, far-flung, boundless, limitless, endless, infinite; shoreless, trackless, pathless.

Adv. extensively; by and large; everywhere, far and near (*or* wide), here, there, and everywhere; from pole to pole, from the four corners of the earth, from all points of the compass; to the four winds, to the uttermost parts of the earth.

181. [Definite space] **REGION.**—*N.* region, sphere, ground, soil, area, realm, hemisphere, quarter, orb, circuit, circle; pale, etc. (*limit*), 233; tract, clearing; domain.

county, shire, canton, province, department, parish, diocese, township, commune, ward, bailiwick; principality, duchy, palatinate, archduchy, dukedom, dominion, colony, commonwealth, territory, country; fatherland, motherland; kingdom, empire.

precinct, arena, district, beat; patch, plot, inclosure, close, enclave, field, paddock, etc. (*inclosure*), 232; street.

clime, climate, zone, meridian, latitude.

Adj. territorial, provincial, regional, insular; local, parochial.

182. [Limited space] **PLACE.**—*N.* place, spot, whereabouts, point; niche, nook, corner, hole, pigeonhole, etc. (*receptacle*), 191; compartment; premises, courtyard, square, place, piazza, plaza, forum; hamlet, village, etc. (*abode*), 189; pen, etc. (*inclosure*), 232; location, site, locality, situation.

Adv. somewhere, in some place, here and there, in various places.

183. SITUATION.—*N.* situation, position, locality, latitude and longitude; footing, status, standing; standpoint; stage; aspect, attitude, posture, pose.

place, site; station, post, seat, whereabouts; environment, ground; bearings, direction, spot, etc. (*limited space*), 182.

topography, geography; map, plan, chart.

V. be situated, be situate, be located; lie; have its seat in.

Adj. situate, situated; local, topical, topographical.

Adv. hereabouts, thereabouts, whereabouts; in place, here, there.

184. LOCATION.—*N.* location, situation; lodgment; stowage; packing, lading; establishment, settlement, installation; insertion, etc., 300.

anchorage, roadstead, mooring.

settlement, plantation, colony; habitation, etc. (*abode*), 189.

domestication; colonization; naturalization.

V. place, situate, locate, localize, put, lay, set, seat; station, park (as, *an automobile*), lodge, quarter, post, install; house, stow, pack; load, lade; establish, fix, root; graft; plant, etc. (*insert*), 300; deposit, store, store away.

billet on, quarter upon, saddle with.

settle, domesticate, colonize, found, people; take root, strike root; anchor, cast anchor, moor, tether, picket; settle down; take up one's abode, establish *or* locate oneself; keep house; squat, burrow, get a footing; bivouac, encamp, pitch one's tent; inhabit, etc., 186.

Adj. placed; situate, ensconced, imbedded, rooted; moored, at anchor.

185. DISPLACEMENT.—*N.* displacement, misplacement, dislocation, derangement, transposition.

ejection, expulsion, eviction; exile, banishment, ostracism.

removal, etc. (*transference*), 270; transshipment, moving, shift.

V. displace, dislodge, disestablish; misplace, unseat, disturb; set aside, remove, take away, cart away, draft off; exile, etc. (*seclude*), 893.

unload, empty, etc. (*eject*), 297; transfer, etc., 270; dispel.

vacate, depart, evacuate.

Adj. displaced; unplaced, unhoused, unsettled; houseless, homeless, out of place; out of a situation.

186. PRESENCE.—*N.* presence, attendance; occupancy, occupation; ubiquity, omnipresence.

permeation, pervasion; diffusion.

bystander, etc. (*spectator*), 444.

V. be present, make one of; look on, attend, remain; find *or* present oneself; lie, stand.

inhabit, occupy, dwell, reside; stay, sojourn; live, abide; lodge, tenant; people.

frequent, resort to, haunt; revisit.

pervade, permeate; overspread; fill, run through.

Adj. present; situate; moored, at anchor; resident, domiciled; ubiquitous, omnipresent.

peopled, inhabited, populous.

Adv. here, there, everywhere; aboard, on board, at home, afield; on the spot; in presence of, before.

187. ABSENCE.—*N.* absence, nonresidence, absenteeism; nonattendance, cut [*colloq.*]; alibi.

emptiness; void, vacuum, vacancy.

interval, hiatus, interruption; interregnum.

truant, absentee.

V. be absent; keep away, play truant, absent oneself, stay away, hold aloof.

withdraw, retreat, retire; go away.

Adj. absent, not present, away, nonresident, gone, from home; missing; lost; wanting; omitted.

empty, void; vacant, vacuous, blank; untenanted, unoccupied, uninhabited, tenantless; desert, deserted, uninhabitable.

Adv. without, minus, nowhere; elsewhere; in default of; sans.

188. INHABITANT.—*N.* inhabitant; resident, dweller, in-dweller, addressee, occupier, occupant, householder; inmate; tenant, incumbent; settler, squatter, backwoodsman, planter, habitant, colonist; islander; denizen, citizen; burgher, townsman, burgess; villager; cottager, cotter; boarder, lodger.

native, aborigine, aboriginal.

people, etc. (*mankind*), 372; population; colony, settlement; household.

V. inhabit, dwell, etc., 186.

Adj. indigenous, native, domestic; domiciled; naturalized; vernacular.

189. HABITATION.—*N.* habitation, abode, dwelling, lodging, domicile, residence, address, berth, housing, quarters, headquarters.

home, fatherland, motherland, country; homestead, hearth, chimney corner; roof, household, housing, native soil, native land.

county, parish, etc. (*region*), 181.

retreat, haunt, habitat, resort; nest, arbor, bower, grotto; lair, den, cave, hole, hiding place, cell, sanctum sanctorum, eyrie, rookery, hive; covert, perch, roost.

anchorage, roadstead, roads; dock, basin, wharf, quay, port, harbor.

camp, bivouac, encampment, cantonment, barracks, quarters; tent, wigwam, tepee; igloo.

farm, farmhouse, grange.

cot, cabin, hut, hovel; shanty, dugout, chalet, log cabin, log house; shack [*colloq*], shed, booth, stall, pen, fold; stable, barn; kennel, sty, cote, dovecote, coop, hutch; cowhouse, cowshed.

house, mansion, place, villa, cottage, lodge, hermitage, rotunda, tower, château, castle, pavilion, hotel, court, manor house, hall, palace; kiosk, bungalow, country seat; apartment (*or* brownstone, duplex, frame, shingle, flat, tenement) house; three-decker; building, buildings.

hamlet, village, dorp [Dutch], rancho [Sp. Amer.].

town, borough, city, capital, metropolis; suburb; province, country; county town, county seat.

street, place, terrace, parade, esplanade, boardwalk, embankment, road, row, lane, alley, court, quadrangle, close, yard, passage.

square, polygon, circus, crescent, block, arcade, colonnade, cloister; market place.

assembly room, auditorium, concert hall, armory, gymnasium; cathedral, church, chapel, meetinghouse, etc. (*temple*), 1000; parliament, etc. (*council*), 696.

inn, hotel, tavern, caravansary, alehouse, saloon, club, clubhouse; grill room, chophouse, coffeehouse, eating house; canteen, restaurant, buffet, café, cabaret, sanatorium, health resort, sanitarium; spa, watering place.

V. inhabit, etc., 186; take up one's abode, etc. (*locate oneself*), 184.

Adj. urban, metropolitan; cosmopolitan; suburban.

provincial, rural, rustic, country, countrified.

190. [Things contained] CONTENTS.—*N.* contents; cargo, lading, freight, shipment, load, bale, burden; cartload, shipload; stuffing.

V. load, lade, ship, pile, fill, stuff.

191. RECEPTACLE.—*N.* receptacle, container; inclosure, etc., 232; recipient, receiver; compartment, cell; hole, corner, niche, recess, nook; crypt; stall; pigeonhole; mouth.

stomach, paunch, belly, crop, craw, maw.

bag, sack, wallet, pocket, pouch; purse; knapsack, haversack, satchel, reticule; saddlebags; portfolio; valise, grip [*colloq.*], suitcase, handbag, schoolbag, brief case, traveling bag, Gladstone bag.

case, chest, box, coffer, caddy, casket; reliquary, shrine; caisson; desk, bureau; trunk, portmanteau, bandbox.

vessel, utensil; vase, canister, jar; basket, pannier, hamper; crate; creel; cradle, bassinet.

For liquids: cistern, reservoir; vat, caldron, barrel, cask, keg, tun, butt, firkin, tub; bottle, jar, decanter, ewer, carafe, canteen, flagon; demijohn; flask, vial, phial; cruet, caster; urn, percolator, coffeepot, teapot, samovar; bucket, pail; pot, tankard, jug, pitcher, mug, porringer; receiver, retort, alembic, crucible; can, kettle; bowl, basin; punch bowl, cup, goblet, beaker, chalice, tumbler, glass.

plate, platter, dish, tray, waiter, salver.

ladle, dipper; shovel, trowel, spatula.

cupboard, closet; locker, bin; buffet, sideboard; drawer, chest of drawers, chiffonier; till, safe; bookcase, cabinet.

chamber, apartment, room, cabin; office, court, hall, suite of rooms, apartment, flat, tenement; parlor, living (*or* sitting, drawing, reception) room; best room [*colloq.*]; boudoir; sanctum; bedroom, dormitory; refectory, dining room; nursery, schoolroom; library, study; studio; smoking room, den.

attic, loft, garret; cellar, vault, hold, cockpit; cubbyhole; basement, kitchen, pantry, scullery; storeroom, lumber room; dairy, laundry; garage; hangar; outhouse, penthouse; lean-to, shed.

portico, porch, stoop, veranda, piazza.

bower, arbor, summerhouse; grotto; conservatory, greenhouse.

II. DIMENSIONS

192. SIZE.—*N.* size, dimensions, proportions; magnitude, bulk, volume; largeness, greatness; expanse, amplitude, mass; capacity; tonnage; cordage; caliber.

lump, block, mass; clod, mountain, mound; heap, etc. (*assemblage*), 72.

corpulence, obesity, plumpness.

immensity, hugeness, monstrosity, enormity.

giant, Titan, Hercules, Gargantua; monster, mammoth, whale, behemoth, leviathan, elephant, jumbo [*colloq.*]; colossus.

V. be large, become large, etc. (*expand*), 194.

Adj. large, big, great, considerable, bulky, voluminous, ample, massive; capacious, comprehensive, spacious; mighty, towering.

stout, corpulent, fat, plump, chubby; portly, burly, brawny, fleshy.

unwieldy, hulky, hulking, lumpish, overgrown; puffy, swollen, bloated.

huge, immense, enormous, titanic, mighty; vast; stupendous; monster, monstrous; gigantic; elephantine, mammoth; giant, colossal, cyclopean, Gargantuan.

193. LITTLENESS.—*N.* littleness, smallness; epitome; microcosm; vanishing point.

dwarf, pygmy, midget; Lilliputian, elf; doll, puppet, manikin; Tom Thumb.

mite, insect, arthropod, ephemerid, ephemera, bug [*pop.*], larva.
atom, monad, animalcule, animalculum (*pl.* animalcula), molecule, microbe, germ, micro-organism, bacterium (*pl.* bacteria), amoeba.

particle, speck, dot, mote; scrap; spark; scintilla; fragment, fraction; grain, powder, dust; minutiæ, etc. (*unimportance*), 643.

V. belittle, lie in a nutshell; become small, decrease; contract, etc., 195.

Adj. little, small, minute, diminutive, microscopic; inconsiderable, petty; limited, cramped; puny, runty, tiny, wee [*colloq.*], elfin, miniature, pocket; undersized, stunted, dwarf, dwarfed, dwarfish, pygmy; Lilliputian; invisible, infinitesimal, homeopathic.

Adv. in a small compass, in a nutshell; on a small scale.

194. EXPANSION.—*N.* expansion, dilation; growth, increase, enlargement, amplification; extension, augmentation, aggrandizement; spread, increment, development, swell, dilatation; obesity, corpulence; dropsy, swelling, distension, puffiness, inflation.

V. enlarge, expand, widen, extend, grow, increase, swell, fill out; dilate, stretch, spread; wax; bud, shoot, sprout, germinate, put forth, open, burst forth; outgrow; overrun.

spread, augment, aggrandize; distend, develop, amplify, spread out, widen, magnify; inflate, blow up; stuff, fatten, pad, cram, bloat; exaggerate.

Adj. **expanded,** larger; swollen, expansive, widespread, overgrown, exaggerated, bloated, fat, tumid, dropsical; corpulent, obese; puffy, distend, bulbous; full-blown, full-grown; big, etc., 192.

195. CONTRACTION.—*N.* **contraction,** reduction, diminution; decrease, etc., 36; lessening, shrinking; atrophy; emaciation, attenuation.

compression, condensation, constraint, compactness; compendium, abstract, epitome; strangulation; astringency.

V. **decrease,** lessen, grow less, dwindle, shrink, contract, narrow, shrivel, collapse, wither, fall away, waste, wane, ebb.

diminish, boil down; deflate, exhaust, empty; constrict, condense, compress, squeeze, crush; pinch, tighten, strangle; cramp; dwarf; shorten, etc., 201; circumscribe, limit, bound, confine.

pare, reduce; attenuate; rub down, scrape, file, grind, chip, shave, shear.

Adj. **contracting,** astringent; shrunk, shrunken, contracted; strangulated; wizened; stunted; waning; compact.

196. DISTANCE.—*N.* **distance,** remoteness; space, etc., 180; far cry to; elongation; drift, offing, background; remote region; reach, span.

outpost, outskirt; horizon, skyline; foreign parts, antipodes.

V. **be distant;** extend to, stretch to, reach to, spread to, stretch away to; range, outreach.

Adj. **distant,** far, far off, far away, remote; telescopic; yon, yonder; ulterior; transatlantic, transalpine; ultramundane, antipodean; inaccessible, out-of-the-way; unapproachable.

Adv. **far off,** far away, afar, afar off; away; beyond range, aloof; wide of, clear of; abroad, yonder, farther, further, beyond; far and wide, from pole to pole; out of range, out of hearing.

apart, asunder; at arm's length.

197. NEARNESS.—*N.* **nearness,** proximity, propinquity; vicinity, vicinage, neighborhood, contiguity, etc., 199.

short distance, short cut; earshot, close quarters, range, stone's throw; gunshot, hair's breadth, span.

purlieus, neighborhood, vicinage, environs, suburbs, confines. **bystander,** spectator; neighbor.

approach, approximation, access; convergence, meeting.

V. **be near,** adjoin, abut, neighbor, trench on; border upon, verge upon; approximate; stand by, hang about; cling to, clasp, hug; huddle; hover over.

bring *or* draw near; converge, etc., 290; crowd, pack, huddle.

Adj. **near,** nigh, close (*or* near) at hand, close, neighboring, bordering upon, contiguous, adjacent, adjoining; proximate, approximate; at hand, handy; intimate.

Adv. **near,** nigh, hard by, close to, close upon; hard upon; at the point of; next door to; within reach (*or* call, hearing, earshot, range); on the verge of; in sight of; at close quarters; beside, alongside, side by side; in juxtaposition; at the heels of.

about; thereabouts; roughly, in round numbers; approximately, as good as, well-nigh.

198. INTERVAL.—*N.* **interval,** space; separation, division; hiatus, cæsura; interruption; interregnum; interstice.

parenthesis; void, vacuum; incompleteness, deficiency.

cleft, break, gap, opening; hole, puncture; chasm, mesh, crevice, chink, cranny, crack, slit, fissure, rift, fault, flaw, breach, fracture, rent, gash, cut.

gorge, defile, pass, ravine, canyon, crevasse; abyss, abysm; gulf; inlet, strait; furrow, etc., 259; gully, gulch, notch.

V. **gape,** yawn; separate, etc., 44.

199. CONTACT.—*N.* **contact,** contiguity, contiguousness, proximity, apposition, abuttal, abutment, juxtaposition, touching, meeting; conjunction, adhesion, etc., 46.

borderland; frontier, etc. (*limit*), 233.

V. **adjoin,** join, abut on, neighbor, border, march with; graze, touch, meet; coincide; coexist; adhere, etc., 46.

Adj. **contiguous,** touching, in contact, conterminous, end to end; close, etc. (*near*), 197.

200. [Linear Dimensions] **LENGTH.**—*N.* **length,** longitude, extent, span; mileage.

line, bar, rule, stripe, streak.

lengthening, prolongation, production, protraction; tension, extension.

Measures of length: line, nail, inch, hand, palm, foot, cubit, yard, ell, fathom, rood, pole, furlong, mile, knot, league; chain; meter, kilometer, centimeter, etc. pedometer, odometer, odograph, viameter, log [*naut.*], speedometer, telemeter, scale.

V. **be long,** stretch out, sprawl; extend to, reach to, stretch to.

lengthen, let out, extend, elongate; stretch; prolong, protract; draw out, spin out.

Adj. **long,** elongate, lengthy, outstretched, extended; lengthened, interminable.

linear, lineal; longitudinal.

lanky, lank, slab-sided [*slang*], rangy; tall; long-limbed.

Adv. **lengthwise,** at length, longitudinally, along; tandem; in a line; from end to end, from stem to stern, from head to foot, from top to toe; fore and aft; over all.

201. SHORTNESS.—*N.* **shortness,** brevity, littleness, etc., 193; a span.

abridgment, shortening, abbreviation, retrenchment, curtailment, epitomization, condensation; reduction, etc. (*contraction*), 195; epitome, etc. (*compendium*), 596.

elision, ellipsis; conciseness, brevity.

V. **shorten,** curtail, retrench, abridge, abbreviate; take in, reduce; compress, contract; epitomize, abstract, summarize, condense; cut, pare down, clip, dock, lop, prune, shear, shave, mow, crop, stunt; nip, check the growth of, foreshorten [*drawing*].

Adj. **short,** brief, curt; compendious, compact; stubby, pudgy, squatty; stumpy [*colloq.*], thickset, chunky, scrub, stocky, squat, dumpy; pug, turned up; little, etc., 193; concise, etc., 572; summary.

202. BREADTH, THICKNESS.—*N.* **breadth,** width, latitude, amplitude.

diameter, bore, caliber; radius.

thickness; corpulence, etc. (*size*), 192; expansion, dilatation.

V. **expand,** etc., 194; thicken, widen.

Adj. **broad,** wide, ample, extended, outspread, outstretched.

thick, dumpy, squat, thickset, stubby, etc., 201.

203. NARROWNESS, THINNESS.—*N.* **narrowness,** slenderness; closeness.

line; hair's breadth.

thinness, tenuity; leanness, lankiness, emaciation.

shaving; strip, etc. (*filament*), 205; thread, skeleton, shadow, scrag, mere skin and bone.

narrowing, tapering; contraction, etc., 195.

V. **narrow,** taper; contract, etc., 195.

Adj. **narrow,** close; slender, thin, fine, delicate, threadlike, finespun, taper, slim; scant, scanty, spare; contracted.

lean, emaciated, skinny, scrawny, meager, gaunt, rawboned, lank, lanky, weedy [*colloq.*]; starved, starveling; attenuated, shriveled, pinched, spindle-legged, spindle-shanked, spindling; worn to a shadow; hatchet-faced; lantern-jawed.

204. LAYER.—*N.* **layer,** stratum, course, bed, coping, substratum, floor, stage, story, tier.

leaf, sheet, flake, scale, coat, peel, membrane, film, slice, shaving, wafer.

stratification, lamination, foliation; scaliness.

V. **slice,** shave, pare, peel.

plate, coat, veneer; cover, etc., 223.

Adj. scaly, filmy, membranous, flaky, foliated, stratified.

205. FILAMENT.—*N.* filament, line; fiber, vein, hair, cobweb, capillary, strand, tendril, gossamer.

thread, yarn, packthread, cotton.

string, twine, twist, cord, rope, tape, ribbon, wire.

strip, shred, slip, band, fillet, lath, splinter.

Adj. fibrous, threadlike, wiry, stringy, ropy; capillary, wire-drawn; hairy, etc. (*rough*), 256.

206. HEIGHT.—*N.* height, altitude, elevation, eminence, pitch; loftiness, sublimity.

tallness, stature; prominence, etc., 250; apex, zenith, culmination.

colossus, etc. (*size*), 192; giant.

height, mount, mountain, hill; headland, foreland, promontory; ridge, dune, rising ground, down, uplands, highlands; knoll, hummock, hillock, mound; bluff, cliff, peak.

tower, pillar, column, obelisk, monument, belfry, steeple, spire, minaret, campanile, turret, dome, cupola; pyramid, pagoda.

pole, pikestaff, Maypole, flagstaff; mast, mainmast, topmast.

high water; high (*or* flood, spring) tide.

V. tower, soar, hover; cap, culminate; overhang, surmount, rise above, command, overtop, rise, ascend.

heighten, uprear, uplift, upraise, elevate.

Adj. high, elevated, eminent, exalted, lofty, sublime; tall, gigantic, big, colossal; towering, beetling, soaring, elevated; higher, superior, upper, supernal; highest, etc. (*topmost*), 210.

lanky, etc. (*thin*), 203.

upland, hilly, mountainous, alpine, heaven-kissing, cloud-capped.

overhanging, impending, incumbent, overlying; superimposed.

Adv. on high, high up, aloft, up, above, overhead; in the clouds.

207. LOWNESS.—*N.* lowness, levelness, flatness; debasement, prostration; depression, hollow; lowlands.

basement, cellar, vault, crypt, cavern; hold; base, etc., 211.

low water, low (*or* ebb, neap) tide.

V. be low, lie low, underlie; crouch, wallow, grovel; lower, etc. (*depress*), 308.

Adj. low, low-lying, level; flat; crouched, squat, prostrate, depressed, debased.

lower, inferior, under, nether.

lowest, nethermost, lowermost.

Adv. under, beneath, underneath, below, down, downward; underfoot, underground; downstairs, belowstairs; at a low ebb; below par.

208. DEPTH.—*N.* depth, profundity, depression, hollow.

pit, shaft, well, crater, chasm, crevasse, deep, abyss, bowels of the earth, bottomless pit.

soundings, draft, submersion, plunge, dive; plummet, lead.

V. deepen, sink, excavate, mine, sap, dig, burrow.

sound, heave the lead, take soundings.

Adj. deep, deep-seated, profound, buried; sunk, submerged, subaqueous, submarine, subterranean, underground.

bottomless, fathomless, unfathomed, unfathomable, abysmal, down-reaching, yawning.

Adv. out of one's depth, beyond one's depth; over head and ears.

209. SHALLOWNESS.—*N.* shallowness, superficiality; shoals.

Adj. shallow, slight, superficial; skin-deep, ankle-deep, knee-deep, shoal.

210. SUMMIT.—*N.* summit, top, vertex, apex, zenith, pinnacle, acme, crown; height, pitch, maximum; goal, consummation; climax, turning point; culmination; turn of the tide, fountainhead.

tip, tiptop; crest, crow's-nest, cap, peak; brow, head.

architrave, frieze, cornice, coping, coping stone, capital, headpiece, capstone, pediment, entablature; attic, loft, garret, housetop, upper story, roof (*covering*), 223.

V. crown, top, cap, crest, surmount, overtop; culminate.

Adj. highest (high, etc., 206), top, topmost, overmost, uppermost, tiptop; capital, head, polar; supreme, supernal.

211. Base.—*N.* base, basement; plinth, dado, wainscot; baseboard, mopboard; bedrock, hardpan; foundation, substructure, substratum, ground, earth, pavement, floor, paving; footing, groundwork, basis.

bottom, nadir, foot, sole, toe, hoof, root; keel.

Adj. bottom, undermost, nethermost; fundamental; founded on, based on.

212. VERTICALITY.—*N.* verticality, perpendicularity, erectness.

cliff, steep, crag, bluff, palisades; wall, precipice.

V. be vertical, stand erect *or* upright, stick up, cock up.

render vertical, set up, raise up, erect, rear, raise, pitch.

Adj. vertical; upright, erect, perpendicular, plumb, bolt upright.

Adv. on end; endwise; at right angles.

213. HORIZONTALITY.—*N.* horizontality; flatness; level, plane, stratum.

recumbency; lying down, reclination, proneness, supination, prostration.

V. be horizontal, lie, recline, lie flat; sprawl, loll.

render horizontal, lay, level, flatten, even, raze, smooth, align.

prostrate, knock down, floor, fell, ground, cut (*or* hew) down, mow down.

Adj. horizontal, level, even, plane, flush; flat, smooth.
recumbent, prone, supine, prostrate.
Adv. on one's back; on all fours; on its beam ends.

214. PENDENCY.—*N.* pendency, dependency; suspension, hanging.

pendant, drop, eardrop, tassel, lobe; tail, train, queue, pigtail; pendulum.

chandelier, gaselier.

V. be pendent; hang, depend, swing, dangle, lower, droop; flap, trail, beetle, jut, overhang.

suspend, hang, sling, hook up, hitch, fasten to, append.

Adj. pendent, pendulous, hanging; dependent; beetling, jutting over, overhanging; lowering; suspended.

215. SUPPORT.—*N.* support, ground, foundation, base, basis, fulcrum, purchase, footing, hold; stage, platform; rest, resting place; groundwork, substratum; floor.

supporter; aid, etc., 707; prop, truss, stand, stalk; bracket; ledge, shelf, table, trestle; rung, round; staff, stick, crook, crutch.

post, pillar, column, pediment, pedestal; caryatid; buttress, jamb, mullion, stile, abutment.
frame, framework; scaffold, skeleton, beam, rafter, girder, lintel, joist; keystone; arch; mainstay.
seat, throne, dais; divan, ottoman, sofa, davenport, couch, daybed; stall; chair, wing chair, armchair, easy chair, elbowchair, rocking chair, Morris chair; settee, form, bench; saddle, sidesaddle, pillion; packsaddle; pommel, horn.
stool, hassock, footstool.
bed, bedstead, four-poster; pallet; cot; hammock, shakedown; crib, trundle bed, cradle; litter, stretcher; bunk, berth; mat, rug, cushion; lap.

V. support, bear, carry, hold, sustain, shoulder; hold up, back up, bolster up, shore up, uphold, brace, truss, stay, prop; maintain; aid, etc., 707.

Adj. supporting, supported; fundamental.

216. PARALLELISM.—*N.* parallelism, equidistance, concentricity.

V. be parallel, parallel, equal.

Adj. parallel, coextensive, equidistant; collateral, concentric, concurrent; abreast, equal, even, alongside.

Adv. alongside, abreast, broadside on.

217. OBLIQUITY.—*N.* obliquity, inclination, incline, slope, slant; leaning, tilt; bias, diagonal, zigzag, list, twist, sag, cant, lurch; distortion, etc., 243; bend, curve.

acclivity, steepness; rise, ascent, pitch, grade, rising ground, hill, bank; cliff, precipice, etc. (*vertical*), 212; shelving beach; declivity, dip, fall.

V. be oblique; slope, slant, lean, cant, incline, shelve, decline, descend, bend; heel over, careen; sag, slouch, sidle, skid.

render oblique; sway, bias; slope, slant, tilt; incline, bend, crook; distort, etc., 243; zigzag, stagger [*mech.*].

Adj. **oblique**, inclined; sloping, tilted; askew, asquint, bias, aslant, diagonal, transverse, athwart; indirect, wry, awry, crooked; sinuous, zigzag; knock-kneed, etc. (*distorted*), 243.

uphill, rising, ascending; steep, abrupt, precipitous.

downhill, falling, descending; declining, shelving, declivitous.

Adv. **obliquely**; on one side, askew, askance, awry, edgewise, at an angle; sidelong, sidewise, slantwise.

218. INVERSION.—*N.* **inversion**, subversion, reversion; opposition, polarity; contrariety, contradiction, reversal, transposition, transposal; turn of the tide; overturn, revolution; somersault; revulsion.

V. **be inverted**, turn (*or* go, wheel) about, turn (*or* tilt, topple) over; capsize, turn turtle.

invert, subvert; reverse; upturn, overturn, upset, overset, turn topsy-turvy; transpose.

Adj. **inverted**, wrong side out (*or* up); inside out, upside down; on one's head, topsy-turvy.

inverse; reverse, etc. (*contrary*), 14; opposite.

Adv. **inversely**, conversely; heels over head, head over heels.

219. CROSSING.—*N.* **crossing**; intersection, grade crossing.

network, reticulation; net, web, mesh, netting, lace, plait; sieve, screen; wicker; mat, matting; trellis, lattice, grating, grille, gridiron, tracery, fretwork, filigree; entanglement.

crucifix, cross, rood, crisscross.

V. **cross**, intersect, interlace, intertwine, intertwist, interweave, interlink, crisscross; twine, entwine, weave, twist, wreathe; dovetail, mortise, splice, link.

plait, pleat, plat, braid; entangle, ravel; net, knot.

Adj. **crossed**, matted, transverse, intersected, cross; crossshaped, cruciform; netlike, retiform, latticed, grated, barred, streaked.

Adv. **cross**, athwart, thwart, transversely; at grade; crosswise, across.

220. EXTERIORITY.—*N.* **exteriority**; outside, exterior; surface, superficies; skin, covering; face, facet.

V. **be exterior**, lie around, environ, encircle.

externalize, objectify, visualize, envisage, actualize.

Adj. **exterior**, external, extraneous; outer, outermost; outward, outlying, outside, outdoor.

outstanding; extrinsic, incidental: superficial, skin-deep.

Adv. **externally**, out, without, over, outwards, out of doors, in the open air.

221. INTERIORITY.—*N.* interiority; inside, interior; interspace, subsoil.

contents, etc., 190; substance, pith, marrow; heart, bosom, breast; recesses, innermost recesses; cave, etc. (*concavity*), 252.

inmate, intern, inhabitant, etc., 188.

V. inclose, etc. (*circumscribe*), 229; intern; embed, etc. (*insert*), 300; place within, keep within.

Adj. interior, internal; inner, intimate, inside, inward, inmost, innermost; deep-seated, inherent, ingrained, innate, inborn, inbred, intrinsic.

home, inland, domestic, family, indoor.

Adv. internally; inwards, within, indoors, withindoors; at home.

222. CENTRALITY.—*N.* centrality; centralization, concentration; center; middle, midst; focus; center of gravity.

core, kernel, nucleus; heart, pole, axis, bull's-eye, nave, hub; marrow, pith; metropolis.

V. centralize, concentrate; bring to a focus; converge, etc., 290.

Adj. central; middle, axial, pivotal, nuclear, focal, concentric; middlemost; metropolitan.

223. COVERING.—*N.* covering, cover; canopy, awning, tent, marquee, wigwam, tepee; umbrella, parasol, sunshade; veil; shield, etc. (*defense*), 717.

roof, ceiling, thatch, tiles, slates, leads, shingles: dome, cupola.

coverlet, counterpane, sheet, quilt, blanket, rug; eiderdown quilt, comforter; pillowcase, pillowslip; linoleum, oilcloth; tarpaulin.

integument: skin, pellicle, fleece, fur, leather, lambskin, sable, beaver, ermine, hide, coat, buff, pelt, peltry [*collective noun*]; cuticle, cutis, epidermis; clothing, etc., 225

peel, rind, crust, bark, husk, shell.

sheath, sheathing, capsule, pod, casing, case, wrapping, wrapper; envelope; cornhusk, corn shuck.

veneer, facing; scale, layer; incrustation, coating, paint, stain, varnish, enamel, whitewash, plaster, stucco.

V. cover, superimpose, overlay, overspread; wrap, incase, face, case, veneer, paper; clapboard, shingle; conceal, etc., 528.

coat, paint, stain, varnish, incrust, crust, cement, stucco, plaster; smear, daub, besmear, bedaub; gild, plate, japan, lacquer, enamel, whitewash.

Adj. covered, hooded, cowled, armored, armor-plated; ironclad; scaly.

224. LINING.—*N.* lining, coating, inner coating; filling, stuffing, wadding, padding; facing, bushing; sheathing.

V. line, stuff, incrust, wad, pad, fill, face, ceil, bush, wainscot, sheathe.

225. CLOTHING.—*N.* clothing, dress; covering, etc., 223; raiment, costume, attire, toilet, habiliment; vesture, vestment;

garment, garb, wardrobe, apparel, wearing apparel, clothes, finery, etc. (*ornament*), 847.

outfit, equipment, trousseau; uniform, khaki; livery, gear, harness, turnout, accouterment, caparison, suit, trappings.

dishabille, undress, tea gown, wrapper, negligee, dressing gown, kimono; rags, tatters, old clothes.

robe, habit, gown, dress, frock; blouse, middy blouse, waist, shirtwaist; suit; coat: toga, tunic, smock.

dress suit, dress clothes, evening dress, dinner coat, dinner jacket; Tuxedo [*colloq.*]; glad rags [*slang*].

cloak, mantle, shawl, veil; cape, plaid [Scot.], muffler, overcoat, greatcoat; oilskins, slicker, mackintosh, waterproof, ulster; poncho; pea-jacket; sweater, blazer, cardigan, jersey; Mackinaw coat.

jacket, vest, waistcoat; gaberdine.

skirt, petticoat, kilt; bloomers.

trousers, breeches, pants [*colloq.*]; overalls; shorts; tights; drawers; knickers [*colloq.*].

headdress, headgear, coiffure [F.], crush hat, opera hat; tam-o'-shanter, topee [India], sombrero; cap, hat, bonnet, panama, leghorn; derby; nightcap, skullcap; hood, coif; wimple: snood; crown, etc., 247; wig, front, peruke, periwig; turban, fez, tarboosh, shako, busby, bearskin; kepi, helmet; mask, domino.

body clothes, underclothing, linen; shirt, undervest, undershirt; smock, shift, chemise; nightgown, nightshirt, pajamas; bedgown.

tie, neckerchief, neckcloth; ruff, collar, cravat, stock, handkerchief, scarf; bib, tucker; boa; girdle, cummerbund [India].

shoe, Oxford shoe, Oxford tie, pump, sneakers, boot, slipper, moccasin, sandal, galosh, arctic, overshoe, rubber; patten, clog; snowshoes, ski.

stocking, hose, sock; hosiery.

glove, gauntlet; mitten, mitt.

V. clothe, array, dress, accouter, rig, fit out, deck, drape, robe, enrobe, gown, attire, apparel, equip; harness, caparison; cover, wrap, shroud, swathe, swaddle.

wear; don; put on, slip on; mantle.

Adj. clothed, clad, invested, habited.

226. DIVESTMENT.—*N.* divestment; nudity, bareness, nakedness: dishabille, etc., 225.

baldness, hairlessness.

V. divest, uncover, expose, lay open, lay bare, denude, bare, strip; undress, disrobe, dismantle; put off, take off, doff.

peel, bare, slough, excoriate, skin, scalp, flay, bark, husk.

Adj. naked, nude, bare, stark-naked, exposed; undressed, undraped, unclad, ungarmented, unclothed.

bald, hairless, beardless; shaven, clean-shaven.

227. ENVIRONMENT.—*N.* environment, encompassment; surroundings, outskirts, suburbs, purlieus, precincts, environs, entourage, neighborhood, vicinage, vicinity.

V. environ, surround, beset, compass, encompass, inclose, encircle, circle, girdle, hedge, embrace, gird, belt, engird; skirt, hem in; circumscribe, etc., 229; beleaguer, invest, besiege, beset, blockade.

Adj. surrounding, begirt; suburban.

Adv. **around,** about: without; on every side, on all sides.

228. INTERLOCATION.—*N.* interlocation, interjacence, interpenetration; interjection, interpolation, interlineation, interspersion, intercalation.

intervention, interference, interposition, intrusion; insinuation; insertion.

intermediary, go-between, interagent, middleman, medium. **partition,** diaphragm, midriff; wall, party wall; panel, bulkhead.

V. **intervene,** come between, get between, interpenetrate.

introduce, import; throw in, edge in, run in, work in; interpose, insinuate, interject, interpolate, insert, intersperse, interlard, dovetail, splice, mortise.

interfere, intrude, obtrude; thrust in, etc. (*insert*), 300.

Adj. **intervening,** parenthetical, episodic; intrusive; embosomed.

Adv. **between,** among; amid, amidst; in the thick of; betwixt and between [*colloq.*]; parenthetically.

229. CIRCUMSCRIPTION.—*N.* circumscription, limitation, inclosure; confinement, etc. (*restraint*), 751; envelope, case.

V. **circumscribe,** limit, bound, confine, inclose; surround, etc., 227; hedge in, rail in, fence round, hedge round; picket; corral; imprison, restrain.

enfold, bury, incase, enshrine, enclasp; clothe, 225; embosom.

Adj. **circumscribed,** begirt, girt; lapped; buried in, immersed in; embosomed, imbedded, mewed up; imprisoned, etc., 751; landlocked.

230. OUTLINE.—*N.* outline, circumference; perimeter, periphery; circuit, lines, contour, profile, silhouette, lineaments, relief; bounds; coast line, horizon.

zone, belt, girdle; girth; band; baldric, zodiac; tire, pale, etc. (*inclosure*), 232; circlet, etc., 247.

V. **outline,** delineate, silhouette, block, sketch, circumscribe, etc., 229.

231. EDGE.—*N.* edge, verge, brink, brow, brim, margin, border, confine, skirt, rim, side; lip.

threshold, door, porch; portal. etc. (*opening*), 260.

shore, coast, strand, bank; quay, wharf, dock, mole, landing.

fringe, flounce, frill, furbelow; valance; trimming, edging, skirting, hem, selvage, welt; frame.

V. **edge,** coast, border, skirt; fringe, flounce, hem.

232. INCLOSURE.—*N.* inclosure, envelope; case, etc. (*receptacle*), 191; wrapper; girdle, etc., 230.

pen, fold; sty, paddock, pasture; pound; corral, yard; net, seine.

fence, pale, paling, balustrade, rail, railing, wall; hedge, hedgerow.

barrier, barricade, cordon, stockade; gate, gateway; weir; door, hatch, prison, etc., 752.

dike, ditch, trench, drain, moat.

V. inclose, circumscribe, etc., 229.

233. LIMIT.—*N.* limit, boundary, bounds, pale, confine, term, bourn, verge; termination, terminus, terminal; stint; frontier, border, marches.

boundary line, landmark; turning point.

V. limit, bound, compass, confine, define, circumscribe.

Adj. definite; terminal; frontier, bordering, border, boundary.

Adv. thus far, thus far and no further.

234. FRONT.—*N.* front, foreground, forefront; face, frontage, façade, proscenium, frontispiece; priority; obverse (*of a medal*).

van, vanguard, advanced guard; front rank; outpost; first line; scout.

brow, forehead; visage, physiognomy, features, countenance; bow, stem, prow; jib; bowsprit.

pioneer, etc. (*precursor*), 64.

V. front, face, confront, brave, dare, defy, oppose; breast; come to the front *or* fore.

Adj. fore, foremost, headmost; forward, anterior, front, frontal.

Adv. before, in front, in the van, in advance; ahead; in the foreground.

235. REAR.—*N.* rear, back; rear rank, rearguard; background, hinterland.

tail, scut (*as of a hare*), brush (*of a fox*).

afterpart; stern, poop; postern door; tailpiece, crupper.

wake; train, retinue, suite, cortege.

reverse; other side of the shield.

V. be behind; fall astern; bring up the rear; heel, tag, shadow, follow, pursue.

Adj. back, rear, hindmost; posterior; after.

Adv. behind, in the rear *or* background; at the heels of; after, aft, abaft, astern, rearward, backward.

236. SIDE.—*N.* side, flank, quarter, lee; wing; profile; gable, gable end; broadside.

points of the compass; East, sunrise, Orient, Levant; West, Occident, sunset.

V. flank, skirt, outflank; sidle; border; be on one side.

Adj. lateral, sidelong; collateral; flanking, skirting.

eastern, eastward, east, Orient, Oriental, auroral, Levantine.

western, west, westerly, westward, Occidental.

Adv. sidewise, sidelong, sideling, broadside on; abreast, along-

side, beside; aside; by, by the side of; side by side; to windward,
to leeward; laterally; right and left.

237. OPPOSITE.—*N.* **opposite**, opposite side, reverse, inverse;
counterpart, antithesis; opposition, polarity; inversion, etc., 218.

antipodes, opposite poles; North and South.

Adj. **opposite**, reverse, converse; antipodal, diametrical, anti-
thetic, counter; fronting, facing.

northern, north, northerly, northward, hyperborean, boreal,
polar, arctic.

southern, south, southerly, southward, austral, antarctic.

Adv. **over**, over the way, over against; against; face to face,
vis-à-vis [F.].

238. RIGHT.—*N.* **right**, right hand; offside, starboard.

Adj. **dextral**, dexterous, right-handed, dexter.

ambidexter, ambidextrous.

239. LEFT.—*N.* **left**, left hand, south paw [*slang*]; near side;
larboard, port.

Adj. **left-handed**, sinistral.

III. FORM

240. FORM.—*N.* **form**, figure, shape, make, formation, frame,
construction, cut, build, contour, outline, stamp, type, cast, mold,
fashion; structure, etc., 329; sculpture, architecture.

feature, lineament, turn; phase, etc. (*aspect*), 448; posture, attitude, pose.

V. **form**, shape, figure, fashion, carve, cut, chisel, hew, cast;
roughhew, sketch, block out; trim, model, knead, mold, sculpture;
cast, stamp; build, etc. (*construct*), 161.

Adj. **structural**; plastic, formative, impressible; creative.

shapely, well proportioned, symmetrical, well made, well
formed, trim, neat.

241. ABSENCE OF FORM.—*N.* **formlessness**, shapelessness,
misproportion, uncouthness; rough diamond; disorder, etc., 59;
deformity, etc., 243; disfigurement, defacement; mutilation.

V. **deface**, disfigure, deform, mutilate, derange, etc., 61;
blemish, mar.

Adj. **formless**, shapeless, amorphous, unshapely, misshapen,
unsymmetrical, malformed, unformed; anomalous.

rough, rude, barbarous, rugged, scraggy; in the rough.

242. [Regularity of form] SYMMETRY.—*N.* **symmetry**, shape-
liness, finish; beauty, etc., 845; proportion, eurythmics, uniformity, parallelism; centrality; radiation; branching, ramification;
regularity, evenness.

Adj. **symmetrical,** shapely, well set, finished; beautiful, etc., 845; classic, chaste, severe.

regular, uniform, balanced; equal, even, parallel.

243. [Irregularity of form] DISTORTION.—*N.* **distortion,** contortion; knot, warp, buckle, screw, twist; crookedness, obliquity; grimace, deformity, malformation; monstrosity, misproportion, ugliness, disfigurement.

V. **distort,** contort, twist, warp, buckle, screw, wrench, wrest, writhe, deform, misshape.

Adj. **distorted,** out of shape, irregular, unsymmetric, awry, wry, askew, crooked, gnarled; not true, not straight; deformed; misshapen, misproportioned, ill-proportioned; ill-made; humpbacked, hunchbacked; bandy-legged, bow-legged; knock-kneed.

244. ANGULARITY.—*N.* **angularity,** bifurcation; fold, etc., 258; notch, etc., 257; fork, crotch, angle, bend, elbow, knee, knuckle; zigzag; right angle, acute angle, obtuse angle; obliquity, etc., 217.

corner, nook, recess, niche.

triangle; rectangle, square; lozenge, diamond; rhomb, rhombus, rhomboid; quadrangle, quadrilateral; parallelogram; polygon, pentagon, hexagon, heptagon, octagon, oxygon, decagon; cube, prism, pyramid.

V. **fork,** branch, ramify, bifurcate, bend hook.

Adj. **angular,** bent, crooked, aquiline, jagged, serrated; forked, bifurcate, crotched, zigzag, hooked; akimbo; oblique, etc., 217.

245. CURVATURE.—*N.* **curvature,** curvedness, incurvature, bend; flexure, crook, hook, bending; deflection, turn; deviation, detour; sweep; curl; sinuosity, etc., 248.

curve, arc, arch, arcade, vault, bow, cresent, half-moon, horseshoe, loop, festoon; parabola, hyperbola; tracery.

V. **be curved,** sweep, sag; deviate, etc., 279; turn; re-enter.

render curved, bend, curve, deflect, inflect; crook; turn, round, arch, arch over, bow, coil, curl, recurve.

Adj. **curved,** curvate, devious; recurved, arched, vaulted; oblique, etc., 217; circular, etc., 247; bell-shaped; bow-shaped; embowed; crescent, crescent-shaped; horned; heart-shaped; cordate; hook-shaped, hooked, hooklike; moon-shaped, lunar, sickleshaped.

246. STRAIGHTNESS.—*N.* **straightness,** directness; inflexibility; straight (*or* bee, right, direct) line; short cut.

V. **be straight,** have no turning, go straight, steer for.

render straight, straighten, rectify; set *or* put straight; unbend, unfold, uncurl, uncoil, unravel.

Adj. **straight,** rectilinear; direct, even, right, true, in a line; undeviating, unswerving, straight as an arrow; inflexible.

perpendicular, plumb, vertical, upright, erect.

247. [Simple circularity] **CIRCULARITY.**—*N.* circularity, roundness; rotundity, etc., 249.

circle, circlet, ring, hoop; bracelet, armlet; loop, wheel, cycle, orb, orbit, disk, circuit, zone, belt, cordon, band; hub, nave; sash, girdle, cestus, cincture, baldric, wreath, garland; crown, coronet, chaplet, snood, fillet; necklace, collar; noose, lasso.

ellipse, oval; ellipsoid, cycloid.

V. round; ring, encircle, etc., 227.

Adj. round, rounded, circular, oval, elliptic, elliptical, egg-shaped.

248. [Complex circularity] **CONVOLUTION.**—*N.* convolution, involution, winding, wave, undulation, sinuosity, sinuousness, meandering, twist, twirl; contortion.

coil, roll, curl, spiral, corkscrew, worm, tendril, scallop, kink; serpent, snake, eel; maze, labyrinth.

V. wind, twine, twirl, wreathe, entwine; wave, undulate, meander; twist, coil, roll; wrinkle; curl, friz, indent, scallop; wring, contort.

Adj. winding, twisted, convoluted; circling, snaky, serpentine, sinuous, undulating, undulated, wavy.

involved, intricate, mazy, tortuous, labyrinthine; circuitous, kinky, curly.

spiral, coiled, screw-shaped.

Adv. in and out, round and round.

249. ROTUNDITY.—*N.* rotundity, roundness, sphericity, globularity.

cylinder, barrel, drum; roll, roller, rolling pin, column.

sphere, globe, ball, spheroid, globule; bulb, bullet, pellet, pill, marble, pea, knob.

V. sphere, form into a sphere, roll into a ball, give rotundity, round.

Adj. rotund; round, etc. (*circular*), 247; cylindrical, conical, spherical, globular, bulbous; egg-shaped, ovoid, ovate; bell-shaped, etc., 245.

250. CONVEXITY.—*N.* convexity, prominence, projection, swelling, swell, bulge, protuberance, protrusion, excrescency.

excrescence, hump; bow; clump, bunch; bulb, bump, knob; knot; boss; tooth, peg; ridge, rib, snag; peak, etc. (*sharpness*), 253; growth, tumor; pimple, wart, wen; fungus, blister; nipple, teat, dug, breast.

proboscis, nose, beak, snout, nozzle.

belly, paunch; abdomen.

arch, cupola, dome, vault.

relief, cameo; low relief, bas-relief, high relief.

point of land, hill, mount, mountain; cape, promontory; foreland, headland; hummock, ledge, spur.

V. project, bulge, protrude; bag, belly, pout, bunch; jut out,
stand out, stick out, stick up; hang over, beetle.

raise, etc., 307; emboss.

Adj. prominent, protuberant, projecting; bossed, bossy, convex, bunchy, hummocky, bulbous; bloated, swollen, distended;
bowed, arched; bold; bellied; gibbous; club-shaped, knobby,
gnarled; salient, in relief, raised.

251. FLATNESS.—*N.* flatness; smoothness.

plane; level, plain, tableland, plateau; stratum; plate, table,
tablet, slab.

V. flatten; level, etc., 213; fell.

Adj. flat, plane, even, smooth; flush; level, horizontal; recumbent, supine, prostrate.

Adv. flat, flatwise. lengthwise, horizontally.

252. CONCAVITY.—*N.* concavity, depression, dip; hollow,
hollowness; indentation, intaglio, cavity, dent, dint, dimple;
honeycomb.

excavation, pit, sap, mine, shaft; caisson; trough, etc. (*furrow*),
259; bay, etc. (*of the sea*), 343.

cup, basin, crater; punch bowl; cell, etc.(*receptacle*), 191; socket.
valley, vale, dale, dell, dingle, glen.

cave, cavern, cove; grot, grotto; hole, burrow, kennel, tunnel;
gully, etc., 198.

excavator, sapper, miner.

V. render concave; depress, hollow, gouge; stave in; scoop,
scoop out; dig, delve, excavate, dent, dint, perforate; mine, sap,
undermine, burrow, tunnel.

Adj. concave, hollow; funnel-shaped; retreating; cavernous;
porous, perforated; honeycombed.

253. SHARPNESS.—*N.* sharpness, acuteness; saliency.

point, spike, spine, spit, needle, pin; prick, barb; spur; horn,
antler; snag; tag; thorn, bristle; tooth, tusk; tine.

beard, porcupine, hedgehog, brier, bramble, thistle, bur; currycomb, comb.

peak, crag, crest, cone, sugar loaf; spire, pyramid, steeple.

cutting edge, knife edge, blade, edge tool, cutlery, knife, penknife, razor; scalpel, lancet; plowshare, colter; hatchet, ax, pick,
cleaver, scythe, sickle, scissors, shears; sword, etc. (*arms*), 727;
bodkin, etc. (*perforator*), 262.

sharpener; hone, strop; grindstone, whetstone, steel, emery,
carborundum.

V. be sharp; taper to a point; bristle with; cut, etc., 44.

sharpen, whet, point, barb, set, strop, grind.

Adj. **sharp,** keen; acute, pointed; tapering; spiked, spiky; studded, peaked, salient; prickly, spiny, thorny, bristling, barbed, spurred, bearded, thistly, briery; craggy, jagged, snaggy; cone-shaped, conical.

keen-edged, cutting; sharp-edged, knife-edged; sharpened.

254. BLUNTNESS.—*N.* **bluntness,** dullness.

V. **be** *or* **render blunt,** dull; take off the point *or* edge; blunt, turn.

Adj. **blunt,** dull, dullish, obtuse, pointless, unpointed; unsharpened.

255. SMOOTHNESS.—*N.* **smoothness;** polish, gloss; lubrication.

smoother; roller, steam roller; sandpaper, emery paper; flatiron, sadiron; burnisher.

V. **smooth;** plane; file; mow, shave; level, roll; macadamize; polish, burnish, sleek, iron, press, mangle; lubricate, oil, grease, wax, anoint.

Adj. **smooth;** polished; even; sleek, glossy, silken, silky; velvety; slippery, glassy, oi'y.

256. ROUGHNESS.—*N.* **roughness,** asperity; corrugation.

hair, mat, thatch, mop; scalp lock; tress, lock, curl, ringlet; shag; mane; eyelashes, lashes; beard, whiskers; mustache; imperial, goatee; fringe; hair shirt.

plumage; plume, crest; feather, tuft.

nap, pile, grain, texture.

V. **roughen,** rough, rough up, crinkle, ruffle, crumple, rumple; corrugate; stroke the wrong way, rub the fur the wrong way.

Adj. **rough,** uneven; rugged, jagged; cross-grained, gnarled, gnarly, knotted, scraggly, scraggy; craggy, cragged; unkempt, unpolished, roughhewn; prickly, etc. (*sharp*), 253.

hairy, bristly, hirsute, tufted, bushy; nappy, bearded, shaggy.

Adv. **against the grain;** in the rough; on edge.

257. NOTCH.—*N.* **notch,** dent, nick, cut, indent, indentation; embrasure, battlement.

saw, tooth, scallop; jag.

V. **notch,** nick, mill, score, cut, dent, indent, jag, scarify, scallop.

Adj. **notched,** dentate, toothed, serrate *or* serrated.

258. FOLD.—*N.* **fold,** crease, flexure, pleat, plait, tuck, gather; joint, elbow, double; wrinkle, pucker, crow's-feet; crinkle, crumple; dog's-ear; ruffle, flounce; corrugation.

V. **fold,** double, pleat, plait, crease, wrinkle, cocker, crinkle, curl, shrivel, rumple, corrugate, ruffle, crumple, pucker; dog's-ear, tuck, ruck, hem, gather.

259. FURROW.—*N.* furrow, groove, rut, scratch, streak, crack, score, incision, slit.

trench, ditch, dike, moat, trough, channel, gutter, ravine, etc., 198; depression.

V. furrow, flute, groove, carve, corrugate, cut, chisel, plow; incise, engrave, etch, grave.

Adj. furrowed, ribbed, striated, fluted, corduroy.

260. OPENING.—*N.* opening, aperture, yawning; chasm, etc., 198.

outlet, inlet; pore; vent, venthole, blowhole, airhole; orifice, mouth, sucker, muzzle, throat, gullet, nozzle.

window, casement, lattice; embrasure; light; skylight, fanlight; bay window, bow window, oriel, dormer.

portal, porch, gate, postern, wicket, trapdoor. hatch, door; cellarway, driveway, gateway, doorway, hatchway, gangway.

way, path, etc., 627; thoroughfare; channel, gully; passage, passageway.

alley, lane, mall, aisle, glade, vista.

tube, pipe, main; water pipe. etc., 350; air pipe, etc., 351; vessel, canal, gut, fistula; smokestack, chimney, flue; bore, caliber.

tunnel, mine, pit, shaft; gallery.

hole, puncture, perforation; pinhole, loophole, peephole, eye, eyelet; slot.

sieve, strainer, colander, riddle, screen.

opener, key, master key; open-sesame.

V. open, gape, yawn, fly open.

perforate, pierce, tap, bore, drill; transpierce, transfix; enfilade, impale, spike, spear, gore, spit, stab, pink, puncture, lance; stick, prick, riddle.

uncover, unclose; punch, stave in; mine, etc. (*scoop out*), 252.

Adj. open; perforated, wide-open, agape, ajar, unclosed; gaping, yawning; patent.

tubular; pervious, permeable; porous, honeycombed.

261. CLOSURE.—*N.* closure, blockade, shutting up, sealing, obstruction; contraction, constipation; impermeability; blind alley; cul-de-sac [F.].

V. close, plug, block up, stop up, fill up, cork up, button up, stuff up, dam up; blockade: obstruct, bar, bolt, stop, seal; choke, throttle; ram down, dam, cram; clinch; shut, slam, snap.

Adj. closed, shut, unopened; unpierced, impervious, impermeable; impenetrable; impassable, pathless, wayless; untrodden.

tight, unventilated, airtight, watertight, hermetically sealed; snug.

262. PERFORATOR.—*N.* perforator, piercer, borer, auger, chisel, gimlet, drill, awl, scoop, corkscrew, dibble, trepan, lancet, probe, bodkin, needle, stiletto; punch, gouge; spear, etc. (*weapon*), 727; puncher; punching machine, punching press.

263. STOPPER.—*N.* stopper, stopple; plug, cork, bung, spike, spill, stopcock, tap, faucet; valve, spigot; rammer; ram, ramrod; piston; stopgap; wadding, stuffing, padding, sponge [*surg.*], tourniquet.

doorkeeper, gatekeeper, janitor, concierge [F.], porter, warder, beadle, usher, guard, sentinel; watchdog.

IV. MOTION

264. MOTION.—*N.* motion, movement; move; mobility, movableness, motive power; mobilization.

stream, flow, flux, run, course, stir.

rate, pace, tread, footfall, step, stride, gait; velocity, clip [*colloq.*]; progress, locomotion.

journey, etc., 266; voyage, sail, cruise, passage; transit, etc., 270.

unrest, restlessness, etc., 149.

V. **move,** go, hie, budge, stir, pass, flit; hover around *or* about; shift, slide, glide, roll, flow, stream, run, drift, sweep along; wander, etc. (*deviate*), 279; walk, etc., 266.

put in motion, set in motion; impel, etc., 276; propel, etc., 284; mobilize.

Adj. **moving,** in motion, traveling; transitional, shifting, movable, mobile, motive, motor; mercurial; restless, etc. (*changeable*), 149; nomadic, etc., 266; erratic, etc., 279; evolutionary.

Adv. **under way;** on the move (*or* wing, fly, tramp, march).

265. REST.—*N.* rest; stillness, quiescence; stagnation, stagnancy, fixity, immobility, catalepsy; quietism.

quiet, tranquility, calm; repose, relaxation; dead calm; silence, peace, hush; sleep, etc. (*inactivity*), 683.

pause, lull, etc. (*cessation*), 142; stand, standstill; deadlock, dead stand; full stop; embargo.

resting place; bivouac; home, abode; bed, etc. (*support*), 215; haven, etc (*refuge*), 666; goal, destination, bourn.

V. **be still,** stand still, stand fast, stand firm, lie still, keep quiet, repose, rest; vegetate, stagnate.

remain, stay; stand, tarry, mark time; pull up, draw up; hold, halt, stop, discontinue, stop short, pause; bring to, heave to, lay to; anchor, cast anchor, come to anchor, ride at anchor, lie to; rest on one's laurels, take breath.

dwell, etc., 186; settle, settle down; alight, dismount, arrive.

quell, becalm, hush, calm, still, tranquilize, stay, lull to sleep, lay an embargo on.

Adj. **quiescent**, still; silent, hushed, quiet; motionless, moveless; fixed; stationary; at rest, at a stand, at a standstill, at anchor; stock-still; sedentary, untraveled, stay-at-home; becalmed, stagnant, quiet; unmoved, calm, restful; immovable, stable; sleeping, etc. (*inactive*), 683.

266. [Locomotion by land] JOURNEY.—*N.* **travel**, traveling, wayfaring; campaigning.

excursion, journey, expedition, tour, trip, circuit, pilgrimage, march, walk, promenade, constitutional [*colloq.*], stroll, saunter, ramble, hike [*colloq.*], tramp, turn, stalk, perambulation; outing, ride, drive, airing, jaunt.

riding, equitation, horsemanship.

roving, vagrancy, nomadism; vagabondism, hoboism; migration; emigration, immigration. *Wanderlust*, [Ger.].

itinerary, route, guide; handbook; roadbook; Baedeker.

procession, parade, cavalcade, caravan, file, cortege, column. **vehicle**, etc., 272.

traveler, etc., 268.

station, stop, stopping place, terminal, terminus, depot, railway station.

V. **travel**, journey, flit, take wing; migrate, emigrate, immigrate; trek; tour, peregrinate.

motor, bicycle, cycle [*colloq.*], spin, speed; trolley [*colloq.*]. **motorize**, electrify.

wander, roam, range, prowl, rove, jaunt, ramble, stroll, saunter, perambulate, meander, straggle; gad, gad about.

take horse, ride, drive, trot, amble, canter, gallop, prance, frisk, caracole.

walk, march, step, tread, pace; plod, trudge, wend; promenade; track; hike [*colloq.*], tramp; stalk, stride; strut, bowl along, toddle; paddle; peg on, jog on, shuffle on.

glide, slide, coast, skim, skate.

file off, march in procession, defile.

go to, repair to, resort to, hie to, betake oneself to.

Adj. **traveling**, journeying; itinerant, peripatetic, roving, rambling, vagrant, migratory, nomadic.

self-moving, automobile, automotive, locomotive.

wayfaring, wayworn; travel-stained.

267. [Locomotion by water or air] NAVIGATION.—*N.* **voyage**, cruise, sail, passage, aquatics; boating, yachting, cruising; ship, etc., 273.

headway, sternway, leeway; fairway.

oar, scull, sweep, pole; paddle, screw, propeller, turbine; sail, canvas.

aeronautics, aerial navigation, balloonery; balloon, etc., 273; ballooning; aviation, airmanship; flying, flight, volplaning, planing [*colloq.*], hydroplaning, volplane, glide, dive, nose-dive, spin, looping the loop; wing; pinion, aileron.

mariner, etc., 269; aviator, etc., 269*a*.

V. sail; embark, etc., 293; spread sail, gather way, make sail, carry sail; ride the waves, ride out the storm.

navigate, scud, boom, drift, course, cruise, steam; coast, hug the shore.

row, paddle, pull, scull, punt.

float, swim, skim, dive, wade.

Aeronautics: fly, soar, drift, hover, aviate; volplane, plane [*colloq.*], glide, dive, fly over, nose-dive, spin, loop the loop, land; take wing, take a flight.

Adj. nautical, maritime, naval; seafaring, seagoing; coasting; afloat; navigable.

aeronautic, aeronautical, aerial.

aquatic, natatory, natatorial.

Adv. under way (*or* sail, canvas, steam), in motion, in progress, on the wing; afloat.

268. TRAVELER.—*N.* traveler, wayfarer, voyager, passenger; commuter, straphanger [*colloq.*].

tourist, excursionist, globe-trotter [*colloq.*]; explorer, adventurer, mountaineer; wanderer, rover, straggler, rambler; landsman, landlubber, vagrant, loafer, tramp, hobo, vagabond, Bohemian, gypsy, nomad, Arab; pilgrim, palmer; immigrant; emigrant.

fugitive, refugee; runaway; renegade.

courier, messenger, runner; Mercury.

pedestrian, walker, foot passenger, hiker [*colloq.*], tramper.

rider, horseman, equestrian, cavalier; jockey, trainer, breaker, roughrider; huntsman, whip; postilion, postboy.

driver, coachman, charioteer, carter, wagoner, drayman, truckman; cabman, cab driver.

Railroad: engineer; fireman, stoker; conductor, motorman.

Automobile: driver, chauffeur, automobilist, motorist.

269. MARINER.—*N.* mariner, navigator; sailor, seaman, seafarer, seafaring man, sea dog [*colloq.*]; tar, bluejacket, gob [*slang*]; marine; midshipman, middy [*colloq.*]; able seaman, hand; crew; captain, commander, master mariner, skipper; mate, boatswain; boatman, ferryman, waterman, lighterman, longshoreman; gondolier; oar, oarsman, rower.

steersman, coxswain, cox [*colloq.*], helmsman, pilot.

269a. AERONAUT.—*N.* aeronaut, aviator, airman, flier, aviatress *or* aviatrix, pilot, observer, spotter [*mil. cant*], scout, bomber, ace; balloonist.

270. TRANSFERENCE.—*N.* transfer, transference; removal; deportation, extradition; conveyance, carriage; contagion, infection; transfusion; transfer, etc. (*of property*), 783.

transit, transition; passage, ferry; portage, carry; carting, cartage; shipment, freight; transmission, transport, transportation; translation; transposition, transposal.

deposit, moraine, drift, alluvium.

gift, bequest, legacy, deed, lease; quitclaim.

freight, cargo, mail, baggage, luggage, goods.

V. transfer, transmit, transport, transplant, transfuse; convey, carry, bear; hand, pass, forward; shift; bring, fetch, reach; conduct, convoy.

send, delegate, consign, relegate, deliver; ship, freight, embark; transpose; drag, etc., 285; mail, post.

Adj. transferable, assignable, negotiable, transmissible, movable, portable; contagious, infectious.

271. CARRIER.—*N.* carrier, porter, redcap, bearer, freighter, expressman; stevedore; coolie; conductor, chauffeur, truck driver; letter carrier, postman; pigeon post, carrier pigeon.

beast of burden, beast, cattle, horse, steed; charger, war horse; hunter; race horse, racer, courser, Arab, barb; blood horse, thoroughbred; palfrey, cob; nag, jade, hack; pack (*or* draft, cart, dray) horse; mare, filly, colt, foal.
pony, Shetland; broncho, cow pony, mustang.
ass, donkey, jackass, burro; mule.
reindeer; camel, dromedary, llama, elephant.

vehicle, etc., 272; ship, etc., 273.

Adj. equine, asinine; electric, motor, express.

272. VEHICLE.—*N.* vehicle, conveyance, carriage, caravan, car, van.

wagon, dray, cart, lorry, truck.

tumbrel, barrow, wheelbarrow, handbarrow; dump cart; baby carriage, gocart, perambulator; wheel chair; police van, patrol wagon, Black Maria [*colloq.*]; Conestoga wagon, prairie schooner; jinrikisha, ricksha [*colloq.*].
equipage, coach, chariot, phaeton, wagonette, break, drag, landau, barouche, victoria, brougham; sulky, runabout.
post chaise, mail stage, diligence, stage, stagecoach; horsecar, omnibus, bus [*colloq.*]; cab, hansom, four-wheeler, hack; dogcart, trap [*colloq.*], buggy, chaise.
team, pair, span, tandem, four-in-hand.
litter, palanquin, sedan; stretcher, hurdle; ambulance.
sled, bob, bobsled; toboggan; sledge, sleigh; ski, snowshoes, skates, roller skates.

cycle, bicycle, tricycle, tandem; machine [*colloq.*], wheel [*colloq.*], motorcycle; velocipede, hobbyhorse.

automobile, motorcar, limousine, sedan, touring car, roadster, coupé, motor [*colloq.*], machine [*colloq.*], car, auto [*colloq.*], autocar, runabout; truck, tractor; taxicab, taxi [*colloq.*], motorbus; flivver [*slang*], jitney [*colloq.*].

Allied automobile terms: tonneau, chassis, hood, top, ignition, spark plug, generator, distributor, magneto, self-starter, gear, gear box, differential, cylinder, manifold, intake, exhaust, carburetor, ammeter, speedometer, oil gauge, primer, clutch, universal joint, crank shaft, transmission, tire, rim; gasoline; trailer; garage; chauffeur, etc., 268.

train; express, mail; car, coach; baggage car; rolling stock; trolley, electric car, electric [*colloq.*].

Adj. vehicular; traveling, etc., 266.

273. SHIP.—*N.* ship, vessel, boat, sail; craft, bottom.

navy, marine, fleet, flotilla.

shipping, man-of-war, etc., 726; merchant ship, merchantman; packet, liner; whaler; slaver; collier; coaster, freight steamer, freighter, lighter; trawler, fishing boat; pilot boat; yacht.

ship, sailing vessel, clipper ship, windjammer [*colloq.*], bark; brig, brigantine, schooner; fore-and-after [*colloq.*]; sloop, cutter, revenue cutter, yawl, ketch, smack, lugger, barge, scow, cat, catboat.

steamer, steamboat, steamship; tug.

boat, rowboat; shallop, skiff, pinnace; launch; lifeboat, longboat, jolly boat, gig, cockboat, tender, cockleshell, dory, canoe, dugout, dinghy, punt, outrigger; float, raft, iceboat.

coracle, gondola, galley, argosy, galleon; junk, sampan [both Chinese]; dhow [Arab.]; trireme; derelict.

Aeronautics: aircraft; balloon, airship, dirigible, zeppelin, air-plane, monoplane, biplane, triplane; air cruiser, flying boat, hydroplane; kite, parachute.

Allied aeronautical terms: fuselage, gondola, wings, controls, aileron, lifting power, rudder; tail, hangar.

Adj. marine, maritime, naval, nautical, seafaring, ocean-going; seaworthy.

aeronautic, aerial; airworthy.

Adv. afloat, aboard; on board, on shipboard.

274. VELOCITY.—*N.* velocity, speed, celerity, swiftness, rapidity; expedition, etc. (*activity*), 682; acceleration; haste, etc., 684.

spurt, sprint, rush, dash, race, steeplechase; round pace; flight.

pace, gallop, canter, trot, round trot, run, hand gallop.

V. speed, hie, hasten, spurt, sprint, scamper, scuttle, trip, post; scud, scurry, whiz; run, dart, swoop, fly, race, shoot, tear, whisk, sweep, skim, scorch [*colloq.*], rush, dash; bolt, run away; ride hard; hurry, hasten, haste; accelerate, quicken; carry sail, crowd sail.

Adj. fast, speedy, swift, rapid, quick, fleet; nimble, agile, expeditious; express; active, brisk, light-footed, nimble-footed; winged.

Adv. apace; at full speed, full gallop; posthaste; in double-quick time; whip and spur; by leaps and bounds; in high (gear *or* speed) [*automobiling*].

275. SLOWNESS.—*N.* slowness, tardiness; languor, etc. (*inactivity*), 683; drawl.

jog trot, dogtrot; amble, rack, pace, single-foot, walk; mincing steps; dead march, slow march.

retardation; slackening; delay, etc. (*lateness*), 133.

slow goer, slowpoke [*colloq.*]; loiterer, sluggard, dawdler; tortoise, snail.

V. move slowly; creep, crawl, lag, walk, linger, loiter, saunter; plod, trudge, lumber; trail, drag; dawdle, etc., 683; worm one's way, inch, inch along, jog on, toddle, waddle, slouch, shuffle, halt, hobble, limp, shamble; flag, falter, totter, stagger; mince, take one's time.

retard, relax, slacken, check, moderate, rein in, curb; reef, shorten *or* take in sail; brake, slacken speed, backwater, back pedal.

Adj. slow, slack; tardy; dilatory, etc. (*inactive*), 683; leisurely; deliberate, gradual; languid, sluggish, apathetic, phlegmatic, lymphatic; moderate.

dull, slow [*colloq.*], prosaic, boring, wearisome, uninteresting, humdrum.

Adv. at half speed, in slow time; with clipped wings; in low (gear *or* speed) [*automobiling*].

gradually, by degrees, step by step, bit by bit.

276. [Motion conjoined with force] IMPULSE.—*N.* impulse, impetus; momentum; push, thrust, shove, boom, boost, explosion, etc. (*violence*), 173; propulsion, etc., 284.

clash, collision, encounter, shock, brunt, crash, bump; impact; charge, onset; percussion, concussion.

blow, stroke, knock, tap, rap, slap, smack, pat, dab; fillip; bang; hit, whack, thwack, cuff, buffet, punch, thump, kick, cut, thrust, lunge; carom, cannon; jab.

Science of mechanical forces: mechanics, dynamics.

V. impel, push; start, set going; drive, urge; boom, boost; thrust, prod; elbow, shoulder, jostle, hurtle, shove, butt, jog, jolt; throw, etc. (*propel*), 284.

strike, knock, thump, beat, bang, slam, dash, punch, thwack, whack; batter, tamp, buffet, cudgel, belabor; lunge, jab, kick; hit, tap, rap, slap, pat.

collide, foul; telescope; bump, butt.

Adj. impulsive, propulsive, dynamic.

277. RECOIL.—*N.* recoil, rebound, ricochet, backlash, boomerang: kick; elasticity, etc., 325; reflex, reflux; reverberation, resonance, repulse; reaction, revulsion.

reactionary, recalcitrant.

V. **recoil**, react; balk, jib; rebound, reverberate, echo; ricochet.

Adj. refluent, recalcitrant, reactionary.

278. DIRECTION.—*N.* **direction**, bearing, course, set, trend, run, drift, tenor; tendency, etc., 176; dip, tack, aim.

points of the compass, cardinal points.

line, path, road, range, line of march, alignment; airline, beeline.

V. **tend toward**, conduct to, go to; point to, bend, verge, incline, dip; steer for, make for, aim at, level at; take aim; hold a course; be bound for; make a beeline for.

Adj. bound for; direct, straight; undeviating, unswerving.

directable, steerable, dirigible, guidable.

Adv. **toward**, on the road to; hither, thither, whither; directly; straight, point-blank; in a bee (*or* direct, straight) line to, as the crow flies; windward, in the wind's eye.

through, via, by way of.

279. DEVIATION.—*N.* **deviation**; warp, refraction; sweep; deflection, zigzag.

diversion, digression, aberration, drift, sheer, divergence, ramification, forking; detour.

Oblique motion: tack, yaw [*both naut.*]; echelon [*mil.*]; knight's move [*chess*].

V. **deviate**, alter one's course, turn, bend, curve, swerve, heel, bear off; jibe, yaw, wear, sheer, tack [*all naut.*]; sidle, edge, veer, diverge; wind, twist; turn aside, wheel, steer clear of; dodge, step aside, shy, jib; glance off.

deflect; divert, shift, switch, shunt; sidetrack.

stray, straggle; digress, wander, meander; go astray, ramble, rove, drift.

Adj. **deviating**, errant; excursive, discursive; devious, desultory, rambling; stray, vagrant, circuitous, roundabout, sidelong, indirect, crooked, zigzag; oblique.

280. PRECEDING.—*N.* **preceding**, leading, heading, precedence, priority, the lead, van, front; precursor, etc., 64.

V. **precede**, go before, forerun; introduce, herald; head, take the lead; lead, steal a march, get ahead, outstrip; take precedence.

Adv. **in advance**, before, ahead, in the van, in front.

281. FOLLOWING.—*N.* **following**, attendance; pursuant; sequence, sequel.

follower, attendant, satellite, pursuer, shadow, dangler, train.

V. **follow**; pursue, etc., 622; go after; attend, dance attendance on, dog; shadow; hang on the skirts of; camp on the trail.

lag, loiter, linger, fall behind.

Adv. behind; in the rear; after, etc. (*order*), 63 (*time*), 117.

282. [Motion forward] PROGRESSION.—*N.* progression, progress, progressiveness; advance, advancement, headway; march, etc., 266; rise, improvement, etc., 658.

V. advance; proceed, go, go on, progress, get on, gain ground, forge ahead, press onward, step forward, make progress (*or* head, headway); go ahead, shoot ahead; distance.

Adj. progressive, advanced, up-to-date; enterprising, go-ahead [*colloq.*].

Adv. forward, onward; forth, on, ahead, under way.

283. [Motion backward] REGRESSION.—*N.* regression, retrogression, retreat, retirement, recession, withdrawal.

reflux, refluence, backwater, ebb, return; reflexion, recoil.

countermotion, countermovement, countermarch; tergiversation, backsliding, fall; deterioration, relapse, reversion.

V. recede, return, revert, retreat, retire; retrograde, back, back out [*colloq.*], back down [*colloq.*], balk; withdraw; recoil, rebound; turn back, fall back, put back; lose ground; drop astern; backwater, put about [*naut.*], veer, shy, double, wheel, countermarch; ebb, regurgitate.

Adj. retrograde, retrogressive; regressive, refluent, reflex, contraclockwise, counterclockwise; balky, perverse, reactionary.

284. PROPULSION.—*N.* propulsion, projection; push, etc. (*impulse*), 276; ejection; throw, fling, toss, shot, discharge, shy.

Science of propulsion: gunnery, ballistics.

missile, projectile; gun, etc. (*arms*), 727.

marksman, rifleman, good shot, dead shot, crack shot; sharpshooter, etc. (*combatant*), 726; gunner; archer, bowman.

V. propel, project, throw, fling, cast, pitch, toss, jerk, heave, shy, hurl.

dart, lance, tilt; drive, sling, pelt, pitchfork.

send; let off, fire off, discharge, shoot; launch, send forth, let fly; dash.

start, put *or* set in motion, set going, trundle, bundle off; impel, etc., 276; expel, eject.

Adj. propulsive, projectile, ballistic.

285. TRACTION.—*N.* traction, draft, pull, haul.

V. draw, pull, haul, lug, rake, trawl, draggle, drag, tug, tow, trail, train; take in tow.

Adj. tractile, tractional, ductile.

286. [Motion toward] APPROACH.—*N.* approach, approximation; access; advent.

pursuit, chase, hunt.

V. approach, converge, near, get (*or* draw) near; move toward, drift; gain upon; pursue, etc., 622; make land.

Adj. approximate, convergent; impending, imminent.

287. [Motion from] RECESSION.—*N.* recession, retirement, withdrawal; retreat; regression, etc., 283; departure, etc., 293; flight.

V. recede, go, go back, move back, retire, withdraw, ebb; shrink; drift away; depart, etc., 293; retreat, retire, fall back; run away, fly, flee.

288. ATTRACTION.—*N.* attraction, attractiveness; pull, magnetism, gravity.

loadstone, lodestar, polestar, magnet.

lure, bait, charm, decoy.

V. attract, pull, drag, draw, magnetize, bait, trap, decoy, charm, lure, allure.

Adj. attractive, attracting, seductive.

289. REPULSION.—*N.* repulsion; antipathy; repulse, abduction.

V. repel, push *or* drive from, etc., 276; chase, dispel; abduct; send away; repulse; keep at arm's length, turn one's back upon.

Adj. repellent, repulsive.

290. [Motion nearer to] CONVERGENCE.—*N.* convergence, confluence, concourse, concurrence, concentration; meeting.

assemblage, etc., 72; resort, etc., 74.

V. converge, concur; come together, unite, meet, close in upon; center, concentrate.

Adj. convergent, confluent, concurrent; centripetal.

291. [Motion farther off] DIVERGENCE.—*N.* divergence, ramification, forking; separation, detachment, dispersion, deviation, etc., 279.

V. diverge, ramify, branch off, fly off; spread, scatter, disperse, etc., 73; part, sever, separate, sunder.

Adj. divergent, radial, centrifugal.

Adv. broadcast.

292. ARRIVAL.—*N.* arrival, advent; landing; debarkation, disembarkation.

destination, bourn, goal; harbor, haven, port; terminus, terminal; home, journey's end; anchorage, refuge.

meeting, joining, encounter, rejoining; return, re-entry.

V. arrive, get to, come to; come; reach, attain; overtake; make, fetch; join, rejoin; return; enter, appear, drop in, visit.

alight, light, dismount, detrain.

land, cast anchor, put in, debark, disembark.

meet, encounter, come across; come (*or* light) upon.

Adv. here, hither.

293. DEPARTURE.—*N.* departure, embarkation; outset, start; removal; exit, etc. (*egress*), 295; exodus, hegira, flight.

leave-taking, adieu, farewell, good-by, Godspeed; valediction, valedictory, valedictorian.

V. depart; go, go away, go off, set out, start, issue, march out, debouch, sally forth; sally, go forth; retire, withdraw, remove; cut [*colloq. or slang*], take flight, take wing; fly, flit; strike tents, decamp, break camp, take leave; disappear, etc., 449; entrain; saddle, bridle, harness up, hitch up [*colloq.*].

quit, vacate, evacuate, abandon.

embark, go abroad; set sail, put to sea, sail, take ship; get under way, weigh anchor.

Adv. hence, whence, thence.

294. [Motion into] INGRESS.—*N.* ingress; entrance, entry; influx, inroad, incursion, invasion, irruption; penetration, infiltration; insinuation, insertion, etc., 300.

immigration, incoming, foreign influx.

import [*used esp. in pl.*], importation.

immigrant, incomer, newcomer, colonist.

inlet; mouth, door, etc. (*opening*), 260; path, etc., 627; conduit, etc., 350.

V. enter; come in, pour in, flow in; set foot on; burst *or* break in upon, invade; penetrate, infiltrate.

Adj. incoming, inbound, inward.

295. [Motion out of] EGRESS.—*N.* egress, exit, issue; emergence; outbreak; outburst, eruption; emanation; evacuation; leakage, percolation, oozing, drain, drainage; gush, outpour, effluence, outflow, discharge.

export [*used esp. in pl.*], exportation; shipment.

emigration, exodus, departure.

emigrant, migrant, colonist.

outlet, vent, spout, faucet, tap, sluice, floodgate; mouth, opening, door; pathway; conduit.

V. emerge, emanate, issue; go (*or* come, pass, pour, flow) out of.

exude, discharge, leak; run through, percolate; strain, distill; perspire, sweat; drain, seep, ooze, filter, infiltrate, gush, spout, flow out; pour, trickle; find vent; escape, etc., 671.

Adj. eruptive, porous, pervious, leaky; outgoing, outbound, outward bound.

296. [Motion into, actively] RECEPTION.—*N.* reception; admission, admittance, entree; importation; initiation, introduction, absorption; suction, sucking; eating, drinking, etc. (*food*), 298; insertion, etc., 300.

V. **give entrance to,** introduce, usher, admit, initiate; receive, import, bring in; absorb, imbibe, instill, implant, induct, inhale; let in, take in.

swallow, gulp; eat, drink, etc., 298.

Adj. **introductory,** initiatory, preliminary.

297. [Motion out of, actively] EJECTION.—*N.* **ejection,** rejection, expulsion, eviction, dislodgment, banishment, exile, deportation, expedition; discharge, evacuation, eruption, eruptiveness; tapping, drainage; emetic; vomiting.

V. **eject,** reject; expel, discard; ostracize, boycott; banish, exile, fire [*slang*], throw away *or* aside, push out *or* off, send off *or* away; discharge, dismiss, turn *or* cast adrift; turn out, throw overboard.

evict, oust, dislodge; turn out of doors, deport, expatriate.

emit, send out, pour out, dispatch, shed, void, evacuate; give vent to; tap, draw off; pour forth; squirt, spurt, spill; breathe, blow, exhale.

empty; drain, sweep off; clear off, draw off; clean out, purge; tap, broach.

root out, root up, unearth, eradicate; weed out, get out; eliminate, get rid of, do away with, shake off.

vomit, spew; cast up, bring up; disgorge.

unpack, unlade, unload, unship; dump.

298. [Eating] FOOD.—*N.* **eating,** mastication, rumination; gastronomy, carnivorousness, vegetarianism, gluttony, etc., 957.

mouth, jaws, mandible [*esp. of birds*], chops.

drinking, potation, draft, libation; carousal, etc. (*amusement*), 840; drunkenness, etc., 959.

food, meat, nourishment, nutriment, sustenance, nurture, subsistence, provender, corn, feed, fodder, provision, ration, board; commissariat, etc. (*provisions*), 637; prey, forage, pasture, pasturage; fare, cheer; diet, dietary; regimen; staff of life, bread.

eatables, victuals, edibles, grub [*slang*], meat; bread, viands, delicacy, dainty, creature comforts, ambrosia; good cheer, good living.

table, cuisine [F.], bill of fare, menu, table d'hôte [F.], à la carte [F.].

meal, repast, feed [*colloq.*], spread [*colloq.*]; mess; refreshment, entertainment; refection, collation, picnic, feast, banquet, potluck.

mouthful, tidbit, morsel.

drink, beverage, liquor, potion, dram, draft.

restaurant, café, eating house.

V. **eat,** feed, fare, devour, swallow, take; gulp, bolt; fall to; dispatch; tuck in [*slang*], dine, banquet, gormandize, etc., 957; crunch, chew, masticate, nibble, gnaw, mumble.

live on; feed upon; browse, graze, crop; bite, champ, munch, ruminate.

drink, quaff, sip, sup; lap; tipple, guzzle, carouse.

cater, purvey, etc., 637.

Adj. **eatable,** edible, esculent; dietetic; culinary; nutritive, nutritious; succulent.

underdone, rare; well done; overdone; high [*of game*]; ripe [*of cheese*].

drinkable, potable; bibulous.

omnivorous, carnivorous, flesh-eating, herbivorous, graminivorous, piscivorous.

299. EXCRETION.—*N.* **excretion,** discharge, emanation, exhalation, secretion, effusion, perspiration, sweat.

hemorrhage, bleeding; outpouring, etc. (*egress*), 295; diarrhea.

saliva, spittle, sputum (*pl.* sputa), spit; catarrh; lava.

V. **excrete,** etc. (*eject*), 297; secrete; exhale, emanate, etc. (*come out*), 295.

300. [Forcible ingress] INSERTION.—*N.* **insertion,** implantation, introduction; interpolation, interlineation, insinuation, etc. (*intervention*), 228; injection, inoculation, infusion; ingress, etc., 294; immersion; submersion, dip, plunge.

V. **insert,** introduce, put in (*or* into), run into; inject; imbed, inlay, inweave; interject, etc., 228; infuse, instill, inoculate, impregnate, imbue.

graft, ingraft, bud, plant, implant.

obtrude; thrust in, stick in, ram in, stuff in, tuck in, press in, drive in; pierce, etc. (*make a hole*), 260.

immerse, merge; bathe, soak, etc. (*water*), 337; dip, plunge, etc., 310.

301. [Forcible egress] EXTRACTION.—*N.* **extraction;** removal, elimination, extrication, eradication, extirpation, extermination; ejection, etc., 297; export, etc. (*egress*), 295; wrench.

V. **extract,** draw; take out, draw out, pull out, tear out, pluck out, pick out, get out; wring from, wrench; extort; root up, weed out; eradicate, uproot, pull up, extirpate.

elicit, evolve, bring forth, draw forth; extricate.

eliminate, etc. (*eject*), 297; remove.

express, squeeze out, press out, distill.

302. [Motion through] PASSAGE.—*N.* **passage,** transmission; permeation, penetration; infiltration; ingress; egress, exit, issue; path, road, way; conduit, opening; journey, voyage, sail, cruise.

V. **pass,** pass through; perforate, penetrate, permeate, thread, cut across; ford, cross; make (*or* work, thread, worm, force) one's way; find a way (*or* vent); transmit, make way, traverse.

303. [Motion beyond] OVERRUNNING.—*N.* overrunning, overrun, inroad, advance, infraction, transgression, encroachment, infringement; transcendence; redundance, etc., 641.

V. overrun, pass, go beyond, go by, shoot ahead of; steal a march upon; gain upon.

outstrip, override, overshoot the mark; outrun, outride, outrival, outdo; beat; distance; throw into the shade; exceed, transcend, surmount; tower above, surpass.

encroach, overstep, transgress, trespass, infringe, intrude, invade.

Adv. ahead, beyond the mark.

304. [Motion short of] SHORTCOMING.—*N.* shortcoming, failure, falling short; default, defalcation; delinquency; fizzle [*colloq.*], slump [*colloq.*]; flash in the pan.

incompleteness, deficiency; defect, imperfection, fault; insufficiency, etc., 640; noncompletion, nonfulfillment; failure, etc., 732.

V. fall short, come short of, not reach; want; keep within bounds (*or* the mark, compass).

collapse, fail, break down, flat out [*colloq.*], come to nothing; fall down, slump, fizzle out [*all colloq.*]; fall through, fall to the ground; cave in [*colloq.*], end in smoke, miss the mark.

Adj. deficient; at fault; short, short of; out of depth; perfunctory, remiss.

305. [Motion upward] ASCENT.—*N.* ascent, ascension; rising, rise, upgrowth, upward flight; upgrade; leap, etc., 309; grade, ramp, acclivity, hill, etc., 217.

stairway, staircase, stairs; flight of steps *or* stairs; ladder, scaling ladder; companionway [*naut.*]; escalator, elevator.

V. ascend, rise, mount, arise, uprise; go up, get up, work one's way up, start up, spring up, shoot up; aspire, aim high.

climb, shin [*colloq.*], swarm [*colloq.*], clamber, scramble, escalade, surmount, wind upward, scale.

tower, soar, spire, go aloft, fly aloft; surge; leap, etc., 309.

Adj. rising; ascendant; upcast; buoyant.

Adv. up, upward, skyward, heavenward; upturned; uphill.

306. [Motion downward] DESCENT.—*N.* descent, inclination, declension, declination; drop; cadence; subsidence, lapse; downcome, comedown, setback, fall; slump [*colloq.*], downfall, tumble, stumble, slip, tilt, trip, lurch.

avalanche, landslide, slide, snowslide, glissade.

declivity, dip, decline, pitch, drop, downgrade.

V. descend, go (*or* drop, come) down, fall, gravitate, drop, slip, skid, slide, settle; decline, sink, subside, droop, slump [*colloq.*].

get down, dismount, alight, light; swoop; stoop, etc., 308; fall prostrate, precipitate oneself; let fall.

tumble, trip, stumble, lurch, pitch, topple; tilt, sprawl.

Adj. steep, sloping, declivitous; beetling, overhanging; bottomless, fathomless, abysmal.

descending; down, downcast, descendent; deciduous.

Adv. downward, downhill.

307. ELEVATION.—*N.* elevation; raising; erection, lift; upheaval; sublimation, exaltation; prominence, relief.

lever, crowbar, crane, derrick, windlass, capstan, winch; dredge, dredger.

elevator, dumbwaiter; escalator.

V. elevate, raise, heighten, lift, erect; set up, tilt up; rear, hoist, heave; uplift, upraise, uprear; buoy, mount, exalt; sublimate.

take up, drag up, fish up; dredge.

Adj. elevated, upturned, stilted, rampant.

308. DEPRESSION.—*N.* depression, lowering; dip, etc. (*concavity*), 252.

overthrow, overturn; upset; prostration, reduction, abasement, subversion.

bow, curtsy, dip [*colloq.*], bob, duck, genuflexion, kowtow, obeisance, salaam.

V. depress, lower, cast down, let drop, let fall; sink, debase, bring low, abase, reduce, precipitate.

overthrow, overturn, overset, upset, prostrate, level, fell; down [*colloq.*], cast (*or* throw, fling, dash, pull, knock, hew) down, raze.

sit, sit down, squat; recline, sprawl.

crouch, stoop, bend, cower.

bow, curtsy, genuflect, kowtow, duck, bob, dip, kneel; incline, make obeisance, salaam, prostrate oneself, bow down.

Adj. depressed; at a low ebb; prostrate, horizontal.

309. LEAP.—*N.* leap, jump, hop, spring, bound, vault.

caper, dance, gambol, frisk, prance, curvet, caracole, buck; hop, skip, and jump.

V. leap, jump, hop, spring, bound, vault, clear, ramp, skip.

prance, dance, caper; buck; curvet, caracole, bob, bounce, flounce; frisk, jump about, romp, frolic, gambol; cavort, cut capers [*colloq.*].

Adj. leaping, saltatorial; frisky, lively, frolicsome.

Adv. on the light fantastic toe.

310. PLUNGE.—*N.* plunge, dip, dive, nose-dive [*aviation*], header [*colloq.*]; submergence, submersion, immersion.

diver; diving bird.

V. plunge, dip, souse, duck; dive, plump; take a header [*colloq.*]; make a plunge; bathe; pitch.

submerge, submerse; immerse; douse, sink, engulf, send to the bottom.

founder, welter, wallow; get out of one's depth; go to the bottom.

Adj. submergible, submersible.

311. CIRCULAR MOTION.—*N.* circulation, turn, excursion, circumnavigation, circumflexion; wheel, compass, lap, circuit; turning, evolution; coil, spiral.

V. turn, bend, wheel; go about, put about [*both naut.*]; go (*or* turn) round, round, turn a corner; double a point [*naut.*]; make a detour.

circle, encircle, circumscribe, circuit, describe a circle, circumnavigate; go the round.

wind, circulate, meander; whisk, twirl, twist, coil.

wallow, welter, roll.

Adj. circuitous, roundabout, devious.

312. ROTATION—*N.* rotation, revolution, gyration, circulation, roll; pirouette, convolution.

eddy, vortex, whirlpool, maelstrom; swirl, surge; whir, whirl; cyclone, tornado; vertiginousness, vertigo.

V. rotate, roll, revolve, spin, turn, turn round, encircle, circulate, swirl, gyrate, wheel, whirl, twirl; roll up, furl; box the compass.

Adj. rotating, rotary; vertiginous.

313. UNFOLDMENT.—*N.* unfoldment, unfolding, development; evolvement, evolution; inversion.

V. evolve; unfold, unroll, unwind, uncoil, untwist, unfurl, untwine, unravel; disentangle; develop.

Adj. evolutional, evolutionary.

314. [Motion to and fro] OSCILLATION.—*N.* oscillation, vibration, undulation, pulsation; pulse, beat, throb.

alternation; coming and going; ebb and flow, flux and reflux, systole and diastole; ups and downs.

fluctuation; vacillation, irresolution, indecision.

swing, wave, beat, shake, wag, seesaw, teeter.

V. oscillate, vibrate, undulate, wave; rock, teeter, sway, swing, dangle; pulsate, beat; wag, waggle; nod, bob, curtsy; wobble.

fluctuate, reel, quake, quiver, quaver, shake, flicker; wriggle; roll, toss, pitch; flounder, stagger, totter.

alternate, pass and repass, shuttle, ebb and flow, come and go; vacillate.

Adj. oscillating; undulatory, vibratory; pendulous.

Adv. to and fro, up and down, back and forth, in and out, seesaw, zigzag, from side to side, shuttlewise.

315. [Irregular motion] AGITATION.—*N.* agitation, stir, tremor, shuffling, shake, ripple, jog, jolt, jar, jerk, shock, trepidation, quiver, quaver, dance; tarantella; twitter, flicker, flutter.

disquiet, perturbation, commotion, turmoil, turbulence; tumult, hubbub, rout, bustle, fuss, racket.

twitching, chorea, St. Vitus' dance; staggers, blind staggers; epilepsy, fits.

spasm, throe, throb, palpitation, convulsion, paroxysm, seizure, grip, cramp.

disturbance, disorder; restlessness, changeableness, instability.

ferment, fermentation, ebullition, effervescence, hurly-burly; tempest, storm, whirlpool, vortex, etc., 312; whirlwind, tornado, cyclone, typhoon.

V. **be agitated**; shake, tremble, flutter, flicker; quiver, quaver, quake; shiver, writhe, toss; shuffle, tumble, stagger, bob, reel, sway; wag, waggle, wriggle; stumble, shamble, flounder, totter, flounce, flop, dance, curvet, prance, cavort; squirm; twitch; bustle.

throb, pulsate, beat, palpitate, go pitapat.

ferment, effervesce, foam, boil, boil over, bubble, bubble up; simmer.

agitate, shake, convulse, toss, tumble, wield, brandish, flap, flourish, whisk, jerk, jolt, jog, joggle, disturb, stir, shake up, churn.

Adj. **agitated**, shaking, tremulous; convulsive, jerky; effervescent, unquiet, restless.

Adv. by fits and starts; in convulsions, in fits, in a flutter.

CLASS III

Words Relating to MATTER

I. MATTER IN GENERAL

316. MATERIALITY.—*N.* materiality, corporality; substantiality, material existence; incarnation, flesh and blood.

matter, body, substance, brute matter, protoplasm, stuff, element, principle, material, substratum.

object, article, thing, something; still life; materials, etc., 635. Science of matter: physics; natural philosophy; physical science. materialist, physicist.

V. **materialize**, substantiate, incorporate, embody, incarnate.

Adj. **material**, bodily, corporeal, corporal, physical, incarnate, materialized, embodied; sensible, tangible, ponderable, palpable, substantial; unspiritual, materialistic.

objective, impersonal, nonsubjective.

317. IMMATERIALITY.—*N.* immateriality, insubstantiality, incorporality, unsubstantiality, spirituality; astral plane.

personality; I, myself, me.

ego, spirit, etc. (*soul*), 450; astral body, etheric double, subliminal self, subconscious self, higher self.

spiritualism, spiritism; animism.

spiritualist, spiritist; animist.

V. dematerialize, disembody, spiritualize.

Adj. immaterial, incorporeal, incorporate, unsubstantial; spiritistic, animistic; discarnate, bodiless, disembodied; extramundane, unearthly; spiritual, etc. (*psychical*), 450.

subjective, personal, nonobjective.

318. WORLD.—*N.* world, creation, nature, universe; earth, globe, sphere, wide world; cosmos, macrocosm.

heavens, sky, empyrean, starry cope (*or* host); firmament.

heavenly bodies, luminaries, stars, asteroids; galaxy, Milky Way; constellations, planets, satellites; comet, meteor, falling (*or* shooting) star; solar system.

sun, orb of day, daystar [*poetic*], Helios, Apollo, Phoebus, etc. (*sun god*), 423.

moon, Diana, Luna, Phoebe, Cynthia, Selene, silver-footed queen.

Adj. cosmic, mundane, terrestrial, earthly, sublunary.

celestial, empyreal, heavenly, solar; lunar; starry, stellar, sidereal, astral; nebular.

Adv. in all creation, on the face of the globe, here below, under the sun.

319. GRAVITY.—*N.* gravity, gravitation; weight, heft, heaviness, ponderousness, specific gravity, pressure, load, burden, ballast, counterpoise; mass.

Weighing instrument: balance, scales, steelyard, beam, weighbridge.

Science of gravity: statics.

V. weigh, load, press; counterweigh, poise; gravitate.

Adj. weighty, heavy, ponderous, ponderable; cumbersome, burdensome, cumbrous, unwieldy, massive; static.

320. LEVITY.—*N.* levity, lightness, imponderability, buoyancy, volatility.

ferment, leaven, yeast, pepsin.

V. be light, float, swim.

render light, lighten.

ferment, work, raise, leaven.

Adj. light, subtle, imponderous, imponderable, ethereal, airy, feathery, gossamery; volatile, vaporous, buoyant, floating, foamy, frothy; portable.

fermenting, fermentative, yeasty.

II. INORGANIC MATTER

(1) Solids

321. DENSITY.—*N.* density, solidity, solidness; impenetrability, impermeability; costiveness, constipation.

condensation; solidification, consolidation, concretion, coagulation; cohesion, etc., 46; petrifaction, etc. (*hardening*), 323; thickening, crystallization, precipitation.

solid body, mass, block, lump; concretion, concrete, conglomerate; stone, rock, cake; card.

sediment, lees, dregs, settlings.

V. **be dense,** compress, squeeze, ram down; solidify; cement, set, consolidate, condense, congeal, coagulate, curd, curdle; fix, clot, thicken, cake, candy, precipitate, deposit, cohere, crystallize; petrify, harden, stiffen.

compress, squeeze, ram down.

Adj. **dense,** solid, solidified; coherent, cohesive, compact; close, serried, thickset; substantial, massive, impenetrable, concrete, hard; crystalline, thick, stodgy.

undissolved, unmelted, unliquefied, unthawed.

indivisible; indissoluble, insoluble.

322. RARITY.—*N.* rarity, tenuity; subtlety.

rarefaction, attenuation, expansion, inflation; ether, etc. (*gas*), 334.

V. **rarefy,** expand, dilate, attenuate, thin.

Adj. **rare,** subtle, thin, fine, tenuous, compressible, flimsy, slight, light, porous; rarefied, unsubstantial.

323. HARDNESS.—*N.* hardness, firmness, rigidity, inflexibility, temper, callosity; induration, petrifaction, ossification; crystallization.

V. **harden,** render hard, temper, stiffen, cement, indurate, petrify, ossify.

Adj. **hard,** rigid, stubborn, stiff, firm; stark, unbending, unyielding, inflexible, tense.

adamantine, stony, granitic, rocky, horny, callous, bony, cartilaginous.

324. SOFTNESS.—*N.* softness, pliableness, flexibility, pliancy, pliability, malleability, ductility, tractility, plasticity, flaccidity, laxity, flabbiness, mollification, softening.

V. **soften,** render soft, mollify, mellow; mash; knead, massage.
bend, give, yield, relent, relax.

Adj. **soft,** tender; mollified; supple, pliant, pliable, flexible,
lithe, lithesome, limber; plastic; ductile, malleable, tractable;
yielding; flabby, flaccid, lax, limp, flimsy; mellow; spongy.

downy, woolly, fluffy, feathery.

325. ELASTICITY.—*N.* **elasticity,** springiness, spring, resili-
ence *or* resiliency, buoyancy; recoil, rebound, reflex.

V. **be elastic;** spring back, recoil.

Adj. **elastic,** springy, resilient, buoyant.

326. INELASTICITY.—*N.* **inelasticity,** flaccidity, laxity; want
of elasticity, etc., 325.

Adj. **inelastic,** flaccid, yielding; not elastic.

327. TENACITY.—*N.* **tenacity,** toughness, strength; cohesiveness, cohesion, adhesion; stubbornness, etc. (*obstinacy*), 606; gumminess, glutinousness, viscidity.

Adj. **tenacious,** cohesive, tough, strong, resisting; adhesive,
stringy, viscid, gummy, glutinous, gristly, cartilaginous; stubborn, etc. (*obstinate*), 606.

328. BRITTLENESS.—*N.* **brittleness,** fragility; frailty; shortness.

V. **break,** crack, snap, split, shiver, splinter, crumble, crash,
crush, burst, give way; fall to pieces; crumble to dust.

Adj. **brittle,** breakable, delicate, fragile, frail; splintery; crisp,
short [*as of pastry*].

329. STRUCTURE.—*N.* **structure,** organization, constitution,
organism, anatomy, frame, mold, fabric, construction; framework,
architecture; stratification.

texture, contexture; tissue, grain, web, surface, nap; roughness;
warp and woof (*or* weft); fineness (*or* coarseness) of grain.

Adj. **structural,** organic; anatomic *or* anatomical.

textile; fine-grained, coarse-grained, ingrained; ingrain; fine,
delicate, subtile, subtle, gossamer, gossamery, filmy; coarse;
homespun, linsey-woolsey.

330. POWDERINESS.—*N.* **powderiness,** grittiness, sandiness,
friability.

powder, dust, sand, shingle; sawdust; grit; meal, bran, flour,
rice, spore; crumb, seed, grain; particle.

Reduction to powder: pulverization, comminution, granulation,
disintegration, abrasion, detrition; mill, grater, rasp, file, pestle
and mortar, grindstone, quern, millstone.

V. **pulverize,** powder, comminute, granulate, reduce to powder;
scrape, file, abrade, grind, grate, rasp, pound, bruise, beat, crush,
craunch, crunch, crumble, disintegrate.

Adj. powdery, granular, mealy, floury, farinaceous, branny, dusty, sandy, gritty.

pulverable *or* pulverizable, friable, crumbly, shivery.

331. FRICTION.—*N.* friction, rubbing, abrasion, rub; massage; erasure; elbow grease [*colloq.*].

eraser, rubber, India rubber.

V. rub, abrade, scratch, scrape, scrub, fray, rasp, graze, curry, scour, polish, rub out, erase, file, grind, etc. (*pulverize*), 330; massage.

332. [Absence or prevention of friction] LUBRICATION.—*N.* lubrication, anointment, oiling.

smoothness, polish, gloss; unctuousness.

lubricant, lubricator; ointment, salve, balm, unguent.

V. lubricate, oil, grease; lather, soap; wax; anoint.

(2) Fluids

333. FLUIDITY.—*N.* fluidity, liquidity, liquidness; liquefaction; solubility; gaseity, etc., 334.

solution; fluid; liquid; juice, sap, lymph, serum.

Science of liquids at rest: hydrostatics, hydrodynamics, hydrokinetics.

V. be fluid; run; flow, etc. (*water in motion*), 348; liquefy, etc., 335.

Adj. liquid, fluid; juicy, succulent, sappy; rheumy; fluent, flowing; liquefied, uncongealed; soluble.

334. GASEITY.—*N.* gaseity, gaseousness, vaporousness; volatility; aeration; gasification; flatulence.

elastic fluid, gas, air, vapor, ether, steam, fume, effluvium; cloud, etc., 353.

Science of elastic fluids: pneumatics, aerostatics, aerodynamics, aerography, aeromechanics.

V. gasify, render gaseous; aerate; vaporize, etc., 336.

Adj. gaseous, ethereal, aery, aerial, airy, vaporous, volatile, flatulent.

335. LIQUEFACTION.—*N.* liquefaction, liquescence; deliquescence; melting, fusion; thaw; solubleness; solution.

mixture, decoction, infusion, solution.

V. dissolve, liquefy; run; melt, thaw, fuse; hold in solution; percolate.

Adj. liquefied; soluble, dissolvable; solvent, dissolvent.

336. VAPORIZATION.—*N.* vaporization, atomization; fumigation, steaming; distillation; gasification; evaporation.

vaporizer, atomizer, spray, evaporator, still, retort.

V. vaporize, gasify, atomize; spray; distill, sublimate, evaporate; exhale, emit vapor; fumigate; fume, smoke, reek, steam.

Adj. volatile, vapory, vaporous, gaseous; volatilized.

337. WATER.—*N.* water, lymph; aqua [L.], *eau* [F.]; fluid, etc., 333.

washing, bathing, bath, immersion; dilution; infiltration, irrigation, seepage.

deluge, etc. (*water in motion*), 348; high water, flood tide, spring-tide.

sprinkler, shower *or* shower bath; nozzle; atomizer, etc., 336.

water, dilute, add water; moisten, etc., 339; steep, soak, drench, wet, dip, immerse, submerge; duck; drown; wash, lave, bathe, sprinkle, dabble; inundate, deluge; irrigate; infiltrate, percolate, seep.

inject; gargle, syringe.

Adj. watery, aquatic, lymphatic; infiltrative, seepy; drenching; diluted, weak; wet, etc. (*moist*), 339.

338. AIR.—*N.* air, etc. (*gas*), 334; atmosphere; ventilation.

the open, open air; sky, blue sky.

weather, climate; rise and fall of the barometer (*or* mercury).

Science of air: aerology, aerometry, aerography; meteorology, climatology; pneumatics; aeronautics, etc., 267.

aeronaut, etc., 269*a*.

barometer, aneroid, weatherglass, weather gauge.

weather vane, weathercock, vane.

V. air, ventilate, fan, etc. (*wind*), 349.

fly, soar, drift, hover; aviate, etc. (*aeronautics*), 267.

Adj. containing air, flatulent, effervescent; windy, etc., 349.

atmospheric, airy; aerial, aeriform; aery, pneumatic.

meteorological, barometric, aerographic, weatherwise.

Adv. in the open air, in the open, under the stars, out of doors, outdoors; alfresco [It.].

339. MOISTURE.—*N.* moisture; moistness, humidity; dew; marsh, etc., 345.

V. moisten, wet, sponge, damp, bedew; infiltrate, saturate; soak, sodden, seethe, sop; drench, etc. (*water*), 337.

perspire, etc. (*exude*), 295.

Adj. moist, damp; watery, etc., 337; undried, humid, wet, dank, muggy; dewy; juicy.

sodden, soppy, soggy, dabbled; reeking, dripping, soaking, saturated, soft, sloppy, muddy: swampy, etc. (*marshy*), 345; irriguous.

340. DRYNESS.—*N.* dryness, aridness, aridity, drought.

desiccation, evaporation; drainage.

V. dry, dry up, soak up; sponge, swab, wipe, drain, parch, sear; desiccate, evaporate.

Adj. dry, rainless, fair, pleasant, fine; arid, sear, droughty, waterless, dried, desiccated; juiceless, sapless; corky; husky, parched; waterproof, watertight.

341. OCEAN—*N.* ocean, sea, main, high seas, deep, salt water; waters, waves, billows; tide, etc. (*water in motion*), 348; offing, watery waste, pond [*humorous for Atlantic*], the seven seas; ocean lane, steamer track.

Neptune, Poseidon, Oceanus, Thetis, Triton, naiad, Nereid; sea nymph, siren, mermaid, merman; trident, dolphin.

oceanography; oceanographer.

Adj. oceanic, marine, maritime; seaworthy, seagoing.

342. LAND.—*N.* land, earth, ground, soil, dry land, terra firma [L.].

continent; mainland, main; peninsula, chersonese; delta; neck of land, isthmus; oasis; promontory, etc. (*projection*), 250; highland, etc. (*height*), 206; plain, etc., 344.

realty, real estate, property, acres.

coast, shore, strand, beach; bank; seaboard, seaside, seacoast, seashore; reclamation, made land.

fatherland, home, country, native land; region, etc., 181.

soil, glebe, clay, loam, marl, gravel, mold, subsoil, clod.

rock, crag, cliff, boulder.

landsman, landlubber, tiller of the soil; agriculturist, etc., 371.

V. land, disembark, debark, come to land, come (*or* go) ashore.

Adj. earthy; continental, midland; earthly, terrestrial; littoral, alluvial; landed, territorial; geographic *or* geographical.

Adv. ashore, on shore, on land, on dry land, on terra firma.

343. GULF, LAKE.—*N.* gulf, bay, inlet, bight, estuary, bayou, fiord, frith *or* firth; mouth; lagoon, cove, creek; natural harbor; roads; sound, strait, narrows.

lake, loch [Scot.], mere, tarn, pond, pool; well, artesian well; ditch, dike, dam, race, millrace; tank, reservoir.

344. PLAIN.—*N.* plain, open country; basin, downs, waste, desert, wild, steppe [*Russia*], grassland; tundra [*Arctic*], pampas [*esp. in Argentina*], savanna [*as in Brazil; also, a treeless plain, as in Florida*], campo [*S. Amer.*], llano [*S. Amer.*], prairie, heath, common, moor, moorland; bush; plateau, tableland, mesa; uplands; reach, stretch, expanse; alkali flat.

meadow, mead, pasture, lea, pasturage, field.

lawn, green, plot, grassplot.

greensward, sward, turf, sod, grass; heather.

grounds; estate, park, common, campus.

345. MARSH.—*N.* marsh, swamp, morass, peat bog, fen, bog, quagmire, slough; mud, slush.

Adj. marsh, marshy, fenny, swampy, boggy, soft; muddy, squashy, spongy.

346. ISLAND.—*N.* island, isle, islet; reef, atoll; archipelago; islander.

V. insulate, island.

Adj. insular, seagirt; archipelagic.

347. [Fluid in motion] STREAM.—*N.* stream, etc. (*of water*), 348 (*of air*), 349.

V. flow, etc., 348; blow, etc., 349.

348. [Water in motion] RIVER.—*N.* running water, jet, squirt, spout, splash, rush, gush, sluice.

waterspout, waterfall; fall, cascade, Niagara; cataract, inundation, deluge; chute, washout.

rain, rainfall; drizzle, shower; downpour, cloudburst; rains, rainy season, monsoon.

stream, course, flux, flow, current, tide, race, millrace, tiderace. spring; fount, fountain; rill, rivulet, streamlet, brooklet; branch; brook, river; reach; tributary.

body of water, torrent, rapids, flood; spring (*or* high, flood, full) tide; bore, eagre; ebb, reflux; undercurrent, undertow; eddy, vortex, whirlpool, maelstrom.

wave, billow, surge, swell, ripple; tidal wave; comber, rollers, ground swell, surf, breakers, white horses.

Science of fluids in motion: hydrodynamics; hydraulics, hydrostatics, hydrokinetics, hydromechanics.

V. flow, run; meander; gush, pour, spout, roll, jet, well, issue; drop, drip, dribble, plash, trickle, distill, percolate; stream, surge, swirl, overflow, inundate, deluge, flow over, splash, swash; murmur, babble, purl, gurgle, spurt, ooze, flow out, etc. (*egress*), 295.

flow into, fall into, open into, drain into; discharge itself, disembogue.

Cause a flow: pour; pour out, etc. (*emit*), 297; shower down; irrigate, drench, etc. (*wet*), 337; spill, splash.

Stop a flow: stanch; dam, plug, stop up, cork, dam up, obstruct, choke, cut off.

rain; pour; shower, sprinkle, drizzle; set in.

Adj. flowing, fluent, meandering, flexuous; choppy, rolling; tidal.

rainy, showery, drizzly, drizzling, wet.

349. [Air in motion] WIND.—*N.* wind, draft, air; breath, puff, whiff, zephyr, blow, stream, current.

gust, blast, breeze, squall, half a gale, gale.

trade wind, trades, monsoon.

storm, tempest, hurricane, whirlwind, tornado, cyclone, typhoon, simoom [as in Asia Minor], harmattan [W. coast of Africa], sirocco [as in W. Africa, Texas, and Kansas], khamsin [Egypt], mistral [Mediterranean]; blizzard, norther, northeaster, northeast gale.

wind gauge, anemometer, anemograph; weathercock, weather vane, vane.

breathing, respiration, inspiration, inhalation, expiration, exhalation; blowing, fanning, inflation; ventilation.

V. blow, waft; storm.

respire, breathe, inhale, exhale; inspire, expire; puff, gasp, wheeze· snuff, snuffle; sniff, sniffle; sneeze, cough, hiccup.

inflate, pump, blow up.

whistle, scream, roar, howl, sing, sing in the shrouds, growl.

Adj. windy, breezy, gusty, squally.

stormy, tempestuous, blustering, cyclonic, typhonic; boisterous, violent.

350. [Channel for the passage of water] CONDUIT.—N. conduit, channel, duct, watercourse, canyon, coulee, water gap, gorge, ravine, chasm; race; aqueduct, canal: flume, dike, main· arroyo, gully, gulch; moat, ditch; gutter, drain, sewer, culvert; scupper; funnel, trough, siphon, pump, hose; pipe, tube; artery; spout, gargoyle; weir, floodgate, water gate, sluice, lock, valve.

Anatomy: artery, vein, blood vessel, pore; aorta; intestines, bowels; esophagus, gullet; throat.

351. [Channel for the passage of air] AIR PIPE—N. air pipe, airhole, blowhole, breathing hole, touchhole, venthole, spilehole, bung, bunghole; shaft, air shaft, smoke shaft, flue, chimney, funnel, vent, ventilator.

nostril, nozzle, throat; windpipe, trachea.

352. SEMILIQUIDITY.—N. semiliquidity; stickiness, pastiness, adhesiveness; thickening, jellification.

mud, slush, slime, ooze; moisture, humidity; marsh, etc., 345.

V. thicken, coagulate, gelatinize; jellify, jelly, jell [colloq.]; emulsify; mash, squash [colloq.], churn, beat up.

Adj. semifluid, semiliquid; half-melted, half-frozen; milky, muddy, curdled; thick, gelatinous, mucilaginous, glutinous, sticky; ropy; clotted.

353. [Mixture of air and water] BUBBLE, CLOUD.—N. bubble; foam, froth, spray, surf; spume, scum; lather, suds, yeast.

effervescence, babbling, fermentation; evaporation.

cloud, vapor, fog, mist, haze, steam; scud, rack, cumulus; nebula, cirrus, curl cloud; thunderhead; stratus.

V. bubble, boil, foam, spume, froth; effervesce, ferment, fizz; aerate.

cloud, overcast, overcloud, befog, becloud, mist, fog, overshadow, shadow.

Adj. bubbling, frothy, effervescent, sparkling, fizzy, heady, cloudy, nebulous; vaporous; overcast.

354. PULPINESS.—*N.* pulpiness; fleshiness; pulp, paste, dough, sponge, batter, curd, pap, jam, poultice.

V. pulp, mash, squash [*colloq.*], macerate; coagulate, etc., 352.

Adj. pulpy; [*of fruit*] fleshy, succulent.

355. UNCTUOUSNESS.—*N.* unctuousness, oiliness; lubrication; unguent, salve, cerate; ointment, etc. (*oil*), 356; anointment; lubricant.

V. oil, anoint, lubricate, etc., 332; smear, salve, grease, lard.

Adj. unctuous, oily, oleaginous, fat, fatty, greasy; waxy, soapy, slippery.

356. OIL.—*N.* oil, fat, butter, cream, grease, tallow, suet, lard, dripping, blubber; glycerin; coconut butter; soap, soft soap; wax; paraffin, benzine, kerosene, naphtha, gasoline, petroleum; ointment, pomade, unguent, liniment.

356a. RESIN.—*N.* resin, rosin, gum; shellac, varnish, mastic, lacquer, sealing wax; amber, ambergris; bitumen, pitch, tar, asphalt.

V. varnish, etc. (*overlay*), 223; rosin, resin.

Adj. resinous, lacquered, tarred, tarry, pitched, pitchy, gummed, gummy, waxed; bituminous, asphaltic.

III. ORGANIC MATTER

(1) Vitality

357. ORGANIZATION.—*N.* organization, structure, organized nature, animated nature; living beings; organic remains; organism; animal and plant life, fauna and flora.

fossils; fossilization, petrifaction; paleontology; paleontologist.

Science of living beings: biology, natural history;[1] zoology, etc., 368, botany; physiology, anatomy, organic chemistry; evolution, Darwinism.

protoplasm, bioplasm; cell, proteid, protein, albumen, germinal matter, germ plasm, germ cell; amoeba, protozoan.

naturalist, biologist, zoologist, botanist, bacteriologist, embryologist.

[1]The term *natural history* is also used as relating to all the objects in nature whether organic or inorganic, and including, therefore, *mineralogy, geology, meteorology*, etc.

V. **organize,** systematize, form, arrange, construct.

fossilize, petrify, mummify.

Adj. **organic,** organized, structural; cellular, protoplasmic.

fossilized, petrified.

358. INORGANIZATION.—*N.* **mineral kingdom,** mineral world; unorganized (*or* inorganic) matter.

Science of the mineral kingdom: mineralogy, geology, metallurgy.

V. **mineralize;** pulverize, turn to dust.

Adj. **inorganic,** inanimate, unorganized, mineral.

359. LIFE.—*N.* **life;** vitality; existence, etc.; animation.

vital spark, vital flame, lifeblood; respiration, breath, breath of life.

vivification; oxygen; life force; vitalization; revival; revivification, etc., 163; life to come, etc. (*destiny*), 152.

Science of life: physiology, biology, embryology.

nourishment, nutriment, etc. (*food*), 298.

V. **live,** be alive, breathe, subsist, exist, walk the earth.

be born, see the light, come into the world; quicken; revive; come to life.

give birth to, etc. (*produce*), 161; bring to life, put life into, vitalize; vivify, reanimate, restore, resuscitate.

Adj. **living,** alive; in life, in the flesh, breathing, quick, animated; lively, etc. (*active*), 682; vital, vivifying.

360. DEATH.—*N.* **death,** decease, demise; mortality; dying, dissolution, departure, release, rest, eternal rest; loss, bereavement.

cessation (*or* loss, extinction) of life.

river of death; Jordan, Stygian shore; the great adventure.

angel of death, death's bright angel; death, doom, fate, destiny.

death song, dirge, requiem, elegy, threnody.

V. **die,** expire, perish; breathe one's last; lose *or* lay down one's life; die a violent death; give (*or* yield) up the ghost.

die for one's country, make the supreme sacrifice, go West [*First World War euphemism*].

Adj. **dead,** lifeless, inanimate; deceased, late; departed, defunct; gone, no more; bereft of life.

deadly, mortal, fatal.

dying, moribund, at the point of death, at death's door, at the last gasp.

361. [Destruction of life; violent death] KILLING.—*N.* **killing;** homicide, manslaughter; murder, assassination; effusion of blood; bloodshed, slaughter, carnage, butchery, massacre.

war, warfare, organized murder; battle; war to the death, etc. (*warfare*), 722; Armageddon; deadly weapon, etc. (*arms*), 727.

deathblow, finishing stroke, *coup de grace* [F.], quietus; execution, etc. (*capital punishment*), 972; martyrdom.

suffocation, strangulation, garrote; hanging, etc., *v.*

slayer, butcher, murderer, Cain, assassin, cutthroat, garroter, thug, gallows, executioner, etc. (*punishment*), 975; apache, gunman [*colloq.*], bandit.

regicide, parricide, fratricide [*these words refer to both doer and deed*].

suicide, self-murder, self-destruction, hara-kiri [Jap.], suttee; immolation, holocaust.

fatal accident, violent death, casualty, disaster, calamity.

Destruction of animals: slaughtering; sport; the chase, venery; hunting, coursing, shooting, fishing; pigsticking.

sportsman, huntsman, hunter, Nimrod; fisherman, angler.

shambles, slaughterhouse.

V. **kill**, put to death, slay, shed blood; murder, assassinate, butcher, slaughter, immolate; massacre, decimate; put an end to; dispatch, do to death, do for [*colloq.*]; hunt, shoot, saber, stab, bayonet, put to the sword.

strangle, garrote, hang, throttle, choke, stifle, suffocate; smother, asphyxiate, drown.

execute; behead, guillotine; hang; electrocute.

die a violent death; commit suicide; kill (*or* make away with, put an end to) oneself.

Adj. **murderous**, slaughterous, sanguinary, bloody-minded, bloodthirsty; homicidal; red-handed, bloody, bloodstained, gory.

mortal, fatal, deadly, lethal; mutually destructive, internecine; suicidal.

362. CORPSE.—*N.* **corpse**, carcass, skeleton, relics, remains, dust, ashes, earth, clay; mummy; carrion.

ghost, shade, phantom, specter, apparition, spirit, revenant, spook [*colloq.*].

363. INTERMENT.—*N.* **interment**, burial, sepulture, entombment; obsequies, funeral, funeral rite, wake; knell, passing bell, death bell, tolling; dirge, etc. (*lamentation*), 839; dead march, muffled drum; pall, bier, litter, hearse, catafalque.

cremation, burning; pyre, funeral pile.

undertaker, funeral director.

mourner, mute; pallbearer, bearer.

graveclothes, shroud, winding sheet; cerecloth, cerements.

coffin, casket; urn; sarcophagus.

burial place, grave, pit, sepulcher, tomb, vault, crypt, catacomb, mausoleum; cemetery, burial ground, graveyard, churchyard; God's acre; potter's field; barrow, tumulus; charnel house, dead-house; morgue, mortuary; burning ghat [India]; crematorium, crematory.

gravedigger, sexton.

monument; gravestone, headstone, tombstone; hatchment, stone, marker, cross; epitaph, inscription.

autopsy, post-mortem examination *or* post mortem [L.].

disinterment, exhumation.

V. inter, bury, entomb; inurn; cremate.

disinter, exhume, unearth.

Adj. funereal, funeral, mortuary, sepulchral, cinerary; burial; elegiac.

364. ANIMAL LIFE.—*N.* animal life, animalism.

human system; breath; flesh, flesh and blood; physique, strength, power, vigor, force; spring, elasticity, tone.

V. incarnate, incorporate.

Adj. fleshly, carnal, human, corporeal.

365. VEGETATION.—*N.* vegetation, vegetable life, growth, herbage, flowerage.

V. vegetate, germinate, sprout, grow, shoot up, luxuriate, grow rank, flourish, flower, blossom; cultivate.

Adj. vegetative, vegetal, vegetable; leguminous, etc., 367.

luxuriant, rank, dense, lush, wild.

366. ANIMAL.—*N.* animal kingdom, fauna, brute creation.

animal, creature, created being, living thing; dumb animal, dumb friend, dumb creature; brute, beast.

mammal, quadruped, bird, reptile, fish, crustacean, shellfish, mollusk, worm, insect, zoophyte; animalcule, etc., 193.

beasts of the field, fowls of the air; flocks and herds, livestock, domestic animals, wild animals, game.

Domestic animals: horse, etc. (*beast of burden*), 271; cattle, ox; bull, bullock; cow, milch cow, Jersey, calf, heifer, shorthorn, yearling, steer; sheep; lamb, ewe, ram; pig, swine, boar, hog, sow; yak, zebu, buffalo.

dog, hound, canine; pup, puppy; whelp, cur [*contemptuous*], mongrel.

cat, feline, puss, pussy, tabby; tomcat *or* tom; mouser; Angora, Persian, Maltese, tortoise-shell; kitten, kitty.

Wild animals: deer, buck, doe, fawn, stag, hart, hind, roe, roebuck, caribou, elk, moose, reindeer, wapiti *or* American elk, fallow deer, red deer.

antelope, gazelle, American antelope *or* pronghorn, chamois.

ape, monkey, gorilla, marmoset, chimpanzee, lemur, baboon, orangutan.

fox, reynard, vixen [*fem.*]; dingo, coyote; wildcat, lynx, bobcat; skunk.

lion, tiger, etc. (*wild beast*), 913.

rat, mouse.

lizard, saurian, iguana, newt, chameleon, Gila monster, dragon; crocodile, alligator.

whale, shark, porpoise, walrus, seal, octopus, devilfish; swordfish; pike; salmon, trout, etc.

Birds: feathered tribes, singing bird, warbler, dickybird [*colloq.*].

canary, vireo, linnet, finch, goldfinch, siskin, crossbill, chewink, peewee, titmouse *or* chickadee, nightingale, lark; magpie, cuckoo, mocking bird, catbird, starling; robin, sparrow, swallow, etc.

swan, cygnet, goose, gander, duck, drake, wild duck, mallard.

gull, sea gull, albatross, petrel, stormy petrel *or* Mother Carey's chicken; owl, bird of night; hawk, vulture, buzzard; eagle, bird of freedom.

game, ruffed grouse, grouse, blackcock, duck, plover, rail, snipe, pheasant.

poultry, fowl, cock, rooster, chanticleer, barndoor fowl, barnyard fowl, hen, chicken, chick; guinea fowl, guinea hen; peafowl, peacock, peahen.

Insects: bee, honeybee, queen bee, drone; ant, white ant, termite; wasp, locust, grasshopper, cicada, cicala, cricket; dragonfly; beetle; butterfly, moth; fly, mosquito; earwig; bug, buffalo bug, gypsy moth, weevil.

vermin, lice, cooties [*slang*], flies, fleas, cockroaches *or* roaches, water bugs, bugs, bedbugs, mosquitoes; rats, mice, weasels.

snake, serpent, viper; asp, adder, coral snake *or* harlequin snake, krait [India], cobra, cobra de capello, king cobra, rattlesnake *or* rattler, copperhead, constrictor, boa constrictor, boa, python.

Mythological: basilisk, cockatrice, salamander; griffin; chimera; Python, Hydra, Cerberus.

Adj. **animal;** zoological; equine; bovine; canine; feline; fishy, piscatorial; ophidian, reptilian, snakelike.

367. VEGETABLE.—*N.* **vegetable,** vegetable kingdom; flora.

organism, plant, tree, shrub, bush, creeper, vine; herb, seedling; exotic; annual, perennial; pulse, greens.

foliage, leafage, verdure; branch, bough, stem, trunk; leaf, spray, leaflet, frond, pad, flag, petal, needle, sepal; spray, runner, shoot, tendril.

flower, blossom, bud, floweret, flowering plant.

tree, sapling, seedling; oak, elm, beech, birch, timber tree, pine, palm, spruce, fir, hemlock, yew, larch, cedar, juniper, chestnut, maple, alder, ash, myrtle, magnolia, walnut, olive, poplar, willow, linden, lime; fruit tree; arboretum, etc., 371.

banyan, teak, acacia, deodar, fig tree, eucalyptus, gum tree.

woodlands, virgin forest, forest primeval, forest, wood, timberland, timber, wood lot; weald, park, greenwood, grove, copse, coppice, thicket, chaparral, jungle, bush.

undergrowth, underwood, brushwood, brake, scrub, heath, heather, fern, bracken, furze, gorse, broom, sedge, rush, bulrush, bamboo; weed, moss, lichen, turf, grass, herbage.

grassland, plain, etc., 344.

seaweed, alga (*pl.* algae), dulse, kelp, rockweed, sea lettuce, gulfweed, sargasso, sargassum; Sargasso Sea.

V. **vegetate,** grow, flourish, bloom, flower, blossom; bud, etc. (*expand*), 194; timber, retimber, plant, trim, graft, prune, cut.

Adj. **vegetable,** vegetative, vegetarian; leguminous, herbaceous, herbal, botanic *or* botanical; arboreous, arboreal, sylvan; grassy, verdant, verdurous; floral; ligneous, wooden, woody; bosky, copsy; mossy, turfy. deciduous, evergreen.

native, domestic, indigenous, native-grown, home-grown.

368. [Science of animals] ZOOLOGY.—*N.* zoology, zoography, morphology, anatomy, histology, embryology; comparative anatomy, animal physiology, comparative physiology, anthropology, ornithology, ichthyology, entomology, paleontology.

zoologist, zoographer, zoographist, anatomist, anthropologist, ornithologist, ichthyologist, entomologist, paleontologist.

Adj. zoological, zoologic; zoographical.

369. [Science of plants] BOTANY.—*N.* botany, phytology, phytobiology, vegetable chemistry; vegetable physiology, dendrology; flora; botanic garden, etc. (*garden*), 371.

botanist, phytologist, phytobiologist, dendrologist; horticulturist, etc., 371; herbalist, herbist, herbarian.

V. botanize, herborize.

Adj. botanic *or* botanical, dendroid, dendriform, herby, herbal; horticultural.

370. MANAGEMENT OF ANIMALS.—*N.* domestication, domesticity, manège, veterinary art; breeding, taming.

menagerie, zoological garden, zoo [*colloq.*]; bear pit; aviary; apiary, beehive, hive; aquarium, fishery, fish hatchery, fish pond; hennery, incubator.
Keeper: herder, cowherd, grazier, drover, cowkeeper; shepherd, shepherdess; gamekeeper; trainer, breeder; cowboy, cowpuncher; horse trainer, bronchobuster [*slang*]; beekeeper, apiarist, apiculturist.

veterinarian, veterinary surgeon, vet [*colloq.*], horse doctor, horseshoer.

inclosure, stable, barn; sheepfold, sty; cage, hencoop.

V. tame, domesticate; corral, round up; break in, gentle, break, bust [*slang*], break to harness, train; ride, drive; spur, prick, lash, goad, whip; yoke, harness, harness up [*colloq.*], hitch, hitch up [*colloq.*], cinch.

groom, tend, rub down, brush, currycomb; water, feed, fodder; bed down, litter.

tend stock, milk, shear; water, etc. (*groom*), *v.*; herd; raise, bring up.

hatch, incubate, sit, brood, cover.

Adj. tame, domestic, domesticated, housebroken, broken, gentle, docile.

371. MANAGEMENT OF PLANTS.—*N.* agriculture, cultivation, husbandry, farming; tillage, gardening, vintage; horticulture, arboriculture, forestry; floriculture; landscape gardening.

husbandman, horticulturist, gardener, florist; agriculturist, yeoman, farmer, granger, cultivator, tiller of the soil, plowman; logger, lumberman, lumberjack, forester, woodcutter, pioneer, backwoodsman.
garden: botanic (*or* flower, kitchen, market, truck) garden; nursery; greenhouse, hothouse, conservatory; grassplot, lawn; shrubbery, arboretum, orchard; vineyard, orangery.

field, meadow, mead, green, common.

V. cultivate, till, till the soil, farm, garden, sow, plant; reap, mow, cut; manure, dress the ground; dig, spade, delve, hoe, plow, harrow, rake, weed; force, seed, turf; transplant, thin out, bed, prune, graft.

Adj. arable, plowable, tillable.

rural, rustic, country, agrarian, pastoral, bucolic, Arcadian.

372. MANKIND.—*N.* mankind, man; human race (*or* species, kind, nature); humanity, mortality, generation.

Science of man: anthropology, ethnology, ethnography.

human being; person, personage; individual, creature, fellow creature, mortal, body, somebody, one, someone; soul, living soul; party [*slang or vulgar*].

people, persons, folk, public, society, world; community, general public; nation, state, realm, republic; commonweal, commonwealth; body politic; the masses, etc. (*commonalty*), 876; population; lords of creation; ourselves.

Adj. human, mortal, personal, individual; national, civic, public social.

373. MAN.—*N.* man, male; gentleman, sir, master; yeoman, chap [*colloq.*], swain, fellow, blade, beau; husband, etc. (*youth*), 129.

mister, Mr., *monsieur* (*abbr.* M., *pl.* Messrs.) [F.], *Herr* [Ger.], *signor* [It., *used before name*], *signore* [It.], *signorino* [It., *dim. of signore*], *señor* [Sp.], *senhor* [Pg.].

Male animal: cock, drake, gander, dog, boar, stag, hart, buck, horse, stallion, gelding; tom, tomcat; he-goat, billy goat [*colloq.*]; ram; bull, bullock; capon; ox, steer.

Adj. male, masculine, manly, virile; unwomanly, unfeminine.

374. WOMAN.—*N.* woman, female, petticoat.

womankind, womanhood; the sex, fair sex, softer sex.

dame [*archaic except as an elderly woman or as slang*], madam, lady, donna, belle, matron, dowager, good woman, squaw; wife.

spinster, old maid, bachelor girl, new woman, girl, etc. (*youth*), 129.

mistress, Mrs., *madame* (*pl.* mesdames) [F.], *Frau* [Ger.], *signora* [It.], *señora* [Sp.], *senhora* [Pg.]; miss, *mademoiselle* (*pl.* mesdemoiselles) [F.], *Fräulein* [Ger.], *signorina* [It.], *señorita* [Sp.], *senhorita* [Pg.].

Effeminacy: betty, molly, mollycoddle, old woman, tame cat [*all contemptuous*].

Female animal: hen; bitch, slut; sow, doe, roe, mare; she-goat, nanny goat [*colloq.*], nanny [*colloq.*]; ewe, cow; lioness, tigress; vixen.

harem, seraglio, purdah [India].

Adj. female, feminine, womanly, ladylike, matronly, girlish, maidenly; womanish, effeminate, unmanly.

(2) Sensation

375. PHYSICAL SENSIBILITY.—*N.* sensibility, sensitiveness, feeling, impressibility, susceptibility.

sensation, impression; consciousness.

V. feel, perceive, be sensitive to.

render sensitive, sharpen, refine, excite, stir, cultivate, tutor. cause sensation, impress, excite (*or* produce) an impression.

Adj. sensitive, sensuous; perceptive, sentient, sensible; conscious, alive, alive to impressions, impressionable, responsive. acute, sharp, keen, vivid, lively.

Adv. to the quick; on the raw [*slang*].

376. PHYSICAL INSENSIBILITY.—*N.* insensibility, obtuseness, paralysis, anesthesia, hypnosis, stupor, coma, sleep.

anesthetic; opium, ether, chloroform, chloral; nitrous oxide, laughing gas; cocaine, novocain; refrigeration.

V. render insensible, blunt, cloy, satiate; benumb, numb, deaden, freeze, paralyze; anesthetize; put to sleep, hypnotize, stupefy, stun.

Adj. insensible, unfeeling, senseless, callous, hard, hardened, casehardened, proof, obtuse, dull; paralytic, palsied, numb, dead.

377. PHYSICAL PLEASURE.—*N.* pleasure, bodily enjoyment, animal gratification, gusto, relish, delight, sensual delight, sensuality; luxuriousness, dissipation, round of pleasure; comfort, ease, luxury, lap of luxury; creature comforts; purple and fine linen; bed of roses.

treat; diversion, entertainment, banquet, refreshment, feast.

happiness, felicity, bliss, beatitude, etc. (*mental enjoyment*), 827.

V. enjoy, relish; luxuriate in, revel in, bask in, wallow in; feast on, gloat over, smack the lips.

please, charm, delight, enchant, etc., 829.

Adj. comfortable, cosy, snug, luxurious, in comfort, at ease, in clover [*colloq.*].

agreeable, etc., 829; grateful, refreshing, comforting, cordial, genial; gratifying, sensuous; palatable, delicious, sweet; fragrant; melodious, harmonious; lovely, etc. (*beautiful*), 845.

Adv. in comfort, on a bed of roses, on flowery beds of ease.

378. PHYSICAL PAIN.—*N.* pain, suffering, dolor, ache, smart; shoot, shooting, twinge, pang, gripe, hurt, cut; sore, soreness; discomfort.

spasm, cramp; crick, stitch; convulsion, throe; throb, colic, gripes.

torment, torture, agony, anguish, rack, crucifixion, martyrdom.

V. **suffer,** feel (*or* suffer, undergo) pain; ache, smart, bleed, tingle, shoot, twinge; writhe, wince.

pain, give pain, inflict pain; lacerate; hurt, chafe, sting, bite, gnaw, stab, grate, gall, fret, prick, pierce, wring, convulse; torment, torture; rack, agonize; crucify; flog, etc. (*punish*), 972.

Adj. **painful,** aching, poignant, excruciating, biting; on the rack; sore, raw.

(1) *Touch*

379. [Sensation of pressure] **TOUCH.**—*N.* **touch,** contact, tangency, impact, feeling; graze, glance, brush, lick; manipulation, rubbing, kneading, massage.

V. **touch,** feel, handle, finger, thumb, paw, fumble, grope; stroke, massage, rub, knead, manipulate, wield; throw out a feeler.

Adj. **tactual,** tangible, palpable, tangent, lambent.

380. SENSATIONS OF TOUCH.—*N.* itching, tickling, titillation.

itch, scabies; mange.

V. **itch,** tingle, creep, thrill, sting; prick, prickle.

tickle, titillate.

Adj. **ticklish,** titillative.

itchy, mangy; creepy, crawly.

381. [Insensibility to touch] **NUMBNESS.**—*N.* **numbness;** physical insensibility, etc., 376; anesthesia.

V. **benumb,** etc., 376; stupefy, drug, deaden, paralyze.

Adj. **numb,** benumbed, insensible, unfeeling, deadened; intangible, impalpable; dazed, comatose, narcotic.

(2) *Heat*

382. HEAT.—*N.* **heat,** caloric; temperature, warmth, incandescence.

summer, dog days, heat wave, broiling sun; sun, etc. (*luminary*), 423.

flush, glow, blush, redness; fever.

fire, spark, scintillation, flash, flame, blaze; bonfire; wildfire; sheet of fire, lambent flame.

hot springs, geysers; thermae, hot baths, Turkish bath; steam.

V. **be hot,** glow, flush, sweat, swelter, bask, smoke, reek, stew, simmer, seethe, boil, burn, singe, scorch, scald, broil, blaze, flame; smolder, parch, pant.

heat, etc. (*make hot*), 384; incandesce.

thaw, fuse, melt, liquefy.

Adj. warm, mild, genial; tepid, lukewarm.

hot, heated, fervid, fervent, baking, ardent, sunny, sunshiny, torrid, tropical, thermal.

close, sultry, stifling, stuffy, suffocating, oppressive, sweltering.

fiery; incandescent, ebullient, glowing, aglow, reeking, smoking; live; on fire, blazing, in flames, in a blaze; alight, afire, ablaze, smoldering.

feverish, febrile, inflamed, burning; in a fever.

383. COLD.—*N.* cold, coldness, frigidity, inclemency.

winter; depth of winter; hard winter; arctic, antarctic.

ice; sleet; hail, hailstone; frost, rime, hoarfrost; icicle, thick-ribbed ice; iceberg, floe, berg, ice field, ice pack, glacier.

snow, snowflake, snowball, snowdrift, snowstorm, snowslip, snow avalanche.

chill, chilliness, shivering, goose flesh, chilblains, frostbite, chattering of teeth.

V. be cold, shiver, quake, shake, tremble, shudder, chill, freeze.

Adj. cold, cool, chill, chilly, frigid; fresh, keen, bleak, raw, inclement, bitter, biting, cutting, nipping, piercing, pinching; shivering, anguish; frostbitten.

icy, glacial, frosty, freezing, wintry, boreal, arctic, snowbound, icebound, frost-bound, frozen.

Adv. with chattering teeth.

384. CALEFACTION.—*N.* calefaction, tepefaction, heating, melting, fusion, liquefaction, combustion; cremation; calcination; incineration; carbonization; cauterization.

ignition, kindling, inflammation, conflagration; incendiarism, arson; auto-da-fé [Pg.], the stake, burning at the stake; suttee.

incendiary, arsonist, pyromaniac, fire bug.

boiling, ebullition, ebullience, decoction; hot spring, geyser.

crematory, crematorium, incinerator; furnace, etc., 386.

wrap, blanket, flannel, wool, fur; wadding, lining, interlining; clothing, etc., 225.

Products of combustion: cinder, ash, embers, slag, clinker; coke, carbon, charcoal.

V. heat, warm, chafe, foment; make hot; sun oneself, bask in the sun.

fire, set fire to, set on fire; kindle, enkindle, light, ignite; rekindle.

melt, thaw, fuse; liquefy, dissolve.

burn, scorch; inflame; roast, toast, fry, grill, singe, parch, bake; brand, cauterize, sear, burn in; corrode, char, carbonize, calcine, incinerate, smelt; reduce to ashes.

take *or* catch fire; blaze, etc. (*flame*), 382.

boil, stew, cook, seethe, scald, parboil, simmer.

Adj. **heated,** warmed; burnt, scorched; molten; volcanic.

inflammable, inflammatory, combustible.

385. REFRIGERATION.—*N.* refrigeration, cooling, congelation, glaciation; solidification; ice; icebox, ice chest; refrigerator.

fire extinguisher, asbestos; fireman, fire brigade, fire department, fire engine.

V. **cool,** fan, refresh; ice, refrigerate, congeal, freeze, benumb, chill, petrify, pinch, nip, cut, pierce, bite.

extinguish, put out, stamp out; damp, slack, quench.

Adj. **incombustible,** asbestic, unflammable, uninflammable; fireproof.

386. FURNACE.—*N.* furnace, stove; cookstove, cooker, oven, brick oven, tin oven, Dutch oven, range, fireless cooker; forge, fiery furnace; volcano; kiln, brickkiln, limekiln.

brasier, tripod, salamander, heater, warming pan, footstove, foot warmer; radiator, register, coil; boiler, caldron, pot; urn, kettle; chafing dish; retort, crucible, alembic, still; flatiron, sadiron; toasting fork, toaster.

galley, caboose; hothouse, conservatory; bakehouse; washhouse, laundry.

fireplace, hearth, grate, firebox; andiron, firedog, fire irons; poker, tongs, shovel, hob, trivet; damper, crane, pothooks, chains, turnspit, spit, gridiron.

hot bath; thermae; Turkish (*or* Russian), vapor, electric, sitz, hip, shower) bath; bathroom, lavatory.

387. REFRIGERATOR.—*N.* refrigerator, icebox, ice chest; cold storage; refrigerating plant; icehouse; ice-cream freezer; freezer; ice bag, ice pack, cold pack; ice pail, cooler, wine cooler.

refrigerant, freezing, mixture, ice, ammonia.

388. FUEL.—*N.* fuel, firing, combustible, coal, anthracite, bituminous coal; carbon, slack, cannel coal *or* cannel, lignite, coke, charcoal; turf, peat; oil, gas, natural gas, electricity; ember, cinder, ash, slag, clinker; tinder, touchwood; punk.

log, backlog, yule log, firewood, fagot, kindling wood, kindlings, brushwood. fumigator, incense, joss stick; smudge; disinfectant.

brand, firebrand, torch; fuse, wick; spill, match, light.

V. **coal,** stoke; feed, fire, etc., 384.

Adj. **carbonaceous;** combustible, inflammable; slow-burning, free-burning.

389. THERMOMETER.—*N.* thermometer, thermometrograph, thermostat, thermoscope; differential thermometer, telethermometer, pyrometer.

(3) *Taste*

390. TASTE.—*N.* taste, flavor, gusto, savor, relish; smack, tang; aftertaste.

palate; tongue; tooth; stomach.

V. taste, flavor, savor, smack; tickle the palate, etc. (*savory*), 394.

Adj. tasty, savory, flavored, spiced; palatable, etc., 394.

391. INSIPIDITY.—*N.* insipidity; tastelessness, unsavoriness.

Adj. insipid; tasteless, unsavory, unflavored, jejune, savorless; weak, stale, flat, vapid, wishy-washy [*colloq.*].

392. PUNGENCY.—*N.* pungency, piquancy, poignancy, tang, nip.

sharpness, acridity; sourness, unsavoriness.

dram, cordial, nip, bracer [*colloq.*], pick-me-up [*colloq.*], potion, liqueur.

tobacco, nicotine; smoke, cigar, cheroot, stogy; cigarette, fag [*slang*], Havana, Cuban tobacco; weed [*colloq.*]; snuff.

V. season, spice, bespice, salt, pepper, pickle, brine, devil, curry.

Adj. pungent, strong, high-flavored, full-flavored, high-seasoned; gamy, high; sharp, piquant, racy; biting, mordant; spicy; seasoned, spiced; hot, peppery; acrid, bitter; sour, acid, etc., 397; unsavory, etc., 395.

salt, saline, brackish, briny.

393. CONDIMENT.—*N.* condiment, flavoring, seasoning, sauce, spice, relish; pickle; chutney; appetizer.

V. season, etc. (*render pungent*), 392.

394. SAVORINESS.—*N.* savoriness, tastiness, palatability; delectability; relish, zest.

appetizer, hors d'oeuvre [F.].

delicacy, titbit, dainty, ambrosia, nectar.

V. be savory; tickle the palate (*or* appetite); tempt the appetite, taste good.

relish, like, smack the lips.

Adj. savory, tasty; good, palatable; pleasing, nice, dainty, exquisite, delicate; delectable, toothsome, appetizing, delicious; rich, luscious, ambrosial, nectareous; distinctive.

395. UNSAVORINESS.—*N.* unsavoriness; acridness, sourness, etc., 397; acerbity; gall and wormwood.

V. be unpalatable, sicken, disgust, nauseate, pall, turn the stomach.

Adj. unsavory, unpalatable, ill-flavored; bitter, acrid, acrimonious.

offensive, repulsive, nasty, sickening, nauseous; loathsome; unpleasant, etc., 830.

396. SWEETNESS.—*N.* sweetness, saccharinity.

sugar, saccharin; preserve, jam, sugar candy, sugarplum.

sweets, confectionery, caramel, lollipop, bonbon, jujube, comfit, sweetmeat, confection; honey, manna; glucose, sirup, treacle, molasses, maple sirup, maple sugar; taffy, butterscotch.

Sweet beverages: nectar; mead, liqueur, sweet wine.

pastry, cake, pie, tart, puff, pudding.

V. sweeten, sugar, sugar off [*local*]; candy.

Adj. sweet, sugary, saccharine, candied, honied, luscious, cloying, honey-sweet, nectareous; dulcet, mellifluous.

397. SOURNESS.—*N.* sourness, acerbity, acidity; acid.

V. render sour, acidify, acidulate, acetify; ferment.

Adj. sour; acid, acidulated; subacid; tart, crabbed; hard, unripe, green; astringent, styptic.

(4) *Odor*

398. ODOR.—*N.* odor, smell, scent; effluvium; emanation, exhalation; fume, trail, redolence.

V. have an odor (*or* scent); smell, exhale; give out a smell (*or* odor); scent.

smell, scent, snuff, sniff, inhale.

Adj. odorous, odoriferous; strong-scented, redolent, pungent.

Relating to the sense of smell: olfactory; quick-scented, keen-scented.

399. INODOROUSNESS.—*N.* inodorousness, absence (*or* want) of smell.

deodorization; deodorizer, deodorant.

V. be inodorous (*or* scentless); not smell.

Adj. inodorous, scentless; without smell (*or* odor).

400. FRAGRANCE.—*N.* fragrance, aroma, redolence, perfume, bouquet; sweet smell (*or* odor), scent.

perfumery; incense, frankincense; musk, myrrh, attar, bergamot, balm, civet, potpourri, tuberose, hyacinth, heliotrope, rose, jasmine, lily, lily of the valley, violet, pomander; toilet water; eau de cologne [F.], cologne, cologne water.

bouquet, nosegay, posy [*colloq.*], boutonniere [F.], buttonhole [*colloq.*].

spray; wreath, garland, chaplet.

Scent containers: smelling bottle, scent bottle, vinaigrette; scent bag, sachet; thurible, censer, incense burner, atomizer, spray.

V. be fragrant (*or* scented); have a perfume (*or* aroma); smell sweet, scent, perfume; embalm.

Adj. fragrant, aromatic, redolent, spicy, balmy, scented; sweet-smelling, sweet-scented; perfumed; incense-breathing, ambrosial.

401. FETOR—*N.* fetor, bad smell (*or* odor), stench, stink, fetidness, fustiness, mustiness; rancidity; foulness.

V. have a bad smell, smell, stink, smell strong, smell offensively.

Adj. fetid; strong-smelling; high, bad, strong, offensive, noisome, rank, rancid, moldy, tainted, musty; smelling, stinking; putrid, rotten, foul; suffocating.

(5) Sound

402. SOUND.—*N.* sound, noise; sonority, sonorousness; strain; accent, twang, intonation; tune, cadence; audibility; resonance, vibration; voice, etc., 580.

Science of sound: acoustics, phonetics, phonology, phonography; telephony, radiophony.

V. sound, make a noise; give out sound, emit sound; resound.

Adj. sounding, sonorous, resonant, audible, distinct; auditory, acoustic.

phonetic, phonic, sonant.

403. SILENCE.—*N.* silence, stillness, quiet, peace, hush, lull; rest [*music*]; muteness; silence of the tomb (*or* grave).

V. silence, still, hush, stifle, muffle, gag, stop; muzzle, put to silence.

Adj. silent; still, stilly; noiseless, quiet, calm, soundless, hushed; speechless; aphonic, surd, mute.

solemn, soft, awful, deathlike.

Adv. in dead silence.

404. LOUDNESS.—*N.* loudness, power, vociferation, uproariousness.

din, loud noise, clang, clangor, clatter, noise, roar, uproar, hubbub, racket, hullabaloo, pandemonium; fracas; outcry, etc., 411; explosion, detonation.

blare, trumpet blast, flourish of trumpets, fanfare, blast, peal, swell, alarum, boom; resonance, etc., 408.

V. be loud (*or* deafening); peal, swell, clang, boom, thunder, roar; deafen, stun, rend the air, awake the echoes; resound, etc., 408; speak up, shout, etc. (*vociferate*), 411; bellow, etc. (*cry as an animal*), 412.

Adj. loud, sonorous, deep, full, powerful; noisy, blatant; clangorous, thundering, deafening, earsplitting, piercing; shrill, etc., 410; obstreperous, uproarious; clamorous, vociferous, fullmouthed, stentorian.

Adv. loudly, noisily; aloud; at the top of one's lungs, lustily, in full cry.

405. FAINTNESS.—*N.* faintness, inaudibility; faint sound, whisper, breath; undertone; murmur, hum, buzz, purr, lap [*of waves*], plash; sough, moan, rustle; tinkle.

hoarseness, huskiness.

silencer, muffler; soft pedal, damper, mute, sordine [*all music*].

V. whisper, breathe; mutter, etc. (*speak imperfectly*), 583.

murmur, purl, hum, gurgle, ripple, babble, flow; rustle; tinkle.

muffle, deaden, mute, subdue.

Adj. **faint,** low, dull; stifled, muffled; inaudible; hoarse, husky; gentle, soft; floating; purling, flowing; muttered; whispered; liquid; soothing; dulcet, etc. (*melodious*), 413.

Adv. **in a whisper,** with bated breath, *sotto voce* [It.]; between the teeth; aside; piano, pianissimo [*both music*]; out of earshot; inaudibly, faintly.

406. [Sudden and violent sounds] SNAP.—*N.* **snap,** etc., *v.*; toot, shout, yell, yap [*dial.*], yelp, bark.

report, thump, knock, clap, thud; burst, thunderclap, thunderburst, eruption, blowout [*tire*], explosion, discharge, detonation, firing, salvo, volley.

V. **snap,** rap, tap, knock; click; clash; crack, crackle; crash; pop; slam, bang, clap; thump, toot, yelp, bark, fire, explode, rattle, burst on the ear.

407. [Repeated and protracted sounds] ROLL.—*N.* **roll,** etc., *v.*; drumming, rumbling, howl, dingdong; ratatat, rubadub, tattoo; pitapat; quaver, clutter, charivari; racket; peal of bells, devil's tattoo; drumfire, barrage; whir, rattle, drone; reverberation.

V. **roll,** drum, boom; whir, rustle, tootle, roar, drone, rumble, rattle, clatter, patter, clack.

hum, trill, shake; chime, peal, toll; tick, beat.

408. RESONANCE.—*N.* **resonance;** ring, chime, ringing, clangor, bell note, tintinnabulation, vibration, reverberation.

bass; basso [It.], basso profundo [It.]; baritone, contralto; pedal point, organ point; snoring, snore.

V. **resound,** reverberate, re-echo; ring, sound; chink, clink; jingle, tinkle; chime; gurgle, mutter, murmur; plash, echo, ring in the ear.

Adj. **resonant,** reverberant, resounding, reverberating; deeptoned, deep-mouthed; hollow, sepulchral; gruff, etc. (*harsh*), 410.

408a. NONRESONANCE.—*N.* **nonresonance,** dead sound; thud, thump, muffled drums, cracked bell; damper, sordine, mute; muffler, silencer.

V. **muffle,** deaden, mute; sound dead; stop (*or* deaden) the sound.

Adj. **nonresonant,** dead, mute; muffled, deadened.

409. [Hissing sounds] SIBILATION.—*N.* **sibilation,** hissing; zip; hiss, buzz; sneezing, sternutation.

V. **hiss,** buzz, whiz; rustle; fizz, fizzle; wheeze, whistle, sizzle, swish.

Adj. **sibilant;** hissing; rustling; wheezy.

410. [Harsh or high sounds] STRIDENCY.—*N.* **stridency;** stridor, harshness, raucousness; sharpness; creak, jar; creaking, grating; discord, dissonance.

high note, shrill note; soprano, treble, tenor, alto, falsetto; head voice, head tone; shriek, yell, cry, wail, pipe.

V. **grate,** creak, saw, snore, jar, burr, pipe, twang, jangle, clank; scream, etc. (*cry*), 411; set the teeth on edge, pierce (*or* split) the ears; yelp, etc. (*animal sound*), 412; buzz, etc. (*hiss*), 409.

Adj. **grating,** creaking, jangling, jarring, strident, harsh, coarse, hoarse, raucous; metallic; rough, rude; gruff, grum, sepulchral, hollow.

high, sharp, acute, shrill; piercing, high-pitched; cracked; discordant.

411. CRY.—*N.* **cry,** shout; shriek; hubbub; bark, etc. (*animal*), 412.

outcry, vociferation, ejaculation, hullabaloo, chorus, clamor, hue and cry, plaint; lungs; stentor.

V. **cry,** roar, shout, bawl; halloo, halloa, yo-ho, whoop; yell, bellow, hoot, boo; howl, scream, screech, shriek; shrill, squeak, squeal, squall; whine, pipe.

cheer, huzza, hurrah, yell.

moan, grumble, groan.

snort, snore; grunt, etc., 412.

vociferate, raise (*or* lift) the voice; yell out, call out, sing out, cry out; exclaim, give cry, clamor; rend the air; make the welkin ring; shout at the top of one's voice.

Adj. **clamorous,** clamant, vociferous; stentorian, etc. (*loud*), 404; open-mouthed; full-mouthed.

412. [Animal sounds] **ULULATION.**—*N.* **ululation,** howling, cry, roar; call, note, howl, bark, yelp, bowwow, belling; woodnote; insect cry; twittering, drone.

V. **ululate,** howl; cry, roar, bellow; bark, yelp; bay, bay the moon; yap, growl, snarl, howl; grunt, snort, squeak; neigh, bray; mew, purr, caterwaul; bleat, low, moo; crow, screech, croak, caw, coo, gobble, quack, cackle, cluck; chirp, cheep, chirrup, peep, sing, twitter; chatter, hoot, wail; hum, buzz; hiss; blat [*colloq.*].

413. MELODY. CONCORD.—*N.* **melody,** rhythm, measure; rhyme, etc. (*poetry*), 597; euphony.

Musical terms: pitch, timbre, intonation, tone, overtone.
orchestration, harmonization, modulation, phrasing.
staff *or* stave, line, space, brace; bar, rest; passage, phrase; trill *or* shake, turn, arpeggio [It.].
note, musical note, notes of a scale; sharp, flat, natural; high note, etc., 410; low note, etc., 408; interval; semitone.
breve, semibreve *or* whole note, minim *or* half note, crotchet *or* quarter note, quaver *or* eighth note, semiquaver *or* sixteenth note, demisemiquaver *or* thirty-second note; sustained note, drone.
scale, gamut; diapason; key, clef, chord.
harmony, concord; tonality; consonance; part; unison; chime.
Science of harmony: harmony, harmonics; thorough bass, counterpoint; composer.

opus (*pl. opera*) [L.], piece of music, etc., 415.

V. **harmonize,** chime, symphonize, transpose, orchestrate; blend, put in tune, tune, accord, string.

Adj. **harmonious,** harmonic, in concord, in tune, in concert, in unison.

melodious, musical, tuneful, tunable; sweet, dulcet, mellow, mellifluous; soft; clear, silvery; euphonious; enchanting, etc. (*pleasure-giving*), 829; fine-toned, silver-toned, full-toned, deep-toned.

414. DISCORD.—*N.* **discord,** dissonance, want of harmony; harshness, etc., 410; charivari, racket; Babel, pandemonium.

V. **be discordant** (*or* harsh); jar, etc. (*sound harshly*), 410.

Adj. **discordant,** dissonant, out of tune, tuneless; unmusical, untunable; unmelodious, inharmonious; singsong; harsh, etc., 410; jarring.

415. MUSIC.—*N.* **music;** minstrelsy; strain, tune, air, melody; piece of music; rondo, rondeau, pastoral; cavatina, fantasia, toccata [It.]; fugue, canon; potpourri, medley; incidental music; variations, roulade, cadenza, cadence, trill; serenade, nocturne.

instrumental music; orchestral score, full score; composition, opus (*pl. opera*) [L.]; concert piece; concerto [It.]; symphony, sonata, symphonic poem, tone poem; chamber music; movement; overture, prelude, voluntary; string quartet (*or* quintet).

lively music, polka, reel, etc. (*dance*), 848; ragtime, jazz; syncopation, martial music, march; allegro, presto.

slow music, Lydian measures; adagio, largo, andante; lullaby, cradle song, berceuse [F.]; dirge, etc. (*lament*), 839; dead march; minuet.

vocal music, vocalism; chant; psalm, psalmody, hymnology; hymn; canticle; oratorio; opera, operetta; cantata; song, lay, ballad, ditty, carol; recitative, aria.

solo, duet, trio, quartet, quintet, sestet, septet, double quartet, chorus; part song, descant, glee, madrigal, catch, round, chorale; antiphon; accompaniment; inside part, second, alto, tenor, bass; score, piano score, vocal score.

concert, musicale, recital, chamber concert, popular concert *or* pop [*colloq.*], open-air concert; serenade; community singing, singsong [*colloq.*].

method, solfeggio [It.], tonic sol-fa, sight singing, sight reading.

V. **compose,** write, etc., 416; attune, tune.

perform, execute, play, etc., 416.

Adj. **musical;** instrumental, vocal, choral, lyric, melodic; operatic; classic, modern, orchestral, symphonic, contrapuntal; program, imitative; harmonious, etc., 413.

416. MUSICIAN. [Performance of music]—*N.* **musician,** virtuoso, performer, player, minstrel; bard, etc. (*poet*), 597; accompanist, instrumentalist, organist, pianist, violinist, fiddler; flutist, harpist, fifer, trumpeter, cornetist, piper, drummer.

orchestra; strings, woodwind, brass; band, brass band, military band, German band, jazz band; street musicians.

vocalist, singer, warbler; songbird; songster, songstress; chorister; chorus singer; choir, chorus.

Orpheus, Apollo, the Muses, Polyhymnia, Erato, Euterpe, Terpsichore.

conductor, choirmaster, bandmaster, concertmaster, drum major, song leader, precentor.

performance, execution, touch, expression.

V. play, tune, tune up, pipe, pipe up, strike up, sweep the chords, fiddle, strike the lyre, beat the drum; blow (*or* wind) the horn; twang, pluck, pick; pound, thump; drum, thrum, strum, beat time; execute, perform; accompany.

compose, set to music, arrange, harmonize, orchestrate.

sing, troll, chant, intone, hum, warble, twitter, carol, chirp, chirrup, lilt, quaver, trill, shake.

Adj. musical; lyric, dramatic; bravura, florid, brilliant.

417. MUSICAL INSTRUMENTS.—*N.* musical instruments; orchestra (*including* strings, woodwind, brass, and percussive instruments); band; string band, military band, brass band.

418. [Sense of sound] HEARING.—*N.* hearing, audition; audibility; acoustics; ear for music.

ear; eardrum, tympanum.

Instruments: ear trumpet, audiphone, dentiphone, speaking trumpet; phonograph, gramophone, graphophone, microphone, victrola; stethoscope; telephone, radiophone, wireless telephone, radio.

hearer, auditor, audience, listener; eavesdropper.

V. hear, overhear; hark, hearken; list, listen; strain one's ears, attend to, give attention, prick up one's ears; give ear, give a hearing to.

Adj. hearing, auditory, acoustic, phonic; auricular; auditive.

419. DEAFNESS—*N.* deafness, hardness of hearing, inaudibility; deaf-mute; deaf-and-dumb alphabet.

V. deafen, render deaf, stun, split the ears (*or* eardrum).

Adj. deaf, hard (*or* dull) of hearing; stunned, deafened; stone-deaf; inattentive.

inaudible, out of earshot (*or* hearing).

(6) *Light*

420. LIGHT.—*N.* light, ray, beam, stream (*of light*), gleam, streak; sunbeam, moonbeam; aurora, dawn, daylight, day, sunshine; glint, glare, glow, afterglow; sun, etc., **423.**

reflection, refraction, dispersion.

halo, glory, nimbus, aureole, aura.

spark, scintilla, scintillation, flash, blaze, coruscation; flame, glare, blaze; lightning; phosphorescence.

luster, sheen, shimmer, gloss, brightness, brilliancy, splendor, effulgence; illumination, radiance, radiation.

Science of light: optics, radiometry; photography; phototelegraphy, radiotelegraphy; actinic rays, radioactivity; Röntgen rays, X rays, ultraviolet rays.

illuminant, gas, etc., 423.

V. shine, glow, beam, glitter, glisten, gleam; flare, blaze, glare, shimmer, glimmer, flicker, sparkle, scintillate, coruscate, flash.

daze, dazzle, bedazzle.

lighten, enlighten, light, irradiate, illume, illumine, illuminate; kindle, etc., 384.

Adj. **luminous,** lucent; light, sunny, bright, vivid, splendid, resplendent, refulgent, lustrous, brilliant, radiant, lambent; aglow.

shiny, glossy, burnished, glassy.

clear, cloudless, unclouded.

421. DARKNESS.—*N.* **darkness,** duskiness; blackness, swarthiness; obscurity, gloom, murk, murkiness; dusk; dimness, etc., 422.

night; midnight; dead of night.

shadow, shade; obscuration, adumbration; eclipse; radiograph.

V. **darken,** obscure, shade, dim; lower, overcast, overshadow, cloud, becloud, bedim.

extinguish, put out, blow out, snuff out.

Adj. **dark,** darkling, obscure; black, etc. (*color*), 431; nocturnal.

somber, dusky; dingy, lurid, gloomy, murky; shady, umbrageous; overcast, etc. (*dim*), 422; cloudy, etc., 426.

422. DIMNESS.—*N.* **dimness,** paleness, dullness, duskiness, mistiness.

twilight, dusk, nightfall, gloaming; dawn, daybreak, break of day, Aurora; moonlight, moonshine [*poetic*], starlight.

V. **cloud over,** gloom, lower.

twinkle, glimmer, flicker.

pale, fade, grow dim.

dim, bedim, obscure, shade, shadow, darken, cloud, becloud.

Adj. **dim,** dull, dingy, dusky, lackluster; cloudy, misty, hazy.

leaden, lurid, dun; overcast, dirty.

423. [Source of light] LUMINARY.—*N.* **luminary;** light, ray, beam; flame, etc. (*fire*), 382; spark, scintilla; phosphorescence.

Heavenly bodies: sun, orb of day, daystar [*poetic*]; star; constellation; galaxy, Milky Way; polestar, Polaris; morning star, Lucifer; evening star, Venus; moon, etc., 318.

sun god, Helios, Phoebus, Apollo, Hyperion, Ra [*Egypt*].

phosphorus; *ignis fatuus* [L.]; jack-o'-lantern, will-o'-the-wisp.

polar lights, northern lights, aurora borealis [L.], aurora australis [L.]; aurora.

Artificial light: gas, gaslight, electric light, electric torch; headlight, searchlight; spotlight, flashlight, limelight, calcium light; lamplight, lamp, lantern, dark lantern, bull's-eye; candle, taper, rushlight; torch, flambeau, brand; gaselier, chandelier; candelabrum, sconce, luster, candlestick; fireworks, pyrotechnics.

signal light, rocket, balefire, beacon fire; lighthouse.

V. illuminate, etc. (*light*), 420.

Adj. self luminous; phosphorescent; radiant, etc. (*light*), 420.

424. SHADE.—*N.* shade; awning, etc. (*cover*), 223.

screen, curtain, portiere [F.]; shutter, blind.

veil, mantle, mask.

cloud, mist, shadow; smoke screen [*mil*.].

blinkers, blinders; smoked glasses, colored spectacles.

V. veil, draw a curtain; cast a shadow, etc. (*darken*), 421.

Adj. shady, umbrageous, shadowy.

425. TRANSPARENCY.—*N.* transparency, transparence, translucence, diaphanousness; lucidity, limpidity; fluorescence; translumination.

V. be transparent (*or* pellucid); transmit light.

Adj. transparent, pellucid, lucid, diaphanous; translucent, limpid, clear, serene, crystalline.

426. OPACITY.—*N.* opacity, opaqueness; cloudiness; film; cloud, etc., 353.

V. be opaque; obstruct the passage of light.

Adj. opaque, impervious to light; dim, etc., 422; turbid, thick, muddy, cloudy, foggy, vaporous; smoky, murky, smeared, dirty.

427. SEMITRANSPARENCY.—*N.* semitransparency, opalescence, milkiness, pearliness; mist, haze, steam.

V. cloud, frost, cloud over; frost over.

Adj. semitransparent, semidiaphanous, semiopaque; opalescent, opaline; pearly, milky; frosted, hazy, misty.

428. [Specific Light] COLOR.—*N.* color, hue, tint, tinge, dye, complexion, shade, tincture; coloration; glow, flush; tone, key.

primary color, complementary color; coloring, keeping, tone, value.

spectrum, spectrum analysis; prism, spectroscope, kaleidoscope.

pigment, coloring matter, paint, dye, wash, distemper, stain; medium.

V. color, dye, tinge, stain, tint, tone; paint, wash, distemper, ingrain, grain, illuminate, emblazon.

Adj. colored, dyed; chromatic, prismatic; double-dyed.

bright, vivid, intense, deep; fresh, rich, gorgeous; bright-colored, gay.

gaudy, florid; garish; showy, flaunting; flashy; many-colored, parti-colored, variegated; raw, crude; glaring, flaring.

mellow, harmonious, pearly, sweet, delicate, subtle, tender.

dull, sad, somber, sad-colored, grave, gray, dark.

429. ABSENCE OF COLOR.—*N.* decoloration, discoloration; pallor, paleness, sallowness.

neutral tint, monochrome, black and white.

V. lose color, fade, become colorless, turn pale; pale, fade out.

deprive of color, decolor, wash out, tone down; whiten, bleach, blanch.

Adj. colorless, uncolored, hueless, pale, pallid; pale-faced, anemic; faint, dull, cold, muddy, leaden, dun, wan, sallow, dingy, ashy, ashen, ghastly, cadaverous, glassy, lackluster; discolored.

light-colored, fair, blond, ash-blond; white, etc., 430; towheaded.

430. WHITENESS.—*N.* whiteness, showiness, hoariness.

whitewash, whiting, whitening, calcimine.

V. whiten, bleach, blanch, silver, frost.

whitewash, calcimine, white.

Adj. white, snow-white, snowy, frosted, hoar, hoary; silvery, silver, milk-white, milky.

whitish, creamy, pearly, ivory, fair, blond, ash-blond; blanched; light.

431. BLACKNESS.—*N.* blackness, darkness, obscurity; swarthiness, swartness; lividness.

Negro, Negress, blackamoor, man of color, colored man, colored woman, nigger [*colloq.*, *usually contemptuous*], darky [*colloq.*], black, Ethiop, Ethiopian, Hottentot, Pygmy, Bushman, African.

V. black, blacken, blot, blotch, smut, smudge, smirch; darken, etc., 421.

Adj. black, sable, somber, livid, dark, inky, ebon, pitchy, sooty; swart, swarthy, dusky, dingy, murky; blotchy, smudgy; low-toned.

432. GRAY.—*N.* gray, etc., *adj.*; grayness; neutral tint, silver, dove color, pepper and salt, chiaroscuro [It.].

V. render gray, gray.

Adj. gray; iron-gray, dun, drab, dingy, leaden, pearly, dove-colored, silver, silvery, silvered; dapple-gray; ashen, ashy; grizzly, grizzled.

433. BROWN.—*N.* brown, etc., *adj.*; brownness.

V. render brown, brown, tan, embrown, bronze.

Adj. brown, nut-brown, seal-brown, mahogany, chocolate; fawn, ecru, tawny; tan, fawn-colored, snuff-colored, liver-colored.

reddish-brown, terra cotta, russet, foxy, bronze, coppery, copper-colored, maroon; bay, roan, sorrel; chestnut, henna, auburn, hazel.

sunburned; tanned, etc., *v.*

434. RED.—*N.* red, etc., *adj.*; flesh color, flesh tint, color, warmth; redness, ruddiness, blush.

V. **redden,** rouge, crimson, incarnadine; ruddle, rust.

blush, flush, color, color up, mantle, redden.

Adj. **red,** scarlet, cardinal, vermilion, carmine, crimson, pink, rose, cerise, cherry, salmon, maroon, carnation, magenta, solferino, damask.

reddish; sanguine, bloody, gory; coral, coralline, rosy, roseate; blood-red, wine-red, wine-colored, ruby, rufous, bricky, reddish-brown, etc., 433; rose (*or* ruby, cherry, claret, flame, flesh, peach, salmon, brick, rust) -colored.

red-complexioned, red-faced, florid, burned, rubicund, ruddy, red, high-colored, glowing, sanguine, blooming, rosy, hectic, flushed, inflamed.

Of hair: sandy, carroty, brick-red, Titian, auburn, chestnut.

435. GREEN.—*N.* green, etc., *adj.*; greenness, verdancy, verdure.

Adj. **green,** verdant, olive; verdurous; emerald (*or* pea, grass, apple, sea, leaf, bottle, Irish, Kelly) green; greenish, aquamarine, blue-green.

436. YELLOW.—*N.* **yellow,** etc., *adj.*; yellowness; jaundice.

V. **render yellow,** yellow, gild.

Adj. **yellow,** aureate, golden, gold, gilt, gilded, lemon, fallow; sallow, jaundiced; tawny, cream, creamy; flaxen, yellowish, buff; gold (*or* saffron, citron, lemon, amber, straw, primrose, cream) -colored.

437. PURPLE.—*N.* **purple,** etc., *adj.*; royal purple; gridelin, amethyst; damson, heliotrope.

V. **render purple,** purple, empurple.

Adj. **purple,** violet, plum-colored, lavender, lilac, puce, mauve, purplish, amethystine, magenta, solferino, heliotrope; livid; purplish.

438. BLUE.—*N.* **blue,** etc., *adj.*; azure [*her.*]; indigo; sapphire, blueness, bluishness; bloom.

Adj. **blue,** azure, cerulean, sky-blue, navy-blue, midnight-blue, cadet-blue, robin's-egg-blue, baby-blue, ultramarine, aquamarine, electric-blue, steel-blue; bluish; cold.

439. ORANGE.—*N.* **orange,** old gold; gold color, etc., *adj.*

Adj. **orange,** orange (*or* gold, brass, apricot) -colored; warm, hot, glowing, flame-colored.

440. VARIEGATION.—*N.* **variegation;** iridescence, play of colors, spottiness; tricolor.

check, plaid, tartan, patchwork; marquetry, parquet, parquetry, mosaic, checkerwork; chessboard, checkers; harlequin.

V. **variegate,** stripe, streak, checker, fleck, speckle, besprinkle,

sprinkle; stipple, dot, tattoo, inlay, tessellate; damascene; embroider, quilt.

Adj. variegated, many-colored, many-hued, divers-colored, parti-colored, polychromatic; kaleidoscopic.

iridescent, opaline, opalescent, prismatic, pearly, shot, tortoise-shell.

mottled, pied, piebald, skewbald; motley, marbled, pepper-and-salt, dappled.

checkered, checked, plaid, mosaic, tessellated.

spotted, spotty; powdered; speckled, freckled, flea-bitten, studded; flecked.

barred, veined, brindled, tabby, watered.

441. [Perception of light] VISION.—*N.* vision, sight, optics, eyesight.

view, look, glance, ken, glimpse, glint, peep, peek; gaze, stare, leer; contemplation, regard, survey; inspection, reconnaissance, watch, espionage, autopsy; sight-seeing, globe-trotting [*colloq.*].

viewpoint, standpoint, point of view; loophole, watchtower.

field of view; theater, amphitheater, arena, vista, horizon; bird's-eye view, panoramic view.

eye, visual organ, organ of vision, naked eye; clear (*or* sharp, quick, eagle) sight.

V. see, behold, discern, perceive, descry, sight, make out; discover, distinguish, recognize, spy, espy, command a view of; witness, contemplate, look on, see at a glance.

look, view, eye, survey, scan, inspect; reconnoiter, glance, cast a glance; observe, etc. (*attend to*), 457; watch, keep watch; watch for, etc. (*expect*), 507; peep, peek, peer, pry, take a peep.

look intently; strain one's eyes; rivet the eyes upon; stare, gaze; pore over, gloat on, gloat over; leer, ogle, glare; goggle; squint, gloat, look askance.

Adj. ocular, visual, optic *or* optical; ophthalmic; visible, etc., 446.

clear-sighted, clear-eyed, farsighted; eagle-eyed, hawk-eyed, lynx-eyed, keen-eyed, Argus-eyed.

Adv. at sight, at first sight, at a glance, at the first blush.

442. BLINDNESS.—*N.* blindness, sightlessness, benightedness, cataract; dim-sightedness, etc., 443; Braille.

V. be blind, not see; lose one's sight; grope in the dark.

blind, blindfold, hoodwink, dazzle; put one's eyes out; throw dust into one's eyes; screen, hide.

Adj. blind, eyeless, sightless, visionless; dark; stone-blind, stark-blind, undiscerning; dim-sighted, etc., 443.

Adv. blindly, blindfold; darkly.

443. DIM-SIGHTEDNESS.—*N*. Imperfect vision: dim (*or* short, near, long) -sightedness; purblindness, bleareredness, myopia, astigmatism; color blindness, snow blindness; ophthalmia; cataract.

squint, cross-eye, cast in the eye, swivel eye, cockeye, goggle-eyes.

Limitation of vision: blinker, blinder; screen, curtain, veil.

Fallacies of vision: refraction, distortion, illusion, mirage, phantasm, phantom; vision; specter, apparition, ghost; will-o'-the-wisp, etc., 423.

V. **be dim-sighted,** see double; see through a glass darkly; wink, blink, squint, look askance, screw up the eyes, glare, glower.

dazzle, glare, swim, blur.

Adj. **dim-sighted,** myopic, nearsighted, shortsighted, astigmatic; blear-eyed, goggle-eyed, one-eyed; half-blind, purblind; cockeyed [*colloq.*], dim-eyed, mole-eyed.

444. SPECTATOR.—*N*. spectator, beholder, observer, looker-on, onlooker, witness, eyewitness, bystander, passer-by; sight-seer; rubberneck [*slang*].

spy, scout; sentinel, etc. (*warning*), 668.

grandstand [*fig.*], bleachers [*fig.*], gallery.

V. **witness,** behold, etc. (*see*), 441; look on, etc. (*be present*), 186.

445. OPTICAL INSTRUMENTS.—*N*. optical instruments; lens, magnifier, microscope; spectacles, glasses, goggles, eyeglass, pince-nez; periscope; telescope, glass, lorgnette, binocular; spyglass, opera glass, field glass; burning glass, convex lens; prism.

camera, hand camera, kodak [*trade name*]; moving-picture machine, magic lantern, stereopticon; stereoscope, kaleidoscope.

mirror, reflector, speculum; looking glass, pier glass, cheval glass.

optics, optician; photography, photographer; optometry, optometrist; microscopy, microscopist.

446. VISIBILITY.—*N*. visibility, perceptibility, conspicuousness, distinctness, appearance, etc., 448; exposure; manifestation, etc., 525; ocular demonstration; field of view, vista, horizon.

V. **appear,** open to the view; catch the eye; present (*or* show, manifest, reveal, expose, betray) itself; stand forth, stand out; materialize; show; arise; peep out, peer out; start up, spring up; gleam, glimmer; glitter, glow, loom; glare; burst forth; burst upon the view; heave in sight [*naut. or colloq.*]; come into view, come out, come forth, come forward; attract the attention, etc., 457.

expose to view, show, display.

Adj. **visible,** perceptible, discernible, apparent; in view, in full view, in sight; exposed to view.

distinct, plain, clear, definite; obvious, etc. (*manifest*), 525; recognizable; glaring, palpable, staring, conspicuous.

Adv. before one, under one's very eyes, in sight of.

447. INVISIBILITY.—*N.* **invisibility,** imperceptibility; indistinctness; mystery; latency, obscurity; concealment, mystification.

V. **be invisible** (*or* imperceptible); be hidden, etc. (*hide*), 528; escape notice.

render invisible; conceal, etc., 528; put out of sight.

Adj. **invisible,** imperceptible; out of sight, not in sight, unseen; viewless; inconspicuous; covert, latent.

indistinct; dim; mysterious, dark, obscure; confused, indistinguishable, shadowy, indefinite, undefined, ill-defined, blurred, out of focus; misty, veiled, concealed.

448. APPEARANCE.—*N.* **appearance,** phenomenon, sight, show, scene, view; lookout, outlook, prospect, vista, perspective, bird's-eye view, scenery, landscape, seascape, picture, tableau; display, exposure, rising of the curtain.

spectacle, pageant; peep show, magic lantern, biograph, cinematograph, cinema [*colloq.*], moving pictures, movies [*colloq.*], photoplay, photodrama; panorama.

aspect, angle, phase, shape, form, guise, look, complexion, color, image, mien, air, cast, carriage, port, demeanor; presence, expression, point of view, light.

lineament, feature, trait, lines; outline, outside; contour, silhouette, face, countenance, visage, profile; physiognomy.

V. **appear,** be visible, seem, look, show; cut a figure, figure; present to the view; show, etc. (*make manifest*), 525; look like, resemble.

Adj. **apparent,** seeming, ostensible; on view.

Adv. **to all appearance,** ostensibly, seemingly, on the face of it, at the first blush, at first sight, to the eye.

449. DISAPPEARANCE.—*N.* **disappearance,** evanescence, eclipse; departure, exit; vanishing point.

V. **disappear,** vanish, dissolve, fade, melt away, pass, go, depart, be gone, leave no trace; be lost to view (*or* sight), pass out of sight.

efface, etc., 552.

Adj. **disappearing,** evanescent; missing, lost; lost to sight.

CLASS IV

Words Relating to the INTELLECTUAL FACULTIES

I. FORMATION OF IDEAS

450. INTELLECT.—*N.* intellect, mind, understanding, reason; rationality; intellectual faculties (*or* powers); senses, consciousness, observation, intellectuality, mentality, intelligence; conception, judgment, wits, brains, parts, capacity, genius; wit; ability; wisdom; ideality, idealism.

ego, soul, spirit; heart, breast, bosom; subconscious self, subliminal consciousness.

seat of thought, brain; head, headpiece; skull, cranium.

Science of mind: psychology, psychoanalysis; psychophysics; metaphysics; philosophy.

psychical research; telepathy, thought transference, thought reading; clairaudience; clairvoyance, mediumship; spiritualism, etc., 992*a*.

V. **reason,** understand, think, reflect, cogitate, conceive, judge, contemplate, meditate; ruminate, etc. (*think*), 451.

note, notice, mark; take notice of; be aware of, realize; appreciate.

Adj. **intellectual,** mental, rational; psychological; conscious, percipient, brainy [*colloq.*].

hyperphysical, subconscious, subliminal; telepathic, clairvoyant; psychic *or* psychical, spiritual, metaphysical, transcendental.

450a. ABSENCE OF INTELLECT.—*N.* want of intellect (*or* mind, understanding); unintellectuality; imbecility, etc., 490.

Adj. unendowed with (*or* void of) reason; unintelligent, etc. (*imbecile*), 499.

451. THOUGHT.—*N.* thought; reflection, cogitation, consideration, meditation, study, speculation, deliberation, brainwork, cerebration; close study, application.

mature thought; afterthought, reconsideration, second thoughts; retrospection, examination.

abstraction, abstract thought, contemplation, musing; reverie, etc., 458; depth of thought.

V. **think,** reflect, cogitate, consider, reason, deliberate: contemplate, meditate, ponder, muse, dream, ruminate, speculate; brood over, con over, study; bend (*or* apply) the mind; digest, discuss, hammer at, hammer out; weigh, realize, appreciate; fancy.

harbor, cherish, entertain, nurture (*as an idea*), imagine; bear in mind; reconsider.

suggest itself, present itself, occur to; come into one's head; strike one, come uppermost; enter (*or* cross, flash across, occupy) the mind.

Adj. **thoughtful,** pensive, meditative, reflective, cogitative, contemplative, speculative, deliberative, studious, introspective, philosophical.

absorbed, rapt; lost in thought; engrossed in, intent.

Adv. **all things considered,** taking everything into consideration (*or* account).

452. ABSENCE OF THOUGHT.—*N.* **vacancy of mind,** poverty of intellect; thoughtlessness, etc. (*inattention*), 458; inanity, fatuity, vacuity.

V. **put away thought;** relax (*or* divert) the mind; make the mind a blank, let the mind lie fallow; indulge in reverie, etc. (*be inattentive*), 458.

Adj. **vacant,** inane, unintellectual, unoccupied, unthinking, irrational, unreasoning, thoughtless, inattentive; diverted; bigoted, narrow-minded.

453. [Object of thought] IDEA.—*N.* **idea,** notion, conception, thought; apprehension, impression, perception; sentiment, reflection, observation, consideration; abstract idea.

view, opinion, theory; conceit, fancy; fantasy, etc., 515.

viewpoint, point of view; aspect, angle; field of view.

454. [Subject of thought] TOPIC.—*N.* **subject,** subject matter; matter, motif, theme, topic, thesis, text, business, affair, matter in hand, argument; motion, resolution, case, point, proposition, theorem; field of inquiry; moot point, point at issue; problem, etc. (*question*), 461.

V. **enter the mind,** etc., 451.

Adv. **under consideration,** under advisement; in question, in the mind; at issue, before the house, on foot, on the carpet.

455. [Desire of knowledge] CURIOSITY.—*N.* **curiosity;** inquisitiveness; interest, thirst for knowledge, mental acquisitiveness; inquiring mind.

investigator, inquirer, etc., 461.

busybody, newsmonger; Peeping Tom, Paul Pry, eavesdropper; gossip.

V. **be curious;** take an interest in, investigate; stare, gape; see the sights.

pry, nose, search, ferret out.

Adj. **curious,** inquiring, etc., 461; inquisitive, burning with curiosity, overcurious, prying; inquisitorial; agape, expectant.

456. [Absence of curiosity] INCURIOSITY.—*N.* **incuriosity;** incuriousness; apathy, unconcern, indifference.

V. **be incurious** (*or* indifferent); have no curiosity, etc., 455; be bored by, take no interest in.

Adj. **incurious,** uninquisitive, indifferent; impassive, etc., 823; uninterested, bored.

457. ATTENTION.—*N.* **attention;** intentness, alertness; thought, etc., 451; observance, observation; consideration, reflection; heed; heedfulness; notice, regard; circumspection, etc. (*care*), 459; study, scrutiny; inspection, revision, revisal.

minuteness, circumstantiality, attention to detail.

V. **attend,** watch, observe, look, see, view, notice, regard, take notice, mark; pay attention to, give heed to; occupy oneself with; contemplate, etc. (*think of*), 451, look to, see to; heed, mind, take cognizance of, entertain, recognize; make (*or* take) note of; note.

examine, scan, scrutinize, consider; overhaul, revise, pore over; inspect, review.

revert to, hark back to; come to the point.

meet with attention; attract notice, fall under one's notice; be under consideration.

call attention to, bring under one's notice; point out (*or* to, at), indicate; direct attention to; show; bring forward.

Adj. **attentive,** mindful, heedful, observant, regardful; alive to, awake to, on the job [*colloq.*], alert; taken up with, occupied with; engrossed in, wrapped in, absorbed, rapt; watchful; intent on, open-eyed; on the watch.

458. INATTENTION.—*N.* **inattention,** inconsideration, want of consideration, inconsiderateness; oversight; inadvertence, disregard; want of thought; heedlessness, etc. (*neglect*), 460; unconcern.

abstraction; absence of mind, absorption, preoccupation, distraction, reverie, brown study [*colloq.*], woolgathering.

V. **be inattentive** (*or* unobservant); overlook, disregard; pass by, neglect; think little of; pay no attention to; dismiss from one's mind; drop the subject, think no more of; turn a deaf ear to.

confuse, disconcert, discompose, perplex, bewilder, fluster, flurry; call off *or* distract the attention (thoughts, mind); put out of one's head.

Adj. **inattentive,** unobservant, undiscerning, unmindful, unheeding, regardless; listless, apathetic; blind, deaf; volatile, scatter-brained, flighty, giddy; unreflecting; inconsiderate, thoughtless; wild, harum-scarum [*colloq.*], heedless, careless, neglectful.

abstracted, absent, distrait [F.], woolgathering, dreamy; dazed, absent-minded; lost in thought; rapt, in the clouds, daydreaming; preoccupied, engrossed; in a reverie; off one's guard; caught napping.

459. CARE. [Vigilance]—*N.* care, solicitude, anxiety; heed, concern, heedfulness; scruple.

vigilance; watchfulness, surveillance, watch, vigil, lookout, watch and ward; espionage, reconnoitering; watching.

alertness, attention, prudence, forethought, circumspection, precaution, caution; accuracy, exactness; minuteness, attention to detail.

watcher, watchman, watchdog.

V. be careful, take care, be cautious; take precautions; pay attention to, etc., 457; take care of; look *or* see to, look after, keep an eye upon; chaperon, matronize, keep watch, mount guard, watch.

Adj. careful, regardful, heedful; prudent, discreet, cautious; considerate, thoughtful; provident; alert; sure-footed.

guarded, on one's guard; on the alert (*or* watch, lookout); awake, vigilant; watchful, wakeful, Argus-eyed, lynx-eyed.

scrupulous, punctilious, conscientious; tidy, orderly; clean; accurate, exact.

Adv. carefully, with care, gingerly.

460. NEGLECT.—*N.* neglect; carelessness; negligence; omission, procrastination; supineness, apathy; inattention, etc., 458; imprudence, improvidence, recklessness; slovenliness, untidiness; dirt; inexactness, inaccuracy.

trifler, waiter on providence; Micawber; slacker.

V. neglect, take no care of, let slip, let go; lose sight of.

delay, defer, procrastinate, postpone, adjourn, pigeonhole, shelve, table, lay on the table.

overlook, disregard; pass over, pass by; let pass; wink at, connive at.

scamp; trifle, slight, slur; skim, skip, take a cursory view of, run over, dip into; slur *or* slip over; push aside, throw into the background, sink; ignore; forget.

Adj. neglectful, negligent, remiss; heedless, careless; thoughtless, inconsiderate; perfunctory, offhand.

unwary, unwatchful, unguarded, off one's guard.

supine, apathetic; inattentive, etc., 458; nonchalant, indifferent; imprudent, reckless; slovenly, disorderly; dirty; inexact, inaccurate; improvident, unthrifty.

neglected, unheeded, uncared for, unattended to; abandoned, shunted, shelved.

461. INQUIRY. [Subject of inquiry. QUESTION.]—*N.* inquiry; request, etc., 765; search, research, quest; pursuit, prosecution.

examination, review, scrutiny, investigation; inquest, inquisition; trial; exploration; exploitation, ventilation; sifting; calculation, analysis, dissection; study, consideration.

reconnoitering, reconnaissance, espionage.

questioning, interrogation, interrogatory; challenge, examination, third degree [*colloq.*], cross-examination; discussion; catechism.

question, query, problem, poser, desideratum, point (*or* matter) in dispute; moot point; issue, question at issue; bone of contention, enigma, etc. (*secret*), 533; knotty point.

inquirer, investigator, inquisitor, inspector, querist, examiner, catechist; scrutator, scrutinizer; analyst.

V. inquire, seek, search, make inquiry, look for, scan, reconnoiter, explore, sound, rummage, ransack, pry, peer, look round; overhaul; look behind the scenes; nose, nose out, trace up; hunt out, fish out, ferret out; unearth.

track, seek a clue; hunt, trail, shadow, mouse, dodge, trace, pursue, experiment, etc., 463.

examine, study, consider, calculate; dip *or* dive into, probe, sound, fathom, scrutinize, analyze, anatomize, dissect, parse, resolve, sift, winnow, thresh out; investigate, look into, discuss, canvass, subject to examination, quiz, pose; audit, tax, pass in review.

question, ask, demand; interrogate, catechize, pump; cross-question, cross-examine; grill [*colloq.*], put through the third degree [*colloq.*].

Adj. inquiring, inquisitive, catechetical, inquisitorial, analytic; interrogative.

undetermined, undecided, tentative; in question, in dispute, in issue, under consideration; moot, proposed; doubtful, etc. (*uncertain*), 475.

462. ANSWER.—*N.* answer, response, reply, rejoinder; retort, repartee; antiphon, acknowledgment; password; echo; counterstatement, countercharge, contradiction.

[Law] defense, plea, reply, rejoinder, rebutter, surrebutter, surrejoinder.

solution, explanation; discovery, disclosure; cause; clue.

oracle, etc., 513.

V. answer, respond, reply, rebut, retort, rejoin; give answer; acknowledge, echo.

[Law] defend, reply, surrejoin, surrebut, plead, rebut.

explain, interpret; solve, etc. (*unriddle*), 522; discover, fathom, hunt out, inquire; satisfy, set at rest, determine.

Adj. responsive, respondent, antiphonal; oracular; conclusive.

463. EXPERIMENT.—*N.* experiment, essay, trial, attempt;

analysis, investigation; verification, probation, proof, criterion, diagnosis, test, crucial test; assay, ordeal.

speculation, random shot, leap in the dark; feeler, pilot balloon.

experimenter, experimentalist, assayer, analyst; prospector, adventurer; speculator, gambler, stock gambler, plunger [*slang*].

V. experiment, essay, try, venture, make an experiment, make trial of; rehearse; put to the test, prove, verify, test.

grope, grope for, feel one's way, fumble, throw out a feeler; send up a pilot balloon; see how the land lies (*or* wind blows); feel the pulse; fish for, angle, trawl, cast one's net.

Adj. experimental, probationary; analytic, speculative, tentative, empirical.

on trial, on examination, on *or* under probation, under suspicion; on one's trial.

464. COMPARISON.—*N.* comparison, contrast, parallelism, balance; identification; simile, similitude, allegory, etc. (*metaphor*), 521.

V. compare, collate, confront, contrast, balance; parallel.

Adj. comparative, relative, contrastive; metaphorical, etc., 521.

Adv. relatively; as compared with.

465. DISCRIMINATION.—*N.* discrimination, distinction, differentiation, diagnosis, nice perception; estimation; nicety, refinement, taste, judgment; tact, discernment, acuteness, penetration.

V. discriminate, distinguish, separate; draw the line, sift; estimate, etc. (*measure*), 466; sum up, criticize; take into account, weigh carefully.

Adj. discriminating, critical, diagnostic, perceptive, discriminative, distinctive; nice, acute.

465a. INDISCRIMINATION.—*N.* indiscrimination, indistinction; want of discernment; uncertainty, etc. (*doubt*), 475.

V. confound, confuse, jumble, heap indiscriminately; swallow whole.

Adj. indiscriminate, indistinguishable, lacking distinction, undistinguished, undistinguishable; promiscuous, undiscriminating.

466. MEASUREMENT.—*N.* measurement, mensuration, survey, valuation, appraisement, assessment, estimate, estimation; dead reckoning [*naut.*]; reckoning, gauging; horsepower, candle power.

measure, gauge; yard measure, standard, rule, foot rule, spirit level, plumb line; square, T-square, steel square, compass, dividers, calipers; log, log line, patent log [*naut.*]; meter, line, rod, check.

flood mark, high-water mark, load-line mark.

scale; graduation, graduated scale; vernier, quadrant, theodolite; beam, steelyard, weighing machine, balance.

latitude and longitude, altitude and azimuth.

geometry; topography, cartography; surveying, land surveying.

surveyor, land surveyor, topographer, cartographer.

V. **measure,** meter; value, assess, rate, appraise, estimate, form an estimate; standardize; span, pace, step, inch, divide, gauge, balance, poise, weigh; plumb, probe, sound, fathom; survey, plot, block in, block out, rule, draw to scale.

Adj. **metrical,** metric; measurable; topographic *or* topographical, cartographic *or* cartographical.

467. [Materials for reasoning] **EVIDENCE.—***N.* **evidence;** facts, premises, data, grounds, proof; confirmation, corroboration, ratification, authentication.

testimony, attestation; affirmation, declaration; deposition.

authority, warrant, credential, diploma, voucher, certificate, document, deed, warranty; autograph, handwriting, signature, seal, countersign; exhibit; citation, reference, quotation; admission, etc. (*assent*), 488.

witness, eyewitness, deponent [*law*]; sponsor.

writ, summons, etc. (*lawsuit*), 696.

V. **evince,** show, betoken, indicate, denote, imply, involve, argue, bespeak.

have weight, carry weight; tell, speak volumes, speak for itself.

testify, bear witness, give evidence, depose, witness, vouch for; certify, attest, acknowledge.

confirm, ratify, corroborate, indorse, support, bear out, vindicate, uphold, warrant.

adduce, evidence, cite, quote; refer to, call, call to witness; bring forward, bring into court; allege, plead.

establish, make out a case; authenticate, substantiate, verify, make good.

Adj. **evidential,** indicative, deducible, inferential, firsthand, authentic, documentary; cumulative, corroborative, confirmatory; significant, weighty, overwhelming, conclusive.

oral, hearsay, circumstantial, presumptive.

Adv. **by inference;** according to, in corroboration of.

468. COUNTEREVIDENCE.—*N.* **counterevidence,** rejoinder, disproof, refutation, negation, denial; plea, etc., 617; vindication.

V. **refute,** rebut, oppose; confute, etc. (*refute*), 479; subvert; destroy, check, weaken; contravene; contradict, deny, alter the case; turn the tables; prove a negative.

Adj. **contradictory,** conflicting; unattested, unauthenticated, unsupported, supposititious, trumped up.

Adv. **on the other hand** (*or* side), in opposition; in rebuttal.

469. QUALIFICATION.—*N.* **qualification,** limitation, modification, coloring; allowance, consideration, extenuating circumstances; mitigation.

condition, proviso, exception; exemption; saving clause.

V. **qualify,** limit, modify, affect, give a color to, narrow, temper; allow for, take into account.

Adj. **qualifying,** extenuating, palliative; conditional; exceptional; hypothetical, contingent.

Adv. **provided,** if, unless, but, yet; according as; conditionally, admitting, supposing; even, although, though.

470. POSSIBILITY.—*N.* possibility, potentiality, practicability, feasibility, workableness; potency; compatibility, etc. (*agreement*), 23.

contingency, chance, etc., 156.

V. **be possible,** stand a chance; admit of, bear.

render possible, put in the way of, bring to bear, bring together.

Adj. **possible,** conceivable, imaginable, credible; compatible, etc., 23; likely.

practicable, feasible, workable, achievable; within reach, accessible, surmountable; attainable, obtainable.

Adv. **possibly,** perhaps, perchance, peradventure, haply.

471. IMPOSSIBILITY.—*N.* impossibility, impracticability, incredibility, hopelessness, infeasibility; discrepancy.

V. attempt impossibilities; square the circle, find the elixir of life, discover the philosopher's stone, discover the grand panacea, find the fountain of youth, discover the secret of perpetual motion; make bricks without straw; weave a rope of sand; be in two places at once; gather grapes from thorns.

Adj. **impossible,** not possible, absurd, contrary to reason, unlikely, unreasonable, incredible, visionary, impractical, inconceivable, improbable, unimaginable, unthinkable.

impracticable, unachievable, infeasible; insuperable, insurmountable, inaccessible, unattainable, unobtainable; out of the question; incompatible, etc., 24; impassable, impervious, self-contradictory.

472. PROBABILITY.—*N.* probability, likelihood, likeness, verisimilitude, plausibility; color, semblance, show of; presumption; credibility; prospect; chance, etc., 156.

V. **be probable,** lend color to; point to; imply, bid fair, promise, stand (*or* run) a good chance.

presume, infer, venture, suppose, take for granted, flatter oneself; expect, etc., 507; count upon, etc. (*believe*), 484.

Adj. **probable,** likely, hopeful, presumable, presumptive, apparent.

plausible, specious, ostensible, colorable, reasonable, credible.

Adv. **in all probability,** most likely, apparently, seemingly, to all appearance.

473. IMPROBABILITY.—*N.* improbability, unlikelihood; bare possibility; long odds; incredibility.

V. **be improbable,** go beyond reason, strain one's credulity; have a small chance.

Adj. **improbable,** unlikely, rare, unheard of, inconceivable; unimaginable, incredible.

474. CERTAINTY.—*N.* **certainty;** necessity, etc., 601; certitude, sureness, surety, assurance; infallibility, reliability, inevitableness; fact; positive fact, matter of fact.

bigotry, positiveness, dogmatism, dogmatization; fanaticism.

dogmatist, doctrinaire, bigot; zealot, fanatic.

V. **render certain,** insure, assure; clinch, make sure; determine, decide; know, etc. (*believe*), 484.

Adj. **certain,** sure, inevitable, assured, solid, well founded.

unqualified, absolute, positive, definite, clear, unequivocal, categorical, unmistakable, decisive.

conclusive, undeniable, unquestionable; indisputable, incontestable, indubitable; irrefutable; final; undoubted, unquestioned, undisputed; questionless.

authoritative, authentic, official.

evident, manifest; self-evident, axiomatic.

infallible, unerring; unchangeable, etc., 150; trustworthy, reliable.

dogmatic, opinionated, dictatorial, doctrinaire; fanatical, bigoted.

Adv. **certainly,** undoubtedly, indubitably; for certain, surely, no doubt, doubtless, to be sure, of course, as a matter of course, in truth, truly, without fail.

475. UNCERTAINTY.—*N.* **uncertainty,** incertitude, doubt, doubtfulness, dubiousness.

hesitation, suspense, perplexity, embarrassment, dilemma, bewilderment; puzzle, quandary; timidity, etc. (*fear*), 860; vacillation, wavering, indetermination.

vagueness, haze, fog, obscurity, ambiguity, open question, blind bargain, pig in a poke, leap in the dark.

fallibility, unreliability, untrustworthiness; precariousness.

V. **hesitate,** flounder, miss one's way, wander aimlessly, beat about; lose oneself, lose one's head.

perplex, pose, puzzle, confuse, confound, bewilder, nonplus. **doubt,** etc. (*disbelieve*), 485.

Adj. **uncertain,** unsure; casual, random, aimless, doubtful, dubious; insecure, unstable, indecisive, irresolute; unsettled, undecided, undetermined, in question; experimental, tentative.

vague, indefinite, ambiguous, equivocal, undefined, confused; mysterious, cryptic, veiled, obscure, undefinable; oracular.

perplexing, enigmatic, paradoxical, apocryphal, problematical.

fallible, questionable, debatable, untrustworthy, unreliable.

puzzled, perplexed; lost, astray, adrift, at sea, at fault, at a loss, at one's wit's end, distracted, distraught.

476. REASONING.—*N.* reasoning, ratiocination; inference, induction, generalization.

logic, art of reasoning, dialectics; deduction, induction; synthesis, analysis; syllogism.

discussion, comment; ventilation; inquiry, etc., 461.

argumentation, controversy, debate; polemics, wrangling, contention.

argument, case, plea, proposition, terms, premises, data, principle.

arguments, reasons, pros and cons.

reasoner, logician, dialectician, casuist; disputant, controversialist; wrangler, arguer, debater.

V. **reason,** argue, discuss, debate, dispute, contend, wrangle; chop logic; controvert, deny; canvass; consider, examine.

Adj. **reasoning,** rational; argumentative, controversial, dialectic, polemical; disputatious.

logical, syllogistic, inductive, deductive, synthetic *or* synthetical, analytic *or* analytical; relevant, germane.

Adv. **for,** because, hence, whence, seeing that, since, then, thence, so; whereas, considering, therefore, wherefore; consequently, *ergo* [L.], thus, accordingly.

finally, in conclusion, in fine, after all, on the whole.

477. [Absence of reasoning] INTUITION. [Specious reasoning] SOPHISTRY.—*N.* intuition; instinct, association of ideas; rule of thumb; presentiment.

sophistry, casuistry, equivocation, evasion, mental reservation, chicanery; perversion, mystification; speciousness; nonsense, etc., 497; hairsplitting, quibbling; begging of the question.

sophism, quibble, quirk, fallacy, subterfuge, shift, subtlety; inconsistency; claptrap.

V. **pervert,** quibble, equivocate, mystify, evade, elude; gloss over, varnish; misteach, etc., 538; mislead, etc. (*error*), 495; misrepresent, etc. (*lie*), 544; cavil, refine, split hairs; misjudge, etc., 481; beg the question, reason in a circle.

Adj. **intuitive,** instinctive, impulsive.

illogical, unreasonable, false, unsound, invalid; unwarranted, gratuitous; incongruous, inconsequent, inconsequential; unconnected; inconsistent; unscientific; untenable, inconclusive, incorrect, fallacious, groundless, unproved.

specious, sophistic *or* sophistical, casuistic; deceptive, illusive, illusory, hollow, plausible; evasive; irrelevant, inapplicable.

weak, feeble, poor, flimsy, loose, vague, irrational; nonsensical, absurd, foolish, etc. (*imbecile*), 499; frivolous; pettifogging, quibbling.

478. DEMONSTRATION.—N. **demonstration,** proof; conclusiveness; evidence, etc., 467; verification, etc., 462.

V. **demonstrate,** prove, establish, make good; show, evince, verify, etc., 467; settle the question.

follow; stand to reason; hold good, hold water [*colloq.*].

Adj. **demonstrative;** demonstrable; unanswerable, conclusive, decisive, convincing; irresistible, irrefutable, undeniable.

demonstrated, proved; unconfuted, unanswered, unrefuted; evident, self-evident, axiomatic.

deducible, inferential, following.

Adv. **of course,** in consequence, consequently, as a matter of course.

479. CONFUTATION.—N. **confutation,** refutation; answer, disproof, conviction, invalidation; exposure, exposé [F.], retort.

V. **confute,** refute, parry, negative, disprove, expose, show up; rebut, defeat, demolish, upset, subvert, overthrow, overturn, confound; invalidate; convince, silence; clinch an argument.

Adj. **confutable,** refutable; capable of refutation.

480. [Results of reasoning] **JUDGMENT.—**N. **judgment,** decision, determination, finding, verdict, sentence, decree; opinion, etc. (*belief*), 484; good judgment.

result, conclusion, upshot; deduction, inference, corollary.

estimation, valuation, appreciation; arbitrament, arbitration; assessment.

estimate, award; review, criticism, critique, notice, report.

plebiscite, voice, casting vote; vote, suffrage, election.

arbiter, arbitrator; judge, umpire; assessor, referee; inspector; censor.

reviewer, critic; connoisseur; commentator, annotator.

V. **judge,** conclude, opine; come to (*or* arrive at) a conclusion; ascertain, determine.

deduce, derive, gather, collect, infer.

estimate, form an estimate, appreciate, value, count, assess, rate, rank, account; regard, consider, think of; size up [*colloq.*].

decide, settle; try, pronounce, rule; find, pass judgment, sentence, doom, decree; give (*or* deliver) judgment; adjudge, adjudicate; arbitrate, award; confirm.

review, comment, criticize; examine, etc., 457; investigate, etc., 461.

Adj. **judicious,** judicial; determinate, conclusive, confirmatory.

critical, hypercritical, hairsplitting, censorious.

Adv. **on the whole,** all things considered, therefore, wherefore.

480a. [Result of search or inquiry] **DISCOVERY.**—*N.* **discovery,** detection, disclosure, find, revelation.

V. **discover,** find, determine, evolve; fix upon; find (*or* trace, make, root) out; spot [*colloq.*], fathom, bring out, draw out, educe, elicit, bring to light, dig up, unearth, disinter.

solve, resolve; unriddle, unravel, find a clue to; interpret; disclose; see through, detect; catch; scent, smell out.

recognize, realize, verify, make certain of, identify.

481. MISJUDGMENT.—*N.* **misjudgment,** obliquity of judgment, warped judgment; miscalculation, misconception, misinterpretation, etc., 523; hasty conclusion.

preconception, prejudgment, foregone conclusion; presumption, preconceived idea; prejudice, predilection, prepossession; presentiment, foreboding; fixed idea, obsession.

partisanship, clannishness; *esprit de corps* [F.], prestige, party spirit, class prejudice, class consciousness, race prejudice, provincialism.

quirk, shift, quibble, equivocation, evasion, subterfuge.

bias, warp, twist; hobby, whim, craze, cult, fad, crotchet, partiality.

V. **misjudge,** misconjecture, misconceive, misunderstand; miscalculate, misreckon; overestimate, etc., 482; underestimate, etc., 483.

prejudge, dogmatize; have a bias, run away with the notion; jump to a conclusion; blunder, etc., 699.

bias, warp, twist; prejudice, prepossess.

Adj. **misjudging,** ill-judging, wrong-headed; superficial; prejudiced, prepossessed; shortsighted, purblind; partial, one-sided; warped.

narrow, narrow-minded, provincial, parochial, insular; mean-spirited, confined, illiberal, intolerant, infatuated, fanatical, positive, dogmatic, dictatorial, pragmatic; egotistical, conceited, opinionated; bigoted, etc. (*obstinate*), 606; unreasonable, stupid, etc., 499; credulous, gullible.

482. OVERESTIMATION.—*N.* **overestimation,** exaggeration, hyperbole; optimism, much ado about nothing; tempest in a teacup; fine writing, rodomontade, gush [*colloq.*], hot air [*slang*].

egoism, egotism, bombast, conceit; vanity; megalomania.

egoist, egoist, megalomaniac; optimist; braggart, boaster, braggadocio, swaggerer.

V. **overestimate,** overrate, overpraise; strain, magnify; exaggerate, etc., 549.

eulogize, gush over [*colloq.*], boost; puff [*colloq.*]; extol.

Adj. inflated, puffed up; grandiose, stilted, pompous, pretentious, bombastic.

483. UNDERESTIMATION.—*N.* underestimation, undervaluation; depreciation, etc. (*detraction*), 934; pessimism; self-detraction, self-depreciation; modesty, etc., 881.

pessimist, depreciator, knocker [*slang*], crapehanger [*slang*].

V. underrate, underestimate, undervalue; depreciate; disparage, detract, decry, ridicule, deride; slight, etc. (*despise*), 930; neglect; slur over.

make light (*or* little) of, belittle, run down [*colloq.*], minimize, set no store by, set at naught, disregard.

Adj. depreciating, depreciative, depreciatory; pessimistic.

depreciated, unappreciated, unvalued, unprized.

484. BELIEF.—*N.* belief, credence; credit; assurance; faith, trust, confidence, presumption; hope.

conviction, principle; persuasion, certainty, opinion, view, conception, impression, surmise; conclusion.

doctrine, tenet, dogma, articles, canons; view, gospel; article (*or* declaration, profession) of faith, creed; assent, avowal, confession; propaganda.

credibility, probability; plausibility.

V. believe, credit, give faith (*or* credit, credence) to; realize; assume, take it; consider, presume; count (*or* depend, rely, build) upon; take for granted.

confide in, believe in, put one's trust in, place reliance on, trust.

think, hold, opine, conceive; have (*or* hold, entertain, adopt, embrace, foster, cherish) a belief *or* an opinion.

persuade, assure, convince, satisfy, bring to reason, convert, indoctrinate; wean, bring round, bring (*or* win) over; carry conviction.

Adj. certain, sure, assured, positive, cocksure [*colloq.*], satisfied, confident, unhesitating, convinced, secure.

confiding, trustful, unsuspecting, unsuspicious; credulous, gullible.

believed, trusted, unsuspected, undoubted.

credible, reliable, trustworthy, accredited, satisfactory; probable.

485. UNBELIEF. DOUBT.—*N.* unbelief, disbelief, incredulity; infidelity, etc. (*irreligion*), 989; wrangling, nonconformity; dissent, change of opinion; retractation, etc., 607.

doubt, uncertainty, skepticism, misgiving, demur; discredit; distrust, mistrust; misdoubt, suspicion, jealousy, scruple, qualm.

incredibility, incredibleness, unbelievability.

agnostic, skeptic; unbeliever, etc., 487.

V. **disbelieve,** discredit, misbelieve, dissent; refuse to believe.

doubt, distrust, mistrust; question, challenge, dispute; deny, etc., 536; cavil, wrangle; suspect, scent, smell, smell a rat [*colloq.*], harbor suspicions; have one's doubts.

demur, stick at, pause, hesitate, shy at, scruple; waver.

stagger, startle; shake one's faith, stagger one's belief.

Adj. **unbelieving,** skeptical, incredulous; distrustful of, suspicious of.

doubtful, etc. (*uncertain*), 475; disputable, questionable, suspicious; incredible, unbelievable, inconceivable.

Adv. with caution, with grains of allowance.

486. CREDULITY.—*N.* **credulity,** credulousness, gullibility; infatuation; self-delusion, self-deception; superstition; bigotry.

credulous person, dupe, gull.

V. **be credulous;** follow implicitly; swallow, swallow whole, gulp down; take on faith.

impose upon, etc. (*deceive*), 545.

Adj. **credulous,** gullible, easily deceived *or* convinced; simple, silly, childish; infatuated, superstitious; confiding, trustful, unsuspicious.

487. INCREDULITY.—*N.* **incredulity,** incredulousness; skepticism, doubt, disbelief, etc., 989; unbelief, etc., 485.

unbeliever, skeptic, doubting Thomas, disbeliever, agnostic, infidel, misbeliever; heretic, etc. (*heterodox*), 984.

V. **be incredulous,** distrust, doubt, suspect, refuse to believe; turn a deaf ear to.

Adj. **incredulous,** skeptical, suspicious; dissenting, unbelieving; heterodox.

488. ASSENT.—*N.* **assent,** acquiescence, admission; nod; consent, compliance; agreement, understanding; affirmation; recognition, acknowledgment, avowal, confession.

unanimity, common consent, consensus, acclamation, chorus; public opinion; concurrence, accord.

ratification, confirmation, corroboration, approval, acceptance; indorsement.

consenter, indorser, subscriber; upholder, etc. (*auxiliary*), 711.

V. **assent,** give assent, acquiesce, agree, accept, accede, accord, concur, consent, coincide, echo, reciprocate, go with; recognize; subscribe to, conform to, defer to; go with the stream; be in the fashion, join in the chorus.

acknowledge, own, admit, confess; concede, yield; abide by; permit, etc., 760.

confirm, ratify, approve, indorse, countersign; corroborate, etc., 467.

Adj. assenting, of one accord (*or* mind); of the same mind, at one with, agreed, acquiescent.

uncontradicted, unchallenged, unquestioned, unanimous.

Adv. yes, yea, aye, true; granted; even so, just so; to be sure, as you say; surely, assuredly; exactly, precisely, certainly, of course, unquestionably, no doubt, doubtless.

unanimously, by common consent, to a man, as one man; with one consent (*or* voice, accord).

489. DISSENT.—*N.* dissent, nonconsent, discordance, disagreement.

nonconformity, heterodoxy, protestantism, schism; disaffection, secession, recantation.

dissension, discord, caviling, wrangling; discontent, etc., 832.

protest, contradiction, denial; noncompliance, rejection.

dissentient, dissenter, nonconformist; sectary; separatist, protestant; heretic, etc., 984.

V. dissent, demur, call in question, disagree, refuse to admit; cavil, wrangle, protest, repudiate; contradict, deny.

secede; recant, etc., 607.

Adj. dissenting, negative; contradictory; dissentient; unconvinced, unconverted.

sectarian, denominational, schismatic; heterodox; intolerant.

Adv. at variance with, at issue with; under protest.

490. KNOWLEDGE.—*N.* knowledge; cognizance; cognition, acquaintance, experience, ken, insight, familiarity; comprehension, apprehension; recognition; appreciation, judgment, etc., 480; intuition, consciousness, perception.

enlightenment, light; impression, perception, discovery, revelation.

learning, erudition, lore, scholarship; letters, literature; book learning, bookishness, general information; education, culture, cultivation, attainments, acquirements, accomplishments, proficiency.

V. know, be aware of; conceive, apprehend, comprehend; realize, understand, appreciate; fathom, make out; recognize, discern, perceive, see, experience.

learn, imbibe knowledge; discover, evolve.

Adj. aware of, cognizant of, conscious of; acquainted with, privy to, in the secret; alive to; apprized of, informed of; undeceived.

educated, erudite, instructed, learned, lettered, well informed, well versed, well read, well grounded, well educated; high-brow [*slang*], bookish, scholastic, profound, deep-read, book-learned, accomplished; self-taught, self-educated, knowing, shrewd.

known, ascertained, well known, recognized, noted, received, notorious, proverbial; familiar, hackneyed, trite, commonplace.

Adv. to the best of one's knowledge; as every schoolboy knows.

491. IGNORANCE.—*N.* ignorance, illiteracy, unlearnedness, unacquaintance, unconsciousness, darkness, blindness; incomprehension, simplicity.

sealed book; virgin soil, unexplored ground; dark ages.

Imperfect knowledge: smattering, superficiality, half learning, shallowness, glimmering; incapacity.

Affectation of knowledge: pedantry, charlatanry, charlatanism.

V. be ignorant (*or* uninformed); be uneducated; know nothing of; ignore, be blind to.

Adj. ignorant; unknowing, unaware, unacquainted, uninformed, uninitiated, unwitting, unconscious; witless, unconversant.

illiterate, unread, low [*slang*], uncultivated, uninstructed, untaught, untutored, unschooled, uneducated, unlearned, unlettered, empty-headed.

shallow, superficial, green, rude, empty, half-learned, half-baked [*colloq.*], unscholarly.

in the dark; benighted, blinded, blindfold, hoodwinked; misinformed.

unknown, unapprehended, unexplained, uninvestigated, unexplored, unheard of; concealed, etc., 528.

Adv. unawares; for aught one knows; not that one knows.

492. SCHOLAR.—*N.* scholar, savant [F.], pundit [India], schoolman, professor, academician, doctor, fellow, don [Eng.], graduate, postgraduate, classicist, philosopher, scientist, linguist, etymologist, philologist, lexicographer; man of learning.

bookworm, bibliophile, bibliomaniac, bluestocking [*colloq.*], high-brow [*slang*].

pedant, doctrinaire; pedagogue, Dr. Pangloss; instructor, etc., 540.

student, learner, pupil, schoolboy, etc. (*learner*), 541.

Adj. learned, etc., 490.

493. IGNORAMUS.—*N.* ignoramus, illiterate, dunce, duffer, numskull [*colloq.*]; no scholar.

smatterer, dabbler, half scholar; charlatan; wiseacre.

novice, greenhorn, plebe [*West Point cant*]; tyro, etc. (*learner*), 541.

Adj. bookless, shallow, simple, dull, dumb [*colloq.*], dense, crass; illiterate, etc., 491.

494. [Object of knowledge] TRUTH.—*N.* truth, verity; fact, reality, authenticity, gospel; veracity, etc., 543.

accuracy, exactitude, exactness, preciseness, precision, regularity, fidelity, nicety.

V. **hold true,** stand the test, have the true ring, hold good.

trace, solve, etc. (*discover*), 480*a*.

Adj. **true,** real, actual, veritable; certain, etc., 474; unimpeachable; veracious, etc., 543.

pure, sound, sterling, true-blue; natural, unsophisticated, unadulterated, simon-pure [*colloq.*], unvarnished, undisguised.

exact, accurate, definite, concrete, precise, well defined, just, right, correct, strict, severe, rigid, rigorous, scrupulous, literal, punctilious, mathematical, scientific, unromantic; faithful, constant, unerring; particular, nice, meticulous, delicate, fine; clean-cut, clear-cut.

authentic, genuine, legitimate; orthodox, etc., 983*a*; official.

valid, well grounded, well founded, solid, substantial, tangible.

Adv. **truly,** verily, indeed, in reality; in very truth, in fact, as a matter of fact, beyond doubt.

495. ERROR.—*N.* **error,** fallacy, misconception, misapprehension, misunderstanding; aberration, inexactness, laxity; misconstruction, misinterpretation; misjudgment, heresy, misstatement, anachronism: fable, etc. (*untruth*), 546.

mistake, fault, blunder, oversight, misprint, erratum (*pl.* errata), slip, blot, flaw, trip, stumble, bungle; slip of the tongue, slip of the pen, clerical error; bull, etc. (*absurdity*), 497; spoonerism, malapropism.

delusion, illusion, false impression; bubble; self-deceit, self-deception; hallucination, mirage, etc., 443; dream, etc. (*fancy*), 515.

V. **mislead,** misguide, lead astray, beguile, misinform, delude; falsify, misstate, deceive, etc., 545; lie, etc., 544.

err, be in error, be mistaken, be deceived; mistake, deceive oneself, blunder, misapprehend, misconceive, misunderstand, miscalculate, misjudge.

trip, stumble, lose oneself, go astray, fail, etc., 732, take the shadow for the substance.

Adj. **erroneous,** untrue, false, faulty, erring, fallacious, unreal, ungrounded, groundless, unsubstantial, unsound, inexact, inaccurate, incorrect.

illusive, illusory, delusive, mock, imaginary, spurious, etc., 545; deceitful, etc., 544; untrustworthy.

exploded, refuted, discarded.

mistaken, in error, deceived, out in one's reckoning; wide of the mark, at fault, at cross-purposes, at sea, bewildered.

496. MAXIM.—*N.* maxim, aphorism, dictum, saying, adage, saw, proverb, motto, epigram, sentence, mot [*Gallicism*], commonplace, moral.

axiom, theorem, formula, truism.

principle, profession of faith, conclusion, etc. (*judgment*), 480.

Adj. aphoristic, proverbial, axiomatic; hackneyed, trite.

Adv. as the saying is, as they say.

497. ABSURDITY.—*N.* absurdity, absurdness, imbecility, etc., 499; nonsense, paradox, inconsistency.

blunder, muddle, Irish bull; anticlimax, bathos.

farce, burlesque, parody, limerick; farrago, extravagance.

pun, sell [*colloq.*], catch [*colloq.*], verbal quibble, joke.

jargon, gibberish, balderdash, bombast, claptrap, twaddle, moonshine, stuff.

tomfoolery, mummery, monkeyshine [*slang*], monkey trick, frisk, practical joke, escapade.

V. **play the fool**, blunder, muddle; be guilty of absurdity; romance, talk nonsense, exaggerate; be absurd, frisk, caper, joke, play practical jokes.

Adj. absurd, nonsensical, farcical, burlesque, preposterous, egregious, senseless, inconsistent, ridiculous, extravagant, self-contradictory, paradoxical; foolish, etc., 499; meaningless, fantastic, bombastic, high-flown.

498. [Faculties] INTELLIGENCE. WISDOM.—*N.* intelligence, capacity, comprehension, understanding; intellect, etc., 450; brains, parts, sagacity, mother wit, wit, gumption [*colloq.*], acuteness, acumen, longheadedness, subtlety, penetration, perspicacity, discernment, good judgment; discrimination, cunning, refinement.

wisdom, sapience, sense, common sense, clear thinking, rationality, reason; reasonableness, judgment, solidity, depth, profundity, caliber.

genius, inspiration, talent, etc., 698.

Wisdom in action: prudence, etc., 864; vigilance, etc., 459; tact, etc., 698; foresight, etc., 510; sobriety, self-possession, ballast, mental poise, balance.

V. have all one's wits about one; be brilliant, scintillate, coruscate; understand, etc. (*intelligible*), 518.

penetrate, see through, see at a glance, discern; foresee, etc., 510; discriminate.

Adj. Applied to persons: intelligent, quick of apprehension, keen, acute, alive, awake, bright, quick, sharp, quick-witted, wide-awake; shrewd, astute; clearheaded, long-sighted, calculating, thoughtful, farsighted, discerning, perspicacious, penetrating, piercing; sharp as a needle; alive to, etc. (*cognizant*), 490; clever, etc. (*apt*), 698.

wise, sage, sapient [*often in irony*], sagacious, rational, sensible, judicious, strong-minded; worldly-wise, sophisticated.

impartial, unprejudiced, unbiased, unbigoted, equitable, fair.

prudent, etc. (*cautious*), 864; sober, staid, solid; watchful; provident, prepared, etc., 673.

Applied to actions: wise, sensible, judicious, well judged, well advised; prudent, politic; expedient, etc., 646.

499. IMBECILITY, FOLLY.—*N.* imbecility, want of intelligence (*or* intellect), shallowness, silliness, foolishness, stupidity, stolidity; incompetence.

simplicity, puerility; senility, dotage, second childhood; fatuity; idiocy.

folly, frivolity, irrationality, trifling, ineptitude, inconsistency, giddiness; eccentricity, etc., 503; extravagance, etc. (*absurdity*), 497; rashness, etc., 863.

V. trifle, drivel, dote; ramble, play the fool, fool, stultify oneself, talk nonsense.

Adj. Applied to persons: unintelligent, unintellectual, unreasoning; mindless, brainless; half-baked [*colloq.*], bovine, thick [*colloq.*], blockish, unteachable; ungifted, unenlightened, unwise; thickskulled, muddleheaded, addleheaded, weak-minded, feebleminded.

stupid, dull, heavy, obtuse, blunt, stolid, asinine, inapt.

childish, childlike; infantine, infantile, babyish, puerile, senile, anile; simple, credulous.

imbecile, fatuous, idiotic, driveling; vacant, bewildered.

foolish, silly, senseless, irrational, insensate, nonsensical, maudlin.

narrow-minded, bigoted, etc., 606; rash, etc., 863; eccentric, odd.

Applied to actions: foolish, unwise, injudicious, improper, unreasonable, ill-advised, ridiculous, silly, stupid, asinine; inconsistent, irrational; extravagant, nonsensical, frivolous, trivial; useless, etc., 645; inexpedient, etc., 647.

500. SAGE.—*N.* sage, wise man; master mind, thinker, philosopher, savant [F.], pundit, etc. (*scholar*), 492; wiseacre [*ironical*]; expert, etc., 700.

authority, oracle, mentor, Solon, Solomon, Buddha, Confucius.

Adj. venerable, venerated, reverenced, revered, honored; authoritative, oracular; wise, erudite, etc., 490.

501. FOOL.—*N.* fool, idiot, tomfool, wiseacre, simpleton,

Simple Simon; donkey, ass, owl, goose, dolt, booby, noodle, imbecile, nincompoop [*colloq.*], oaf, lout, blockhead, bonehead [*slang*], calf [*colloq.*], colt, numskull [*colloq.*], clod, clodhopper; soft or softy [*colloq. or slang*], mooncalf, saphead [*slang*], gawk, rube [*slang*].

greenhorn, etc. (*dupe*), 547; dunce, etc. (*ignoramus*), 493; lubber, etc. (*bungler*), 701; madman, etc., 504; dotard, driveler, old fogy [*colloq.*].

502. SANITY.—*N.* **sanity,** soundness, rationality, sobriety, lucidity, senses, common sense, horse sense [*colloq.*], sound mind.

V. **become sane,** come to one's senses, sober down, cool down, see things in proper perspective.

render sane, bring to one's senses, sober, bring to reason.

Adj. **sane,** rational, normal, wholesome, right-minded, reasonable, sound, sound-minded, in possession of one's faculties.

Adv. **sanely,** in reason, within reason, within bounds.

503. INSANITY.—*N.* **insanity,** lunacy; madness, mania, dementia, idiocy; delirium tremens, d.t.'s, the horrors [*colloq.*]; frenzy, raving, wandering, delirium, delusion, obsession, hallucination, derangement, unsoundness of mind.

vertigo, dizziness, swimming, sunstroke.

oddity, eccentricity, twist, monomania; fanaticism, infatuation, craze.

V. **be** or **become insane,** lose one's senses (or reason), go mad, rave, dote, ramble, wander; lose one's head, drivel.

derange, render or drive mad, madden, infatuate, obsess, befool; turn the brain, turn one's head.

Adj. **insane,** mad, lunatic; crazy, crazed, crackbrained, cracked [*colloq.*], touched; bereft of reason; unhinged, insensate, beside oneself, demented, maniacal, daft, frenzied, deranged, maddened, moonstruck, off one's head.

giddy, vertiginous, wild, flighty, distracted, distraught, bewildered.

odd, fanatical, infatuated, eccentric.

delirious, lightheaded, rambling, wandering, frantic, raving, stark mad.

504. MADMAN.—*N.* **madman,** lunatic, maniac; crank [*colloq.*], nut [*slang*].

dreamer, visionary, rhapsodist, seer, enthusiast, fanatic; Don Quixote, Ophelia.

idiot, etc., 501.

505. [The Past] MEMORY.—*N.* **memory,** remembrance; retention, retentiveness; retentive (or tenacious, trustworthy, ready) memory.

recollection, retrospect, reminiscence; recognition; afterthought.

reminder, hint, suggestion, memorandum (*pl.* memoranda), token, memento, souvenir, keepsake, relic; memorial, monument; commemoration, jubilee.

mnemonics; art of memory, artificial memory; Mnemosyne.

fame, celebrity, renown, reputation; repute, notoriety.

V. **remember**, retain the memory of, keep in mind; bear in mind, haunt one's mind (*or* thoughts); rankle; keep the wound open, brood over.

recollect, recall, call up, conjure up, retrace; look back upon, review; call (*or* bring) to mind.

remind, suggest, hint, prompt; put (*or* keep) in mind; bring to mind, call up, summon up, renew; redeem from oblivion; commemorate.

memorize, commit to memory; con, con over; fix in the mind, engrave upon the memory; learn by heart, know by rote, have at one's fingers' ends.

make a note of, put down, record.

Adj. **remembering**, mindful, reminiscent; fresh, still vivid; enduring, unforgotten; never to be forgotten, indelible; within one's memory; memorable, suggestive.

Adv. **by heart**, by rote, without book, word for word.

506. OBLIVION.—*N.* oblivion; forgetfulness; Lethe; obliteration of the past; short (*or* treacherous, untrustworthy, slippery, failing) memory; decay (*or* failure, lapse) of memory; amnesia.

amnesty, general pardon.

V. **forget**, be forgetful; fall (*or* sink) into oblivion; have a short memory; lose, lose the memory of, lose sight of.

efface, from the memory; unlearn; consign to oblivion, think no more of; let bygones be bygones.

Adj. **forgotten**, unremembered, out of mind; buried (*or* sunk) in oblivion.

forgetful, oblivious; heedless, deaf to the past; Lethean.

507. [The Future] EXPECTATION.—*N.* expectation, expectancy, anticipation, prospect, contingency, reckoning, calculation; foresight; suspense; abeyance.

assurance, confidence, reliance, hope, trust, presumption; prognostication; prediction, etc., 511.

V. **expect**; look for, look out for, look forward to; hope for, anticipate; have in prospect, keep in view; contemplate; wait for, watch for, await; foresee, prepare for, forestall.

predict, prognosticate, forecast.

Adj. **expectant**; expecting, in expectation, vigilant; open-eyed, open-mouthed; agape, gaping, on tenterhooks, on tiptoe; ready, prepared, provided for, provident.

expected, foreseen; in prospect, prospective, provisional; future, coming; in view, on the horizon; impending.

Adv. **expectantly,** on the watch, with muscles tense, on edge [*colloq.*], with eyes (*or* ears) strained, with bated breath.

soon, shortly, forthwith, presently.

508. NONEXPECTATION.—*N.* **nonexpectation,** unforeseen contingency, the unforeseen; miscalculation, false expectation; disappointment; disillusion.

surprise, blow, shock; bolt out of the blue; astonishment, amazement; wonder, bewilderment.

V. **be unexpected,** come unawares, turn up, burst *or* flash upon one; take by surprise, catch unawares.

surprise, startle, stun, stagger, astound; throw off one's guard; spring upon, astonish, etc. (*strike with wonder*), 870.

Adj. **nonexpectant,** surprised; unwarned, unaware; off one's guard.

unexpected, unanticipated, unlooked for, unforeseen; unheard of; startling; sudden.

Adv. **unexpectedly,** abruptly, suddenly, unawares; without notice *or* warning.

509. DISAPPOINTMENT.—*N.* **disappointment,** blighted hope, disillusion, balk; blow, false (*or* vain) expectation; miscalculation; fool's paradise.

V. **be disappointed;** look blank, look *or* stand aghast; find to one's cost.

disappoint, crush (*or* dash, blight) one's hope, balk *or* disappoint one's expectation, balk, tantalize; dumfounder, dumfound, disconcert, disillusionize; dissatisfy; disgruntle.

Adj. **aghast;** disgruntled; out of one's reckoning.

510. FORESIGHT.—*N.* **foresight,** prevision, long-sightedness, farsightedness; anticipation; prudence; forethought.

foreknowledge, prescience; presentiment, foreboding; second sight.

prospect; foregone conclusion; forecast.

V. **foresee;** look forward to, look ahead *or* beyond; look into the future; see one's way; see how the land lies.

anticipate, expect, surmise, contemplate; predict; forewarn.

Adj. **foreseeing,** prescient, anticipatory; farseeing, farsighted, long-sighted; provident; weatherwise; prospective; expectant.

Adv. against the time when; for a rainy day.

511. PREDICTION.—*N.* **prediction,** announcement; program;

platform; premonition, presage, foreboding; phophecy, prognostication, augury, forecast; omen, etc., 512; horoscope; soothsaying, fortunetelling, divination; oracle, etc., 513.

astrology; spell, charm, etc., 993; sorcery, magic, etc., 992.

V. **predict,** forecast, prognosticate, prophesy, divine, foretell; tell fortunes, cast a horoscope (*or* nativity); forewarn.

presage, augur, bode, forebode; foretoken, betoken; portend, signify, point to.

herald, usher in, announce; lower; threaten.

Adj. **prophetic,** oracular, sibylline; weatherwise.

ominous, portentous; auspicious; premonitory, significant of.

512. OMEN.—*N.* **omen,** portent, presage, augury; sign, token; harbinger; bird of ill omen; halcyon birds; signs of the times; warning, etc., 668.

Adj. **auspicious,** favorable, halcyon, of good omen.

inauspicious, ill-boding, ill-omened, ill-starred.

513. ORACLE.—*N.* **oracle;** prophet, seer, soothsayer, prophetess, witch, sibyl; augur, haruspex; medium, clairvoyant, palmist; fortuneteller; sorcerer, etc., 994; interpreter, etc., 524.

Delphic oracle; Cumaean Sibyl, Sibyl, Cassandra, Witch of Endor, Sphinx.

weather prophet, weather bureau.

514. [Creative Thought] SUPPOSITION.—*N.* **supposition,** assumption, presumption, condition, hypothesis, postulate, theory, data; thesis, theorem; conjecture, guess, guesswork, speculation; surmise, suspicion, inkling, suggestion, hint.

theorist, theorizer, doctrinaire, doctrinarian.

V. **suppose,** conjecture; surmise, suspect, guess, divine; theorize, speculate; presume, presuppose, assume, predicate; believe, take for granted.

propound, propose, put forth; put a case, submit; move, make a motion; hazard *or* put forward a suggestion (*or* supposition); suggest, allude to, hint.

Adj. **assumed,** given; conjectural, presumptive, hypothetical; theoretical, academic.

suggestive, allusive, stimulating.

Adv. **if,** if so be; on the supposition, in case, in the event of; as if, provided; perhaps, for aught one knows.

515. IMAGINATION.—*N.* **imagination,** originality, invention; fancy; inspiration.

ideality, idealism; romanticism, utopianism, castle-building, dreaming; frenzy, rhapsody, ecstasy, reverie, daydream.

conception; flight of fancy; creation of the brain; imagery; word painting.

fantasy, conceit; figment, myth; romance, extravaganza; dream, vision; shadow, chimera, phantasm, illusion, phantom, fancy, whim, vagary; bugbear, nightmare; flying Dutchman, great sea serpent, man in the moon, castle in the air, castle in Spain, Utopia, fairyland; land of Prester John.

Creative works: work of fiction, etc. (*novel*), 594; poetry, etc., 597; drama, etc., 599; music, etc., 415; painting, sculpture, architecture; art.

idealist, romanticist, visionary, romancer, daydreamer, dreamer, castle-builder; creative artist.

V. imagine, fancy, conceive; idealize, realize; dream, dream of; indulge in reverie; fancy (*or* represent, picture, figure) to oneself.

create, originate, devise, invent, make up, coin, fabricate; improvise.

Adj. imaginative, original, inventive, creative, productive.

extravagant, romantic, high-flown, flighty, preposterous; unreal; unsubstantial.

ideal; intellectual, impracticable, imaginary, visionary, utopian, quixotic.

fanciful; fantastical; fictitious; fabulous, legendary, mythic *or* mythical, mythological, chimerical; whimsical; fairy, fairylike.

II. COMMUNICATION OF IDEAS

516. MEANING.—*N.* meaning [*idea to be conveyed*], signification, significance; sense, import, purport; pith, essence; force; drift, bearing, tenor, spirit; allusion; suggestion, interpretation; acceptation.

Thing signified: matter, subject, subject matter, substance, gist, argument.

V. mean, signify, denote, express; import, purport; convey, imply, indicate; tell of, speak of; touch on; point to, allude to; drive at; involve; declare; affirm, state.

paraphrase, state differently; express by a synonym.

Adj. meaning, expressive, significant, pithy; intelligible, explicit, clear; suggestive; allusive.

literal, word-for-word, verbatim; exact, real.

synonymous; tantamount, equivalent.

implied; understood, tacit.

Adv. to that effect; that is to say.

517. UNMEANINGNESS.—*N.* unmeaningness, absence of meaning, drivel, senselessness; empty sound.

nonsense, jargon, gibberish, mere words, rant, bombast, balderdash, babble, inanity, twaddle, trash, rubbish; absurdity; imbecility, folly; ambiguity, vagueness, etc., 519.

V. mean nothing; be unmeaning; gibber; jabber, twaddle, rant, babble.

scribble, scrawl, scratch.

Adj. **unmeaning,** meaningless, senseless; nonsensical; inexpressive; vague; not significant.

trashy, inane, trumpery, trivial, insignificant.

518. INTELLIGIBILITY.—*N.* **intelligibility;** comprehensibility; clearness, clarity, explicitness, lucidity, perspicuity; precision; plain speaking.

V. **render intelligible,** popularize, simplify, elucidate, explain, interpret.

understand, comprehend; take in, catch, grasp, follow; master.

Adj. **intelligible;** clear, lucid; perspicuous, transparent.

plain, distinct, clear-cut, hard-hitting, to the point, explicit; positive; definite, precise; unequivocal, legible, obvious, etc., 525.

graphic, telling, vivid; expressive.

519. UNINTELLIGIBILITY.—*N.* **unintelligibility,** incomprehensibility, vagueness, obscurity, ambiguity, confusion; mystification; jargon.

enigma, riddle; sealed book.

V. **render unintelligible,** conceal, darken, confuse, mystify, perplex.

Adj. **unintelligible,** incomprehensible, unaccountable, undecipherable, unfathomable, inexplicable, inscrutable, insoluble, impenetrable; puzzling, enigmatic; indecipherable, illegible.

obscure, crabbed, dark, muddy, dim, nebulous, mysterious, hidden, latent, occult; abstruse; indefinite, vague, loose, ambiguous.

inexpressible, unutterable, ineffable.

520. [Having a double sense] EQUIVOCALNESS.—*N.* **equivocalness,** equivocation, double meaning; ambiguity; quibble; conundrum, riddle; pun, word play; sphinx, Delphic oracle.

equivocation, etc. (*duplicity*), 544; white lie, mental reservation, etc., 528.

V. **equivocate,** etc. (*palter*), 544; prevaricate; have a double meaning.

Adj. **equivocal,** ambiguous; double-tongued; enigmatical; indeterminate, doubtful.

521. FIGURE OF SPEECH.—*N.* **figure,** trope, phrase, expression; euphemism; image, imagery; personification, metaphor; simile, satire, irony.

allegory, apologue, parable, fable.

V. **employ figures of speech;** personify, allegorize, fable, shadow forth, allude to.

Adj. **figurative,** metaphorical, euphuistic, allusive; allegoric *or* allegorical, ironic, ironical, satiric *or* satirical; euphemistic.

522. INTERPRETATION.—*N.* **interpretation,** definition, explanation; elucidation, diagnosis; solution, answer; meaning, etc., 516; clue.

translation; rendering, rendition; metaphrase, literal (*or* word-for-word) translation; free translation; key; crib, horse, pony, trot [*school cant*].

comment, commentary; exegesis, exposition; inference, deduction; illustration, exemplification; gloss, annotation, note, construction, version, reading.

equivalent, equivalent meaning, synonym; paraphrase, convertible terms.

dictionary, etc., 562.

prediction, etc., 511; chiromancy, palmistry; astrology.

V. **interpret,** explain, define, construe, translate, render; decipher, make out, unravel, disentangle, solve; read between the lines.

elucidate, account for, throw *or* shed light upon; clear up, popularize, simplify; illustrate, exemplify; unfold, expound, comment upon, annotate.

Adj. **explanatory,** expository; interpretative, elucidative, inferential, illustrative.

equivalent, convertible, synonymous.

metaphrastic, literal, word-for-word.

Adv. **in explanation;** that is to say, to wit, namely.

literally, strictly speaking; in plain terms (*or* words).

523. MISINTERPRETATION.—*N.* **misinterpretation,** misapprehension, misconception, misunderstanding, misconstruction; misapplication; cross-purposes; mistake, etc., 495.

misrepresentation, perversion, misstatement, exaggeration; abuse of terms; play upon words, pun, parody, travesty; falsification, etc. (*lying*), 544.

V. **misinterpret,** misapprehend, misunderstand, misconceive; misjudge, misspell; mistranslate, misconstrue, misapply; mistake, etc., 495.

misrepresent, pervert, misstate, garble, falsify, distort; travesty, play upon words; stretch (*or* strain, twist, wrest) the sense *or* meaning.

Adj. **misinterpreted,** mistranslated; confused, tangled, snarled, mixed.

dazed, perplexed, bewildered, rattled [*slang*], benighted.

Adv. **at cross-purposes,** at sixes and sevens [*colloq.*]; in a maze.

524. INTERPRETER.—*N.* **interpreter,** translator, expositor, expounder, exponent; demonstrator; commentator, annotator; oracle, etc., 513.

spokesman, speaker, mouthpiece, foreman of the jury, mediator, advocate, delegate, representative, diplomatic agent, ambassador, plenipotentiary.

guide, courier, cicerone, showman, barker [*colloq.*].

525. MANIFESTATION.—*N.* manifestation, indication, expression; plain speaking, candor, openness; showing, exposition, demonstration; séance, materialization; exhibition, production, display, show.

Thing shown: exhibit, exhibition, exposition, show [*colloq.*], performance.

publicity, etc., 531; disclosure, etc., 529; openness, candor; saliency, prominence.

V. make manifest, materialize, express, represent, set forth, evidence, exhibit, produce, show, show up, expose; hold up, show forth, unveil, display, demonstrate, lay open; draw out, bring out; manifest oneself; speak out, proclaim, publish.

indicate, point out; disclose, discover; translate, transcribe, decipher, decode; elicit, bring to light, disinter.

be manifest *or* plain, appear, etc., 446; transpire, come to light, be disclosed; go without saying, be self-evident.

Adj. manifest, apparent; salient, striking, prominent, in the foreground, ostensible, notable, pronounced.

plain, intelligible, clear, defined, definite, distinct, conspicuous, obvious, evident, unmistakable; conclusive, indubitable, palpable, self-evident; open, patent, express, explicit; naked, bare, literal, downright, unreserved, frank, plain-spoken.

barefaced, brazen, bold, shameless, daring, flaunting, loud [*colloq.*]; flagrant, arrant, notorious; glaring.

Adv. manifestly, openly, plainly, above board, in plain sight, in the open, in broad daylight; without reserve.

526. LATENCY.—*N.* latency, hidden meaning; obscurity, ambiguity; secret, mystery, occultism, mysticism, symbolism; reserve, reticence; concealment, mystification, suppression, evasion; Delphic oracle; undercurrent; snake in the grass.

allusion, insinuation, implication; innuendo.

latent influence, power behind the throne, friend at court, wirepuller [*colloq.*], kingmaker.

V. lurk, smolder, underlie, make no sign; escape observation (*or* detection, recognition); lie hid, lie in ambush.

keep back, etc. (*conceal*), 528.

involve, imply, connote, import, allude to, leave an inference; symbolize.

Adj. latent, lurking; dormant, secret, occult; esoteric, recondite, veiled, symbolic, cryptic, mystic, mystical.

unapparent, unknown, unseen, unsuspected; invisible; unexpressed, undisclosed, tacit.

indirect, crooked, underhand, underground; by inference, by implication; implied, implicit, understood, tacit; allusive, covert, undercover, concealed.

Adv. **secretly,** stealthily, incognito; in the background; behind the scenes, between the lines; below the surface.

527. INFORMATION.—*N.* **information,** enlightenment, acquaintance, knowledge; publicity, notoriety.

mention; instruction, communicativeness, intercommunication.

notification, intimation, communication, notice, annunciation, announcement, communiqué; representation; message, etc., 532.

report, advice, monition; news, tidings, return, record, account, description; statement, estimate, specification.

informant, authority, teller, harbinger, herald, reporter, exponent, mouthpiece; spokesman, etc. (*interpreter*), 524; spy, informer, eavesdropper, detective, sleuth [*colloq.*]; newsmonger; messenger, etc., 534.

guide, cicerone; pilot; guidebook, handbook; map, plan, chart, gazetteer; itinerary.

hint, suggestion, insinuation, innuendo, inkling, whisper, cue, byplay; gesture; word to the wise.

V. **tell,** inform, acquaint, impart, apprise, advise, instruct, enlighten.

mention, express, intimate, represent, communicate, make known; publish, disseminate; notify, signify, specify; retail, describe; state, declare, assert, affirm.

announce, report, bring (*or* send, leave) word; telegraph, wire [*colloq.*], telephone, phone [*colloq.*].

disclose, etc., 529; explain.

hint, insinuate, allude to, glance at, let fall, indicate; suggest, prompt, give the cue.

undeceive, set right, correct, disabuse.

Adj. **informational,** advisory.

expressive, explicit, plain-spoken; declaratory; expository; communicative.

528. CONCEALMENT.—*N.* **concealment,** mystification; reticence, reserve, reservation; mental reservation, aside; suppression, evasion, white lie; silence, closeness, secretiveness, mystery.

screen, cloak; ambush, ambuscade; stowaway; blind baggage [*slang*].

cipher, code, sympathetic ink.

stealth, stealthiness, slyness, caution, cunning.

secrecy, privacy, secretness; disguise, mask, masquerade; incognito (*fem.* incognita).

masquerader, masker, mask, domino.

V. conceal, hide, secrete; lock up; cover, screen, cloak, veil, shroud; curtain, muffle; mask, camouflage, disguise; ensconce.

keep from, keep to oneself, keep secret; bury; sink, suppress; keep in the background; stifle, hush up; withhold, reserve.

code, use a code *or* cipher, reduce to a code.

hoodwink, blind, blindfold; mystify, puzzle, deceive, lead astray.

be concealed, hide oneself, couch; lie in ambush, lurk, sneak, skulk, slink, prowl, gumshoe [*slang*].

Adj. concealed, hidden, secret, private, privy; recondite, mystic, mystical, occult, dark, cryptic; in secret, tortuous; close, inviolate, confidential, behind a screen, undercover, in ambush, in hiding, in disguise; undisclosed, untold, covert, mysterious.

furtive, stealthy, skulking, surreptitious, underhand, sly, cunning, evasive; secretive, clandestine; reserved, reticent, uncommunicative, close, taciturn.

Adv. secretly, in secret, in private, incognito.

behind closed doors, under the rose, *sub rosa* [L.]; on the sly [*colloq.*]; in a whisper.

confidentially, in strict confidence, between ourselves, between you and me.

underhand, by stealth, like a thief in the night; stealthily.

529. DISCLOSURE.—*N.* disclosure, revelation, divulgence, exposition, exposure, publication, exposé.

acknowledgment, avowal, confession, confessional.

narrator, etc., 594; talebearer, etc., 532; informant, etc., 527.

V. disclose, discover, unmask, unveil, unfold, uncover, unseal, lay bare, expose, bare, bring to light, disabuse, open the eyes of, turn informer.

divulge, reveal, let into the secret, tell, etc. (*inform*), 527; breathe, utter, peach [*slang*]; let slip *or* drop, betray; blurt out, vent, whisper about, speak out, break the news, publish, etc., 531.

acknowledge, allow, concede, grant, admit, own, confess, avow, make a clean breast, unbosom oneself; turn informer.

be disclosed, transpire, come to light, become known, escape the lips; ooze out, leak out, come to one's ears.

530. AMBUSH. [Means of concealment]—*N.* ambush, ambuscade, lurking place, trap, snare, pitfall, etc., 667.

hiding place, secret place, recess, hole, cubbyhole, crypt; safe, safe-deposit box, safety-deposit box.

screen, cover, shade, blinker; veil, curtain, blind, cloak, cloud.

mask, visor, disguise, masquerade, domino.

V. **ambush,** ambuscade, lie in ambush, lie in wait for; set a trap for, ensnare.

531. PUBLICATION.—*N.* **publication,** public announcement, promulgation, propagation, proclamation, pronouncement, edict.

publicity, notoriety, currency, flagrancy, cry, hue and cry, bruit; report, etc. (*news*), 532; telegram, etc., 532.

the press, the fourth estate, public press; newspaper, journal, gazette.

advertisement, placard, bill, flier [*cant*], leaflet, handbill, poster; circular, notice, program, manifesto.

V. **publish,** make public, broach, utter, circulate, propagate, promulgate, spread, spread abroad, rumor, diffuse, disseminate; issue; bring before the public; give to the world; report, voice, bruit; proclaim, herald, blazon, noise abroad, advertise.

telegraph, cable, wireless [*colloq.*], broadcast, wire [*colloq.*].

Adj. **published,** current; public, notorious, flagrant.

Adv. **publicly,** in public, in open court, with open doors.

532. NEWS—*N.* **news,** information, etc., 527; intelligence, tidings; beat *or* scoop [*newspaper cant*], story, copy [*cant*].

message, word, advice, communication, bulletin, broadcast, dispatch; telegram, cable [*colloq.*], wire [*colloq.*], radio, radiogram, wireless telegram, wireless [*colloq.*]; telephone, radiophone, wireless telephone.

report, rumor, hearsay, cry, bruit, fame; talk, scandal, gossip; tittle-tattle.

narrator, historian; newsmonger, scandalmonger; talebearer, telltale, gossip, tattler, tattletale; chatterer, busybody; informer.

V. **transpire,** etc. (*be disclosed*), 529; rumor, etc. (*publish*), 531.

Adj. **rumored,** rife, current, in circulation.

533. SECRET.—*N.* **secret,** mystery; problem, etc. (*question*), 461; unintelligibility, etc., 519.

enigma, riddle, puzzle, conundrum, charade, rebus.

maze, labyrinth, intricacy.

Adj. **secret,** concealed, etc., 528; involved, tortuous, circuitous, labyrinthine; enigmatic *or* enigmatical.

534. MESSENGER.—*N.* **messenger,** intermediary, go-between; envoy, emissary, legate, nuncio, delegate; angel; Gabriel, Hermes, Mercury.

courier, runner; commissionaire, errand boy; herald, crier, trumpeter, bellman.

mail, post, post office; air mail; postman, mailman, letter carrier; carrier pigeon.

telegraph, cable, wire [*colloq.*], radiotelegraph, wireless telegraph, wireless [*colloq.*], radio.

telephone, phone [*colloq.*], radiotelephone, radiophone, wireless telephone.

reporter, newspaperman, journalist; gentleman (*or* representative) of the press; special correspondent; scout, spy, informer.

535. AFFIRMATION.—*N.* affirmation, statement, allegation, profession, assertion, declaration; confirmation; asseveration, swearing, oath, affidavit, deposition; assurance, protest, protestation.

positiveness, emphasis, peremptoriness, dogmatism, weight.

vote, voice; ballot, suffrage.

remark, observation, saying, dictum, sentence.

V. **assert,** say, affirm, declare, state; protest, profess; acknowledge; put forward; advance, allege, propose, propound; announce, enunciate, broach, set forth, maintain, contend, pronounce.

depose, aver, avow, avouch, asseverate, swear, affirm; take one's oath; make an affidavit; vow, vouch, warrant, certify, assure; attest; adjure.

emphasize, insist upon, lay stress on; lay down the law; dogmatize, repeat, reassert, reaffirm.

Adj. **affirmative,** declaratory, positive; unmistakable, clear; certain, etc., 474; express, explicit, absolute, emphatic, decided, insistent, dogmatic, formal, solemn, categorical, peremptory.

Adv. with emphasis, ex cathedra, without fear of contradiction.

536. NEGATION.—*N.* **negation,** denial; disavowal, disclaimer; contradiction, protest; dissent, etc., 489.

qualification, etc., 469; repudiation, rejection, recantation, revocation; retractation, rebuttal, confutation; refusal, etc., 764.

V. **deny;** contradict, contravene; controvert, gainsay, negative, give the lie to, belie.

disclaim, disown, repudiate, disaffirm, disavow, abjure, forswear, renounce; recant, revoke.

dispute, impugn, confute, rebut, join issue upon; bring (*or* call) in question, set aside, ignore; refuse, etc., 764.

Adj. **contradictory;** negative; recusant, dissentient, at issue upon.

Adv. **no,** nay, not, nowise, not at all, not in the least, quite the contrary, by no means.

537. TEACHING.—*N.* **teaching,** pedagogics, pedagogy, instruction, edification, education, tuition, tutorship, tutelage; direction, guidance.

preparation, qualification, training, schooling, discipline; drill, practice.

lesson, lecture, recitation, sermon, homily, harangue, disquisition; apologue, parable; discourse; explanation; exercise, task; curriculum; course.

V. **teach,** instruct, educate, edify, school, tutor, cram [*colloq.*], grind [*colloq.*], prime, coach; enlighten, inform, etc., 527; direct, guide.

inculcate, infuse, instill, imbue, impregnate, implant; disseminate, propagate.

expound, etc. (*interpret*), 522; lecture; hold forth, preach; sermonize, moralize.

train, discipline, form, ground, prepare, qualify, drill, exercise, practice, familiarize with, inure, initiate, graduate.

Adj. **educational,** scholastic, academic, disciplinary, instructive, pedagogic, didactic; cultural, humanistic, humane; pragmatic, practical, utilitarian.

538. MISTEACHING.—*N.* **misteaching,** misinformation, misguidance, misdirection, perversion, sophistry; the blind leading the blind.

V. **misinform,** misteach, misinstruct, misdirect, misguide, pervert; deceive, mislead, misrepresent, lie.

render unintelligible, bewilder, mystify, conceal.

539. LEARNING.—*N.* **learning,** acquisition of knowledge, acquirement, attainment; mental cultivation, scholarship, erudition; lore; wide reading; study, grind [*colloq.*]; inquiry, etc., 461.

apprenticeship, tutelage, novitiate.

V. **learn,** acquire (*or* gain, imbibe, pick up, obtain) knowledge *or* learning; master, grind [*college slang*], cram [*colloq.*], get up, learn by heart.

study, read, peruse; con, pore over, wade through, plunge into. burn the midnight oil; be taught.

Adj. **studious;** industrious, etc., 682; scholastic, scholarly, well read, widely read, erudite, learned.

540. TEACHER.—*N.* **teacher,** preceptor, instructor, master, tutor, schoolmaster, dominie, pedagogue; kindergartner, governess, mistress; coach [*colloq.*], crammer [*colloq.*]; professor, don [*Univ. cant*], lecturer, reader, preacher; pastor, etc. (*clergy*), 996; schoolmistress.

guide, counselor, adviser, mentor, pioneer, apostle, missionary, propagandist; example.

professorship, chair, fellowship, tutorship, mastership, instructorship.

Adj. **pedagogic,** tutorial, professorial; scholastic, etc., 537.

541. LEARNER.—*N.* **learner,** scholar, student, alumnus (*pl.* alumni; *fem.* alumna, *pl.* alumnae), pupil, schoolboy, schoolgirl;

monitor, prefect; undergraduate, freshman; **graduate student,** postgraduate student.

class, form, grade, room; promotion, graduation.

disciple, follower, apostle, proselyte.

classmate, fellow student, schoolmate, schoolfellow, fellow pupil.

novice, beginner, tyro, recruit, tenderfoot [*slang or colloq.*], neophyte, probationer; apprentice.

Adj. in leading strings, pupillary, probationary.

542. SCHOOL.—*N.* **school,** academy, lyceum, seminary, college, educational institution, institute; university, varsity [*colloq.*], alma mater [L.].

General: day (*or* boarding, preparatory, elementary, denominational, secondary, military, naval, technical, library, secretarial, business, correspondence) school; kindergarten, nursery school; Sunday (*or* Sabbath, Bible) school.

United States: district (*or* grade, parochial, public, primary, grammar, junior high, high, Latin) school; private school, normal school, kindergarten training school; summer school; military academy (West Point); naval academy (Annapolis); college, fresh-water college [*colloq.* or *slang*], state university; graduate school, postgraduate school.

class, division, form, etc., 541; seminar.

classroom, room, schoolroom, recitation room; lecture room, lecture hall, theater, amphitheater.

desk, reading desk, pulpit, forum, stage, rostrum, platform.

schoolbook, textbook; grammar, primer, reader.

Adj. **scholastic,** academic, collegiate; educational, cultural; gymnastic, athletic, physical, eurythmic.

543. VERACITY.—*N.* **veracity,** truthfulness, frankness, truth, sincerity, candor, honesty, fidelity, love of truth; probity, etc., 939.

V. **speak the truth,** tell the truth; speak on oath; speak without equivocation (*or* mental reservation), make a clean breast, disclose, etc., 529; speak one's mind.

Adj. **truthful,** true; veracious, scrupulous, punctilious; sincere, candid, frank, open, outspoken, straightforward, unreserved, truth-telling, honest, trustworthy; guileless, pure, truth-loving; true-blue, as good as one's word; unfeigned, ingenuous.

544. FALSEHOOD.—*N.* **falsehood,** falseness, falsity, falsification, misrepresentation, deception, etc., 545; untruthfulness, lying; untruth, etc., 546; mendacity, guile, perjury, false swearing; forgery, invention, fabrication; perversion, distortion, exaggeration, prevarication, equivocation, evasion, fraud; simulation, dissimulation, dissembling; deceit; sham, pretense; malingering.

duplicity, double dealing, insincerity, hypocrisy, cant, pharisaism; casuistry, Machiavellism; lip service, hollowness, mere show; quackery, charlatanism, charlatanry; humbug; cajolery, flattery; Judas kiss; perfidy, etc., 940; cunning, etc., 702; misstatement, false report.

V. **lie,** tell a lie (*or* an untruth), fib, swear falsely, forswear, perjure oneself, bear false witness.

falsify, misstate, misquote; misrepresent, etc., 523; belie; garble, gloss over, disguise, color, varnish, doctor [*colloq.*], dress up, embroider; exaggerate, etc., 549.

prevaricate, equivocate, quibble; trim, shuffle, fence, beat about the bush.

fabricate, invent; trump up; forge; coin; hatch, concoct; romance.

dissemble, dissimulate; feign, assume; pretend, make believe; play false, play a double game; coquet; act *or* play a part; affect, pose; simulate, pass off for; counterfeit, sham; malinger; deceive, etc., 545.

Adj. **false,** untrue, deceitful, mendacious, lying, untruthful, fraudulent, dishonest; faithless, forsworn; evasive, disingenuous, hollow, insincere; artful, cunning, tricky, wily, sly; perfidious, treacherous, perjured; spurious, etc., 545; falsified.

hypocritical, canting, pharisaical; Machiavellian, double-tongued, double-dealing; two-faced, double-faced; smooth-spoken, smooth-tongued; plausible, mealy-mouthed; affected, canting, insincere.

545. DECEPTION.—*N.* **deception;** falseness, etc., 544; untruth, etc., 546; imposition, imposture; fraud, deceit, guile, fraudulence, misrepresentation, bluff; trickery, knavery, sharp practice, collusion, chicanery; treachery, double-dealing.

delusion, jugglery, sleight of hand, legerdemain, conjuring.

trick, cheat, wile, blind, feint, chicane, juggle, swindle; stratagem, artifice; hoax; bunk [*slang*], gold brick [*colloq.*].

snare, trap, pitfall, gin; bait, decoy duck, stool pigeon; cobweb, net, meshes, toils; ambush, ambuscade.

disguise, false colors, camouflage, masquerade, mask, mummery, borrowed plumes; dissembler, hypocrite, etc., 548.

sham, mockery, copy, counterfeit, make-believe, forgery, fraud, untruth, etc., 546; hollow mockery; whited sepulcher, tinsel, paste.

illusion, delusion, self-deception, *ignis fatuus* [L.], mirage, etc., 443.

V. **deceive,** mislead, lead astray, take in, defraud, cheat, cozen, swindle, victimize; betray, play false; lie, etc., 544: mystify; blind, hoodwink; throw dust into the eyes; impose upon, practice upon, palm off on; bluff.

outwit, circumvent, overreach, steal a march on.

insnare, ensnare, entrap, decoy, waylay, lure, beguile, delude, inveigle, trick.

fool, befool, dupe, gull, hoax, humbug, stuff [*slang*], sell [*slang*]; trifle with, cajole, flatter; dissemble, dissimulate, sham, counterfeit.

practice chicanery, live by one's wits, juggle, conjure, play off, palm off, foist off.

Adj. deceptive, deceitful, tricky, cunning, etc., 702; elusive, insidious; delusive, illusory.

make-believe; untrue, etc., 546; mock, sham, counterfeit, pseudo, spurious, so-called, pretended, feigned, bogus [*colloq.*], fraudulent, surreptitious, illegitimate, contraband; adulterated, disguised; unsound, meretricious, jerry-built; tinsel.

Adv. under false colors, under cover of.

546. UNTRUTH.—*N.* untruth, falsehood, lie, story, fib, whopper [*colloq.*].

fabrication, forgery, invention; misstatement, misrepresentation, perversion, falsification, false coloring, exaggeration.

fiction, fable, nursery tale, fairy tale, romance, extravaganza; canard; yarn [*colloq.*], fish story [*colloq.*], traveler's tale, cock-and-bull story, myth, moonshine, bosh [*colloq.*].

half truth, white lie, pious fraud; suppression; irony.

pretense, pretext, subterfuge, evasion, shift, shuffle, make-believe, sham, etc., 545; profession, Judas kiss, cajolery, flattery; disguise, etc., 530.

V. feign, make-believe, pretend, sham, counterfeit; lie, etc., 544.

Adj. untrue, false, trumped up; unfounded, invented, fictitious, fabulous, fabricated, fraudulent, forged; evasive.

547. DUPE.—*N.* dupe, gull, victim, April fool; sucker [*slang*]; laughingstock, etc., 857; greenhorn; fool, etc., 501; puppet, cat's-paw.

V. be deceived, be the dupe of; fall into a trap; swallow *or* nibble at the bait; swallow whole; bite.

Adj. credulous, gullible, etc., 486.

mistaken, etc. (*error*), 495.

548. DECEIVER.—*N.* deceiver, dissembler, hypocrite, Pharisee; sophist; serpent, snake in the grass, Judas, wolf in sheep's clothing.

liar, storyteller, perjurer, false witness, faker [*slang*], fraud, four-flusher [*slang*], confidence man, decoy, stool pigeon; rogue, knave, cheat, swindler.

impostor, pretender, malingerer, humbug; adventurer, adventuress.

trickster, conjurer, juggler, necromancer, sorcerer, magician, wizard, medicine man, witch doctor; quack, charlatan, mountebank.

549. EXAGGERATION.—*N.* exaggeration, expansion, amplification; fringe, embroidery; extravagance, hyperbole, stretch, high coloring, caricature; yarn [*colloq.*], traveler's tale, fish story [*colloq.*]; tempest in a teacup; much ado about nothing; puffery, etc. (*boasting*), 884; rant, etc.. 577.

V. exaggerate, magnify, pile up, aggravate; amplify, expand, overestimate, overstate, overdraw, overshoot the mark, overpraise; stretch a point; draw a long bow [*colloq.*], out-Herod Herod; overcolor, heighten; embroider, color; puff, etc. (*boast*), 884.

Adj. exaggerated, overwrought; bombastic, etc. (*magniloquent*), 577; hyperbolical, extravagant; preposterous, egregious.

550. [Means of communication] INDICATION.—*N.* indication, sign, symbol; index, indicator, pointer, cue, note, token, symptom; type, figure, emblem, cipher, device; motto, epitaph.

means of recognition; lineament, feature, trait, trick, earmark, characteristic.

gesture, gesticulation; pantomime; wink, glance, leer; nod, shrug, beck; touch, nudge; byplay, dumb show; deaf-and-dumb alphabet, dactylology.

track, spoor, trail, footprint, scent; clue, key.

signal, rocket, watch fire, beacon fire, watchtower; telegraph, semaphore; fiery cross; calumet, peace pipe; heliograph; searchlight, flashlight.

mark, line, stroke, score, streak, scratch, tick, dot, notch, nick, blaze; red letter, underlining, impression.

Map drawing: hachure, contour line; isobar, isopiestic line, isobaric line; isotherm, isothermal line; latitude, longitude, meridian, equator.

For identification: badge, countercheck, countersign, counterfoil, stub, duplicate, tally; label, ticket, counter, check, chip, voucher, stamp; trade-mark, hallmark; card, visiting card; credentials; handwriting, sign manual, autograph, signature; monogram, seal, signet; fingerprint; brand; caste mark; mortarboard [*colloq.*], cap and gown, hood; shibboleth; watchword, catchword, password, cue; sign, countersign, pass, grip; open-sesame.

Insignia: banner, flag, colors, streamer, pennant, pennon, ensign, standard; eagle, oriflamme, blue peter, jack, Union Jack; Old Glory [*colloq.*], Stars and Stripes.

Heraldry: crest, arms, coat of arms, armorial bearings; hatchment, escutcheon *or* scutcheon; shield, supporters; livery, uniform; cockade, brassard, epaulet, chevron; garland, chaplet, love knot, favor.

Of locality: beacon, flagstaff, hand, pointer, vane, cock, weathercock, weather vane; guidepost, signpost; sign, signboard; North Star, polestar; landmark, seamark; lighthouse; address, direction, name.

Of the future: warning, premonition; omen, portent, sign.

Of the past: trace, record.

Of danger: warning, alarm, fire alarm, burglar alarm.

Of authority: scepter, etc., 747.

Of triumph: trophy, etc., 783.

Of mourning: mourning, etc., 839.

Of quantity: gauge, etc., 466.

Of distance: milestone, milepost.

Of disgrace; brand, foolscap, mark of Cain, stigma, stripes, broad arrow.

call, word of command; bugle call, trumpet call; bell, alarum, battle cry, reveille, taps, last post; sacring bell, Sanctus bell, angelus; dirge.

V. indicate, denote, betoken, connote, signify; represent, stand for; typify, symbolize; mark, note, stamp, nick, blaze; label, ticket.

make a sign, signalize; beckon, nod, wink, glance, leer, nudge, shrug, gesticulate.

sign, seal, attest, underscore, underline; call attention to.

Adj. indicative, indicatory; connotative, denotative, representative, typical, individual, symbolic *or* symbolical, symptomatic, characteristic, significant, diagnostic, emblematic, armorial.

551. RECORD.—*N.* trace, vestige, relic, remains; scar, cicatrix; footstep, footmark, footprint; track, mark, wake, trail, scent, spoor.

monument, hatchment; escutcheon *or* scutcheon; slab, tablet, trophy, obelisk, pillar, column, monolith; memorial; memento; testimonial, medal, Congressional medal; cross, Victoria cross [Eng.], iron cross [Ger.]; ribbon, garter; commemoration, etc. (*celebration*), 883.

record, note, minute; register, registry; roll, list; entry, memorandum, endorsement, inscription, copy, duplicate, docket; mark, etc., 550; deed; document; deposition, affidavit; certificate.

notebook, memorandum book; bulletin, bulletin board, scoreboard, score sheet; card index, file, letter file, pigeonholes.

newspaper, daily, gazette, magazine, paper [*colloq.*].

calendar, diary, log, journal, daybook, ledger, cashbook.

archive, scroll, state paper, return, bluebook; almanac, gazetteer, census report; statistics; Congressional Records; minutes, chronicle, annals; legend; history, biography, etc., 594.

registration; registry, enrollment, tabulation; entry, booking; signature, sign manual; recorder, etc., 553; journalism.

mechanical record, recording instrument; phonograph, etc., 418; speedometer, pedometer, patent log [*naut.*]; ticker, tape; time clock; turnstile; cash register.

V. record, put *or* place upon record, chronicle, calendar, hand down to posterity; commemorate, etc. (*celebrate*), 883; report, commit to writing, note, put *or* set down; mark, etc. (*indicate*), 550; sign, etc. (*attest*), 467; enter, book, post, insert; mark off, tick off; register, list, enroll, inscroll; file.

552. [Suppression of sign] OBLITERATION.—*N.* obliteration, erasure, cancellation, deletion; blot; effacement, extinction.

V. efface, obliterate, erase, expunge, cancel; blot (*or* rub, scratch, strike, wash, wipe) out; deface, render illegible; rule out.

be effaced, leave no trace.

Adj. obliterated, erased; unrecorded, unregistered.

553. RECORDER.—*N.* recorder, notary, clerk; registrar, register; amanuensis, secretary, recording secretary, stenographer, bookkeeper, scribe.

annalist, historian, historiographer, chronicler; biographer, etc.

(*narrator*), 594; antiquary, antiquarian, archeologist; memorialist.

journalist, newspaperman, reporter, interviewer; publicist, author, editor.

554. REPRESENTATION.—*N.* representation, depiction, imitation, illustration, delineation, imagery, portraiture; design, designing; art, fine arts; painting, etc., 556; sculpture, etc., 557; engraving, etc., 558.

photography; radiography, X-ray photography, skiagraphy.
personation, impersonation; personification; drama, etc., 599.

drawing, picture, sketch, draft; tracing; copy, etc., 21.
photograph, photo [*colloq.*], daguerreotype, print, cabinet, snapshot.
image, effigy, icon, portrait, likeness, facsimile.
figure, figurehead, puppet, doll, manikin, lay figure, model, marionette, statue, statuette, bust.
map, plan, chart; diagram; ground plan, projection, elevation; atlas; outline, view.
radiograph, radiogram, skiagraph, skiagram, X-ray photograph, Xray [*colloq*].
delineator, draftsman; artist, etc., 559; photographer, radiographer, X-ray photographer, skiagrapher, daguerreotypist.

V. represent, delineate, depict, portray, picture, limn, photograph, snapshot; figure, shadow forth, adumbrate; describe, etc., 594; trace, copy; mold; illustrate, symbolize; paint, etc., 556; sculpture, etc., 557; engrave, etc., 558.

personate, impersonate, dress up [*colloq.*], pose as, act; personify; play, etc. (*drama*), 559; mimic, etc. (*imitate*),19.

Adj. representative; illustrative; imitative, figurative; similar, like, etc., 17; descriptive, etc., 594.

555. MISREPRESENTATION.—*N.* misrepresentation, misstatement, falsification, exaggeration, distortion; bad likeness, daub, scratch.

burlesque, travesty, parody, take-off, caricature, extravaganza.

V. misrepresent, distort, overdraw, exaggerate, daub; falsify, understate, overstate, stretch.

burlesque, travesty, parody, caricature.

556. PAINTING. BLACK AND WHITE.—*N.* painting, depicting, drawing; design; perspective; composition; treatment; arrangement, values, atmosphere, tone, technique.

palette; easel; brush, pencil, stump, black lead, charcoal, crayons, chalk, pastel; paint, etc. (*coloring matter*), 428; water (*or* oil) colors: oils, oil paint; varnish; distemper, fresco, enamel, mosaic, encaustic painting; batik.
style, school; the grand style, high art; futurist, cubist, vorticist.
picture, painting, piece, tableau, canvas; fresco, cartoon; drawing, draft; still life, genre (*or* landscape) painting; sketch, outline, study.
portrait; head; miniature; silhouette; profile.

view, landscape, seascape, sea view, seapiece; scene, prospect; interior; panorama, bird's-eye view.

picture gallery, art gallery, art museum; studio, atelier [F.].

photograph, radiography, etc., 554; photograph, radiograph, etc., 554.

V. **paint,** design, limn, draw, sketch, pencil, color; stencil; depict, etc. (*represent*), 554.

Adj. **pictorial,** graphic; picturesque, historical; futurist, cubist, vorticist; in the grand style.

557. SCULPTURE.—*N.* **sculpture,** carving, modeling, statuary; ceramics.

marble, bronze, terra cotta; ceramic ware, pottery, porcelain, china, earthenware; cloisonné, enamel, faïence.

relief, low relief, bas-relief, high relief; intaglio; cameo; medal, medallion.

statue, statuette, bust; cast.

V. **sculpture,** carve, cut, chisel, model, mold; cast.

558. ENGRAVING.—*N.* **engraving,** etching, chiseling; plate (*or* copperplate, steel, half-tone, wood) engraving; lithography, chromolithography, photolithography.

printing; color printing, lithographic printing; type printing; three-color process.
impression, print, engraving, plate; steel-plate, copperplate; etching; aquatint, mezzotint; cut, woodcut; lithograph, chromolithograph, photolithograph.
illustration, illumination; half-tone; photogravure; rotogravure; vignette, initial letter, tailpiece.

V. **engrave,** grave, etch; bite; bite in; lithograph; print.

559. ARTIST.—*N.* **artist;** painter, drawer, sketcher, designer, engraver, graver, line engraver, draftsman; chaser; copyist; enameler, enamelist; cartoonist, caricaturist.

historical (*or* landscape, marine, flower, portrait, genre, miniature, scene) painter; carver, modeler, statuary, sculptor.

(1) Language generally

560. LANGUAGE.—*N.* **language;** phraseology, etc., 569; speech, etc., 582; tongue, lingo [*chiefly humorous or contemptuous*], vernacular, mother (*or* vulgar, native) tongue; king's English; dialect, brogue, patois, idiom.

confusion of tongues, Babel; universal language, Esperanto, Ido; pantomime, dumb show.

literature, letters, polite literature, belles-lettres [F.], muses, humanities, republic of letters, dead languages, classics.

linguist, etc. (*scholar*), 492.

V. **express,** say, express by words.

Adj. **lingual,** linguistic; dialectal, dialectic; vernacular, current; bilingual; polyglot; literary; colloquial, slangy.

561. LETTER.—*N.* **letter;** character; hieroglyphic; alphabet,

ABC; consonant, vowel, diphthong, mute, surd, sonant, liquid, labial, palatal, cerebral, dental, guttural.

syllable; monosyllable, dissyllable, polysyllable; prefix, suffix.

spelling, orthography; phonetic spelling, phonetics.

cipher, code; monogram, anagram; acrostic, double acrostic.

V. spell; transliterate.

cipher, decipher; code, decode.

Adj. literal; alphabetical, syllabic.

phonetic, voiced, tonic, sonant; voiceless, surd; mute, labial, palatal, cerebral, dental, guttural, liquid.

562. WORD.—N. word, term, vocable; name, etc., 564; phrase, etc., 566; root, derivative; part of speech.

dictionary, lexicon, vocabulary, wordbook, index, glossary, thesaurus.

Science of language: etymology, philology; terminology; pronunciation, orthoëpy; lexicography.

verbosity, verbiage, wordiness; loquacity, etc., 584.

V. vocalize; etymologize, derive; index; translate.

Adj. verbal, literal; derivative.

verbose, wordy, etc., 573; loquacious, etc., 584.

563. NEOLOGY.—N. neology, neologism; barbarism; corruption.

dialect, brogue, patois, provincialism, broken English, Anglicism, Briticism, Gallicism, Americanism; gypsy lingo, Romany.

lingua franca, pidgin English, Hindustani; Esperanto, Ido.

jargon, dog Latin, gibberish; confusion of tongues, Babel; lingo, slang, cant, argot, billingsgate.

pseudonym, pen name; nickname; alias.

neologist, word coiner, coiner of words.

V. coin words; Americanize, Anglicize, Gallicize.

Adj. neologic, neological; slang, cant, barbarous.

564. NOMENCLATURE.—N. nomenclature; naming, nicknaming; baptism.

name, appellation, appellative, designation, denomination; nickname, etc., 565; epithet; title, head, heading; style, proper name, cognomen, patronymic, surname; title, handle to one's name; namesake.

term, expression, noun; technical term; cant.

V. name, call, term, denominate, designate, style, entitle, dub [colloq. or humorous], christen, baptize, nickname, characterize, specify, label.

Adj. named, yclept [humorous]; known as; titular, nominal.

565. MISNOMER.—N. misnomer; malapropism, Mrs. Malaprop.

nickname, sobriquet, pet name, assumed name, alias; stage name; *nom de guerre* [F.], nom de plume [English formation], pen name, pseudonym.

V. **misname,** miscall, nickname; take an assumed name.

Adj. **misnamed;** self-styled; so-called, quasi.

nameless, anonymous; unacknowledged; pseudo.

566. PHRASE.—*N.* **phrase,** expression, locution; sentence, paragraph; paraphrase, metaphor, euphemism, euphuism; motto, proverb; figure of speech; idiom, turn of expression; phraseology, etc., 569.

V. **express,** phrase; word, voice; put into (*or* express by) words; call, denominate, designate, dub.

Adv. in round (*or* set) terms; in set phrases; by the card.

567. GRAMMAR.—*N.* **grammar,** accidence, syntax, analysis, parts of speech; inflection, case, declension, conjugation; philology.

V. **parse,** analyze, conjugate, decline.

Adj. **grammatical,** syntactic *or* syntactical, inflectional, declensional, synthetic *or* synthetical.

568. SOLECISM.—*N.* **solecism;** grammatical blunder; error, slip; slip of the pen, slip of the tongue, bull; barbarism, impropriety.

V. **solecize,** commit a solecism; murder the king's English.

Adj. **ungrammatical,** incorrect, inaccurate, faulty; improper.

569. STYLE.—*N.* **style,** diction, phraseology, wording; manner, strain; composition; mode of expression, idiom, choice of words; mode of speech, literary power, command of language; authorship, artistry.

V. **word,** phrase, express by words, write; apply the file.

Various Qualities of Style

570. PERSPICUITY.—*N.* **perspicuity,** perspicacity, explicitness, lucidness, lucidity, limpidity, clearness; plain speaking, expression, definiteness, definition; exactness, etc., 494.

Adj. **lucid,** intelligible, etc., 518; limpid, pellucid, clear, explicit; exact, etc., 494.

571. OBSCURITY.—*N.* **obscurity,** unintelligibility, involution, confusion; hard words; ambiguity, indefiniteness, vagueness, inexactness, inaccuracy; darkness of meaning.

Adj. **obscure,** involved, confused.

572. CONCISENESS.—*N.* **conciseness,** terseness, brevity, laconicism, abridgment, compression, condensation, epitome, etc., 596.

Portmanteau word [Lewis Carroll]; brunch [breakfast + lunch], slithy, *adj.* [slimy + lithe], torrible, *adj.* [torrid + horrible].

V. **be concise,** telescope, compress, condense, abridge, abbreviate, abstract, etc., 596; come to the point.

Adj. **concise,** brief, short, laconic, succinct, curt, compact, summary, compendious, etc., 596; terse, to the point; compressed, condensed, pointed; pithy, crisp, trenchant, epigrammatic, sententious.

Adv. **briefly,** summarily; in brief, in short, in a word.

573. DIFFUSENESS.—*N.* **diffuseness,** profuseness, amplification, verbosity, wordiness; verbiage, flow of words, etc. (*loquacity*), 584; looseness; tautology, exuberance, redundance, prolixity, periphrase, expletive; padding [*editors' cant*]; drivel, twaddle.

V. **expand,** expatiate, enlarge, dilate, amplify, inflate, pad [*editors' cant*], rant; maunder, prose; harp upon, dwell on.

digress, ramble, beat about the bush, protract.

Adj. **diffuse,** profuse, wordy, verbose, copious, exuberant; lengthy, long, long-winded, protracted, prolix, diffusive, roundabout, digressive, discursive, loose; rambling, frothy.

574. VIGOR.—*N.* **vigor,** power, force; boldness, intellectual force; spirit, punch [*slang*], point, piquancy, raciness; verve, ardor, enthusiasm, glow, fire, warmth; gravity, weight.

loftiness, elevation, sublimity, grandeur.

eloquence; command of words, command of language.

Adj. **vigorous,** nervous, powerful, forcible, forceful; mordant, biting, trenchant, incisive; graphic, impressive.

spirited, lively, glowing, sparkling; racy, bold, pungent, piquant, pithy.

lofty, elevated, sublime, poetic, grand, weighty, ponderous; eloquent.

vehement, passionate, burning, impassioned, petulant.

575. FEEBLENESS.—*N.* **feebleness,** baldness, enervation, flaccidity, vapidity, poverty.

Adj. **feeble,** tame, meager, insipid, watery, nerveless, vapid, trashy, poor, dull, dry, languid; bald, colorless, enervated; prosy, prosaic, weak, slight; careless, slovenly, loose, lax; slipshod, inexact; puerile, childish; rambling, etc. (*diffuse*), 573.

576. PLAINNESS.—*N.* **plainness,** homeliness, simplicity, severity; household words.

V. **speak plainly,** waste no words, come to the point.

Adj. **plain,** simple, unornamented, unadorned, unvarnished; homely, homespun; neat; severe, chaste, pure, Saxon; commonplace, matter-of-fact, natural, prosaic, sober.

Adv. **point-blank**; in plain English; in common parlance.

577. ORNAMENT.—*N.* **ornament,** floridness, grandiloquence, magniloquence, declamation, well-rounded periods; elegance, etc., 578; flourish, trope; euphuism, euphemism.

bombast, inflation, pretension; rant, fustian, highfalutin [*slang*], buncombe, balderdash; fine writing; purple patches.

V. **ornament,** overcharge, overload; euphuize, euphemize.

Adj. **ornate;** ornamented, beautified, florid, rich, flowery; euphuistic, euphemistic; sonorous, inflated, swelling, tumid; turgid, pedantic, pompous, stilted, high-flown, sententious, rhetorical, declamatory; grandiose; grandiloquent, magniloquent, bombastic; frothy, flashy, flamboyant.

578. ELEGANCE.—*N.* **elegance,** distinction, clarity, purity, grace, felicity, ease; gracefulness, euphony; taste, good taste, restraint, propriety, correctness.

purist, classicist, stylist.

Adj. **elegant,** polished, classic *or* classical, correct, artistic; chaste, pure; graceful, easy, fluent, unaffected, natural, mellifluous, euphonious; restrained.

felicitous, happy, neat; well expressed.

579. INELEGANCE.—*N.* **inelegance,** impurity, vulgarity; poor diction, poor choice of words; loose construction; ill-balanced sentences; barbarism, slang; solecism, mannerism, affectation.

Adj. **inelegant,** graceless, ungraceful; harsh, abrupt; dry, stiff, cramped, formal, forced, labored; artificial, mannered, affected, ponderous, awkward; unpolished; turgid, barbarous, uncouth, rude, crude, halting, vulgar.

(2) Spoken Language

580. VOICE.—*N.* **voice;** intonation; utterance; vocalization; cry, exclamation, expletive, ejaculation; vociferation, enunciation, articulation; distinctness; clearness; delivery, attack.

accent, accentuation; emphasis, stress; pronunciation; euphony, etc. (*melody*), 413.

V. **speak,** utter, breathe; cry, etc. (*shout*), 411; ejaculate, rap out; articulate, enunciate, vocalize, pronounce, accentuate, deliver, emit; whisper, murmur.

Adj. **vocal,** phonetic, oral; ejaculatory, articulate, distinct, euphonious, melodious.

581. DUMBNESS.—*N.* **dumbness;** silence, etc. (*taciturnity*), 585; deaf-mutism, deaf-muteness, deaf-dumbness, mute, dummy, deaf-mute.

V. silence, muzzle, muffle, suppress, smother, gag, strike dumb, dumfound.

Adj. dumb, mute, mum; tongue-tied; voiceless, speechless, wordless; silent, etc. (*taciturn*), 585; inarticulate.

582. SPEECH.—*N.* speech, locution, talk, parlance, word of mouth, prattle.

oration, recitation, delivery, speech, address, discourse, lecture, harangue, sermon, tirade, soliloquy, etc., 589; conversation, etc., 588; salutatory; valedictory.

oratory, elocution, eloquence, rhetoric, declamation; grandiloquence.

speaker, spokesman, mouthpiece, orator, rhetorician, lecturer, preacher, elocutionist, reciter, reader; spellbinder.

V. speak, talk, say, utter, pronounce, deliver, breathe, let fall, rap out, blurt out.

soliloquize, etc., 589; tell, etc. (*inform*), 527; address, etc., 586; converse, etc., 588.

declaim, hold forth, harangue, stump [*colloq.*], spout, rant; recite, lecture, sermonize, discourse, expatiate.

Adj. oral, lingual, phonetic, unwritten, spoken.

eloquent, oratorical, rhetorical, elocutionary, declamatory, grandiloquent.

583. [Imperfect Speech] STAMMERING.—*N.* inarticulateness; stammering, hesitation, impediment in one's speech; lisp, drawl, nasal accent; twang; falsetto, brogue.

V. stammer, stutter, hesitate, falter.

mumble, mutter, maunder; mince, lisp; jabber, gabble, gibber; splutter, sputter; drawl, mouth; croak.

murder the language, murder the king's English; mispronounce.

Adj. inarticulate; stammering, guttural, throaty, nasal; tremulous.

584. LOQUACITY.—*N.* loquacity, loquaciousness, effusion; talkativeness, garrulity.

gabble, gab [*colloq.*], jaw [*low*], hot air [*slang*]; jabber, chatter; prate, prattle, twaddle, small talk.

fluency, volubility, flow of words; verbosity, etc. (*diffuseness*), 573; eloquence.

talker; chatterer, chatterbox; babbler, ranter, proser, driveler, gossip, magpie.

V. be loquacious, talk glibly, pour forth, prate, palaver, prose, maunder, chatter, blab, gush, prattle, jabber, jaw [*low*], babble, gabble; expatiate, gossip, talk at random, talk nonsense.

Adj. loquacious, talkative, garrulous, chattering, chatty, declamatory, fluent, voluble, effusive, glib, flippant.

585. TACITURNITY.—*N.* taciturnity, silence, muteness, curtness; reserve, reticence.

man of few words; Spartan.

V. be silent, keep silence; hold one's tongue, say nothing; render mute.

Adj. silent, mute, mum, still, dumb.

taciturn, laconic, concise, sententious, close, close-mouthed, curt; reserved; reticent.

586. ADDRESS.—*N.* address, allocution; speech, etc., 582; appeal, invocation, salutation, salutatory.

V. address, speak to, accost, apostrophize, appeal to, invoke; hail, salute; call to, halloo.

lecture, preach, harangue, spellbind.

587. RESPONSE, etc., *see* **Answer 462.**

588. CONVERSATION.—*N.* conversation, colloquy, converse, interlocution, talk, discourse, dialogue, duologue.

chat, tattle, gossip, tittle-tattle; babble.

conference, parley, interview, audience, reception; congress, etc. (*council*), 696; powwow.

debate, palaver, war of words, controversy.

talker, gossip, tattler; chatterer, etc. (*loquacity*), 584; speaker, etc., 582; conversationalist.

V. converse, talk together, hold (*or* carry on, join in, engage in) a conversation; parley; palaver; chat, gossip, tattle; prate, etc., 584.

confer with, discourse with, commune with, talk it over.

Adj. conversational, conversable; chatty, colloquial.

589. SOLILOQUY.—*N.* soliloquy, monologue, apostrophe.

V. soliloquize, monologize, talk to oneself; think aloud, apostrophize.

Written Language

590. WRITING.—*N.* writing, chirography, penmanship; typewriting; manuscript; script; character, letter, etc., 561.

shorthand, stenography, phonography; secret writing, cipher, cryptography.

handwriting; signature, mark, autograph, hand, fist [*colloq.*]; calligraphy.

composition, authorship; lucubration, production, work, screed, article, paper; book, etc., 593; essay, theme, thesis; novel, text-book; poem, book of poems (*or* verse), anthology.

writer, scribe; author, etc., 593; amanuensis, secretary, clerk, penman, copyist; stenographer, typewriter, typist.

V. write, pen, typewrite, type [*colloq.*]; copy, engross; transcribe; scribble, scrawl, scratch; note down, write down, record.

compose, indite, draw up, draft, formulate; dictate; inscribe.

Adj. written, in writing, in black and white; stenographic.

591. PRINTING.—*N.* printing, typography; type, linotype, monotype; composition, print, letterpress, text, context, matter; copy, impression, proof, galley, galley proof, page proof.

printer, compositor; reader, proofreader, corrector of the press; printer's devil; copyholder, copyeditor.

V. print; compose; go to press; publish, issue, bring out.

Adj. typographical, printed, in type.

592. CORRESPONDENCE.—*N.* correspondence, letter, epistle, missive, note, post card, postal card; dispatch; bulletin, circular.

correspondent, writer, letter writer.

V. correspond, write to, send a letter to; communicate, communicate by writing (*or* letter); circularize, follow up, bombard; reply.

593. BOOK.—*N.* book, booklet; writing, work, volume, tome, tract, treatise, brochure, monograph, pamphlet, libretto; handbook, manual, novel, etc. (*composition*), 590; publication; magazine, periodical.

work of reference, encyclopedia, cyclopedia, dictionary, thesaurus, concordance, anthology, compilation.

writer, author, essayist, contributor; hack writer, hack; journalist, publicist, reporter, correspondent; editor, scribe, etc., 590; playwright, etc., 599; poet, etc., 597.

publisher, bookseller; librarian; bookworm.

bookstore, bookshop, bookseller's shop, publishing house.

library, public library, lending library.

594. DESCRIPTION.—*N.* description, account, statement, report, record; brief, etc. (*abstract*), 596; delineation, sketch, pastel, vignette; monograph; narration, recital, rehearsal, relation.

narrative, history, memoir; annals, etc., (*chronicle*), 551; journal, letters, biography, autobiography, life, adventures.

Fiction· novel, romance, story, tale, short story, anecdote; detective story, fairy tale, fable, parable, allegory.

narrator, historian, biographer, novelist, storyteller, romancer, anecdotist, word painter; writer, etc , 593.

V. describe, set forth, picture, portray, characterize, delineate, narrate, relate, recite, recount, romance, tell, report; detail, particularize.

Adj. descriptive, graphic, narrative, epic, romantic, historic *or* historical, biographical, autobiographical; traditional, legendary, mythical, fabulous; anecdotic, idealistic; realistic, true to life.

595. DISSERTATION.—*N.* dissertation, treatise, essay, thesis, theme; tract, discourse, memoir, disquisition, lecture, sermon, homily, investigation, study, discussion, exposition.

commentary, review, critique, criticism, article, leader, editorial.

commentator, critic, essayist, publicist, reviewer, leader writer, editor.

V. **comment**, explain, interpret, criticize, illuminate; treat of (*or* ventilate, discuss, deal with, go into) a subject.

596. COMPENDIUM.—*N.* compendium, abstract, précis, epitome, analysis, digest, brief, condensation, abridgment, abbreviation, etc., 201; summary, draft, minute, note; excerpt, extract; synopsis, textbook, outlines, syllabus, contents, heads, prospectus.

fragments, extracts, cuttings; fugitive pieces, anthology, miscellany, compilation.

recapitulation, résumé, review; symposium.

V. **abridge**, abstract, epitomize, summarize; abbreviate, etc. (*shorten*), 201; condense, etc. (*compress*), 195.

compile, etc. (*collect*), 72; note down, collect, edit.

recapitulate, review, skim, run over, sum up.

Adj. **compendious**, synoptic, abridged, analytic *or* analytical.

Adv. **in short**, in substance, in few words, in a nutshell.

597. POETRY.—*N.* poetry, poetics, poesy, muse, Apollo, Parnassus, inspiration, fire of genius.

poem; epic, ballad, lyric, ode, idyl, eclogue, pastoral, sonnet, elegy; dramatic (*or* didactic, satirical, narrative, lyric) poetry; satire; anthology.

versification, rhyming, prosody; scansion, scanning.
canto, stanza, verse, line, couplet, triplet, quatrain; refrain, chorus, burden; octave, sextet.
verse, rhyme, assonance, alliteration, meter, measure; foot, numbers, rhythm; ictus, beat, accent, accentuation, iambus, iambic, dactyl, spondee, trochee, anapest, etc.; hexameter, pentameter; Alexandrine; blank verse, heroic verse; doggerel.

poet, genius, creator; poet laureate; laureate; bard, lyrist, sonneteer, rhapsodist, satirist, troubadour; minstrel; minnesinger, Meistersinger; jongleur, versifier, rhymer, rhymester, minor poet, poetaster.

V. **poetize**, sing, write poetry; string verses together, versify, make verses, rhyme.

Adj. **poetic** *or* poetical; lyric *or* lyrical; tuneful; metrical; elegiac, iambic, dactylic, spondaic, trochaic, anapestic.

598. PROSE.—*N.* prose, prosaicness; poetic prose; narrative, etc., 594.

prose writer, essayist, novelist, etc., 594.

V. **prose**; write prose (*or* in prose).

Adj. **prosaic**, prosy, unpoetical, unrhymed, in prose.

599. THE DRAMA.—*N.* the drama, the stage, the theater, the play; theatricals, histrionic art.

play, drama, piece, tragedy, comedy, opera, vaudeville, curtain raiser, interlude, afterpiece, farce, extravaganza, harlequinade, pantomime, burlesque, ballet, spectacle, masque, melodrama; comedy of manners; charade, mystery, miracle play, morality play.

act, scene, tableau, curtain; introduction, prologue, exposition, epilogue; libretto, book, text, prompter's copy.

performance, representation, show [*colloq.*], stage setting, stagecraft; acting; impersonation, stage business; slapstick [*slang*]. buffoonery.

theater, playhouse, amphitheater, moving-picture theater, moving pictures, movies [*colloq*]; puppet show, marionettes, Punch and Judy.

cast, dramatis personae [L.], role, part, character; repertoire, repertory.

actor, player, performer; masker, mime, mimic; star, headliner; comedian, tragedian.

buffoon, mummer, pantomimist, clown; pantaloon, harlequin, columbine; punch.

company, first tragedian, prima donna, leading lady; lead; leading man; comedian, comedienne; juvenile lead, juvenile; villain, heavy lead, heavy, heavy father; ingenue, soubrette; character man, character woman, extra, mute, supernumerary, super [*theat. cant*].

dramatist, playwright, playwriter; dramatic author (*or* writer). audience, house; orchestra, gallery.

V. act, play, perform; put on the stage, dramatize, stage, produce, set; personate, mimic, enact; rehearse, spout, rant; tread the stage (*or* boards); make one's debut, take a part, star.

Adj. dramatic; theatrical; scenic, histrionic, comic, tragic, farcical, tragicomic, melodramatic, operatic; stagy, spectacular.

Adv. on the stage, on the boards; in the limelight, in the spotlight; before the footlights, before an audience; behind the scenes.

CLASS V

WORDS RELATING TO THE VOLUNTARY POWERS

I. INDIVIDUAL VOLITION

600. WILL.—*N.* will, volition, free will; freedom, etc., 748; discretion; choice, inclination, intent, purpose, option, etc. (*choice*), 609; spontaneity, spontaneousness; originality.

determination, etc. (*resolution*), 604; force of will, will power, autocracy, bossiness [*colloq.*].

wish, desire, pleasure, mind, disposition, etc., 602; intention, etc., 620.

V. will, see fit, think fit; determine, etc. (*resolve*), 604; enjoin; settle, etc. (*choose*), 609; volunteer; do what one chooses, etc. (*freedom*), 748; have one's own way; use one's discretion; boss, [*colloq.*]; originate.

Adj. **voluntary**, volitional, willful; free, etc., 748; optional, discretionary; autocratic, dictatorial, bossy [*colloq.*].

willing, etc., 602; unbidden, spontaneous; original.

Adv. **voluntarily**, at will, at pleasure.

of one's own accord, on one's own responsibility; by choice, purposely, intentionally.

601. NECESSITY.—*N.* **necessity**, obligation; compulsion, etc., 744; subjection, etc., 749; stern (*or* dire) necessity, last resort.

instinct, blind impulse, natural tendency (*or* impulse), predetermination.

destiny, fatality, fate, kismet, doom, election, predestination; lot, fortune; fatalism.

Fates, God's will, heaven, will of heaven; stars; planets; wheel of fortune.

V. **be obliged**, be forced, be driven; be fated, be doomed, be destined, have no alternative.

destine, doom, foredoom, devote; predestine, preordain; necessitate; compel, etc., 744.

Adj. **necessary**, needful, etc. (*requisite*), 630; compulsory, etc. (*compel*), 744; inevitable, unavoidable, irresistible, irrevocable, inexorable, binding.

fated; destined, fateful, set apart, devoted, elect.

involuntary, instinctive, automatic, blind, mechanical; unconscious, unwitting, unthinking; unintentional.

Adv. **necessarily**, of necessity, of course; willy-nilly.

602. WILLINGNESS.—*N.* **willingness**, disposition, inclination, liking, turn, propensity, leaning, frame of mind, humor, mood, vein, bent, aptitude.

geniality, cordiality, good will; alacrity, readiness, zeal, enthusiasm, earnestness, eagerness.

assent, etc., 488; compliance, etc., 762.

volunteer, unpaid worker, amateur, nonprofessional.

V. **be willing**, incline, lean to, mind, hold to, cling to; desire, etc., 865; acquiesce, assent, comply with; jump at, catch at; take up, plunge into, have a go at [*colloq.*].

volunteer, offer, proffer.

Adj. **willing**, fain, disposed, inclined, favorable, content, well disposed; ready, forward, earnest, eager, zealous, enthusiastic; bent upon, desirous.

docile, amenable, easily persuaded, facile, easygoing, tractable, genial, gracious, cordial.

voluntary, gratuitous, free, unconstrained, spontaneous, unasked, unforced.

Adv. **willingly**, fain, freely, with pleasure, of one's own accord; graciously, with a good grace, without demur.

603. UNWILLINGNESS.—*N.* **unwillingness**, indisposition, disinclination, aversion, averseness, reluctance; indifference, etc., 866; backwardness, slowness; obstinacy, etc., 606.

scruple, scrupulousness, delicacy, qualm, shrinking, recoil; hesitation, fastidiousness.

dissent, etc., 489; refusal, etc., 764.

V. **be unwilling**, dislike, etc., 867; demur, stick at, scruple, stickle; hang fire, shirk, slack, recoil, shrink, hesitate; avoid, etc., 623; oppose, etc., 708; dissent, etc., 489; refuse, etc., 764.

Adj. **unwilling**, loath, disinclined, indisposed, averse, reluctant, opposed, adverse, laggard, backward, remiss, slack, indifferent, scrupulous; repugnant, restive; grudging, forced, under compulsion, irreconcilable.

Adv. **unwillingly**, grudgingly, with an ill grace; against one's will, against the grain; under protest.

604. RESOLUTION.—*N.* **determination**, will, decision, resolution; backbone; clear grit, grit; sand [*slang*]; strength of mind, resolve, firmness, energy, manliness, vigor, resoluteness; zeal, devotion.

self-control, self-mastery, self-command, self-reliance, self-restraint, self-denial.

tenacity, perseverance, etc., 604a; obstinacy, etc., 606; pluck.

V. **resolve**, will, determine, decide, form a resolution, conclude, fix, bring to a crisis, take a decisive step, take upon oneself.

take one's stand, stand firm, insist upon, make a point of, set one's heart upon; stick at nothing, make short work of, not stick at trifles; persevere, etc., 604a.

Adj. **resolved**, determined; strong-willed, strong-minded; resolute, self-possessed, earnest, serious; decided, peremptory, unflinching, firm, iron, game, plucky, tenacious, gritty, indomitable, inexorable, relentless; obstinate, etc., 606; unyielding; grim, stern, inflexible, irrevocable.

Adv. **resolutely**, in earnest, earnestly; on one's mettle, manfully, like a man.

604a. PERSEVERANCE.—*N.* **perseverance**, continuance, constancy, steadiness, persistence, patience; pertinacity, industry.

grit, bottom, pluck, stamina, backbone, sand [*slang*]; tenacity, staying power, endurance; bulldog courage.

V. **persevere**, persist, hold on, hold out; stick to, cling to, adhere to; keep on, carry on, hold on; bear up, keep up, hold up; plod; continue, die in harness, die at one's post.

Adj. **persevering**, constant; steady, steadfast, unwavering, unfaltering, unflinching, unflagging, plodding; industrious, etc., 682; strenuous, pertinacious, persistent; indomitable, indefatigable.

Adv. **without fail**, through thick and thin, through fire and water; sink or swim, rain or shine, fair or foul.

605. IRRESOLUTION.—*N.* irresolution, indecision, indetermination, instability, uncertainty; demur, suspense, hesitation, hesitancy, vacillation, changeableness, fluctuation; caprice, etc., 608; lukewarmness.

fickleness, levity, pliancy, weakness, timidity; cowardice, etc., 862.

waverer, shilly-shally, turncoat, opportunist, timeserver.

V. **be irresolute**, remain neuter; dilly-dally, hesitate, hover, shilly-shally, hem and haw, demur, debate, balance; dally with, coquet with; go halfway, compromise, be afraid.

vacillate, falter, waver, fluctuate, change, alternate, shuffle, palter, shirk, trim.

Adj. **irresolute**, drifting, halfhearted; undecided, undetermined, uncertain, at a loss; fickle, unreliable, irresponsible, unstable; capricious, etc., 608.

weak, feeble-minded, frail, timid, cowardly, pliant.

Adv. **irresolutely**, in faltering accents; off and on.

606. OBSTINACY.—*N.* obstinacy, tenacity, cussedness; perseverance, etc., 604*a*; immovability, inflexibility, obduracy, doggedness, stubbornness, self-will, contumacy, perversity; resolution, etc., 604.

bigotry, intolerance, dogmatism; fixed idea, fanaticism, zealotry, infatuation, monomania.

bigot, dogmatist, zealot, fanatic, bitter-ender [*colloq.*]; mule.

V. **be obstinate**, stickle, take no denial, be wedded to an opinion, persist, die hard, not yield an inch, stand out.

Adj. **obstinate**, tenacious, stubborn, obdurate, inflexible, balky; immovable, unchangeable, inexorable, determined, mulish, dogged; sullen, sulky; unmoved.

arbitrary, dogmatic, positive, bigoted, opinionated, stiff-necked, hidebound, unyielding; incorrigible.

willful, self-willed, perverse; ungovernable, wayward, refractory, unruly, headstrong; contumacious; cross-grained.

Adv. **with set jaw**; no surrender.

607. APOSTASY.—*N.* apostasy, recantation; renunciation; abjuration, defection, retraction, withdrawal, disavowal, revocation, tergiversation, reversal; backsliding.

turncoat, apostate, renegade, pervert, deserter, backslider, crawfish [*slang*].

timeserver, trimmer, double-dealer; weathercock.

V. **apostatize,** veer round, turn round; change one's mind, abjure, renounce, relinquish, back down, shift one's ground, change sides, go over, recant, retract, revoke, rescind, forswear.

trim, shuffle, blow hot and cold, be on the fence, straddle.

Adj. **changeful,** irresolute, ductile, slippery, trimming, timeserving.

608. CAPRICE.—*N.* **caprice,** fancy, humor, whim, fit, crotchet, quirk, freak, fad, vagary, prank, escapade.

V. **be capricious,** take it into one's head, blow hot and cold, play fast and loose.

Adj. **capricious,** erratic, eccentric, fitful, inconsistent, fanciful, whimsical, crotchety, freakish, wayward, wanton; contrary, captious, unreasonable, arbitrary; fickle, etc. (*irresolute*), 605.

Adv. by fits, by fits and starts, without rhyme or reason.

609. CHOICE.—*N.* **choice,** option, selection, pick; discretion, alternative, preference, adoption, decision.

Scylla and Charybdis.

election, poll, ballot, vote, voice, suffrage, plebiscite, referendum; electioneering; voting, elective franchise; ticket, ballot box.

voter, elector, constituent, electorate, constituency.

V. **choose;** elect, make one's choice; make choice of, fix upon, settle, decide, make up one's mind; adopt, take up, embrace, espouse.

vote, poll, hold up one's hand, give a (*or* the) voting sign; divide.

select, pick, cull, glean, winnow; pitch upon, indulge one's fancy; set apart, mark out for.

prefer, fancy, have rather, had (*or* would) as lief; reserve.

Adj. **optional,** discretional, at choice, on approval.

chosen, choice, elect, select, popular; preferential.

Adv. **optionally,** at pleasure, at the option of.

by choice, by preference; in preference; rather, before.

609a. ABSENCE OF CHOICE.—*N.* **no choice;** Hobson's choice; first come first served; necessity, etc., 601.

neutrality, indifference; indecision, etc. (*irresolution*), 605.

V. **be neutral,** have no preference, waive, not vote.

Adj. **neutral,** neuter; indifferent; undecided, etc. (*irresolute*), 605.

610. REJECTION.—*N.* **rejection,** repudiation, exclusion; refusal, etc., 764.

V. **reject,** set (*or* lay) aside, give up; decline, etc. (*refuse*), 764; exclude, except; pluck up, spurn, cast out, repudiate, scout, disclaim, discard.

Adv. neither, neither the one nor the other.

611. PREDETERMINATION.—*N.* predetermination, predestination, premeditation, foregone conclusion; resolve, project; intention, etc., 620; fate, necessity.

list, schedule, calendar, docket, slate [*pol. cant*], register, roster, poll, muster, draft.

V. predetermine, predestine, premeditate, resolve beforehand.

list, schedule, docket, slate, register, poll, empanel, draft.

Adj. premeditated, predesigned, prepense [*as,* malice *prepense*], studied, designed, calculated, aforethought; foregone.

well laid, well devised, well weighed; maturely considered; cut-and-dried.

Adv. deliberately, with eyes open, in cold blood; intentionally.

612. IMPULSE.—*N.* impulse, sudden thought; impromptu, improvisation; inspiration, flash, spurt.

V. improvise, extemporize; say what comes uppermost, act on the spur of the moment, rise to the occasion; spurt.

Adj. extemporaneous, impulsive, snap, improvised, unpremeditated, unprompted, natural, unguarded; spontaneous.

Adv. extempore, extemporaneously; offhand, impromptu.

613. HABIT.—*N.* habit, addiction, wont, run, way, matter of course, beaten path, second nature; trick, knack, skill.

custom, use, usage, prescription, practice; prevalence, observance; conventionalism, conventionality, mode, fashion, vogue, etiquette.

rule, standing order, precedent, routine, red tape, rut, groove.

V. habituate, inure, harden, season, caseharden; accustom, familiarize; acclimatize.

cling to, adhere to; acquire a habit; follow the beaten track (*or* path), move in a rut.

prevail; come into use, become a habit, take root; grow upon one.

Adj. habitual, customary, accustomed, wonted, usual, general, ordinary, common, frequent, everyday, household, familiar, trite, hackneyed, commonplace, conventional, regular, set, stock, established, stereotyped; fixed, rooted, permanent, inveterate, besetting, ingrained, current.

wont; used to, given to, addicted to, in the habit of; seasoned, imbued with, devoted to, wedded to.

Adv. as usual, as things go, as the world goes; as you were [*mil.*].

as a rule, for the most part, generally, most frequently.

614. DESUETUDE.—*N.* desuetude, disusage; disuse, etc., 678; want of practice.

V. **be unaccustomed,** leave off (*or* break off, shake off, violate) a habit *or* custom; be weaned from; disuse, etc., 678; wear off.

Adj. **unaccustomed,** unused, unwonted, unseasoned, untrained; new, fresh, original; unskilled.

unconventional, unfashionable, unusual; disused, etc., 678.

615. MOTIVE.—*N.* **motive,** reason, ground, call, principle, mainspring, pro and con, reason why; ulterior motive; intention, etc., 620.

inducement, consideration; attraction, loadstone, magnet, magnetism, temptation, enticement, allurement, glamour, witchery; charm, spell; fascination, blandishment, cajolery; seduction.

influence, prompting, dictate, instance; impulse, incitement, press, insistence, instigation; inspiration, persuasion, encouragement, exhortation, advice, solicitation, pull [*slang*].

incentive, stimulus, spur, fillip, whip, goad, provocative, whet.

bribe, lure, sop, decoy, bait, bribery and corruption.

tempter, prompter, instigator, coaxer, wheedler, siren; firebrand.

V. **induce,** move, draw, inspire; put up to [*slang*], prompt; stimulate, rouse, arouse, animate, whet, incite, provoke, instigate, actuate, encourage, advocate.

influence, bias, sway, incline, dispose, predispose; lead, lobby.

persuade, prevail upon, overcome, carry, bring round, conciliate, win (*or* talk) over; enlist, engage; invite, court.

tempt, overpersuade, entice, allure, captivate, fascinate, bewitch, hypnotize, charm, magnetize, wheedle, coax, lure, inveigle.

bribe, tamper with, suborn, grease the palm, corrupt.

enforce, force, impel, propel, whip, lash, goad, spur, prick, urge, egg on, hound on, hurry on.

Adj. **persuasive,** inviting, tempting, suasive, seductive, attractive, fascinating; provocative.

Adv. **because,** therefore, for, by reason of, for the sake of, on account of; out of, from, as, forasmuch as.

615a. ABSENCE OF MOTIVE.—*N.* **absence of motive;** caprice, etc., 608; chance, etc. (*absence of design*), 621.

V. **scruple,** etc. (*be unwilling*), 603; have no motive.

Adj. **aimless,** capricious, without rhyme or reason.

Adv. **capriciously,** out of mere caprice.

616. DISSUASION.—*N.* **dissuasion,** expostulation, remonstrance; deprecation, etc., 766; discouragement, damper, wet blanket.

curb, restraint, constraint, check.

V. **dissuade,** cry out against, remonstrate, expostulate, warn.

disincline, indispose, shake, stagger; discourage, dishearten, disenchant; deter, hold back, restrain, repel, turn aside, damp, cool, chill, blunt, calm, quiet, quench.

Adj. averse, etc. (*unwilling*), 603; repugnant, etc. (*dislike*), 867.

617. [Ostensible motive, ground, or reason] PLEA.—*N.* plea, pretext; allegation, excuse, vindication, justification; color; gloss, guise.

pretense, subterfuge, dust thrown in the eye; blind, lame excuse, makeshift, shift.

V. **plead,** allege, excuse, vindicate; color, gloss over, make a pretext of, use as a plea, take one's stand upon; pretend.

Adj. ostensible, alleged, pretended.

Adv. ostensibly; under the plea of, under the pretense of.

618. GOOD.—*N.* good, benefit, advantage; improvement, etc., 658; interest, service, behoof, behalf; commonweal; gain, profit, harvest; boon, etc. (*gift*), 784; good turn, blessing, prize, windfall, godsend, good fortune; happiness, etc., 827; goodness, etc., 648.

V. **benefit,** profit, advantage, serve, help, avail, do good to.

gain, prosper, flourish, thrive.

Adj. commendable, etc., 931; useful, etc., 644; good, beneficial, etc., 648.

Adv. **well,** aright, satisfactorily, favorably, in one's interest.

619. EVIL.—*N.* evil, ill, harm, hurt, mischief, nuisance, drawback, disadvantage; ills that flesh is heir to, mental suffering, pain; bane, etc., 663.

badness, etc., 649; painfulness, etc., 830; evildoer, etc., 913.

blow, buffet, stroke, scratch, bruise, wound, gash, mutilation; mortal blow (*or* wound); damage, loss.

disaster, accident, casualty, mishap, misfortune, calamity, woe, fatal mischief, catastrophe, tragedy, ruin; adversity, etc., 735.

outrage, wrong, injury, foul play; bad turn, disservice, grievance.

V. **harm,** injure, hurt, do disservice to.

Adj. **disastrous;** hurtful, etc., 649; disadvantageous, injurious, harmful.

Adv. amiss, wrong, ill; to one's cost.

620. INTENTION.—*N.* intention, intent, purpose; project, etc., 626; undertaking, design, ambition; view, proposal; contemplation.

object, aim, end; drift, tendency; destination, mark, point, goal, target, prey, quarry, game.

decision, determination, resolve; fixed purpose, resolution; ultimatum.

V. **intend,** purpose, design, mean, have in view, bid for, labor for, aspire to, aim at; contemplate, meditate, think of, dream of, talk of; premeditate, destine, propose; project, etc. (*plan*), 626; desire, etc., 865; pursue, etc., 622.

Adj. intentional, advised, express, determinate; bound for; disposed, inclined, bent upon, at stake; in prospect.

Adv. intentionally, advisedly, wittingly, knowingly, designedly, purposely, on purpose, by design, studiously, pointedly; deliberately.

621. [Absence of purpose] CHANCE.[1]—N. chance, etc., 156; lot, destiny, etc., 601; luck; hoodoo [*colloq.*], jinx [*slang*], Jonah, voodoo; wheel of chance, fortune's wheel; mascot.

speculation, venture, random shot, blind bargain, leap in the dark; fluke [*sporting cant*], flier [*slang*]; flutter [*slang*]; futures.

gambling, betting, drawing lots; wager; gamble, risk, stake, bet.

gambler, gamester, speculator; bookmaker, man of the turf.

V. chance, etc., 156; toss up, cast (*or* draw) lots; tempt fortune; speculate.

risk, venture, hazard, stake; wager, bet, gamble, game, play for.

Adj. chance; fortuitous, etc., 156; unintentional, unintended, accidental; random, undesigned, purposeless.

Adv. at random, at a venture, by chance, as it may happen.

622. [Purpose in action] PURSUIT.—N. pursuit, prosecution; pursuance, enterprise, undertaking, business, etc., 625; adventure, quest, hobby.

chase, hunt, race, steeplechase; hunting, coursing, sport, shooting, angling, fishing.

pursuer; hunter, huntsman, the field; sportsman, Nimrod; hound.

V. pursue, prosecute, follow, shadow; carry on, undertake, engage in, set about, endeavor, seek, trace, aim at, fish, fish for; press on, follow up, take up; go in for.

chase, give chase, stalk, course, hunt, hound.

Adj. in quest of, in pursuit, in full cry, on the scent.

623. [Absence of pursuit] AVOIDANCE.—N. avoidance, evasion, flight; escape, retreat, recoil, departure.

abstention, abstinence; forbearance; inaction, etc., 681; neutrality.

shirker, slacker [*colloq.*], shirk, quitter, truant; fugitive, refugee, runaway, deserter, renegade, backslider.

V. abstain, refrain, spare; eschew, keep from, let alone.

avoid, shun, steer (*or* keep) clear of; fight shy of, evade, elude, shirk.

shrink, hang (*or* hold, draw) back; recoil, retire, flinch, shy, dodge, parry.

[1] See note on 156.

beat a retreat; turn tail, take to one's heels; run, run away, cut and run [*colloq.*]; fly, flee, take flight; desert, make off, sneak off, sheer off; slip, play truant, decamp, flit, bolt, abscond; escape, etc., 671; abandon, etc., 624.

Adj. **elusive,** evasive; fugitive, runaway; shy, wild.

624. RELINQUISHMENT.—*N.* **relinquishment,** abandonment; desertion, defection, secession, withdrawal; discontinuance, renunciation, abrogation, resignation, retirement; cession, etc. (*of property*), 782.

V. **relinquish,** give up, abandon, desert, forsake, leave in the lurch; go back on [*colloq.*]; leave, quit, vacate, resign.

renounce, forego, have done with, drop, discard, give up the point (*or* argument), table, table the motion.

625. BUSINESS.—*N.* **business,** occupation, employment, undertaking, pursuit; affair, concern, matter, case.

task, work, job, chore, errand, commission, mission, charge, duty; avocation, hobby.

function, part, role, capacity, province, department, sphere, field, line; walk, round, routine; race, career.

office, place, position, post, incumbency, living; situation, berth, billet, appointment, engagement; undertaking, etc., 676.

vocation, calling, profession; cloth, faculty; craft, handicraft; trade.

V. **occupy oneself with;** employ oneself in *or* upon; undertake, etc., 676; turn one's hand to; be engaged in, be occupied with, be at work on; have in hand; ply one's trade.

officiate, serve, act, do duty; discharge (*or* perform) the duties of; hold (*or* fill) an office; hold a portfolio.

Adj. **businesslike;** workaday; professional, official, functional; busy.

in hand, on hand, afoot, on foot, going on; acting.

626. PLAN.—*N.* **plan,** scheme, design, project, proposal, proposition, suggestion; resolution, motion; organization, arrangement, system.

outline, sketch, skeleton, draft, rough draft, copy; forecast, program, prospectus; order of the day, memoranda, platform, plank, slate, ticket; role; policy.

contrivance, invention, expedient, receipt, nostrum, artifice, device; stratagem, trick; shift.

measure, step; stroke, master stroke; trump, trump card.

intrigue, cabal, plot, conspiracy, machination; mine.

promoter, designer, organizer, founder, projector; author, artist.

V. **plan,** scheme, design, frame, contrive, project, forecast, sketch, devise, invent, hatch, concoct; hit upon; map out, shape out a course; prepare, etc., 673.

systematize, organize; cast, recast, arrange; digest, mature.

plot, intrigue; counterplot, mine, countermine, lay a train.

Adj. under consideration, on the carpet, on the table.

627. METHOD. [Path]—*N.* method, way, manner, form, mode, fashion, guise; procedure.

path, road, route, course, tack; trajectory, orbit, track, beat.

means of access, entrance, approach, passage, cloister, covered way, lobby, corridor, aisle; alley, lane, avenue, artery, channel; gateway, door; secret passage; covert way.

roadway, thoroughfare; highway, turnpike, state road, causeway, king's highway; parkway, boulevard, speedway; walk, footpath, pathway, pavement, sidewalk, byroad, crossroad; railroad, railway, trolley track, tramway; towpath; street, etc. (*abode*), 189; bridge, viaduct.

Adv. how; in what way, in what manner; by what mode; so, thus; anyhow.

628. MID-COURSE.—*N.* mid-course, middle way, middle course; moderation; mean, etc., 29; golden mean.

compromise, half measures, neutrality.

V. keep the golden mean, steer a middle course; go straight.

compromise, make a compromise, concede half, go halfway.

Adj. neutral, average, even; impartial, moderate; straight.

Adv. in the mean; in moderation.

629. CIRCUIT.—*N.* circuit, roundabout way, digression, detour, loop, winding.

V. go round about, make a circuit, make a detour; meander, deviate.

Adj. circuitous, indirect, roundabout; zigzag.

Adv. in a roundabout way; by an indirect course.

630. REQUIREMENT.—*N.* requirement, need, wants, necessities; stress, exigency, pinch, case of need; desideratum; necessity, indispensability, urgency.

requisition, demand, request, claim; run, call for.

charge, command, injunction, precept, mandate, order, ultimatum.

V. require, need, want, stand in need of, lack; desire, etc., 865.

Adj. necessary, requisite, needful, imperative, essential, indispensable, called for; in demand, in request.

urgent, exigent, pressing, instant, crying.

Adv. of necessity; at a pinch.

631. INSTRUMENTALITY.—*N.* instrumentality; aid, etc., 707; subservience, mediation, intervention; pull [*slang*], influence; medium, intermediary, vehicle, tool, agency; instrument, expedient; means, etc., 632.

minister, handmaid, servant; friend at court, go-between.

V. **mediate,** minister, intervene, come (*or* go) between; interpose; use one's influence, be instrumental; subserve.

Adj. **instrumental;** useful, etc., 644; subservient, serviceable; intermediary, intermediate, intervening; conducive.

Adv. **through,** by, whereby, thereby, hereby; by the agency of, by dint of; by (*or* in) virtue of; by means of.

somehow, by fair means or foul; somehow or other; by hook or by crook.

632. MEANS.—*N.* **means,** resources, wherewithal, ways and means; capital, etc. (*money*), 800; revenue, income; stock in trade, provision, reserve, remnant, last resource, appliances, conveniences; expedients, wheels within wheels; sheet anchor; aid, etc., 707; medium, etc., 631.

V. **provide the wherewithal,** find (*or* possess) means, have powerful friends, have friends at court; have something to draw on.

Adj. **instrumental,** etc., 631; **mechanical,** etc., 633.

trustworthy, reliable, efficient; honorable, etc. (*upright*), 939.

Adv. **by means of,** with; wherewith, herewith, therewith; wherewithal.

633. INSTRUMENT.—*N.* **instrument,** organ, tool, implement, utensil, machine, engine, lathe, gin, mill; motor; machinery, mechanism.

equipment, gear, tackle, tackling; rigging, apparatus, appliances; plant, harness, trappings, fittings, accouterments, appointments, furniture, upholstery; chattels; paraphernalia.

mechanical powers; leverage; fulcrum, lever, crow, crowbar, jimmy, marline spike, handspike; arm, limb, wing; wheel and axle; wheelwork, clockwork; wheels within wheels; pinion, crank, winch, capstan, wheel, flywheel, turbine, water wheel, pump; pulley, crane, derrick; inclined plane; wedge; screw; jack; spring, mainspring; loom, shuttle, jenny.

handle, hilt, haft, shaft, shank; tiller, rudder, helm; treadle, pedal.

Adj. **mechanical;** propulsive, driving, hoisting, elevating, lifting.

useful, labor-saving, ingenious; well made, well fitted, well equipped.

634. SUBSTITUTE.—*N.* **substitute,** etc., 147; proxy, alternate, understudy; deputy, etc., 759.

635. MATERIALS.—*N.* **material,** raw material, stuff, stock, staple; ore.

636. STORE.—*N.* **store,** accumulation, hoard; stock, fund, mine, vein, lode, quarry; spring, fount, fountain; well; orchard, garden, farm; stock in trade, supply; treasure; reserve, reserve fund, savings.

crop, harvest, vintage, yield, product, gleaning.

storehouse, storeroom, store closet; depository, depot, cache, warehouse, magazine; garner, granary, grain elevator, silo; safe-deposit vault; armory; arsenal; stable, barn.

reservoir, cistern, tank, pond, millpond; gasometer.

V. **store,** put by, lay by, set by, stow away, store up, hoard up, treasure up, lay up, save, preserve, save up, bank; cache, deposit; stow, stack, load; harvest; accumulate, amass, hoard.

reserve; keep back, hold back; husband, husband one's resources.

Adj. in store, in reserve, spare, supernumerary.

Adv. for a rainy day, for a nest egg, to fall back upon; on deposit.

637. PROVISION.—*N.* provision, supply; grist, resources, etc. (*means*), 632; groceries, purveyance, commissariat.

caterer, purveyor, commissary, quartermaster, steward, purser, housekeeper; innkeeper, landlord, mine host; grocer, fishmonger, provision merchant.

V. **provide,** make provision, lay in, lay in a stock (*or* store).

supply, furnish; cater, victual, provision, purvey, forage; stock, make good, replenish, fill; recruit, feed.

store, etc., 636; conserve, keep, preserve, lay by, gather into barns.

638. WASTE.—*N.* consumption, expenditure, exhaustion; dispersion, leakage, loss, wear and tear, waste; prodigality.

V. **consume,** spend, expend, use, swallow up; exhaust, spill, drain, empty, deplete; disperse, etc., 73; waste; squander.

labor in vain, etc. (*useless*), 645; cast pearls before swine; waste powder and shot.

run to waste; ebb, leak, melt away, run dry, dry up.

Adj. **wasted,** gone to waste, useless, run to seed; dried up.

wasteful, etc. (*prodigal*), 818; penny wise and pound foolish.

639. SUFFICIENCY.—*N.* sufficiency, adequacy, enough, wherewithal, competence.

abundance, plenitude, plenty, copiousness, amplitude, profusion, full measure; fill; luxuriance, affluence, fat of the land.

rich man, etc. (*wealth*), 803; financier, banker, plutocrat.

V. **suffice,** do, just do [*both colloq.*], satisfy, pass muster; have enough, have one's fill.

abound, teem, flow, stream, rain, shower down; pour, pour in; swarm; bristle with.

Adj. **sufficient,** enough, adequate, up to the mark, commensurate, competent, satisfactory; ample; plenty, plentiful, plenteous; copious, abundant; replete, unstinted, inexhaustible.

rich, affluent, etc. (*wealthy*), 803; luxuriant, etc. (*fertile*), 168.

Adv. without stint; to the good.

640. INSUFFICIENCY.—*N.* insufficiency, inadequacy, incompetence, deficiency, imperfection, shortcoming; paucity, stint, bare subsistence; poverty, etc., 804.

scarcity, dearth; want, need, lack, poverty, starvation, famine, drought.

dole, mite, pittance; short allowance; half rations.

depletion, emptiness, vacancy; ebb tide; low water; insolvency, etc. (*nonpayment*), 808.

poor man, pauper, etc., 804; bankrupt.

V. **want,** lack, need, require; be in want, etc. (*poor*), 804; live from hand to mouth.

impoverish, drain, drain of resources; stint, etc., 819.

Adj. **insufficient,** inadequate, too little, not enough; incompetent, perfunctory, deficient, wanting; imperfect; ill-furnished, ill-provided, ill-stored.

short of, out of, destitute of, devoid of, bereft of, slack, at a low ebb; empty, vacant, bare; dry, drained.

unprovided, unsupplied, unfurnished; unfed; empty-handed.

meager, poor, thin, spare, stinted, starved, emaciated, undernourished, underfed, half-starved, famine-stricken, famished.

scarce, scant, not to be had, scurvy, stingy, etc., 819; at the end of one's tether; without resources, in want.

Adv. in default of, for want of; failing.

641. REDUNDANCE.—*N.* redundance, too much, too many, superabundance, superfluity, exuberance, profuseness; profusion, plenty, repletion, plethora, glut, congestion, surfeit, overdose, oversupply, overflow; excess, surplus, remainder.

V. **superabound,** overabound, swarm; bristle with, overflow, run over; run riot; overrun, overstock, overdose, overfeed, overload, overburden, overwhelm, overshoot the mark; gorge, glut, load, drench, inundate, deluge, flood; send (*or* carry) coals to Newcastle.

cloy, choke, suffocate; pile up, lay on thick, lavish.

Adj. **redundant,** turgid; exuberant, inordinate, superabundant, excess, overmuch, replete, profuse, lavish, prodigal; exorbitant, extravagant, overflowing; gorged, stuffed.

superfluous, unnecessary, needless, over and above, supernumerary, spare, duplicate, supererogatory.

Adv. **over and above;** over much, too much; too far; over, too; over head and ears, over one's head; up to one's eyes; extra.

642. IMPORTANCE.—*N.* importance, consequence, moment, prominence, consideration, mark; weight, influence; value, usefulness; greatness, etc., 31; superiority, etc., 33; notability.

salient point, outstanding feature; cardinal point; substance, gist, sum and substance, cream, salt, core, kernel, heart, nucleus; key, keynote; keystone.

import, significance, concern; emphasis, interest.

gravity, seriousness, solemnity; pressure, urgency, stress.

V. **be important,** be somebody, be something; import, signify, matter, carry weight; come to the front, lead the way, take the lead.

value, care for, set store upon *or* by.

accentuate, emphasize, lay stress on; mark, underline, underscore.

Adj. **important,** of importance, momentous, material, considerable, weighty, influential, notable, prominent, salient, signal; memorable, remarkable; stirring, eventful.

grave, serious, earnest, grand, solemn, impressive, commanding, imposing.

urgent, pressing, critical, crucial, instant.

foremost, principal, leading, chief, main, prime, primary; capital; superior, etc., 33; marked, rare; paramount, essential, vital, radical, cardinal.

significant, telling, trenchant, emphatic, pregnant.

Adv. **in the main;** above all, in the first place, before everything else.

643. UNIMPORTANCE.—*N.* **unimportance,** insignificance, nothingness, immateriality.

triviality, levity, frivolity, paltriness, smallness, matter of indifference; no object.

nothing, small (*or* trifling) matter; joke, jest, snap of the fingers, fudge, fiddlestick, incident, mere nothing, nonentity.

toy, plaything, gewgaw, bauble, trinket, bagatelle, kickshaw, knickknack.

trumpery, trash, rubbish, stuff, frippery; chaff, dross, froth, scum, bubble, smoke; weed; refuse.

trifle, straw, pin, fig, button, feather, continental, jot, mote, rap, old song; cent, red cent; picayune [*colloq*].

nine days' wonder, flash in the pan, much ado about nothing, tempest in a teapot.

minutiae, details, minor details.

V. **be unimportant,** not matter, matter (*or* signify) little, not matter a straw.

make light of, catch at straws, make mountains out of molehills.

Adj. **unimportant,** immaterial; nonessential, unessential, irrelevant; indifferent, mediocre, passable, fair, tolerable, commonplace; mere, common, ordinary, insignificant.

trifling, trivial; slight, slender, light, airy, flimsy, idle, shallow, weak, powerless, frivolous, petty, finical.

paltry, poor, pitiful, contemptible, puerile; sorry, mean, meager, shabby, miserable, wretched, vile, niggardly, scurvy, beggarly, worthless, two-by-four [*colloq.*], cheap, trashy, catchpenny, gimcrack, trumpery; one-horse [*colloq.*]

Adv. rather, somewhat, fairly, fairly well, tolerably.

644. UTILITY.—*N.* utility, usefulness, efficacy, efficiency, adequacy; helpfulness, service, use, help, aid, applicability, subservience; value, worth, productiveness, utilization.

commonweal, public good; utilitarianism.

V. avail, serve, conduce, tend, answer (*or* serve) one's turn; benefit, bear fruit, profit, remunerate.

act a part, etc. (*action*), 680; discharge a function, render a service; bestead, stand one in good stead; help, etc., 707.

Adj. useful, of use, serviceable, subservient, conducive, helpful.

advantageous, beneficial, profitable, gainful, remunerative, valuable; invaluable, beyond price; prolific.

adequate; efficient, efficacious; effective, effectual.

applicable, available, ready, handy, at hand, commodious, adaptable.

645. INUTILITY.—*N.* inutility, uselessness, inefficacy, futility; ineptitude, inadequacy, unfitness; inefficiency, incompetence, unskillfulness, labor in vain; worthlessness; triviality, etc., 643.

rubbish, junk, lumber, litter, odds and ends, shoddy; rags, leavings, dross, trash, refuse, sweepings, offscourings, waste, rubble, debris; chaff, stubble, dregs, weeds, tares.

V. labor in vain; seek (*or* strive) after impossibilities; use vain efforts, beat the air, pour water into a sieve, bay at the moon; cast pearls before swine, carry coals to Newcastle.

render useless, dismantle, dismast, disqualify; disable, hamstring, cripple, lame; spike guns, clip the wings; put out of gear.

Adj. useless, inutile, futile, unavailing, bootless; inoperative, inadequate, inept, inefficient, ineffectual, incompetent.

worthless, valueless, unsalable; not worth a straw, good for nothing, dear at any price; vain, empty, inane; gainless, profitless, fruitless; unserviceable, unprofitable; ill-spent; effete, barren, sterile, impotent, worn out, unproductive; uncalled for; unnecessary, unneeded, superfluous.

646. EXPEDIENCE.—*N.* expedience, desirability, fitness, propriety, utility, advantage, opportunity; opportunism; pragmatism.

V. be expedient, suit, befit; suit (*or* befit) the occasion.

Adj. expedient, desirable, advisable, acceptable; convenient; worth while, meet; fit, fitting, due, proper, eligible, seemly, be-

coming, befitting; opportune, advantageous, etc., 644; suitable.
practical, practicable, effective, pragmatic, pragmatical.

Adv. in the nick of time; in the right place.

647. INEXPEDIENCE.—*N.* inexpedience, undesirability, impropriety, unfitness, inutility, disadvantage, inconvenience, inadvisability.

V. be inexpedient, come amiss, embarrass, put to inconvenience.

Adj. inexpedient, undesirable; inadvisable, ill-advised, unsuitable, troublesome, objectionable, ineligible, inadmissible, inconvenient, discommodious, disadvantageous; inappropriate, unfit; unsatisfactory, unprofitable, inept, inopportune, improper, unseemly.

clumsy, awkward; cumbrous, cumbersome, lumbering, unwieldy, hulky.

648. [Good qualities] GOODNESS.—*N.* goodness, excellence, merit; beneficence, benevolence, etc., 906; virtue, etc., 944; value, worth, price.

perfection, quintessence; superiority, etc., 33; prime, flower, cream, elite, pick, A 1 *or* A number 1 [*colloq.*], pick of the crop, salt of the earth; prodigy, wonder; gem of the first water, treasure, one in a thousand.

good man, etc., 948.

V. be beneficial, produce (*or* do) good, profit, benefit, improve, be the making of, make a man of; do a good turn, confer an obligation.

be good, be pure gold, look good to [*colloq.*]; excel, transcend, stand the test; pass muster, pass an examination.

vie, challenge, comparison, emulate, rival.

Adj. beneficial, valuable, of value; useful, etc., 644; advantageous, profitable; edifying, salutary.

harmless, innocuous, innocent, inoffensive.

favorable; propitious, etc. (*hope-giving*), 858; fair.

good, excellent; better; superior, etc., 33; above par; nice, fine; genuine, etc. (*true*), 494.

choice, best, select, picked, elect, rare, priceless, matchless, peerless, unequaled, unparalleled, inimitable, crack [*colloq.*], crackajack [*slang*], gilt-edge [*colloq.*]; superfine, of the first water; first-rate, first-class; high-wrought, exquisite, admirable, capital, estimable, precious, priceless, invaluable, inestimable.

satisfactory, up to the mark, unexceptionable, unobjectionable.

Adv. for one's benefit.

649. [Bad qualities] BADNESS.—*N.* badness, hurtfulness, virulence; abomination, pestilence, guilt, depravity, vice, etc., 945; malignity, malevolence.

bane, etc., 663; plague spot, evil star, ill-wind; hoodoo [*colloq.*], jinx [*slang*], Jonah; snake in the grass, skeleton in the closet; thorn in the flesh.

ill-treatment, annoyance, molestation, abuse, oppression, persecution, outrage, misusage, scathe, injury.

bad man, etc., 949; evildoer, etc., 913.

V. **hurt,** harm, scathe, injure; pain, etc., 830.

wrong, aggrieve, oppress, persecute, trample upon; overburden, weigh down; victimize.

maltreat, abuse; ill-use, ill-treat; buffet, bruise, scratch, maul; smite, molest, do violence; stab, pierce.

Adj. **hurtful,** harmful, baneful, baleful, injurious, deleterious, detrimental, noxious, pernicious, mischievous, mischief-making, malignant, prejudicial; oppressive, burdensome, onerous; malign.

corrupting, virulent, venomous, corrosive; poisonous, deadly, destructive.

bad, ill, arrant, dreadful; horrid, horrible; dire; rank, foul, rotten.

unsatisfactory, indifferent, deteriorated, below par, imperfect, ill-conditioned.

deplorable, wretched, sad, grievous, lamentable, pitiful, pitiable, woeful.

evil, wrong; depraved, wicked, etc., 945; shocking; reprehensible.

hateful, abominable, vile, base, villainous, detestable, execrable, cursed, accursed, damnable, diabolic.

Adv. to one's cost; where the shoe pinches.

650. PERFECTION.—*N.* **perfection;** paragon, pink, pink (*or* acme) of perfection.

model, standard, pattern, mirror.

masterpiece, master stroke, prize winner, prize; superexcellence.

V. **perfect,** bring to perfection, ripen, mature; consummate, crown, put the finishing touch to (*or* upon); complete.

Adj. **perfect,** faultless, immaculate, spotless, impeccable, unblemished, sound, scathless, intact; consummate, finished.

best, model, standard; inimitable, unparalleled, beyond all praise.

Adv. clean as a whistle; with a finish; to the limit.

651. IMPERFECTION.—*N.* **imperfection;** deficiency, inadequacy, defection, badness, immaturity.

fault, defect, weak point; screw loose; flaw, taint, blemish, weakness, shortcoming, drawback.

V. **be imperfect,** have a defect, lie under a disadvantage; not pass muster, fall short.

Adj. **imperfect,** deficient, defective, faulty, unsound, tainted, out of order; warped, injured; inadequate, crude, incomplete, below par.

indifferent, middling, ordinary, mediocre, average, tolerable, fair, passable; decent; not bad, not amiss; admissible, bearable.

inferior, secondary, second-rate, one-horse [*colloq.*]; two-by-four [*colloq.*].

Adv. to a limited extent, pretty, moderately, considering.

652. CLEANNESS.—*N.* cleanness, purity, purification, purgation; ablution, lavation; disinfection, drainage, sewerage.

bath, bathroom, swimming pool, swimming bath, public bath, baths, bathhouse, lavatory; laundry, washhouse.
cleaner, washerwoman, laundress, laundryman, washerman; scavenger, sweeper; street sweeper, white wing [*local*]; dustman.
brush; broom, vacuum cleaner, carpet sweeper; mop, swab, hose.

cathartic, purgative, aperient, laxative.

V. clean, cleanse; rinse, flush, mop, sponge, scour, swab, scrub; wash, lave, launder; purify; purge, expurgate, clarify, refine.

strain, separate, filter, filtrate, drain; percolate.

sift, winnow, sieve, bolt, screen, riddle; pick, weed.

comb, rake, scrape, rasp; card.

sweep, brush, brush up, rout out; clean house, spruce up [*colloq.*].

disinfect, fumigate, ventilate, deodorize; whitewash.

Adj. clean, cleanly, pure, immaculate, spotless, stainless, unspotted, unsoiled, unsullied, untainted, sweet.

neat, spruce, tidy, trim, cleaned.

653. UNCLEANNESS.—*N.* uncleanness, impurity; defilement, contamination, abomination; taint.

decay, putrefaction; corruption; mold, mildew, dry rot, caries [*med.*].

squalor, squalidness, slovenliness.

dirt, filth, soil, slop; dust, smoke, soot, smudge, smut, grime.
dregs, grounds, lees, sediment, heeltap; dross, ashes, cinders; scum, froth.

sty, pigsty, lair, den, Augean stable, sink of corruption; slum, rookery.

mud, mire, quagmire, silt, slime, slush.

V. rot, putrefy, fester, rankle, reek; mold, molder, go bad.

soil, smoke, tarnish, spot, smear; daub, blot, blur, smudge, smutch, smirch; drabble, besmear, befoul, splash, stain, sully.

pollute, defile, debase, contaminate, taint, corrupt.

Adj. unclean, dirty, filthy, grimy, soiled, dusty, smutty, sooty; mussy [*colloq.*].

uncleanly, slovenly, slatternly, untidy, frowzy, sluttish, unkempt, unwashed, squalid.

offensive, nasty, coarse, foul, impure, abominable, beastly, reeky, fetid; moldy, musty, rancid, bad, touched, rotten, corrupt, tainted, putrid; gory, bloody.

654. HEALTH.—*N.* health, sanity; soundness, vigor; good (*or* perfect, excellent, robust) health; bloom, convalescence, strength, poise.

V. **be in health**, bloom, flourish, enjoy good health.

return to health; recover, etc., 660; get better, convalesce, be convalescent, recruit; restore to health, cure.

Adj. **healthy**, healthful, in health, well, sound, whole, strong, blooming, hearty, hale, fresh, green, florid, hardy, robust, vigorous, in fine fettle; chipper [*colloq.*].

uninjured, unscathed, unmarred, without a scratch, safe and sound.

655. DISEASE.—*N.* disease; illness, sickness; infirmity, ailment, indisposition; complaint, disorder, malady, loss of health, delicacy, delicate health, invalidism, malnutrition, want of nourishment; prostration, decline, collapse, decay.

visitation, attack, seizure, stroke, fit, epilepsy, apoplexy, palsy, paralysis; shock; shell shock.

taint, virus, pollution, infection, contagion; epidemic, plague, pestilence.

Science of disease: pathology, therapeutics; diagnostics, diagnosis.

V. **ail**, suffer, be affected with, droop, flag, languish, sicken, pine, dwindle; waste away, fail, lose strength, be laid by the heels; lie helpless.

Adj. **sick**, ill, not well, indisposed, ailing, squeamish, poorly, seedy [*colloq.*], laid up, confined, bedridden, in hospital, on the sick list; out of health, out of sorts [*colloq.*], under the weather [*colloq.*]; valetudinary.

sickly, infirm, unsound, unhealthy, weakly, drooping, flagging, lame, halt, crippled, halting.

diseased, morbid, tainted, poisoned, septic; mangy, leprous, cankered; rotten, withered; palsied, paralytic; consumptive, tubercular, tuberculous.

656. HEALTHINESS.—*N.* healthiness, wholesomeness; healthfulness, salubrity.

Preservation of health: hygiene, pure air, exercise, nourishment, tonic; immunity; sanitarium, sanatorium.

V. **be salubrious**, make for health, conduce to health; be good for, agree with.

Adj. **healthy**, healthful; salubrious, salutary, wholesome, sanitary, prophylactic; benign, bracing, tonic, invigorating, nutritious; hygienic.

innocuous, innocent; harmless, uninjurious, immune.

657. UNHEALTHINESS.—*N.* unhealthiness, plague spot; malaria, insalubrity; contagion; poisonousness.

V. be unhealthy, disagree with; shorten one's days.

Adj. unhealthy, insalubrious, unwholesome, noxious, noisome; pestiferous, pestilential; virulent, venomous, poisonous, septic, toxic, deadly.

infectious, contagious, catching, communicable, epidemic, sporadic, endemic; epizootic [*of animals*].

658. IMPROVEMENT.—*N.* improvement, amelioration, betterment; recovery, mend, amendment, emendation; advancement, advance, promotion, preferment, elevation, increase.

cultivation, culture, march of intellect, civilization.

reform, reformation; revision, radical reform; correction, refinement, elaboration; purification, repair.

reformer, progressive, radical.

V. improve, mend, amend, better, ameliorate, relieve; correct, repair, restore.

improve upon; rectify; enrich, mellow, elaborate, fatten.

refresh, revive; invigorate, strengthen, recruit, renew, revivify, freshen.

promote, cultivate, advance, forward, enhance, bring forward, foster.

revise, edit, review, make corrections, make improvements.

reform, remodel, reorganize, reclaim, civilize, lift, uplift, inspire.

Adj. better, better off, all the better for; improving, progressive, improved.

corrigible, improvable, curable.

Adv. on consideration, on reconsideration, on second thought.

659. DETERIORATION.—*N.* deterioration, debasement; wane, ebb, recession, retrogradation, decrease.

degeneracy, degeneration, degradation, depravation, depravity, demoralization.

injury, damage, loss, detriment, harm, impairment, outrage, havoc, inroad, ravage, vitiation, discoloration, pollution, poisoning, contamination, canker, corruption, adulteration, alloy.

decline, declension, declination; decadence, falling off; senility, decrepitude.

decay, dilapidation, wear and tear, erosion, corrosion, rottenness; moth and rust, dry rot, blight, atrophy.

V. deteriorate, degenerate, fall off, wane, ebb; retrograde, decline, droop, run to seed *or* waste, lapse, break down, crack, shrivel, fade, wither, molder, rot, rankle, decay, go bad; rust, crumble, shake, totter, perish.

corrupt, taint, infect, contaminate, poison, envenom, canker, blight, rot, pollute, defile, vitiate, debase, deprave, degrade; alloy, adulterate, tamper with, prejudice; pervert, demoralize, brutalize.

embitter, exasperate, irritate.

injure, impair, damage, harm, hurt, spoil, mar, despoil, waste; overrun, ravage, pillage

wound, stab, pierce, maim, lame, cripple, hamstring, mangle, mutilate, disfigure, blemish, deface, warp.

Adj. deteriorated, unimproved, injured, degenerate, imperfect; battered, weathered, weather-beaten, stale, dilapidated, faded, worn, wasted, wilted, shabby, threadbare, frayed.

decayed, moth-eaten, worm-eaten, mildewed, rusty, moldy, seedy [*colloq.*], timeworn, effete, crumbling, moldering, rotten, cankered, blighted, tainted; decrepit, broken-down, worn-out, used up [*colloq.*].

stagnant, backward, unprogressive.

Adv. on the downgrade, on the downward track; beyond hope.

660. RESTORATION.—*N.* restoration, replacement, rehabilitation, reconstruction, reproduction, renovation, renewal, revival, resuscitation, reanimation, reorganization; redemption, restitution, relief, redress, retrieval, reclamation, recovery, convalescence, resumption.

renaissance, renascence, rebirth, new birth, regeneration, regeneracy, resurrection.

repair, repairing, reparation, mending; recruiting.

mender, repairer, tinker, cobbler.

V. recover, rally, revive; come to, come round, come to oneself; pull through, weather the storm, be oneself again; get well, survive, reappear.

restore, put back, reinstate, replace, rehabilitate, re-establish, reconstruct, rebuild, reorganize, convert, recondition, renew, renovate; regenerate; rejuvenate.

redeem, reclaim, recover, retrieve; rescue, etc. (*deliver*), 672.

cure, heal, remedy, doctor, bring round, set on one's legs.

resuscitate, revive, reanimate, revivify, reinvigorate, refresh.

repair, mend, put in repair, retouch, tinker, cobble, patch up, darn; stanch, calk, splice.

Adj. restored, convalescent, rejuvenated, renascent.

restorative, recuperative, curative, remedial.

restorable, remediable, retrievable, curable.

661. RELAPSE.—*N.* relapse, lapse; falling back, retrogradation; deterioration, etc., 659; backsliding.

V. relapse, lapse, fall (*or* slip) back, have a relapse, be overcome, be overtaken, yield again to, fall again into, return, retrograde.

Adj. backsliding, retrograde.

662. REMEDY.—*N.* remedy, help, redress, febrifuge; antipoison, antidote, emetic; stimulant, tonic; prophylactic, antiseptic, germicide, disinfectant; restorative; specific; cure, sovereign remedy, panacea.

materia medica, pharmacy, pharmaceutics; pharmacopoeia.

narcotic, opium, morphine, cocaine, hashish, dope [*slang*]; sedative.

physic, medicine, simples, drug, potion, draft, dose, pill, medicament; recipe, receipt, prescription; patent medicine, nostrum; elixir, balm, balsam, cordial.

salve, ointment, oil, lenitive, lotion, embrocation, liniment.

treatment, regimen, diet; dietary, dietetics; operation, the knife [*colloq.*], surgical operation; major operation.

healing art, practice of medicine, therapeutics; allopathy, homeopathy, osteopathy, eclecticism, surgery; faith cure, faith healing, mind cure, psychotherapy, psychotherapeutics; vocational therapy; dentistry.

hospital, surgery, infirmary, clinic, sanitarium, sanatorium; springs, baths, spa; asylum, home; Red Cross; ambulance.

dispensary, drugstore.

doctor, physician, medical man, general practitioner; specialist, consultant; surgeon.

intern, anesthetist, aurist, oculist, dentist, dental surgeon; osteopath, osteopathist; nurse, sister, nursing sister; apothecary, druggist, pharmacist, pharmaceutical chemist, Hippocrates, Galen; masseur (*fem.* masseuse), rubber.

V. **apply a remedy,** doctor [*colloq.*], dose, physic, nurse, minister to, attend, dress the wounds; relieve, palliate, heal, cure, remedy, restore.

Adj. **remedial,** restorative, corrective, palliative, healing; sanatory, sanative; prophylactic; medical, medicinal; therapeutic, surgical; tonic, sedative, lenitive; allopathic, homeopathic, eclectic; aperient, laxative, cathartic, purgative; septic; aseptic, antiseptic.

dietetic, dietary, alimentary; nutritious, nutritive; digestive, digestible.

663. BANE.—*N.* **bane,** curse, thorn in the flesh; bête noir [F.], bugbear; evil, scourge; fungus, mildew; dry rot; canker, cancer; poison, virus, venom; stench, fetor, poison gas.

sting, fang, thorn, bramble, brier, nettle.

Science of poisons: toxicology.

Adj. **baneful,** poisonous, etc. (*unwholesome*), 657.

664. SAFETY.—*N.* **safety,** security, surety, impregnability, invulnerability, escape, means of escape; safeguard, palladium; sheet anchor; rock, tower.

guardianship, wardship, wardenship; tutelage, custody, safekeeping, protection; auspices.

protector, guardian; warden, warder: preserver, lifesaver, custodian, duenna, chaperon.

safe-conduct, escort, convoy; guard, shield, guardian angel; tutelary deity (*or* saint).

watchman, patrolman, policeman, police officer, officer [*colloq.*]; cop, copper [*both slang*], bluecoat [*colloq.*], constable; detective, spotter [*slang*]; sheriff, deputy; sentinel, sentry, scout.

armed force, garrison, lifeguard, state guard, militia, regular army, navy; volunteer; marine, etc , 726; battleship, man-of-war, etc., 726.

judge, justice, judiciary, magistrate, justice of the peace.

V. **protect,** watch over, take care of, preserve, cover, screen, shelter, shroud, flank, ward, guard; defend, take precautions.

escort, support, accompany, convoy.

watch, mount guard, patrol, scout, spy.

Adj. **safe,** secure, sure, on terra firma [L.]; on the safe side; undercover, under lock and key; out of danger, protected; at anchor, high and dry, above-water; safe and sound.

snug, seaworthy, watertight, weatherproof, waterproof, fireproof; bombproof, shellproof.

defensible, tenable, proof against, invulnerable, unassailable, impregnable.

guardian, tutelary, protective.

Adv. with impunity.

665. DANGER.—*N.* **danger,** peril, insecurity, jeopardy, risk, hazard, venture, precariousness, instability; exposure, vulnerability, vulnerable point, heel of Achilles; forlorn hope.

Sense of danger: apprehension, etc., 860.

V. **endanger,** expose to danger, imperil, jeopardize, beard the lion in his den; sail too near the wind.

risk, hazard, venture, adventure, stake, set at hazard; run the gantlet.

Adj. **dangerous,** hazardous, perilous, unsafe, unprotected, insecure.

defenseless, guardless, unsheltered, unshielded; vulnerable, exposed; at bay.

precarious, critical, ticklish; slippery, between Scylla and Charybdis, between two fires; under fire; at stake, in question.

unsteady, unstable, shaky, tottering, top-heavy, tumble-down, ramshackle, crumbling, helpless, trembling in the balance; nodding to its fall.

threatening, ominous, ill-omened, alarming.

666. [Means of safety] REFUGE.—*N.* **refuge,** sanctuary, retreat, fastness, stronghold, fortress, castle, keep; asylum, shelter, covert, ark, home, hiding place.

anchorage, roadstead; breakwater, port, haven, harbor, pier, jetty, embankment, quay, wharf.

anchor, sheet anchor, grapnel, grappling iron, mainstay, support, safeguard.

667. [Source of danger] PITFALL.—*N.* pitfall, ambush, trap, snare, mine, spring gun.

rocks, reefs, sunken rocks, snags; sands, quicksands; breakers, shoals, shallows, lee shore, rockbound coast.

abyss, abysm, pit, void, chasm.

whirlpool, eddy, vortex, rapids, undertow; current, tiderace, maelstrom; eagre, bore, tidal wave.

pest, ugly customer, incendiary, firebug [*slang*]; firebrand; hornet's nest.

sword of Damocles; wolf at the door, snake in the grass, snake in one's bosom.

668. WARNING.—*N.* warning, caution, notice, premonition, prediction; symptom; lesson, admonition; handwriting on the wall, monitor, warning voice; stormy petrel, bird of ill omen, gathering clouds.

watchtower, beacon, signal post; lighthouse, etc., 550.

sentinel, sentry; watch, watchman; watch and ward; watch-dog; patrol, picket, scout, spy, lookout, flagman.

V. warn, caution; forewarn, admonish, forbode, give warning; put on one's guard; sound the alarm.

beware, take warning, look out, keep watch and ward.

Adj. premonitory, cautionary; ominous, threatening, lowering, minatory; symptomatic.

Adv. with alarm, on guard, after due warning, with one's eyes open.

669. [Indication of danger] ALARM.—*N.* alarm; alarum, alarm bell, tocsin, beat of drum, sound of trumpet, hue and cry; signal of distress, SOS; fog signal, siren; yellow flag; danger signal; red light, red flag; fire alarm, still alarm; burglar alarm; police whistle.

V. alarm, give (*or* raise, sound) an alarm, warn, ring the tocsin.

670. PRESERVATION.—*N.* preservation, safekeeping, conservation, economy, maintenance, support, salvation, deliverance, etc., 672.

Means of preservation: prophylaxis; preserver, preservative; hygiene, hygienics; ensilage; dehydration, evaporation, drying, canning, pickling.

V. preserve, maintain, keep, sustain, support; save, rescue, make safe, take care of, guard; husband, economize.

embalm, dry, cure, salt, pickle, season, bottle, pot, tin, can; dehydrate, evaporate.

Adj. preserved, unimpaired, unbroken, uninjured, unhurt, unmarred; safe, safe and sound, intact, with a whole skin.

671. ESCAPE.—*N.* escape, flight, evasion, loophole, retreat; narrow (*or* hairbreadth) escape; close call [*colloq.*]; impunity.

refugee, etc. (*fugitive*), 623.

V. escape, make one's escape; break jail; get off, get clear off, elude, make off, give one the slip; wriggle out of; break loose, break away.

Adj. stolen away; fled; scot-free.

672. DELIVERANCE.—*N.* deliverance, extrication, rescue, ransom, reprieve, respite; armistice, truce; liberation, emancipation; redemption, salvation.

V. deliver, extricate, rescue, save, free, liberate, set free, release, emancipate, redeem, ransom; come to the rescue.

673. PREPARATION.—*N.* preparation, provision, arrangement, anticipation, precaution, forecast, rehearsal; dissemination, propaganda.

groundwork, steppingstone; foundation; scaffold, scaffolding.

elaboration, ripening, evolution; concoction, digestion; hatching, incubation.

Preparation of men: training, education, equipment, inurement; novitiate.

Preparation of food: cooking, cookery, culinary art; brewing.

Preparation of the soil: tilling, plowing, sowing, cultivation.

preparedness, readiness, ripeness, mellowness; maturity.

preparer, trainer, coach, teacher, pioneer; prophet; forerunner, etc. (*precursor*), 64; sappers and miners.

V. prepare, prime, get (*or* make) ready, arrange, make preparations, settle preliminaries, get up; prepare the ground, lay the foundations, erect the scaffolding.

elaborate, mature, ripen, mellow, season, bring to maturity; nurture; cook, brew.

equip, arm, man; fit out, fit up; furnish, rig, dress, accouter, array.

prepare for, guard against, forearm; make provision for; provide, provide against; set one's house in order, make all snug; clear decks, clear for action.

be prepared, be ready, watch and pray, keep one's powder dry, lie in wait for, anticipate, foresee.

Adj. preparatory, precautionary, provident; provisional, preliminary; in embryo, in hand, in train; afoot, afloat; on foot, brewing, hatching, forthcoming.

prepared, ready, cut and dried; available, at one's elbow, ready for use, all ready; handy.

ripe, mature, mellow; seasoned, practiced, experienced.

elaborate, labored, high-wrought, worked up.

Adv. **in preparation,** in anticipation of; afoot, astir, abroad.

674. NONPREPARATION.—*N.* **nonpreparation,** unpreparedness; improvidence.

immaturity, crudity, rawness; disqualification.

Absence of art: nature, state of nature; virgin soil, unweeded garden; rough diamond; raw material.

improvisation, etc. (*impulse*), 612.

V. **be unprepared;** lie fallow; live from hand to mouth.

extemporize, improvise; cook up, fix up.

surprise, drop in [*colloq.*], take (*or* catch) unawares; take by surprise.

Adj. **unprepared,** incomplete, premature, rudimental, embryonic, immature, unripe, callow, unfledged, unhatched; uncooked, raw, green, crude; coarse; rough, roughhewn; in the rough.

untaught, uneducated, untrained, untutored, unlicked.

fallow, unsown, untilled, uncultivated.

unfitted, disqualified, unqualified, ill-digested; unready, unorganized, unfurnished, unprovided, unequipped.

shiftless, improvident, unthrifty, thriftless, happy-go-lucky; slack, remiss.

Adv. **inadvertently,** by surprise, without premeditation; extempore.

675. ESSAY—*N.* **essay,** trial, endeavor, attempt; aim, struggle, venture, adventure, speculation, probation, experiment.

V. **try,** essay; experiment, etc., 463; endeavor, strive; tempt, attempt, venture, adventure, speculate, tempt fortune.

Adj. **tentative,** experimental, empirical, problematic, probationary.

Adv. **on examination,** on trial, at a venture; by rule of thumb.

676. UNDERTAKING.—*N.* **undertaking,** adventure, venture, engagement, compact, enterprise; pilgrimage.

V. **undertake,** engage in, embark in, launch (*or* plunge) into, volunteer; apprentice oneself to; engage, contract, devote oneself to, take up, take on, take in hand; tackle [*colloq.*]; set about; launch forth; betake oneself to, turn one's hand to, have in hand, begin, broach, institute.

Adj. **energetic;** full of pep [*slang*]; enterprising, adventurous, venturesome.

677. USE.—*N.* **use,** employ, exercise, application, appliance; disposal; consumption; agency, usefulness, etc., 644; benefit, recourse, resort, avail.

Conversion to use: utilization, utility, service, wear.

Way of using: usage, employment, *modus operandi* [L.].

user, consumer, market, demand.

V. **use,** make use of, employ, put to use, apply, put in action, set in motion, set to work; ply, work, wield, handle, manipulate; exert, exercise, practice, avail oneself of, profit by; resort to, have recourse to, recur to, take up, try.

utilize, turn to account (*or* use); exploit; administer, apply, bring into play; task, tax, put to task; devote, dedicate, consecrate.

consume, use up, devour, swallow up; absorb, expend; wear.

Adj. **useful,** etc., 644; instrumental, subservient, utilitarian, pragmatic.

678. DISUSE.—*N.* disuse; forbearance, abstinence; relinquishment, abandonment; desuetude, disusage.

V. **not use;** do without, dispense with, let alone, forbear, abstain, spare, waive, neglect; keep back, reserve.

disuse; lay up, lay by, shelve; set aside, lay aside, leave off, have done with; supersede, discard, throw aside, relinquish; destroy, make away with, cast (*or* throw) overboard; dismantle.

Adj. **disused,** done with, run down, worn out; unemployed, unapplied, unexercised, uncalled for, not required.

679. MISUSE.—*N.* misuse, misusage, misapplication, misappropriation; abuse, profanation, desecration; waste.

V. **misuse,** misemploy, misapply; exploit; misappropriate; desecrate, abuse, profane.

overtask, overtax, overwork; squander, waste.

680. ACTION.—*N.* action, performance, perpetration, exercise, movement, operation, evolution, work, employment; labor, exertion, execution; procedure, conduct; handicraft; business, agency.

deed, act, stitch, touch, transaction, job, doings, dealings, proceeding, measure, step, maneuver, bout, passage, move, stroke, blow; feat, exploit, achievement; handiwork, craftsmanship, workmanship; manufacture; stroke of policy.

doer, worker, agent, etc., 690.

V. **do,** perform, execute, achieve, transact, enact: commit, perpetrate, inflict; exercise, prosecute, carry on, work, labor, practice, play; employ oneself, ply one's task; officiate, have in hand; shape one's course.

act, operate, take action, take steps, take in hand, put in practice, carry into execution, act upon.

Adj. **in action,** acting, in harness, on duty; at work; operative.

Adv. **in the act,** in the midst of; red-handed.

681. INACTION.—*N.* inaction, passiveness, watchful waiting; noninterference; neglect, etc., 460; inactivity, etc., 683; stagnation, vegetation, rest, loafing, want of occupation, unemployment; sinecure; soft snap, cinch [*both slang*].

V. **not do,** not act, not attempt; be inactive, abstain from doing, do nothing, hold, spare; leave (or let) alone; let be, let pass, let things take their course, live and let live; rest upon one's oars; stand aloof; refrain, relax one's efforts; desist, stop, pause, wait; waste time.

undo, do away with; take down, take to pieces; destroy, etc., 162.

Adj. passive; unoccupied, unemployed, out of employ (or work, a job); uncultivated, fallow.

Adv. at a stand.

682. ACTIVITY.—*N.* activity, animation, life, vivacity, spirit, verve, pep [*slang*], dash, go [*colloq.*], energy, snap, vim.

smartness, nimbleness, agility; quickness, velocity, alacrity, promptitude; dispatch, expedition, haste, etc., 684; punctuality.

eagerness, zeal, ardor, enthusiasm, earnestness, intentness, vigor, devotion, exertion.

industry, assiduity, assiduousness, sedulousness, laboriousness, drudgery, diligence, perseverance, etc., 604a.

vigilance, etc., 459; wakefulness; sleeplessness, restlessness; insomnia.

bustle, hustle [*colloq.*], movement, stir, fuss, ado, bother, fidget, flurry.

officiousness, dabbling, meddling; interference, intermeddling; butting in [*slang*], intrusiveness, intrigue.

man of action, busy bee; new broom; devotee, enthusiast, fanatic, zealot, hustler [*colloq.*], live wire, human dynamo [*both colloq.*].

meddler, intriguer, busybody.

V. be active, busy oneself in; stir, stir about, bestir oneself; speed, hasten, bustle, fuss; push, go ahead, push forward; make progress; toil, moil, drudge, plod, persist, persevere, hustle [*colloq.*], push [*colloq.*], keep moving, seize the opportunity, lose no time, dash off, make haste.

have a hand in, take an active part, put in one's oar, have a finger in the pie, dabble, intrigue; agitate.

meddle, tamper with, interfere, interpose; obtrude; butt in, horn in [*both slang*].

Adj. active, brisk, lively, animated, vivacious, alive, frisky, spirited; nimble, agile, light-footed, nimble-footed.

quick, prompt, instant, ready, alert, spry [*colloq. and dial.*], sharp, smart; fast, etc. (*swift*), 274; capable, expeditious, awake, go-ahead [*colloq.*], live [*colloq.*], hustling [*colloq.*], wide-awake.

enterprising, eager, ardent, strenuous, zealous, resolute.

industrious, assiduous, diligent, sedulous, painstaking, intent, indefatigable, persevering, unwearied, sleepless; busy, occupied; hard at work, hard at it; plodding, hard-working, businesslike.

bustling, restless, fussy, fidgety, pottering.

meddlesome, pushing, officious.

astir, stirring, afoot, on foot, in full swing; on the alert.

Adv. with life and spirit, with might and main, full tilt.

683. INACTIVITY.—*N.* inactivity; inaction, etc., 681; inertness, lull, quiescence; rust.

idleness, remissness, sloth, indolence, dawdling, puttering, relaxation.

languor, dullness, sluggishness, procrastination, torpor, stupor, somnolence, drowsiness, heaviness, hypnotism, lethargy.

sleep, slumber; Morpheus; coma, trance, catalepsy, hypnosis, dream; nap, doze, siesta; hibernation.

idler, drone, dawdler, truant; dead one [*slang*], dummy, bum [*slang*], tramp, hobo, beggar, lounge lizard [*slang*], lounger, loafer, slow-poke, laggard, sluggard.

V. **be inactive,** do nothing; dawdle, drawl, lag, hang back, slouch, loll, lounge, loaf, loiter; sleep at one's post; take it easy.

dally, dilly-dally, idle (*or* fritter, fool) away time; putter, dabble.

sleep, slumber, be asleep, oversleep, hibernate; doze, drowse, nap, take a nap; fall asleep, drop asleep; get sleepy, nod, go to bed, turn in.

languish, expend itself, flag, hang fire; relax.

Adj. **inactive,** motionless; unoccupied, unemployed.

indolent, lazy, slothful, idle, remiss, slack, inert, torpid, sluggish, logy, languid, listless; lackadaisical, maudlin; heavy, dull, leaden; dilatory, laggard, slow, flagging; puttering.

sleeping, asleep, comatose; in the arms (*or* lap) of Morpheus.

sleepy, dozy, drowsy, somnolent, lethargic, heavy, heavy with sleep; soporific, hypnotic; dreamy.

Adv. with half-shut eyes, half asleep; in dreams, in dreamland.

684. HASTE.—*N.* haste, urgency, dispatch, acceleration, spurt, forced march, rush, scurry, scuttle, dash; velocity, etc., 274; precipitancy, precipitation, impetuosity; hurry, drive, scramble, bustle, fidget, flurry.

V. **haste,** hasten, make haste, dash on, push on, press on *or* forward, hurry, scurry, bustle, flutter, scramble, plunge, dash off, rush, express; bestir oneself, etc. (*be active*), 682; lose no time, make short work of; work against time, work under pressure.

quicken, accelerate, expedite, precipitate, urge, whip, spur, flog, goad.

Adj. **hasty,** hurried, cursory, precipitate, headlong, furious, boisterous, impetuous, hotheaded; feverish, pushing.

in haste, in a hurry, in hot haste, breathless, hard-pressed, urgent.

Adv. **with haste,** with speed, in haste, apace, amain; at short notice, immediately, posthaste; by cable, by telegraph, by wireless [*colloq*.], by airplane, by return mail, by forced marches.

hastily, precipitately, helter-skelter, hurry-scurry, slapdash, slap-bang; full-tilt, full-drive; heels over head, headlong.

685. LEISURE.—*N.* **leisure,** convenience; spare time, vacant hour; time, time to spare; holiday, ease.

V. **have leisure,** take one's time (*or* leisure, ease); repose, etc., 687; move slowly, while away the time, be master of one's time, be an idle man.

686. EXERTION.—*N.* **exertion,** effort, strain, stress, tug, pull, throw, stretch, struggle, spell, spurt; dead lift, heft [*dial*.]; trouble, pains, duty; energy, etc. [*physical*], 171.

exercise, practice, play, gymnastics, field sports; breather [*colloq*.].

labor, work, toil, manual labor, sweat of one's brow, drudgery, slavery.

worker, plodder, laborer, drudge, slave; man of action; Hercules.

V. **labor,** work, toil, sweat, fag, drudge, slave, strive, strain; pull, tug, ply; ply the oar; exert oneself, bestir oneself (*be active*), 682.

work hard; rough it; put forth one's strength, buckle to, set one's shoulder to the wheel, do double duty; burn the candle at both ends, work (*or* fight) one's w y; do one's best, do one's utmost; take pains; strain every nerve; spare no efforts *or* pains.

Adj. **laborious,** elaborate; strained; toilsome, wearisome, burdensome; uphill; herculean.

hard-working, painstaking, strenuous, energetic, never idle.

Adv. with might and main, with all one's might, to the best of one's abilities, tooth and nail, hammer and tongs, heart and soul.

687. REPOSE.—*N.* **repose,** rest, sleep, etc., 683; relaxation, breathing time; halt, stay, pause, respite.

day of rest, Sabbath, Lord's day, Sunday; holiday, red-letter day, gala day; vacation, recess.

V. **repose,** rest, take rest, take one's ease; lie down, recline, go to rest (*or* bed, sleep).

relax, unbend, slacken, take breath, rest upon one's oars; pause, etc. (*cease*), 142; stay one's hand.

take a holiday, shut up shop; lie fallow.

Adj. **holiday,** festal; sabbatic *or* sabbatical.

688. FATIGUE.—*N.* **fatigue;** weariness, etc., 841; yawning, drowsiness, lassitude, tiredness, sweat.

faintness, fainting, swoon, exhaustion, collapse, prostration.

V. **be fatigued,** yawn, droop, sink; flag; gasp, pant, puff, blow, drop, swoon, faint, succumb.

fatigue, tire, bore, weary, flag, jade, harass, exhaust, wear out, prostrate.

tax, task, strain; overtask, overwork, overburden, overtax, overstrain, fag, fag out.

Adj. fatigued; weary, etc., 841; drowsy, haggard, toilworn, wayworn, footsore, faint; done up [*colloq.*], exhausted, prostrate, spent, ready to drop, all in [*slang*], dog-tired, tired to death, played out.

worn, worn out; battered, shattered, seedy [*colloq.*], enfeebled.

breathless, short of (*or* out of)breath, blown, puffing and blowing, short-breathed, broken-winded.

689. REFRESHMENT.—*N.* recuperation; recovery of strength, restoration, revival, etc., 660; repair, refreshment; relief, etc., 834.

V. refresh, brace, strengthen, reinvigorate; air, freshen up, recruit, regale, repair, restore, revive; get better, recover (*or* regain) one's strength, recuperate.

Adj. refreshing, recuperative.

690. AGENT.—*N.* agent, doer, actor, performer, perpetrator, operator; executor, executrix; practitioner, worker; minister, etc. (*instrument*), 631; representative, etc. (*commissioner*), 758, (*deputy*), 759; factor, steward; servant, etc., 746; factotum.

workman, artisan, craftsman, handicraftsman, mechanic, operative; workingman, laboring man; hewers of wood and drawers of water; laborer; hand, man, day laborer, journeyman, hack, drudge, roustabout.

maker, artificer, artist, wright, manufacturer, architect, contractor, builder, smith.

machinist, engineer, electrician.

workwoman, charwoman, dressmaker, modiste, seamstress, needlewoman, milliner, laundress, washerwoman.

coworker, associate, fellow worker, co-operator, colleague, confrere; force, staff, personnel.

691. WORKSHOP.—*N.* workshop, laboratory, manufactory, armory, arsenal, mill, factory, studio, atelier; hive, hive of industry, beehive; bindery; dock, dockyard, slip, yard, wharf; foundry, forge, furnace.

melting pot, crucible, caldron, mortar, alembic; matrix.

692. CONDUCT.—*N.* conduct, behavior; deportment, carriage, demeanor, guise, bearing, manner; course of conduct, line of action; role; process, ways, practice, procedure, method; dealing, transaction, business.

policy, tactics, game, generalship, statesmanship, strategy, plan.

management; government, etc., 693; stewardship, husbandry; housekeeping, ménage, regime, regimen, economy; economics, political economy.

career, life, course, walk, province, race, record; execution, treatment; campaign.

V. **transact,** execute; dispatch, proceed with, discharge; carry on (*or* through, out, into effect); work out; go through, get through; enact.

adopt a course, shape one's course, play one's part; shift for oneself, paddle one's own canoe; conduct; manage, etc. (*direct*), 693.

behave, conduct (*or* acquit, carry, comport, bear, demean) oneself.

Adj. **directive,** methodical, businesslike, practical, executive, strategic, economic.

693. DIRECTION.—*N.* **direction;** management, government, conduct, legislation, regulation, guidance, reins; steerage, pilotage, helm, rudder, needle, compass; guiding star, lodestar, polestar, cynosure.

ministry, administration; stewardship, proctorship; chair; agency.

supervision, superintendence; surveillance, oversight; eye of the master; control, charge; auspices; command, etc. (*authority*), 737.

statesmanship, statecraft, kingcraft, reins of government; director, etc., 694; seat, portfolio.

V. **direct,** manage, govern, conduct; order, prescribe, head, lead, regulate, guide, steer, pilot, take the helm, be at the helm; hold the reins, drive.

superintend, supervise; overlook, oversee, control, handle, look after, see to, administer, patronize; rule, etc. (*command*), 737; hold office.

Adj. **directing,** executive, gubernatorial, supervisory; statesmanlike.

Adv. **in charge of,** under the guidance of, under the auspices of; in control of, at the helm, at the head of.

694. DIRECTOR.—*N.* **director,** manager, governor, controller, superintendent, supervisor, overseer, supercargo, inspector, foreman, surveyor, taskmaster; master, etc., 745; leader, ringleader, agitator, demagogue, conductor, precentor, bellwether, file leader.

guide, pilot; helmsman, steersman; adviser, etc., 695.

driver, whip, charioteer; coachman, carman, cabman; postilion, muleteer, teamster; chauffeur, motorman, engine driver.

head, headman, chief, principal, president, speaker; chair, chairman; captain, etc. (*master*), 745; superior; prime minister, premier.

officer, functionary, minister, official, bureaucrat, officeholder.

statesman, strategist, legislator, lawgiver, politician, boss [*slang*], political dictator, wirepuller [*colloq.*], power behind the throne, kingmaker.

steward, factor, agent, bailiff, factotum, major-domo, seneschal, housekeeper, shepherd; proctor, curator, librarian.

695. ADVICE.—*N.* advice, counsel, word to the wise, suggestion, recommendation, advocacy; consultation; exhortation, expostulation, dissuasion, admonition; guidance.

instruction, charge, injunction, message, speech from the throne.

adviser, prompter; counsel, counselor; monitor, mentor, sage, wise man; teacher, etc., 540; physician; arbiter, referee, judge.

consultation, conference, parley, powwow; reference.

V. advise, counsel, suggest, prompt, recommend, prescribe, advocate, exhort, persuade.

enjoin, enforce, charge, instruct, call, call upon, request, dictate.

expostulate, dissuade, admonish, warn.

confer, consult, refer to, call in; follow, take (*or* follow) advice.

696. COUNCIL.—*N.* council, committee, privy council, court, chamber, cabinet, board, directorate, syndicate, bench, staff.

Ecclesiastical: convocation, synod, congregation, church, chapter, vestry; consistory, conventicle, conclave, convention.

legislature, parliament, congress, national council, states-general, diet.

Duma [Russia], Storthing *or* Storting [Norway], Rigsdag [Denmark], Riksdag [Sweden], Cortes [Spain], Reichsrath *or* Reichsrat [Austria], Volksraad [Dutch], Dail Eireann [Sinn Fein].

upper house, upper chamber, first chamber, senate, legislative council, House of Lords, House of Peers; Bundesrath *or* Bundesrat [Ger.], federal council, Lagting [Nor.], Landsthing [Den.].

lower house, lower chamber, second chamber, house of representatives, House of Commons, the house, legislative assembly, chamber of deputies; Odelsting [Nor.], Folkething [Den.], Reichstag [Ger.].

assembly, caucus, clique; meeting, sitting, séance, conference, hearing, session, palaver; council fire, powwow.

Representatives: congressman, M.C., senator, representative; member, member of parliament, M.P., assemblyman, councilor.

Adj. curule, congressional, senatorial, parliamentary; synodic *or* synodical.

697. PRECEPT.—*N.* precept, direction, instruction, charge; prescript, prescription; recipe, receipt; golden rule; maxim, etc., 496.

rule, canon, law, code, convention; unwritten law; canon law; act, statute, rubric, stage direction, regulation; model, form, formula, technicality.

order, etc. (*command*), 741.

698. SKILL.—*N.* skill, skillfulness, address, dexterity, adroitness, expertness, proficiency, competence, craft; facility, knack, trick, sleight; mastery, excellence, sleight of hand, etc. (*deception*), 545.

accomplishment, acquirement, attainment; art, science; finish, technique.

worldly wisdom, knowledge of the world, *savoir-faire* [F.]; tact; mother wit, discretion, finesse; management.

cleverness, talent, ability, ingenuity, capacity, talents, faculty, endowment, forte, turn, gift, genius, intelligence, sharpness, readiness, aptness, aptitude, resourcefulness; felicity, capability, qualification.

expert, adept, etc., 700.

masterpiece, masterwork, chef-d'oeuvre [F.].

V. **be skillful,** excel in, be master of; have a turn for.

take advantage of, make the most of, profit by, make a hit, make a virtue of necessity, make hay while the sun shines.

Adj. **skillful,** dexterous, adroit, expert, apt, handy, quick, deft, ready, smart, proficient, good at, at home in, master of, conversant with; masterly, crack [*colloq.*], crackajack [*slang*], accomplished.

experienced, practiced, skilled, up in, in practice, competent, efficient, qualified, capable, fitted, fit for, trained, initiated, sophisticated, prepared, primed, finished.

clever, able, ingenious, felicitous, gifted, talented, resourceful, inventive; shrewd, sharp, cunning; neat-handed, fine-fingered; nimble-fingered, ambidextrous, sure-footed.

technical, artistic, scientific, workmanlike, businesslike, statesmanlike.

Adv. **skillfully,** artistically, with skill, with fine technique, with consummate skill; like a machine.

699. UNSKILLFULNESS.—*N.* **unskillfulness,** want of skill, incompetence, inability, infelicity, clumsiness, inaptitude, inexperience; disqualification.

mismanagement, misconduct, bad policy, impolicy; maladministration; misrule, misgovernment.

blunder, act of folly, bungle, botch, bad job, sad work.

bungler, etc., 701; fool, etc., 501.

V. **bungle,** blunder, muff [*esp. baseball*], boggle, fumble, botch, mar, spoil, flounder, stumble, trip; mismanage, misdirect, misapply.

mistake, take the shadow for the substance, bark up the wrong tree; be in the wrong box [*colloq.*]; lose one's way, miss one's way; fall into a trap.

Adj. **unskillful,** unskilled, inexpert, incompetent, bungling, awkward, clumsy, gawky, unhandy, maladroit; stupid, ill-qualified, unfit; raw, green, inexperienced; rusty, out of practice.

unaccustomed, unused, untrained, uninitiated; unbusinesslike, unpractical, shiftless; unstatesmanlike.

ill-advised, misadvised; ill-devised, ill-judged, ill-contrived, ill-conducted; misguided, foolish, wild; infelicitous.

700. EXPERT.—*N.* expert, adept, proficient, connoisseur, master, master hand; top sawyer; prima donna, first fiddle; past master.

picked man; medalist, prizeman.

veteran, old stager, old campaigner, man of business, man of the world.

genius; mastermind, master spirit; prodigy of learning, walking encyclopedia, mine of information.

man of cunning, diplomatist, diplomat, Machiavellian; politician, tactician strategist.

701. BUNGLER.—*N.* bungler, blunderer, blunderhead; fumbler, lubber, clown, lout, duffer [*colloq.*]; butter-fingers, muff, muffer [*all colloq.*]; awkward squad; novice, greenhorn.

landlubber, fresh-water sailor, fair-weather sailor, horse marine.

sloven, slattern, slut.

702. CUNNING.—*N.* cunning, craft, subtlety, maneuvering, temporization; circumvention; chicane, chicanery; sharp practice, knavery, jugglery, concealment, guile, duplicity, foul play.

diplomacy, politics, Machiavellianism; gerrymander, jobbery, back-stairs influence.

artifice, art, device, machination; plot, maneuver, stratagem, dodge, wile, trick, trickery, ruse, finesse, subterfuge, evasion, white lie, gold brick [*colloq.*], imposture, deception, net, trap.

schemer, trickster, sly boots [*humorous*], fox, reynard; intriguer, man of cunning.

V. intrigue, live by one's wits; maneuver, gerrymander, finesse, double, temporize, circumvent, outdo, get the better of, throw off one's guard; surprise, waylay, undermine, flatter; have an ax to grind.

Adj. cunning, crafty, artful, skillful; subtle, feline, deep, profound, designing, timeserving, tricky, wily, sly, insidious, stealthy, underhand, double-faced, shifty, deceptive; deceitful, crooked; shrewd, acute; sharp, canny, astute, knowing.

703. ARTLESSNESS.—*N.* artlessness, unsophistication, simplicity, innocence, candor, sincerity, singleness of purpose, honesty.

rough diamond, matter-of-fact man; *enfant terrible* [F.].

V. be artless, think aloud; speak one's mind; be free with one, call a spade a spade; tell the truth, the whole truth, and nothing but the truth.

Adj. artless, natural, pure, confiding, simple, plain, unsophisticated, unaffected, naïve; sincere, frank, open, candid, ingenuous, guileless; unsuspicious, honest, childlike; innocent, straightforward, aboveboard; single-minded.

matter-of-fact, plain-spoken, outspoken; blunt, downright, direct, unflattering, unvarnished.

Adv. in plain words (*or* English); without mincing the matter.

704. DIFFICULTY.—*N.* difficulty, hardness, impracticability, uphill work, herculean task; dead weight, dead lift.

dilemma, predicament, fix [*colloq.*], quandary, embarrassment, deadlock, perplexity, intricacy, entanglement, knot, Gordian knot, maze, coil, strait, pass, pinch, rub, critical situation, exigency, crisis, trial, emergency, scrape, slough, quagmire, hot water [*colloq.*], pickle, stew, imbroglio, mess, muddle, botch, hitch, stumbling block.

vexed question, poser, puzzle, knotty point, paradox; hard nut to crack, crux.

V. be difficult, go against the grain, try one's patience, go hard with one, pose, perplex, bother, nonplus.

flounder, boggle [*local*], struggle, stick fast; come to a deadlock.

render difficult, enmesh, encumber, embarrass, entangle; spike one's guns.

Adj. difficult, hard, tough [*colloq.*]; troublesome, toilsome, irksome; laborious, onerous, arduous, herculean, formidable.

awkward, unwieldy, unmanageable, intractable, stubborn, perverse, refractory, knotted, knotty, thorny; pathless, trackless, intricate.

embarrassing, perplexing, delicate, ticklish, critical, thorny.

in difficulty, in hot water [*colloq.*], in a fix [*colloq.*], in a scrape, between Scylla and Charybdis; on the horns of a dilemma; on the rocks; reduced to straits; hard-pressed; run hard; pinched, straitened; hard up [*slang*]; puzzled, at a loss, at one's wits' end, at a standstill; nonplused, stranded, aground.

Adv. with much ado; uphill, upstream; in the teeth of; against the grain.

705. FACILITY.—*N.* facility, ease, easiness, capability, feasibility, practicability; flexibility, pliancy, smoothness, plain sailing; mere child's play; cinch, snap [*both slang*].

V. be easy, run smoothly; have full play, obey the helm, work well, work smoothly.

facilitate, smooth, ease, lighten, free, clear, disencumber, disembarrass, disentangle, extricate, unravel, unknot; humor, leave a loophole, leave the matter open; give full play, make way for, pave the way, bridge over.

Adj. easy, facile; feasible, practicable, within reach, gettable, accessible.

manageable, tractable; submissive; yielding, ductile, tractable, pliant.

unburdened, unencumbered, unloaded, unobstructed, untrammeled; unrestrained, free, at ease, light.

Adv. **easily,** readily, expertly, adroitly, smoothly, swimmingly, with no effort.

706. HINDRANCE.—*N.* **prevention,** obstruction, stoppage, interruption, interception, hindrance, embarrassment, constriction, restriction, restraint, etc., 751.

interference, interposition, obtrusion; discouragement, disapproval, disapprobation, opposition.

impediment, obstacle, obstruction, knot, snag, hitch, contretemps, stumbling block, lion in the path.

check; encumbrance; clog, brake, anchor; bit, snaffle, curb; drag, load, burden, onus, impedimenta; dead weight; lumber, pack; nightmare, incubus; stay, stop; preventive, prophylactic.

drawback, objection; difficulty, etc., 704; obstacle; ill-wind, head wind; trammel, tether.

damper, wet blanket, kill-joy, dog in the manger, usurper, interloper, opponent; filibusterer.

V. **hinder,** impede, filibuster, embarrass.

avert, keep off, stave off, ward off; obviate; turn aside, draw off, prevent, nip in the bud; retard, slacken, check, counteract, countercheck, preclude, debar, inhibit, restrict.

obstruct, stop, stay, bar, bolt, lock; block, barricade; dam up, put on the brake, put a stop to, interrupt, intercept, oppose, interfere, interpose.

encumber, cramp, hamper; clog, cumber, handicap; choke, saddle with, load with, overload, overwhelm, lumber, entrammel, trammel, incommode, discommode, discompose, corner.

thwart, frustrate, disconcert, balk, foil; circumvent, baffle, override, defeat, spoil, mar, clip the wings of, cripple, damp, dishearten, discountenance, undermine.

Adj. **obstructive,** intrusive, meddlesome; onerous, burdensome; cumbrous, cumbersome.

Adv. **in the way,** with everything against one, through all obstacles, under many difficulties.

707. AID.—*N.* **aid,** assistance, help, succor; support, lift, advance, furtherance, promotion.

patronage, auspices, countenance, favor, interest, advocacy.

sustenance, maintenance, nutrition, nourishment; manna in the wilderness, food, means, subsidy, bounty.

relief, rescue; ministry, ministration; supernatural aid; *deus ex machina* [L.].

supplies, re-enforcements, contingents, recruits, support, ally.

V. **aid,** assist, help, succor, lend a hand; contribute, subscribe to;

take by the hand, take in tow; relieve, rescue; set on one's legs, give new life to, be the making of; re-enforce, recruit; promote, further, forward, advance; speed, expedite, quicken, hasten.

support, sustain, uphold, prop, hold up, bolster.

nourish, nurture, nurse, cradle, dry-nurse, suckle, foster, cherish, cultivate.

serve; do service to, tender to, pander to, minister to; tend, attend, wait on; take care of; entertain, regale.

oblige, accommodate, consult the wishes of; humor, cheer, encourage.

second, stand by, back, back up; abet, work for, stick up for [*colloq.*], stick by, take up (*or* espouse) the cause of; advocate, countenance, patronize, smile upon, favor, befriend, side with.

Adj. **aiding,** auxiliary, adjuvant, helpful, subservient, accessary, accessory, subsidiary.

friendly, amicable, favorable, propitious, well disposed, neighborly, obliging, at one's beck.

Adv. in aid of, on (*or* in) behalf of, in favor of, in the name of, in furtherance of, on account of, for the sake of.

708. OPPOSITION.—*N.* **opposition,** antagonism, contrariness, contrariety; contravention, counteraction; resistance, etc., 719; hindrance, restraint, etc., 751.

collision, conflict, discord, want of harmony; filibuster, clashing.

competition, rivalry, emulation, race, contest; tug of war.

V. **oppose,** counteract, withstand, etc. (*resist*), 719; hinder, restrain; obstruct, etc., 706; antagonize, cross, thwart, pit against, face, confront, cope with; protest (*or* vote) against; disfavor; contradict, contravene, belie.

encounter, meet, stem, breast, resist, grapple with, kick against the pricks; contend with (*or* against), do battle with (*or* against).

compete, emulate, rival; force out, drive one out of business.

Adj. **adverse,** antagonistic, oppugnant, contrary, at variance, at issue, at war with, in opposition, at daggers drawn.

unfavorable, unpropitious, unfriendly, hostile, inimical, cross.

competitive, emulous, cutthroat; in rivalry with, in friendly rivalry.

Adv. **against,** counter to, in conflict with, at cross-purposes.

in spite, in despite, in defiance; in the teeth (*or* face) of; across; athwart.

709. CO-OPERATION.—*N.* **co-operation,** concert, concurrence, complicity, collusion; participation; union, combination.

association, alliance, joint stock, partnership, pool, gentleman's agreement; confederation, coalition, federation, fusion; logrolling; freemasonry.

unanimity, *esprit de corps* [F.], party spirit, school spirit; clanship, partisanship; concord.

V. co-operate, concur; conduce, combine, pool, unite one's efforts, pull together, stand shoulder to shoulder; act in concert, join forces, fraternize; conspire, concert.

side with, take sides with, go along with, join hands with, make common cause with, unite with, join with, take part with, cast in one's lot with; rally round.

participate, be a party to, lend oneself to; chip in [*colloq.*], bear part in, second, espouse a cause.

Adj. co-operating, in league, hand in glove with; favorable to, unopposed.

Adv. unanimously, as one man, shoulder to shoulder.

710. OPPONENT.—*N.* opponent, antagonist, adversary; opposition; assailant, enemy, etc., 891.

oppositionist, wrangler, disputant; filibuster, filibusterer, extremist, bitter-ender, irreconcilable, obstructionist.

malcontent; demagogue, reactionist; anarchist, Red.

rival, competitor, contestant: the field.

711. AUXILIARY.—*N.* auxiliary, recruit, assistant, help, helper, helpmate, helping hand; colleague, partner, confrere, co-operator, coadjutor, collaborator, associate, right hand, right-hand man.

ally; friend, etc., 890; confidant (*fem.* confidante), alter ego [L.], pal [*slang*], chum [*colloq.*], mate.

puppet, cat's-paw, creature, tool; satellite, adherent, parasite, dependent.

confederate; accomplice; accessory.

upholder, seconder, backer, supporter, abettor, advocate, partisan, champion, patron, friend at court, mediator.

friend in need, special providence, guardian angel, fairy godmother, tutelary genius.

712. PARTY.—*N.* party, faction, denomination, class, communion, side, crew, team; band, horde, posse, phalanx; caste, family, clan.

community, body, fellowship, party spirit, solidarity, freemasonry; fraternity, sodality, brotherhood, sisterhood, sorority; fraternal order.

gang, tong [Chin.], bolsheviki, bolshevists, ring, machine, junto, cabal.

clique, knot, circle, set, coterie; club, casino.

corporation, corporate body, guild, company, partnership, firm, house; combine [*colloq.*], trust; holding company, merger.

society, association; institute, institution; union; trade-union;

league, syndicate, alliance, combination, coalition, federation, confederation, confederacy.

staff; cast, dramatis personae [L.].

V. unite, join, band together, club together, co-operate, etc., 709; associate, federate, federalize.

Adj. joint, federal, corporate, confederated, organized, leagued, syndicated; fraternal, Masonic, institutional, denominational; cliquish, cliquy.

Adv. side by side, hand in hand, shoulder to shoulder, in the same boat.

713. DISCORD.—*N.* discord, dissidence, dissonance, disagreement, jar, clash, break, shock.

variance, difference, dissension, misunderstanding, cross-purposes, odds, division, split, rupture, disruption, disunion, breach, schism, feud, faction.

polemics; litigation, strife, warfare, outbreak, open rupture, declaration of war.

quarrel, dispute, tiff, bicker, squabble, altercation, words, high words, family jars.

broil, brawl, row [*colloq.*], racket, hubbub, imbroglio, fracas, scrimmage, rumpus [*colloq.*], squall, riot, disturbance, commotion.

subject of dispute, ground of quarrel, battleground, disputed point, bone of contention, apple of discord, question at issue.

V. disagree, clash, jar, conflict, misunderstand, live like cat and dog; differ; dissent, etc., 489.

quarrel, fall out, dispute, litigate; controvert, squabble, altercate, row [*colloq.*], wrangle, bicker, nag, spar, brawl.

split, break with; declare war, try conclusions, join issue, pick a quarrel; sow dissension, embroil, entangle, disunite, widen the breach; set (*or* pit) against.

Adj. discordant, dissident, out of tune, dissonant, harsh, grating, jangling, unmelodious; on bad terms, dissentient, unreconciled, unpacified; inconsistent, contradictory, incongruous.

quarrelsome, heated, unpacific, controversial, polemic, disputatious, factious.

at strife, at odds, at loggerheads, at daggers drawn, at variance, at issue, at cross-purposes, at sixes and sevens, embroiled, torn, disunited.

714. CONCORD.—*N.* concord, accord, harmony, homologue, correspondence, agreement, sympathy, response; union, unison, unity, peace, unanimity; happy family.

amity, etc. (*friendship*), 888; alliance, *entente cordiale* [F.], good understanding, conciliation, arbitration, reunion.

peacemaker, intercessor, interceder, mediator.

V. **agree,** accord, harmonize with, fraternize, go hand in hand, run parallel, concur, co-operate, pull together, sing in chorus.

side with, sympathize with; go with, chime in with, fall in with; assent, etc., 488; reciprocate.

smooth, pour oil on the troubled waters, keep in good humor, meet halfway; mediate, intercede.

Adj. **concordant,** congenial; in accord, harmonious, united, cemented, allied, friendly, fraternal, conciliatory, of one mind.

Adv. **unanimously,** with one voice, in concert with, hand in hand.

715. DEFIANCE.—*N.* **defiance,** dare, defial; challenge; threat, etc., 909; war cry, war whoop.

V. **defy,** dare, beard, brave, set at defiance, set at naught, hurl defiance at; laugh to scorn; disobey, etc., 742; threaten; challenge.

Adj. **defiant,** rebellious, bold, insolent, reckless, contemptuous, greatly daring, regardless of consequences.

Adv. in the teeth of; under one's very nose; in open rebellion.

716. ATTACK.—*N.* **attack,** assault, onset, onslaught, charge.

aggression, offense; incursion, inroad, invasion; irruption, outbreak; sally, sortie, raid, foray.

storm, storming, boarding, escalade; siege, investment, bombardment, cannonade, barrage; zero hour.

fire, volley, fusilade; sharpshooting, broadside, cross-fire.

thrust, lunge, pass, home thrust; cut.

assailant, aggressor, invader; sharpshooter, dead shot.

V. **attack,** assault, assail; set upon, pounce upon, fall upon, charge; enter the lists.

show fight, take the offensive; strike at, thrust at; aim (*or* deal) a blow at; be the aggressor, strike the first blow, fire the first shot; advance (*or* march) against, march upon, invade, harry.

close with, come to close quarters, bring to bay, come to blows.

fire upon, fire at, draw a bead on, shoot at, pop at, level at, open fire, pepper, bombard, shell, fire a volley.

besiege, beset, beleaguer, invest; sap, mine; storm, board, scale the walls, go over the top.

cut and thrust, bayonet, butt; kick, strike, etc., 276; horsewhip, whip.

Adj. **aggressive,** offensive; up in arms; amuck.

Adv. on the warpath; over the top; at bay.

717. DEFENSE.—*N.* **defense,** protection, guard, ward; guardianship.

self-defense, self-preservation; resistance, etc., 719.

safeguard, screen, fortification, bulwark, trench, mine, dugout;

moat, ditch, intrenchment; rampart, dike; parapet, battlement, bastion, redoubt, embankment, mound, bank, breastwork, earthwork, fieldwork; buttress, abutment, fence, wall, paling, palisade, stockade; barrier, barricade, boom; portcullis, barbed-wire entanglements.

stronghold, hold, fastness, asylum, keep, donjon, citadel, capitol, castle; tower, fortress, fort, barrack; blockhouse.

[**protective devices**] buffer, fender, cowcatcher, armor; mail, shield, buckler.

defender, protector, guardian, bodyguard, champion; knight-errant, paladin; garrison.

V. **defend,** guard, ward (*or* beat) off, shield, screen, shroud; garrison, man; fence, intrench, arm, accouter.

repel, parry, put to flight; hold (*or* keep) at bay; resist invasion, stand siege, stand (*or* act) on the defensive, show fight; stand one's ground, hold, stand in the gap.

Adj. **defensive;** armed, armed at all points (*or* to the teeth); panoplied, accoutered; iron-plated, ironclad; bulletproof, bombproof; protective.

Adv. on the defensive, in defense, in self-defense; at bay.

718. RETALIATION.—*N.* **retaliation,** reprisal, retort; counterstroke, counterblast; retribution.

requital, desert; tit for tat, give-and-take, blow for blow, an eye for an eye; boomerang.

recrimination, accusation; revenge, etc., 919; compensation.

V. **retaliate,** retort, turn upon; pay, pay off, pay back; cap, match; reciprocate, turn the tables upon, return the compliment; exchange blows; give and take, be quits, be even with; pay off old scores.

Adj. **retaliatory,** retaliative, retributive, recriminatory, reciprocal.

719. RESISTANCE.—*N.* **resistance,** stand, front, opposition, recalcitrance, repugnance, repulsion.

repulse, rebuff, snub.

insurrection, revolt, etc., 742; strike, lockout; boycott; riot.

V. **resist;** withstand; stand, stand firm (*or* fast, one's ground), stick it out [*colloq.*].

face, confront, breast the wave, stem the tide; grapple with; show a bold front, make a stand.

oppose, etc., 708; fly in the face of; withstand an attack, rise up in arms, strike, turn out, boycott; revolt, rebel; repel, repulse.

Adj. **resistant,** resistive, refractory, repugnant, recalcitrant, repulsive, repellent; up in arms.

unconquerable, stubborn, unconquered; indomitable, unyielding.

720. CONTENTION.—*N.* contention, strife, contest, struggle; belligerency, pugnacity, opposition.

controversy, polemics; debate, war of words, paper war, high words, quarrel, litigation.

competition, rivalry, match, race; athletics, athletic sports; games of skill.

conflict, skirmish; encounter, rencounter, rencontre, collision, affair, brush, fracas, etc. (*discord*), 713; clash of arms; tussle, scuffle, bout, broil, fray, affray, fight, battle, combat, action, engagement, joust, tournament, tourney; pitched battle; guerrilla (*or* irregular) warfare; death struggle, Armageddon.

duel, single combat, satisfaction, passage of arms, affair of honor; hostile meeting, appeal to arms.

V. contend, contest, strive, struggle, scramble, wrestle; spar, exchange blows, tussle, tilt, box, fence; skirmish, fight; wrangle; oppose, etc., 708; join issue.

compete (*or* cope, vie, race) with, emulate, rival; run a race.

Adj. contentious, combative, bellicose, belligerent, warlike, quarrelsome, pugnacious, pugilistic.

athletic, gymnastic, competitive, rival.

721. PEACE.—*N.* peace, amity, etc. (*friendship*), 888; harmony, concord, tranquillity, truce, pipe of peace, calumet.

piping time of peace, quiet life; neutrality; pacifism.

V. be at peace, keep the peace, make peace, pacify; be a pacifist.

Adj. pacific; peaceable, peaceful; calm, tranquil, untroubled, halcyon; bloodless; neutral, pacifistic.

722. WARFARE.—*N.* warfare, fighting, hostilities; war, arms, the sword, bloodshed; Mars.

appeal to arms (*or* the sword); ordeal (*or* wager) of battle; declaration of war.

battle array, campaign, crusade, expedition; warpath.

art of war, rules of war, the war game, tactics, strategy, generalship.

battle, conflict, etc. (*contention*), 720; service, campaigning, active service, tented field; war to the death (*or* knife).

war medal, military medal, Congressional Medal, Victoria Cross, V. C. [Eng.], *Croix de guerre* [F.], *Médaille militaire* [F.], Iron Cross [Ger.].

V. war, make war, go to war, declare war, wage war, arm, take up (*or* appeal to) arms; take the field, give battle, engage, fight, combat, contend, battle with.

serve; enroll, enlist; be on service (*or* active service), campaign;

smell powder, be under fire; be on the warpath, keep the field; take by storm; go over the top [*colloq.*]; sell one's life dearly.

Adj. armed, in (*or* under) arms, in battle array, in the field; embattled; battled.

warlike, belligerent, combative, bellicose, martial, military, militant; soldierly, chivalrous; civil, internecine; irregular, guerrilla.

Adv. in the thick of the fray, in the cannon's mouth; at the sword's point, at the point of the bayonet.

723. PACIFICATION.—*N.* pacification, conciliation, reconciliation, reconcilement; accommodation, arrangement, adjustment; terms, compromise; amnesty.

peace offering; olive branch; calumet, peace pipe.

truce, armistice; suspension of arms (*or* hostilities); truce of God; flag of truce, white flag.

V. pacify, tranquillize, compose, allay, reconcile, propitiate, placate, conciliate, meet halfway, hold out the olive branch, heal the breach, make peace, restore harmony, bring to terms.

raise a siege, sheathe the sword, bury the hatchet, lay down one's arms, turn swords into plowshares.

Adj. conciliatory, pacificatory.

724. MEDIATION.—*N.* mediation, mediatorship, intervention, interposition, interference, intercession; parley, negotiation, arbitration, good offices.

mediator, intercessor, peacemaker, negotiator, go-between, diplomatist, propitiator; umpire, arbitrator.

V. mediate, intercede, interpose, interfere, intervene; step in, negotiate; meet halfway; arbitrate, propitiate.

Adj. mediatory, propitiatory, diplomatic.

725. SUBMISSION.—*N.* submission, yielding, acquiescence, compliance, submissiveness, deference, nonresistance, obedience.

surrender, cession, capitulation, resignation, backdown [*colloq.*].

obeisance, homage, kneeling, genuflection, curtsy, kowtow [Chinese], salaam [Oriental], prostration.

V. submit, succumb, yield, defer to; bend, stoop; accede, resign oneself.

surrender, cede, capitulate, come to terms, lay down one's arms, strike one's flag, give way (*or* ground, in, up); obey.

yield obeisance, kneel to, bow to, pay homage to, cringe to, truckle to; kneel, bow submission, curtsy, kowtow [Chinese].

Adj. submissive, resigned, crouching, prostrate; unresisting, humble.

untenable, indefensible, insupportable, unsupportable.

726. COMBATANT.—*N.* combatant; belligerent, assailant, swashbuckler, duelist, swordsman; competitor, rival.

fighter, fighting man, prize fighter, pugilist, bruiser; gladiator.

soldier, warrior, brave, man at arms, guardsman, gendarme [F.]; campaigner, veteran; military man; knight; myrmidon, mercenary, irregular, free lance, franctireur; private, Tommy Atkins [Brit.], doughboy [slang], rank and file; sepoy [India], spearman, pikeman; archer, bowman; musketeer, rifleman, sharpshooter, skirmisher; grenadier, fusileer, infantryman, foot soldier, chasseur, zouave, artilleryman, gunner, cannoneer, engineer; cavalryman, trooper, dragoon; cuirassier, hussar, lancer; recruit, rookie [slang], conscript, drafted man, enlisted man.

officer, etc. (commander), 745; subaltern, ensign, standard-bearer.

horse and foot; cavalry, horse, light horse; infantry, foot, rifles; artillery, horse artillery, field artillery, gunners; military train.

armed force, troops, soldiery, military, forces, the army, standing army, regulars, the line; militia, national guard, state guard, yeomanry, volunteers, minutemen [Am. hist.]; posse; guards, yeomen of the guard, beefeaters [Eng.], lifeguards, household troops, bodyguard.

levy, draft; raw levies, awkward squad.

army, army corps; division, column, wing, detachment, garrison, flying column, brigade, regiment, battalion, squadron, company, battery, section, platoon, squad; picket, guard, legion, phalanx, cohort.

navy, first line of defense, wooden walls, naval forces, fleet, flotilla, armada, squadron; man-of-war's man, etc. (sailor), 269; marines.

man-of-war, line-of-battle ship, ship of the line, battleship, warship, ironclad, war vessel, superdreadnought, dreadnought, cruiser; torpedo boat, destroyer, gunboat, submarine, submersible, U-boat [Ger.]; submarine chaser, monitor; frigate, sloop of war, corvet, flagship; privateer; troopship, transport, tender.

airplane, hydroplane, seaplane, flying boat; glider; divebomber, bomber, Flying Fortress; dirigible, blimp [cant]; zeppelin, etc. (aeronautics), 273.

727. ARMS.—N. arms; arm, weapon, deadly weapon; armament; armor.

side arms, sword, cold steel, naked steel, steel, blade; broadsword, saber, cutlass, scimitar, rapier, foil, dagger, poniard, dirk, stiletto, bowie knife, bayonet.

ax, battle-ax, poleax, halberd, tomahawk, bill, partisan.

spear, lance, pike, assagai, javelin, dart, arrow; harpoon, boomerang; oxgoad, ankus.

club, war club, mace, truncheon, staff, bludgeon, cudgel, shillelagh, quarterstaff; billy, life preserver, blackjack.

bow, crossbow, long bow; catapult, sling.

firearms; gun, piece; artillery, ordnance; park, battery; cannon, fieldpiece, field gun, siege gun, mortar, howitzer, pompom, seventy-five [French rapid-fire 75-mm. field gun]; Lewis gun.

small arms; musketry; musket, firelock, fowling piece, rifle, carbine, blunderbuss, matchlock, harquebus, shotgun, breechloader, muzzle-loader, magazine rifle, automatic pistol, automatic, revolver, repeater; shooting iron [slang], six-shooter [colloq.], gun [colloq. for revolver or pistol], pistol.

missile, bolt, projectile, shot, ball, slug; grape, shrapnel, grenade, shell, bomb, depth bomb, smoke bomb, gas bomb; bullet; dumdum (or explosive, expanding) bullet; torpedo.

ammunition; powder, powder and shot; explosive; gunpowder; dynamite, cordite; cartridge; poison gas, mustard gas, chlorine gas, tear gas, etc.

728. ARENA.—N. arena, field, platform; scene of action, theater, walk, course; hustings; stage, boards, amphitheater,

coliseum, colosseum; hippodrome, circus, race course, turf, cockpit, bear garden, gymnasium, ring, lists; campus, playing field, playground.

battlefield, battleground, field of battle; no man's land [*First World War*]; theater (*or* seat) of war.

729. COMPLETION.—*N.* completion; accomplishment, achievement, fulfillment, performance, execution; dispatch, consummation, culmination; finish, conclusion; limit, close, finale, denouement, issue, upshot, result.

V. complete, perfect, effect, accomplish, achieve, compass, consummate, bring to maturity (*or* perfection); elaborate.

do, execute, make, work out, enact, dispatch, knock off [*colloq.*], finish off, dispose of, perform, discharge, fulfill, realize; carry out (*or* into effect).

do thoroughly, not do by halves, drive home; carry through, deliver the goods [*colloq.*].

finish, bring to a close, wind up, clinch, seal, put the last (*or* finishing) touch to; crown, crown all; cap.

Adj. conclusive, final, crowning, exhaustive, complete, mature, perfect, consummate, thorough.

Adv. to crown all, as a last stroke, as a fitting climax.

730. NONCOMPLETION.—*N.* noncompletion, nonfulfillment, nonperformance, neglect, etc., 460; shortcoming, incompleteness; drawn battle, drawn game.

V. leave unfinished, leave undone, neglect, etc., 460; let alone, let slip; lose sight of.

fall short of, do things by halves, hang fire; collapse.

Adj. incomplete, uncompleted, unfinished, unaccomplished, unperformed, unexecuted; sketchy; sterile.

Adv. without (*or* lacking) the final touches.

731. SUCCESS—*N.* success, successfulness; progress; advance; good fortune, prosperity, etc., 734; profit.

trump card; hit, stroke, master stroke; ten-strike [*colloq.*]; checkmate; prize.

mastery, advantage over; upper hand, whip hand; ascendancy, conquest, victory, walkover [*colloq.*], triumph.

victor, conqueror, master, champion, winner; master of the situation (*or* position).

V. succeed, be successful, gain one's end (*or* ends); crown with success; gain (*or* attain, carry, secure) a point *or* an object; get there [*slang*]; manage to, contrive to; accomplish, effect; come off successfully, take (*or* carry) by storm; gain the day (*or* prize, palm); carry all before one, score a success.

make progress, etc. (*advance*), 282; win (*or* make, work) one's way; speed; turn to account, prosper, etc., 734; strike oil [*slang*], make one's fortune.

triumph, be triumphant, gain a victory (*or* an advantage); surmount (*or* overcome) a difficulty, stem the torrent, weather the storm, master; distance, surpass, win.

defeat, conquer, discomfit, vanquish, overcome, overthrow, overpower, overmaster, outwit, outdo, outmaneuver, outgeneral, checkmate, beat, rout, floor, worst, lick to a frazzle [*colloq.*]; settle [*colloq.*], do for [*colloq.*], subdue, subjugate, reduce.

quell, silence, put down, confound, nonplus, baffle, circumvent, elude; drive to the wall.

avail, answer, answer the purpose; prevail, take effect, do, turn out well, take [*colloq.*], tell, bear fruit.

Adj. **successful;** prosperous, etc., 734; triumphant, crowned with success, victorious; unbeaten.

Adv. **successfully,** with flying colors, in triumph, swimmingly.

732. FAILURE.—*N.* failure, unsuccess, nonsuccess, nonfulfillment; labor in vain, no go [*colloq.*], inefficacy; vain attempt; frustration, disappointment.

blunder, error, etc., 495; fault, omission, miss, oversight, slip, trip, stumble; step, *faux pas* [F.]; scrape, mess, muddle, botch, fiasco.

mishap, etc. (*misfortune*), 735; split, collapse, smash, blow, explosion.

repulse, rebuff, defeat, rout, overthrow, discomfiture; beating, drubbing; subjugation, checkmate.

fall, downfall, ruin, perdition, wreck; deathblow; bankruptcy.

V. **fail,** be unsuccessful, make vain efforts, labor in vain; flunk [*colloq.*]; bring to naught, make nothing of, fall short of, go to the wall [*colloq.*], lick the dust; be defeated, have the worst of it, lose the day, lose; succumb.

miss, miss one's aim (*or* the mark), slip, trip, stumble, blunder, miscarry.

flounder, falter, limp, halt, hobble, fall, tumble, run aground, split upon a rock, break down, sink, drown, founder, come to grief.

come to nothing, end in smoke; flat out [*colloq.*]; fall through, hang fire, flash in the pan, collapse, go to wrack and ruin.

Adj. **unsuccessful,** successless, at fault; unfortunate, etc., 735; abortive, sterile, fruitless, bootless; ineffectual, ineffective, inefficient, lame, insufficient, unavailing.

stranded, aground, grounded, swamped, wrecked, shipwrecked, foundered, capsized.

undone, lost, ruined, broken, bankrupt, played out; done up, done for [*colloq.*]; broken down, overborne, overwhelmed; all up with [*colloq.*].

frustrated, thwarted, crossed, disconcerted; unhorsed, hard hit, stultified, befooled, dished [*colloq.*], foiled, defeated, victimized, sacrificed.

Adv. to little or no purpose, in vain.

733. TROPHY.—*N.* trophy; medal, prize, palm. laurel, laurels, bays, crown, chaplet, wreath; eulogy, citation; scholarship; garland; triumphal arch: war medal, etc., 722; Carnegie medal, Nobel prize; blue ribbon; decoration, etc., 877.

734. PROSPERITY.—*N.* prosperity, welfare, well-being; affluence, etc. (*wealth*), 803; success, etc., 731; luck, good fortune, good luck, blessings, godsend; bed of roses; fat of the land.

upstart, parvenu, *noureau riche* [F.], mushroom.

V. prosper, thrive, flourish, swim with the tide: rise (*or* get on) in the world; light on one's feet; bask in the sunshine; have a run of luck; make one's fortune, feather one's nest, make one's pile [*slang*].

flower, blossom, bloom, fructify, bear fruit; fatten, batten.

Adj. prosperous, thriving, well off, well to do, at one's ease; rich, etc., 803; fortunate, lucky; palmy, halcyon.

auspicious, propitious, providential.

Adv. prosperously, swimmingly; as good luck would have it.

735. ADVERSITY.—*N.* adversity, evil, etc., 619; failure, etc., 732; bad (*or* ill, evil, adverse, hard) fortune *or* luck, frowns of fortune; broken fortunes; slough of despond; evil day, hard times, rainy day, cloud, gathering clouds, ill-wind; affliction, trouble, hardship, curse, blight, load, pressure, humiliation.

misfortune, mishap, mischance, misadventure, disaster, calamity, catastrophe; accident, casualty, blow, trial, sorrow, visitation, infliction, reverse, check, setback, contretemps [F.].

downfall, fall; losing game; ruin, undoing, extremity.

V. come to grief, go downhill, go to wrack and ruin, go to the dogs [*colloq.*]; fall, decay, sink, decline, go down in the world; have seen better days; be all up with [*colloq.*].

Adj. unfortunate, unblest, unhappy, unlucky, unprosperous, hoodooed [*colloq*], luckless, hapless, out of luck; under a cloud; badly off; in adverse circumstances; poor, etc., 804; decayed, undone, on the road to ruin.

ill-fated, ill starred, ill-omened; devoted, doomed; inauspicious, ominous, sinister, unpropitious, unfavorable.

adverse, untoward; disastrous, calamitous, ruinous, dire, deplorable.

Adv. from bad to worse, out of the frying pan into the fire.

736. MEDIOCRITY.—*N.* mediocrity, golden mean, moderation; moderate (*or* average) circumstances; respectability.

middle classes, *bourgeoisie* [F.].

V. strike the golden mean; preserve a middle course.

jog on, get along [*colloq.*], get on tolerably (*or* respectably).

Adj. middling, so-so, fair, medium, moderate, mediocre, ordinary.

Adv. with nothing to brag about.

II. INTERSOCIAL VOLITION[1]

737. AUTHORITY.—*N.* authority; influence, patronage, power, prestige, prerogative, jurisdiction.

right, divine right, authoritativeness, royalty, absolutism, despotism, tyranny.

command, empire, sway, rule; dominion, domination; sovereignty, supremacy, suzerainty, kingship; lordship, headship, leadership, mastership, government, dictation, control, hold, grasp; grip, iron sway, rod of empire.

reign, dynasty, administration; dictatorship, protectorate, presidency, presidentship, consulship, magistracy.

Governments: empire; monarchy; limited (*or* constitutional) monarchy; aristocracy; oligarchy, democracy, republic; triumvirate; autocracy; dictatorship, totalitarian state.

representative government, constitutional government, home rule, dominion rule [Brit.], colonial government; self-government, autonomy, self-determination; republicanism, federalism; socialism; communism; authoritarianism; totalitarianism; bureaucracy; martial law; feudal system, feudalism.

state, realm, commonwealth, country, power, body politic.

ruler, person in authority, lord, etc., 745; judicature, etc., 965; cabinet, etc. (*council*), 696; seat of government, headquarters.

V. authorize, empower, etc., 760; warrant, dictate.

rule, sway, command, control, administer, govern, direct, lead, preside over, be at the head of, reign.

dominate, have the upper (*or* whip) hand; preponderate, boss [*colloq.*]; override, overrule, overawe; lord it over, keep under, bend to one's will, have it all one's own way, be master of the situation, take the lead, lay down the law.

Adj. ruling, regnant, dominant, paramount, supreme, predominant, preponderant, in the ascendant, influential; imperious, dictatorial, peremptory; authoritative, executive, administrative, official, gubernatorial, bureaucratic, departmental.

sovereign; regal, royal, royalist, monarchical, kingly; dynastic, imperial, autocratic; oligarchic, democratic, republican.

[1] Implying the action of the will of one mind over the will of another.

Adv. in the name of, by the authority of, at one's command, in virtue of, under the auspices of.

738. [Absence of authority] LAXITY.—*N.* **laxity**; laxness, looseness, slackness; toleration, lenity, etc., 740; relaxation; freedom, etc., 748.

anarchy, interregnum; misrule, license, insubordination, mob rule, mob law, lynch law, nihilism, reign of violence.

Deprivation of power: dethronement, impeachment, deposition, abdication; usurpation.

V. **be lax**, hold a loose rein; give the reins to, give rope enough, give free rein to; tolerate; relax; misrule.

have one's fling, act without authority, act on one's own responsibility, usurp authority.

dethrone, depose; abdicate.

Adj. **lax**, loose; slack, remiss, negligent, etc., 460; weak.

relaxed, licensed, unbridled; anarchic *or* anarchical, nihilistic; unauthorized.

739. SEVERITY.—*N.* **severity**; strictness, harshness, rigor, stringency, austerity, inclemency; arrogance, etc., 885.

arbitrary power; absolutism, despotism; dictatorship, autocracy, tyranny, domination, oppression, assumption, usurpation; inquisition, reign of terror, iron rule, coercion, etc., 744; martial law.

bureaucracy, red-tapism, officialism.

tyrant, disciplinarian, martinet, stickler, despot, autocrat, oppressor, inquisitor, extortioner.

V. **arrogate**, assume, usurp, take liberties; domineer, bully, tyrannize, put on the screw, be hard upon, ill-treat, rule with a rod of iron, oppress, override, trample under foot, ride roughshod over; coerce, etc., 744.

Adj. **severe**, strict, hard, harsh, dour [Scot.], rigid, stern, rigorous, uncompromising, exacting, searching, inexorable, inflexible, obdurate, austere, relentless, stringent, strict, strait-laced, peremptory, absolute, arbitrary, imperative, coercive, tyrannical, extortionate, oppressive, cruel, arrogant: formal, punctilious.

Adv. with a high (*or* strong, tight, heavy) hand.

740. MILDNESS.—*N.* **mildness**, lenity, moderation, temperateness; tolerance, toleration, mildness, gentleness; favor; indulgence, clemency, mercy, forbearance, quarter, compassion, etc., 914.

V. **be lenient**, tolerate, bear with; spare the vanquished, give quarter; indulge, spoil.

Adj. **lenient**, mild, gentle, tolerant, indulgent, easy, moderate, complaisant, easygoing; clement, compassionate, forbearing; long-suffering.

741. COMMAND.—*N.* command, order, ordinance, act, fiat, bidding, word, call, beck, nod; direction, injunction, charge, instructions; dispatch, message.

demand, exaction, imposition, requisition, claim, requirement, ultimatum; request, etc., 765.

decree, dictate, dictation, mandate, precept; prescript, writ, ordination, bull, edict, dispensation, prescription, enactment, law, act; warrant, passport, summons, subpoena, citation; word of command, order of the day.

V. command, order, decree, enact, ordain, dictate, direct, give orders, issue a command; call to order; assume the command.

prescribe, set, appoint, mark out; set (*or* prescribe, impose) a task; set to work.

bid, enjoin, charge, instruct; require, demand, exact, impose, tax.

claim, lay claim to, reclaim.

cite, summon, call for, send for; subpoena; beckon.

Adj. commanding, authoritative, imperative, decisive, final.

Adv. in a commanding tone; by a stroke (*or* dash) of the pen; by order.

742. DISOBEDIENCE.—*N.* disobedience, insubordination, contumacy; infraction, infringement, violation.

revolt, rebellion, mutiny, outbreak, rising, uprising, insurrection, riot, tumult, strike.

sedition, treason; lese majesty; defection, secession, revolution; bolshevism.

insurgent, mutineer, rebel, traitor, communist, Fenian, Sinn Feiner, Red, Bolshevist, seceder, Secessionist [esp., U. S. hist.] *or* Secesh [*colloq. or slang*, U. S.]; apostate, renegade, anarchist.

V. disobey, violate, infringe; shirk, slack; defy, set at defiance, run riot, take the law into one's own hands; kick over the traces; refuse to support, bolt [*politics*].

resist, strike, rise, rise in arms; secede, mutiny, rebel.

Adj. disobedient, unruly, ungovernable; insubordinate, restive, refractory, defiant, contumacious; recusant, recalcitrant.

lawless, riotous, mutinous, seditious, insurgent, revolutionary.

743. OBEDIENCE.—*N.* obedience, observance, compliance; submission, subjection; nonresistance, passivity, resignation, submissiveness, ductility, obsequiousness, servility.

allegiance, loyalty, fealty, homage, deference, devotion; constancy, fidelity.

V. obey, submit, etc., 725; comply, do one's bidding, attend to orders, serve faithfully (*or* loyally, devotedly, without question); be resigned to, be submissive to; serve, etc., 746; play second fiddle.

Adj. **obedient,** law-abiding, complying, compliant; loyal, faithful, devoted; under beck and call, under control.

resigned, passive; submissive, etc., 725; unresisting, pliant.

Adv. as you please, if you please; in compliance with, in obedience to.

744. COMPULSION.—*N.* **compulsion,** coercion, constraint; restraint, etc., 751; enforcement, draft, conscription; eminent domain.

force; brute (*or* main, physical) force; the sword; mob law, martial law.

necessity, etc., 601; spur of necessity, Hobson's choice.

V. **compel,** force, make, drive, dragoon, coerce, constrain, enforce, necessitate, oblige.

extort, wring from, force upon, drag into; bind, pin down; require; tax, put in force; commandeer; restrain, etc., 751.

Adj. **compelling,** coercive, inexorable, compulsory, obligatory, stringent, peremptory, binding.

Adv. **forcibly,** by force, by force of arms; on compulsion, perforce, under protest, in spite of, in one's teeth; against one's will.

745. MASTER.—*N.* **master,** lord, commander, commandant, captain, chief, chieftain; paterfamilias [*Rom. law*], patriarch; sahib [India], head, senior, governor, ruler, dictator, leader, director, boss; sachem, sagamore.

potentate; liege, liege lord, suzerain, overlord, sovereign, monarch, crowned head, emperor, king, majesty, protector, president; autocrat, despot, tyrant, oligarch, dictator.

caesar, kaiser, czar, sultan, caliph, mogul, great mogul, mikado, inca; prince, duke, etc. (*nobility*), 875; archduke, doge; maharaja, raja, emir, nizam, nawab [*Indian ruling chiefs*].

empress, queen, sultana, czarina, princess, infanta, duchess, maharani, rani [both Hindu], begum [Moham.].

regent, viceroy, khedive, pasha, bey, mandarin.

the authorities, the powers that be, the government; staff, official, man in office, person in authority.

Military authorities: marshal, field marshal, generalissimo; commander in chief, general, brigadier general, brigadier, lieutenant general, major general, colonel, lieutenant colonel, major, captain, lieutenant, sublieutenant; officer, staff officer, aide-de-camp, adjutant, ensign, cornet, cadet, subaltern; noncommissioned officer; sergeant, top sergeant, corporal.

Civil authorities: mayor, prefect, chancellor, magistrate, syndic; burgomaster, seneschal, alderman, warden, constable.

Naval authorities: admiral, admiralty; commodore, captain, commander, lieutenant; skipper, master, mate.

746. SERVANT.—*N.* **servant,** retainer, follower, henchman, servitor, domestic, menial, help [*local*], employee; attaché [F.], official.

subject, liege, liegeman.

retinue, suite, cortege, staff, court; office force, clerical staff, clerical force, workers, associate workers, employees, the help.

attendant, squire, usher, apprentice; page, buttons [*colloq.*]; trainbearer, cupbearer; waiter, butler, lackey, footman, flunky [*colloq.*]; boy [*any colored male servant, as in the Orient, South Africa, etc*]; valet, equerry, groom, jockey, hostler or ostler, orderly, messenger, caddie; secretary, stenographer, clerk, agent, underling, understrapper; man.

maid, maidservant; girl, help [*local*], handmaid, lady's maid, nurse, ayah [India], nursemaid; cook, scullion, Cinderella; general servant [Brit.], general-housework maid [U. S.], general [*colloq.*]; washerwoman, laundress, charwoman.

dependent, hanger-on, satellite, parasite, protégé [F.], ward, hireling, mercenary, puppet, creature; serf, vassal, thrall, slave, Negro, helot; bondsman, bondswoman; bondslave; villein [*hist.*], churl [*hist.*].

V. serve, minister to, help, co-operate; wait (*or* attend, dance attendance) upon; squire, valet, tend, do for [*colloq.*].

Adj. serviceable, useful, helpful, co-operative; at one's call.

servile, slavish, subject, thrall, bond; subservient, obsequious, base, fawning, truckling, sycophantic, parasitic, cringing.

747. [Insignia of authority] SCEPTER.—*N.* Regal: scepter, orb; pall; robes of state, ermine, purple; crown, coronet, diadem; triple plume; flail [Egyptian]; signet seal.

Ecclesiastical: tiara, triple crown; ring, keys; miter, crozier, crook, staff; cardinal's hat; bishop's apron (*or* sleeves, lawn, gaiters), fillet.

Military: epaulet, star, bar, eagle, crown [Brit.], oak leaf, Sam Browne belt; chevron, stripe.

caduceus; Mercury's staff (*or* rod, wand); mace, fasces, ax, truncheon, staff, baton, wand, rod; flag, etc. (*insignia*), 550; regalia; toga, mantle; decoration, title, etc., 877; portfolio.

throne, divan; woolsack [*seat of English Lord Chancellor in the House of Lords*], chair, seat, dais.

talisman, amulet, charm, sign.

748. FREEDOM.—*N.* freedom, liberty, independence; license, indulgence.

scope, range, latitude, play, free play (*or* scope), swing, full swing, elbowroom, margin, rope, wide berth.

franchise; prerogative, etc., 924.

freeman, freedman, citizen, denizen.

immunity, exemption; emancipation, etc., 750; right, privilege.

autonomy, self-government; free trade; self-determination, noninterference; Monroe Doctrine [U. S.].

independent, free lance, freethinker, free trader.

V. be free, have scope (*or* one's own way), do what one likes, go at large, feel at home, stand on one's rights.

free, liberate, set free, etc., 750; give the reins to; make free of, enfranchise.

Adj. free, independent, at large, loose, scot-free; unconstrained, unconfined, unchecked, unhindered, unobstructed, uncontrolled, ungoverned, unchained, unshackled, unfettered, unbridled, uncurbed, unmuzzled, unvanquished.

unrestricted, unlimited, unconditional; absolute; with unlimited power (*or* opportunity); discretionary.

unbiased, unprejudiced, uninfluenced; spontaneous.

free and easy, at ease, at one's ease; quite at home.

exempt, immune, freed, freeborn; autonomous, freehold.

gratuitous, gratis, etc., 815; for nothing, for love.

Adv. **freely,** at will, with no restraint.

749. SUBJECTION.—*N.* subjection; dependence, subordination; thrall, thralldom, subjugation, bondage, serfdom; feudalism, vassalage, slavery, enslavement; conquest.

service; servitude, employ, tutelage, constraint, yoke, submission, obedience.

V. **be subject,** be at the mercy of, depend upon; fall a prey to, fall under, play second fiddle; serve, etc., 746; obey, etc., 743; submit, etc., 725.

subjugate, subject, tame, break in; master, tread down, weigh down, keep under, enthrall, enslave, lead captive, rule, etc., 737; hold in bondage (*or* leading strings).

Adj. **subject,** dependent, subordinate; feudal, feudatory; under control; in leading strings, in harness; servile, slavish, enslaved, downtrodden; henpecked; under one's thumb, tied to one's apron strings, at one's beck and call; liable.

Adv. **under;** under orders (*or* command), at one's orders.

750. LIBERATION.—*N.* liberation, disengagement, release, emancipation, Emancipation Proclamation; enfranchisement, manumission; discharge, dismissal.

deliverance, etc., 672; redemption, extrication, acquittance, absolution, acquittal, escape.

V. **liberate,** free, set free, emancipate, release; enfranchise, manumit; demobilize, disband, discharge, dismiss; let go, let loose, let out, deliver, etc., 672; absolve, acquit.

unfetter, untie, loose, loosen, relax; unbolt, unbar, unhand, unbind, unchain, disengage, disentangle; clear, extricate; reprieve.

Adj. **liberated,** freed; foot-loose, one's own master.

Adv. **at large,** at liberty; adrift.

751. RESTRAINT.—*N.* restraint; hindrance, etc., 706; coercion, compulsion, constraint, repression; discipline, control; limitation, restriction, protection, monopoly; prohibition, economic pressure.

confinement, durance, duress; imprisonment, incarceration, thrall, thralldom, limbo, captivity; blockade.

keep, care, charge, custody, ward.

repressionist, monopolist, protectionist.

V. **restrain,** check, restrict, debar, hinder, constrain, coerce, compel, curb, harness, control; hold in leash, withhold, repress, suppress, keep under; smother, pull in, rein in, hold, prohibit.

fasten, enchain, fetter, shackle, trammel; bridle, muzzle, gag, pinion, manacle, handcuff, hobble, bind, swathe, swaddle; tether, picket, tie, secure.

confine, shut up (*or* in), lock up, box up, bottle up, cork up, seal up, blockade, hem in, bolt in, wall in, rail in; impound, pen, coop; inclose, cage, imprison, immure, incarcerate, entomb; put in irons, cast into prison.

arrest, take into custody; take (*or* make) prisoner, lead captive, send to prison, commit; give in charge (*or* custody).

Adj. **restrained,** constrained, repressive, suppressive; imprisoned, pent up, wedged in; on parole; doing time [*colloq. or slang*], in custody.

stiff, narrow, prudish, strait-laced, hidebound.

Adv. **under restraint** (*or* lock and key, hatches), under discipline; in prison, in jail, in durance vile, in confinement; behind bars, in captivity, under arrest.

752. [Means of restraint] **PRISON.**—*N.* **prison,** prisonhouse; jail, cage, coop, den, cell; stronghold, fortress, keep, donjon, dungeon, Bastille, penitentiary, state prison, lockup, station house, station [*colloq.*], pen [*also slang for penitentiary*], pound; penal settlement; workhouse [U. S.; *in England, a workhouse is a poorhouse*], reformatory, reform school.

Restraining devices: shackle, bond, gyve, fetter, irons, pinion, manacle, handcuff, straight jacket, stocks, pillory; vise, bandage, splint, strap; yoke, collar, halter, harness; muzzle, gag, bit, curb, snaffle, bridle; rein, reins, lines [U. S. and dial. Eng.], ribbons [*colloq.*]; tether, picket, band, chain, cord.

bar, bolt, lock, padlock; rail, paling, palisade; wall, fence, barrier, barricade.

drag, brake, check, etc. (*hindrance*), 706.

753. KEEPER.—*N.* **keeper,** custodian, ranger, gamekeeper, warder, jailer, turnkey, castellan, guard; watch, watchdog, watchman, concierge [F.], sentry, sentinel; coastguard.

escort, bodyguard; convoy.

guardian, protector, governor; duenna, governess, nurse.

754. PRISONER.—*N.* **prisoner,** convict, captive, close prisoner.

V. stand committed; be imprisoned.

Adj. **imprisoned,** in prison, in custody, in charge, behind bars, under lock and key, under hatches.

755. [Vicarious authority] **COMMISSION.**—*N.* **commission,**

delegation; consignment, assignment; proxy, power of attorney, deputation, legation, mission, embassy; agency.

errand, charge, brevet, diploma, permit.

appointment, nomination, charter; ordination; installation, inauguration, investiture; accession, coronation, enthronement.

V. commission, delegate, depute; consign, assign, commit, charge, intrust, authorize.

accredit, engage, hire, bespeak, appoint, name, nominate, return; ordain, install, induct, inaugurate, invest, crown; enroll, enlist; employ, empower.

Adv. instead of, in one's stead, in one's place; as proxy for.

756. ANNULMENT.—*N.* annulment, nullification, cancellation, abrogation, revocation, repeal.

dismissal, *congé* [F.], sack [*slang*], deposition, dethronement; disestablishment, disendowment.

countermand, repudiation, retractation, recantation; abolition, abolishment; dissolution.

V. annul, cancel, destroy, abolish, abrogate, revoke, repeal, rescind, reverse, retract, recall; overrule, override; set aside; disannul, dissolve, quash, nullify, nol-pros [*law, short for nolle prosequi*], disestablish; countermand, counterorder, throw overboard.

disclaim, deny, ignore, repudiate; recant, break off.

dismiss, discard; turn out, cast off (*or* adrift, aside, away); send off, send away, discharge, get rid of, bounce [*slang*]; fire, sack [*both slang*].

cashier, oust, unseat, dethrone, depose, unfrock, strike off the roll, disbar.

757. RESIGNATION.—*N.* resignation, retirement, abdication; renunciation, retractation, retraction, disclaimer, abandonment, relinquishment.

V. resign, give up, throw up, lay down, abjure, renounce, forego, disclaim, retract, deny, desert.

vacate, abdicate, retire, tender (*or* hand in) one's resignation.

758. CONSIGNEE.—*N.* consignee, trustee, nominee; committee.

functionary, curator; treasurer, etc., 801; agent, factor, steward, bailiff, clerk, secretary, attorney, solicitor, proctor, broker, underwriter, commission agent, factotum, caretaker, employee; servant, etc., 746.

negotiator, go-between; middleman.

delegate, commissioner; emissary, envoy, messenger.

diplomatist, diplomat, ambassador, plenipotentiary, diplomatic agent, representative, resident, consul, legate, etc., 534; attaché [F.].

salesman, traveler, traveling salesman, commercial traveler, drummer, traveling man.

759. DEPUTY.—*N.* deputy, substitute, proxy, delegate, representative, alternate; vice-president.

regent, vicegerent, viceroy, minister, premier, chancellor, provost, warden, lieutenant, consul, ambassador; delegate, etc., 758.

team, eight, nine, eleven; captain, champion.

V. represent, stand for, appear for, hold a brief for, answer for; stand in the shoes of; stand in the stead of.

delegate, depute, empower, commission, substitute, accredit.

Adj. acting, vice, viceregal; accredited to; delegated, representative.

Adv. in behalf of, in the place of, as representing, by proxy.

760. PERMISSION.—*N.* permission, leave, allowance, sufferance, tolerance, toleration, connivance; liberty, law, license, concession, grace; indulgence, favor, dispensation, exemption, release; authorization, accordance, admission.

permit, warrant, sanction, authority, pass, passport; license, carte blanche [F.], grant, charter, patent.

V. permit, let, allow, admit; suffer, tolerate, recognize; concede, etc., 762; accord, vouchsafe, favor, humor, gratify, indulge, wink at, connive at.

grant, empower, charter, enfranchise, privilege, license, authorize, warrant, sanction; intrust, commission.

absolve, release, exonerate, dispense with.

Adj. permitted, permissible, allowable, lawful, legitimate, legal, legalized, chartered, unforbidden.

Adv. by (*or* with) leave, under favor of, by all means.

761. PROHIBITION.—*N.* prohibition, inhibition; veto, interdict, interdiction, injunction, embargo, ban, taboo, proscription, restriction; contraband; forbidden fruit; Volstead Act, 18th amendment [all U. S.].

V. prohibit, inhibit, forbid, disallow; bar, debar, hinder, restrain, etc., 751; withhold, limit, circumscribe, clip the wings of, restrict; interdict, taboo, proscribe; exclude, shut out.

Adj. prohibitive, prohibitory; proscriptive; restrictive, exclusive.

prohibited, unlicensed, contraband, taboo, illegal, unauthorized.

762. CONSENT.—*N.* consent; assent, etc., 488; acquiescence, approval, compliance, agreement, concession, accession, acknowledgment, acceptance; permit, etc. (*permission*), 760; promise, etc., 768.

settlement, adjustment, ratification, confirmation.

V. consent; assent, etc., 488; yield assent, admit, allow, concede, grant, yield; acknowledge, give consent, comply with, acquiesce, agree to, accede, accept, close with, satisfy, settle, come to terms; deign, vouchsafe, promise.

Adj. willing, compliant, agreeable [*colloq.*], eager.

763. OFFER.—*N.* offer, proffer, tender, bid, overture, proposal, proposition; motion, invitation, offering.

V. offer, proffer, present, tender; bid; propose, move, make a motion, start, invite, place at one's disposal; make possible, put forward, press, urge upon, hold out.

volunteer, come forward, be a candidate, offer (*or* present) oneself, stand for, bid for; seek; be at one's service.

Adj. in the market, for sale, to let, disengaged, on hire; at one's disposal.

764. REFUSAL.—*N.* refusal, rejection, denial, declension, flat (*or* point-blank) refusal; repulse, rebuff; discountenance, disapprobation.

negation, abnegation, protest, renunciation, disclaimer; dissent, etc., 489; revocation, annulment.

V. refuse, reject, deny, decline, turn down [*slang*], dissent, etc., 489; negative, withhold one's assent, grudge, begrudge; stand aloof, be deaf to, turn one's back upon, discountenance, forswear, set aside.

resist, repel, repulse, rebuff, deny oneself, discard, repudiate, rescind, disclaim, protest.

Adj. uncomplying, deaf to, noncompliant, unconsenting; recusant, dissentient.

Adv. on no account, not for the world, not on your life! [*colloq.*].

765. REQUEST.—*N.* request, requisition; claim, demand, etc., 741; petition, suit, prayer, solicitation, invitation, entreaty, importunity, supplication, invocation.

motion, overture, application, canvass, address, appeal, imprecation; proposal, proposition.

V. request, ask, beg, crave, sue, pray, petition, solicit, canvass, invite, beg leave, beg a boon, apply to, call to, call for; make a request, make application, claim, demand; offer up prayers.

entreat, beseech, plead, supplicate, implore; conjure, adjure; apostrophize, cry to, kneel to, appeal to; invoke, evoke; press, urge, importune, dun, clamor for, cry aloud, cry for help.

Adj. importunate, clamorous, urgent, solicitous; cap in hand.

Adv. please, prithee, do, pray; be so good as, be good enough; have the goodness, vouchsafe, will you, I pray thee, if you please.

766. [Negative request] **DEPRECATION.**—*N.* deprecation, expostulation; intercession, mediation, protest, remonstrance.

V. deprecate, protest, expostulate, enter a protest, remonstrate.

Adj. deprecatory, expostulatory, intercessory.

unsought, unbesought; unasked.

767. PETITIONER.—*N.* petitioner, solicitor, applicant, suppliant, supplicant, suitor, candidate, claimant, aspirant, competitor, bidder; place hunter.

salesman, drummer, etc., 758; canvasser.

beggar, mendicant, panhandler [*slang*], cadger.

hotel runner, runner [*both cant*], steerer [*colloq.*], barker [*colloq.*].

sycophant, parasite, etc. (*servility*), 886.

768. PROMISE.—*N.* promise, undertaking, word, troth, plight, pledge, parole, word of honor, vow, oath, profession, assurance, warranty, guarantee, insurance, obligation, contract, stipulation.

engagement, affiance, betrothal, marriage contract (*or* vow); plighted faith.

V. promise, undertake, engage; make (*or* form, enter into) an engagement; bind (*or* pledge) oneself; vow, swear, give (*or* pledge) one's word; betroth, plight faith.

assure, warrant, guarantee, covenant, agree, vouch for, attest; answer for, be answerable for; secure, give security, underwrite.

Adj. promissory, votive, under hand and seal, upon oath, upon affirmation.

promised, affianced, pledged, bound, committed, compromised.

Adv. as true as I live; in all soberness; upon my honor; my word for it.

769. COMPACT.—*N.* compact, contract, specialty, deal [*colloq.*], agreement, bargain; pact, bond, covenant, indenture [*law*]; stipulation, settlement, convention; compromise, negotiation.

treaty, protocol, concordat, charter, Magna Charta, pragmatic sanction.

ratification, completion, signature, seal, bond.

V. contract, covenant, agree for; engage, etc. (*promise*), 768.

negotiate, treat, stipulate, make terms; bargain.

conclude, close, close with, complete, strike a bargain; come to terms (*or* an understanding); compromise, settle; confirm, ratify, clinch, subscribe, underwrite; indorse, sign, seal.

Adj. contractual, complete, agreed; signed, sealed, and delivered.

Adv. as agreed upon, as promised, according to the contract.

770. CONDITIONS.—*N.* conditions, terms, articles, articles of agreement; memorandum, clauses, provisions, proviso, covenant, stipulation, obligation, ultimatum.

V. condition, stipulate, insist upon, make a point of; bind, tie up; fence in, hedge in, make (*or* come to) terms.

Adj. **conditional,** provisional, guarded, fenced, hedged in.

Adv. conditionally, provisionally, on condition; with a string to it [*colloq.*], with a reservation.

771. SECURITY.—*N.* **security,** guaranty, guarantee; gage, bond, tie, pledge, mortgage, debenture; bill of sale, lien, collateral, bail, stake, deposit, earnest.

promissory note; bill, bill of exchange; I O U; personal security, covenant.

acceptance, indorsement, signature, execution, stamp, seal.

sponsor, surety, bail, hostage; godchild, godfather, godmother.

authentication, verification, warrant, certificate, voucher, receipt.

deed, instrument, title deed, indenture; charter, paper, parchment, settlement, will, testament, codicil.

V. **give security,** give bail, go bail; pawn, put in pawn, pledge, mortgage.

guarantee, warrant, assure; accept, indorse, underwrite, insure.

execute, stamp; sign, seal.

Adj. **pledged,** pawned, in pawn, at stake, on deposit, as earnest.

772. OBSERVANCE.—*N.* **observance,** performance, compliance, acquiescence, concurrence; obedience, etc., 743; fulfillment, satisfaction, discharge; acquittance, acquittal; adhesion, ackowledgment; fidelity.

V. **observe,** comply with, respect, acknowledge, abide by; cling to, adhere to, be faithful to, act up to; meet, fulfill, carry out, execute, perform, discharge, keep one's word (*or* pledge).

Adj. **observant,** faithful, true, loyal, honorable, etc., 939; punctual, punctilious, scrupulous, as good as one's word.

Adv. to the letter.

773. NONOBSERVANCE.—*N.* **nonobservance,** noncompliance, evasion, failure, omission, neglect, slackness, laxness, laxity, informality; lawlessness, disobedience, etc., 742; bad faith, etc., 940.

infringement, infraction; violation, transgression; piracy, literary theft.

V. **evade,** fail, neglect, omit, elude, cut [*colloq.*], set aside, ignore; shut (*or* close) one's eyes to.

infringe, transgress, violate, steal, pirate [*a book, etc.*].

discard, repudiate, protest, nullify, declare null and void, cancel, forfeit.

Adj. **elusive,** evasive, slack, lax, casual, slippery; nonobservant.

774. COMPROMISE.—*N.* **compromise,** composition, middle term, compensation, adjustment, mutual concession.

V. **compromise,** commute, compound, split the difference, meet one halfway, give and take, come to terms, submit to arbitration, patch up, arrange, straighten out, adjust, agree, make the best of, make a virtue of necessity.

POSSESSIVE RELATIONS[1]

(1) Property

775. ACQUISITION.—*N.* acquisition, procurement; purchase, inheritance; gift, etc., 784.

recovery, redemption, salvage, find.

gain, thrift, money-making, pelf, lucre, filthy lucre, the main chance.

profit, earnings, wages, salary, emolument, income, remuneration; winnings, pickings, perquisite; proceeds, produce, product; outcome, output; return, fruit, crop, harvest; benefit; prize; wealth, etc., 803.

V. acquire, get, gain, win, earn, obtain, procure, gather; collect, pick, pick up, glean, find, light upon, come across, come at; scrape up (*or* together); get in, net, bag, secure; derive, draw, get in the harvest.

profit, turn to profit (*or* account), make capital out of, make money by, obtain a return, reap the fruits of; gain an advantage; make (*or* coin, raise) money, raise funds; realize, clear, produce, take, receive, come by, inherit.

recover, get back, regain, retrieve, redeem.

Adj. profitable, productive, advantageous, gainful, remunerative, paying, lucrative.

Adv. in the way of gain; for money; at interest.

776. LOSS.—*N.* loss, forfeiture, lapse; privation, bereavement, deprivation, riddance; damage, squandering, waste.

V. lose, incur a loss, miss, mislay, let slip, be deprived of, be without, forfeit.

squander, lavish, get rid of, waste.

Adj. bereft, bereaved, deprived of, shorn of, denuded, minus [*colloq., exc. in math.*], cut off; rid of, quit of, out of pocket, lost.

777. POSSESSION.—*N.* possession, ownership, proprietorship, occupancy, hold, holding, tenure, tenancy, dependency.

exclusive possession, monopoly, retention, corner.

future possession, heritage, inheritance, heirship, reversion; primogeniture.

V. possess, have, hold, occupy, enjoy, be possessed of, own, command, inherit.

[1]That is, relations which concern property.

monopolize, corner, engross, forestall, appropriate.

belong to, appertain to, pertain to; be in one's possession, vest in.

Adj. possessing, worth, possessed of, master of, in possession of; endowed (*or* blest, fraught, laden, charged) with.

possessed, on hand, in hand, in store, in stock; at one's command, at one's disposal.

777a. EXEMPTION.—*N.* exemption, exception, immunity, privilege, release.

V. not have, not possess, not own, be without.

Adj. devoid of, exempt from, without, unpossessed of, unblest with; immune from.

unpossessed; untenanted, vacant, without an owner.

778. [Joint possession] PARTICIPATION.—*N.* participation, joint tenancy; joint (*or* common) stock: partnership; communion; community of possessions, communism, collectivism, socialism; co-operation.

participator, sharer, partner; shareholder; joint tenant; tenants in common; coheir.

communist, communalist, collectivist, socialist.

V. participate, partake, share, share in, join in, go shares, go cahoots [*slang*], go halves; share and share alike.

communize, communalize; have (*or* possess) in common.

Adj. communistic, socialistic; co-operative, profit-sharing.

Adv. in common, share and share alike; on shares.

779. POSSESSOR.—*N.* possessor, holder, occupant, occupier, tenant, tenant at will, lessee, lodger.

owner; proprietor, proprietress, master, mistress, lord.

landholder, landowner, landlord, landlady; lord of the manor, laird [*Scot.*], landed gentry.

Future possessor: heir, heir apparent, heir presumptive; inheritor, heiress, inheritrix.

780. PROPERTY.—*N.* property, possession, tenure; ownership, etc., 777.

estate, interest, right, title, claim, demand, holding, vested interest; use, trust, benefit; term, lease, settlement; remainder, reversion.

dower, dowry, jointure, inheritance, heritage, patrimony, legacy.

assets, belongings, means, resources, circumstances; wealth, etc., 803; money, etc., 800; estate and effects.

realty, real estate, land, lands, landed (*or* real) property; tenements; plant, fixtures; ground; freehold, copyhold, leasehold.

manor, domain, demesne; farm, plantation, ranch.

territory, state, kingdom, principality, realm, empire, protectorate, dependency, sphere of influence, mandate.

personalty, personal property (*or* estate, effects), chattels, goods, effects, movables: stock, stock in trade, things, paraphernalia, equipage, appurtenances; income, etc., 810.

baggage, luggage [esp. in Eng.], impedimenta, bag and baggage; cargo.

V. **possess,** etc., 777; be the possessor, own; inherit.

Adj. **landed,** hereditary, entailed, real, personal.

Adv. **to one's credit,** to one's account; to the good.

781. RETENTION.—*N.* **retention,** detention, custody; tenacity, firm hold, grasp, gripe, grip, clutches, talon, claw, fang, tentacle.

captive, prisoner, bird in hand.

V. **retain,** keep, hold, hold fast, clinch, clench, clutch, grasp, gripe, hug; secure, withhold, detain; hold (*or* keep) back; husband, reserve; have (*or* keep) in stock; entail, tie up, settle.

Adj. **retentive,** tenacious.

782. RIDDANCE.—*N.* **riddance,** relinquishment, abandonment, renunciation, dereliction; cession, surrender, dispensation; resignation.

derelict, jetsam; abandoned farm [U. S.]; waif, foundling.

V. **relinquish,** give up, surrender, yield, cede; let go, let slip; spare, drop, resign, forego, renounce, abandon, give away, dispose of, part with; lay aside, set aside, discard, cast off, dismiss; maroon.

cast (*or* throw, fling) away, jettison.

supersede, give notice to quit, give warning; be (*or* get) rid of; eject.

divorce, cut off, desert, disinherit; separate.

Adj. **relinquished,** cast off, derelict; disowned, disinherited, divorced.

783. TRANSFER [of property].—*N.* **transfer,** conveyance, assignment, alienation, conveyancing, transmission, sale, lease, release, exchange, barter; succession, reversion.

V. **transfer,** convey, alienate, assign, grant, consign; make over, hand over, transmit, negotiate; hand down; exchange.

change hands, devolve, succeed; require, come into possession.

disinherit; dispossess, etc., 789; substitute.

Adj. **transferable,** alienable, negotiable, reversional, transmissive; inherited.

784. GIVING.—*N.* **giving,** bestowal, presentation, concession, cession; delivery, consignment, dispensation, endowment; investment, investiture; award, recompense, etc., 973.

charity, almsgiving, liberality, generosity.

gift, donation, present, boon, favor, benefaction, grant, offering, bonus, oblation, sacrifice.

allowance, contribution, subscription, subsidy, tribute.

bequest, legacy, devise, will, dot, dowry, dower.

gratuity, alms, largess, bounty, dole, help, offertory, honorarium, Christmas box, tip, baksheesh, consideration.

bribe, bait, peace offering; graft [*colloq.*].

giver, grantor, donor, testator; investor, subscriber, contributor; fairy godmother.

V. **deliver**, hand, pass, assign, hand (*or* make, deliver, turn) over.

pay, etc., 807; render, impart, communicate.

concede, cede, yield, part with, shed; spend, sacrifice.

give, bestow, donate, confer, grant; accord, award, assign, offer; present, give away, dispense, dispose of; give (*or* deal) out, fork out [*slang*]; allow, contribute, subscribe.

invest, endow, settle upon; bequeath, leave, devise.

furnish, supply, help, administer to, afford, spare, accommodate with, indulge with, favor with; lavish, pour on, thrust upon.

bribe, tip; grease the palm [*slang*].

Adj. **charitable**, eleemosynary, tributary; gratis, etc., 815; donative.

785. RECEIVING.—*N.* **receiving**, acquisition, etc., 775; reception, acceptance, admission.

recipient, receiver; assignee, legatee, grantee, lessee; beneficiary, pensioner.

income, etc. (*receipt*), 810.

V. **receive**; take, etc., 789; pocket; acquire, etc., 775; admit, take in, catch, accept.

be received; come in, come to hand, go into one's pocket; fall to one's lot (*or* share), accrue.

Adj. **receiving**, recipient; stipendiary, pensionary.

received, given, allowed; secondhand.

786. APPORTIONMENT.—*N.* **apportionment**, allotment, consignment, assignment, allocation, appropriation; distribution, division, deal; partition, administration.

portion, dividend, share, allotment, lot, measure, dose; dole, meed, pittance; ration; ratio, proportion, quota, modicum, allowance.

V. **apportion**, divide; distribute, administer, dispense; allot, allocate, detail, cast, share, mete; portion (*or* parcel, dole) out; deal, carve.

partition, assign, appropriate, appoint.

Adv. **respectively**, each to each; by lot; in equal shares.

787. LENDING.—*N.* **lending**, loan, advance, accommodation, mortgage, etc., 771; investment.

lender, pawnbroker, my uncle [*slang*], moneylender, usurer, Shylock.

V. **lend,** advance, accommodate with; lend on security; loan; pawn.

invest, intrust, place (*or* put) out to interest; place, put; embark, risk, venture, sink.

let, lease, sublet, sublease.

Adv. in advance; on loan, on security.

788. BORROWING.—*N.* borrowing, pledging, pawning.

V. **borrow,** pledge, pawn, put up the spout [*slang*], raise money, raise the wind [*slang*]; run into debt.

hire, rent, farm; take a lease.

appropriate, adopt, apply, imitate, make use of, take; plagiarize, pirate.

789. TAKING.—*N.* taking, reception, appropriation, capture, apprehension, seizure; abduction, abstraction.

dispossession; deprivation, bereavement, disinheritance; attachment, execution, sequestration, confiscation, eviction.

rapacity, rapaciousness, extortion, bloodsucking; theft, etc.,791.

taker, captor, capturer; extortioner *or* extortionist; vampire.

V. **take,** catch, hook, bag, sack, pocket, receive, accept.

reap, crop, cull, pluck, gather, draw.

appropriate, assume, possess oneself of; commandeer [*colloq.*]; help oneself to, make free with, lay under contribution; intercept, scramble for; deprive of.

seize, snatch, abstract, take away (*or* off), run away with; abduct, kidnap, capture, steal, pounce (*or* spring) upon; swoop down upon; take by storm; take prisoner; grapple, embrace, grip, gripe, clasp, grab [*colloq.*], clutch, collar, throttle, claw.

dispossess, take from, take away from; tear from, tear away from, wrench (*or* wrest, wring) from, extort; deprive of, bereave; disinherit, oust, evict, eject, divest; levy, distrain [*law*], confiscate; sequester, sequestrate, usurp; despoil, strip, fleece, bleed [*colloq.*].

Adj. **predatory,** wolfish, rapacious, ravening, ravenous; parasitic; all-devouring, all-engulfing.

790. RESTITUTION.—*N.* restitution, return, restoration, reinstatement, reinvestment, rehabilitation, reparation, atonement; compensation, indemnification; recovery.

V. **restore,** return, give back, render, give up, let go, release, remit; disgorge, recoup, reimburse, compensate, indemnify, reinvest, reinstate, rehabilitate, repair, make good.

recover, get back, retrieve, redeem; take back again.

Adj. **compensatory,** indemnificatory; reversionary, redemptive.

Adv. in full restitution; as partial compensation; to atone for.

791. STEALING.—*N.* **stealing,** theft, thievery, robbery, rapacity, thievishness, abstraction, appropriation, plagiarism, depredation; kidnaping.

pillage, spoliation, plunder, sack, rapine, brigandage, highway robbery, holdup [*slang*]; raid, foray, piracy, privateering, buccaneering, filibustering; burglary, housebreaking; shoplifting, blackmail.

peculation, embezzlement, fraud, forgery, larceny, pilfering; kleptomania.

V. **steal,** thieve, rob, purloin, pilfer, filch, bag, crib [*colloq.*], palm; abstract; appropriate, plagiarize.

abduct, convey away, carry off, kidnap, impress, make (*or* run) off with, run away with, spirit away, seize.

plunder, pillage, filibuster, rifle, sack, loot, ransack, spoil, despoil, strip, sweep, gut, forage, levy blackmail, maraud, poach, smuggle, bunko; hold up.

swindle, peculate, embezzle; sponge, pluck, fleece, defraud, obtain under false pretenses.

counterfeit, forge, coin, circulate bad money.

Adj. **thievish,** light-fingered, piratical; predatory, raptorial.

792. THIEF.—*N.* **thief,** robber, spoiler, depredator, pillager, marauder; pilferer, plagiarist; harpy, shark [*slang*], smuggler, poacher, kidnaper; crook [*slang*], shoplifter.

pirate, corsair, viking, buccaneer, privateer.

brigand, bandit, filibuster, freebooter, thug, cattle thief, bushranger, mosstrooper [*hist.*], highwayman, footpad, strong-arm man.
pickpocket, cutpurse, light-fingered gentry; sharper; cardsharper, trickster.
swindler, peculator, forger, coiner, counterfeiter; fence, receiver of stolen goods.
burglar, housebreaker, yegg [*slang*], cracksman [*slang*], sneak thief; second-story thief (*or* man).

793. BOOTY.—*N.* **booty,** spoil, plunder, prize, prey, loot, swag [*cant*]; perquisite, boodle [*polit. cant*], graft [*colloq.*], pork barrel [*polit. cant*], pickings; blackmail; stolen goods.

Adj. **looting,** plundering, spoliative.

794. BARTER.—*N.* **barter,** exchange, interchange, Indian gift [*colloq.*].

trade, commerce, buying and selling, traffic, business, custom, transaction, negotiation, bargain; speculation, jobbing, stock-jobbing.

free trade [*opp. to* protection].

V. **barter,** exchange, truck, swap *or* swop [*colloq. and dial.*]; interchange.

trade, traffic, buy and sell, give and take, carry on (*or* ply) a trade; deal in, speculate.

bargain; drive (*or* make, strike) a bargain; negotiate, bid for; haggle, stickle, dicker, cheapen, beat down, underbid; outbid.

Adj. **commercial**, mercantile, trading; marketable, staple, in the market, for sale; at a bargain, marked down; retail; wholesale.

Adv. across the counter; in the marts of trade.

795. PURCHASE.—*N.* **purchase**, buying, purchasing, shopping.

buyer, purchaser, client, customer, patron, clientele.

V. **buy**, purchase, invest in, procure; shop, market, go a-shopping; rent, hire, repurchase, buy in.

796. SALE.—*N.* **sale**, disposal; auction, custom.

salableness, salability, marketability, vendibility.

seller, vender, vendor [*law*]; merchant, auctioneer.

salesmanship, selling ability.

V. **sell**, vend, dispose of, make a sale, effect a sale; auction, sell at auction, put up to (*or* at) auction; hawk, dump, unload, place, undersell; dispense, offer, retail; deal in, sell off (*or* out), turn into money, realize.

Adj. **salable**, marketable, staple, in demand, popular.

unsalable, unpurchased, unbought, on the shelves, on one's hands.

797. MERCHANT.—*N.* **merchant**, trader, dealer, salesman; money-changer, shopkeeper, shopman; tradesman, tradespeople, tradesfolk.

peddler, hawker, huckster, sutler, vivandière; costermonger; canvasser, solicitor; faker [*slang*].

moneylender, usurer, banker; money-changer, money broker.

jobber, broker; buyer, seller; bear, bull [*Stock Exchange*].

firm, company, house, corporation, concern, trust.

798. MERCHANDISE.—*N.* **merchandise**, ware, commodity, effects, goods, article, stock, produce, staple commodity; stock in trade, cargo.

799. MART.—*N.* **mart**, market, market place; fair, bazaar, exchange, stock exchange, Wheat Pit [*Chicago*]; bourse, curb.

shop, store, department store, chain store, warehouse, depot, emporium, establishment; stall, booth; office, chambers, counting-house, bureau; counter.

(2) Monetary Relations

800. MONEY.—*N.* **money**, finance, funds, treasure, capital, stock; assets, wealth, etc., 803; supplies, ways and means, wherewithal *or* wherewith, sinews of war, almighty dollar, cash.

solvency, responsibility, reliability, solidity, soundness.

sum, amount; balance, balance sheet; sum total; proceeds, receipts.

currency, circulating medium, specie, coin, piece, hard cash; dollar, sterling; pounds, shillings, and pence, £ s. d.; guinea; wallet, roll, wad [slang], purse, ready money.
precious metals, gold, silver, copper, bullion, ingot, bar, nugget.
petty cash, pocket money, pin money, spending money, change, small coin.
wampum.
great wealth, money to burn [colloq.]; power or mint of money [colloq.], good sum, millions, thousands.
Science of coins: numismatics.
paper money; bill, money order; note, note of hand; bank note, promissory note; I O U, bond; bill of exchange; draft, check, order, warrant, coupon, debenture, greenback.

V. total, amount to, come to, mount up to.
issue, utter, circulate; fiscalize, monetize.
demonetize, deprive of standard value; cease to issue.
Adj. monetary, pecuniary, fiscal, financial; sterling.
solvent, sound, substantial, good, reliable, responsible, solid, having a good rating; able to pay 100 cents to the dollar.

801. TREASURER.—*N.* treasurer, bursar, purser, banker, financier; receiver, liquidator, steward, trustee, accountant, expert accountant, almoner, paymaster, cashier, teller; money-changer.

802. TREASURY.—*N.* treasury, bank, exchequer, bursary; strongbox, stronghold, strong room; coffer, chest, safe, depository, cash register, cashbox, money box, till.
purse, moneybag, pocketbook, wallet; pocket.
securities, stocks; public stocks (*or* funds, securities); bonds, government bonds, Liberty bonds [U. S.], gilt-edged securities.

803. WEALTH.—*N.* wealth, riches, fortune, opulence, affluence; easy circumstances; independence, competence.
capital, money; great wealth, bonanza, El Dorado; philosopher's stone; the golden touch.
pelf, mammon, lucre, filthy lucre.
means, resources, substance, command of money; property, income, livelihood.
rich man, moneyed man, man of substance; capitalist, millionaire, multimillionaire, plutocrat; nabob, Croesus, Midas.
V. be rich, roll (*or* wallow) in wealth, have money to burn [colloq.]; afford, well afford, command money.
become rich, fill one's pocket, feather one's nest, make a fortune; make money; worship mammon, worship the golden calf.
Adj. wealthy, rich, affluent, opulent, moneyed, well-to-do, well off, rolling in riches.

804. POVERTY.—*N.* poverty, indigence, penury, pauperism, destitution, want; need, neediness; lack, necessity, privation, dis-

tress, difficulties, wolf at the door, straits; low water [*slang*], impecuniosity.

mendancy, beggary, mendicity; broken (*or* loss of) fortune; insolvency.

poor man, pauper, mendicant, beggar.

V. **be poor,** want, lack, starve, live from hand to mouth, have seen better days, go to rack and ruin; beg one's bread, run into debt.

impoverish, reduce, reduce to poverty, pauperize, fleece, ruin.

Adj. **poor,** indigent; poverty-stricken, badly off, moneyless, penniless; impecunious, short of money, hard up, seedy [*colloq.*]; barefooted, beggarly, beggared, destitute, reduced, needy, necessitous, distressed, pinched, straitened, embarrassed, involved, insolvent.

805. CREDIT.—*N.* credit, trust, score, tally, account.

paper credit, letter of credit, circular note; duplicate; mortgage. lien, draft, securities.

creditor, lender, lessor [*law*], mortgagee; dun, usurer.

V. **credit,** accredit, intrust, keep (*or* run up) an account with; place to one's credit (*or* account); give (*or* take) credit.

Adj. **accredited;** of good credit, of unlimited credit; well rated; credited.

Adv. on credit, to the account of, to the credit of.

806. DEBT.—*N.* debt, obligation, liability, debit, score.

arrears, deferred payment, deficit, default, insolvency; bad debt.

interest; premium, usury.

debtor; mortgagor, defaulter, borrower.

V. **be in debt,** owe; incur (*or* contract) a debt, run up a bill, (*or* an account); borrow, run into debt, be in difficulties.

answer for, go bail for; back one's note.

Adj. **liable,** chargeable, answerable for.

indebted, in debt, in embarrassed circumstances, in difficulties; encumbered, involved; insolvent.

unpaid; unrequited, unrewarded; owing, due, in arrear, outstanding.

807. PAYMENT.—*N.* payment, discharge, settlement, clearance, liquidation, satisfaction, reckoning, arrangement.

acknowledgment, release; receipt, voucher.

repayment, reimbursement, retribution; pay, money paid.

V. **pay,** defray, make payment; pay one's way, expend, put down, lay down; discharge, settle, foot the bill [*colloq.*]; settle with, satisfy, pay in full, clear, liquidate, pay up; cash, honor a bill, acknowledge; redeem.

repay, refund, reimburse, disgorge, make repayment.

Adj. out of debt, owing nothing, all clear, clear of debt, abovewater; solvent.

Adv. money down, cash down, cash on delivery, C.O.D.

808. NONPAYMENT.—*N.* nonpayment; default, defalcation; protest, repudiation.

insolvency, bankruptcy, failure; run upon a bank; overdrawn account.

defaulter, bankrupt, insolvent, insolvent debtor; absconder, welsher [*slang*].

V. **not pay,** fail, break, stop payment; become insolvent (*or* bankrupt), swindle, run up bills.

protest, dishonor, repudiate, nullify.

Adj. in debt, behindhand, in arrear; beggared, insolvent, bankrupt, ruined.

809. EXPENDITURE.—*N.* **expenditure,** outgoings, outlay, expenses, disbursement; circulation.

Money paid: payment, etc., 807; pay, etc. (*remuneration*), 973; fee, footing, subsidy, tribute, ransom, bribe, donation, gift; investment; purchase.

deposit, earnest, installment.

V. **expend,** spend; run (*or* get) through, pay, disburse; lay out, fork out [*slang*]; invest, sink money.

reward, fee, remunerate; give, subscribe, subsidize; bribe.

Adj. lavish, free, liberal; beyond one's income.

expensive, costly, dear, high-priced, precious, high.

810. RECEIPT.—*N.* **receipt,** value received, income, revenue, return, proceeds; earnings.

rent, rent roll; rental.

premium, bonus, prize, drawings, handout [*slang*].

pension, annuity, pittance, jointure, alimony.

V. **receive,** get, be in receipt of, have coming in; take money; draw from, derive from; acquire, take.

yield, bring in, afford, pay, return; accrue.

Adj. **remunerative,** profitable, gainful, well paying, interest-bearing, well invested.

Adv. within one's income.

811. ACCOUNTS.—*N.* **accounts,** money matters, finance, budget, bill, score, reckoning, account.

bookkeeping, audit, single entry, double entry; ledger, cashbook, journal; balance sheet; receipts, assets; expenditure, liabilities; profit and loss account (*or* statement).

accountant, auditor, actuary, bookkeeper; expert accountant, certified accountant; bank examiner.

V. **keep accounts,** enter, post, post up, book, credit, debit, balance.

812. PRICE.—*N.* **price,** amount, cost, expense, charge, figure, demand, fare, hire; wages.

dues, duty, toll, tax, impost, tariff, levy; capitation, poll tax; custom, excise, assessment, taxation, tithe, ransom, salvage, towage; brokerage, wharfage, freightage.

worth, rate, value, par value, valuation, appraisement, money's worth; price current, market price, quotation.

V. **price,** set (*or* fix) a price, appraise, assess, charge, demand, ask, require, exact.

fetch, sell for, cost, bring in, yield, afford.

Adj. **taxable,** dutiable, assessable.

813. DISCOUNT.—*N.* **discount,** abatement, concession, reduction, depreciation, allowance, qualification, setoff, drawback, percentage. rebate.

V. **discount.** bate, rebate, abate, deduct, strike off, mark down, reduce, take off, allow, give, make allowance; depreciate.

Adv. **at a discount,** at a bargain, below par.

814. DEARNESS.—*N.* **dearness,** expensiveness, costliness, high price; overcharge, extravagance, exorbitance, extortion.

V. **overcharge,** bleed [*colloq.*], skin [*slang*], fleece, extort, profiteer.

pay too much, pay dearly, pay through the nose [*colloq.*].

Adj. **dear,** high, high-priced, expensive, costly, precious; extravagant, exorbitant, extortionate.

at a premium. beyond price, above price; priceless, of priceless value.

Adv. **dear,** dearly: at great cost, at heavy cost, at a high price.

815. CHEAPNESS.—*N.* **cheapness,** low price, depreciation, bargain, drug in the market.

V. **be cheap,** cost little; come down (*or* fall) in price, be marked down.

buy at a bargain, buy dirt-cheap, have one's money's worth; beat down, cheapen.

Adj. **cheap,** low-priced, low, moderate, reasonable, inexpensive, cheap at the price; dirt-cheap, catchpenny.

reduced, half-price, depreciated, shopworn, marked down, unsalable.

gratuitous, gratis, free, for nothing; costless, without charge, scot-free, complimentary, honorary.

Adv. **at a bargain,** for a mere song; at cost price, at prime cost.

816. LIBERALITY.—*N.* **liberality,** generosity, munificence;

bounty, bounteousness, hospitality, charity, open (*or* free) hand, open (*or* large) heart.

cheerful giver, free giver, patron; benefactor.

V. be liberal, spend freely; shower down upon, spare no expense, give with both hands; keep open house.

Adj. liberal, free, generous. charitable, hospitable; bountiful, bounteous, ample, handsome; unsparing, ungrudging; unselfish; open-handed. large-hearted; munificent, princely.

Adv. ungrudgingly; with open hands, with both hands.

817. ECONOMY.—*N.* economy, frugality; thrift, thriftiness, care, husbandry, retrenchment.

savings; prevention of waste, save-all; parsimony, etc., 819.

V. economize, save; retrench, cut down expenses; make both ends meet, meet one's expenses, pay one's way; husband, save (*or* invest) money; provide against a rainy day.

Adj. economical, frugal, careful, thrifty, saving, chary, spare, sparing; parsimonious, etc., 819; sufficient; plain.

818. PRODIGALITY.—*N.* prodigality, wastefulness, unthriftiness, waste; profusion, profuseness; extravagance, lavishness.

prodigal, spendthrift, waster, high roller [*slang*], squanderer, spender, prodigal son.

V. squander, lavish, sow broadcast, pay through the nose, spill, waste. dissipate, exhaust, drain, overdraw, spend money like water.

Adj. prodigal, profuse, thriftless, unthrifty, improvident, wasteful, extravagant, lavish, dissipated; penny-wise and pound-foolish.

Adv. with an unsparing hand.

819. PARSIMONY.—*N.* parsimony, parsimoniousness, stinginess, stint, illiberality, avarice, avidity, rapacity, extortion, venality, cupidity, selfishness.

miser, niggard, churl, screw, skinflint, curmudgeon, harpy, extortioner, extortionist, usurer.

V. grudge, begrudge, stint, pinch, gripe, screw, dole out, hold back, withhold, starve, famish.

drive a bargain, cheapen, beat down; have an itching palm, grasp, grab.

Adj. parsimonious, penurious, stingy, miserly, mean, shabby, near, niggardly, close, sparing, grudging, illiberal, ungenerous, churlish, sordid, mercenary, venal, covetous, avaricious; greedy, grasping, extortionate, rapacious.

Adv. with a sparing hand.

CLASS VI

WORDS RELATING TO THE SENTIENT AND MORAL POWERS

I. AFFECTIONS IN GENERAL

820. AFFECTIONS.—*N.* character, qualities, disposition, affections, nature, spirit, temper, temperament, idiosyncrasy, predilection, turn of mind, bent, bias, predisposition, proneness, proclivity, propensity, vein, humor, mood, sympathy.

soul, heart, bosom, inner man; inmost recesses of the heart.

passion, pervading spirit; ruling passion, fullness of the heart.

energy, fervor, fire, verve, force.

Adj. characterized, affected, formed, molded, cast, tempered; framed.

prone, predisposed, disposed, inclined; having a bias.

inborn, inbred, ingrained; deep-rooted, congenital, inherent.

Adv. at heart; in the vein, in the mood.

821. FEELING.—*N.* feeling, suffering, endurance, sufferance, response; sympathy, impression, inspiration, affection, sensation, emotion, pathos.

fervor, unction, gusto, vehemence, heartiness, cordiality, earnestness, eagerness, gush [*colloq.*], ardor, warmth, zeal, passion, enthusiasm, ecstasy.

excitement; thrill, shock, agitation, quiver, flutter, flurry, fluster, twitter, tremor, throb, throbbing, pulsation, palpitation, panting; blush, flush.

V. feel, receive an impression, be impressed with, respond, enter into the spirit of.

bear, suffer, support, sustain, endure, brook, brave, stand, abide, experience, taste, prove.

be agitated, be excited, glow, flush, blush, crimson, change color, mantle; darken, whiten, pale, tingle, thrill, heave, pant, throb, palpitate, tremble, quiver, flutter, shake, stagger, reel; wince.

Adj. sentient, sensuous, emotional; of (*or* with) feeling.

keen, sharp, lively, quick, acute, cutting, piercing, incisive, trenchant, pungent, racy, piquant, poignant, caustic.

impressive, deep, profound, indelible, deep-felt, heartfelt, soul-stirring, electric, thrilling, rapturous, ecstatic, rapt; pervading, penetrating, absorbing.

earnest, wistful, eager, fervent, fervid, gushing [*colloq.*], warm, passionate, hearty, cordial, sincere, zealous, enthusiastic, glowing, ardent.

rabid, raving, feverish, fanatical, hysterical, impetuous.

Adv. **heartily,** heart and soul, from the bottom of one's heart, devoutly.

822. SENSITIVENESS.—*N.* **sensitiveness,** sensibleness, sensibility, impressibility, susceptibility, vivacity, tenderness, sentimentality. sentimentalism.

excitability, etc., 825; physical sensibility, etc., 375.

V. **be sensitive,** have a tender heart; take to heart, shrink, wince, blench, quiver.

Adj. **sensitive,** sensible, impressible, impressionable; susceptive, susceptible; warmhearted, tenderhearted, softhearted, tender; sentimental, romantic; enthusiastic, impassioned, spirited, mettlesome, vivacious, lively, expressive, mobile, excitable, oversensitive, thin-skinned, fastidious.

Adv. to the quick, on the raw.

823. INSENSITIVENESS.—*N.* **insensitiveness,** insensibility, insensibleness, inertness, inertia, impassibility, impassivity, apathy, dullness, insusceptibility, lukewarmness.

coldness, coolness, frigidity, stoicism, nonchalance, unconcern, indifference, callousness, heart of stone.

torpor, torpidity, lethargy, coma, trance; sleep, stupor, stupefaction; paralysis, numbness.

stoic, Indian, man of iron.

V. **be insensitive,** not mind, not care, not be affected by; take no interest in; disregard.

blunt, numb, benumb, paralyze, deaden, stun, stupefy; brutalize.

inure; harden, steel, caseharden, sear.

Adj. **insensitive,** insensible, unconscious, impassive, insusceptible, unimpressible; passionless, spiritless, heartless, soulless, unfeeling.

apathetic, unemotional, phlegmatic; dull, frigid, cold, coldblooded, coldhearted; inert, supine, sluggish, torpid, sleepy, languid, halfhearted; numb, numbed; comatose.

indifferent, lukewarm, careless, mindless, inattentive, unconcerned, nonchalant.

unaffected, unruffled, unimpressed, unexcited, unmoved, unstirred, untouched, unshocked, unblushing.

callous, thick-skinned, impervious, hard, hardened, inured, casehardened; impenetrable, unfelt.

Adv. in cold blood; with dry eyes.

824. EXCITEMENT.—*N.* **excitement,** excitation, stimulation, piquancy, provocation, inspiration, animation, agitation, perturbation; fascination, intoxication, impressiveness; irritation, passion, thrill.

emotional appeal, melodrama, sensationalism, yellow journalism.

V. **excite**, affect, touch, move, impress, strike, interest, animate, inspire, smite, infect, awake, wake; awaken, waken; call forth; evoke, provoke; raise up, summon up, call up, wake up, raise; rouse, arouse, stir, fire, kindle, enkindle, illumine, illuminate, inflame.

stimulate, inspirit; stir up, infuse life into, give new life to; introduce new blood, quicken; sharpen, whet, fillip; fan, foster, heat, warm, foment, revive, rekindle.

penetrate, pierce; go to one's heart, touch to the quick, possess the soul, rivet the attention; prey on the mind.

agitate, perturb, ruffle, fluster, flutter, flurry, shake, disturb, startle, shock, stagger, strike dumb, stun, astound, electrify, galvanize, petrify.

irritate, sting, cut, pique, infuriate, madden, lash into fury.

flare up, flash up, seethe, boil, simmer, foam, fume, flame, rage, rave.

Adj. **excited**, wrought up, overwrought, hot, red-hot, flushed, feverish; raging, flaming, ebullient, seething, foaming, fuming, stung to the quick; wild, raving, frantic, mad, distracted, beside oneself.

exciting, impressive, telling, warm, glowing, fervid, spirit-stirring, thrilling; soul-stirring, heart-stirring, agonizing, sensational, yellow [*colloq.*], melodramatic, hysterical; overpowering, overwhelming.

piquant, spicy, appetizing, stinging, provocative, tantalizing.

Adv. at a critical moment, under a sudden strain.

825. [Excess of sensitiveness] EXCITABILITY.—*N.* excitability, impetuosity, vehemence, boisterousness, turbulence; impatience, intolerance, irritability; disquiet, disquietude, restlessness, fidgets, agitation.

trepidation, perturbation, ruffle, hurry, fuss, flurry, fluster, flutter; ferment; whirl; stage fright, thrill.

passion, excitement, flush, heat, fever, fire, flame, fume, tumult, effervescence, ebullition; gust, storm, tempest; burst, fit, paroxysm, explosion, outbreak, scene, outburst; agony.

fury; violence, fierceness, rage, furor, desperation, madness, distraction, raving, delirium; frenzy, hysterics; intoxication; towering rage, anger, etc., 900.

fixed idea, monomania; fascination, infatuation; fanaticism; quixotism, quixotry.

V. fidget, fuss.

fume, rage, foam; bear ill, wince, chafe, champ the bit, lose one's temper, break out, burst out, fly out, explode, flare up, flame up, fire up, boil, rave, rant, tear, go into hysterics; run riot, run amuck; raise Cain [*slang*].

Adj. **excitable,** easily excited, mettlesome, high-mettled, skittish, high-strung, nervous, irritable, hasty, impatient, intolerant, moody; feverish, hysterical, delirious, mad.

restless, unquiet, mercurial, galvanic, fidgety, fussy.

vehement, demonstrative, violent, wild, furious, fierce, fiery, hotheaded; overzealous, enthusiastic, impassioned, fanatical; rabid, rampant, clamorous, uproarious, turbulent, tempestuous, boisterous.

impulsive, impetuous. passionate, uncontrolled, uncontrollable, ungovernable, irrepressible. volcanic.

Adv. in confusion, pellmell.

826. INEXCITABILITY.—*N.* inexcitability, imperturbability, even temper, tranquil mind, dispassion; toleration, tolerance, patience; passiveness, inertia, etc., 172; impassibility, etc. (*insensibility*), 823; stupefaction.

calmness, composure, placidity, *sang-froid* [F.], coolness, tranquillity, serenity, content; quiet, quietude; peace of mind.

equanimity, poise, staidness, gravity, sobriety, philosophy, stoicism, self-possession, self-control, self-command, self-restraint; presence of mind.

resignation, submission, sufferance, endurance, long-sufferance, forbearance, longanimity, fortitude, patience of Job, moderation, restraint.

V. **endure,** bear, go through, support, brave, disregard; tolerate, suffer, stand, bide; abide, bear with, put up with, acquiesce, submit, resign oneself to, brook, digest, eat, swallow, pocket, stomach; carry on, carry through; make light of, make the best of, put a good face on.

compose, appease, assuage, propitiate, repress, restrain, master one's feelings, set one's mind at ease (*or* rest), calm down, cool down.

Adj. **inexcitable,** imperturbable; unsusceptible, dispassionate, cold-blooded, enduring, stoical, philosophical, staid, sober, grave; sedate, demure, coolheaded, levelheaded.

easygoing, peaceful, placid, calm; quiet, tranquil, serene, cool, undemonstrative.

composed, collected, temperate, unstirred, unruffled, unperturbed.

meek, mild, tame, subdued, unoffended, unresisting, submissive, gentle, patient, tolerant, clement, long-suffering.

Adv. in cold blood; more in sorrow than in anger.

II. PERSONAL AFFECTIONS[1]

827. PLEASURE.—*N.* pleasure, gratification, enjoyment, delectation, relish, zest, gusto, satisfaction, complacency; well-being; good, etc., 618; comfort, ease, luxury: physical pleasure, etc., 377.

joy, gladness, delight, glee, cheer, sunshine; cheerfulness, etc., 836; treat, luxury; amusement, etc., 840.

happiness, felicity, bliss, beatitude, enchantment, transport, rapture, ecstasy; paradise, heaven.

V. enjoy oneself, joy, be in clover [*colloq.*], tread on enchanted ground; go into raptures; feel at home, breathe freely, bask in the sunshine.

enjoy, like, relish, be pleased with, derive pleasure from, take pleasure in, delight in, rejoice in, indulge in, gloat over, love; take to, take a fancy to [*both colloq.*].

Adj. pleased, gratified, glad, gladsome; comfortable, etc. (*physical pleasure*), 377; at ease; content, etc., 831.

happy, blessed, blissful, beatified, joyful, in raptures, in ecstasies.

overjoyed, entranced, enchanted; raptured, enraptured, ravished, transported; fascinated, captivated.

pleasing, delightful, ecstatic, beatific, painless, unalloyed, cloudless.

828. PAIN.—*N.* pain, mental suffering, dolor, suffering, ache; physical pain, etc., 378.

displeasure, dissatisfaction, discomfort, discomposure, disquiet; inquietude, uneasiness, discontent.

annoyance, irritation, worry; infliction, visitation; plague, bore; bother, vexation, mortification, chagrin.

care, anxiety, solicitude, concern, trouble, trial, ordeal, shock, blow, fret, burden, load.

grief, sorrow, distress, affliction, woe, bitterness, heartache, heavy (*or* aching, bleeding, broken) heart.

misery, unhappiness, infelicity, tribulation, wretchedness, desolation; despair, etc., 859; extremity, prostration, depth of misery, slough of despond; nightmare, incubus.

anguish, pang, agony, torture, torment; crucifixion, martyrdom, rack, hell upon earth; reign of terror.

sufferer, victim, prey, martyr, wretch, shorn lamb.

V. suffer, ail, feel (*or* suffer, undergo, bear, endure) pain, smart, ache, bleed, bear the cross; fall on evil days, come to grief.

fret, chafe, sit on thorns, wince, worry oneself, fret and fume; take to heart.

[1]Or those which concern one's own state of feeling.

grieve, mourn, lament, etc., 839; yearn, repine, pine, droop, languish, sink, despair, break one's heart.

Adj. pained, afflicted, suffering, worried, displeased, aching, griped, sore, raw, on the rack.

uneasy, uncomfortable, ill at ease; disturbed; discontented; weary, etc., 841.

unfortunate, etc., 735; doomed, devoted, accursed, undone, crushed, lost, stranded; victimized, ill-used.

unhappy, infelicitous, poor, wretched, miserable, woebegone, comfortless, cheerless, etc. (*dejected*), 837; careworn; heavy-laden, stricken.

sorry, concerned, sorrowful, cut up [*colloq.*], chagrined, horrified, horror-stricken; heartbroken, brokenhearted.

829. [Capability of giving pleasure] PLEASURABLENESS.—
N. pleasurableness, pleasantness, agreeableness, pleasure giving, amusement, etc., 840; treat, etc. (*physical pleasure*), 377; dainty titbit, sweets, sweetmeats, nuts, salt, savor.

attraction, attractiveness, charm, fascination, captivation, enchantment, witchery, seduction, winning ways, winsomeness; loveliness, beauty, etc., 845.

V. delight, charm, gladden, bless, captivate, fascinate; enchant, entrance, enrapture, transport, bewitch, ravish.

please, satisfy, gratify, satiate, quench, indulge, humor, flatter, tickle; tickle the palate, refresh, enliven, treat, amuse, take one's fancy; attract, allure; stimulate, excite, interest.

Adj. pleasurable, pleasure-giving, pleasing, pleasant, amiable, agreeable, grateful, gratifying: acceptable; dear. beloved, welcome, favorite.

refreshing, comfortable, cordial, genial, glad. gladsome; sweet, delectable, nice, dainty. delicate. delicious.

attractive, inviting. prepossessing, engaging. winning, winsome, magnetic, fascinating, seductive, alluring. enticing, appetizing, cheering, bewitching, enchanting, entrancing.

delightful, charming, felicitous, exquisite, lovely, ravishing, rapturous; heartfelt, thrilling, ecstatic. heavenly.

Adv. to one's delight, in utter satisfaction; at one's ease; in clover [*colloq.*].

830. [Capability of giving pain] PAINFULNESS.—*N.* painfulness, trouble, care, trial, affliction, infliction, misfortune, mishap; cross, blow, stroke, burden, load, curse.

annoyance, pique, grievance, nuisance, vexation, mortification, worry, bore, bother, hornet's nest, plague, pest, wound; sore subject, skeleton in the closet; thorn in the flesh.

V. pain, hurt, wound, cause (*or* occasion, give, inflict) pain;

pierce, prick, cut, etc. (*physical pain*), 378; pierce (*or* break, rend) the heart; make the heart bleed.

sadden, make unhappy, grieve, afflict, distress; cut up [*colloq.*], cut to the heart.

annoy, incommode, displease, discompose, trouble, disturb, cross, thwart, perplex, molest; tease, tire, irk, fret, vex, mortify, worry, plague, bother, pester, bore, harass, harry, badger, heckle [*Brit.*], bait, beset, infest, persecute.

torment, wring, harrow, torture, rack, crucify, convulse, agonize.

irritate, provoke, sting, nettle, pique, fret, roil, rile [*colloq. & dial.*], chafe, gall; aggrieve, affront, enrage, ruffle, give offense.

maltreat, bite, snap at, assail, smite, etc., 972.

repel, revolt, sicken, disgust, nauseate, disenchant, offend, shock, rankle, gnaw, corrode, horrify, appall.

Adj. **painful,** hurtful, dolorous; distressing, cheerless, dismal, disheartening, depressing, dreary, melancholy, grievous, piteous, woeful, mournful, deplorable, pitiable, lamentable, sad; affecting, touching, pathetic.

unpleasant, unpleasing, displeasing, disagreeable, unpalatable, bitter, distasteful, uninviting, unwelcome, undesirable, obnoxious; unacceptable.

inauspicious, unlucky, ill-starred, unsatisfactory; untoward.

irritating, provoking, annoying, aggravating [*colloq.*], exasperating, galling, vexatious; troublesome, tiresome, irksome, wearisome.

importunate, pestering, bothering, harassing, worrying, tormenting.

insufferable, intolerable, insupportable, unbearable, unendurable.

shocking, terrific, grim, appalling, crushing; dreadful, fearful, frightful, tremendous, dire, heartbreaking, heart-rending, harrowing, rending.

odious, hateful, execrable, repulsive, repellent, horrid, horrible; offensive; nauseous, disgusting, revolting, nasty, loathsome, vile, hideous.

acute, sharp, sore, severe, grave, hard, harsh, cruel, biting, caustic; cutting, corroding, consuming, excruciating, agonizing.

cumbrous, cumbersome, burdensome, onerous, oppressive.

desolating, withering, tragical, disastrous, calamitous, ruinous.

Adv. in agony, out of the depths.

831. CONTENT.—*N.* content, contentment, contentedness; complacency, satisfaction, ease, peace of mind, serenity, cheerfulness; comfort.

patience, moderation, endurance; conciliation, reconciliation; resignation.

V. be content, rest satisfied, let well enough alone; take in good part; be reconciled to, take heart, take comfort.

content, set at ease, comfort; conciliate, reconcile, win over, propitiate, disarm, beguile; content, satisfy; gratify, etc., 836.

Adj. content, contented, satisfied, at ease, at one's ease, easygoing, not particular; conciliatory, unrepining, resigned, cheerful, serene, at rest; snug, comfortable.

satisfactory, adequate, sufficient, ample, equal to; satisfying.

Adv. to one's heart's content.

832. DISCONTENT.—*N.* discontent, dissatisfaction; disappointment, mortification; cold comfort; regret, repining, inquietude, vexation of spirit, soreness; heartburning.

malcontent, grumbler, growler, grouch [*slang*], croaker, faultfinder.

the opposition; bitter-enders [*politics*, U. S.], die-hards.

V. be discontented, repine, regret, take to heart, make a wry face, look blue, look black, look glum.

grumble, take ill, take in bad part; fret, chafe, croak; lament. dissatisfy, disappoint, mortify, put out [*colloq.*], disconcert, dishearten.

Adj. discontented, dissatisfied, unsatisfied, regretful, dejected, etc., 837; dissentient, malcontent, exacting.

glum, sulky, in high dudgeon, in a fume, in the sulks (*or* dumps), in bad humor; sour, soured, sore; out of humor, out of temper.

833. REGRET.—*N.* regret, repining; homesickness, nostalgia; bitterness, heartburning; lamentation, penitence, etc., 950.

V. regret, deplore, bewail, lament, etc., 839; repine, rue, rue the day; repent, etc., 950; leave an aching void.

Adj. regretful, rueful; homesick.

834. RELIEF.—*N.* relief, deliverance, alleviation, mitigation, palliation, solace, consolation, comfort, unction; encouragement.

V. relieve, ease, alleviate, mitigate, palliate, soothe; salve; soften, assuage, allay; remedy, cure, restore, refresh.

cheer, comfort, console; enliven; encourage, give comfort, inspirit, invigorate.

Adj. soothing, assuaging, balmy, lenitive, palliative, curative.

835. AGGRAVATION.—*N.* aggravation, heightening, intensification, overestimation, exaggeration.

V. aggravate, render worse, heighten, embitter, sour, intensify, enhance [*Note*: aggravate *in the sense of* provoke *is colloquial*].

Adj. aggravated, worse, unrelieved, aggravative.

Adv. from bad to worse, worse and worse.

836. CHEERFULNESS.—*N.* cheerfulness, geniality, gayety, cheer, good humor, spirits; high spirits, animal spirits, glee, high glee, light heart.

liveliness, life, alacrity, vivacity, animation, joviality, jollity, levity, jocularity.

mirth, merriment, hilarity, exhilaration, laughter, merrymaking, rejoicing, etc., 838.

optimism, hopefulness, etc., 858.

V. be cheerful, have the mind at ease, smile, keep up one's spirits, cheer up, take heart, cast away care, perk up; rejoice, etc., 838; carol, chirp, chirrup, lilt.

cheer, enliven, elate, exhilarate, gladden, delight, inspirit, animate, inspire.

Adj. cheerful; happy, etc., 827; cheery, sunny, smiling; blithe, in good spirits, chipper [*colloq.*], gay, debonair, light, lightsome, lighthearted; buoyant, bright, airy, jaunty, sprightly, spirited, lively, animated, vivacious, sparkling, sportive.

merry, joyful, joyous, jocund, jovial; jolly, blithesome, gleeful, hilarious.

winsome, bonny, hearty, buxom.

playful, tricksy, frisky, frolicsome, jocose, jocular, waggish, mirthful, rollicking.

elate, elated; exulting, jubilant, flushed, rejoicing.

cheering, inspiriting, exhilarating, pleasing, palmy, flourishing.

Adv. cheerfully, cheerily, with relish, with zest.

837. DEJECTION.—*N.* dejection, depression, mopishness, low (*or* depressed) spirits; heaviness, gloom; weariness, disgust of life; prostration, broken heart; despair, hopelessness.

melancholy, sadness, melancholia, blue devils [*colloq.*], blues [*colloq.*], dumps [*chiefly humorous*], doldrums, horrors, hypochondria, pessimism; despondency, slough of despond; disconsolateness, hope deferred.

gravity; demureness, solemnity; long face, grave face.

hypochondriac, self-tormentor, croaker, pessimist, damper, wet blanket.

V. be dejected, grieve, mourn, lament, give way, lose heart, despond, droop, sink, despair.

lower, frown, pout; look blue, lay to heart, take to heart.

mope, brood over, fret, sulk, pine, pine away; yearn, repine.

depress, discourage, dishearten, dispirit, damp, dull, deject, sink, dash, unman, prostrate, break one's heart; sadden, dash one's hopes, prey on the mind, damp the spirits.

Adj. cheerless, joyless, spiritless; unhappy, etc., 828; melancholy, dismal, dreary, depressing, somber, dark, gloomy, lowering, frowning, funereal, mournful, lamentable, dreadful.

downcast, downhearted, down in the mouth [*colloq.*], down on one's luck [*colloq.*], heavyhearted; sullen, mopish, moody, glum; sulky, etc. (*discontented*), 832; out of heart (*or* spirits); lowspirited; weary, etc., 841; discouraged, disheartened, despondent, crestfallen.

sad, pensive, doleful, woebegone, melancholic, bilious, jaundiced, saturnine, lackadaisical.

serious, sedate, staid, earnest, grave, sober, solemn, demure, grim, grim-faced, rueful, wan, long-faced.

disconsolate, forlorn, comfortless, desolate, sick at heart, heartsick.

overcome, broken-down, prostrate, cut up [*colloq.*], unnerved, unmanned; downfallen, downtrodden; brokenhearted; careworn.

Adv. with a long face, with tears in one's eyes.

838. [Expression of pleasure] REJOICING.—*N.* rejoicing, exultation, triumph, jubilation, heyday, flush, reveling, merrymaking, pæan, *Te Deum* [L.]; congratulation.

smile, simper, smirk, grin; broad grin, sardonic grin.

laughter, giggle, titter, snicker, snigger, crow, cheer, chuckle, shout; guffaw, burst (*or* fit, shout, roar, peal) of laughter.

cheer, huzza, hurrah, cheering; shout, yell [U. S. and Can.], college yell; tiger [*colloq.*].

V. rejoice, congratulate oneself, hug oneself, clap one's hands; skip; sing, carol, chirrup, chirp, hurrah, cry for joy, leap with joy; exult, triumph; make merry.

smile, simper, smirk, grin, laugh in one's sleeve.

laugh, giggle, titter, snigger, snicker, chuckle, cackle; burst out, shout, roar, shake (*or* split) one's sides.

Adj. rejoicing, jubilant, exultant, triumphant, flushed, elated; laughing, convulsed with laughter.

laughable, ludicrous, etc. 853.

Adv. in fits of laughter; in triumph.

839. [Expression of pain] LAMENTATION.—*N.* lamentation, lament, wail, complaint, plaint, murmur, mutter, grumble, groan, moan, whine, whimper, sob, sigh; frown, scowl.

cry, scream, howl; outcry, wail of woe.

weeping, flood of tears, fit of crying, crying; melting mood. plaintiveness; languishment; condolence, etc., 915.

mourning, weeds [*colloq.*], widow's weeds, crape, deep mourning; sackcloth and ashes; death song, dirge, requiem, elegy, threnody, jeremiad, keen [Ir.].

mourner, keener [Ir.]; Niobe.

V. **lament,** mourn, deplore, grieve, keen [Ir.], weep over; bewail, bemoan, condole with, etc., 915; fret.

sigh, give (*or* heave) a sigh; wail.

cry, weep, sob, blubber, snivel, whimper, shed tears, burst into tears.

scream, groan, moan, whine, yelp, howl, yell, roar; rend the air.

complain, murmur, mutter, grumble, growl, clamor, croak, grunt.

Adj. **lamenting,** in mourning, in sackcloth and ashes, clamorous, sorrowing, sorrowful, mournful, lamentable, tearful, lachrymose, plaintive, querulous; in tears.

840. AMUSEMENT.—*N.* **amusement,** entertainment, diversion, recreation, relaxation, solace; pastime, sport; labor of love; pleasure, etc., 827.

fun, frolic, merriment, jollity, joviality, laughter, etc., 838; pleasantry, quip, jocoseness; drollery, buffoonery, tomfoolery; mummery, pageant.

play, game, gambol, romp, prank, antic, lark [*colloq.*], spree, skylarking, vagary, monkey trick, escapade, practical joke.

dance, hop [*colloq.*]; ball, masquerade, ballet; step dance, skirt dance, folk dance, morris dance; gavot, minuet, Highland fling, reel, jig, hornpipe, sword dance, cakewalk; country dance, Scotch reel, Virginia reel, quadrille, lancers, cotillion; waltz, polka, mazurka, schottische, one-step, fox-trot.

festivity, fete, festival, merrymaking; party, etc. (*social gathering*), 892; revels, revelry, reveling, carnival, saturnalia, jollification [*colloq.*], junket, picnic.

holiday, red-letter day, play day; high days and holidays; high holiday.

place of amusement, theater; concert hall, ballroom, dance hall, assembly room; moving-picture theater; movies [*colloq.*]; music hall; vaudeville theater; circus, hippodrome.

Sports and games: athletic sports, track events, gymnastics; tournament.
skating, tobogganing; cricket, tennis, lawn tennis, rackets, squash, fives; croquet, golf, curling, hockey, polo, football, Rugby, rugger [*colloq.*]; association, soccer [*colloq.*]; quoits, discus, putting the weight (*or* shot), tug of war; baseball, basketball, pushball, lacrosse.
billiards, pool, pyramids, bagatelle; bowls, skittles, ninepins, tenpins; chess, draughts, checkers, dominoes, dice; card games, etc.

toy, plaything, doll, bauble.

sportsman (*fem.* sportswoman), hunter, Nimrod.

gamester, sport, gambler; dicer, punter, plunger.

devotee, enthusiast, follower, fan [*slang*], rooter [*slang or cant*].

V. **amuse,** entertain, divert, enliven, raise a smile, excite (*or* convulse with) laughter; cheer, rejoice, solace, please, interest.

amuse oneself, sport, disport, revel, junket, feast, carouse.

banquet, make merry; frolic, gambol, frisk, romp, caper, dance.

Adj. **amusing,** entertaining, diverting, recreative, pleasant, laughable, etc. (*ludicrous*), 853; witty, etc., 842; festive, festal, jovial, jolly, roguish, arch, playful, sportive.

Adv. at play, in sport.

841. WEARINESS.—*N.* **weariness,** ennui, boredom, lassitude, fatigue, etc., 688; drowsiness, languor.

disgust, nausea, loathing, sickness; satiety, repletion.

tedium, wearisomeness, tediousness, monotony.

bore, buttonholer, proser, dry-as-dust, fossil [*colloq.*], wet blanket.

V. **weary,** tire, fatigue, bore, send to sleep; buttonhole.

pall, sicken, nauseate, disgust; harp on the same string.

Adj. **wearying,** wearing, wearisome, tiresome, irksome, uninteresting, stupid, monotonous, dull, dry, arid, tedious, humdrum, flat; prosy, prosing; slow, soporific, somniferous.

weary, tired, drowsy, sleepy, etc., 683; uninterested, flagging, used up, worn out, blasé [F.].

842. WIT.—*N.* **wit,** wittiness, Attic salt, Atticism; point, fancy, whim, humor, drollery, pleasantry.

buffoonery, fooling, farce, tomfoolery, broad farce, fun.

jocularity, jocoseness, facetiousness, waggishness, comicality.

smartness, ready wit, banter, persiflage, retort, repartee.

witticism, smart saying, sally, flash, scintillation, flash of wit; jest, joke, epigram, conceit.

wordplay, play upon words, pun, riddle, conundrum, quibble.

V. **joke,** jest, cut jokes; crack a joke, pun; make merry with.

retort, flash back, flash, scintillate; banter, etc. (*ridicule*), 856.

Adj. **witty,** clever, keen, keen-witted, brilliant, pungent, quick-witted, smart, jocular, jocose, funny, waggish, facetious, comic, whimsical, humorous, sprightly, sparkling, epigrammatic.

843. DULLNESS.—*N.* **dullness,** heaviness, flatness, stupidity, want of originality, dearth of ideas; matter of fact, commonplace, platitude.

V. **be dull,** hang fire, fall flat, platitudinize, prose.

depress, damp, throw cold water on, lay a wet blanket on.

Adj. **dull,** jejune, dry, uninteresting, heavy-footed, elephantine; insipid, tasteless, unimaginative; prosy, prosaic, matter-of-fact, commonplace, platitudinous, pointless.

stupid, slow, flat, humdrum, monotonous, stolid.

844. HUMORIST.—*N.* **humorist,** wag, wit, epigrammatist, punster; life of the party; joker, jester, buffoon, comedian, merry-andrew, mime, tumbler, acrobat, mountebank, harlequin, pantaloon, punch, punchinello, clown; motley fool; caricaturist.

845. BEAUTY.—*N.* **beauty,** form, elegance, grace, symmetry, bloom, delicacy, refinement, charm, style; comeliness, fairness, polish, gloss; good effect, good looks.

brilliancy, radiance, splendor, gorgeousness, magnificence; sublimity.

beau ideal, Venus, Aphrodite, Hebe, the Graces, peri, houri, Cupid, Apollo, Hyperion, Adonis; Helen of Troy, Cleopatra; Venus de Milo, Apollo Belvedere.

loveliness, pleasurableness, etc., 829.

beautifying, decoration, ornamentation, etc., 847.

V. **beautify,** set off, grace; decorate, etc., 847.

Adj. **beautiful,** beauteous, handsome; pretty; lovely, graceful, elegant, exquisite, delicate, dainty.

comely, fair, goodly, bonny, good-looking, well favored, well formed, well proportioned, shapely, symmetrical, harmonious.

bright, bright-eyed; rosy-cheeked, rosy, ruddy, blooming, in full bloom.

trim, trig, tidy, neat, spruce, smart, jaunty, dapper.

brilliant, shining, sparkling, radiant, splendid, resplendent, dazzling, glowing, glossy, sleek; rich, gorgeous, superb, magnificent, grand, fine.

artistic, aesthetic, picturesque, pictorial, enchanting, attractive, becoming, ornamental.

perfect, unspotted, spotless, immaculate; undeformed, undefaced.

passable, presentable, tolerable, not amiss.

846. UGLINESS.—*N.* **ugliness,** deformity, inelegance, disfigurement, blemish, want of symmetry, distortion; squalor.

eyesore, object, figure, sight [*colloq.*], fright, scarecrow, hag, harridan, satyr, witch, monster.

V. **deface,** disfigure, deform, distort, blemish, injure, spoil; soil.

Adj. **ugly,** inartistic, unsightly, unseemly, uncomely, unshapely, unlovely; unbeautiful; coarse, plain, homely.

misshapen, misproportioned, shapeless, monstrous, gross; ill-made, ill-shaped, ill-proportioned, crooked, distorted.

unprepossessing, hard-featured, ill-favored, ill-looking; squalid, haggard; grim, grisly, ghastly, cadaverous, gruesome.

uncouth, ungainly, graceless, inelegant, ungraceful, stiff, rough, gross, rude, awkward, clumsy, gawky, lumbering, unwieldy.

repellent, forbidding, frightful, hideous, odious, repulsive; horrid, horrible, shocking.

disfigured, tarnished, smeared, besmeared, discolored, spotted, spotty.

showy, specious, pretentious, garish.

847. ORNAMENT.—*N.* ornament, ornamentation, ornateness, adornment, decoration, embellishment.

embroidery, needlework; lace, trimming, drapery; tapestry, arras; millinery.
wreath, festoon, garland, chaplet, flower, nosegay, bouquet, posy [*colloq.*].
tassel, knot; shoulder knot, epaulet, star, rosette, bow; feather, plume, fillet, snood.
jewelry: tiara, crown, coronet, diadem; jewel, gem, precious stone, trinket.

finery, frippery, tinsel, spangle, excess of ornament; pride, show, ostentation.

illustration, illumination; purple patches.

virtu, article of virtu, work of art, bric-a-brac, curio; rarity, a find.

V. ornament, embellish, enrich, decorate, adorn, beautify; garnish, furbish, polish, gild, varnish, enamel, paint.

spangle, bespangle, bead, embroider, chase, tool; emblazon, blazon, illuminate.

smarten, trim, bedizen, prink, trick up, trick out, deck, bedeck, array; spruce up [*colloq.*]; smarten up, dress, dress up.

Adj. ornamental, ornate, ornamented, rich, gilt, begilt, festooned.

smart, gay, flowery, glittering, new-spangled, fine, well groomed.

showy, gorgeous, flashy, gaudy, garish, tawdry, etc., 851.

848. BLEMISH.—*N.* blemish, disfigurement, deformity, defect, flaw, injury, eyesore.

stain, blot, spot, speck, speckle, blur, freckle, patch, blotch, smudge, birthmark, scar, mole, pimple, blister.

V. disfigure, etc. (*injure*), 659.

Adj. disfigured, imperfect, injured; discolored, specked, speckled, freckled, pitted, bruised.

849. SIMPLICITY.—*N.* simplicity, plainness, homeliness; chasteness, chastity, restraint, severity, naturalness, unaffectedness.

V. simplify, reduce to simplicity, strip of ornament, chasten, restrain.

Adj. simple, plain, homelike, homely, homespun [*fig.*], ordinary.

unaffected, natural, native; inartificial, free from affectation; chaste, severe; unadorned, unornamented.

simple-minded, childish, credulous, etc., 486.

850. [Good taste] TASTE.—*N.* taste, good (*or* refined, cultivated) taste; delicacy, refinement, fine feeling, discrimination, tact, polish, elegance, grace, culture, cultivation.

Science of taste: aesthetics.

man of taste, connoisseur, judge, critic, virtuoso, amateur, dilettante; purist, precisian.

V. display taste, appreciate, judge, criticize, discriminate.

Adj. in good taste, tasteful, unaffected, pure, chaste, classical, cultivated; graceful, attractive, charming, aesthetic, artistic.

refined, elegant, prim, precise, formal.

Adv. with quiet elegance; with elegant simplicity; without ostentation.

851. [Bad taste] VULGARITY.—*N.* **vulgarity,** vulgarism, barbarism, vandalism, bad taste; want of tact; ill-breeding, coarseness, indecorum, misbehavior, boorishness.

lowness, low life, brutality, blackguardism, rowdyism, ruffianism; ribaldry.

Excess of ornament: gaudiness, tawdriness, cheap jewelry; flashy clothes (*or* dress), finery, frippery, trickery, tinsel.

vulgarian, rough diamond, clown, Goth, vandal; snob, cad [*colloq.*], cub; parvenu, upstart; frump [*colloq.*], dowdy, slattern.

V. be vulgar, misbehave; show a want of tact (*or* consideration); be a vulgarian.

Adj. in bad taste, vulgar, unrefined, coarse, indecorous, ribald, gross; unseemly, unpresentable, ungraceful; dowdy, slovenly; low, extravagant, monstrous, horrid, shocking.

ill-mannered, ill-bred, underbred, snobbish, uncourtly, uncivil, discourteous, ungentlemanly, unladylike.

uncouth, unkempt, unpolished, plebeian; rude, awkward; homely, homespun, provincial, countrified, rustic; boorish, clownish; savage, brutish, blackguardly, rowdy, wild; barbarous, barbaric, outlandish; uncultivated.

antiquated, obsolete, out of fashion, old-fashioned, out of date, unfashionable.

newfangled, fantastic, fantastical, odd, affected.

tawdry, gaudy, meretricious, obtrusive, flaunting, loud, crass, showy, flashy, garish.

852. FASHION.—*N.* **fashion,** style, society, good (*or* polite) society, civilized life, civilization; court, high life, world, fashionable world; upper ten [*colloq*], elite, smart set [*colloq.*], the four hundred; Vanity Fair; Mayfair.

manners, breeding, politeness; air, demeanor, *savoir-faire* [F.], gentility, decorum, propriety, Mrs. Grundy; convention, conventionality, the proprieties, punctiliousness, form, formality, etiquette.

mode, vogue, style, the latest thing, the rage, prevailing taste; custom.

V. **be fashionable,** be the rage, have a run, pass current, follow the fashion, go with the stream

Adj. **fashionable,** in fashion, *à la mode* [F.], presentable; punctilious, genteel, decorous, conventional; well bred, gentlemanly, ladylike.

polished, refined, thoroughbred, gently bred, courtly, distinguished, aristocratic, self-possessed, poised, easy, frank, unconstrained.

modish, stylish, swell [*slang*], all the rage, all the go [*colloq.*].

Adv. for fashion's sake; in the latest style (*or* mode).

853. RIDICULOUSNESS.—*N.* ridiculousness, comicality, oddity, drollery; farce, comedy, burlesque, buffoonery, bull, Irish bull, spoonerism; bombast, anticlimax, bathos; absurdity, laughingstock.

V. be ridiculous, play the fool, make a fool of oneself, commit an absurdity.

Adj. ridiculous, ludicrous, comic *or* comical, waggish, quizzical, droll, funny, laughable, farcical, seriocomic, tragicomic.

odd, grotesque, whimsical, fanciful, fantastic, queer, quaint, bizarre, eccentric, strange, outlandish, out-of-the-way.

extravagant, monstrous, preposterous, absurd, bombastic, inflated, stilted, burlesque, mock heroic.

854. FOP.—*N.* fine gentleman, fop, swell [*colloq.*], dandy, exquisite, coxcomb, beau, man about town, spark, popinjay, puppy [*contemptuous*], prig, jackanapes, carpet knight; dude [*colloq.*].

fine lady, belle, flirt, coquette, toast.

855. AFFECTATION.—*N.* affectation, affectedness, pretense, pretension, airs, pedantry, stiffness, formality, mannerism, euphuism; boasting, charlatanism, quackery.

prudery, demureness, mock modesty, false shame; sentimentalism.

foppery, dandyism, coxcombry, puppyism, conceit; coquetry.

poser, actor; pedant, pedagogue, doctrinaire, purist, euphuist, mannerist; bluestocking, prig, charlatan; prude, puritan, precisian, formalist.

V. affect, act a part, give oneself airs, boast, simper, mince, attitudinize, pose, languish; overact, overdo.

Adj. affected, pretentious, pedantic, stilted, stagy, theatrical, canting, insincere, unnatural; self-conscious, artificial; overdone, overacted.

stiff, formal, prim, smug, complacent; demure, puritanical, prudish.

priggish, conceited, foppish, finical, finicking, mincing, simpering, namby-pamby, sentimental, languishing.

856. RIDICULE.—*N.* ridicule, derision, snicker *or* snigger, grin, scoffing, mockery, banter, irony, persiflage, raillery, chaff.

squib, satire, skit, quip.

burlesque, parody, travesty, farce, caricature.

buffoonery, practical joke, horseplay, roughhouse [*slang*].

V. **ridicule, deride;** laugh at, grin at, smile at; snicker **or** snigger; banter, chaff, joke, guy [*colloq.*], rag [*slang*], haze [*colloq.*].

burlesque, satirize, parody, caricature, travesty.

Adj. **derisive,** sarcastic, ironical, satirical, quizzical, burlesque, mock.

Adv. as a joke, to raise a laugh.

857. [Object and cause of ridicule] LAUGHINGSTOCK.—*N.* laughingstock, butt, game, fair game, April fool, original, oddity; queer fish [*colloq.*], figure of fun [*colloq.*]; monkey; buffoon.

858. HOPE.—*N.* hope; desire, etc., 865; trust, confidence, reliance, faith, assurance, security; reassurance.

hopefulness, buoyancy, optimism, enthusiasm, aspiration; assumption, presumption; anticipation.

optimist, utopian.

daydream, castles in the air, utopia, millennium; golden dream, airy hopes, fool's paradise, fond hope.

mainstay, anchor, sheet anchor; staff.

V. **hope,** trust, confide, rely, lean upon; live in hope, rest assured.

hope for, etc. (*desire*), 865; anticipate; presume, aspire; promise oneself; expect.

be hopeful, look on the bright side of, make the best of it, hope for the best; hope against hope, take heart, flatter oneself.

encourage, hearten, inspirit, hold out hope, cheer, assure, reassure, buoy up, embolden; promise, bid fair, augur well.

Adj. **hopeful,** confident, in hopes, secure, sanguine, buoyant, elated, flushed, exultant, enthusiastic.

fearless, unsuspecting, unsuspicious, undespairing, self-reliant; dauntless, etc. (*courageous*), 861.

propitious, promising; probable, auspicious, reassuring; encouraging, cheering, inspiriting, bright, roseate.

859. HOPELESSNESS.—*N.* hopelessness, despair, desperation; despondency, dejection, etc., 837; pessimism, hope deferred, dashed hopes.

pessimist, hypochondriac; bird of ill omen.

V. **despair;** lose (*or* give up, abandon) all hope, give up, give over, yield to despair; falter; despond.

Adj. **hopeless,** desperate, despairing, gone, in despair, forlorn, inconsolable, brokenhearted.

undone, ruined; incurable, cureless, incorrigible; irreparable, irrecoverable, irretrievable, irreclaimable, irredeemable, irrevocable.

unpropitious, unpromising, inauspicious, ill-omened, threatening, lowering, ominous.

860. FEAR.—*N.* **fear,** timidity, diffidence, apprehensiveness, fearfulness, solicitude, anxiety, care, apprehension, misgiving, mistrust, suspicion, qualm; hesitation.

trepidation, flutter, fear and trembling, perturbation, tremor, quivering, shaking, trembling, palpitation, nervousness, restlessness, disquietude, funk [*colloq.*].

fright, alarm, dread, awe, terror, horror, dismay, consternation, panic, scare; stampede [*of horses*].

intimidation, bullying; terrorism, reign of terror; terrorist, bully.

V. **fear,** be afraid, apprehend, dread, distrust; hesitate, falter, funk [*colloq.*], cower, crouch, skulk, take fright, take alarm; start, wince, flinch, shy, shrink, fly.

tremble, shake, shiver, shudder, flutter, quake, quaver, quiver, quail.

frighten, fright, terrify, inspire (*or* excite) fear, bulldoze [*colloq.*], alarm, startle, scare, dismay, astound; awe, strike terror, appall, unman, petrify, horrify.

daunt, intimidate, cow, overawe, abash, deter, discourage; browbeat, bully, threaten, terrorize.

haunt, obsess, beset, besiege; prey (*or* weigh) on the mind.

Adj. **afraid,** frightened, alarmed, fearful, timid, timorous, nervous, diffident, fainthearted, tremulous, shaky, afraid of one's shadow, apprehensive; aghast, awe-struck, awe-stricken, horror-stricken, panic-stricken.

dreadful, alarming, redoubtable, perilous, dread, fell, dire, direful, shocking, frightful, terrible, terrific, tremendous; horrid, horrible, ghastly, awful, awe-inspiring, revolting.

861. [Absence of fear] COURAGE.—*N.* **courage,** bravery, valor, resoluteness, boldness, spirit, daring, gallantry, intrepidity, prowess, heroism, chivalry, audacity, rashness, dash, defiance, confidence, self-reliance; manhood, manliness, nerve, pluck, mettle, grit, virtue, hardihood, fortitude, firmness, backbone, resolution, tenacity.

exploit, feat, deed, act, achievement.

brave man, man of courage, a man, hero, demigod; Hercules, Achilles, Sir Galahad.

brave woman, heroine; Amazon, Joan of Arc.

V. **dare,** venture, make bold; face (*or* front, confront, brave, defy, despise) danger; face; meet, brave, beard, defy.

nerve oneself, summon up (*or* pluck up) courage, take heart, stand to one's guns, bear up, hold out; present a bold front, show fight, face the music.

hearten, inspire courage, reassure, encourage, embolden, inspirit, cheer, nerve, rally.

Adj. **courageous,** brave, valiant, valorous, gallant, intrepid, spirited, high-spirited, mettlesome, plucky; manly, manful, stout-hearted, lionhearted, bold, daring, audacious, fearless, dauntless, undaunted, undismayed, unflinching, unshrinking, confident, self-reliant.

enterprising, adventurous, venturous, venturesome; dashing, chivalrous, warlike, soldierly, heroic.

fierce, savage, pugnacious, bellicose.

strong-minded, strong-willed, hardy, doughty [*archaic or humorous*]; firm, resolute, determined, dogged, indomitable.

862. [Excess of fear] COWARDICE.—*N.* **cowardice,** pusillanimity, cowardliness, timidity, effeminacy; baseness, abject fear, funk [*colloq.*]; fear, etc., 860; white feather, cold feet [*slang*], yellow streak [*slang*].

coward, poltroon, dastard, sneak, recreant, cur [*contemptuous*], craven.

alarmist, terrorist, pessimist.

shirker, slacker; fugitive, etc., 623.

V. **quail,** funk [*colloq.*], cower, skulk, sneak; flinch, shy, fight shy, slink, run away; show the white feather.

Adj. **cowardly,** coward, fearful, shy, timid, timorous, spiritless, soft, effeminate, fainthearted; white-livered; dastard, dastardly, base, craven, sneaking, recreant; unwarlike.

Adv. with fear and trembling, in fear of one's life, in a blue funk [*colloq.*].

863. RASHNESS.—*N.* **rashness,** temerity, imprudence, indiscretion; overconfidence, presumption, audacity, precipitancy, impetuosity, foolhardiness, heedlessness, thoughtlessness, carelessness, desperation.

gaming, gambling; blind bargain, leap in the dark.

desperado, madcap, daredevil; scapegrace, Don Quixote, knight-errant, adventurer; fire-eater, bully, bravo.

gambler, gamester, etc. (*chance*), 621.

V. **be rash,** stick at nothing, play a desperate game, run into danger, play with fire (*or* edged tools); rush on destruction, tempt providence, go on a forlorn hope.

Adj. **rash,** incautious, indiscreet, injudicious, imprudent, improvident, uncalculating, impulsive, heedless, careless, without ballast.

reckless, wild, madcap, desperate, devil-may-care, death-defying, hotheaded, headlong, headstrong; breakneck, foolhardy, harebrained, precipitate.

overconfident, overweening; venturesome, venturous, adventurous, quixotic.

Adv. posthaste, headforemost.

864. CAUTION.—*N.* caution, cautiousness, discretion, prudence, heed, circumspection, calculation, deliberation, foresight, etc., 510; vigilance, etc., 459; warning, etc., 668.

worldly wisdom; safety first, Fabian policy, watchful waiting.

coolness, self-possession, self-command; presence of mind, *sang-froid* [F.].

V. be cautious, take care, take heed, mind, be on one's guard; think twice, look before one leaps, count the cost, feel one's way, see how the land lies; pussyfoot [*colloq.*], keep out of harm's way, stand aloof; keep (*or* be) on the safe side.

warn, caution, etc., 668.

Adj. cautious, wary, guarded, on one's guard, suspicious, vigilant, careful, heedful, chary, sure-footed, circumspect, prudent, noncommittal, canny [Scot.], discreet, politic, strategic.

unenterprising, unadventurous, cool, steady, self-possessed; overcautious.

865. DESIRE.—*N.* desire, wish, fancy, inclination, leaning, bent, mind, whim, partiality, predilection, propensity, liking, love, fondness, relish.

longing, hankering, yearning, aspiration, ambition, eagerness, zeal, ardor, solicitude, anxiety.

need, want, exigency, urgency, necessity.

appetite, keenness, hunger, stomach, thirst, drought.

avidity, greed, greediness, covetousness, ravenousness, grasping, craving, rapacity, voracity.

mania, passion, rage, furor, frenzy, itching palm, cupidity, kleptomania, dipsomania; monomania.

Person desiring: lover, votary, devotee, aspirant; parasite, sycophant.

attraction, magnet, loadstone, lure, allurement, fancy, temptation, fascination; hobby.

V. desire, wish, wish for, care for, affect, like, take to, cling to, fancy; prefer, have an eye to, have a mind to; have a fancy for, have at heart, be bent upon; set one's heart (*or* mind) upon, covet, crave, hanker after, pine for, long for; hope, etc., 858.

woo, court, ogle, solicit; fish for.

want, miss, need, lack, feel the want of.

attract, allure, whet the appetite; appetize, take one's fancy, tempt, tantalize, make one's mouth water.

Adj. desirous, desiring, appetitive, inclined, fain, wishful, longing, wistful; anxious, solicitous, sedulous.

eager, keen, burning, fervent, ardent; agog; breathless; impatient.

ambitious, aspiring, vaulting.

craving, hungry, sharp-set, peckish [*colloq.*], ravening, famished; thirsty, athirst, dry [*colloq. when meaning thirsty*], droughty.

greedy, voracious, ravenous, omnivorous, covetous, rapacious, grasping, extortionate, exacting, sordid, insatiable, insatiate.

desirable, desired, in demand, popular, pleasing, appetizing.

Adv. fain; with eager appetite.

866. INDIFFERENCE.—*N.* indifference, neutrality; unconcern, nonchalance, apathy, supineness, disdain, inattention, coldness.

V. be indifferent, stand neuter, take no interest in, have no desire for, have no taste for, not care for, care nothing for (*or* about); not mind; spurn, disdain.

Adj. indifferent, cold, frigid, lukewarm; cool, neutral, unconcerned, phlegmatic, easygoing, careless, listless, halfhearted, unambitious, undesirous, unsolicitous.

unattractive, unalluring, undesired, undesirable, unwished.

867. DISLIKE.—*N.* dislike, distaste, disrelish, disinclination, unwillingness, reluctance, backwardness.

repugnance, disgust, nausea, loathing, aversion, abomination, antipathy, abhorrence, horror, hatred, detestation; hate, etc., 898.

V. dislike, disrelish; mind, object to, have no taste for, shudder at, turn up the nose at, look askance at; shun, avoid, eschew, shrink from.

loathe, abominate, detest, abhor; hate, etc., 898.

repel, disincline, sicken, pall, nauseate, disgust, shock, make one's blood run cold.

Adj. loath, averse; shy of, sick of, disinclined, heartsick.

repugnant, repulsive, repellent, abhorrent, insufferable, fulsome, nauseous, loathsome, offensive, disgusting.

unpopular, undesirable, uncared for, disliked, out of favor.

uneatable, inedible, unappetizing, unsavory.

Adv. to satiety, to one's disgust.

868. FASTIDIOUSNESS.—*N.* fastidiousness, nicety, hypercriticism, epicurism.

discrimination, discernment, perspicacity, keenness, sharpness, insight.

epicure, gourmet.

Excess of delicacy: prudery, prudishness, primness.

V. be fastidious, split hairs; mince the matter; turn up one's nose at, disdain.

discriminate, have nice discrimination; have exquisite taste; be discriminative.

Adj. fastidious, nice, delicate, meticulous, finicking *or* finicky, exacting, hard to please, difficult, dainty, squeamish, thin-skinned; querulous; particular, scrupulous; critical, hypercritical, overcritical.

prudish, strait-laced, prim.

discriminative, discriminating, discerning, judicious, keen, sharp, perspicacious.

869. SATIETY.—*N.* satiety, satisfaction, saturation, repletion, glut, surfeit, satiation.

V. sate, satiate, satisfy, saturate, cloy, quench, slake, pall, glut, gorge, surfeit; bore, tire, spoil.

Adj. satiated, overgorged, overfed, blasé [F.], sick of.

870. WONDER.—*N.* wonder, astonishment, amazement, wonderment, bewilderment, admiration, awe; stupor, stupefaction, fascination, surprise.

V. wonder, marvel, admire, be surprised, start, stare; gape, hold one's breath, stand aghast.

astonish, surprise, amaze, astound; dumfound, dumfounder, startle, dazzle, daze, strike, electrify, stun, stupefy, petrify, confound, bewilder, stagger, fascinate, take away one's breath, strike dumb.

Adj. astonished, surprised, aghast, breathless, agape, openmouthed, thunderstruck, spellbound; lost in amazement (*or* wonder, astonishment).

wonderful, wondrous, surprising, striking, marvelous, miraculous; unexpected, mysterious, monstrous, prodigious, stupendous, inconceivable, incredible, strange.

indescribable, inexpressible, ineffable; unutterable, unspeakable.

Adv. for a wonder, strange to say, to one's great surprise.

871. [Absence of wonder] EXPECTANCE.—*N.* expectance, expectancy, expectation, etc., 507.

calmness, imperturbability, *sang-froid* [F.], coolness, steadiness, lack of nerves, want of imagination.

V. expect, etc., 507; not wonder, make nothing of, take it coolly.

Adj. expecting, unamazed, astonished at nothing, blasé [F.], expected, foreseen.

calm, imperturbable, nerveless, cool, coolheaded, unruffled, steady, unimaginative.

common, ordinary, etc. (*habitual*), 613.

872. PRODIGY.—*N.* prodigy, phenomenon, wonder, wonderment, marvel, miracle; freak, freak of nature, monstrosity, monster; curiosity, infant prodigy, lion, sight, spectacle; sign, portent.

873. REPUTE.—*N.* **repute,** reputation, distinction, mark, name, figure, note, notability, éclat, vogue, celebrity, fame, renown, popularity; credit, prestige, account, regard, respect, fair name.

dignity, stateliness, solemnity, grandeur, luster, splendor, nobility, majesty, sublimity, glory, honor.

rank, standing, precedence, station, place, status, position, order, degree, caste, condition.

eminence, greatness, height, importance, pre-eminence, supereminence, elevation, exaltation.

celebrity, worthy, hero, man of mark (*or* rank), lion, notability, somebody.

scholar, savant; paragon, star; elite.

ornament, honor, feather in one's cap, halo, aureole, nimbus; laurels.

posthumous fame, memory, celebration, canonization, enshrinement, glorification, immortality, immortal name.

V. **be distinguished,** shine, etc. (*light*), 420; shine forth, figure, cut a figure, flourish, flaunt, play first fiddle, bear the palm, take precedence; win laurels (*or* golden opinions).

surpass, outshine, outrival, outvie, eclipse; throw into the shade, overshadow.

rival, emulate, vie with.

honor, give (*or* do, pay) honor to, accredit, dignify, glorify, pledge, toast, look up to, exalt, aggrandize, elevate, enthrone, signalize, immortalize, deify.

consecrate; dedicate to, devote to; enshrine, inscribe, blazon, lionize.

Adj. **distinguished,** noted, of note, honored, popular, remarkable, notable, celebrated, renowned, famous, famed, far-famed, conspicuous, foremost.

reputable, in good odor, in favor, in high favor, respectable, creditable, worthy.

imperishable, deathless, immortal, never fading, fadeless.

illustrious, glorious, splendid, brilliant, radiant; bright, etc.,420.

eminent, prominent, high, etc., 206; peerless, pre-eminent, great, dignified, proud, noble, honorable, lordly, grand, stately, august, princely, imposing, solemn, transcendent, majestic, sacred, sublime.

874. DISREPUTE.—*N.* **disrepute,** discredit, ill-repute, illfavor, ingloriousness, derogation, abasement, debasement, degradation; odium, obloquy, opprobrium, ignominy, dishonor, disgrace, shame, humiliation, scandal, infamy.

stigma, brand, reproach, imputation, slur, stain, blot, spot, blur, tarnish, taint, badge of infamy.

V. **be inglorious**, have a bad name; disgrace oneself, lose caste; fall from one's high estate, cut a sorry figure.

shame, disgrace, put to shame, dishonor; tarnish, stain, blot, sully, taint; discredit, degrade, debase, expel.

stigmatize, vilify, defame, slur, brand, post, send to Coventry, snub, show up [*colloq.*], reprehend.

disconcert, put out [*colloq.*], upset, discompose; put to the blush.

Adj. **disgraced**, overcome, downtrodden, in bad repute, under a cloud, in the shade (*or* background); down in the world, down and out [*colloq.*].

inglorious, nameless, obscure, unknown to fame, unnoticed, unnoted, unhonored, unglorified.

discreditable, questionable, shameful, disgraceful, disreputable, despicable; unbecoming, unworthy, derogatory, degrading, humiliating, scandalous, infamous, opprobrious, arrant, shocking, outrageous, notorious, ignominious, base, abject, vile.

beggarly, pitiful, mean, petty, shabby.

875. NOBILITY.—*N.* nobility, rank, condition, distinction, blood, birth, high descent, order, quality.

high life, upper classes, upper ten [*colloq.*], the four hundred; elite, aristocracy, fashionable world.

celebrity, bigwig [*humorous*], magnate, great man, star, great gun [*colloq.*].

The nobility: peerage, baronage; House of Lords (*or* peers); lords, noblesse.
peer, noble, nobleman; lord, grandee, don, hidalgo; aristocrat, swell [*colloq.*], gentleman, squire, patrician.
gentry, gentlefolk, magnates.
king, etc., 745; prince, duke, marquis, earl, viscount, baron, baronet, knight, chevalier, count, esquire, laird [Scot.]; signior, seignior; *signor* [It.], *señor* [Sp.], *senhor* [Pg.]; sheik, pasha, sahib
empress, queen, princess, duchess, marchioness, viscountess, countess; lady, *doña* [Sp.], *dona* [Pg.]; *signora* [It.], *señora* [Sp.], *senhora* [Pg.].
Hindu titles: raja, rana (*fem.* rani), maharaja, maharana (*fem.* maharani), Gaekwar [*lit.* cowherd; *Baroda*].
Mohammedan titles: nawab, sultan (*fem.* sultana), amir.
Rank or office: kingship, dukedom, marquisate, earldom; viscountship, county, lordship, baronetcy, knighthood.

Adj. **noble**, exalted, princely, titled, patrician, aristocratic; highborn, well born, courtly.

Adv. in high quarters.

876. THE PEOPLE.—*N.* the people, commonalty, democracy; obscurity; *bourgeoisie* [F.], the four million; lower classes (*or* orders), common herd, rank and file, the many, the general, the crowd, the ruck, the populace, the multitude, the million, the masses, the mobility [*humorous*], the peasantry, proletariat; *hoi polloi* [Gr.].

rabble, horde, canaille, dregs of society, mob, trash, riffraff, ragtag and bobtail.
commoner, one of the people, democrat, plebeian, republican, bourgeois [F.].
peasant, countryman, boor, churl, serf; swain, clown, clodhopper, yokel, lout,
bumpkin; plowman, hayseed [*slang*], rustic, lunkhead [*colloq.*], rube [*slang*]; tiller
of the soil; hewers of wood and drawers of water; gamin, street Arab.
rough, rowdy, roughneck [*slang*], ruffian, tough [*colloq.*], scullion, low fellow, cad.

upstart, parvenu, nobody, snob, mushroom, adventurer, *nouveau riche* (*pl. nouveaux riches*) [F.].

vagabond, beggar, caitiff, ragamuffin, pariah, outcast, tramp, panhandler [*slang*], bum [*slang*], hobo.

Adj. ignoble, common, mean, low, base, vile, sorry, scrubby, beggarly; vulgar, low-minded; snobbish, parvenu, low-bred; menial, servile.

plebeian, proletarian, lowborn, baseborn, risen from the ranks, obscure, untitled.

rustic, country, uncivilized; loutish, boorish, clownish, churlish, rude.

barbarous, barbarian, barbaric.

Adv. below the salt.

877. TITLE.—*N.* title, honor; earldom, etc. (*nobility*), 875.

highness, excellency, grace, lordship, reverence; reverend; esquire, sir, master, Mr., *signor* [It.], *señor* [Sp.], etc., 373; your (*or* his) honor.

madam, etc. (*mistress*), 374; empress, queen, etc., 875.

decoration, laurel, palm, wreath, garland, bays; medal, ribbon, cordon, cross, crown, coronet, star, garter; epaulet, chevron, colors, cockade; livery; order, arms, coat of arms, shield, escutcheon *or* scutcheon, crest; handle to one's name.

878. PRIDE.—*N.* pride, haughtiness, high notions, hauteur, vainglory, arrogance, self-importance, pomposity, side [*slang*], swagger, toploftiness [*colloq.*].

dignity, self-respect, self-esteem, decorum, stateliness, seemliness.

V. be proud, presume, swagger, strut, hold one's head high, look big, carry with a high hand; ride the high horse, give oneself airs.

Adj. dignified, stately, lordly, lofty-minded, high-souled, high-minded, high-mettled, high-flown.

proud, haughty, lofty, high, mighty, swollen, puffed up, flushed, vainglorious; purse-proud, fine.

supercilious, disdainful, bumptious, magisterial, imperious, high and mighty, overweening, consequential; pompous, toplofty [*colloq.*]; arrogant.

stiff, stiff-necked; starched, stuck up [*colloq.*]; strait-laced, prim, affected, etc., 855.

Adv. with head erect, with nose in air, with nose turned up; with a sneer, with curling lip.

879. HUMILITY.—*N.* humility, humbleness, meekness, lowliness, abasement, self-abasement, submission, resignation.

modesty, timidity; confusion, humiliation, mortification.

V. **be humble,** deign, vouchsafe, condescend, humble oneself, stoop, submit, yield the palm, sing small [*colloq.*], hide one's face.

be humiliated, be put out of countenance, be shamed, be put to the blush, receive a snub, eat humble pie.

humble, humiliate, snub, abash, abase, strike dumb, lower, cast into the shade, put to the blush, confuse, shame, mortify, disgrace, crush.

Adj. **humble,** lowly, meek, modest, etc., 881; humble-minded, sober-minded; submissive, servile.

humbled, bowed down, abashed, ashamed, dashed, crestfallen, shorn of one's glory.

Adv. with downcast eyes, with bated breath, on bended knee.

880. VANITY.—*N.* vanity, conceit, conceitedness, self-conceit, self-sufficiency, self-praise, self-glorification, self-applause, self-admiration; selfishness, etc., 943.

pretension, airs, affected manner, mannerism; egoism, egotism, priggishness; vainglory, arrogance, pride, ostentation.

egoist, egotist; peacock; coxcomb.

V. **be vain,** pique oneself, have too high opinion of oneself, strut, put oneself forward; give oneself airs, boast, etc., 884.

render vain, inflate, puff up, turn one's head.

Adj. **vain,** conceited, overweening, forward, vainglorious, high-flown, ostentatious, etc., 882; puffed up, inflated, flushed, elate.

self-satisfied, complacent, self-confident, self-sufficient, self-admiring, pretentious, priggish, egotistic *or* egotistical, arrogant, assured.

881. MODESTY.—*N.* modesty; humility, etc., 879; diffidence, demureness, timidity, bashfulness, retiring disposition, unobtrusiveness; blush, blushing; reserve, constraint.

V. **be modest,** retire, give way to, hide one's face; keep in the background; hide one's light under a bushel.

Adj. **modest,** diffident, retiring, humble, etc., 879; timid, timorous, bashful, shy, coy, demure, sheepish, shamefaced, blushing.

unpretending, unpretentious, unobtrusive, unassuming, unostentatious, reserved, constrained.

Adv. **modestly,** quietly, privately; without ceremony.

882. OSTENTATION.—*N.* ostentation, display, show, flourish, parade, pomp, magnificence, splendor, pageantry, array, state, solemnity; dash [*colloq.*], splash [*colloq.*], glitter, pomposity, pretense, pretensions.

demonstration, pageant, spectacle, exhibition, exposition, procession, turnout [*colloq.*]; fete, field day, review, march past, promenade.

ceremony, ceremonial, ritual, form, formality, etiquette, punctilio.

V. **flaunt,** show off, parade, display, exhibit, brandish, blazon forth; dangle, emblazon.

Adj. **ostentatious,** showy, dashing, pretentious, grand, pompous; garish, gaudy, flaunting, glittering, gay.

splendid, magnificent, sumptuous, palatial.

theatrical, theatric, dramatic, spectacular, scenic.

ceremonial, ceremonious, ritualistic; solemn, stately, majestic, formal, punctilious.

Adv. with flourish of trumpet, with beat of drum, with flying colors.

883. CELEBRATION.—*N.* **celebration,** solemnization, commemoration; jubilation, ovation, triumph; inauguration, installation, presentation; coronation; debut, coming out [*colloq.*].

birthday, anniversary, biennial, triennial, etc.; centenary, centennial; bicentenary, bicentennial; tercentenary, tercentennial, etc.; festivity, festival, fete, holiday.

triumphal arch; salute, salvo, salvo of artillery; flourish of trumpets, fanfare; colors flying; illuminations.

jubilee, 50th anniversary; diamond jubilee.

V. **celebrate,** keep, signalize, do honor to, commemorate, solemnize; rejoice, etc., 838; paint the town red [*colloq.*].

inaugurate, install, instate, induct, chair.

Adj. **commemorative,** celebrated, kept in remembrance; immortal.

Adv. **in honor of,** in commemoration of, in celebration of, in memory of, in memoriam [L.].

884. BOASTING.—*N.* **boasting,** boast, vaunt, pretensions, braggadocio, puff [*colloq.*], flourish, bluff, highfalutin, swagger, jingoism, chauvinism, brag, bounce, bluster, bravado, buncombe [*cant or slang*]; rodomontade, bombast, hot air [*slang*], tall talk [*colloq.*], exaggeration, magniloquence, heroics.

boaster, braggart, pretender, bluffer, hot-air artist [*slang*]; chauvinist, jingo, jingoist; blusterer, swaggerer.

V. **boast,** brag, vaunt, puff, show off, flourish, strut, swagger, bluff; talk big, draw the long bow, blow one's own trumpet.

exult, crow [*colloq.*], triumph, glory, rejoice, cheer; gloat, gloat over, chuckle.

Adj. **boastful,** braggart, pretentious, vainglorious, highfalutin.

elate, elated, jubilant, triumphant, exultant: in high feather.

885. [Undue assumption of superiority] INSOLENCE.—*N.* insolence, brazenness, haughtiness, arrogance, airs; bumptiousness, assumption, presumption; disdain, insult, bluster, swagger.

impertinence, cheek [*colloq. or, slang*], nerve [*slang*], sauce [*colloq.*], abuse; flippancy.

impudence, self-assertion, assurance, audacity, hardihood, gall [*slang*], shamelessness, effrontery.

V. **be insolent,** bluster, swagger, give oneself airs, arrogate, assume, presume; make bold, make free, take a liberty.

outface, outlook, outstare, outbrazen, brazen out; look big.

domineer, bully, dictate, hector; lord it over; snub, browbeat, intimidate; dragoon, bulldoze [*colloq.*], terrorize.

Adj. **insolent,** haughty, arrogant, imperious, dictatorial, arbitrary, highhanded, supercilious, overbearing, toplofty [*colloq.*], intolerant, domineering, overweening, bumptious.

pert, flippant, fresh [*slang*], saucy, forward, impertinent, assuming, impudent, audacious, presumptuous.

brazen, shameless, unblushing, unabashed; barefaced, brazen-faced; lost to shame.

blustering, swaggering, hectoring, rollicking, roistering, devil-may-care.

jingo, jingoistic, chauvinistic.

Adv. with nose in air; with arms akimbo; with a high hand.

886. SERVILITY.—*N.* servility, slavery, obsequiousness, toadying, subserviency; abasement, prostration, toadeating, fawning, flunkyism, sycophancy; humility, etc., 879.

sycophant, parasite, toady, toadeater, flunky, hanger-on, timeserver, flatterer, tool; beat [*slang*], dead beat [*slang*]; heeler, ward heeler [*both polit. cant*]; sponge, sponger, truckler.

V. **cringe,** bow, stoop, kneel; fawn, crouch, cower, sneak, crawl, sponge, toady, grovel; be servile.

go with the stream, follow the crowd, worship the rising sun; be a timeserver.

Adj. **servile,** obsequious, oily, pliant, cringing, fawning, slavish, groveling, sniveling, mealy-mouthed; sycophantic, parasitical; abject, prostrate, base, mean, sneaking, timeserving.

887. BLUSTERER.—*N.* blusterer, swaggerer, braggart; roisterer, brawler, bully, terrorist, rough, ruffian, roughneck [*slang*], tough [*colloq.*], rowdy, hoodlum [*colloq.*], hooligan [*slang*], swashbuckler; desperado, daredevil, fire-eater [*colloq.*], jingo.

dogmatist, doctrinaire, stump orator.

III. SYMPATHETIC AFFECTIONS

888. FRIENDSHIP.—*N.* friendship, amity, friendliness; harmony, concord, peace, etc., 721; cordiality, *entente cordiale* [F.], good understanding, sympathy, fellow feeling, response; affection, etc. (*love*), 897; benevolence, good will; partiality, favoritism.

brotherhood, fraternization, association; acquaintance, familiarity, intimacy, intercourse, fellowship.

fraternity, sodality; sisterhood, sorority, sorosis.

V. **be friendly,** be friends, be acquainted with, know; have dealings with, sympathize with, have a leaning to, bear good will, love, befriend.

become friendly, make friends with, break the ice, be introduced to, make (*or* scrape) acquaintance with, get into favor, gain the friendship of; shake hands with, fraternize.

Adj. **friendly,** amicable, neighborly; brotherly, fraternal, sisterly; ardent, devoted, sympathetic, harmonious, hearty, cordial, warmhearted.

friends with, at home with, on good (*or* friendly, amicable, cordial, familiar, intimate) terms, on speaking terms, on visiting terms.

acquainted, familiar, intimate, hail fellow well met, free and easy; welcome.

Adv. with open arms; arm in arm.

889. ENMITY.—*N.* enmity, hostility, antagonism, unfriendliness; discord, etc., 713; bitterness, rancor; heartburning, animosity; malevolence, etc., 907.

alienation, estrangement; dislike, aversion, hate, etc., 898.

V. **be unfriendly,** keep (*or* hold) at arm's length; be at loggerheads, bear malice, fall out; take umbrage; alienate, estrange.

Adj. **unfriendly,** inimical, hostile; at enmity, at variance, at daggers drawn, up in arms against.

on bad terms, not on speaking terms; cool, cold, estranged, alienated, disaffected, irreconcilable.

890. FRIEND.—*N.* **friend,** alter ego [L.], other self; intimate, confidant (*masc.*), confidante (*fem.*); best (*or* bosom, fast) friend, well-wisher; neighbor, acquaintance.

patron, backer, tutelary saint, good genius, advocate, partisan, sympathizer; ally, friend in need.

associate, comrade, mate, companion, confrere, colleague, partner, consort, chum [*colloq.*], pal [*slang*], buddy [*slang, First World War*]· playfellow, playmate, schoolmate, schoolfellow, classmate; bedfellow, bunkie [*colloq.*], roommate, shopmate, shipmate, messmate; fellow (*or* boon) companion.

Famous friendships: Pylades and Orestes, Castor and Pollux, Achi'les and Patroclus, Damon and Pythias, David and Jonathan; Soldiers Three, the Three Musketeers.

host, hostess (*fem.*).

guest, visitor, frequenter, habitué, protégé.

compatriot, countryman, fellow countryman; fellow townsman.

891. ENEMY.—*N.* enemy, antagonist, foe, foeman, open (*or* bitter) enemy, opponent; mortal aversion (*or* antipathy); snake in the grass.

public enemy, enemy to society; anarchist, seditionist, traitor, traitress (*fem.*).

892. SOCIALITY.—*N.* sociality, sociability, social intercourse, intercourse, companionship, comradeship, fellowship; urbanity, intimacy, familiarity, condescension, *esprit de corps* [F.]; morale.

conviviality, good fellowship, joviality, jollity, festivity, merrymaking; hospitality, heartiness; cheer.

welcome, greeting; hearty (*or* warm) reception; hearty welcome (*or* greeting), the glad hand [*slang*].

social gathering, social reunion, assembly, barbecue; bee; cornhusking, corn shucking [U. S.]; husking, husking-bee [U. S.]; hen party [*colloq.*]; house raising, housewarming, hanging of the crane, smoker [*colloq.*]; Dutch treat [*colloq.*]; stag, stag party [*both colloq.*]; sociable [U. S.], party, entertainment, reception, levee, at home, soiree, matinee; garden party, coming-out party [*colloq.*], surprise party; ball, hunt ball, dance festival.

Social meals: breakfast, wedding breakfast, hunt breakfast; luncheon, lunch; picnic lunch, basket lunch, picnic; tea, afternoon tea, five-o'clock tea, cup of tea, dish of tea [esp. Brit.], coming-out tea [*colloq.*]; tea party, tea fight [*slang*]; dinner, potluck, bachelor dinner, stag dinner [*colloq.*], hunt dinner; church supper, high tea, banquet.

visit, visiting; round of visits; call, morning call, interview; tryst, appointment.

V. be sociable, know, be acquainted, associate with, consort with, club together, join; make advances, fraternize.

visit, pay a visit, call at, call upon, leave a card, drop in, look in.

entertain, give a party; see one's friends, keep open house, do the honors, receive, welcome; kill the fatted calf.

Adj. sociable, companionable, clubbable [*colloq.*], cozy, chatty, conversational; convivial, festive, festal, jovial, jolly, hospitable.

free and easy, hail fellow well met, familiar, intimate, social, neighborly.

Adv. en famille [F.], in the family circle; on terms of intimacy; in the social whirl.

893. SECLUSION. EXCLUSION.—*N.* seclusion, privacy, retirement, concealment, rustication, solitude, isolation, loneliness, voluntary exile, aloofness.

retreat, cell, hermitage, cloister, convent; sanctum sanctorum [L.], study, library, den [*colloq.*].

exclusion, excommunication, banishment, exile, ostracism, cut.

unsociability, unsociableness, inhospitality, domesticity, self-sufficiency.

recluse, hermit; caveman, cave dweller, troglodyte, cynic, Diogenes.

outcast, pariah, leper; outsider, rank outsider; castaway, foundling.

V. **seclude oneself,** keep aloof, shut oneself up; deny oneself, rusticate, retire, retire from the world; take the veil.

exclude, repel, cut; send to Coventry, turn one's back upon, shut the door upon; blackball, excommunicate, exile, expatriate; banish, outlaw, maroon, ostracize, keep at arm's length; boycott, embargo, blockade, isolate.

Adj. **secluded,** sequestered, retired, private, out of the world.

unsociable, unsocial, inhospitable; domestic, stay-at-home.

excluded, unfrequented, unvisited, uninvited, unwelcome, under a cloud.

friendless, homeless, desolate, lorn, forlorn; solitary, lonely, lonesome, isolated, single, estranged; derelict, outcast, deserted, banished.

uninhabited, unoccupied, untenanted, tenantless, abandoned.

894. COURTESY.—*N.* **courtesy;** respect, etc., 928; good manners (*or* behavior, breeding); manners, politeness, urbanity, gentility, breeding, gentle breeding, cultivation, culture, polish, civility, amenity, suavity; good temper, good humor, amiability, complacency, affability, complaisance, compliance, gallantry, chivalry.

pink of courtesy, pink of politeness; flower of knighthood; Chesterfield; Lancelot.

ceremonial; salutation, reception, presentation, introduction, welcome, greeting; respects, regards, remembrances; deference, love.

Forms of greeting: bow, curtsy, salaam, kowtow [China], obeisance, bowing and scraping; kneeling, genuflection; capping, pulling the forelock, nod, shaking hands; embrace, hug, squeeze, kiss; salute, accolade.

V. **be courteous,** show courtesy; behave oneself, conciliate, speak one fair, take in good part.

do the honors, usher, usher in, receive, greet, hail, bid welcome, welcome; bid Godspeed; speed the parting guest.

salute; nod to; smile upon; uncover, touch (*or* raise) the hat, doff the cap, bow, make one's bow, curtsy, bob a curtsy, kneel; bow (*or* bend) the knee; salaam, kowtow [China], prostrate oneself.

Adj. **courteous,** polite, civil, mannerly, urbane; well behaved, well mannered, well bred, gently bred, of gentle breeding; polished, cultivated, refined; gallant, chivalrous, chivalric, knightly.

tactful, ingratiating, winning; gentle, mild; good-humored, cordial, gracious, amiable, familiar; neighborly; obliging, complacent, conciliatory.

bland, suave, affable, honey-tongued; oily, unctuous, obsequious.

Adv. with a good grace; with open arms, with outstretched arms, with perfect courtesy, in good humor.

895. DISCOURTESY.—*N.* discourtesy, ill-breeding, bad manners; tactlessness; discourteousness, rusticity, incivility, lack (*or* want) of courtesy, disrespect, impudence, misbehavior, barbarism, barbarity; vulgarity, brutality, blackguardism, conduct unbecoming a gentleman.

bad temper, ill-temper, peevishness, surliness, churlishness, perversity; moroseness, etc., 901*a*; sternness, austerity; moodishness, captiousness, tartness, acrimony, asperity.

scowl, black looks, frown; sulks, short answer, rebuff; hard words, unparliamentary language, personality.

bear, brute, blackguard, beast; unlicked cub; crosspatch [*colloq.*], grouch [*slang*].

V. **be rude,** insult, treat with discourtesy, make bold with, make free with; take a liberty; stare out of countenance, ogle, point at.

sulk, frown, scowl, glower, pout; snap, snarl, growl.

cut; turn one's back upon, turn on one's heel; give the cold shoulder, keep at a distance.

Adj. **discourteous,** uncourteous, uncourtly, ill-bred, ill-mannered, ill-behaved, unmannerly, uncivil, impolite, unaccommodating, unneighborly, ungallant, ungracious, unpolished; ungentlemanly; unladylike; vulgar.

pert, forward, obtrusive, impudent, rude, saucy, flippant.

rough, rugged, bluff, blunt, short, gruff; churlish, boorish, bearish; brutal, brusque, stern, harsh, austere; cavalier.

bad-tempered, ill-tempered, ill-humored, crusty, tart, sour, crabbed, sharp, trenchant, sarcastic, caustic, virulent, bitter, acrimonious, venomous, contumelious, snarling, surly, perverse, grim, sullen, peevish, bristling, thorny.

Adv. with a bad grace.

896. CONGRATULATION.—*N.* **congratulation,** felicitation, compliment; compliments of the season; good wishes, best wishes.

V. **congratulate,** felicitate, wish one joy, compliment, tender (*or* offer) one's congratulations; wish many happy returns of the day.

897. LOVE.—*N.* **love,** affection, sympathy, fellow feeling; tenderness, heart, brotherly love; charity, good will, benevolence; attachment, fondness, liking, inclination; regard, admiration, fancy.

yearning, tender passion, gallantry, passion, flame, devotion, fervor, enthusiasm, rapture, enchantment, infatuation, adoration, idolatry.

mother love, maternal love, natural affection.

attractiveness, charm; popularity; idol, favorite, etc., 899.

god of love, Cupid, Eros, Venus; myrtle.

lover, suitor, fiancé [F.], follower [*colloq.*], admirer, adorer, wooer, beau, sweetheart, swain, young man [*colloq.*], flame [*colloq.*], love, truelove.

ladylove, sweetheart, mistress, inamorata, darling, idol, angel, goddess: betrothed, fiancée [F.].

flirt, coquette.

V. **love,** like, fancy, care for. take an interest in, sympathize with: be in love with, regard, revere, take to, set one's affections on, adore, idolize, dote on (*or* upon), make much of, hold dear, prize; hug, cling to, cherish, caress, fondle, pet.

charm, attract, attach, fascinate, captivate, bewitch, enrapture, turn the head.

Adj. **loving,** affectionate, tender, sympathetic, amorous, lovesick, fond, ardent, passionate, rapturous, devoted, motherly.

loved, beloved, well beloved, dearly beloved; dear, precious, darling, pet; favorite, popular.

lovable, adorable, lovely, sweet, attractive, winning, winsome, charming, enchanting, captivating, fascinating, bewitching, amiable.

898. HATE.—*N.* **hate,** hatred, vials of hate; hymn of hate; disaffection, disfavor; alienation, estrangement, coolness; enmity, etc., 889; animosity, malice, implacability.

umbrage, pique, grudge, spleen, bitterness, bitterness of feeling; ill-blood, bad blood; acrimony.

repugnance, etc. (*dislike*), 867; odium, unpopularity; detestation, abhorrence, loathing, execration, abomination, aversion, antipathy.

object of hatred, an abomination, an aversion, bête noire [F.]; enemy, etc., 891; bitter pill.

V. **hate,** detest, abominate, abhor, loathe; recoil at, shudder at; shrink from, revolt against, execrate; dislike, etc., 867.

alienate, estrange, repel, horrify, set against, sow dissension, set by the ears, envenom, incense, irritate, ruffle, vex.

Adj. **abhorrent,** averse from, set against; bitter, etc. (*acrimonious*), 895; implacable.

unloved, unbeloved, unlamented, undeplored, unmourned, uncared for, unvalued: disliked.

lovelorn, jilted, crossed in love, forsaken, rejected.

hateful, obnoxious, odious, abominable, repulsive, offensive, shocking; disgusting, reprehensible.

invidious, spiteful; malicious, etc., 907.

899. FAVORITE.—*N.* favorite, pet, idol, jewel, spoiled child, apple of one's eye, man after one's own heart.

love, dear, darling, duck, honey, sweetheart, etc. (*ladylove*), 897.

general (*or* universal) favorite; idol of the people; matinee idol.

900. RESENTMENT.—*N.* resentment, displeasure, animosity, anger, wrath, ire, indignation; exasperation, vexation, wrathful, indignation.

pique, umbrage, huff, soreness, acerbity, virulence, bitterness, acrimony, asperity; irascibility, etc., 901; sulks, etc., 901*a*; hate, etc., 898; revenge.

irritation; warmth, ferment, excitement, ebullition; angry mood, pet, tiff, passion, fit, tantrum [*colloq.*].

rage, fury, towering rage, passion; outburst, explosion, paroxysm, storm, violence, vials of wrath; hot blood, high words.

Furies, Erinyes (*sing.* Erinys), Eumenides.

provocation, affront, offense, indignity, insult, grudge; last straw, sore subject; ill-turn, outrage; buffet, blow, box on the ear, rap on the knuckles.

V. **resent,** take amiss, take offense (*or* umbrage, exception); pout, frown, scowl, lower, snarl, growl, gnash, snap; redden, color; look black, look daggers.

be angry, fly into a rage, bridle up, fire up, flare up; chafe, mantle, fume, kindle, fly out, boil, boil with indignation (*or* rage); rage, storm, foam; hector, bully, bluster; lose one's temper; raise Cain [*slang*]; breathe revenge.

anger, affront, offend, give offense (*or* umbrage); hurt the feelings; insult, ruffle, heckle [Brit.], nettle, huff, pique; excite, irritate, fret, sting, provoke, chafe, wound, incense, inflame, enrage, envenom, embitter, exasperate, infuriate, madden; rankle.

Adj. **angry,** wroth, irate, ireful, wrathful; irascible, etc., 901; bitter, virulent, acrimonious, offended, indignant, hurt, sore.

fuming, raging, hot under the collar [*slang*]; convulsed with rage; fierce, wild, furious, fiery, rabid, savage, violent.

Adv. in the height (*or* heat) of passion; in an ecstasy of rage.

901. IRASCIBILITY.—*N.* irascibility, temper; crossness, petulance, irritability, tartness, acerbity, acrimony, asperity, pugnacity, excitability.

shrew, vixen, virago, dragon, scold, spitfire, fury.

V. **be irascible,** have a temper, be possessed of the devil, have the temper of a fiend; fire up, flare up.

Adj. **irascible,** bad-tempered, irritable, excitable; thin-skinned, sensitive; hasty, quick, warm, hot, testy, touchy, huffy, pettish, petulant, fretful, querulous, captious, moody, cross, fractious, peevish.

quarrelsome, contentious, disputatious, pugnacious, cantankerous [*colloq.*], cross-grained; waspish, peppery, fiery, passionate, choleric, shrewish.

901a. SULLENNESS.—*N.* sullenness, moroseness, spleen; churlishness, irascibility, moodiness, perversity, obstinacy, crabbedness.

sulks, dudgeon, dumps [*humorous*], doldrums; black looks, scowl; grouch [*slang*], huff.

V. sulk, frown, scowl, lower, glower, pout, grouch [*slang*].

Adj. sullen, sulky, ill-tempered, ill-humored, ill-disposed; crusty, crabbed, sour, sore, surly, moody, cross, cross-grained; perverse, wayward, refractory, restive, ungovernable, cussed [*vulgar or euphemistic*]; grumpy, glum, grum, grim, morose, grouchy [*slang*].

902. [Expression of affection] ENDEARMENT.—*N.* endearment, caress, blandishment, fondling, billing and cooing, dalliance, caressing, embrace, salute, kiss, smack, osculation.

courtship, wooing, suit, addresses, love-making; calf love [*colloq.*]; amorous glances, ogle, side glance, sheep's eyes, goo-goo eyes [*slang*].

flirting, flirtation, gallantry; coquetry, spooning [*slang*].

engagement, betrothal; marriage, etc., 903; honeymoon; love letter, billet-doux; valentine.

flirt, coquette; male flirt, philanderer; spoon [*slang*].

V. **caress,** fondle, pet; smile upon, coax, wheedle, coddle, make much of, cherish, foster.

clasp, hug, cuddle; fold to the heart, press to the bosom, fold in one's arms; snuggle, nestle, nuzzle; embrace, kiss, salute.

court, make love, bill and coo, spoon [*slang*], toy, dally, flirt, coquet, philander, pay court to; serenade; woo.

propose, make (*or* have) an offer, pop the question [*colloq.*]; become engaged, become betrothed; plight one's troth.

Adj. lovesick, spoony [*slang*].

903. MARRIAGE.—*N.* marriage, matrimony, wedlock, union, intermarriage; nuptial tie, nuptial knot; match; betrothment.

wedding, nuptials, Hymen, bridal, espousals; leading to the altar; honeymoon.

bridesmaid, maid of honor, matron of honor; attendant, usher, best man, bridesman, groomsman; bride, bridegroom.

married man, partner, spouse, mate, husband, man [*dial.*], consort.

married woman, wife, wedded wife, spouse, helpmeet, helpmate, better half, lady [*obs. or uncultivated*]; squaw; matron.

married couple, man and wife, wedded pair, wedded couple, Darby and Joan.

Kinds of marriage: monogamy, bigamy, polygamy, polyandry; Mormonism; morganatic (*or* left-handed) marriage, *mésalliance* [F.].

matchmaker, matrimonial agency (*or* agent, bureau).

V. **marry,** wive, take to oneself a wife; be married, be spliced [*colloq.*]; wed, espouse, lead to the altar, join, couple, be made one.

Adj. **engaged,** betrothed, plighted, affianced.

Matrimonial, marital, conjugal, connubial, wedded; nuptial, hymeneal, spousal, bridal.

904. CELIBACY.—*N.* **celibacy,** singleness, single blessedness; bachelorhood, bachelorship; misogyny.

virginity, maidenhood, maidenhead.

unmarried man, bachelor, old bachelor; misogamist, misogynist; monk, priest, celibate, religious.

unmarried woman, maid, maiden, virgin, spinster, old maid; nun, sister, vestal, vestal virgin; Diana.

Adj. **unmarried,** unwedded; wifeless, spouseless; single, celibate, virgin.

905. DIVORCE. WIDOWHOOD.—*N.* **divorce,** divorcement; separation, judicial separation, separate maintenance.

widowhood, weeds.

widow, relict, dowager; divorcée; grass widow.

widower; grass widower.

V. live separate; separate, divorce, put away.

906. BENEVOLENCE.—*N.* **benevolence,** Christian charity; God's grace; good will, philanthropy, unselfishness, kindness, kindliness, good nature, loving-kindness, benignity, brotherly love, charity, humanity, kindly feelings, fellow feeling, sympathy, goodness of heart, warmheartedness, kindheartedness, amiability, tenderness, love, friendship; tolerance, consideration; mercy.

charitableness, bounty, almsgiving; good works, beneficence, generosity, a good turn.

philanthropist, salt of the earth; good Samaritan, sympathizer, well-wisher, altruist.

V. **bear good will,** wish well, take (*or* feel) an interest in; be interested in, sympathize with, feel for; treat well, give comfort, do good, do a good turn, benefit, assist, render a service, render assistance, aid.

enter into the feelings of others, practice the golden rule, do as you would be done by.

Adj. **benevolent,** kind, kindly, well meaning, amiable, cordial, obliging, accommodating, indulgent, gracious, tender, considerate, warmhearted, kindhearted, tenderhearted, largehearted, softhearted, merciful; sympathizing, sympathetic.

full of natural affection, fatherly, motherly, brotherly, sisterly; paternal, maternal, fraternal; friendly.

charitable, beneficent, philanthropical, generous, humane, benignant, unselfish, altruistic, bountiful.

Adv. with the best intentions; out of deepest sympathy.

907. MALEVOLENCE.—*N.* **malevolence,** bad intent, bad intention, unkindness, uncharitableness, ill-nature, ill-will, enmity, hate, malice, malignance, malignity, maliciousness; spite, resentment; gall, venom, rancor, virulence, hardness of heart, heart of stone, obduracy; evil eye, cloven foot (*or* hoof).

ill-turn, bad turn; affront, indignity; tender mercies (*ironical*).

cruelty, brutality, savagery, ferocity; outrage, atrocity, ill-usage, persecution; barbarity, inhumanity, truculence, ruffianism; inquisition, torture.

V. **bear malice,** harbor a grudge; hurt, annoy, injure, harm, wrong, outrage, malign; molest, worry, harass, harry, bait, hound, persecute, oppress, grind, maltreat, ill-treat; give no quarter, have no mercy.

Adj. **malevolent,** ill-disposed, ill-intentioned, ill-natured, ill-conditioned, evil-minded, evil-disposed, venomous, malicious, malign, malignant, maleficent; rancorous, spiteful, treacherous, caustic, bitter, envenomed, acrimonious, virulent; grinding, galling, harsh; disobliging, unkind, unfriendly; ungracious, churlish, surly, sullen.

cold-blooded, coldhearted, hardhearted, stonyhearted, cold, unnatural; ruthless, pitiless, relentless.

cruel, brutal, brutish, savage, ferocious, inhuman; barbarous, fell, truculent, bloodthirsty, atrocious, fiendish, diabolic *or* diabolical, devilish, infernal, hellish.

Adv. with bad intent; with the ferocity of a tiger.

908. MALEDICTION.—*N.* **malediction,** malison, curse, imprecation, denunciation, execration; anathema, ban, proscription, excommunication, commination, fulmination; disparagement, vilification, vituperation.

abuse, evil speaking, foul (*or* bad, strong, unparliamentary) language, billingsgate, blackguardism, cursing, profane, swearing, expletive, oath, foul invective, ribaldry, scurrility, invective.

V. **curse,** imprecate, damn, swear at; execrate, vituperate, scold; anathematize, denounce, proscribe, excommunicate, fulminate, thunder against.

909. THREAT.—*N.* **threat**, menace, defiance, abuse, intimidation, denunciation, fulmination, etc., 908; gathering clouds.

V. **threaten**, threat, menace; snarl, growl, mutter, bully; defy, intimidate, shake the fist at; thunder, fulminate, bluster.

Adj. **threatening**, menacing, minatory, abusive; ominous, defiant.

910. PHILANTHROPY.—*N.* **philanthropy**, altruism, humanity, humanitarianism, benevolence; public welfare.

public spirit, patriotism, nationality, love of country.

philanthropist, altruist, etc., 906; humanitarian, patriot.

Adj. **philanthropic**, altruistic, humanitarian, public-spirited, patriotic; humane, largehearted, benevolent, etc., 906; generous, liberal, etc., 942.

911. MISANTHROPY.—*N.* **misanthropy**, hatred of mankind; selfishness, egoism, egotism; sullenness, moroseness, cynicism; want of patriotism.

misanthrope, misanthropist, egoist, egotist, cynic, man hater. woman hater, misogynist.

Adj. **misanthropic**, antisocial, unpatriotic; egoistical, egotistical, selfish; morose, sullen, cynical, etc., 901*a*.

912. BENEFACTOR.—*N.* **benefactor**, savior, protector, good genius, tutelary saint, guardian angel, good Samaritan; friend in need; salt of the earth; philanthropist, etc., 910; fairy godmother.

913. [Maleficent being] EVILDOER.—*N.* **evildoer**, evil worker, wrongdoer, etc., 949; mischiefmaker, marplot; oppressor, tyrant; incendiary, etc., 384; anarchist, nihilist,⁻ destroyer, vandal, iconoclast, terrorist.

savage, brute, ruffian, barbarian, desperado; apache, gunman, hoodlum [*colloq.*], redskin, tough [*colloq.*], bully, rough, hooligan [*slang*], dangerous classes; thief, etc., 792; cutthroat.

wild beast, tiger, leopard, panther, hyena, catamount [U. S.], catamountain, lynx, cougar, jaguar, puma; bloodhound, hellhound, sleuthhound; gorilla; vulture.

cockatrice, adder; snake, serpent, cobra, asp, viper, rattlesnake, boa; alligator, crocodile, octopus.

hag, hellhag, beldam, Jezebel.

monster, fiend, demon, etc., 980; devil incarnate, Frankenstein's monster; cannibal; bloodsucker, vampire, ogre, ghoul.

914. PITY.—*N.* **pity**, compassion, commiseration, sympathy, fellow feeling, tenderness, softheartedness, yearning forbearance, humanity, mercy, clemency; leniency, lenity, charity, ruth, longsuffering; quarter, grace.

sympathizer; advocate, friend, partisan, patron, well-wisher, defender; champion.

V. **pity,** have (*or* take) pity, commiserate, condole, sympathize, feel for, be sorry for.

forbear, relent, relax, give quarter.

excite pity, touch, soften, melt, melt the heart; propitiate.

Adj. **pitying,** pitiful, compassionate, sympathetic, touched. merciful, clement, humane, humanitarian; tender, tender-hearted, softhearted, lenient, forbearing.

914a. PITILESSNESS.—*N.* pitilessness, inclemency, inexorability, inflexibility, hardness of heart; want of pity, severity, malevolence, etc., 907.

V. **be pitiless,** turn a deaf ear to; claim one's pound of flesh; have no mercy, give no quarter.

Adj. **pitiless,** merciless, ruthless, unpitying, unmerciful, inclement, grim-faced, grim-visaged; inflexible, relentless, inexorable, harsh, cruel, etc., 907.

915. CONDOLENCE.—*N.* condolence, sympathy, consolation; lamentation, etc., 839.

V. **condole with,** console, sympathize, express pity; afford consolation; lament with, express sympathy for, feel for, send one's condolences; share one's sorrow.

916. GRATITUDE.—*N.* gratitude, gratefulness, thankfulness; sense of obligation; acknowledgment, recognition, thanksgiving, giving thanks.

thanks, praise, benediction; paean; *Te Deum* [L.], grace, requital, thank offering.

V. **be grateful,** thank; give (*or* render, return, offer, tender) thanks, acknowledge, requite; lie under an obligation; never forget, overflow with gratitude.

Adj. **grateful,** thankful, obliged, beholden, indebted to, under obligation.

917. INGRATITUDE.—*N.* ingratitude, thanklessness, unthankfulness; thankless task, thankless office.

V. **be ungrateful,** feel no obligation, owe one no thanks, forget benefits, have a short memory for.

Adj. **ungrateful,** unmindful, unthankful; thankless, ingrate. forgotten; unacknowledged, unthanked, unrequited, unrewarded; ill-requited; ill-rewarded.

918. FORGIVENESS.—*N.* forgiveness, pardon, grace, remission, absolution, amnesty, oblivion; reprieve.

conciliation; reconciliation, forbearance, propitiation.

exoneration, excuse, quittance, release, indemnity; acquittal, exculpation.

V. **forgive,** pardon, think no more of, let bygones by bygones, bury the hatchet. start afresh.

remit, exculpate, exonerate, absolve, give absolution; blot out one's sins (*or* offenses, transgressions), wipe the slate clean; reprieve, acquit.

excuse, pass over, overlook; condone, wink at; bear with, allow for, make allowances for; pocket the affront.

conciliate, propitiate, placate; beg (*or* ask) pardon, make up a quarrel.

Adj. forgiving, placable, conciliatory.

919. REVENGE.—*N.* revenge, vengeance; vendetta, death feud, eye for an eye, tooth for a tooth, retaliation; day of reckoning.

rancor, vindictiveness, implacability, ruthlessness; malevolence, etc., 907.

avenger, nemesis, Eumenides.

V. revenge, avenge, take revenge, have one's revenge; breathe vengeance; give no quarter, take no prisoners.

keep the wound open, harbor revenge, bear malice; rankle, rankle in the breast.

Adj. revengeful, vengeful, vindictive, rancorous; pitiless, ruthless, rigorous, avenging, retaliative; unforgiving, unrelenting; inexorable, implacable, relentless, remorseless.

920. JEALOUSY.—*N.* jealousy, distrust, mistrust, heartburn; envy, etc., 921; doubt, suspicion; green-eyed monster.

V. be jealous, view with jealousy, grudge, begrudge.

doubt, distrust, mistrust, suspect, misdoubt.

Adj. jealous, jaundice, yellow-eyed, envious.

921. ENVY.—*N.* envy, enviousness; rivalry; ill-will, spite; jealousy, etc., 920.

V. envy, covet, grudge, begrudge, break the tenth commandment.

Adj. envious, invidious, covetous, grudging, begrudged; belittling.

IV. MORAL AFFECTIONS

922. RIGHT.—*N.* right; what ought to be, what should be; fitness.

justice, equity, equitableness, propriety, fairness, fair play, square deal [*colloq.*], impartiality; lawfulness, legality.

morals, etc. (*duty*), 926; law, etc., 963; honor, etc., 939; virtue, etc., 944.

V. be right, stand to reason.

do right, see justice done, see fair play; do justice to, recompense, hold the scales even, give everyone his due.

Adj. **right**, good; just, reasonable; fit, etc., 924; equal, equable, equitable; even-handed, fair, square.

legitimate, justifiable, rightful, as it ought to be; lawful, legal.

Adv. in justice, in equity, in reason; upon even terms.

923. WRONG.—*N.* **wrong**, iniquity; what ought not to be, what should not be; unreasonableness, grievance; shame.

injustice, unfairness, foul play, partiality, leaning, favor, favoritism, partisanship; undueness, unlawfulness, illegality.

dishonor, etc., 939; vice, etc., 945.

V. **do wrong**, be inequitable, show partiality, favor, lean toward; encroach; impose upon; reap where one has not sown.

Adj. **wrong**, wrongful, iniquitous, bad, unjust, unfair, inequitable, unequal, partial, one-sided; injurious.

unjustifiable, unreasonable, unwarrantable, objectionable, improper, unfit, unjustified; unlawful; illegal, immoral.

924. AUTHORIZATION.—*N.* **authorization**, sanction, authority, charter, warrant; constitution; bond.

right, dueness, due, privilege, prerogative, prescription, title, claim, pretension, legality, demand, birthright.

immunity, license, liberty, franchise; vested interest (*or* right).

deserts, merits, dues.

claimant, appellant; plaintiff, etc., 938.

V. **deserve**, merit, be worthy of, make good.

demand, claim, lay claim to, reclaim, exact; insist on (*or* upon), make a point of, require, assert, assume, arrogate.

entitle, give (*or* confer) a right, authorize, sanction, legalize, ordain, prescribe, allot.

Adj. **privileged**, allowed, sanctioned, warranted, authorized; ordained, prescribed, constitutional, chartered, enfranchised.

prescriptive, presumptive, absolute, inalienable, inviolable, sacrosanct.

merited, due to, deserved, condign [*archaic, except of punishment*].

right, creditable, fit, fitting, correct, square, due, proper, meet, befitting, becoming, seemly; decorous.

lawful, legitimate, legal, legalized, allowable.

Adv. by right, by divine right; on the square [*colloq.*].

925. [Want of authorization] IMPROPRIETY.—*N.* **impropriety**, undueness, unrightfulness, illegality, unlawfulness; falseness, invalidity of title; illegitimacy.

loss of right, disfranchisement, forfeiture.

assumption, usurpation, tort [*law*], violation, breach, encroachment, seizure, exaction, imposition.

usurper, pretender, impostor.

V. **infringe,** encroach, trench on, exact, arrogate, usurp, violate; get under false pretenses, sail under false colors.

disentitle, disfranchise, disqualify; invalidate.

Adj. **undue,** unlawful, illegal, illicit, unconstitutional, unauthorized, unwarranted, unsanctioned, unjustified; disqualified, unqualified; unprivileged, unchartered.

undeserved, unmerited, unearned.

illegitimate, bastard, spurious, false; usurped.

improper, unfit, unbefitting, unseemly, unbecoming, misbecoming; preposterous, pretentious, would-be.

926. DUTY.—*N.* **duty,** moral obligation, accountability, liability, onus, responsibility.

allegiance, fealty, tie; engagement; function, part, calling.

observance, fulfillment, discharge, performance, acquittal, satisfaction, redemption; good behavior.

morality, morals, decalogue; conscientiousness, conscience, inward monitor, still small voice within, sense of duty.

propriety, fitness, seemliness, decorum, the thing, the proper thing.

Science of morals: ethics, moral (*or* ethical) philosophy, casuistry, polity.

V. **behoove,** become, befit, beseem; belong to, pertain to; rest with, fall to one's lot, devolve on.

take upon oneself, be (*or* become) sponsor for, incur a responsibility; perform (*or* discharge) a duty *or* an obligation; act one's part, redeem one's pledge, be at one's post, do one's duty.

impose a duty, enjoin, require, exact; bind, bind over; saddle with, prescribe, assign, call upon, look to, oblige.

Adj. **obligatory,** binding, imperative, peremptory, stringent, incumbent on.

amenable, liable, accountable, responsible, answerable.

right, meet, etc. (*due*), 924; moral, ethical, conscientious.

Adv. with a safe conscience, as in duty bound, on one's own responsibility, at one's own risk.

927. DERELICTION OF DUTY.—*N.* **dereliction,** nonobservance, nonperformance, nonco-operation; indolence, neglect, infraction, violation, transgression, failure, evasion; fault, etc. (*guilt*), 947.

slacker, loafer, time killer; eyeserver, eyeservant; striker; nonco-operator.

V. **violate,** break, break through; infringe, set aside, set at naught; encroach upon, trench upon, trample on; slight, get by [*slang*], neglect, evade, escape, transgress, fail.

927a. EXEMPTION.—*N.* **exemption,** freedom, irresponsibility, immunity, liberty, license, release, discharge, excuse, dispensation, absolution, exculpation, exoneration.

V. exempt, release, acquit, discharge, remit; free, set at liberty, let off [*colloq.*], pass over, spare, excuse, dispense with, license; absolve, exonerate.

Adj. exempt, free, immune, at liberty, scot-free, released, unbound; irresponsible, not accountable, excusable.

928. RESPECT.—*N.* respect, regard, consideration, courtesy, attention, deference, reverence, honor, esteem, estimation, veneration, admiration; approbation, etc., 931.

homage, fealty, obeisance, genuflection, kneeling, prostration; salaam, etc., 894.

V. respect, regard; revere, reverence, honor, venerate, hallow; esteem, think much of, entertain respect for, look up to, defer to, pay attention to, pay respect to, do honor to; do the honors, hail, show courtesy, pay homage to.

command respect, inspire respect; awe, impose, overawe, dazzle.

Adj. respectful, deferential, decorous, reverential, ceremonious, bareheaded, cap in hand; prostrate.

respected, estimable; time-honored, venerable.

Adv. in deference to; with all respect, with due respect, with the highest respect: with submission.

929. DISRESPECT.—*N.* disrespect, disfavor, disrepute, want of esteem, low estimation, disparagement, detraction, irreverence, slight, indignity, contumely, affront, dishonor, insult, outrage, discourtesy, scoffing; hiss, hissing, hoot, derision; mockery.

gibe, flout, jeer, scoff, taunt, sneer, fling.

V. slight, disregard, undervalue, humiliate, depreciate, trifle with, pass by, push aside, overlook, be discourteous.

disparage, call names; throw mud at; point at, indulge in personalities.

dishonor, desecrate; insult, affront, browbeat, outrage.

deride, scoff, sneer, laugh at, ridicule, gibe, mock, jeer, taunt, twit, flout, roast [*colloq.*], guy [*colloq.*], rag [*dial. Eng.* and *college slang*], burlesque, scout, hiss, hoot.

Adj. disrespectful, disparaging, etc., 934; insulting, supercilious, rude, derisive, sarcastic, scurrilous, contemptuous, insolent, disdainful; irreverent.

unrespected, unregarded, disregarded, unenvied, unsaluted.

930. CONTEMPT.—*N.* contempt, disdain, scorn, contemptuousness, derision, etc. (*disrespect*), 929; contumely; slight, sneer, spurn, byword.

V. despise, contemn, scorn, disdain, disregard, scout, slight, pass by, look down upon, sneer at, laugh at, curl up one's lip, think nothing of, make light of, underestimate, esteem slightly, care nothing for, set no store by; pooh-pooh; damn with faint praise.

spurn, turn one's back upon, trample underfoot; kick; fling to the winds, repudiate.

Adj. **contemptuous,** disdainful, scornful, withering, supercilious, cynical, haughty, cavalier; derisive; with the nose in air.

contemptible, despicable, despised, pitiable, pitiful, down-trodden.

931. APPROBATION.—*N.* **approbation,** approval, sanction, advocacy; esteem, estimation, good opinion, admiration; love, etc., 897; appreciation, regard, account, popularity, credit, repute.

commendation, compliment, praise, laud, laudation; good word; encomium, eulogy, eulogium, panegyric, blurb [*slang*]; benediction, blessing, benison.

applause, plaudit, clap, clapping, acclaim, acclamation; cheer; paean, shout (*or* peal, chorus, thunders) of applause.

V. **approve,** esteem, value, prize, set great store by; honor, hold in esteem, look up to, admire, like, appreciate: stand up for, stick up for [*colloq.*], uphold, countenance, sanction, indorse, recommend.

commend, praise, laud, compliment, applaud, clap, cheer, acclaim, encore; eulogize, boost [*colloq.*], root for [*slang*], cry up, puff; extol, magnify, glorify, exalt, sing the praises of.

Adj. **commendatory,** complimentary, laudatory, panegyrical, eulogistic, lavish of praise, uncritical.

approved, praised, popular, in good odor; in high esteem, in favor, in high favor.

praiseworthy, commendable, worthy of praise, good, meritorious, estimable, creditable, unimpeachable.

Adv. with credit, to admiration.

932. DISAPPROBATION.—*N.* **disapprobation,** disapproval, disesteem, odium, dislike, black list, blackball, ostracism, boycott.

disparagement, depreciation, dispraise, detraction, etc., 934; denunciation, condemnation, stricture, objection, exception, criticism; blame, censure, obloquy, sarcasm, satire, insinuation, innuendo, sneer, taunt.

reproof, reprehension, remonstrance, expostulation, reprobation, admonition, reproach; rebuke, reprimand, lecture, curtain lecture; wigging, dressing down [*both colloq.*]; rating, scolding, correction, rebuff, home thrust, hit; frown, scowl, black look.

abuse, personalities, personal remarks, vituperation, invective, contumely, hard words; bad language.

diatribe, tirade, philippic.

clamor, outcry, hue and cry; hiss, hissing, catcall; execration.

V. **disapprove,** dislike, object to, take exception to, think ill of, view with disfavor, frown upon, look askance, look black upon, set one's face against.

blame, censure, reproach, reprobate, impugn, impeach, accuse, denounce, expose, brand, gibbet, stigmatize; show up [*colloq.*].

reprove, reprehend, chide, admonish, berate, take to task, overhaul, lecture, rebuke, blow up [*colloq.*], correct, reprimand, snub; chastise, castigate, lash, trounce.

remonstrate, expostulate, recriminate.

abuse, scold, rate, upbraid, fall foul of; jaw [*low*], rail, rail at, call names, execrate, revile, vilify.

decry, cry down, run down, backbite; insinuate, damn with faint praise; hiss, hoot, catcall, mob; ostracize, blacklist, boycott, blackball.

disparage, depreciate, knock [*colloq.*], dispraise, deprecate, speak ill of, condemn, scoff at, sneer at, satirize, lampoon, defame, criticize.

incur blame, scandalize, shock, revolt; get a bad name, forfeit one's good opinion, be under a cloud.

Adj. **disparaging,** condemnatory, denunciatory, reproachful, abusive, vituperative, defamatory.

critical, satirical, sarcastic, sardonic, cynical, dry, sharp, cutting, biting, severe, withering, trenchant, censorious, captious, hypercritical.

blameworthy, reprehensible, blamable, answerable, bad; vicious, etc., 945.

Adv. with a wry face.

933. FLATTERY.—*N.* **flattery,** adulation, cajolery, fawning, wheedling, obsequiousness, sycophancy, flunkeyism, toadyism.

honeyed words, flummery, buncombe [*cant or slang*]; blarney, soft soap [*both colloq.*].

V. **flatter,** overpraise, puff, wheedle, cajole, fawn upon, humor, pet, coquet, butter [*colloq.*], jolly [*slang or colloq.*]; truckle to, pander to, court, curry favor with.

Adj. **flattering,** adulatory; mealy-mouthed, honeyed, smooth, smooth-tongued; oily, unctuous, specious, plausible, servile, sycophantic, fulsome.

934. DETRACTION.—*N.* **detraction,** disparagement, depreciation, vilification, obloquy, scandal, defamation, slander, calumny, evil-speaking, backbiting; sarcasm, cynicism, criticism; invective.

personality, libel, lampoon, skit, squib.

V. **detract,** derogate, decry, depreciate, disparage, run down, cry down, belittle, criticize, pull to pieces, asperse, bespatter, blacken, vilify, brand, malign, backbite, libel, lampoon, traduce, slander, defame, calumniate.

Adj. **detracting**, defamatory, detractory, derogatory, disparaging, libelous; scurrilous, abusive, foul-mouthed; slanderous, calumnious.

935. FLATTERER.—*N.* **flatterer**, adulator, eulogist, euphemist; optimist; puffer, booster [*colloq.*], whitewasher.

toady, sycophant, parasite, hanger-on; courtier.

936. DETRACTOR.—*N.* **detractor**, censor, censurer; cynic, critic, caviler, carper.

defamer, knocker [*colloq.*], backbiter, slanderer, lampooner, satirist, traducer, libeler, calumniator, reviler, vituperator.

Adj. defamatory, etc., 934.

937. VINDICATION.—*N.* **vindication**, justification, warrant; exoneration, exculpation, acquittal; whitewashing, extenuation, palliation, softening, mitigation.

plea, apology, gloss, varnish; excuse, extenuating circumstances; allowance; reply, defense; recrimination.

apologist, vindicator, justifier; defendant, etc., 938.

V. **justify**, warrant, lend a color, vindicate, exculpate, acquit, clear, exonerate, whitewash.

extenuate, palliate, excuse, soften, apologize.

advocate, defend, plead one's cause; contend for, speak for; bear out, make good; support, plead, say in defense.

Adj. **vindicative**, vindicatory, vindicating, palliative, extenuating, exculpatory, apologetic.

excusable, defensible, pardonable; venial, plausible, justifiable.

938. ACCUSATION.—*N.* **accusation**, charge, imputation, slur, incrimination, recrimination, denunciation.

libel, challenge, citation, arraignment, impeachment, indictment, true bill, lawsuit, condemnation.

accuser, prosecutor, plaintiff, complainant, libelant, informant, informer.

accused, defendant, prisoner, respondent, litigant.

V. **accuse**, charge, tax, impute, twit, taunt with, reproach, stigmatize, slur; incriminate, inculpate, implicate.

inform against, indict, denounce, arraign; charge with, saddle with; impeach, show up [*colloq.*], challenge, cite, prosecute; blow upon [*colloq.*], squeal [*slang*].

Adj. **accusatory**, denunciatory, recriminatory.

inexcusable, indefensible, unpardonable, unjustifiable.

939. PROBITY.—*N.* **probity**, integrity, rectitude, uprightness, respectability, honesty, faith, honor, good faith; constancy, faithfulness, fidelity, loyalty, trustworthiness, truth, veracity, candor, singleness of heart.

fairness, fair play, justice, equity, impartiality, principle.

punctiliousness, punctilio, delicacy, scrupulosity, scrupulousness, scruple; point of honor.

man of honor, man of his word, gentleman, trump [*slang*], brick [*slang or colloq.*].

V. **be honorable,** speak the truth, draw a straight furrow, make a point of: do one's duty, play the game [*colloq.*]; redeem one's pledge, keep one's promise (*or* word), keep faith with.

Adj. **upright,** honest, veracious, truthful, virtuous, noble, honorable, reputable, respectable; fair, right, just, equitable, impartial, square, white [*slang*].

manly, straightforward, frank, candid, openhearted.

loyal, constant, faithful, stanch; true; trusty, trustworthy; incorruptible.

conscientious, right-minded, high-principled, high-minded, scrupulous, religious, strict; nice, punctilious.

stainless, unstained, unsullied, inviolate, untainted, incorrupt, innocent, pure, undefiled, undepraved.

chivalrous, jealous of honor, high-spirited.

Adv. on the square [*colloq.*], in good faith, in all honor, by fair means, with clean hands.

940. IMPROBITY.—*N.* **improbity,** dishonesty, dishonor, disgrace; fraud, lying; bad faith, infidelity, faithlessness; Judas kiss, betrayal, perfidy, treachery, double-dealing; villainy, baseness, degradation, turpitude, moral turpitude.

breach of trust (*or* faith), disloyalty, divided allegiance, hyphenated allegiance [*cant*], treason, high treason; apostasy.

knavery, roguery, rascality, foul play; jobbing, jobbery, graft [*colloq.*], venality, corruption, sharp practice.

V. **play false;** break one's word (*or* promise), jilt, betray, forswear; grovel, sneak, lose caste; sell oneself, squeal [*slang*], go back on [*colloq.*].

Adj. **dishonest,** dishonorable; unconscientious, unscrupulous; fraudulent, knavish, falsehearted; unfair, one-sided; double, double-tongued, double-faced; timeserving, crooked, slippery; fishy [*colloq.*], questionable.

infamous, arrant, foul, base, vile, low, ignominious, perfidious, treacherous, perjured; contemptible, abject, mean, shabby, paltry, dirty, sneaking, groveling, rascally, corrupt, venal.

derogatory, degrading, undignified, unbefitting, ungentlemanly, unchivalric, unmanly, recreant, inglorious.

faithless, false, unfaithful, disloyal; untrustworthy; trustless, lost to shame, dead to honor.

Adv. like a thief in the night, by crooked paths, by foul means.

941. KNAVE.—*N.* **knave,** rogue, villain, rascal, etc., 949; shyster.

traitor, betrayer, archtraitor, conspirator, Judas; reptile, serpent, snake in the grass, wolf in sheep's clothing, sneak, squealer [*slang*], telltale, mischiefmaker; renegade, recreant, slacker.

942. DISINTERESTEDNESS.—*N.* **disinterestedness,** unselfishness, generosity; liberality, altruism, benevolence, loftiness of purpose, exaltation, magnanimity; honor, chivalry, heroism, sublimity.

self-denial, self-control, stoicism, self-abnegation, self-sacrifice, devotion, self-devotion; labor of love.

Adj. **disinterested,** unselfish, self-denying, self-sacrificing, altruistic.

magnanimous, high-minded; princely, great, high, elevated, lofty, exalted, greathearted, largehearted; generous, liberal; chivalrous, heroic, sublime.

943. SELFISHNESS.—*N.* **selfishness,** self-love, self-indulgence, self-worship, self-seeking, self-interest; egotism, egoism; illiberality, meanness.

self-seeker, timeserver, fortune hunter, monopolist, dog in the manger, trimmer; hog, roadhog [*colloq.*].

V. **be selfish,** feather one's nest; have an eye to the main chance, live for oneself alone.

Adj. **selfish,** self-seeking, self-indulgent, self-interested; self-centered; egotistic, egoistic.

illiberal, mean, ungenerous, narrow-minded; mercenary, venal; covetous.

worldly, unspiritual, earthly, earthly-minded, mundane, worldly-minded, worldly-wise; timeserving, interested.

Adv. from selfish motives.

944. VIRTUE.—*N.* **virtue,** morality, moral rectitude; integrity, probity, nobleness, well-doing, good actions, good behavior, well-spent life, innocence.

merit, worth, desert, excellence, credit; self-control, self-denial.

morals; ethics, duty, etc., 926; cardinal virtues.

V. **be virtuous,** practice virtue, do one's duty, fight the good fight; acquit oneself well, keep in the right path.

Adj. **virtuous,** good, innocent, meritorious, deserving, worthy, dutiful, duteous; moral, right, righteous, right-minded; creditable, laudable, commendable, praiseworthy; sterling, pure, noble; whole-souled.

exemplary; matchless, peerless; saintly, saintlike; angelic, godlike.

945. VICE.—*N.* vice, evildoing, wrongdoing, wickedness, viciousness, iniquity, sin, immorality, want of principle, knavery, obliquity, backsliding, infamy, brutality.

depravity, demoralization, corruption, profligacy, flagrancy.

weakness, infirmity, frailty, imperfection, error; foible; failing, failure; besetting sin; defect, defection.

fault, crime; guilt, etc., 947.

reprobate; sinner, etc., 949.

V. be vicious, sin, commit sin, err, transgress; misconduct oneself, misbehave; fall, lapse, slip, trip, offend, trespass, go astray; sow one's wild oats.

demoralize, brutalize; corrupt, degrade, etc., 659.

Adj.[1] vicious, sinful; wicked, iniquitous, immoral, unrighteous, wrong, criminal; unprincipled, lawless, disorderly, disgraceful, recreant, disreputable; demoralized, corrupt, depraved, degenerate; evil-minded, heartless, graceless, shameless, abandoned.

base, sinister, foul, gross, vile, black, felonious, nefarious, shameful, scandalous, infamous, villainous, heinous; flagrant, atrocious.

diabolic *or* diabolical, devilish, fiendish, fiendlike, demoniacal, Mephistophelian, satanic, hellish, infernal, hellborn.

incorrigible, irreclaimable, obdurate, reprobate, reprehensible.

unjustifiable, indefensible, inexcusable, inexpiable, unpardonable.

improper, unseemly, indecorous, indiscreet, unworthy, blameworthy, discreditable; incorrect, undutiful, naughty.

weak, frail, lax, infirm, imperfect; spineless, invertebrate [*both fig.*].

946. INNOCENCE.—*N.* innocence; guiltlessness, incorruption, impeccability; clean hands, clear conscience.

innocent, newborn babe; lamb, dove.

Adj. innocent, not guilty, unguilty; guiltless, faultless, sinless, stainless, spotless, clear, immaculate, unerring, undefiled, inculpable, blameless, above suspicion, irreproachable, unimpeachable; virtuous, etc., 944.

harmless, inoffensive, innocuous, pure.

Adv. with clean hands; with a clear conscience.

947. GUILT.—*N.* guilt, guiltiness, culpability, criminality; vice, sinfulness, misconduct, misbehavior, misdeed; fault, sin, error, transgression; dereliction, delinquency.

indiscretion, lapse, slip, trip, flaw, blot, omission, failing, failure, blunder, break [*colloq.*].

[1] Most of these adjectives are applicable both to the act and to the agent.

offense, trespass; misdemeanor, malefaction, malversation, corruption, malpractice; crime, felony, capital crime.

enormity, atrocity, outrage; deadly sin, mortal sin.

Adj. guilty, blamable, culpable, reprehensible, blameworthy.

Adv. in the very act, red-handed.

948. GOOD MAN. GOOD WOMAN.—*N.* good man, worthy, model, paragon, pattern, good example; hero, demigod, angel, saint; benefactor, etc., 912; philanthropist, etc., 910.

salt of the earth; one in ten thousand; a man among men, white man [*slang*].

good woman, virgin, innocent; goddess, queen, Madonna, ministering angel, heaven's noblest gift.

949. BAD MAN. BAD WOMAN.—*N.* bad man, wrongdoer, worker of iniquity; evildoer, etc., 913; sinner, transgressor; bad example.

rascal, scoundrel, villain, knave, etc., 941; miscreant, wretch, reptile, viper, serpent, monster, devil, demon, devil incarnate, fallen angel, lost sheep, black sheep, castaway, prodigal.

bad woman, jade, Jezebel, hellcat.

ruffian, rowdy, bully, etc., 887; thief, murderer.

culprit, delinquent, criminal, malefactor, felon, convict, outlaw.

riffraff, scum of the earth; blackguard, loafer, sneak, vagabond.

scamp, scapegrace, ne'er-do-well, good for nothing, reprobate, scalawag [*colloq.*], limb [*colloq.*], rapscallion [*all the words in this paragraph are commonly applied jocularly or lightly*].

950. PENITENCE.—*N.* penitence, contrition, compunction, repentance, remorse, regret, self-reproach, self-reproof, self-accusation, self-condemnation, qualms of conscience.

acknowledgment, confession, apology, recantation; penance.

penitent, Magdalen, prodigal son, returned prodigal.

V. repent, be sorry for, rue, regret, think better of, recant; plead guilty, acknowledge, confess, humble oneself, beg pardon, apologize; turn over a new leaf.

reclaim, reform, regenerate, redeem, convert, amend, make a new man of, restore self-respect.

Adj. penitent, repentant, contrite, softened, melted, touched, conscience-stricken; self-accusing, self-convicted.

951. IMPENITENCE.—*N.* impenitence, irrepentance, recusancy, hardness of heart, heart of stone, seared conscience, obduracy.

V. be impenitent, steel the heart, harden the heart; die and make no sign.

Adj. impenitent, obdurate, hard, hardened, seared, recusant, unrepentant; relentless, remorseless, graceless.

lost, incorrigible, irreclaimable; unreclaimed, unreformed.

952. ATONEMENT.—*N.* atonement, reparation, compromise, composition, compensation, quittance, expiation, redemption, reclamation, conciliation, propitiation; indemnification, redress, amends, apology, satisfaction; sacrifice.

penance, fasting, sackcloth and ashes, shrift, purgation, purgatory.

V. atone, atone for, expiate, propitiate, make amends; reclaim, redeem, repair, ransom, absolve, purge, shrive, do penance, pay the penalty.

apologize, express regret, beg pardon, give satisfaction.

Adj. propitiatory, expiatory, sacrifice, sacrificial.

953. [Moral Practice] TEMPERANCE.—*N.* temperance, moderation, frugality, sobriety, soberness, forbearance, abnegation; self-denial, self-restraint, self-control.

abstinence, abstemiousness, asceticism; vegetarianism, prohibition, teetotalism, total abstinence.

abstainer; teetotaler, etc., 958; vegetarian, fruitarian; ascetic.

V. be temperate, abstain, forbear, refrain, deny oneself, spare.

Adj. temperate, moderate, sober, frugal, sparing, abstemious.

954. INTEMPERANCE.—*N.* intemperance, sensuality, animalism, pleasure, luxury, luxuriousness, freeliving, indulgence, high living, dissipation, self-indulgence; voluptuousness, debauchery.

revel, revels, revelry, orgy; drunkenness, debauch, carousal, drinking bout, saturnalia.

V. be intemperate, indulge, exceed; live high (*or* on the fat of the land), dine not wisely but too well; plunge into dissipation, revel, carouse, run riot, sow one's wild oats.

Adj. intemperate, excessive; sensual, self-indulgent, voluptuous, wild, dissipated, dissolute, fast.

brutish, swinish, piggish, hoggish, beastlike, beastly.

luxurious, epicurean, sybaritical; nursed in the lap of luxury; indulged, pampered; full fed, high fed.

intoxicated, drunk, etc., 959.

954a. SENSUALIST.—*N.* sensualist, sybarite, voluptuary, man of pleasure, epicure, epicurean, gourmet; gourmand, glutton, pig, hog; free liver, hard liver.

955. ASCETICISM.—*N.* asceticism, puritanism, austerity; total abstinence; mortification, sackcloth and ashes, penance, fasting; martyrdom.

ascetic, anchorite, hermit, recluse; puritan, yogi [Hindu]; dervish, fakir [both Moham.]; martyr.

Adj. ascetic, austere, puritanical.

956. FASTING.—*N.* fasting, famishment, starvation.

fast, fast day, Lent, spare (*or* meager) diet, lenten diet, Barmecide feast; short rations.

V. **fast**, starve, famish, perish with hunger.

Adj. **fasting**, lenten, unfed; starved, half-starved, hungry.

957. GLUTTONY.—*N.* **gluttony**; greed, greediness, voracity; epicurism, gastronomy; high living; guzzling.

feast, banquet, good cheer, blow out [*slang*].

glutton, gormandizer, cormorant, hog, etc. (*sensualist*), 954a.

epicure, *bon vivant* [F.], gourmand [*obs. as* glutton], gourmet.

V. **gormandize**, gorge; overeat, glut, satiate, indulge, eat one's fill, cram, stuff, guzzle, bolt, devour, gobble up, gulp, raven, eat out of house and home.

Adj. **gluttonous**, greedy, gormandizing, omnivorous, voracious, devouring, overfed, gorged.

958. SOBRIETY.—*N.* **sobriety**; total abstinence, teetotalism.

water drinker; prohibitionist, dry [*slang*], teetotaler, total abstainer.

V. take the pledge; abstain, etc., 953.

Adj. **sober**, temperate, moderate, abstemious.

959. DRUNKENNESS.—*N.* **drunkenness**, intemperance, drinking, inebriety, inebriation, intoxication, winebibbing; bacchanalia; libations.

alcoholism, dipsomania; delirium tremens, d.t.'s [*colloq.*].

drink, alcoholic drinks, alcohol, blue ruin [*slang*], booze [*colloq.*]; grog, punch; punchbowl, cup, rosy wine, flowing bowl; liquor, dram, beverage, beer, etc.; cocktail, highball, peg [*slang*, orig. India]; stirrup cup, parting cup.

illicit distilling; bootlegging [*slang*], moonshining, moonshine *or* moonshine whisky [*colloq.*], hooch [*slang*], home-brew; moonshiner [*colloq.*]; bootlegger [*slang*].

drunkard, sot, toper, tippler, winebibber, hard drinker, soaker [*slang*], sponge [*slang*], boozer [*colloq.*], bum [*slang*]; reveler, carouser; dipsomaniac.

V. **get** (*or* be) **drunk**, see double; take a drop (*or* glass) too much; drink, tipple, booze [*colloq.*], soak [*slang*], have a jag on [*slang*], carouse; drink hard (*or* deep, like a fish).

liquor, liquor up [*both slang*], wet one's whistle [*colloq. or humorous*]; raise the elbow, hit the booze [*slang*], crack a bottle.

inebriate, fuddle [*colloq.*], befuddle.

sell illicitly, bootleg [*slang*].

Adj. **drunk**, tipsy, intoxicated, inebriate, inebriated; in a state of intoxication, overcome, fuddled [*colloq.*], boozy [*colloq.*], full [*vulgar*], lit up [*slang*], elevated [*colloq.*]; groggy [*colloq.*]; screwed, tight, primed [all slang], muddled, maudlin; blind drunk, dead drunk.

960. PURITY.—*N.* purity; decency, decorum, delicacy; continence, chastity, virtue, modesty; virginity.

virgin, vestal, prude; Diana.

Adj. pure, undefiled, modest, delicate, clean, decent, decorous; chaste, continent, virtuous, honest.

961. IMPURITY.—*N.* impurity, uncleanness; immodesty; grossness; indelicacy, indecency, obscenity; dissipation.

Adj. impure, unclean; immodest, shameless, indelicate, indecent, coarse, gross.

962. LIBERTINE.—*N.* libertine, voluptuary, rake, roué [F.], fast man.

5. Institutions

963. LEGALITY.—*N.* legality, legitimacy, legitimateness; legitimization.

law, code, constitution, charter, act, enactment, statute, rule, canon, ordinance, institution, regulation, bylaw, decree, standing order.

equity, common law; unwritten law; law of nations, international law; constitutionality; justice, etc., 922; jurisprudence; legislation.

V. legalize, legitimize; enact, ordain, decree, authorize, pass a law, legislate; codify, formulate, regulate.

Adj. legal, legitimate; according to law; vested, constitutional, chartered, legalized, lawful, statutory; legislative; judicial, juridical.

Adv. in the eye of the law.

964. [Absence or violation of law] ILLEGALITY.—*N.* lawlessness, illicitness; breach (*or* violation) of law; disobedience, violence, brute force, despotism, tyranny, outlawry; mob (*or* lynch) law.

illegality, informality, unlawfulness, illegitimacy; smuggling.

V. violate the law, set the law at defiance, make the law a dead letter, take the law into one's own hands.

smuggle, run, poach, bootleg [slang].

Adj. illegal, prohibited, unlawful, illegitimate, illicit, contraband, actionable.

unchartered, unconstitutional, lawless, unwarranted, unauthorized; unofficial.

arbitrary, despotic, summary, irresponsible.

Adv. with a high hand, in violation of law.

965. JURISDICTION. [Executive]—*N.* jurisdiction, judicature, administration of justice; judge, etc., 967; tribunal, etc., 966.

city government, municipal government, commission government, Oregon plan [U. S.]; municipality, corporation; police, police force, constabulary.

executive, officer, commissioner, lord lieutenant [Brit.], city manager, mayor, alderman, councilor, selectman; bailiff, beadle; sheriff, constable, policeman, police constable, police sergeant, patrolman, gendarme [F.].

bureau, department, portfolio, secretariat.

V. **judge,** adjudge, adjudicate, sit in judgment; have jurisdiction over.

Adj. **executive,** administrative; municipal; judiciary, judicial, juridical.

966. TRIBUNAL.—*N.* **tribunal,** court, board, bench, judicature, court of justice (*or* law); judgment seat, mercy seat; bar, bar of justice; town hall, statehouse, townhouse, courthouse; forum; sessions.

United States courts: U. S. Supreme Court, U. S. District Court, U. S. Circuit Court of Appeal; Federal Court of Claims, Court of Private Land Claims; Supreme Court, Superior Court, court of sessions, criminal court, police court, juvenile court.

court-martial, (*pl.* courts-martial), drumhead court-martial.

Adj. **judicial,** etc., 965; appellate; curial.

967. JUDGE.—*N.* **judge,** justice, justice (*or* judge) of assize; magistrate, police magistrate, beak [*slang*]; his worship [Eng.], his honor, his lordship [Brit.]; the court.

Lord Chancellor, Master of the Rolls, Vice-Chancellor, Lord Chief Justice [all Brit.], Chief Justice.

arbiter, arbitrator; moderator, receiver, master; umpire, referee; censor.

jury, grand jury, petty jury, inquest, panel.

juror, juryman, talesman; grand juror, grand juryman; petty juror, petty juryman.

V. **adjudge,** etc. (*determine*), 480; try a case, try a prisoner.

Adj. **judicial,** etc., 965.

968. LAWYER.—*N.* **lawyer,** jurist, legal adviser, advocate; barrister, barrister-at-law [Eng.]; counsel, counselor; king's counsel [Eng.]; pleader, special pleader.

attorney, solicitor; conveyancer, notary, notary public; pettifogger, shyster.

bar, legal profession; Inns of Court [Eng.].

V. **practice law;** practice at (*or* within) the bar, plead; be called to (*or* within) the bar; admitted to the bar.

disbar, degrade.

Adj. learned in the law; at the bar; forensic.

969. LAWSUIT.—*N.* **lawsuit,** suit, action, cause; litigation; suit in law.

writ, summons, subpoena, citation; habeas corpus [L.].

arraignment, prosecution, impeachment, accusation; present-
ment, true bill, indictment.

arrest, apprehension, committal, commitment; imprisonment.

pleadings; declaration, bill, claim; affidavit, libel; answer, plea,
demurrer, rebutter, rejoinder; surrebutter, surrejoinder.

litigant, suitor, libelant; plaintiff, defendant, etc., 938.

hearing, trial; judgment, sentence, finding, verdict; appeal,
writ of error.

case, decision, decided case, precedent.

V. litigate, go to law, appeal to the law; bring to justice (*or*
trial, the bar), put on trial, accuse, prefer (*or* file) a claim.

cite, summon, summons, serve with a writ, arraign; sue, prosecute, indict, impeach; attach, distrain; commit, apprehend, arrest, give in charge.

try, hear a cause; sit in judgment; adjudicate, etc., 480.

970. ACQUITTAL.—*N.* acquittal, exculpation, acquittance,
clearance, exoneration, discharge, release, absolution, reprieve,
respite, pardon.

Exemption from punishment: impunity, immunity.

V. acquit, exculpate, exonerate, clear; absolve, whitewash, discharge, release, liberate, reprieve, respite, pardon.

Adj. acquitted, uncondemned, unpunished; recommend to
mercy.

971. CONDEMNATION.—*N.* condemnation, conviction, judgment, penalty, sentence; death warrant.

V. condemn, convict, find guilty, damn, doom, sentence, pass
sentence on, attaint, confiscate, sequestrate.

proscribe, interdict; disapprove, etc., 932; accuse, etc., 938.

Adj. condemnatory, damnatory, condemned, self-convicted.

972. PUNISHMENT.—*N.* punishment, punition, chastise-
ment, chastening, correction, castigation; discipline, infliction,
trial; judgment, penalty, retribution, nemesis, retributive justice.

Forms of punishment: lash, scaffold, etc. (*instrument of punishment*), 975; imprisonment; transportation, banishment, expulsion, exile, involuntary exile, ostracism, penal servitude, hard labor, galleys; beating, flagellation, bastinado, blow,
stripe, cuff, kick, buffet, pummel; torture, rack.

capital punishment, execution; hanging, shooting, electrocution, decapitation,
strangling, strangulation, crucifixion, impalement, martyrdom, auto-da-fé (*pl.*
autos-da-fé) [Pg.], hara-kiri [Jap.], happy dispatch [*jocular*], lethal chamber,
hemlock.

V. punish, chastise, chasten, castigate, correct, inflict punishment; tar and feather; masthead, keelhaul.

visit upon, pay, settle, settle with, do for [*colloq.*], get even with,
make an example of; give it one [*both colloq.*].

strike, etc., 276; smite; spank, thwack, thump, beat, buffet,
thrash, pommel, drub, trounce, belabor; trim [*colloq.*], cowhide,

lambaste [*slang*], lash, flog, scourge, whip, birch, cane, switch, horsewhip, lay about one, beat black and blue; sandbag, blackjack; pelt, stone.

execute; bring to the block (*or* gallows), behead, decapitate, guillotine; hang [*p. p.* hanged, *not* hung, *for the death penalty*], electrocute, shoot, burn, crucify, impale, lynch.

torture, agonize, rack, put on (*or* to) the rack, martyr, martyrize.

banish, exile, transport, deport, expel, ostracize; rusticate; drum out; dismiss, disbar; unfrock [*as a priest*].

Adj. punitive, penal, punitory, inflictive, castigatory.

973. REWARD.—*N.* reward, recompense, remuneration, prize, meed, guerdon, indemnity, indemnification; quittance, compensation, reparation, redress, acknowledgment, requital, amends, sop, consideration, return; atonement.

perquisite, perks [*slang*]; donation, etc., 784; tip, bribe, hush money, blackmail.

allowance, salary, stipend, wages; pay, payment, emolument; tribute; premium, fee, honorarium; hire; mileage.

V. reward, recompense, repay, requite, remunerate, compensate; fee, tip, bribe; pay, etc., 807; make amends, indemnify, redress, atone, satisfy, acknowledge.

Adj. remunerative, compensatory; retributive.

974. PENALTY.—*N.* penalty; retribution, etc. (*punishment*), 972; pain, penance.

fine, mulct, forfeit, forfeiture, damages, sequestration, confiscation.

V. penalize, fine, mulct, confiscate, sequestrate, sequester; forfeit.

975. [Instrument of punishment] SCOURGE.—*N.* scourge, whip, lash, strap, thong, cowhide, knout, cat, cat-o'-nine-tails; rope's end; black snake, bullwhack, quirt, rawhide.

rod, cane, stick, rattan, birch, birch rod; rod in pickle; switch, ferule, cudgel, truncheon.

Various instruments: pillory, stocks, whipping post, ducking stool, iron maiden; thumbscrew, boot, rack, wheel; treadmill, crank, galleys; bed of Procrustes.

scaffold; block, ax, guillotine; stake; cross, gallows, gibbet, tree; noose, rope, halter, bowstring; death chair, electric chair.

prison, jail, etc., 752; jailer.

executioner; electrocutioner, headsman, hangman; lyncher, torturer.

malefactor, criminal, culprit, felon, victim, gallows bird [*slang*].

V. RELIGIOUS AFFECTIONS

976. DEITY.—*N.* **Deity,** Divinity, Godhead, Omnipotence, Omniscience, Providence.

GOD, Lord, Jehovah, The King of Kings, The Lord of Lords, The Almighty, The Supreme Being, The Absolute, The First Cause, Author of all things, Creator of all things, The Infinite, The Eternal, The All-powerful, The Omnipotent, The All-wise, The All-merciful, The All-knowing, The Omniscient.

Deus [L.], *Theos* [Gr. Θεος], *Dieu* [F.], *Gott* [Ger.], *Dio* [It.], *Dios* [Sp.], *Deos* [Pg.], *Gud* [Nor., Sw., and Dan.], *God* [Du.], *Bog* Russ.], *Brahma* [Skr.], *Deva* [Skr.], *Khuda* (Hind.), *Allah* (Ar.).

THE TRINITY, The Holy Trinity, The Trinity in Unity, Triunity, Threefold Unity.

I. GOD THE FATHER, The Maker, The Creator, The Preserver.

Functions: creation, preservation, divine government, thearchy.

II. GOD THE SON, Jesus Christ; The Messiah, The Anointed, The Saviour, The Redeemer, The Mediator, The Intercessor, The Advocate, The Judge; The Son of God, The Son of Man; The Only-Begotten, The Lamb of God, The Word, Logos; The Man of Sorrows; Jesus of Nazareth, King of the Jews, The Son of Mary, The Risen, Immanuel, The King of Kings and Lord of Lords, The King of Glory, The Prince of Peace, The Good Shepherd, The Way, The Door, The Truth, The Life, The Bread of Life, The Light of the World, The Vine, The True Vine.

The Incarnation, The Word made Flesh.

Functions: salvation, redemption, atonement, propitiation, mediation, intercession, judgment.

III. GOD THE HOLY GHOST, The Holy Spirit, Paraclete, The Comforter, The Consoler, The Intercessor, The Spirit of God, The Spirit of Truth, The Dove.

Functions: inspiration, regeneration, sanctification, consolation, grace.

The Deity in other religions: Brahmanism *or* **Hinduism: Brahma** (*neuter*), the Supreme Soul *or* Essence of the Universe; Trimurti *or* Hindu trinity *or* Hindu triad: (1) Brahma (*masc.*), the Creator; (2) Vishnu, the Preserver; (3) Siva, the Destroyer and Regenerator.

Buddhism: the Protestantism of the East; Buddha, the Blessed One, the Teacher.

Zoroastrianism: Zerâna-Akerana, the Infinite Being; Ahuramazda *or* Ormazd, the Creator, the Lord of Wisdom, the King of Light (*opposed by* Ahriman, the King of Darkness).

Mohammedanism *or* **Islam:** Allah.

V. **create,** fashion, make, form, mold, manifest.
preserve, uphold, keep, perpetuate, immortalize.
atone, redeem, save, propitiate, expiate; intercede, mediate.

predestinate, predestine, foreordain, preordain; elect, call, ordain.

bless, sanctify, hallow, justify, absolve, glorify.

Adj. **almighty,** all-powerful, omnipotent; omnipresent, all-wise, all-seeing, all-knowing, omniscient, supreme.

divine, heavenly, celestial; holy, hallowed, sacred, sacrosanct.

supernatural, superhuman, spiritual, ghostly, unearthly.

Adv. **by God's will,** by God's help, *Deo volente* [L.], God willing; in Jesus' name, in His name, to His glory.

977. [Beneficent spirits] ANGEL.—*N.* **angel,** archangel, messenger of God, guardian angel; ministering spirits, invisible helpers, choir invisible, heavenly host, sons of God; saint; seraphim (*sing.,* seraph, *E. pl.,* seraphs), Cherubim (*sing.,* cherub, *E. pl.,* cherubs· cherubim *or* cherubin *are often treated as sing.*).

Madonna, Our Lady, *Notre Dame* [F.], Holy Mary, The Virgin, The Blessed Virgin, The Virgin Mary.

Adj. **angelic,** seraphic, cherubic, archangelic.

978. [Maleficent spirits] SATAN.—*N.* **Satan,** the Devil, Lucifer, Belial, Beelzebub, Mephistopheles, Mephisto, Asmodeus, *le Diable* [F.], Deil [Scot.].

fallen angels, unclean spirits, devils; rulers of darkness, the powers of darkness; demon, etc.,980.

Moloch, Mammon; Belial, Beelzebub; Loki [*Norse Myth*].

diabolism, devil worship, demonism, demonology; Black Mass, black magic, demonolatry, witchcraft.

diabolist, demonologist.

V. **demonize;** bewitch, bedevil, etc. (*sorcery*), 992; possess, obsess.

Adj. **satanic,** diabolic *or* diabolical, devilish, demoniac *or* demoniacal, infernal, hellborn.

979. MYTHIC AND PAGAN DEITIES.—*N.* **god,** goddess; heathen gods and goddesses; pantheon.

Greek and Latin: Zeus, Jupiter *or* Jove (*King*); Apollo *or* Phoebus Apollo (*the sun*); Ares, Mars (*war*); Hermes, Mercury (*messenger*); Poseidon, Neptune (*ocean*); Hephaestus, Vulcan (*smith*); Dionysus, Bacchus (*wine*); Hades [Gr.], Pluto *or* Dis [L.] (*King of the lower world*); Kronos, Saturn (*time*); Eros, Cupid (*love*); Pan, Faunus (*flocks, herds, forests, and wild life*).

Hera, Juno (*Queen*); Demeter, Ceres (*fruitfulness*); Persephone, Proserpina *or* Proserpine (*Queen of the lower world*); Artemis, Diana (*the moon and hunting*); Athena, Minerva (*wisdom*); Aphrodite, Venus (*love and beauty*); Hestia, Vesta (*the hearth*); Rhea *or* Cybele ("Mother of the gods," *identified with* Ops, *wife of Saturn*); Gaea *or* Ge, Tellus (*earth goddess, mother of the Titans*).

Norse: Ymir (*primeval giant*), Odin *or* Woden (*the All-father* = Zeus); the Æsir: Thor (*the Thunderer*), Balder (= *Apollo*), Freyr (*fruitfulness*), Tyr (*war*), Bragi (*poetry and eloquence*), Höder (*blind god of the winter*), Heimdall (*warder of Asgard*), Loki (*evil*).

the Vanir: Njorth (*the winds and the sea*), Frey (*prosperity and love*), Freya (*goddess of love and beauty* = *Venus*).

Frigg or Frigga (*wife of Odin*), Hel (*goddess of death = Persephone*), Idun (*goddess of spring, wife of Bragi*), Sigyn (*wife of Loki*).

Egyptian: Ra or Amon-Ra (*the sun god*), Osiris (*judge of the dead*), Isis (*wife of Osiris*), Horus (*the morning sun; son of Osiris and Isis*), Anubis (*jackal-god, brother of Horus, a conductor of the dead*), Nephthys (*sister of Isis*), Set (*evil deity, brother of Osiris*), Thoth (*clerk of the underworld*), Bast or Bubastis (*a goddess with head of a cat*), the Sphinx (*wisdom*).

Various: Baal [Semitic]; Astarte or Ashtoreth (*goddess of fertility and love*) [Phoenician]; Bel [Babylonian]; The Great Spirit [N. Amer. Indian].

nymph, dryad, hamadryad, wood nymph; naiad, fresh-water nymph; oread, mountain nymph; nereid, sea nymph; Oceanid, ocean nymph; Pleiades, Hyades.

fairy, fay, sprite; nix (*fem.* nixie), water sprite; the good folk, brownie, pixy, elf (*pl.* elves), banshee; the Fates; kobold, troll, hobgoblin, gnome, kelpie; faun; peri, undine, sea maid, mermaid (*masc.* merman); Mab, Oberon, Titania, Ariel; Puck, Robin Goodfellow.

familiar spirit, familiar, genius, guide, good genius, daimon, demon.

mythology, mythical lore, folklore, fairyism, fairy mythology.

Adj. **mythical,** mythic, mythological, fabulous, legendary.

fairylike, sylphlike, elfin, elflike, elfish, nymphlike.

980. EVIL SPIRITS.—*N.* demon, fiend, devil, etc. (*Satan*), 978; evil genius, familiar, familiar spirit; bad (*or* unclean) spirit; incubus; ogre, ogress, ghoul, vampire, harpy; Fury, the Furies, the Erinyes, the Eumenides.

imp, bad fairy, sprite, jinni (*pl.* jinn), genius (*pl.* genii), dwarf. changeling, elf child, werewolf; satyr.

elemental, sylph, gnome, salamander, nymph [*Rosicrucian*]. siren, nixie, undine, Lorelei.

bugbear, bugaboo, bogy, goblin, hobgoblin.

Adj. **demoniac,** demoniacal, fiendish, fiendlike, evil, ghoulish; pokerish [*colloq.*], bewitched.

980a. SPECTER.—*N.* specter, ghost, apparition, vision, spirit, sprite, shade, shadow, wraith, banshee, spook [*now humorous*], phantom, phantasm, materialization [*spiritualism*], double.

will-o'-the-wisp, etc., 423.

Adj. **spectral,** ghostly, ghostlike, spiritual, wraithlike, weird, uncanny, eerie, spooky [*colloq.*] haunted; unearthly, supernatural.

981. HEAVEN.—*N.* heaven; kingdom of heaven (*or* God), heavenly kingdom; heaven of heavens, God's throne, throne of God; Paradise, Eden, Zion, Holy City, New Jerusalem, Heavenly City, City Celestial, abode of the blessed.

Mythological heaven or paradise: Olympus; Elysium, Elysian fields, Islands (*or* Isles) of the Blessed, Happy Isles, Fortunate Isles, garden of the Hesperides; third heaven, seventh heaven; Valhalla [Scandinavian]; Nirvana [Buddhist]; happy hunting grounds [N. Amer. Indian].

future state, life after death, eternal home, resurrection, translation; apotheosis, deification.

Adj. **heavenly,** celestial, supernal, unearthly, paradisaic, beatific; Elysian, Olympian.

982. HELL.—*N.* **hell,** bottomless pit, place of torment; pandemonium; hell-fire, everlasting fire (*or* torment); worm that never dies.

purgatory, limbo, Gehenna, abyss.

Mythological hell: Tartarus, Hades, Avernus; infernal regions, inferno, shades below, realms of Pluto.

Pluto, Rhadamanthus, Erebus, Charon, Cerberus; Persephone, Proserpina; Minos, Osiris.

Rivers of hell: Styx, Acheron, Cocytus, Phlegethon, Lethe.

Adj. **hellish,** infernal, stygian.

983. [Religious Knowledge] THEOLOGY.—*N.* **theology,** theosophy, divine wisdom, divinity, hagiography; monotheism, theism, religion; religious persuasion (*or* sect, denomination, affiliation); creed, articles (*or* declaration, profession, confession) of faith.

theologian, scholastic, divine, schoolman, the Fathers; monotheist, theist.

Adj. **theological,** religious, divine, canonical; denominational; sectarian.

983a. ORTHODOXY.—*N.* **orthodoxy;** strictness, soundness, religious truth, true faith; truth, etc., 494; soundness of doctrine; Christianity, Catholicism.

the church, Holy Church, Church Militant, Church Triumphant; Catholic (*or* Universal, Apostolic) Church; Established (*or* State) Church; The Bride of the Lamb; temple of the Holy Ghost; Church of Christ; Christians, Christendom.

canons; thirty-nine articles; Apostles' (*or* Nicene, Athanasian) Creed.

Adj. **orthodox,** sound, strict, faithful, catholic, Christian, evangelical, scriptural, literal, divine, monotheistic, true, etc., 494.

984. HETERODOXY. [Sectarianism]—*N.* **heterodoxy;** error, false doctrine, heresy, schism, recusancy, backsliding, apostasy; materialism, atheism; idolatry, superstition.

bigotry, fanaticism, iconoclasm; precisianism; sabbatarianism, puritanism, bibliolatry.

sectarianism, nonconformity, dissent, secularism; religious sects, the clash of creeds, the isms.

[*Generally speaking, each sect is* orthodox *to itself and* heterodox *to others.*]

paganism, heathenism, heathendom; animism, polytheism, pantheism; dualism.

pagan, heathen, paynim; kafir, non-Mohammedan; gentile; pantheist, polytheist, animist.

misbeliever, heretic, apostate; backslider; antichrist; idolater; skeptic, etc., 989.

bigot, dogmatist, fanatic, dervish, iconoclast.

sectarian, sectary; seceder, separatist, recusant, dissenter, non-conformist.

materialist, positivist, deist, agnostic, atheist, etc., 989.

Adj. **heterodox,** heretical, unorthodox, unscriptural, uncanonical, unchristian, apocryphal; antichristian; schismatic, recusant, iconoclastic; sectarian, dissenting, secular; agnostic, atheistic; skeptical, etc., 989.

bigoted, dogmatical, fanatical; superstitious, credulous; idolatrous.

pagan, heathen, heathenish, gentile, paynim; polytheistic, pantheistic, animistic.

985. REVELATION. [Biblical]—*N.* **revelation,** inspiration.

The Bible, the Book, the Book of Books, The Good Book, the Word, the Word of God, Scripture, the Scriptures, Holy Writ, Holy Scriptures, inspired writings, Gospel.

Old Testament, Septuagint, Vulgate, Pentateuch; the Law, the Prophets; Apocrypha.

New Testament; Gospels, Evangelists, Acts, Epistles, Apocalypse, Revelation; Good Tidings, Glad Tidings.

inspired writers, prophet, evangelist, apostle, disciple, saint; the Fathers, the Apostolic Fathers; Holy Men of old.

Adj. **scriptural,** biblical, sacred, prophetic; evangelical, evangelistic, apostolic, apostolical; inspired, apocalyptic, revealed; ecclesiastical, canonical.

986. SACRED WRITINGS. [Non-Biblical]—*N.* The Vedas, Upanishads, Puranas, Sutras, Bhagavad Gita [all Brahmanic]; Zendavesta, Avesta [Zoroastrian]; The Koran *or* Alcoran [Mohammedan]; Tripitaka, Dhammapada [Buddhist]; Granth, Adigranth [*Sikh*]; the Kings [Chinese]; the Eddas [Scandinavian].

Non-Biblical prophets and religious founders: Gautama (Buddha); Zoroaster, Confucius, Mohammed.

987. PIETY.—*N.* **piety,** religion, theism, faith; religiousness, religiosity, holiness, saintship; reverence, humility, veneration, devotion, worship, grace, sanctity, consecration.

beatification, regeneration, conversion, sanctification, salvation, inspiration, bread of life; Body and Blood of Christ.

believer, convert, theist, Christian, devotee, pietist, saint.

V. **be pious,** have faith, believe, receive Christ; venerate, adore, worship, revere, be converted, be on God's side, stand up for Jesus, fight the good fight, keep the faith, let one's light shine.

regenerate, convert, edify, sanctify, hallow, keep holy, beatify, inspire, consecrate, enshrine.

Adj. pious, religious, devout, devoted, reverent, godly, humble, pure, pure in heart, holy, spiritual, saintly, saintlike; believing, faithful, Christian.

regenerated; inspired, consecrated, converted, unearthly. elected, adopted, justified, sanctified.

988. IMPIETY.—*N.* impiety, sin, irreverence; profaneness, profanity, blasphemy, profanation; desecration, sacrilege; scoffing.

Assumed piety: hypocrisy, pietism, cant, pious fraud; lip devotion, lip service; formalism, austerity; sanctimony, sanctimoniousness, pharisaism, sabbatarianism; sacerdotalism; bigotry; blue laws.

apostasy, recusancy, backsliding, perversion, reprobation.

bigot, pharisee, sabbatarian, formalist, pietist, precisian, devotee, ranter, fanatic.

sinner, scoffer, blasphemer, sabbath breaker; worldling; hypocrite.

the wicked, the evil, the unjust, the reprobate.

V. profane, desecrate, blaspheme, revile, scoff, swear; commit sacrilege.

dissemble, simulate, play the hypocrite, snuffle.

Adj. impious, irreligious, etc., 989; profane, irreverent, sacrilegious, blasphemous.

unhallowed, unsanctified, unregenerate; hardened, perverted, reprobate.

hypocritical, canting, pietistical, sanctimonious, unctuous, pharisaical, overrighteous.

bigoted, fanatical, hidebound, narrow, narrow-minded, illiberal, prejudiced, little; provincial, parochial, insular.

989. IRRELIGION.—*N.* irreligion, impiety, ungodliness, laxity, apathy, indifference.

skepticism, doubt; unbelief, disbelief, incredulity, agnosticism, freethinking; materialism, rationalism, positivism; atheism, infidelity.

unbeliever, infidel, atheist, heretic, heathen, alien, gentile, Nazarene; freethinker, skeptic, rationalist; materialist, positivist, nihilist, agnostic.

V. disbelieve, lack faith; doubt, question, deny the truth.

Adj. irreligious; undevout, godless, graceless, ungodly; unholy, unsanctified, unhallowed; atheistic.

skeptical, freethinking, unbelieving, unconverted; incredulous, faithless.

worldly, mundane, earthly, carnal, worldly, worldly-minded, unspiritual.

990. WORSHIP.—*N.* worship, cult, adoration, devotion, vow, aspiration, homage, service; kneeling, genuflection, prostration.

prayer, invocation, supplication, intercession, orison, petition; collect, litany, Lord's prayer, paternoster; *Ave Maria* [L.], Hail, Mary.

thanksgiving; grace, praise, glorification, paean, benediction, doxology, hosanna, hallelujah, alleluia, *Te Deum* [L.], *Gloria* [L.].

psalm, hymn, chant, response, anthem.

offering, oblation, sacrifice, incense, libation, offertory, collection.

divine service, office, duty; exercises; morning prayer; Mass, matins, evensong, vespers, vigils, lauds.

worshiper, congregation, communicant, celebrant.

V. **worship,** lift up the heart, aspire; revere, adore, do service, pay homage, offer one's vows, vow; bow down and worship.

pray, invoke, supplicate; beseech; offer up prayers, say one's prayers, tell one's beads, recite the rosary.

give thanks, say grace, bless, praise, laud, glorify, magnify, sing praises.

Adj. devout, devotional, reverent, solemn, fervid.

991. IDOLATRY.—*N.* idolatry, idolatrousness, demonism, demonology, devil worship, fetishism.

idolization, deification, apotheosis, canonization; hero worship.

sacrifice, hecatomb, holocaust; human sacrifices, immolation, self-immolation, suttee.

idol, golden calf, graven image, fetish, joss [Chinese], *lares et penates* [L.]; god (*or* goddess) of one's idolatry; Baal, Moloch, Juggernaut.

idolater, idolatress, idolizer, fetishist.

V. **idolize,** idolatrize, worship idols, worship, put on a pedestal, prostrate oneself before; make sacrifice to, deify, canonize.

Adj. **idolatrous,** idolistic, prone before, prostrate before, in the dust before, at the feet of.

992. SORCERY.—*N.* sorcery, magic, black magic, the black art, necromancy, demonology, witchcraft, witchery, wizardry, fetishism, hoodoo, voodoo, voodooism; fire worship, incantation, enchantment, bewitchment, glamour; obsession, possession.

divination, etc. (*prediction*), 511; sortilege, ordeal, hocus-pocus.

V. **practice sorcery,** cast a nativity (*or* horoscope), conjure, charm, enchant, bewitch, bedevil, witch, voodoo, hoodoo [*colloq.*]; entrance, fascinate, hypnotize, cast a spell; call up spirits.

Adj. **magic,** magical, witching, weird, cabalistic, talismanic.

992a. **PSYCHICAL RESEARCH.**—*N.* **psychical research,** psychical (*or* psychic) investigation; abnormal (*or* mediumistic) phenomena; mysticism.

the **subconscious,** the subconscious self, the subliminal self, the higher self, ego, astral body; aura; subconsciousness, subliminal consciousness; intuition; dual personality, multiple personality, obsession, possession.

psychotherapy, psychotherapeutics, psychoanalysis; hysteria, neurasthenia, dreams, visions, apparitions, hallucinations.

mesmerism, animal magnetism; mesmeric trance; hypnotism; hypnosis.

Phenomena: **telepathy,** thought transference, thought transmission, telepathic transmission; second sight, clairvoyance, clairaudience, psychometry.

premonitions, previsions, premonitory apparition, fetch, wraith, double; death lights, ominous dreams.

automatism, automatic writing, planchette, ouija board, trance writing, spirit writing; trance speaking, inspirational speaking.

spiritualism, spiritism, spirit manifestations; trance, spirit control, spirit possession; mediumistic communications; séance; materialization.

medium, seer, clairvoyant, clairaudient, telepathist; guide, control; mesmerist, hypnotist.

V. **psychologize;** investigate the abnormal (*or* supernormal, subconscious, subliminal), traverse the borderland, know oneself.

mesmerize, magnetize, hypnotize, place under control, subject to suggestion, place in a trance, induce hypnosis.

Adj. **psychical,** psychic, psychological; spiritistic, spiritualistic, spiritual; subconscious, subliminal, supernormal, abnormal; mystic *or* mystical.

993. **SPELL.**—*N.* **spell,** charm, incantation, exorcism, abracadabra, open-sesame; evil eye.

talisman, amulet, phylactery, philter, fetish, wishbone; mascot, rabbit's foot, hoodoo [*colloq.*], jinx [*slang*], scarabaeus *or* scarab; veronica, swastika.

wand, caduceus, rod, divining rod, witch hazel, Aaron's rod.

Magic wish-givers: Aladdin's lamp, Aladdin's casket, magic casket, magic ring, magic belt, magic spectacles, wishing cap, Fortunatus' cap; seven-league boots; magic carpet; cap of darkness.

994. **SORCERER.**—*N.* **sorcerer,** magician, wizard, necromancer, conjuror, prestidigitator; charmer, exorcist. voodoo medicine man, witch doctor; astrologer, soothsayer, etc., 513.

sorceress, witch, hag; siren, harpy.

Cagliostro, Merlin; Circe, weird sisters, witch of Endor.

995. **CHURCHDOM.**—*N.* **churchdom;** church, ministry, priesthood, prelacy, hierarchy, church government; clericalism, sacerdotalism, episcopalianism.

monasticism, monkhood, monachism; celibacy.

Ecclesiastical offices and dignities: cardinalate, cardinalship; primacy, archbishopric, archiepiscopacy; prelacy, bishopric, episcopate, episcopacy, see, diocese; benefice, incumbency, living, cure, charge, cure of souls; rectorship, vicariate, vicarship; pastorate, pastorship, pastoral charge; deaconry, deaconship; curacy; chaplaincy, chaplainship, presbytery.

holy orders, ordination, institution, consecration, induction, installation, preferment, translation, presentation.

papacy, pontificate, See of Rome, the Vatican, the apostolic see.

V. **call,** ordain, induct, install, translate, consecrate, present, elect, bestow.

Adj. **ecclesiastical,** clerical, sacerdotal, priestly, pastoral, ministerial, hierarchical, episcopal, canonical; pontifical, papal, apostolic.

996. CLERGY.—*N.* **clergy,** clericals, ministry, priesthood, presbytery, the cloth, the pulpit, the desk.

clergyman, divine, ecclesiastic, priest, pastor, shepherd, minister, preacher, clerk in holy orders, parson, sky pilot [*slang*]; father, padre, *abbé* [F.], *curé* [F.]; reverend.

Dignitaries of the church: Pope, pontiff, Holy Father; cardinal, primate, metropolitan, archbishop, bishop, prelate, dean, archdeacon, canon, rector, vicar, beneficiary, incumbent, chaplain, curate; elder, deacon.

religious, abbot, prior, monk, friar, lay brother, pilgrim, palmer.

nun, sister, priestess, abbess, prioress, canoness; mother superior, the reverend mother; novice.

Adj. **ordained,** in orders, in holy orders, called to the ministry.

997. LAITY.—*N.* **laity,** flock, fold, congregation, assembly, brethren, people; society [U. S.]; class [Methodist].

layman, parishioner, catechumen.

V. **laicize,** secularize.

Adj. **secular,** lay congregational, civil, temporal, profane.

998. RITE.—*N.* **rite,** ceremony, observance, function, duty, form, solemnity, sacrament; service, ministry, ministration.

sermon, preaching, preachment, exhortation, religious harangue, homily, lecture, discourse.

worship, etc., 990; invocation of saints, confession, the confessional; absolution, remission of sins; reciting the rosary, telling one's beads.

Seven Sacraments: (1) baptism, immersion, christening; baptismal regeneration; font.

(2) confirmation, laying on of hands.

(3) Eucharist, Mass, Lord's supper, communion; the sacrament, the holy sacrament; consecrated elements, bread and wine, celebration; transubstantiation, real presence.

(4) penance, fasting, sackcloth and ashes, flagellation.

(5) **extreme unction,** last rites, viaticum.

(6) **holy orders,** ordination, etc. (*churchdom*), 995.

(7) **matrimony,** marriage, wedlock, etc., 903.

Sacred articles: relics, rosary, beads, reliquary, host, cross, rood, crucifix; pyx, censer, thurible; prayer wheel [Buddhist]; Sangraal, Holy Grail.

ritual, liturgy, rubric, canon, ordinal, missal, breviary, Mass book, beadroll, litany, prayer book, Book of Common Prayer; psalter, psalmbook, hymnbook, hymnal.

ritualism, ceremonialism; sabbatism, sabbatarianism; ritualist, sabbatarian.

V. **perform service,** do duty, minister, officiate, celebrate.

excommunicate; ban with bell, book, and candle.

preach, sermonize, address the congregation.

Adj. ritual, ritualistic, ceremonial, liturgic *or* liturgical; paschal.

999. CANONICALS.—*N.* canonicals, vestments, robe, gown, surplice, etc.

1000. TEMPLE.—*N.* temple, fane, place of worship; house of God, house of prayer; cathedral, minster, church, kirk [Scot.], chapel, meetinghouse.

synagogue, tabernacle; mosque [Moham.]; pagoda, Chinese temple, joss house [*colloq.*]; pantheon, shrine.

monastery, priory, abbey, friary, convent, nunnery, cloister.

parsonage, rectory, vicarage, manse, deanery, clergy house; bishop's palace; Vatican.

Adj. **churchly,** cloistered, monastic, monasterial, conventual.

INDEX

The numbers refer to the headings under which the words or phrases occur. When the same word or phrase can be used in various senses, the several headings under which it or its synonyms will be found are indicated by *italics*.

When the word given in the Index is itself the title or heading of a category, the word is printed in capitals and the reference number in bold-faced type, thus: **ACTIVITY 682.** When the word is the keyword to a group of synonyms, the reference number is also in bold-faced type.

Derivatives likewise have been sparingly admitted, since the allied or basic term will serve as a key to the various derived forms; thus *alarm* is given, but not *alarmed* or *alarming*. Adverbs ending in *-ly* should be looked for under the adjective, if not found in the Index.

IMPORTANT NOTE

The numbers following all references in this Index Guide refer to the *section* numbers in the text, and *not* to pages.

INDEX

A

abandon 624, 782
abandoned
  forsaken 893
  vicious 945
abandonment 757, 782
abase 879
abasement 874
abash 879
abashed 879
abatement 36
abbess 996
abbey 1000
abbot 996
abbreviation 201
abdicate 757
abdomen 250
abduct *repel* 289
  steal 791
aberration 83
abet 707
abhor 867, 898
abhorrence 867, 898
abhorrent *painful* 830
  hateful 898
abide *endure* 1, 106
  remain 110
  dwell 186
ability 157, 698
abject *vile* 874
  servile 886
abjure *deny* 536
  renounce 607
ablaze 382
able *capable* 157
  skilful 698
able-bodied 159
ablution 652
abnormal 83
aboard *present* 186
  afloat 273
abode 189
abolish 756
abolition 2, 162, 756
abominable *bad* 649
  hateful 898
abominate *dislike* 867
  hate 898
abomination 867
aboriginal 66, 124
aborigine 188
abound 639
about *nearly* 32, **197**
  around 227

above 206
abracadabra 993
abrade 330,331
abrasion 330,331
abreast 216, 236
abridge 36, 201
  in writing 596
abridgment 35, **201**
abroad 57, 196
abrupt *sudden* 113
  steep 217
abscond 623
ABSENCE 187
  -of mind 458
  -of time 107
absent 187, 458
absentee 187
absent-minded 458
absolute *not relative* 1
  great 31
  certain 474
absolution 918
absolve 918, 952
absorb *combine* 48
  take in 296
absorbed 451
absorption 296
abstain *refrain* 623
  be temperate 953
abstainer 953, 958
abstemious 953, 958
abstention 623
abstinence 623, **953**
abstract, *v. take* 789
abstract, *n. epitome* 195, 596
abstracted *inattentive* 458
abstraction 38, 451, **458**
absurd 471, **497**, 583
ABSURDITY
  impossibility 471
  nonsense **497**
  ridiculousness 853
abundance 31, **639**
abundant *great* 31
  enough 639
abuse, *v. illtreat* 649
  misuse 679
abuse, *n. in-vective* **908**, 932
abusive 909, 932
abut 197
abysmal *deep* 208

abyss 198, 667
academic 537
academy 542
accede *assent* 488
  submit 725
  consent 762
accelerate **132**, 274, 684
accent 402, 580
accentuate 580, **642**
accept *assent* 488
  receive 785
acceptable
  expedient 646
  agreeable 829
acceptance *security* **771**
access *approach* 286
accessible *possible* 470
  easy 705
accession *increase* 35
accessory *extrinsic* 6
  adjunct 37, 39
  accompanying 88
accident 151, 619, **735**
accidental *extrinsic* 6
  occasional 134
  fortuitous 156
acclaim 931
acclamation 488, **931**
acclivity 217
accommodate *suit* 23
  aid 707
accommodation
  adaptation 23
  space 180
ACCOMPANIMENT
  adjunct 37, 39
  coexistence 88
  musical 415
accompany
  coexist 88
  escort 664
accomplice 711
accomplish *execute* **161**
  complete 729
accomplishment
  learning 490
  talent 698
accord
  agree 23
  assent 488
  grant 760, 784
accordance 16, 23
accordingly **8**, 476

311

accost 586
account
  description 594
  credit 805
  repute 873
  -for 155
accountable 177, 926
accountant 801, 811
ACCOUNTS 811
accouple 43
accouter 225, 717
accredit 873
accretion 35
accrue 785
accumulate 72
accumulation 35, 72
accuracy 494
accurate 494
ACCUSATION 938
accusatory 938
accuse 938
accuser 938
accustom *habit* 613
ace *aviator* 269a
ache 378
achieve *produce* 161
  do 680
  accomplish 729
achievement
  feat 861
acid 397
acidify 397
acknowledge
  assent 488
  disclose 529
  consent 762
  pay 807
  thank 916
  reward 973
acme 210
acoustic 402
acoustics 402
acquaintance
  knowledge 490
  friend 890
acquiesce
  assent 488, 602
  consent 762
acquiescence *assent* 488
  consent 762
  submission 725
acquire 775
acquirement *learning* 539
  talent 698
ACQUISITION 775
acquit *liberate* 750
  exempt 927a
  absolve 970
ACQUITTAL 970
acquittance 970
acrobat 159
across 219
act, *v.*
  operate 170
  personate 599
  do 680

act, *n. play* **599**
  statute 741
acting *deputy* **759**
ACTION 680
  battle 720
  lawsuit 969
active *physical* **171**
  voluntary 682
ACTIVITY 682
actor *player* **599**
  affectation 855
actual *existing* 1
  present 118
  real 494
actuality [*see* actual]
actuate 175
acumen 498
acute *physically violent*
  173
  pointed 253
  physically sensible **375**
  discriminative 465
  perspicacious 498
  piercing 821
  morally painful **830**
acuteness 253, 465
adage 496
adamantine 159, 323
adapt *agree* 23
adaptable 82, 644
add *increase* 35, **39**
  join 37
addendum 39
ADDITION *increase* 35,
  37
  thing added 39
  arithmetic 85
address, *v. speak to* 582,
  586
ADDRESS, *n. residence*
  189
  speech 586
adduce 467
adept 700
adequate *sufficient* 639
  for a purpose 644
  content 831
adhere *stick* 46
adherent 65, 711
adhesive 46
adieu 293
adjacent 197
adjoin 197, **199**
adjourn 133, 460
adjudge 480
adjudicate 480
ADJUNCT *addition* 37
  thing added 39
  accompaniment 88
adjure *request* 765
adjust *adapt* 23
  equalize 27
  regulate 58
adjustment 762
adjutant 745
administer 693, 737

administrative 737, 965
admirable 648
admiral 745
admiration *wonder* 870
  respect 928
admissible 23, 651
admission [*see* admit]
admit *composition* 54
  include 76
  let in 296
  assent 488
  acknowledge 529
  concede 762
admittance 296
admixture 41
admonish 932
ado 682
ADOLESCENCE 131
adopt *choose* 609
  appropriate 788
adoration 990
adore *love* 897
  worship 990
adorn 847
adrift 475
adroit 698
adulation 933
adult 131
adulterate *mix* 41
  deteriorate 659
advance *increase* 35
  elapse 109
  progress **282**
  lend 787
advancement [*see*
  advance]
advantage *superiority* 33
  increase 35
  influence 175
advantageous **644, 648**
advent 292
adventure *event* 151
  risk 665
adventurer 548, 863
adventurous 861
adversary 710
adverse *contrary* 14
  opposed 708
  unprosperous 735
ADVERSITY 735
advertise 531
advertisement 531
ADVICE *notice* 527
  counsel 695
advisable 646
advise 695
adviser 695
advisory 527
advocate, *v. recommend*
  695
advocate, *n. counselor* 968
aeon 109, 110
aerial *aeronautic* 273
  airy 334
AERONAUT 269a
aeronautic 267, **273**

aeronautics 267, **273**
aerostatics 267
aesthetic 845
afar 196
affable 894
affair *event* **151**
  battle 720
affect *relate to* 9
  qualify 469
  touch 824
  simper 855
  desire 865
AFFECTATION 579, **855**
affected 579, **855**
affection 879
affectionate 897
AFFECTIONS 820
affianced 903
affiliated 9, 11
affinitive 9
affinity *relation* 9
  similarity 17
affirm 535
AFFIRMATION 535
affirmative 535
affix *addition* **37**
  sequel 39
  precedence 62
afflict 830
affliction 828, 830
affluence 734, 803
afford 803
affront 900, 929
afield 186
afire 382
afloat 267, **273**
afoot *ready* 673
aforesaid 104
afraid 860
afresh *repeated* 104
  new 123
aft 235
after *in order* 63
  in time 117
  rear 235
  in pursuit 281
aftermath 154
afternoon 126
afterpart 235
afterthought 451
afterward 117
again 104
  -and again 136
against 708
  -the grain 256, **704**
agape 455, 507
AGE *period* 108
  course 109
  long time 110
  oldness 124
  advanced life **128**
aged 128
AGENCY 170
AGENT 690
aggrandize 35
aggravate *increase* 35

heighten **835**
AGGRAVATION 35, **835**
aggregate 50
aggression 716
aggrieve 830
aghast 860
agile 274
agitate *move* **315**
  excite 821, **824**
AGITATION
  [see agitate]
  energy 171
  motion 315
aglow 382, 420
agnostic 485, 984, 989
agnosticism 989
ago 122
agonizing 830
agony *physical* 378
  mental 828
agree *accord* **23, 714**
  concur 178
  assent 488
  -to 762
agreeable 82, 377
AGREEMENT 23, 82, 178
agriculture 371
agriculturist 342
aground *fixed* 150
  failure 732
ahead 234, 282, **303**
AID 707, 906
ail 655
aileron 267
ailment 655
aim *direction* 278
  purpose 620
aimless 615a
air *gas* 334
ATMOSPHERIC 338, 349
  tune 415
  appearance 448
aircraft 273
air line 278
airman 269
AIR PIPE 351
airplane 273, 726
airs *affectation* 855
  vanity 880
airwoman 269a
airy [see air]
  visionary 4
  light 320
aisle 260
ajar 260
akimbo 244
akin *related* 11
alacrity 682, 836
ALARM
  notice of danger **669**
  fear 860
alarmist 862
alarum 550, 669
album 593, 596
alcohol 959
alcove 191

alert *watchful* 457, 459
  active 682
alertness 457, 459
alias 18
alibi 187
alien *irrelevant* 10
  foreigner 57
alienate *disjoin* 44
  estrange 889
  set against 898
alight, *v. arrive* **292**
  descend 306
alight, *adv. on fire* 382
align 278
alike 17
alive *living* 359
  intelligent 498
  active 682
all *whole* 50
  complete 52
allay 174, 834
allege 467, 535
allegiance *obedience* **743**
  duty 926
alleviate 174, 834
alleviation **174**
alley 260
alliance *relation* 9
  kindred 11
  co-operation 709
allied 11, 48
alliteration 104
allot 786
allow *admit* **529**
  permit 760
allowable 760
allowance
  qualification 469
  gift 784
  salary 973
alloy *mixture* 41
  combine 48
allude 521, 526
allure 865
allusion **526**
ally, *v.* 48
ally, *n.*
  auxiliary 711
  friend 890
almanac 86, 114
almighty 157, 976
Almighty, the 976
almost 32
alms 784
aloft 206
alone 87
along 200
alongside *near* 197
  parallel 216
  laterally 236
aloof *distant* 196
  secluded 893
aloud 404
alphabet 561
already 118
also 37

altar 903
alter 15, 140
alteration *difference* 15
  variation 20a
  change 140
alternate *reciprocal* 12
  vary 20a
  periodic 138
  substitute 147
  oscillate 314
alternation 12, 138, **314**
alternative 147
although 179, 469
altitude 206
altogether 50, 52
altruism 910, 942
altruist 906, 910
alumnus 541
always *uniformly* **16**
  generally 78
  perpetually 112
amain *violent* 173
amalgamate 41, 48
amass 50, 72
amateur 602
amateurish 643
amaze 870
amazement 870
ambassador 534, 758
ambidexter 238
ambiguous *uncertain* 475
  unintelligible 519
  equivocal 520
ambition 620, 865
ambitious 865
amble 266
ambuscade 530
AMBUSH *hiding* **530**
  pitfall 667
amenable 602, **926**
amend *improve* 658
amendment 658
amends 952
amenity 894
amiable 894, 906
amicable 888
amidst 41, 228
amiss 619
amity 714, 888
ammunition 727
amnesty 918
among 41, 228
amorous 897
amount *quantity* 25
  sum of money 800
amphitheater 728
ample *much* 31
  spacious 180
  large 192
  broad 202
amplify 194, 549
amputate 38
amulet *talisman* **747**
  charm 993
amuse 840
AMUSEMENT 840

ANACHRONISM 115,
135
anemia 160
anesthesia 376, 381
anesthetic 376
anesthetize 376
analogous 17
analogy 9, 17
analysis
  decomposition 49
  inquiry 461
  reasoning 476
analyst 463
analytical [*see* analysis]
analyze [*see* analysis]
anarchist 891, 913
anarchy *disorder* 59
  social 738
anathema 908
anathematize 908
anatomize *dissect* 44
  investigate 461
anatomy 44, 329
ancestor 166
ancestral 166
ancestry 69, **122**, 166
anchor *moor* 184
  stop 265
  safeguard 666
  hope 858
anchorage *location* 184
  roadstead 189
  refuge 666
anchorite 893, 955
ancient *old* 124
and 37
anecdote 594
anew 104, 123
ANGEL 977
angelic 977
anger 900
angle 244, 448
angry 900
anguish *physical* 378
  moral 828
angular 244
ANGULARITY 244
ANIMAL 366, **370**
  -life 364
animalcule 193
animalism 954
animate 824, 836
animation *activity* 682
  vivacity 836
animosity 889, 900
annalist 553
annals 594
annex 37, 43
annihilate 2, 162
annihilation 2
anniversary **138**, 883
annotation 522
announce *predict* 511
  inform 527
announcement
  [*see* announce]

annoy *molest* 907
  disquiet 830
annoyance 828, **830**
annual 138
annul 756
ANNULMENT 756
anoint 332, 355
anointment 332, 355
anomaly 83
anonymous 565
another 15
ANSWER *reply* **462**
  go bail 806
answerable 177, 926
ant 366
antagonism *different* 24
  enmity 889
antagonist 710
antagonistic 14, 24, **179**
antecedence 62
antecedent 64
antedate 115
antediluvian 124
antelope 366
anthem 990
anthology *collection* 596
anthropology 368, 372
antic 840
anticipate
  foresee 121, **510**
  be early **132**
  expect 507
  hope 858
anticipation 115, 121
  [*see* anticipate]
anticlimax 853
antipathy *contrariety* 14
  repulsion 289
  dislike 867
  enemy 891
  hate 898
antipodes 14, 237
antiquary 122
antiquated
  aged 122, **124**, 128
  out of fashion 851
antique 124
antiquity 122, 124
antiseptic 662
antisocial 911
antithesis 14, 15
anxiety *solicitude* 459
  pain 828
  fear 860
anxious [*see* anxiety]
any 25
anybody 78
anyhow 627
apace 132
apache 361, 913
apart *irrelative* 10
  separate 15, 44
  singleness 87
  asunder 96
apartment 191
apathetic 275, 462, **823**

apathy 823
ape *monkey* 366
ape, *v. imitate* 19
aperient 652
aperture 260
apex 206, 210
aphorism 496
apiary 370
apiece 79
Apocalypse 985
Apocrypha 985
apocryphal 475
apologetic 937
apologist 937
apology *substitution* 147
   vindication 937
   penitence 950
apostasy *recantation* 607
   impiety 988
apostate *turncoat* 607
   heretic 984
apostatize 607
apostle 985
apostolic 985, 995
apostrophe 589
apostrophize 765
apothecary 662
apotheosis 981, 991
appall *pain* 830
   terrify 860
apparatus 633
apparel 225
apparent *visible* 446
   appearing 448
   probable 472
   manifest 525
apparition
   phantom 4, 362
   spirit 980a, 992a
appeal *address* 586
   request 765
appear *arrive* 292
   come in sight 446, 448
APPEARANCE 448
appease 174, 826
append 37, 63
appendage *addition* 37
   adjunct 39
   sequel 65
   accompaniment 88
appendix 65
appertain 777
appetite 865
appetizer 394
appetizing 394
applaud 931
applause 931
appliance *use* 677
appliances 632
applicable *relevant* 9, 23
   useful 644
applicant 767
application *study* 457
   request 765
apply *appropriate* 788
appoint 755, 786

appointment *business* 625
   charge 755
   interview 892
appointments *gear* 633
apportion 786
APPORTIONMENT 786
apposition 23, 199
appraise 466
appreciate *realize* 450
   know 490
apprehend *know* 490
   fear 860
   seize 969
apprehension *idea* 453
   fear 860
apprehensive 860
apprentice 541
apprenticeship 539
APPROACH 286
   of time 121
   nearness 197
   path 627
approbation 931
appropriate *fit* 23
   peculiar 79
   timely 134
   borrow 788
   take 789
appropriation
   allotment 786
   taking 789
approval *assent* 488
   commendation 931
approve 488, 931
approved 931
approximate
   related to 9
   resemble 17
   near 197
   nearing 286
appurtenance 780
apt *consonant* 23
   clever 698
aquatic 267
aqueduct 350
aquiline 244
arable 371
arbiter *critic* 480
   judge 967
arbitrament 480
arbitrary 10
   willful 606
   severe 739
   lawless 964
arbitrate 480, 724
arbitration 480
arbitrator 724
arbor 191
arboreal 367
arc 245
arcade 189
arch *curve* 245
   convexity 250
   roguish 840
archeologist 122
archeology 122

archaic *old* 124
archaism 122, 124
archangel 977
archbishop 996
archer 284, 726, 840
archetype 22
archipelago 346
architect 164, 690
architecture 161
archive 551
arctic 237, 383
arctics 225
ardent *eager* 682
   loving 897
ardor *vigor* 574
   feeling 821
arduous 704
area 181
ARENA *space* 180
   field of battle 728
argosy 273
argot 563
argue 467, 476
argument 476
argumentation 476
arid 169, 340
aright 618
arise *begin* 66
   happen 151
   mount 305
aristocracy 875
aristocrat 875
aristocratic 852
arithmetic 85
ark 666
arm *part* 51
   power 157
   prepare 673
   weapon 727
armada 726
armament 727
armchair 215
armed 722
   -force 664, 726
armful 25
armistice 142, 723
armor 727
armorial 550
armory 636
ARMS 727 [*see* arm]
   heraldry 550
army *collection* 72
   multitude 102
   troops 726
aroma 400
around 227
arouse *move* 615
   excite 824
arraign *accuse* 938
   indict 969
arraignment 969
arrange *set in order* 60
   organize 357
   harmonize 416
   plan 626
   compromise 774

ARRANGEMENT 60
[see arrange]
arrant *great* 31
  base 940
array *order* 58
  multitude 102
  dress 225
arrears *debt* 806
arrest *stop* 142
  restrain 751
  in law 969
ARRIVAL 292
arrive 265, 292
arrogance 878, 880, 885
arrogant *proud* 878
  vain 880
  insolent 885
arrogate *assume* **739**, 885
  claim 924
arrow 727
arsenal 691
arson 384
art *representation* 554
  skill 698
  cunning 702
artery 350, 627
artful 702
article *thing* 3
  review 595
articulation *junction* 43
  speech 580
artifice *plan* 626
  cunning 702
artificer 690
artificial *fictitious* 545
  affected 855
  -light **420**
artillery 727
artilleryman 726
artisan 690
ARTIST 559
artistic *skilful* 698
  beautiful **845**
artistry 569
artless 703
ARTLESSNESS 703
as *motive* 615
ascend *increase* 35
  rise 305
ascendancy *power* 157
  influence 175
ascension [see ascend]
ASCENT *gradient* 217
  rise 305
ascertain 480
ascertained 490
ascetic 953, 955
ASCETICISM 953, 955
ascribe 155
aseptic 662
ashamed 879
ashen 429
ashes *corpse* 362
  dirt 653
ashore **342**
ashy 429

aside *laterally* 236
  in a whisper 405
ask *inquire* 461
  request 765
askance 217
askew 217, 243
aslant 217
asleep 683
aspect *feature* **5**
  situation 183
  appearance 448
asperity *roughness* 256
  discourtesy 895
asphyxiate 361
aspirant *candidate* 767
aspire *hope* 858
  worship 990
asquint 217
ass *beast of burden* 271
  fool 501
assail *attack* 716
assailant 716, 726
assassin 361
assault 716
ASSEMBLAGE 72
assembly *assemblage* 72
  council 696
assembly room **189**
ASSENT *agreement* **488**
  be willing 602
assert *affirm* **535**
assess *measure* 466
  determine 480
  tax 812
assessor *judge* 967
assets 780
asseverate 535
assiduous 682
assign *commission* 755
  give 784
  allot 786
assignable 270
assignee 785
assignment 155, 755
assimilate 16
assimilation 23, 161
assist 707, 906
assistant 711
assize *tribunal* 966
associate, *n.* 690, 890
associate, *v. relate* 9
  mix 41
  unite 43
  combine 48
  accompany 88
association
  [see associate]
  relation 9
  co-operation 709
assonance 597
assort *arrange* 60
assortment 72
assuage *moderate* 174
  relieve 834, 826
assume *suppose* 514
  take 789

assumed 514
assuming *insolent* 885
assumption [see assume]
  seizure 925
assurance
  certainty 474
  belief 484
  confidence 507
  promise 768
assure *render certain* 474
  convince 484
  promise 768
assuredly *assent* 488
astern 235
asteroid 318
astigmatism 443
astir *active* 682
astonish 870
astonishment 870
astound *excite* 824
  frighten 860
astral 318
  -body 317, 992*a*
astray 475
astute 498
asunder *separate* 44
  distant 196
asylum *retreat* 666
atheism 989
atheist 984
athirst 865
athlete 159
athletic *strong* 159
  gymnastic 720
athletics 159, 720
athwart 219
at large 750
atlas 86
atmosphere *air* 338
  painting 556
atmospheric 338
atom 32, 193
atomize 336
atone 952, 976
ATONEMENT
  expiation 952
  propitiation 976
atrocious 907, 947
atrophy 195
attach *join* 43
  legal 969
attaché 746, 758
attachment 43, 969
ATTACK 716
attain *arrive* 292
  succeed 731
attainable 470
attainment *knowledge* 490
attempt 675
attend *accompany* 88
  be present 186
  follow 281
  apply the mind **457**
  treat medically 662
  serve 746
attendance [see attend]

attendant 88, 281, **746**
ATTENTION 457
attentive *mindful* 457 [*see*
attend]
attenuate *decrease* 36
   reduce 195
   make rare 322
attenuated 203
attest *bear testimony* 467
   guarantee 768
attic 191, 210
attire 225
attitude 240
attitudinize 855
attorney 968
attract *bring towards* 288
   allure 865
   excite *love* 897
ATTRACTION *pull* 288
   pleasure 829
   lure 865
attractive [*see* attract]
   pleasing 829
attribute 88
attribute to 155
attribution 155
attune *music* 415
   prepare 673
attuned to *habit* 613
auburn 433
auction 796
audacity *courage* 861
   rashness 863
   insolence 885
audible 402
audience *hearers* 418
   drama 599
audit 85, 461, 811
auditor *hearer* 418
   accountant 811
auditorium 189
auditory 402
auger 262
aught 51
augment *increase* 35, 37
   expand 194
augur *soothsayer* 513
augury 512
august 31
aura 992a
aureole 873
auricular 418
aurist 662
aurora 125, 423
auspices 175, 664
auspicious *opportune* 134
   favorable 512
   prosperous 734

hopeful 858
austere 739, 955
austerity 739, 955
authentic *well founded* 1
   evidential 467
   certain 474
   true 484
authentication
   evidence 467
   security 771
author *writer* 593
   projector 626
authoritative *certain* 474
   commanding 741
authorities 745
AUTHORITY *power* 737
   influence 157, 175
   testimony 467
   sage 500
   informant 527
   permission 760
   right 924
AUTHORIZATION 924
authorize *empower* 737
   permit 760
   entitle 924
authorized 924
authorship
   composition 54
   production 161
   writing 590
auto 272
autocar 272
autocracy 737
autocrat 739, 745
autocratic *will* 600
   ruling 737
auto-da-fé *burning* 384
   execution 972
autograph *evidence* 467
   signature 550
   writing 590
automatic 601
   pistol 727
automatism 992a
automobile 266, **272**
automobilist 268
autonomy 748
autopsy 363
autumn 126
AUXILIARY 711
   extra 37
   aiding 707
avail *be useful* **644**
   succeed 731
available 673
avalanche 306
avarice 819

Ave Maria 900
avenge 919
avenger **919**
avenue 627
aver 535
average *balance* 29
   mediocre 651
averse *contrary* 14
   unwilling 603, 867
aversion *dislike* 867
avert 706
aviate 267
aviation 267
aviator 269
avidity *avarice* 819
   desire 865
avocation 625
avoid 623, 867
AVOIDANCE 623
avouch 535
avow 535
avowal 535
await *foresee* 121
   be kept waiting **133**
   expect 507
awake *attentive* 457
   intelligent 498
   excite 824
awaken *excite* 824
award *adjudge* 480
   give 784
aware 490
away *distant* 196
awe *fear* 860
   wonder 870
awe-struck 860, **870**
awful *fearful* 860
awhile 111
awkward *inexpedient* 647
   unskillful 699
   difficult 704
   ugly 846
awkwardness
   [*see* awkward]
awning 223
awry *oblique* 217
   distorted 243
ax *edge tool* 253
   weapon 727
axiom 496
axiomatic 496
axis 222
axle 312
ay 488
aye *ever* 112
   yes 488
azure 438

B

babble *gurgle* 348
   jabber 517, 584
babe 129

Babel 560, 563
baby 129, 167
babyhood 127

babyish 499
bachelor 904
back, *n. rear* 235

battleship 726
baubel *trifle* 643
　　toy 840
bawl 411
bay, *n. gulf* 343
bay, *adj. brown* 433
bay, *v. cry* 412
bayonet 716, 727
bays *trophy* 733
bay window 260
be 1
beach 342
beacon 550
beadle *law officer* 965
beam *support* 215
　　light 420
bear, *n. brute* 895
　　stock exchange 797
bear, *v. endure* 151, 826
　　produce 161
　　sustain 215
　　carry 270
　　admit of 470
　　suffer 821
　　-fruit *prosper* 734
　　-upon *be relevant* 9
bearable 651
beard 253, 256
bearded 256
beardless 226
bearer 271
bearing *relation* 9
　　direction 278
　　meaning 516
　　demeanor 692
bearings *situation* 183
bearish 895
beast *animal* 366
　　brute 895
　　-of burden 271
beastly *unclean* 653
beat, *n. periodicity* 138
　　verse 597
　　path 627
beat, *v. be superior* 33
　　surpass 303
　　oscillate 314
　　agitate 315
　　strike 972
　　-a retreat 623
　　-down *cheapen* 819
beaten track *habit* 613
beatific 827, 981
beatification 987
beau *fop* 854
　　admirer 897
　　-ideal *perfect* 650
　　beauty 845
beautiful 845
beautify 845, 847
BEAUTY 845
becalm 265
because 476, 615
beckon 550
becloud *befog* 353
become *change to* 144

behove 926
becoming *beautiful* 845
　　due 924
bed 215
bedaub 223
bedazzle 420
bedeck 847
bedevil *derange* 61
　　bewitch 992
bedizen 847
bedridden 655
bedrock 211
bee 366
beehive *for bees* 370
　　workshop 691
beeline 278
Beelzebub 978
beer 298
befall 151
befit *agree* 23
　　behoove 924
befitting 924
before *in order* 62
　　in space 234
　　ahead 280
beforehand 132
befriend 707, 888
beg *ask* 765
　　-pardon 950
　　-the question 477
beggar *petitioner* 767
　　poor man 804
　　low person 876
beggarly *vile* 874
begin 66
beginner 541
BEGINNING 66
begrudge 819
beguile *mislead* 495
behalf *advantage* 618
behave 692
　　-oneself 894
behavior 692
behead 361, 972
behind *in space* 235
　　in sequence 281
behindhand *late* 133
behold *see* 441
beholden *grateful* 916
behoove 926
being *abstract* 1
　　concrete 3
belated *late* 133
belie *deny* 536
　　falsify 544
BELIEF *credence* 484
　　religious creed 983
believe 484, 987
believer 484, 987
belittle *decrease* 36
　　underestimate 483
　　detract 934
bell *alarm* 550
belle 854

belligerent
　　contentious 720
　　warlike 722
　　combatant 726
bellow *cry* 411
belly 250
belong to *related* 9
　　compose 56
　　property 777
beloved 897
below 207
belt *outline* 230
　　ring 247
bemoan 839
bench *support* 215
　　tribunal 966
bend *fork* 244
　　curve 245
　　turn 311
　　give 324
beneath 207
benediction *gratitude* 916
　　approval 931
benefaction 784
BENEFACTOR 912
beneficent 906
beneficial 648
beneficiary 785
benefit *profit* 618
　　do good 644, 648
　　assist 906
BENEVOLENCE
　　kindness 906, 910
benevolent 906
benighted *ignorant* 491
benignant 906
bent, *n. tendency* 176, 820
　　desire 865
bent, *adj. angular* 244
benumb *deaden* 381
　　blunt 823
bequeath 784
bequest 270, 784
berate 932
bereavement *death* 360
　　loss 776
bereft 776
berth *lodging* 189
　　office 625
beseech 765
beset *surround* 227
　　attack 716
beside 197, 236
besides 37
besiege *surround* 227
　　attack 716
besmear 653
bespeak 755
best *good* 648
　　perfect 650
bestir oneself 682
bestow *give* 784
betimes 132
betoken 467
betray *disclose* 529
　　deceive 545

betroth 768, 903
betrothal 902
betrothed 897, 903
better *improve* 658
between 228
betwixt 228
beverage 298
bevy 102
bewail 839
beware 668
bewilder *put out* 458
  perplex 475
  astonish 870
bewitch *fascinate* 615
  diabolize 978
  hoodoo 992
beyond *superior* 33
  further 196
bias *influence* 175
  tendency 176
  slope 217
  prepossession 481
bib *pinafore* 225
Bible 985
bicentenary 98, 138
bicentennial 98, 138
bicker *quarrel* 713
bicycle 272
bid *order* 741
  offer 763
bide *wait* 133
  remain 141
biennial 138
bier 363
big *in degree* 31
  in size 192, 206
bigot *dogmatist* 474
  mule 606
  heterodox 984
  impious 988
bigoted 988
bigotry 474, 606, 984
bill *money account* 811
  -of fare 86, 298
billet, *n. office* 625
billet, *v. locate* 184
billingsgate 908
billows 341
bind *connect* 43
  compel 744
biography 594
biologist 357
biology 357, 359
biplane 273
bird 366
birth *beginning* 66
  production 161
birthday 138
birthright 924
bisect 91
bisection 91
bishop 996
bishopric 995
bit *small quantity* 32
  part 51
  curb 752

bite *eat* 298
biting *cold* 383
  pungent 392
bitter *cold* 383
  acrid 395
  malevolent 907
bitterness [*see* bitter]
bivouac 265
bizzare 83, 853
black *color* 431
  -sheep 949
blackball 893, 932
blacken 431
  defame 934
blacklist 932
blackmail 793
BLACKNESS 431
blade *edge tool* 253
blamable 932, 947
blame 155, **932**
blameless 946
blameworthy **932**, 947
blanch 429, 430
bland 894
blandishment 902
blank *inexistent* 2
  unsubstantial 4
blanket 223
blare 404
blarney 933
blasé 869, 871
blasphemy 988
blast, *n. destroy* 162
  explosion 173
blast, *v. wind* 349
blatant *loud* 404
blaze *heat* 382
  mark 550
blazer *coat* 225
blazon *publish* 531
  inscribe 873
  -forth 882
bleach 429
bleachers 444
bleak 383
blear-eyed 443
bleat 412
bleed *extort money* 814
  suffer 828
bleeding *hemorrhage* 299
BLEMISH *deface* 241
  imperfection 651
  defect 848
blench *shrink* 821
blend *mix* 41
  combine 48
  harmonize 413
bless *sanctify* 976
blessed 827
blessing 618, 931
blight 659
blighted 659
blind, *n. shade* 530
  pretext 617
blind, *adj. sightless* 442
blind, *v. conceal* 528

blinders 443
blindfold 442, 491, 528
BLINDNESS 442
blink *wink* 443
blinker **424**, 443, 530
bliss 827
blister 848
blithe 836
blithesome 836
blizzard 349
bloat *inflate* 194
bloated *expanded* 194
  convex 250
block, *n. houses* 189
  mass 192
block, *v. hinder* 706
  execution 975
blockade *surround* 227
  close 261
  seclude 893
blockhead 501
blonde 429
blood *consanguinity* 11
  -relation 11
bloodlessness 160
bloodshed 361
bloodthirsty 361
bloody *killing* 361
bloom *blossom* 367
  health 654
  flower 734
blossom
  flower 161, 365, 367
  flower 734
blot *blacken* 431
  blemish 848
  disgrace 874
blotch *black* 431
  blemish 848
blotchy 431
blouse 225
blow *knock* 276
  waft 349
  disappointment 509
  evil 619
  -up *explode* 173
  inflate 194, 349
  objurgate 932
blowhole 260, 351
bludgeon 727
BLUE *color* 438
bluestocking 492
bluff *high* 206
  brag 884
blunder *error* 495
  absurdity 497
  bungle 699
  failure 732
  indiscretion 947
blunt *obtuse* 254
  benumb 376
  plain-spoken 703
BLUNTNESS 254
blur *dim* 443
  blemish 848
blurred *invisible* 447

budge 264
budget *finance* **811**
buff *color* 436
buffer 717
buffet *strike* 276
  smite 972
buffet *café* 189
  cupboard 191
buffoon *actor* 599
  humorist 844
  butt 857
buffoonery
  humor **840, 842, 853**
  horseplay **856**
bug 193, 366
bugaboo 980
bugbear 980
build *construct* 161
  form 240
building 189
bulb 249, 250
bulge 250
bulk, *n. quantity* 25
  whole 50
  size 192
bulk, *v.* 31
bulkhead 228
bulky 31, 192
bull *animal* 366
  absurdity 495, 497
  stock exchange 797
bulldoze 860
bullet 727
bulletin *list* 86
  news 532
bullion 800
bully, *n.* 863, 887
bully, *v. frighten* 860
  bluster 885
  threaten 909
bulwark 717
bump, *n.* 250
bump, *v.* 276

bumptious *proud* 878
bunch *collection* 72
  protuberance 250
buncombe *bombast* 577
  boast 884
  flattery 933
bundle *packet* 72
bung 263
bungle 495, 699
bungler 701
bunkum
  [see buncombe]
buoy *raise* 307
buoyant
  floating 305
  light 320
  elastic 325
  hopeful 858
bur 53
burden *clog* 706
bureau *chest* 191
  department 965
bureaucracy 737
burgess 188
burgher 188
burglar 792
burglary 791
burial 363
  -place **363**
burlesque, *n.*
  travesty 555, 853
  absurdity 497
  ridicule 856
burlesque, *v. imitate* 19
  ridicule 856
burn *heat* 382
  consume 384
burnish *polish* 255
burrow *excavate* 208, 252
burst, *n. sound* 406
  paroxysm 825
burst, *v.*
  -forth *begin* 66

expand 194
be seen 446
bury 229, 363
bush *shrub* 367
bushy 256
BUSINESS 151, **625**
businesslike
  orderly 58
  business **625**
  practical 692
bustle *energy* 171
  agitation 315
  activity **682**
bustling **682**
busy 625, **682**
busybody 455
but 30
butcher *kill* 361
butchered 53
butler 746
butt, *n. cask* 191
  laughingstock 857
butt, *v.* 276
butter 356
button *fasten* 43
buttonhole, *n.*
  bouquet 400
buttonhole, *v.*
  to bore 841
buttress 717
buxom 836
buy 795
buyer 795
buzz 409
by 236, 631
  -and by 132
  -means of **632**
  -the by 134
  -the way 134
bygone *past* 122
byplay 550
bystander 197, 444
byword, *contempt* 930

C

cab 272
cabin *room* 189
cabinet *receptacle* 191
  council 696
cable, *n. link* 45
  dispatch 532
cable, *v.* 534
cabman 268
cackle (*of geese*) 412
  laugh 838
cad 851
cadaverous *pale* 429
  hideous 846
cadence *sound* 402
  music 415
cadet *junior* 129
  officer 745
caesura 44, 198

café 189, 298
cage, *n. prison* 752
cage, *v. restrain* 751
caisson 191, 252
cajole *flatter* 933
  [see cajolery]
cajolery *imposition* 544
  persuasion 615
  flattery 933
cake, *n.* 396
cake, *v. stick* 46
  consolidate 321
calamitous
  adverse 735, 935
  disastrous 830
calamity *killing* 361
  evil 619
  adversity 735

calcine 384
calculate 85
calculation 85
caldron 191
CALEFACTION 384
calendar *list* 86, 611
  chronicle 114
calf *animal* 366
  fool 501
caliber *measure* 26, 192
  intellectual capacity **498**
calipers 466
calisthenics 159
calk 660
call *signal* 550
  name 564
  visit 892
  ordain 995

-upon *visit* 892
calling *business* 625
callous *hard* 323
  insensible 823
callow *young* 127
  bare 226
  immature 674
calm, *adj. quiet* 265
  silent 403
  serene 826
  imperturbable 871
calm, *v. soothe* 174
  dissuade 616
calmness
  composure **826, 871**
  [see *calm*]
calumet 721
calumniator 936
calumny 934
cameo 250
camera 445
camouflage 528, 545
camp, *n.* 189
camp, *v.* 184
campaign 692, 722
campaigner 726
campanile 206
campus 344
can, *n. receptacle* 191
can, *v. preserve* 670
canal 260, 350
cancel *destroy* 162
  obliterate 552
  abrogate 756
candid *sincere* 543
  ingenuous 703
candidate 767
candle 423
candle power 466
candor 543
candy *sweet* 396
cane, *n. weapon* 727
cane, *v. punish* 972
  scourge 975
cannibal 913
cannon *arms* 727
cannonade 716
canny 702
canoe 273
canon *belief* 983a
  precept 697
CANONICALS 999
canonization 873
canopy 223
  -of heaven 318
canorous 413
cant *hypocrisy* 544
  impiety 988
canter 274
canting 855
canton 181
cantonment 189
canvas *sail* 267
  picture 556
canvass *investigate* 461
  discuss 476

solicit 765
canvasser 767, 797
canyon *ravine* 198, 350
cap *hat* 225
capability *skill* 698
capable 682, 698
capacious 180, 192
capacity *power* 157
  space 180
  size 192
  intellect 450
cape *protection* 250
caper *leap* 309
capital, *n. city* 189
capital, *adj.*
  money 800
  wealth 803
  important 642
  excellent 648
  -punishment **972**
capitalist 803
capitulate 725
CAPRICE 608
capricious *irregular* 139
  changeable 149, 608
capriciously 615a
  [see *capricious*]
capsize 218, 252
captain *mariner* 269
  master 745
captious *capricious* 608
  irascible 901
captivate *please* 829
captivation *attraction* 829
captive *prisoner* 754
captivity 751
captor 789
capture 789
car 272
caravan *vehicle* 272
carbine 727
carbon 388
carbonize 384
card, *n.* 550
card, *v. comb* 652
cardinal *red* 434
CARE *attention* **459**
  adversity 735
  custody 751
  pain 828
  -for *love* 897
career *conduct* 692
careful *heedful* **459, 864**
  frugal 817
careless 460, 863
carelessness 460
caress 897, 902
careworn 828, 837
cargo 190, 270
caricature, *n. copy* 19, 21
caricature, *v. misrepresent*
  555
  ridicule 856
caricaturist 844
caries 49
carnage 361

carnal *fleshly* 364
  irreligious 989
carnival 840
carnivorous 298
carol *music* 415, 416
carouse *feast* 840
  revel 954
carriage *aspect* 448
CARRIER 271
carry *support* 215
  transfer 270
cart 272
carter 268
cartoon 21
cartridge 727
carve *cut* 44
  form 240
  furrow 259
  sculpture 557
cascade 348
case *box* 191
  sheath 223
  topic 454
  argument 476
  lawsuit 969
casehardened *callous* 823
casement 260
cash *money* 800
cashbox 802
cashier 801
casing 223
cask 191
casket *box* 191
  coffin 363
cast, *n. role* 51, **599**
  aspect 448
cast, *v. mold* 21
  form 240
  throw 284
  -away *waste* 638
  -lots 621
  -up *add* 37, 85
castaway *exile* 893
caste *class* 75
  lose- 940
castigate *reprove* 932
  punish 972
castle *defense* 717
casual *incidental* 6
  accidental 156
casualty *misfortune* 735
casuistry 926
cat *animal* 366
cataclysm *convulsion* 146
  destruction 162
catalepsy 265, 683
catalogue 60, 86
cataract *waterfall* 348
catastrophe *disaster* 619
  misfortune 735
catcall *disapproval* 932
catch *imitate* 19
  detect 480a
  gather the meaning 518
  take 789
catching *infectious* 657

clash, v. disagree 24
  cross 179
  -of arms 720
clashing contrariety 14
clasp fasten 43
  stick 46
  embrace 902
CLASS, n. category 75
  learners 541
  school 542
  party 712
  laity 997
class, v. arrange 60
classfellow 890
classic old 124
  symmetry 242
classics 560
classification 60
classify 60
classmate 541
classroom 542
clatter noise 404
  rattle 407
clause 51
claw 781
clay earth 342
clean perfect 650
  unstained 652
  -cut 494
cleaner 652
cleanly 652
cleanness 652
cleanse 652
clear simple 42
  light 420
  transparent 425
  certain 474
  intelligible 518
  manifest 525
  distinct 535
  perspicuous 570
clear, v. leap 309
  vindicate 937, 970
clear-cut true 494
clear-sighted 441
clearness [see clear]
cleavage cutting 44
cleave sunder 44
  adhere 46
  bisect 91
clef 413
cleft chink 198
clement lenient 740
  compassionate 914
CLERGY 996
clergyman 996
clerical 995
clerk recorder 553
  writer 590
clever 698
cleverness 698
click 406
client dependent 711
  customer 795
clientele 795
cliff height 206

verticality 212
  steep 217
  crag 342
climate 338
climax supremacy 33
  summit 210
climb 305
clime 181
clinch fasten 43
cling adhere 46
  -to
  persevere 604a
  desire 865
  love 897
clink resound 408
clip shorten 201
clique 75, 712
cliquish 712
cloak, n. dress 225
cloak, v. conceal 528
  disguise 530
clock 114
clod lump 192
  earth 342
  fool 501
clog hinder 706
cloister arcade 189
  seclusion 893
close, n. end 67
close, adj. similar 17, 21
  tight 43
  near 197
  dense 321
  warm 382
  taciturn 585
  stingy 819
close, v. shut 261
  conclude 769
closely [see close]
closet 191
CLOSURE 261
clot 321
clothe 225
CLOTHING 225
cloture 142
CLOUD, n. mist 353
cloud, v. darken 421
  dim 422, 427
  -over 422, 427
cloudy dim 422
  opaque 426
clown 599, 844
cloy 641, 869
club, n. place of meeting 74
  association 712
  weapon 727
club, v. combine 48, 892
clue answer 462
  indication 550
clump 72, 250
  -of trees 367
clumsiness [see clumsy]
clumsy unfit 647
  awkward 699
cluster 72
clutch seize 781

throttle 789
clutter 59
coach, n. carriage 272
  tutor 540
coach, v. teach 537
coachman 268
coagulate cohere 46
  densify 321
coal 388
coalesce 13, 48
coalition 709, 712
coarse harsh 410
  vulgar 851
coast, n. border 231
coast, v. glide 266
  navigate 267
  land 342
coat layer 204
  paint 223
  dress 225
  -of arms 550
coating, inner - 224
coax persuade 615
  wheedle 902
cobble mend 660
cobbler 660
cobra 366
cobweb 205
cock vane 338
  bird 366
cockeyed 443
cockle 258
cocksure 484
coddle 902
code concealment 528
  cipher 561
  law 963
codicil addition 37
  testament 771
codify arrange 60
  legalize 963
coequal 27
coequality 27
coerce compel 744
  restrain 751
coeval 120
coexist exist 1
  concur 120
coexistence 120
coffer chest 191
  money chest 802
coffin 363
cog tooth 253
cogency 157
cogent powerful 157
cogitate 450, 451
cogitative 451
cognate related 9
  similar 17
cognition 490
cognizance 490
cohere 46
COHERENCE 46
coherent 23
cohesion 46
cohesive 46

convenient 646
convent 1000
conventicle *council* 696
convention *assembly* 72
  canon 80
  law 697
  compact 769
  social rule 852
conventional 82, 613, 852
conventionalism 613
conventionalist 82
conventionality 82, 852
conventionalize 82
conventual *monastic* 1000
converge 290
CONVERGENCE 290
convergent 286, 290
conversant 698
CONVERSATION 588
conversational 588
  sociable 892
converse *reverse* 14
  talk 588
conversely 148
conversible 144
CONVERSION 144, 987
convert, *n.* 987
convert, *v.*
  change 140
  change to 144, 484
  reclaim 950
convertible 13, 27
convex 250
CONVEXITY 250
convey *transfer* 270
  assign 783
conveyance
  transference 270
  vehicle 272
convict, *n. prisoner* 754
  condemned man 949
convict, *v. condemn* 971
conviction *belief* 484
  guilt 971
convince *confute* 479
  assure 484
convivial 892
conviviality 892
convocation
  assemblage 72
convoke 72
CONVOLUTION
  coil 248
convoy *accompany* 88
  transfer 270
  guard 664
convulse 315, 378
convulsion *revolution* 146
  fit 173, 315, 378
cook, *n. servant* 746
cook, *v. heat* 384
  prepare 673
cool, *adj. cold* 383
  refrigerate 385
  inexcitable 826
  cautious 864

indifferent 866
imperturbable 871
unfriendly 889
cool, *v. moderate* 174
coolheaded
  unexcitable 871
coolness [see cool]
caution 864
  calmness 871
coop *restrain* 751
co-operate 709, 746
CO-OPERATION
  physical 178
  voluntary 709
  participation 778
co-operative
  concurring 178
  helpful 746
co-ordinate *equal* 27
cope with *oppose* 708
  contend 720
copious *productive* 168
  abundant 639
copper *money* 800
copperish 433
coppice 367
copse 367
COPY, *n. facsimile* 21
  prototype 22
  duplicate 90
copy, *v. imitate* 19
copyist *imitator* 19
coquet, *v. lie* 544
  change one's mind 607
  flirt 902
coquetry 855
coquette *belle* 854
  flirt 902
cord *tie* 45
  filament 205
cordial, *n. dram* 392
cordial, *adj.*
  pleasurable 377
  willing 602
  fervid 821
  grateful 829
cordiality *good will* 602
  fervor 821
cordon 232, 247
core *center* 68, 222
  gist 5, 642
cork *plug* 263
corkscrew 248
corky *dry* 340
corner *plight* 7
  place 182
  angle 244
  monopoly 777
corollary *adjunct* 39
coronation
  enthronement 755
  celebration 883
coronet 247, 747
corporal, *n.* 745
corporal, *adj. corporeal*
  316

corporate *joined* 43
corporation
  association 712, 797
  jurisdiction 965
corporeal 3, 316
corps *assemblage* 72
  troops 726
CORPSE 362
corpulence 192
corpulent 192
corral, *n. inclosure* 232
corral, *v. circumscribe* 229
  round up 370
correct, *adj. true* 494
correct, *v. inform* 527
  improve 658
  censure 932
  punish 972
correction [see correct]
  house of - 752
correctness [see correct]
CORRELATION
  relation 9
  reciprocity 12
correlative 9, 12, 17
correspond *agree* 23
  write 592
CORRESPONDENCE
  correlation 12
  similarity 17
  agreement 23
  writing 592
correspondent
  letter writer 592
  journalist 593
corridor 627
corrigible 658
corroboration *evidence* 467
  assent 488
corrode *burn* 384
corrosion [see corrode]
corrosive [see corrode]
  caustic 171
  destructive 649
corrugate *roughen* 256
  rumple 258
  furrow 259
corrupt 659, 940
corrupting *noxious* 649
corruption
  decomposition 49
  improbity 940
  vice 945
cortege *suite* 746
cosmic 318
cosmopolitan *urban* 189
cost 812
costly 809, 814
costume 225
cosy *snug* 377
  sociable 892
cot *abode* 189
  bed 215
coterie *class* 75
  junto 712
cottage 189

cottager 188
couch, *n. bed* 215
couch, *v. lurk* 528
cough 349
COUNCIL *senate* **696**
councilor 696
counsel *advice* 695
　lawyer 968
count, *n. item* 79
　lord 875
count, *v.*
　compute 37, 85
　estimate 480
countenance, *n. face* 234
　appearance 448
　favor 707
countenance, *v. approve* 931
counter, *n. token* 550
counter, *adj. contrary* 14
　reverse 237
counteract 179, 706
COUNTERACTION 179
counterbalance 30, 179
countercharge 462
counterclaim 30
COUNTEREVIDENCE 468
counterfeit *imitate* 19
　copy 21
　sham 545
　swindle **791**
counterfeiter 792
countermand 756
countermarch 283
countermotion 283
counterpane 223
counterpart *identity* 13
　complement 14
　match 17
　copy 21
counterpoise
　compensate 30
countersign *n.*
　evidence 467
　mark 550
countersign, *v.* 488
countess 875
countless 105
countrified 189
country *region* 181
　abode 189
　land 342
　state 737
countryman 876
county 181
coupé 272
couple, *n. two* 89
couple, *v. unite* 43
　combine 48
COURAGE 861
courageous 861
courier *traveler* 268
　messenger **534**
COURSE *order* 58
　continuity 69

time 106, **109**
layer 204
locomotion 267
direction 278
lesson 537
pursue 622
courser *horse* 271
court, *n. house* 189
　hall 191
　retinue 746
court, *v. invite* 615
　tribunal 966
　woo **902**
　flatter 933
courteous **894**
COURTESY
　politeness **894**
courtier 935
courtly 852
court-martial **966**
courtship **902**
courtyard 182
cousin 11
cove *hollow* 252
　bay 343
covenant *compact* 769
　condition 770
　security 771
cover, *n. dress* 225
　lid 223
cover, *v. include* 76
　superpose 223
　conceal 528
　keep safe 664
covered 223
COVERING 220, **223**
coverlet 223
covert *abode* 189
　invisible 447
　latent 526
　refuge 666
coverture 903
covet *desire* 865
　envy 921
covetous *miserly* 921
covey 102
cow, *n. animal* 366
cow, *v. intimidate* 860
coward 862
COWARDICE **862**
cowardly 862
cowboy 370
cower *stoop* 308
　fear 860
　quail 862
　fawn 886
cowherd 370
cowhide, *n. whip* 975
cowhide, *v. lash* 972
coworker 690
cowpuncher 370
coxcomb 854, 880
coxcombry *affectation* 855
coxswain 269
coy 881
cozy 377, **892**

crabbed *sour* 397
　unintelligible 519
　uncivil 895
crack, *n. fissure* 44, 198
　furrow 259
crack, *v. split* 44
　crush 328
　sound 406
crack, *adj. excellent* 648
crack-brained *insane* 503
cracked *unmusical* 410
　mad 503
crackle 406
cracksman 792
cradle *beginning* 66
　infancy 127
　origin 153
　bed 215
　aid 707
craft *shipping* 273
　calling 625
　cunning 702
craftsman 690
craftsmanship 680
crag *cliff* 212, 253, 342
craggy *rough* 256
crake 884
cram *stuff* 194
　choke 261
　teach 537
　learn 539
　gorge 957
cramp, *n. spasm* 315
cramp, *v. paralyze* 158
　weaken 160
　hinder 706
crane *lever* 307
cranium 450
crank *fanatic* 504
　instrument 633
cranny 198
crash, *n. collision* 276
　sound 406
crash, *v. destroy* 162
　crack 328
crass *unintelligent* 493
　bad taste 851
cravat 225
crave *ask* 765
　desire 865
craven *cowardly* 862
craving 865
craw 191
crawl *elapse* 109
　creep 275
　cower 886
crazy *weak* 160
　mad 503
creak 410
cream, *n.* 356
　important part 642
　best 648
cream, *adj. yellow* 436
creamy 430
crease 258
create *cause* 153

compress 195
shatter 328
humble 879
crushed *unhappy* 828
crust 223
crusty *discourteous* 895
crutch *support* 215
crux *difficulty* 704
CRY *stridor* 410
   human 411
   animal 412
   weep 839
crying [*see* cry]
   urgent 630
crypt *cell* 191
   grave 207, 363
cryptic *uncertain* 475
   concealed 528
crystalline *dense* 321
   transparent 425
crystallization 321, 323
crystallize 321
cub *cad* 851
cubicle 191
cubist 556
cuddle 902
cudgel, *n.* 727
cudgel, *v. beat* 276
cue *hint* 527
   watchword 550
cuff *blow* 276
cuirass 717
cuisine 298
cul-de-sac 261
culinary 298
cull *choose* 609
   take 789
culminate *cap* 33
   tower 206
   crown 210
culprit 949, 975
cult 481, 990
cultivate *till* 371
   improve 658, 707
cultivated *courteous* 894
cultivation *tillage* 371
   knowledge 490
   improvement 658
   courtesy 894
cultivator 371
cultural 537, 542
culture *knowledge* 490
   improvement 658
   courtesy 894
cumber 706
cumbersome *heavy* 319
   disagreeable 830
cumbrous 319, 830
cumulative 467
CUNNING *artfulness* 702
cup *vessel* 191

hollow 252
cupboard 191
cupidity *avarice* 819
   desire 865
cupola *dome* 223, 250
cupping 662
cur *dog* 366
curable 658, 660
curate 996
curb, *n. bit* 752
curb, *v. moderate* 174
   slacken 275
   check 706
   restrain 751
curd 321
curdle *condense* 321
cure *reinstate* 660
   remedy 662
curio 847
CURIOSITY 455
   phenomenon 872
curious *exceptional* 83
   inquisitive 455
curl *bend* 245
   convolution 248
   hair 256
curly 248
currency *publicity* 531
   money 800
current, *n.*
   of air 349
current, *adj. existing* 1
   general 78
   present 118
   happening 151
   rife 531, 532
currycomb 253
curse, *n. bane* 663
   adversity 735
curse, *v. execrate* 908
cursory *transient* 111
   hasty 684
curt *short* 201
   concise 572
curtail *retrench* 38
   shorten 201
curtailment
   decrease 36
   [*see* curtail]
curtain *shade* 424
   screen 530
curtsy 308
CURVATURE 245
curve 245, 252, 279
curved 245
curvet *leap* 309
cushion *pillow* 215
cussedness 606
custodian 753
custody 664, 751
custom, *rule* 80

habit 124, **613**
barter 794
sale 796
fashion 852
customary [*see* custom]
   regular 80
customer 795
cut, *n. bit* 51
   notch 257
   blow 276
   path 627
cut, *v. divide* 44
   absent 187
   curtail 201
   form 240
   depart 293
   reap 371
   carve 557
   ignore 893
   snub 895
   –across 302
   –adrift 44
   –away 38
   –off *subduct* 38
   disjoin 44
   bereft 776
   divorce 782
   –out *surpass* 33
   substitute 147
   –short *stop* 142
cuticle 223
cutlass 727
cutlery 253
cutter 273
cutthroat 361, 913
cutting *sharp* 253
   affecting 821
   painful 830
   –edge **253**
cuttings 596
cycle *period* 138
   circle 247
   vehicle 272
cyclic 138
cyclist 268
cyclone *rotation* 312
   wind 349
cyclonic 349
cyclopedia 593
cylinder 249, 272
cylindrical 249
cynic *recluse* 893
   misanthrope 911
   detractor 936
cynical *morose* 911
   contemptuous 930
   censorious 932
cynicism
   misanthropy 911
   discourtesy 895
czar 745

D

dab *morsel* 32
  slap 276
dabble *meddle* 682
  potter 683
dad 166
daft 503
dagger *weapon* 727
Dail Eireann 696
daily, *n. newspaper* 531
daily, *adj.*
  frequent 136
  periodic 138
dainty, *n. food* 298
dainty, *adj. savory* 394
  pleasing 829
  delicate 845
  fastidious 868
dais *support* 215
  throne 747
dale *valley* 252
dally *delay* 133
  idle 683
  fondle 902
dam, *n. parent* 166
dam, *v. close* 261, 348
  obstruct 706
damage, *n. loss* 776
damage, *v. injure* 659
dame 374
damn *curse* 908
  condemn 976
damoiselle 129
damp, *adj. moist* 339
damp, *v. dissuade* 616
  depress 837
damper *muffler* 405
  hindrance 706
damsel 129
dance, *n.* 840
dance, *v. jump* 309
  agitate 315
dancer 840
dandy *fop* 854
dandyism 855
DANGER 665
dangerous 665
dangle *hang* 214
  swing 314
  display 882
dangler 281
dank 339
dapper *elegant* 845
dapple-gray 432
dappled 432
dare *confront* 234
  defy 715
  face danger 861
dare-devil 863
daring 861
dark *obscure* 421
  dim 422
  invisible 447

  unintelligible 519
darken
  obscure 421, 422
DARKNESS [*see* dark]
  421
darling *beloved* 897
darn 660
dart, *n. missile* 727
dart, *v.* 274
Darwinism 357
dash, *n. race* 274
  mark 550
  courage 861
dash *mix* 41
  speed 274
  -**off** *be active* 682
  haste 684
dashing *brave* 861
  ostentatious 882
dastard 862
data *evidence* 467
  reasoning 476
date 106, 114
datum [*see* data]
daub 223
daughter 167
daunt 860
dauntless 861
dawdle 133, 275
dawn, *n.* 125, 420, 422
dawn, *v. begin* 66
daybreak 125, 422
daydream *fancy* 515
  hope 858
daylight 125, 420
daze 420, 870
dazed *confused* 523
dazzle *daze* 420
  blind 443
  awe 928
deacon 996
dead *lifeless* 360
  mute 408a
  -**of night**
    midnight 126
    dark 421
deaden *weaken* 158
  numb 381
  muffle 405, 408a
deadened 381
deadlock *cessation* 142
  difficulty 704
deadly 361
deaf 419
deafen 419
DEAFNESS 419
deal, *n. much* 31
deal, *v. compact* 769
  allot 786
  -**with** *treat of* 595
dealings 680
dean *elder* 128

  clergyman 996
dear *high priced* 809, **814**
  loved 897
DEARNESS **814**
dearth 640
DEATH 360
deathblow *end* 67
  killing 361
deathless *perpetual* 112
  famous 873
debar *hinder* 706
  restrain 751
  prohibit 761
debark 292, 342
debase *depress* 308
  deteriorate 659
  degrade 874
debased *lowered* 207
debatable 475
debate, *n.* **588**
debate, *v. reason* 476
  hesitate 605
debility 160
debit *debt* 806
debonair 836
debouch 293
debris 645
DEBT 806
debtor 806
debut 883
decade *ten* 98
decadence 659
decamp 293, 623
decapitate 361, 972
decay, *n.*
  putrefaction 49, **653**
  deterioration 659
decay, *v. decrease* 36
  rot 49
  decline 124
decayed 160
  deteriorated **659**
decease 360
deceit *falsehood* 544
  deception 545
deceitful 544
deceive 545
deceived *in error* 495
  duped 486
DECEIVER **548**
decennial 108
decennium 108
decent *mediocre* 651
  pure 960
DECEPTION 545, 702
deceptive *sophistical* 477
  deceiving 545
decide *turn the scale* 153
  judge 480
  resolve 604
  choose 609
decided *great* 31

resolved 604
deciduous *transitory* **111**
  falling 306
decimal 99
decimate *kill* 361
decipher 522, 525
decision *judgment* 480
  resolution 604
  intention 620
decisive *certain* 474
  convincing 478
deck, *n. floor* 211
deck, *v. clothe* 225
declaim 582
declamatory 582
declaration *evidence* 467
  affirmation 535
  -of faith
  belief 484
  theology 983
  -of war 722
declare 535
declension [see decline]
  decrease 36
declination [see decline]
decline, *n. old age* **124**
  descent 306
  deterioration 659
decline, *v. decrease* 36
  grow old 128
  reject 610
  refuse 764
declivity *slope* 217
  descent 306
decode 525
decoloration 429
decompose 49
DECOMPOSITION 49
decoration *ornament* 847
  title 877
decorous [see decorum]
  proper 924
  respectful 928
decorum *fashion* 852
  dignity 878
  purity 960
decoy, *n.* 548
decoy, *v. deceive* 545
  entice 615
DECREASE *in degree* 36
  in size 195
decree *judgment* 480
  order 741
  law 963
DECREMENT
  decrease 36
  thing deducted **40a**
decrepit *old* 128
  impotent 158
  weak 160
decrepitude 128, 158
decrescendo 36
decry *underrate* 483
  censure 932
  detract 934
dedicate 677, 873

deduce *infer* **480**
deducible 478
deduct *retrench* **38**
deduction
  decrement 38, 40*a*
  reasoning 476
  inference 480
deed *record* 551
  act 680
  security **771**
  exploit 861
deem 484
deep *great* 31
  profound 208
  sonorous 404
  cunning 702
deepen *increase* 35
  excavate 208
deeply [see deep]
deer 366
deface *destroy form* **241**
  injure 659
  render ugly 846
defalcation 808
defamation 934
defamatory 932, 934
defame *shame* 874
  censure 932
  detract 934
defamer 936
default *shortcoming* 304
  debt 806
  nonpayment 808
defaulter *nonpayer* **808**
defeat *confute* 479
  succeed **731**
  failure 732
defect *decrement* 40*a*
  incompleteness 53
  shortcoming 304
  imperfection 651
  failing 945
defection
  disobedience 742
defective *incomplete* **53**
  imperfect 651
defend 462
defendant 938
defender 717, 914
DEFENSE *answer* 462
  resistance 717
  vindication 937
defenseless *impotent* 158
  exposed **665**
defensible *safe* **664**
  excusable 937
defensive 717
defer *put off* 133
  neglect 460
  -to assent 488
  submit 725
  respect 928
deference *submission* 725
  obedience 743
  courtesy 894
  respect 928

deferment 460
DEFIANCE 715
defiant 715, 742
deficiency
  [see deficient]
deficient *unequal* 28
  inferior 34
  incomplete 53
  remiss 304
  imperfect 651
deficit *incompleteness* **53**
  debt 806
defile, *n. gorge* 198
defile, *v. march* 266
  spoil 659
define *limit* 233
  explain 522
definite *special* 79
  limited **233**
  certain 474
  exact 494
  manifest 525
definition
  interpretation 521
deflate 195
deflect *curve* 245
  deviate 279
deform 243, 846
deformed 243
deformity *distortion* 243
  ugliness 846
defraud *cheat* 545
  swindle 791
defray 807
deft *clever* 698
defunct 360
defy *confront* 234, 861
  set at defiance 715
degeneracy 659
degenerate
  deteriorate 659
  vice 945
degradation *shame* 874
  dishonor 940
degrade 874
DEGREE 26
deification 981
deify *honor* 873
  idolatry 991
deign *condescend* 879
deities 979
DEITY 976
DEJECTION
  melancholy **837**
delay 133, 460
delectable *savory* 394
  agreeable 829
delegate, *n.* 524, 755, **758**
delegate, *v. depute* 759
delegation 755
deliberate, *adj. slow* 275
deliberate, *v.* 451
deliberately 133, 275
deliberation 451
delicacy *weakness* 160
  dainty 298, **394**

beauty 845
taste 850
honor 939
delicate [*see* delicacy]
dainty 394, 829
delicious 829
delight *pleasure* 377, 827
charm 829
delightful 829
delineate *outline* 230
represent 554
describe 594
delineator 554
delinquency 304
delinquent 949
delirious 503
delirium *raving* 503
passion 825
-*tremens* 959
deliver *transfer* 270
utter 580
rescue 672
liberate 750
give 784
DELIVERANCE 672, 750
delivery [*see* deliver]
dell 252
delude *beguile* 495
deceive 545
deluge 337, 348
delusion 495, **545**
delve *dig* 252
demagogue
malcontent 710
demand, *n. request* 630
user 677
demand, *v. inquire* 461
order **741**
ask 765
claim 924
dematerialize 317
demean oneself 692
demeanor 692, 852
demigod *hero* 861
demise *death* 360
demobilize 750
democracy 737, **876**
democratic 737
demolish 162
demon *devil* 980
demonetize 800
demoniac 980
demonize 978
DEMONSTRATION
proof 478
manifest 525
ostentation 882
demonstrative
conclusive 478
manifest 525
vehement 825
demoralize *unnerve* 158
brutalize 945
demur *disbelieve* **485**
be unwilling 603
hesitate 605

demure *grave* 826
sad 837
affected 855
modest 881
den *abode* 189
seclusion 893
denial *negation* 536
refusal 764
denizen 188
denomination *class* 75
name 564
sect 712
denote *specify* 79
indicate 457, 550
mean 516
denouement *end* 67
denounce *curse* 908
disapprove 932
accuse 938
dense *crowded* **72**
close **321**
rank 365
ignorant 493
DENSITY 321
dent *hollow* 252
notch 257
denude 226
denunciation 908, 909, 938
deny *doubt* 485
dissent 489
negative **536**
refuse 764
-*oneself*
be temperate 953
depart **293,** 449
departed *nonexistent* 2
department *class* 75
business 625
bureau 965
DEPARTURE 293, 449
depend *hang* 214
be contingent 475
-*upon*
trust 484
dependence 749
dependency
property 777, 780
dependent, *n. servant* **746**
subject 749
dependent, *adj.*
liable 177
hanging 214
depict *represent* 554
describe 594
deplete 638
depletion 640
deplorable 649
deplore *regret* 833
complain 839
deport 972
deportation *removal* 270
emigration 297
deportment 692
depose *testify* 467
declare **535**
dethrone 738, 756

deposit, *n. transference* **270**
security 771
payment **809**
deposit, *v.* 184
deposition
[*see* depose, deposit]
record 551
depot *station* 266
store 636
shop 799
deprave *spoil* 659
depraved *vicious* 945
depravity 945
deprecate 766
DEPRECATION 766
depreciate *discount* 36
underrate 483
slight 929, 932
depreciation
[*see* depreciate]
discount 813
detraction 934
depredation 791
depress 252, **308,** 837
[*see* depression]
depressed 308
DEPRESSION
lowness 207
depth 208
concavity 252
lowering **308**
dejection 837
deprivation 789
deprive 38, 789
DEPTH *physical* **208**
mental 498
deputation 755
depute 755, 759
DEPUTY 759
derange *disorganize* **61**
madden 503
deranged 503
DERANGEMENT 61
derelict 782
dereliction
relinquishment 782
guilt 947
-*of duty* 927
deride *ridicule* 856, **929**
contempt 930
derisive 856
derivate 155
derivation
origin 153, 154, 155
derivative 154
derive *attribute* 155
deduce 480
acquire 775
derogate 934
derogatory
shameful 874, 934
dishonorable 940
derring do 860
descend *slope* 217
go down **306**
descendant 167

DESCENT 69
 lineage 166
 fall 306
describe 594
DESCRIPTION *kind* 75
 narration 594
descriptive 594
desecrate *misuse* 679
 profane 988
desert, *n. waste* 169, 180,
 344
 merit 924
desert, *v. run away* 187
 relinquish 624
deserted *empty* 187
 outcast 893
deserter 623
DESERTION 624
deserve *be entitled to* **924**
deserving **924**
deshabille
 [*see* dishabille]
desiccate 340
desideratum 630
design *prototype* 22
 delineation 554
 painting 556
 intention 620
 plan 626
designate *specify* 79
 call 564
designation *kind* 75
designer 559, 626
designing *cunning* 702
desirability 646
desirable 646, **865**
DESIRE 865
 will 600
desirous *desiring* 865
desist *discontinue* 142
desk *box* 191
 school - **542**
desolate, *adj. dejected* 837
 secluded 893
desolate, *v. ravage* 162
desolating *painful* 830
desolation
 [*see* desolate]
despair *grief* 828
 hopelessness 859
despatch [*see* dispatch]
desperado 863, 887
desperate *great* 31
 violent 173
 hopeless 859
 rash 863
despicable *shameful* 874
 contemptible 930
despise 930
despite 30
despoil *injure* 659
 take 789
 rob 791
despond *despair* 859
 fear 860
despot 739, 745

despotism *severity* 739
 tyranny 964
destination *end* 67
 rest 265
 arrival 292
destine 152, 601, 620
DESTINY *chance* 152
 fate 601
destitute 640, 804
destroy 2, 162
DESTROYER 165
 naval 726
DESTRUCTION 21, **162**
destructive *ruinous* 162
 bad 649
DESUETUDE 614
desultory *fitful* 70
 irregular in time 139
 changeable 149
 deviating 279
detach 44
detached *irrelated* 10
 loose 47
detachment *separation* 44
 part 51
 army 726
detail, *n. item* 79
detail, *v. describe* 594
 allot 786
 in - 51
details *minutiae* 32
 particulars 79
detain 781
detect 480a
detective 527
detention 781
deter *dissuade* 616
deteriorate 659
DETERIORATION 659
determine *define* 79
 cause 153
 satisfy 462
 make sure 474
 judge 480
 discover 480a
 resolve 604
determinant 153
determined *resolute* 604
detest *dislike* 867
 hate 898
detestable 649
dethrone 738
dethronement 738, 756
detour 279, 629
detract *subduct* 38
 underrate 483
 defame 934
DETRACTION 934
DETRACTOR 936
detriment 619, 659
detrimental 649
devastate *destroy* 162
 make havoc 659
 depopulate 893
devastation 162
develop *produce* 161

evolve 313
development 35, 154
deviate *change* 140
 turn 279
DEVIATION 20a, 140, **279**
device *motto* 550
 expedient 626
 artifice 702
devil *Satan* 978
 -worship 978
devious *changeful* 140
 deviating 279
 circuitous 311
devise *imagine* **515**
 plan 626
 bequeath 784
devoid 777a
devolve 783
devote *destine* 601
 employ 677
 consecrate 873
devoted *ill-fated* **735**
 obedient 743
 loving 897
devotee *zealot* 682
 enthusiast **840**
 fanatic 988
devotion *obedience* **743**
 love 897
 piety 987
 worship 990
devour *destroy* 162
 eat 298
 cram 957
devout 987, 990
dew 339
dewy 339
dexter 238
dexterous 238, 698
dextral 238
dextrality 238
diabolic *malevolent* 907
 wicked **945**
 satanic 978
diabolism 978
diabolist 978
diadem 747, 847
diagnosis 465, 522, **655**
diagnostic 15, 465, 550
diagonal 217
diagram 554
dial 114
dialect 560, **563**
dialogue 588
diameter 202
diametrical 237
diamond *lozenge* 244
diaphragm 68, 228
diary *journal* 114
diatribe 932
dichotomy 91
dicker *haggle* 794
dictate *write* 590
 advise 695
 command 741
dictator 745

disclaim *deny* **536**
  repudiate **756**
disclaimer **536**
disclamation
  [see disclaim]
disclose **529**
DISCLOSURE **529**
  discovery **480a**
discoloration **429**
discolored **848**
discomfiture **732**
discomfort *physical* **378**
  mental **828**
discommode *hinder* **706**
discompose *derange* **61**
  put out **458**
  pain **830**
  disconcert **874**
disconcert *derange* **61**
  distract **458**
  dishearten **832**
  confuse **874**
disconnect **44**
disconnected
  unrelated **10**
  interrupted **70**
disconnection
  irrelation **19**
  disjunction **44**
  discontinuity **70**
disconsolate **837**
DISCONTENT **832**
discontinuance **142**
DISCONTINUITY **70**
discontinuous **44, 70**
DISCORD
  disagreement **24**
  of sound **414**
  dissension **713**
discordance **414, 713**
DISCOUNT *decrease* **36**
  decrement **40a**
  money **813**
discountenance **706**
discourage *dissuade* **616**
  dishearten **837**
  frighten **860**
discourse, *n. speech* **582**
  talk **588**
discourse, *v. speak* **582**
  talk **588**
discourteous **895**
DISCOURTESY **895**
discover *perceive* **441**
  find **480a**
  disclose **529**
DISCOVERY **480a**
discredit *disbelieve* **485**
  dishonor **874**
discreditable **874**
discreet **459, 864**
discrepancy **20a, 24**
discretion *will* **600**
  choice **609**
  caution **864**
discriminate **15, 465, 868**

DISCRIMINATION
  difference **15**
  nice perception **465**
  fastidiousness **868**
discriminative **868**
discursive *wandering* **279**
discuss *inquire* **461**
  reason **476**
discussion **476**
disdain, *n. pride* **878**
  contempt **930**
disdain, *v. spurn* **866**
disdainful *proud* **878**
  disrespectful **929**
DISEASE **655**
diseased **655**
disembark **342**
disembody
  spiritualize **317**
disembogue
  flow out **348**
disencumber **705**
disengage *detach* **44**
  liberate **750**
disengaged *to let* **763**
disentangle *separate* **44**
  arrange **60**
  facilitate **705**
  liberate **750**
disestablish *displace* **185**
  abrogate **756**
disfavor *oppose* **708**
  disrespect **929**
disfigure *deface* **241**
  deform **846**
  blemish **848**
disfranchise **925**
disgorge *emit* **297**
  restore **790**
disgrace *shame* **879**
  dishonor **940**
disgraceful **945**
disgruntle **509**
disgruntled **509**
disguise, *n. mask* **530**
  deception **545**
disguise, *v. conceal* **528**
disgust, *n.*
  weariness **841**
  dislike **867**
disgust, *v. nauseate* **395**
  offend **830**
disgusting **867**
dish *plate* **191**
dishabille *undress* **225**
dishearten *dissuade* **616**
  disappoint **832**
  deject **837**
dishevel *disorder* **61**
dishonest *false* **544**
  base **940**
dishonor *protest* **808**
  disrepute **874**
  disrespect **929**
  baseness **940**
disillusion **509**

disinclination **867**
disincline *dissuade* **616**
  dislike **867**
disinclined **603, 867**
disinfect *purify* **652**
disinfectant **388, 662**
disinherit **782, 783**
disintegrate *separate* **44**
  decompose **49**
disintegration **49**
disinter *exhume* **363**
  discover **480a**
disinterment **363**
disinterested **942**
DISINTERESTEDNESS
  542
disjoin **44**
DISJUNCTION **10, 44**
disjunctive **44**
disk **247**
DISLIKE **867**
dislocate *separate* **44**
  put out of joint **61**
dislodge *displace* **185**
  eject **297**
disloyal **940**
dismal *depressing* **830**
  dejected **837**
dismantle *destroy* **162**
  divest **226**
  render useless **645**
dismast **645**
dismay **860**
dismember **44**
dismiss *discharge* **297**
  liberate **750**
  abrogate **756**
dismissal **746**
dismount **306**
DISOBEDIENCE **742**
disobey **742**
DISORDER, *n.*
  confusion **59**
  turbulence **173**
  disease **655**
disorder, *v. derange* **61**
disorderly **59, 945**
disorganize *derange* **61**
disown **536**
disparage
  underrate **483, 929**
  dispraise **932**
  detract **934**
disparagement **908, 934**
disparate **15, 18**
disparity *difference* **15**
  dissimilarity **18**
  disagreeing **24**
  inequality **28**
dispassionate **826**
dispatch, *n. message* **527**
  news **532**
  epistle **592**
  expedition **682**
  haste **684**
  command **741**

dispatch, v. eject 297
 kill 361
dispel scatter 73
 destroy 162
 repel 289
dispensation
 [see dispense]
 command 741
 license 760
 exemption 927a
dispense disperse 73
 give 784
 apportion 786
 retail 796
 -with disuse 678
 exempt 927a
disperse separate 44, 49
 scatter 73
DISPERSION 44, 73
dispirit 837
displace annihilate 2
 derange 61
 remove 185
DISPLACEMENT
 derangement 61
 removal 185
display show 525
 parade 882
displease 830
displeasure 828
 anger 900
disport 840
disposal [see dispose]
dispose arrange 60
 tend 176
 induce 615
 -of relinquish 782
 give 784
 sell 796
disposition temperament 5
 arrangement 60
 inclination 602
 mind 820
dispossess 789
disproof 479
disproportion
 irrelation 10
 disagreement 24
disprove 479
disputable uncertain 475
 doubtful 485
disputant 476
dispute disagree 24
 discuss 476
 doubt 485
 deny 536
 discord 713
disqualification 158, 699,
 925
disqualify 158, 925
disquiet changeability 149
 agitation 315
 uneasiness 828
disquietude 860
disregard overlook 458
 neglect 460

make light of 483
 disrespect 929
disrelish dislike 867
disreputable 874
 vicious 945
DISREPUTE 874, 929
DISRESPECT 929
disrespectful 929
disrobe 226
disruption disjunction 44
 destruction 162
dissatisfaction 828, 832
dissatisfied 832
dissatisfy 832
dissect anatomize 44, 49
 investigate 461
dissemble 544, 988
dissembler 548
disseminate scatter 73
 publish 531
 teach 537
dissemination
 [see disseminate]
dissension 489, 713
DISSENT 489
 heterodoxy 984
dissenter 489, 984
dissentient 24, 489
dissenting 487
DISSERTATION 595
dissever 44
DISSIMILARITY 15,
 16a, 18
dissimilitude 15, 16a, 18,
 24
dissimulate 544
dissimulation 544
dissipate destroy 162
dissipated 954, 961
dissociate 10, 44
dissociation 10, 44
dissoluble 51
dissolution
 [see dissolve]
 decomposition 49
 end 67
 destruction 162
 death 360
dissolvable 51
dissolve vanish 2, 4, 49
 destroy 162
 liquefy 335
 abrogate 756
dissonance
 disagreement 24
 discord 414, 713
dissonant 414
dissuade 616
DISSUASION 616
DISTANCE 196
 overtake 282
 go beyond 303
distant 196
distaste 867
distemper color 428
distend 194
distended 192, 250

distill extract 301
 evaporate 336
distillation 336
distinct audible 402
 visible 446
 intelligible 518
 manifest 525
distinction difference 15
 greatness 31
 discrimination 465
 elegance 578
 fame 873
distinctive 15
distinguish perceive 441
 discriminate 465
distinguished superior 33
 noted 873
distinguishing 15
distort 243, 523
DISTORTION twist 243
 of vision 443
 misinterpretation 523
 falsehood 544
distract 458
distracted confused 475
 excited 824
distraction passion 825
distrain take 789
 attach 969
distraught 475, 503
distress, n. poverty 804
 affliction 828
distress, v.
 cause pain 830
distressing 830
distribute arrange 60
 disperse 73
 allot 786
distribution
 [see distribute]
district 181
distrust disbelief 485
 fear 860
 mistrust 920
distrustful 487
disturb derange 61
 displace 185
 agitate 315
 distress 830
disturbance
 disorder 59, 61, 315
disunion disagreement 24
 separation 44
disunite separate 44
DISUSE 614, 678
disused 678
ditch inclosure 232
 trench 259
 conduit 350
ditto 13, 104
ditty 415
divarication 16a
dive 267, 310
diver 310
diverge 291
 [see divergence]

down-hearted 837
downhill *sloping* 217
  descent 306
downpour 348
downright *absolute* 31
  sincere 703
downs *uplands* 180
downtrodden *subject* 749
  dejected 837
  disgraced 874
downward 306
downy *soft* 324
dowry 780, 784
doze 683
dozen 98
drab *color* 432
draft, *n. depth* 208
  drink 298
  wind 349
  drawing 554
  abstract 596
  list 611
  physic 662
  troops 726
  cheque 800
draft, *v. write* 590
drafted man 726
draft horse 271
drag, *n.*
  impediment 706
drag, *v. elapse* 109
  crawl 275
  draw 285
  -on *endure* 106, 110
draggle 285
dragon *monster* 83
dragoon, *n. soldier* 726
dragoon, *v. compel* 744
drain, *n. conduit* 232, 350
drain, *v. flow out* 295
  empty 297
  waste 640, 688
  exhaust 789
drainage [*see* drain]
dram *drink* 298
  cordial 392
DRAMA 599
dramatic 599
dramatist 599
dramatize 599
drape 225
drapery 225
drastic 171
draught [*see* draft]
draw *compose* 54
  pull 285, 288
  delineate 556
  -near *time* 121
  approach 286
  -out *protract* 110
  extract 301
  -up *write* 590
drawback *hindrance* 706
drawers *garment* 225
drawing 554, 556
drawing room

assembly 72
  room 191
drawl 583
drawn -battle 730
dread 860
dreadful *dire* 830
  fearful 860
dreadnought *battleship* 726
dream *unsubstantial* 4
  fancy 515
  psychotherapy 992a
  -of 620
dreamer 504
dreamlike 4
dreamy *unsubstantial* 4
  sleepy 683
drear 16
drearisome 16
dreary *uniform* 16
  melancholy 830, 837
dredge *raise* 307
dregs 40, 321, 653
drench *drink* 298
  wet 337
dress, *n. clothes* 225
dress, *v. equalize* 27
  equip 673
  -down *berate* 527
  -wounds 662
dress clothes 225
dress suit 225
dribble 348
driblet 25
drift, *n.*
  trend 176
  moraine 270
  direction 278
  meaning 516
drift, *v. accumulate* 72
  float 267
  deviate 279
  approach 286
drill, *n. auger* 262
drill, *v. bore* 260
  teach 537
drink, *n. liquor* 298
  tipple 959
drink, *v.* 298
drinkable 298
drinking 298
drip 295, 348
dripping *wet* 339
drive *take horse* 266
  propel 284
  urge 615
  compel 744
  -a bargain 794, 819
drivel, *n.* 573
drivel, *v.* 499
driver *coachman* 268
  director 694
drizzle 348
drollery 842, 853
drone, *n. idler* 683
drone, *v. sound* 407

droop, *v. hang* 214
  sink 306
  decline 659
drop, *n. small quantity* 32
drop, *v. discontinue* 142
  be powerless 158
  fall 306
  trickle 348
  relinquish 624
  - in *arrive* 292
  let - 308
dross *trash* 643
  rubbish 645
  dirt 653
drought *dryness* 340
  thirst 865
droughty 340
drove *multitude* 102
drown 337
  kill 361
drowsy *sleepy* 683
drub *punish* 972
drudge, *n. worker* 690
drudge, *v. plod* 682, 686
drudgery 686
drug *remedy* 662
  -store 662
druggist 662
drum, *n.* 249
drum, *v. repeat* 104
  sound 407
  -out 972
drunk 959
drunkard 959
DRUNKENNESS 955, 959
dry, *adj. arid* 340
  tedious 841
  dull 843
  thirsty 865
  cynical 932
dry, *v. preserve* 670
DRYNESS 340
dual 89, 90
dualism 89, 984
DUALITY 89
dub 564, 566
dubiosity 475
dubious 475
duchess 875
duck, *n. zero* 101
  bird 366
duck, *v. stoop* 308
  plunge 310
  water 337
duct 350
ductile *tractile* 285
  flexible 324
ductility [*see* ductile]
dude 854
due, *adj. expedient* 646
  owing 806
due, *n. privilege* 924
duel 720
duelist 726
dues 812

duet 415
duffer *ignoramus* 498
   bungler 701
dugout *boat* 273
   defense 717
duke 875
dukedom 877
dulcet *sweet* 396
   melodious 413
dull *unintelligent* 493
   inert 172
   blunt 254
   slow 275
   somber 428
   stolid 499
   weary 841
   prosing 843
dullard 501
DULLNESS 254, **843**
duma 696
dumb *voiceless* 581
   -*animal* 366
   strike - *astonish* 870
DUMBNESS 581
dumfound *disappoint* 509
   astonish 870
dummy *substitute* 147
   idle 683

dump *unload* 297
dumps 837, 901*a*
dumpy *short* 201
   thick 202
dun, *n. creditor* 805
dun, *adj. gray* 432
dun, *v. importune* 765
dunce 493
dungeon 752
duologue 588
DUPE, *n.* 547
dupe, *v. deceive* 545
duplex 90
duplicate *copy* 21
   double 90
DUPLICATION 19, **90**,
   104
duplicity 544
DURABILITY 110, 141
durable 110, 141
duration 106
duress *restraint* 751
during 106
dusk 126, 422
dusky *dark* 421
   dim 422
dust *powder* 330
   dirt 653

throw - in the eyes
   blind 442
   deceive 545
dusty 330, 653
dutiable 812
dutiful 944
DUTY
   business 625
   work 686
   tax 812
   obligation **926**
dwarf, *n.* 193
dwarf, *v. lessen* 36
dwell *reside* 186, 188
   abide 141, 265
   -*upon repeat* 573
dweller 188
dwelling *location* 184
   abode 189
dwindle *lessen* 36
   shrink 195
dye 428
dying 360
dyke *see dike*
dynamic 157, 276
dynamite 727
dynasty 106, **737**

E

each 79
eager *willing* 602
   active 682
   ardent 821
   desirous 865
eagerness 682
eagle *bird* 366
ear *hearing* 418
earl 875
earldom 877
EARLINESS 132
early 121, **132**
earn 775
earnest, *n. pledge* 771
earnest *willing* 602
   determined 604
   emphatic 642
   eager 821
   serious 837
earnings 775
earsplitting 404
earth *ground* 211
   world 318
   land 342
earthenware 384
earthly 318, 342
earthquake 146
earthwork 717
earthly 342
ease, *n. leisure* 377, 685
   facility 705
ease, *v. abate* 36
easel *support* 215

easily [*see easy*] 705
east 236
eastern 236
easy *gentle* 275
   facile 705
easy-going
   inexcitable 826
   contented 831
   indifferent 866
eat 298
eatable 298
eatables 298
eating 298
eaves 250
eavesdropper 455
ebb, *n. decline* 36
   tide 348
ebb, *v.*
   decrease 36
   regress 283
   recede 287
ebb tide 36, 207
ebullient *hot* 382
ebullition *violence* 173
   ferment 315
   boiling 384
eccentric *irregular* 83
   crazed 503
   capricious 608
ecclesiastical 995
echelon 279
echo, *n. similarity* 17
   copy 21

   resonance 408
echo, *v. imitate* 19
   repeat 104
   recoil 277
éclat 873
eclipse, *n.* 421
eclipse, *v. surpass* 33
   outshine 873, 527
economical 817
economics 692
economize 817
ECONOMY *order* 58
   management 692
   frugality 817
ecstasy *frenzy* 515
   rapture 827
ecstatic 827, 829
EDDY *whirlpool* 348
   current 312
Eden *heaven* 827
EDGE *brink* 231
   -*in* 228
edible 298
edict 531, 741
edification 537
edifice 161
edifying 648
edit *publish* 531
   compile 596
   revise 658
edition 531
editor 593, 595
editorial 595

educate *teach* 537
educated 490
education *teaching* 537
    knowledge 490
educational 537
educe *extract* 301
efface *destroy* 162
    obliterate 552
EFFECT *consequence* 154
    complete 729
effective *capable* 157
    influential 175
    useful 644
effects *property* 780
    goods 798
effectual 157, 175
effectually 52
effeminacy
    [*see* effeminate]
effeminate *weak* 160
    womanish 374
    timorous 862
effervesce 173, 353
effervescence 353
effervescent 338, 353
effete *old* 128
    weak 160
    useless 645
efficacious [*see* efficient]
efficient *powerful* 157
    operative 170
    reliable 632
    useful 644
effigy *copy* 21
efflorescence 161
effluence 295
effluvium *vapor* 334
    odor 398
efflux *egress* 295
effort 686
effrontery 885
effulgence 420
effusion
    loquacity 584
    -of blood 361
effusive 584
egg *embryo* 153
    -on 615
egg-shaped 247
ego 317, 450, 980a
egoism 482, 880, 911
egoist 482, 880, 911
egotism *overestimation* 482
    vanity 880
    cynicism 911
    selfishness 943
egotist 482, 880, 911
egotistical [*see* egotism]
    narrow 481
egregious *exceptional* 83
    absurd 497
EGRESS 295
Egyptian -deities **979**
eight *number* 98
ejaculate *utter* 580
eject 284, 297

EJECTION
    displacement 185
    propulsion 284
    emission 297
eke
    -out *complete* 52
    spin out 110
elaborate, adj. 686
elaborate, v. *improve* 658
    prepare 673
    work out 729
elaboration 673
elapse *flow* 109
    pass 122
elastic 325
    [*see* elasticity]
ELASTICITY
    strength 159
    energy 171
    spring 325
elate, adj. *exulting* **836**
    vain 880
    boastful 884
elate, v. *gladden* 836
elated 838
    [*see* elate]
elbow, n. *angle* 244
elbow, v. *push* 276
elbowroom 180, 748
elder, adj. 124, 128
elder, n. 996
elderly 128
elect *choose* 609
    predestinate 976
election 609
elector 609
electorate 609
electric *swift* 274
electricity 388
electrify *strengthen* **157**
    motorize 226
    excite 824
    astonish 870
electron 32
ELEGANCE *in style* **578**
    beauty 845
elegy *poetry* 597
element *component* 56
    beginning 66
    cause 153
elemental, adj. *simple* 42
elemental, n.
    Rosicrucian 980
elementary *simple* 42
elephantine *huge* 192
elevate 307
elevated 206
ELEVATION
    height 206
    raising 307
    repute 873
elevator 307
elf *fairy* 979
elicit *cause* 153
    draw out 301
    discover 480a

eligible 646
eliminate *subduct* 38
    simplify 42
    exclude 55
    weed out 103, 297
    extract 301
elimination 42
eliminative 299, 350
elision 201
elixir 5
ellipse 247
ellipsis 201
elliptic 247
elocution 582
elocutionist 582
elongate 200
elongation 200
eloquence *style* 569, **574**
    speech 582
eloquent 574, **582**
elsewhere 187
elucidate 522
elude *avoid* 623
    escape 671
    palter 773
elusive 623, **773**
elysian 981
Elysium 981
emaciated 203, 640
emaciation 203
emanate 295
emanation *egress* 295
    odor 398
emancipate *deliver* 672
    free 750
embalm 400
embankment
    esplanade 189
    fence 717
embargo 761
embark *sail* 267
    depart 293
    -in *engage in* 676
embarrass 704
embarrassed *poor* 804
    in debt 806
embarrassing 704
embarrassment 704
embassy 755, 758
embellish 847
embers 384
embezzle 791
embitter *deteriorate* 659
    aggravate 835
emblazon *color* 428
    ornament 847
emblem 550
embody *join* 43
    combine 48
    form a whole 50
    include 76
    materialize 316
embolden 861
emboss 250
embrace, n. 892, 902
embrace, v. *compose* 54

erudite 490, 500, 539
erudition 490, 539
eruption *revolution* 146
  violence 173
  egress 295
  ejection 297
  explosion 406
eruptive [*see* eruption]
escalade 305
escalator 305, 307
escapade 608, 840
ESCAPE, *n. flight* 671
escape, *v.* 671, 927
eschew *avoid* 623
  dislike 867
escort *companion* 88
  safeguard 664
  keeper 753
esculent 298
escutcheon 550, 551
esophagus 350
esoteric 528
especial 79
especially 33
espionage 441, 461
esplanade 189
espouse *choose* 609
  marry 903
  -a cause *aid* 707
  co-operate 709
esprit de corps 709
espy 441
esquire 875
essay, *n.*
  experiment 463
  dissertation 595
ESSAY, *v.*
  endeavor 675
essence *being* 1
  nature 5
  meaning 516
essential *real* 1
  intrinsic 5
  inherent 56
  important 642
establish *settle* 150
  create 161
  place 184
  evidence 467
  demonstrate 478
established 141
  church 983a
establishment
  fixture 150
  location 184
  shop 799
estate *condition* 7
  property 780
esteem 928, 931
estimable 648
estimate *number* 85
  measure 466
  adjudge 480
estimation 480, 928, 931
estrange *disjoin* 44
  alienate 889

hate 898
estuary 343
etch 259, 558
etching 558
Eternal, The - 976
eternal 112
eternalize 112
eternity 112
  an - 110
ether *space* 180
  vapor 334
  anaesthetic 376
ethereal 4, 820
etheric body 980a
ethical 926
ethics 926
ethnology 372
etiquette *custom* 613
  fashion 852
etymology 562
Eucharist 998
eulogist 935
eulogize 482
eulogy 931
Eumenides 173, 900
euphemism *metaphor* 521
  phrase 566
  style 577
euphemist 935
euphony *melody* 413
  elegant style 578
euphuism 579, 855
eurythmic 542
eurythmics 242
evacuate *vacate* 185
  quit 293
  emit 297
evade *elude* 477
  not observe 773
  exempt 927
evanescent 111
evangelical 983a, 985
Evangelists 985
evaporate *vanish* 4
  vaporize 336
  dry up 340
evaporation
  vaporization 336
  dryness 340
evasion *sophistry* 477
  quirk 481
  concealment 528
  falsehood 544
  avoidance 623
evasive [*see* evasion]
eve 126
even, *adj.*
  uniform 16
  equal 27
  level 213
  parallel 216
  straight 246
  flat 251
  smooth 255
even, *v. level* 213
even, *adv.* 469

EVENING 126
evenness
  [*see* even]
  symmetry 242
evensong 126, 990
event 151
  in the - of
  circumstance 8
  eventuality 151
  destiny 152
  supposition 514
  justified by the - 937
eventful 151, 642
eventide 126
eventual 121
EVENTUALITY 151
eventually 121, 151, 154
eventuate 151
ever 16, 112
everlasting 112
evermore 16, 112
every 78, 138
  -other 138
everybody 78
every one 78
everywhere 180, 186
evict 297, 789
EVIDENCE 467
evident *visible* 446
  certain 474
  proved 478
  manifest 525
evidential 467
EVIL *harm* 619
  badness 649
  -spirits 980
  -star 649
EVILDOER 913, 949
evildoing 945
evil-minded 907, 945
evil speaking 908, 934
evince *show* 467
  prove 478
evoke *cause* 153
  call upon 765
  excite 824
evolution 161, 311, 313
evolutionary 313
evolve 161, 313
ewer 191
exact, *adj. similar* 17
  copy 21
  true 494
  literal 516
exact, *v. require* 741
  claim 924, 926
exacting *discontented* 832
  fastidious 865
exaction 741
exactly *literally* 19
exactness [*see* exact]
  repetition 13
exaggerate *increase* 35
  overestimate 482
  magnify 549
  misrepresent 555

EXAGGERATION 549
   [see exaggerate]
exalt *increase* 35
   elevate 307
   extol 931
exalted *high* 206
   noble 875
   magnanimous 942
examination 461
examine *attend to* 457
   inquire 461
example *pattern* 22
   instance 82
exasperate
   irritate 173
   enrage 900
excavate 208, 252
excavation 252
excavator 252
exceed *surpass* **33**
   remain 40
   transgress 303
exceedingly 31
excel *surpass* 33, 648
excellence 648
except, *v. exclude* 55, 610
except, *adv. without* 38
   unless 83
exception *exclusion* 55
   uncomformity 83
   disapproval 932
   take - *resent* 900
exceptional *unimitated* 20
   special 79
   uncomformable 83
   in an - degree 31
excess 33, 40, 641
excessive *great* 31
exchange *reciprocity* 12
   interchange 148
   barter 794
   mart 799
exchequer 802
excise, *v.* 38
excision 38
EXCITABILITY
   excitement 825
   irascibility 901
excitable 825
excite *energize* 171
   be violent 173
   impassion 824
excited 173, 824
EXCITEMENT 821, 824
   825
exclaim 411
exclamation 580
exclude *sift* 42
   leave out 55
   reject 610
   banish 893
EXCLUSION 55, 77, 893
exclusive *omitting* 55
   special 79
   irregular 83
   forbidding 761

   -of 38
excommunicate 908, 998
excrescence 250
EXCRETION 299
excruciating
   physical pain 378
   mental pain 830
exculpate *forgive* 918
   vindicate 937
   acquit 970
excursion 266
excursionist 268
excursive *deviating* 279
excusable 937
excuse, *n. plea* 617
excuse, *v. forgive* **918**
   exempt 927a
   vindicate 937
execrable *bad* 649
   offensive 830
execrate *hate* 898
   curse 908
execute *kill* 361, 972
   complete 771
execution *music* 416
   action 680
   signing 771
   punishment 972
executioner 975
executive, *n.* 965
executive, *adj.*
   directive 693, 737, **965**
executor 690
exemplar 22
exemplary 944
exemplify *quote* 82
   illustrate 522
exempt *free* 748
   dispense 927a
EXEMPTION
   exception 83
   permission 760
   nonpossession 777a
   nonliability **927a**
exercise, *n.*
   operation 170
   task 537
   use 677
   exertion 686
exercise, *v. teach* 537
   use 677
   act 680
exert *use* 677
EXERTION 686
exhale 299, 349
exhaust *paralyze* 158
   deflate 195
   waste 638
   fatigue 688
   drain 789
exhausted 158
exhaustion 158, 638
exhaustive *complete* 52
exhibit *show* 525
   display 882
exhibition 525, 882

exhilarate 836
exhort 695
exhortation
   [see exhort]
exhume *disinter* 363
exigency *crisis* 8
   difficulty 704
   need 865
exile *transport* 185
   banish 297, 893
   punish 972
exist *be* 1, 359
EXISTENCE *being* **1**
   -*in time* 118
   -*in space* 186
existent **1**
exit *departure* 293
   egress 295
   disappearance 449
exodus 293, 295
exonerate *forgive* 918
   vindicate 937
   acquit 970
exoneration **918**
exorbitant
   redundant 641
   dear 814
exordium 64, 66
exotic, *n. plant* 367
exotic, *adj. alien* 10
   exceptional 83
expand *increase* 31, **35**
   swell 194
   rarefy 322
expanse *space* 180
   plain 344
EXPANSION 35, **194**, 202
expansive 194
expatiate *range* 266
   be diffuse 573
expatriate 296, 893
expect *anticipate* 121, 133
   look forward to 507
   hope 858
   not wonder 871
EXPECTANCE 871
expectancy 507, 871
expectant 121, 507
EXPECTATION 507, 871
expected 507, 871
EXPEDIENCE 646
expedient, *n. plan* 626
   means 631, 632
expedient, *adj. useful* 646
expedite 132, 684
expedition *promptitude*
   132
   march 266
   alacrity 682
   campaign 722
expel *push* 284
   eject 297
   banish 972
expend *waste* 638
   use 677
   pay 809

F

fantastic *odd* 83
  absurd 497, 853
  imaginative 515
fantasy 515
far 196
  -and near 180
  -and wide 180, 196
farce *absurdity* 497, 853
  drama 599
  wit 842
farcical 497, 853
fare, *n. food* 298
  price 812
fare, *v. do* 7
farewell 293
far-famed 31, 873
farfetched 10
far-flung 180
far-gone *much* 31
  insane 503
  spoiled 654
farinaceous 330
farm, *n. land* 780
farm, *v. till* 371
  rent 788
farmer 371
farmhouse 189
farsighted 441, 510
farther 196
  [*see further*]
farthing *coin* 800
fascinate *please* 829
  astonish 870
  love 897
  conjure 992
fascination [*see* fascinate]
  infatuation 825
  charm 829
  desire 870
FASHION, *n. state* 7
  custom 613
  mode 852
fashion, *v. form* 240
  create 976
fashionable 852
fast, *adj. joined* 43
  steadfast 150
  rapid 274
  intemperate 954
fast, *v.* 956
fasten *join* 43
  restrain 751
fastening 45
fastidious 868
FASTIDIOUSNESS 868
FASTING *penance* 952
  abstinence 956
fastness *defense* 717
fat, *n.* 356
fat, *adj. corpulent* 192
  bloated 194
  unctuous 355
fatal 361
fatalism 601
fatality 601
fate, *future* 152

  doom 360, 611
  necessity 601
fateful 601
Fates 601
father 166
  priest 996
Father, God the - 976
fatherland 189, **342**
fatherly 906
Fathers, the - 983
fathom, *n.* 466
fathom, *v. investigate* 461
  solve 462
  discover 480a
fathomless 208
FATIGUE 688
fatness [*see* fat]
fatten *expand* 194
  improve 658
  prosper 734
  -upon *feed* 298
fatuity 499
faucet 263, 295
fault *break* 70
  defect 304
  error 495
  imperfection 651
  failure 732
  at - *uncertain* 475
faultfinder 832
faultless *perfect* 650
  innocent 946
faulty *imperfect* 651
fauna 366
favor, *n. badge* 550
  indulgence 740
  gift 784
  partiality 923
favor, *v. resemble* 17
  aid 707
  permit 760
favorable *lucky* 134
  good 648
  aiding 707
  -to 709
FAVORITE 897, **899**
favoritism *friendship* 888
  wrong 923
fawn, *n. animal* 366
fawn, *adj. brown* 433
fawn, *v. cringe* 886
  flatter 933
fawning *servile* 746
fay 979
fealty *obedience* 743
  respect 928
FEAR 860
fearful *painful* 830
  timid 862
fearless 858, 861
feasible *possible* 470
feast *period* 138
  banquet 298, **957**
  revel 840
feat 680, 861
feather *class* 75

  tuft 256
  ornament 847
  -in one's cap
    honor 873
feathery 324
feature *character* 5
  form 240
  appearance 448
  lineament 234, 550
federal 712
federate 48
federation 709, 712
fee *pay* 809
  reward 973
feeble *weak* 160, **575**
  illogical 477
feeble-minded
  imbecile 499
  irresolute 605
FEEBLENESS *style* 575
feed *eat* 298
  fodder 370
  supply 637
feel *sense* 375
  touch 379
  respond 821
  -for 914
feeler *antenna* 379
  experiment 463
FEELING 821
feign 544, **546**
feint 545
felicitate 896
felicitous *agreeing* 23
  happy 578
  pleasant 829
felicity 578, 827
feline, *n. cat* 366
feline, *adj. cunning* 702
fell, *v. destroy* 162
  lay flat 213
  lay low 308
fell, *adj.*
  dire 860
  malevolent 907
fellow *counterpart* 17
  equal 27
  companion 88
  man 373
  scholar 492
fellow countryman 890
fellow creature 372
fellow feeling
  friendship 888
  love 897
  benevolence 906
  pity 914
fellowship *friendship* 888
fellow student 541
felon 949, 975
felonious 945
felony 947
female 374
feminine 374
femininity 374
fen 345

fence, n. *enclosure* **232,**
  752
  thief 792
  on the - 607
fence, v. *evade* 544
  fight 720
fender 717
ferment, n. *disorder* 59
  agitation 171, **315**
  lightness 320
  excitement 825
ferment, v. *effervesce* 353
  sour 397
fermentation
  [see ferment]
fern 367
ferocity *violence* **173**
  brutality **907**
ferret
  -out *be curious* 455
ferry 270
ferryman 269
fertile 168
fertilization 161, 168
fertilize 168
ferule 975
fervent *hot* 382
  desirous 865
fervid *hot* 382
  heartfelt 821
fervor *passion* 820
  animation **821**
festal 687, 840
fester *corrupt* 653
festival 138, 883
festivity 840, 883
festoon 245
fetch *bring* 270
  sell for 812
fete 840, 882
fetid 401
fetish 991, 993
FETOR 401, 663
fetter *restrain* 43, **751**
  shackle 752
feud *discord* 713
feudal 749
feudatory 749
fever *heat* 382
  disease 655
  excitement 825
feverish *hot* **382**
  hurry 684
  excited 824
few 103, 137
FEWNESS 32, **103**
fez 225
fiancée 897
fiasco 732
fiat 741
fib *falsehood* 546
fiber *filament* 205
fibrous
fickle *changeable* 149
  irresolute 605
fickleness 605

fiction *untruth* 546
  work of - **594**
fictitious 515, 546
fiddle 417
fiddler 416
fidelity *identity* **13**
  truth 494
  veracity 543
  obedience 743
  honor 939
fidget 682, 825
field *scope* 180
  region 181
  plain 344
  agriculture **371**
  business 625
field day 882
field glass 445
field marshal 745
fiend *ruffian* 913
  demon 980
fiendish 907, 945, 980
fierce *violent* 173
  daring 861
  angry 900
fiery *violent* **173**
  hot 382
  excitable 825
  angry 900
fifer 416
fight *contention* 720
  warfare 722
  -shy *avoid* 623
  turn tail 862
fighter 726
figment 515
figurative **521**
FIGURE, n. *number* 84
  form 240
  metaphor 521
  price 812
  cut a - *repute* 873
  - of speech **521**
figure, v. *represent* **554**
figurehead *sign* 550
  representation 554
FILAMENT **205**
filch 791
file, v. *pare* 38
  arrange 60
  smooth 255
  pulverize 330
  record 551
  -off *march* **266**
file, n. *row* 69
  list 86
  on - 60
filial 167
filibuster, n.
  obstructionist 710
  freebooter 792
filibuster, v. *delay* 133
  impede 706
  pillage 791
filibusterer 706, 710
filigree 219

fill *complete* 52
  occupy 186
  load 190
  stuff 224
  -up *complete* 52
  close 261
fillet *band* 45
  filament 205
  ornament 847
filling *stuffing* 224
fillip *impulse* 276
  stimulus 615
film *layer* 204
  opacity 426
filmy *scaly* 204
filter *percolate* 295
  clean 652
filth 653
filthy 653
final 67, 729
finale *end* 67, 729
finality 67, 729
finally *eventually* 151
  on the whole **476**
finance 800
financier 639
find *experience* 151
  adjudge 480
  discover 480a
  -out 480a
finding *judgment* 480
fine, adj. *rare* 322
  not raining 340
  delicate 329
  exact 494
  good 648
  beautiful 845
  adorned 847
  proud 878
  -arts 554
  -gentleman *fop* **854**
  -lady 854
  -writing 482, 577
  in *end* 67
  after *all* 476
fine, v. *mulct* 974
fineness [see fine)]
finery 847
finesse *tact* 698
  artifice 702
finger *touch* 379
finical 855, 868
finicking 855, 868
finis 67
finish, n. *end* 67
  symmetry 242
finish, v. *complete* 729
finished *symmetrical* 242
  perfect 650
  skilled 698
finite 32
fire, n. *energy* 171
  heat 382
  fuel 388
fire, v. *make hot* **384**
  shoot 716

dismiss 756
  excite 824
  -at 716
  -up *rage* 825
firearms 727
firebrand *fuel* 388
  instigator 615
fire bug 384, 949
fire-eater 863, 887
fire extinguisher 385
fireman *stoker* 268
  extinguisher 385
fireplace 386
fireproof 385
firm, *n. partnership* 712
  797
firm, *adj. fast* **43**
  steadfast 150
  hard 323
  resolute 604
firmness [*see* firm]
first 66
firstborn 124, 128
first-class *best* 648
first fruits 154
first-rate 648
firth 343
fiscal 800
fish, *n.* 366
fish, *v.* 622
  -for *pursue* 622
  desire 865
  -out *inquire* 461
  -up *raise* 307
fisherman 361
fissure 44, 198
fit, *n. paroxysm* **173**
  caprice 608
  disease 655
fit, *adj. expedient* 646
  right 922, 924
fit, *v. agree* 23
  -out *dress* 225
  prepare 673
fitful *irregular* 139
  changeable 149
fitness 23, 926
fitting 924
FIVE 98
fix, *n. dilemma* 7, 704
fix, *v. join* 43
  arrange 60
  establish 150
  place 184
fixed *intrinsic* 5
  durable 110
  permanent 141
  stable 150
  -idea 825
fixity 141, 265
fixture 150
fizz 353
fizzle 304, 353
flabby 324
flaccid 324, 326
flaccidity 326

flag, *n.* 550, 747
flag, *v. be weak* 160
  falter 275
  languish 683
  fatigue 688
flagon 191
flagrant *manifest* 525
  notorious 531
  atrocious 945
flagstaff 206
flake 204
flamboyant 577
flame *fire* 382
  light 420
  passion 824, 825
flank *side* 236
flap, *v. hang* 214
  move to and fro 315
flapper *girl* 129
flare *flash* 173
  glare 420
  -up *be excited* 824
  get angry 900
flash *flare* 173
  fire 382
  light 420
flashy *gaudy* 428
  tawdry 851
flask 191
flat, *n. house* 191
  note 413
flat, *adj. low* 207
  horizontal 213
  even 251
  vapid 391
  dull 843
flatiron 255
flatness 213, 251
flatten 213, 251
flatter *deceive* 545
  please 829
  adulate **933**
  -oneself 472, 858
FLATTERER 935
flattering 938
FLATTERY 933
flaunt *flourish* 873
  display 882
flaunting 882
flavor 390
flavoring 393
flaw *break* 70, 198
  error 495
  imperfection 651
  blemish 848
flaxen 436
flay 226
flea *insect* 366
fleck 440
fled *escaped* 671
flee 287
fleece, *n.* 223
fleece, *v. strip* 789
  rob 791
  surcharge 814
fleet, *n.* 273, 726

fleet, *adj. transient* 111
  swift 274
fleeting 111
flesh 364
flesh color 434
fleshy *of fruit* 354
flexible *pliant* 324
flicker *waver* 314
  flutter 315
  glimmer 420, 422
flier *aviator* 269a
  advertisement 531
flight *flying* 267
  swiftness 274
  departure 287, 293
  escape 671
flighty *inattentive* 458
  fanciful 515
flimsy *weak* 160
  slight 322
  soft 324
  sophistical 477
  trifling 643
finch *fear* 860, 862
fling *propel* 284
flippant *pert* 885
  discourteous 895
flirt 854, **902**
flirtation 902
flit *elapse* 109, 111
  move 264
  depart 293
  run away 623
flivver 272
float *navigate* **267**
  buoy up 305
  be light 320
flock *multitude* 72, 102
  laity 997
floe *ice* 383
flog 684, 972
flood 337, 348
floodgate 350
flood tide 206, 337
floor, *n.* 211
floor, *v. overthrow* 731
flop 315
flora 367, 369
floral 367
floriculture 371
florid 428, 434
  (*style*) 577
florist 371
flotation [*see* float]
flotilla 273, 726
flounce, *n. trimming* 231
flounce, *v. jump* 309
flounder *toss* 315
  be uncertain 475
  bungle 699
  fail 732
flourish *brandish* 315
  vegetate 365, 367
  prosper 734
  flaunt 872
  boast 884

front 234
　important **642**
forenoon 125
forensic 968
foreordain *destine* 152
forerun 62, 116, 280
forerunner 64, 673
foresee *expect* 121, **507**
　foreknow 510
foreseen 871
foreshadow 511
foreshorten 201
FORESIGHT **510**
forest 367
forestall 132
forester 371
forestry 371
foretaste 510
foretell 511
forethought 510
forever 16, 112
forewarn *predict* 511
　warn 668
foreword 64
forfeit, *n.* **974**
forfeit, *v. lose* **776**
forgather 72
forge *imitate* 19
　swindle **791**
　-ahead 282
forger **792**
forgery 21, **791**
forget **506**
forgetful 506
forgive **918**
FORGIVENESS **918**
forgo [*see* forego]
forgotten 122, **506**
fork *divide* **91**
　branch **244**
forlorn *dejected* 837
　hopeless 859
　deserted 893
　-hope 859
FORM, *n. state* **7**
　likeness 21
　bench 215
　shape **240**
　school class 541
　manner 627
　beauty 845
　fashion 852
　etiquette 882
form, *v. make up* **54**
　compose **56**
　order 58
　arrange 60
　convert 144
　produce 161
　shape **240**
　organize 357
formal [*see* form]
　regular 82
　severe 739
　affected 855
　stately 882

formalism 739, **988**
formalist 82, **988**
formality [*see* formal]
　ceremony 882
formation
　composition 54, 76
　production 161
　shape 240
formative *causal* 153
former *in order* 62
　prior in time 116
　past **122**
formerly 119, **122**
formidable **704**
formless **241**
formula 80, **697**
formulate 590
forsake **624**
forsaken **898**
forswear *deny* **536**
　lie 544
　refuse 764
fort 666, 717
forth 282
forthwith 132
fortification **717**
fortify 159
fortitude *endurance* 826
　courage 861
fortress 666, 717
fortuitous 6, 156, 621
fortuity 156
fortunate *opportune* 134
　prosperous **734**
fortune *destiny* 152, 601
　chance 156
　wealth 803
fortune teller 513
forum *place* 182
　tribunal 966
forward, *adj. early* 132
　front 234
　onward **282**
　active 682
　insolent 885
　uncourteous 895
forward, *v. transmit* 270
　improve 658
　help 707
fossil 40, **357**
fossilize **357**
foster *aid* 707
　excite 824
　caress 902
foul, *adj. bad* 649
　dirty 653
　ugly 846
　base 940
　vicious 945
　-play *wrong* 923
　improbity 940
foul, *v. collide* 276
foul-mouthed 895
foulness [*see* foul]
foul-spoken 934
found *cause* 153

colonize 184
foundation *stability* **150**
　base 211
　support 153, 215
founder, *n.* 164, 626
founder, *v. sink* **310**
　fail 732
foundling 782, 893
fountain 153, 348
four 95
fourfold 96
Four Hundred 852, **875**
fowl 366
fox *animal* 366
fox trot *dance* 840
fracas *noise* 404
　discord 713
FRACTION *part* 51
　less than one **100a**
fractional 51, 100a
fractious 901
fracture *disjunction* 44, 70
　fissure 198
fragile *weak* 160
　brittle 328
fragment *small part* **32**
　part 51. 100a
　extract 596
fragmentary 100a
FRAGRANCE **400**
fragrant **400**
frail *weak* 160
　brittle 328
　irresolute 605
　failing 945
frailty [*see* frail]
frame, *n. condition* **7**
　support 215
　border 231
　form 240
　structure 329
frame, *v. make* 161
framework 215, 329
franchise *freedom* **748**
　right 924
frangible 328
frank *open* 525
　sincere 543
　artless 703
frantic *violent* 173
　delirious 503
　excited 824
fraternal *brotherly* 11
　leagued 712
　friendly 888
　-order 711
fraternity *brothers* 11
　party 712
　friends 888
fraternize *combine* 48, **709**
　sympathize 888
　associate 892
fraud *deception* 545
　impostor 548
fraudulent [*see* fraud]
fraught *full* 52

possessing 777
fray, *n. battle* 720
fray, *v.* 331
frayed *worn* 659
freak 83, 608
freckle 848
freckled 848
free, *adj. detached* 44
  unconditional 52
  unobstructed 705
  gratis 815
  liberal 816
  -and easy 748, 888
free, *v. deliver* 672
  liberate 748
  exempt 927a
freebooter 792
freeborn 748
freedman 748
FREEDOM 748
freehold 780
freely *willingly* 602
freeman 748
Freemason 711
freethinker 989
freeze 383, 385
freezing 383
freight *cargo* 190
  transfer 270
freighter *vessel* 273
frenzy *madness* 503
  furor 865
frequency 136
frequent *in number* 104
  in time 136
  habitual 613
frequenter 613
fresh *extra* 37
  new 123
  cold 383
  color 428
  unaccustomed 614
  healthy 654
  pert 885
freshen 689
freshet 348
freshman 492, 541
freshness [*see* fresh]
fret *suffer* 378
  grieve 828
  gall 830
  mope 837
  irritate 900
fretful 901
fretwork 219
friable 330
friar 996
friary 1000
FRICTION *obstacle* 179
  rubbing 331
FRIEND 711, 890
  -in need 711
friendless 893
friendliness 888
friendly *favorable* 707
  amicable 888

FRIENDSHIP 888
frieze 210
frigate 726
fright *alarm* 860
frighten 860
frightful *dreadful* 830, 860
  ugly 846
frigid *cold* 383
frill *border* 231
fringe *border* 231
frippery *ornament* 847
  finery 851
frisk *leap* 309
frisky *brisk* 682
  in spirits 836
fritter
  -away *time* 683
frivolity 499
frivolous *foolish* 499
  trivial 643
friz *curl* 248
frock *dress* 225
frolic 309, 840
frolicsome 836
frond 367
FRONT, *n.* 66, **234**
front, *v. resist* 719
frontage 234
frontal 220, 234
frontier *vicinity* 199
  limit 233
frontispiece 64, 234
frost, *adj. cold* 383
frost, *v. whiten* 430
froth 353
frothy 353
frown *lower* 837
  scowl 839
  disapprove 932
frowzy 653
frozen 383
fructify 168
frugal 817, 953
fruit *result* 154
  profit 775
fruitful 168
fruition 161
fruitless *unproductive* 169
  useless 645
frustrate 179, 706
frustrated 732
fry *shoal* 102
  heat 384
FUEL *combustible* 388
fugitive, *n.* 623
fugitive, *adj.* 111
fulcrum 215, 633
fulfill *complete* 729, 772
full *much* 31
  complete 52
full-blown 194
full-grown 131, 194
fullness [*see* full]
fully 31, 52
fulminate *rage* 173
  threaten 908

fulsome *abhorrent* 867
  adulatory 933
fumble *handle* 379
  grope 463
  botch 699
fumbler 701
fume, *n. exhalation* 334
  odor 398
fume, *v. rage* 173
  exhale 336
  flare up 824
  be impatient 825
fumigate 336, 652
fumigator 388
fun *amusement* 840
function *business* 625
  duty 926
functionary 694, 758
fund 636
fundamental *intrinsic* 5
  base 211
funds 800
funeral 363
funerary 363
funereal 363
funk *fear* 860
  cowardice 862
funnel 350, 351
funny 842, 853
fur *covering* 223
furbelow 231
furbish 847
Furies 900, 913
furiosity 173
furious *violent* 173
  angry 900
furl 312
furlough 760
FURNACE 386
furnish *provide* 637
  prepare 673
  give 784
furniture 633
  (*property*) 780
furor *passion* 825
  desire 865
FURROW 259
further *extra* 37
  distant 196
furthermore 37
furtive *clandestine* 528
fury *violence* 173
  anger 825, 900
fuse *combine* 48
  dissolve 335
  heat 384
  torch 388
fuselage 273
fusileer 726
fusillade 716
fusion *union* 48
  heat 384
fuss *agitation* 315
  activity 682
  excitement 825
fussy 481, 682

futile 645
futility 499, 645
FUTURE 117, **121**, 152

expected 507
-events **152**
-state *destiny* 152

heaven **981**
futurity 121

G

gab 584
gabble 584
gable *side* 236
gad 266
gag 403, 581
  muzzle 751
gage *measure* 466
gain *increase* 35
  prosper **618**
  acquisition **775**
  -time *protract* 110
  -upon *approach* 286
  pass 303
gainsay 536
gairish [*see* garish]
gait *walk* 264
galaxy *multitude* 102
  stars 318
gale 349
gall, n. *bitterness* 395
  insolence 885
gall, v *hurt* 378
  annoy 830
gallant *brave* 861
  courteous 894
gallantry 861, 902
gallery *room* 191
  passage 260
  spectators 444
galley *ship* 273
  cookroom 386
  printing 591
gallop 266, 274
gallows 361, 975
galore 102
galvanic *excitable* 825
galvanize 157
gamble 156, 621, 840
gambler 463, **621**, **863**
gambling *chance* **621**
  rashness 863
gambol 309
game, n. *animal* **366**
  amusement **840**
game, *adj. resolute* 604
game, v. *gamble* 621
gamester 840
gaming 156
gang 72, **712**
gangway 260
gaol [*see* jail]
gap 70, 198
gape, *yawn* **198**, 260
  stare 455
garage 191, 272
garb 225
garble *misinterpret* 523
  falsify 544

garden 371
gardener 371
gargle 337
garish 851
garland *circle* 247
  fragrance 400
  ornament 847
garment 225
garner *store* 636
garnish 847
garret 210
garrison 717, 726
garrote 361
garrulity 584
garter *fastening* 45
gas *gaseity* 334
GASEITY 334
gaseous *unsubstantial* 4
  vaporous **334**, 336
gash *cut* 44
  interval 198
gasify 334
gasoline 356
gasp 688
gastronomy 957
gate 66, 232, 260
gather *collect* 72
  fold 258
  conclude 480
gathering *assemblage* 72
gaudy 428, 851
gauge 466
gaunt 203
gauntlet *glove* 225
gawky *awkward* 699
  ugly 846
gay *bright* 428
  cheerful 836
  showy 882
gayety [*see* gay] 836
gaze 441
gazelle 366
gazette 531
gazetteer 86
gear *clothes* 225
  harness 633
gelatinous 352
gem *excellence* 648
  ornament 847
gendarme 726, 965
gender 75
genealogy 69
general, *adj. generic* **78**
  habitual 613
general, n. 745
GENERALITY 78
generalize 78, 476
generally 16, 78

generalship 692, 722
generate 161, 168
generation
  consanguinity 11
  period 108
  production 161
generic 78
generosity *liberality* 816
  benevolence 906
  disinterestedness 942
generous [*see* generosity]
genesis *beginning* 66
  production 161
genial *cordial* 377
  warm 382
  willing 602
geniality 602
  [*see* genial]
genius *intellect* 450
  talent **498**
  skill 698
  adept **700**
  familiar spirit 979
genteel 852
gentile *heterodox* 984
gentility 852
gentle *moderate* 174
  lenient 740
  meek 826
  courteous 894
  -breeding 894
gentlefolk 875
gentleman 373, 939
gentleness [*see* gentle]
gentry 875
genuflexion 308
genuine *true* 494
  good 648
genus 75
geography 183
geometry 466
germ *origin* 66
  cause 153
  stem 193
  -cell 357
germane *relevant* 23
germinate 194, 365
gesticulate 550
gesture 550
get *acquire* 775
  -back *regain* 775
  -down *descend* **306**
  -in 775
  -on *advance* 282
  prosper 734
gewgaw *trifle* 643
geyser 382, 384
ghastly *pale* 429

hideous 846
ghost 362, 980a
ghoul *demon* 980
giant 192, 206
gibber *stammer* 583
gibberish 563
gibbet 975
gibbous 249, 250
gibe *disrespect* 929
giddy *inattentive* 458
   wild 503
gift *power* 157
   transference 270
   talent 698
   thing given 784
gifted 698
gigantic *large* 192
   tall 206
giggle 838
gild 223, 436
gilt 436
gimcrack *weak* 160
   trifling 643
gimlet 262
gingerly 459
gipsy 268
gird *bind* 43
   strengthen 159
   surround 227
girder *beam* 215
girdle *bond* 45
   tie 225
   circumference 230
   circle 247
girl 129
   servant 746
girlhood 127
girlish 374
girt 229
girth 45, 230
gist *essence* 5
   meaning 516
give *yield* 324
   bestow 784
  -up *relinquish* 624
   surrender 782
   restore 790
giver 784
GIVING 784
glacial 383
glacier 383
glad *pleased* 827
   pleasing 829
gladden 836
glade 260
gladiator 726
glamour 615, 992
glance *touch* 379
   look 441
  -at *take notice of* 457
   allude to 527
  -off 279
glare *light* 420
   stare 441
glaring [*see* glare]
   great 31

gaudy 428
   manifest 525
glass 255
   vessel 191
   lens 445
glassy 255
glaze 255
gleam *light* 420
   shine 446
glean *choose* 609
   acquire 775
glee 827, 836
glen 252
glib *voluble* 584
   facile 705
glide *lapse* 109
   move 264
   travel 266
   aviation 267
glimmer *light* 420
   flicker 422
   be visible 446
glimpse *sight* 441
glint 420, 441
glisten 420
glitter *shine* 420
   be visible 446
gloaming 126
gloat
  -over *delight* 827
   brag 884
globe *sphere* 249
   world 318
globe-trotter 268
globularity 249
gloom *darkness* 421
   dimness 422
   sadness 837
gloomy *dark* 421
   sad 837
glorification
   [*see* glorify]
glorify *honor* 873
   worship 976, 990
glorious 873
glory *light* 420
   honor 873
gloss *smoothness* 255
   sheen 420
  -over 477
glossary *list* 86
   dictionary 562
glossy [*see* gloss]
glove 225
glow *warm* 382
   shine 420
   appear 446
glower *glare* 443
   be sullen 901a
glowing [*see* glow]
   red 484
   exciting 824
glue *cement* 46
glum *discontented* 832
   sulky 901a
glut 957

glutinous 327, 352
glutton 954a 957
GLUTTONY 957
gnarled *crooked* 243
   rough 250, 256
gnaw 298
go, *n. energy* 171, 682
go, *v. move* 264
   progress 282
   depart 293
   disappear 449
  -about *turn around* 311
  -by *elapse* 109
   outrun 303
  -off *explode* 173
   depart 293
  -on *continue* 143
   advance 282
  -through *meet with* 151
   endure 826
  -to *travel* 266
goad, *n.* 370
goad, *v. quicken* 684
go-ahead 171, 282, 682
goal *end* 67, 292
   haven 265
   object 620
gob *sailor* 269
gobble *cry* 412
   gormandize 957
go-between
   intermediary 228, 758
   instrument 631
goblet 191
goblin 980
GOD 976
god 979
goddess 979
Godhead 976
godly 944
godsend 618, 734
Godspeed *farewell* 293
goggle 441
gold, *adj. yellow* 436
gold, *n. money* 800
golden 436
  -mean 628
gondola 273
gondolier 269
gone [*see* go]
   extinct 2
   past 122
   absent 187
   dead 360
  -by 124
GOOD, *n.* 618
  for - *permanent* 141
good, *adj. palatable* 394
   beneficial 648
   virtuous 944
   pious 987
  -at 698
  -humor 836
  -looks 845
  -luck 734
  -man *worthy* 948

-nature 906
-offices *mediation* 724
-taste 578, 850
-turn *kindness* 906
-will *benevolence* 906
-woman **948**
-word 931
make - *restore* 790
  substantiate 924
  vindicate 937
good-for-nothing 158, **949**
good-looking 845
goodly *great* 31
  handsome 845
good-natured 906
GOODNESS 648
goods *effects* 780
  merchandise 798
goose *bird* 366
gore, *n. gusset* 43
  blood 361
gore, *v.* 260
gorge, *n. ravine* **198**
gorge, *v. glut* 869
  gormandize 957
gorgeous *gay* 428
  beautiful 845
gorilla 366
gormandize **957**
gorse 367
gory *murderous* 361
  red 434
gospel *doctrine* 484
  truth 494
Gospels 985
gossamer 205
gossamery 320
gossip *news* 532
  babbler 584
  conversation 588
gouge 262
gourmand *glutton* 957
gourmet 868, **954a**
govern 693, 737
governess 540
government 737, 745, **965**
governor *director* 694
  ruler 745
gown *dress* 225
grab *take* 789
grace *elegance* 845
  polish 850
  pity 914
  forgiveness 918
  worship 990
graceful *elegant* 578
  beautiful 845
  tasteful 850
graceless *inelegant* 579
  ugly 846
  impenitent 951
Graces 845
gracious *courteous* **894**
  kind 906
gradation *degree* 26
  order 58

grade *degree* 26
  classify 60
  term 71
  obliquity 217
  ascent 305
  class 541
  crossing 219
gradual *degree* 26
  continuous 69
  slow 275
gradually **275**
graduate, *n.* 492
graduate, *v. adjust* 23
  measure 26
  arrange 60
  initiate 537
graduation 541
graft, *v. insert* **300**
graft, *n. loot* 784
  improbity 940
grain *humor* 5
  tendency 176
  roughness 256
  texture 329
  powder 330
  against the-704
GRAMMAR 567
grammatical 567
gramophone 418
grand *august* 31
  important 642
  handsome 845
  glorious 873
  ostentatious 882
  -juror 967
grandee 875
grandeur *greatness* 31
  repute 873
grandfather 130, 166
grandmother 166
grandness [*see* grand]
granny 30
grant *admit* 529
  permit 760
  consent 762
  confer 784
granular 330
graphic *intelligible* **518**
  vigorous 574
  descriptive 594
graphophone 418
grapnel 666
grapple 789
  -with
  -a *question* 461
  -*difficulties* 704
  oppose 708
  resist 719
grasp, *n. power* 737
grasp, *v. comprehend* 518
  retain 781
  -at 865
grasping *miserly* 819
  covetous 865
grass 367
  -widow 905

grassland 367
grassplot 371
grassy 367
grate, *n. fireplace* 386
grate, *v. rub* 330
  -on the ear
  harsh sound 410
grateful *enjoyable* 377
  agreeable 829
  thankful 916
gratification 377, 827
gratify *permit* 760
  please 829
grating *lattice* 219
  stridor 410
gratis 815
GRATITUDE 916
gratuitous
  inconsequent 477
  free 748, 815
gratuity *gift* 784
grave, *n.* 363
grave, *adj. somber* 428
  important 642
  distressing 830
  sad 837
graveclothes 363
gravedigger 363
gravestone 363
gravitate *descend* 306
  weigh 319
  -towards 176
GRAVITY *weight* **319**
  importance 642
  seriousness **837**
  [*see* grave]
GRAY *old* 128
  color 428, **432**
graybeard 130
graze *touch* 199, **379**
  browse 298
  rub 331
grease *lubricate* **332**
  oil 355, 356
greasy 355
great *much* **31**
  big 192
  glorious 873
greater 33
greatness 33
GREATNESS 31
greed *desire* 865
  gluttony 957
greedy 819, **865**, **957**
Greek - deities **970**
GREEN, *n. lawn* 344, **371**
  color **435**
green, *adj. new* **123**
  young 127
  sour 397
  credulous 486
  novice 701
  immature 674
greenhorn *novice* 493
  bungler 701
greenness **435**

greensward **344**
greet *hail* **894**
greeting **894**
gregarious **892**
grenade **727**
grenadier **726**
grey [*see* gray]
gridiron *crossing* **219**
grief **828**
grievance **830, 923**
grieve *mourn* **828**
   pain **830**
   complain **839**
grievous *bad* **649**
   painful **830**
grievously *very* **31**
grill **384**
   question **461**
grim *resolute* **604**
   painful **830**
   doleful **837**
   sullen **901a**
grimace **243**
grimy **652**
grin *laugh* **838**
grind *reduce* **195**
   sharpen **253**
   pulverize **330**
   learn **539**
   oppress **907**
grip *bag* **191**
   paroxysm **315**
   indication **550**
   power **737**
   clutch **789**
gripe [*see* grip] **378**
grisly **846**
grist **637**
grit *strength* **159**
   resolution **604, 861**
   stamina **604a**
gritty **323, 330**
grizzled *gray* **432**
groan *cry* **411**
   lament **839**
grocer **637**
groceries **637**
groin, **244**
groom, *n.* **746**
groom, *v.* **370**
groomsman **903**
groove *furrow* **259**
   habit **613**
grope *feel* **379**
   experiment **463**
gross *huge* **31**
   whole **50**
   ugly **846**
   vulgar **851**
grossness [*see* gross]
grotesque *odd* **83**
   ridiculous **853**
grotto **252**
grouch **901a**
ground *cause* **153**
   situation **183**

base **211**
support **215**
land **342**
evidence **467**
teach **537**
motive **615**
stand one's-
   defend **717**
   resist **719**
grounded *stranded* **732**
groundless
   unsubstantial **4**
   illogical **477**
   erroneous **495**
grounds *estate* **344**
   dregs **653**
groundwork *substance* **3**
   cause **153**
   basis **211**
   support **215**
   preparation **673**
group, *n.* **72**
group, *v.* **60**
grove *group* **72**
   wood **367**
grovel *wallow* **207**
   cringe **886**
grow *increase* **31, 35**
   become **144**
   expand **194**
   vegetation **365, 367**
grower **164**
growl *cry* **412**
   complain **839**
   resent **900**
   threat **909**
grown up **131**
growth [*see* grow]
   increase **35**
   conversion **144**
   development **161**
   -*in size* **194**
   vegetation **365**
grub
   food **298**
grudge *begrudge*
   refuse **764**
   stint **819**
   envy **921**
gruesome **846**
gruff *harsh* **410**
   discourteous **895**
grum *morose* **901a**
grumble *cry* **411**
   complain **832, 839**
grumpy **901a**
Grundy, Mrs. **852**
grunt *animal sound* **412**
   complain **839**
guarantee **768, 771**
guaranty **771**
guard *stopper* **263**
   defense **717**
   soldier **726**
guardian *safety* **664**
   keeper **753**

-*angel* **912**
guardianship **664**
guardsman **726**
guerdon **973**
guerrilla **722**
guess **514**
guesswork **514**
guest **890**
guffaw **838**
guidable **278**
guide, *n. model* **22**
   itinerary **266, 527**
   courier **524**
   teacher **540**
   director **694**
guide, *v. teach* **537**
   indicate **550**
   direct **693**
   advise **695**
guidebook **527**
guidepost **550**
guiding star **693**
guild *society* **712**
guile *deceit* **554, 545**
   cunning **702**
guileless *veracious* **543**
   artless **703**
guillotine **975**
GUILT **947**
guiltless **946**
guilty **947**
guinea **800**
guise *state* **7**
   dress **225**
   appearance **448**
GULF **343**
gull, *n. bird* **366**
   dupe **547**
gull, *v. deceive* **545**
gullet **260**
gullible **486**
gully *gorge* **198**
gulp *swallow* **296**
gum *fasten* **46**
gumminess **327**
gummy *tenacious* **327**
   resinous **356a**
gumption **498**
gun *weapon* **727**
gunboat **726**
gunman **913**
gunner **284, 726**
gunnery **284**
gunpowder **727**
gunshot **197**
gurgle *flow* **348**
   faint sound **405**
gush, *n. ardor* **821**
gush, *v. flow out* **295**
gushing *emotional* **821**
gusset **43**
gust *wind* **349**
gusto
   physical pleasure **377**
   emotion **821**
gusty **349**

gut, *n.* 260
gut, *v. destroy* 162
gutter *groove* 259
guttural 561
guy *chaff* 856

guzzle *gourmandize* 957
gybe 279
gymnasium 189, 728
gymnast 159
gymnastic *strong* 159

athletic 720
gymnastics 159
gypsy 268
gyrate 312
gyve 752

H

habiliment 225
HABIT, *n. dress* 225
　custom 613
habitat 189
HABITATION 189
habitual *normal* 80
　ordinary 82
　customary 136, 613
habituate 613
habitude 613
hack, *n. horse* 271
　vehicle 272
　writer 593
hack, *v. cut* 44
hackneyed *trite* 496
　habitual 613
Hades 982
haft 633
hag 846, 913
haggard *tired* 688
　ugly 846
haggle *chaffer* 794
ha-ha *ditch* 198
hail, *n.* 383
hail, *v. welcome* 292
　call 586
　greet 894
hair 205, 256
hairless 226
hair-splitting 480
hairy 256
halcyon *calm* 174
　prosperous 734
hale 654
half 91
　-truth 546
half-baked *ignorant* 491
half-blood *mixture* 41
half-breed 41
half-caste 41
halfhearted
　irresolute 605
　insensible 823
　indifferent 866
half-starved 640, 956
halfway 68
half-witted 499, 501
hall *chamber* 189
hallelujah 990
halloo 411, 586
hallow 976, 987
hallowed 976
hallucination 495, 992a
halo *light* 420
　glory 873
halt *cessation* 142

rest 265
halt, *adj. lame* 655
halter 752
halve 91
hamadryad 979
hamlet 189
hammer *repeat* 104
hammock 215
hamper, *n. basket* 191
hamper, *v. obstruct* 706
hand, *n. side* 236
　mariner 269
　man 372
　organ of touch 379
　indicator 550
　writing 590
　at - *present* 118
　　destined 152
　　near 197
　in - *incomplete* 53
hand, *v. transfer* 270
　grasp 781
handbag 191
handbook *travel* 266
　information 527
　book 593
handcuff 751
handful 25
handicap, *n. race* 720
handicap, *v. equalize* 27
　incumber 706
handicraft 625
handiwork 154, 680
handkerchief 225
handle, *n.* 633
handle, *v. touch* 379
　use 677
　manage 693
handmaid 631, 746
handsome *liberal* 816
　beautiful 845
handwriting 590
handy *near* 197
　useful 644
　ready 673
　dexterous 698
hang *loiter* 133
　be pendent 214
　kill 361
　execute 972
　-back 623
　-fire *be late* 133
　not finish 730
　fail 732
　-together 178
hangar 273

hanger-on
　accompaniment 88
　dependent 746
　flunky 886
hangman 975
hanker 865
hansom 272
hap 156
haphazard 156
hapless 735
haply *possibly* 470
happen, 1, 151
happening 151
happiness 377, **827**
　[see *happy*]
happy *fit* 23
　opportune 134
　glad 827
　cheerful 836
harangue *speech* 582
harass *vex* 830
　worry 907
harbinger *precursor* 64
　omen 512
harbor, *n. haven* 189, 292
　refuge 666
harbor, *v. cherish* **451**
hard *strong* 159
　firm 323
　difficult 704
　severe 739
　grievous 830
　impenitent 951
　-by 197
　-pressed 684, 704
　-up 704, 804
harden 323 [see *hard*]
　strengthen 159
　accustom 613
hardened *impenitent* **951**
hardheaded 498
hardhearted 907
hardihood *courage* 861
　insolence 885
hardiness [see *hardy*]
hardly *scarcely* 32, **137**
　-ever 137
HARDNESS 323
hardpan 211
hardship 735
hard-working 686
hardy *strong* 159
　brave 861
harebrained 863
harem 374
hark *hear* 418

help *benefit* **618**
  utility **644**
  aid **746**
helper 711
helpful 746
helpless *incapable* **158**
helpmate *wife* **903**
helter-skelter 684
hem *edge* **231**
  fold **258**
  -in **751**
hemisphere 181
hemorrhage 299
hen *bird* **366**
hence *arising from* **155**
  departing **293**
  therefore **476**
henchman 746
henpecked 749
herald, *n.* **64, 527**
herald, *v. precede* **280**
  predict **511**
  proclaim **531**
heraldry 550
herb 367
herbaceous 367
herculean *strong* **159**
  difficult **704**
herd 72, 102
here 183, 186
hereabouts 183
hereafter 121, 152
hereditary *intrinsic* **5**
  derivative **154, 167**
heredity 167
heresy 984
heretic 984, 989
heretical 984
hereupon 106
heritage 121
hermit *recluse* **893**
  ascetic **955**
hermitage *house* **189**
hero 861, 873
heroic 861
  magnanimous **942**
heroics 884
heroine 861
heroism 861, 942
hesitate *flounder* **475**
  demur **485**
  be reluctant **603**
  be irresolute **605**
heterodox 984
HETERODOXY 984
heterogeneity 10, 15, 16a
heterogeneous
  unrelated **10**
  different **15**
  mixed **41**
  multiform **81**
  exceptional **83**
hew *cut* **44**
  -down **213, 308**
hiatus *interval* **198**
hibernate 683

hidden 528
hide, *n. skin* **223**
hide, *v conceal* **528**
hidebound
  strait-laced **751**
  bigoted **988**
hideous 846
hiding place *ambush* **530**
  refuge **666**
hie *go* **264**
  speed **274**
hierarchy 995
high *lofty* **206**
  gamy **298**
  treble **410**
  -life **875**
  -note **410**
  -principled **939**
  -tide **106, 348**
  -time **134**
  -words *quarrel* **713**
  anger **900**
  on - **206**
highborn 875
high-brow 490
higher 33
highest 210
high-flown *absurd* **497**
  imaginative **515**
  vain **880**
highlands 206
high-minded 898, 942
high-priced 809
high-spirited *brave* **861**
  honorable **939**
high-strung 825
highway 627
highwayman 792
hike 260
hilarity 836
hill *height* **206**
hillock 206
hilly 206
hilt 633
hind *deer* **366**
hind, *adj. back* **235**
hinder *impede* **706**
Hinduism 976
HINDRANCE 706
hinge *fastening* **43**
  cause **153**
  -upon *depend upon* **154**
hint, *n. reminder* **505**
hint, *v. inform* **527**
hire, *n. reward* **973**
hire, *v.* **788**
hireling 746
hirsute 256
hiss *sound* **409**
  disrespect **929**
  disapprobation **932**
historian 553
historic 594
history 122, 594
  natural - **357**
histrionic 599

hit *chance* **156**
  strike **276**
  reach **292**
hitch, *n. stoppage* **142**
  difficulty **704, 706**
hitch, *v. fasten* **43**
  hang **214**
  -a horse **370**
hither 278
hitherto 122
hive 184
  apiary **370**
hoar *aged* **128**
hoard 636
hoarse *husky* **405**
hoary 124, 128, 430
hoax 545
hobble *limp* **275**
  fail **732**
  shackle **751**
hobby 481, 625
hobgoblin 980
hobo 268, 876
Hobson's choice 609a
hodgepodge 41
hog *animal* **366**
  selfishness **943**
  glutton **957**
hoist 307
hold, *n. influence* **175**
  storage **191**
  power **737**
hold, *v. cohere* **46**
  contain **54**
  cease **142**
  support **215**
  believe **484**
  defend **717**
  restrain **751**
  possess **777**
  retain **781**
  -forth *declaim* **537, 582**
  -good **478, 494**
  -on *continue* **141, 143**
  persevere **604a**
  -out *persevere* **604a**
  offer **763**
  -true **494**
  -up *support* **215**
  aid **707**
holder 779
holding
  tenancy **777**
  property **780**
holdup 791
hole *hovel* **189**
  cave **251**
  opening **260**
holiday *anniversary* **138**
  leisure **685**
  vacation **687**
  amusement **840**
  celebration **883**
holiness *God* **976**
  piety **987**
holloa 411

hollow, *n.* 207, 252
hollow, *adj.*
  unsubstantial 4
  resonant 408
  gruff 410
  specious 477
hollowness [*see* hollow]
holocaust 991
Holy *of God* 976
  pious 987
  -Ghost 976
  -orders 995, 998
  -Scriptures 985
homage *submission* 725
  respect 928
home *habitation* 189
  interior 221
  country 342
  refuge 666
  -rule 737
  -thrust
    attack 716
    censure 932
homeless *unhoused* 185
  banished 893
homelike 849
homeliness 851
  [*see* homely]
homely *unadorned* 849
  common 851
homesick 833
homestead 189
homicide 361
homily *teaching* 537
  sermon 998
homogeneity *relation* 9
  identity 13
  uniformity 16
  simplicity 42
hone 253
honest 939
honeycomb 252
honeymoon, 902, 903
honor, *n. glory* 873
  respect 928
  approbation 931
  probity 939
honor, *v.* 873
honorable 873, 939
honorarium 784, 973
honorary 815
honored 873
hood *cap* 225
hoodoo 621, 992, 993
hoodwink *blind* 442
  hide 528
hoof 211
hook *fasten* 43
  hang 214
  fork 244
  curve 245
hooligan 887, 913
hoop *circle* 247
  cry 411
hoot *cry* 411, 412
  deride 929

  censure 932
hop *leap* 309
HOPE 858
hopeful 858
hopeless 859
HOPELESSNESS 859
horde 72
horizon 196, 230
horizontal 213, 251, 308
HORIZONTALITY 213
horny 323
horoscope 511
horrible *noxious* 649
  dire 830
  ugly 846
  fearful 860
horrid 649, 830, 846
horrify *terrify* 860
horror *fear* 860
  dislike 867
horror-stricken 828
horse *animal* 271
  translation 539
  cavalry 726
horseman 268
horsemanship 266
horseplay 856
horse power 466
horticulture 371
horticulturist 369
hosanna 990
hose *stockings* 225
  pipe 350
hospitable 816, 892
hospital 662
hospitality 816, 892
host *multitude* 102
  army 726
  friend 890
hostage 771
hostel 189
hostess 890
hostile 14, 24, 889
hostility 889
hot *warm* 382
  pungent 392
  excited 824
  irascible 901
  -air *bombast* 884
  -bath 386
  -springs 382
hotbed 153
hotel 189
  -runner 767
hotheaded 825, 863
hothouse *conservatory* 371
hound, *n. animal* 366
hound, *v. hunt* 622
  persecute 907
hourglass 114
house *lineage* 69
  family 166
  abode 189
  council 696
  firm 712
  -of Commons 966

  -of Lords 875
  -of Representatives 696
house, *v.* 184
housebreaker 792
housebreaking 791
household *inhabitants* 188
  abode 189
householder 188
housemaid 746
housing *lodging* 189
hovel 189
hover *soar* 206, 267
  vacillate 605
how 627
however 30
howitzer 727
howl *cry* 411, 412
  lamentation 839
hoyden *tomboy* 129
hub 222, 247
hubbub 315, 404
huddle 72, 197
hue 428
huff 900
hug, *v. clasp* 46
  border on 197
  love 897
huge 192
hulking 193
hulky *big* 192
  unwieldy 647
hullabaloo *noise* 404
hum *sound* 405, 407
  sing 416
human 364, 372
humane *benevolent* 906
  merciful 914
humanitarian 910
humanitarianism 910
humanity 906, 910
humble *inferior* 34
  meek 879
humbug, *n. falsehood* 544
  deceiver 548
humbug, *v.* 545
humdrum *dull* 843
humid 339
humiliate 879, 929
humiliation 735, 879
HUMILITY
  meekness 879
hummock 206, 250
humor, *n. essence* 5
  tendency 176
  disposition 602
  caprice 608
  wit 842
humor, *v. indulge* 760
  please 829
  flatter 933
HUMORIST 844
humorous 842
hump 250
humpbacked 243
Hun *destroyer* 165
hunch 250

hunchbacked 243
hundred 98
hunger 865
hungry 865, 956
hunt *pursuit* 286, 622
  inquiry 461
hunter *horse* 271
  pursuer 622
hurl 284
hurrah 838
hurricane *tempest* 349
hurry 274, 684
hurt, *n. physical pain* 378
  evil 619
hurt, *v.*
  cause (physical) pain 378
  maltreat 649
  injure 659, 907
  pain 830
  more frightened than-
  860
hurtful 649
hurtle 276
hurtless 648

husband *store* 636
  director 694
  spouse 903
husbandman 371
husbandry *agriculture* 371
  conduct 692
  economy 817
hush *moderate* 174
  stop 265
  silence 403
  taciturn 585
 -up *conceal* 528
  pacify 723
husk *covering* 223
husky *strong* 159
  hoarse 405, 581
hussar 726
hustings 728
hustle 682
hustler 682
hut 189
hybrid 41
hydroplane 273
hydroplaning 267

hygiene 656
hygienic 656
hygienics 670
Hymen 903
hymeneal 903
hymn *song* 415
  worship 990
hyperbole 549
hypercriticism 868
hyperphysical 450
hyphen 45
hypnosis 376, 992a
hypnotic 683
hypnotism 683, 992a
hypnotize 615, 992
hypochondriac 837, 859
hypocrisy 544, 988
hypocrite 548
hypocritical 544, 988
hypothesis 514
hypothetical 514
hysteria 992a
hysterical 821
hysterics 173

I

ice 383, 387
iceberg 383
ice chest 385
icon 554
iconoclasm 984
iconoclast 165
icy 383
IDEA *notion* 453
ideal 515
idealism 450, 515
idealist 515
ideality 450, 515
idealize 515
identical 13
identification 13
IDENTITY 13, 27
idiocy 503
idiom 560, 566
idiosyncrasy 5, 79, 83
idiot 501
idiotic *foolish* 499
idle *trivial* 643
  slothful 683
idler 683
idol *favorite* 899
  fetich 991
idolater 991
IDOLATRY 991
idolize *love* 897
  idolatrize 991
idyl 597
if 8, 469, 514
igneous 382
ignis fatuus 4, 443
ignite 384
ignition *calefaction* 384
ignoble 876

ignominious 940
ignominy *shame* 874
  dishonor 940
IGNORAMUS 493
IGNORANCE 491
ignorant 491
ignore *neglect* 460
  not known 491
ill, *n. evil* 619
  badness 649
  sick 655
ill, *adj. bad* 649
  -usage 807
 -will 907, 921
ill-adapted 24
ill-advised *inexpedient* 647
  unskillful 699
ill-assorted 24
ill-behaved 895
ill-bred *vulgar* 851
  rude 895
ill-disposed 907
illegal 964
ILLEGALITY 964
illegible 519
illegitimate 925, 964
ill-fated 135, 735
ill-favored 846
illiberal *stingy* 819
  selfish 943
  bigoted 988
illicit 925, 964
illiteracy 491
illiterate 491, 493
ill-made 243
ill-mannered 851
ill-natured 907

illness 655
illogical 477
ill-omened 135, 735
ill-proportioned 846
ill-spent 645
ill-starred 135
ill-timed 24, 135
ill-treat 649, 907
ill-treatment 649
illuminant 420
illuminate *enlighten* 420
  comment 595
illumine *lighten* 420
  excite 824
ill-use 649
illusion
  fallacy of vision 443
  error 495
  deception 545
illusive 4, 495
illusory 4, 495
illustrate *exemplify* 82
  interpret 522
  represent 554
illustration 558
illustrious 873
image *likeness* 17
  appearance 448
  metaphor 521
imagery *fancy* 515
  metaphor 521
imaginable 470
imaginary 2, 4, 515
IMAGINATION 515
imaginative 515
imagine 515
imbecile, *adj. ignorant* 493

foolish 499
imbecile, *n. fool* 501
IMBECILITY 499
imbed *insert* 300
imbibe 296
imbroglio *disorder* 59
discord 713
imbue *mix* 41
impregnate 300
imburse 803
imitate *copy* 19
appropriate 788
IMITATION *copying* 19
copy 21
imitative 19
imitator 19
immaculate *perfect* 650
clean 652
innocent 946
immanence 5
immanent 5
immaterial 4, 317
IMMATERIALITY 317
immature *incomplete* 53
new 123
unprepared 674
immeasurable *infinite* 105
immediate 69, 132
immediately 113, 132
immemorial 124
immense *great* 31
infinite 105
-size 192
immensity *greatness* 31
infinity 105
size 192
immerge 300, 337
immerse *insert* 300
submerge 310
dip 337
immersion [*see* immerse]
baptism 998
immigrant 57, 268, 294
immigration 266, 294
imminent 121, 132, 152, 286
immobility 150, 265
immoderately 31
immodest 961
immoral *wrong* 923
vicious 945
immortal
perpetual 110, 112, 143
glorious 873
celebrated 883
immortalize 112, 873
immovable *stable* 150
quiescent 265
obstinate 606
immune *innocuous* 656
[*see* immunity]
immunity *freedom* 748
exemption 777a, 927a
acquittal 970
immure *imprison* 751
immutable *stable* 150
imp *child* 167

demon 980
impact *contact* 43
impulse 276
impair 659
impairment 659
impale *transfix* 260
impalpable 381
impart *inform* 527
give 784
impartial *judicious* 498
neutral 628
just 922
impassable 261
impassioned 822, 825
impassive 823
impatient 825
impeach 938, 969
impeachment 938
[*see* impeach]
impeccability 946
impecunious 804
impede 179, 706
impediment 706
-in speech 583
impel *push* 276
induce 615
impend *destiny* 152
overhang 206
impending 132, 152
[*see* impend]
impenetrable *closed* 261
solid 321
unintelligible 519
IMPENITENCE 951
impenitent 951
imperative 630, 741
imperceptible *minute* 193
invisible 447
imperfect *incomplete* 53
failing 651
IMPERFECTION 304,
651
inferiority 34
imperfectly 32
imperial 737
imperil 665
imperious 737, 878
imperishable *eternal* 112
stable 150
glorious 873
impermeable 261
impersonal 316
impersonate 19, 554
impertinent *insolent* 885
imperturbable
inexcitable 826
unamazed 871
impervious *closed* 261
insensible 823
impetuosity 173, 863
impetuous *boisterous* 173
hasty 684
excitable 825
rash 863
impetus 276
IMPIETY 988, 989

impious 988
implacable 898, 919
implant *insert* 296
teach 537
implanted 5, 6
implement 633
implicate *involve* 54, 526
accuse 938
implication *meaning* 516
latency 526
implicit 526
implied 516
implore 765
imply *evidence* 467
mean 516
involve 526
impolite 895
imponderable 4
import, *n. importation* 294
significance 642
import, *v. put between* 228
take in 296
mean 516
involve 526
IMPORTANCE 62, 642,
873
important 642
importunate 765, 830
importune *ask* 765
pester 830
impose *awe* 928
-upon deceive 545
be unjust 923
imposing *important* 642
glorious 873
imposition [*see* impose]
seizure 925
-of hands 998
IMPOSSIBILITY 471
impossible 471
impost 812
impostor 548, 925
imposture 702
impotence 158
impotent 158
impound *imprison* 751
impoverish *weaken* 160
drain 640
render poor 804
impracticable 471
impracticality 471
imprecation *prayer* 765
curse 908
impregnable 159, 664
impregnate *combine* 48
insert 300
teach 537
impress, *v.* 375, 824
impressible 822
impression *sensation* 375
idea 453
mark 550
engraving 558
emotion 821
impressionable 822
impressive *important* 642

deep-felt **821**
imprint **550**
imprison **229, 751, 972**
imprisoned **754**
imprisonment **972**
IMPROBABILITY **473**
improbable **473**
IMPROBITY **940**
impromptu **612**
improper *incongruous* **24**
  inexpedient **647**
  wrong **923**
  unmeet **925**
  vicious **945**
IMPROPRIETY **24, 925**
  [*see* improper]
improve **658**
  -the occasion **134**
IMPROVEMENT **658**
improvident *careless* **460**
  not preparing **674**
  prodigal **818**
improvise **612**
improviser **612**
imprudent **460, 863**
impudence *insolence* **885**
  discourtesy **895**
impudent *insolent* **885**
impugn *deny* **536**
  blame **932**
IMPULSE *push* **276**
  sudden thought **612**
  motive **615**
impulsive *impelled* **276**
  improvised **612**
  excitable **825**
  rash **863**
impunity *escape* **671**
  acquittal **970**
  with - safety **664**
impure **961**
IMPURITY *inelegance* **579**
  foulness **653**
  immodesty **961**
imputation *attribution* **155**
  slur **874**
  accusation **938**
inability **158, 699**
inaccessible **196, 471**
inaccurate **495**
INACTION *inertness* **172**
  not doing **681**
inactive **683**
INACTIVITY **683**
  inertness **172**
inadequacy
  [*see* inadequate]
inadequate *unequal* **28**
  powerless **158**
  insufficient **640**
  useless **645**
inadmissible *excluded* **55**
  inexpedient **647**
inadvertence **458**
inadvertently **674**
inadvisable **647, 649**

inalienable **924**
inane **4, 452**
inanimate **358, 360**
inanity **452**
inapplicable **10, 24**
inapposite **10, 24**
inappreciable
  in degree **32**
inappropriate **24, 647**
inapt *incongruous* **24**
  useless **645**
  inexpedient **647**
  unskillful **699**
inarticulate **583**
inartistic **846**
INATTENTION **458**
inattentive **419, 458**
inaudible **403, 419**
inaugural **64**
inaugurate *begin* **66**
  celebrate **883**
inauspicious
  untimely **135**
  untoward **830**
  adverse **512, 735**
  hopeless **859**
inborn *intrinsic* **5**
  inbred **820**
inbound **294**
inbred **5, 820**
incalculable *much* **31**
  infinite **105**
incandescence **382**
incantation **765, 993**
incapable **158**
incapacitate **158**
incapacity **158**
incarcerate **751**
incarnate, *adj. intrinsic* **5**
incarnate, *v.* **316, 364**
incarnation **316, 976**
incase **223, 229**
incautious *rash* **863**
incendiary **162, 384**
incense, *n.* **400**
incense, *v. hate* **898**
  anger **900**
incentive **615**
inception **66**
incertitude **475**
incessant *repeated* **104**
  ceaseless **112**
  frequent **136**
inch, *n.* **200**
inch, *v. move slowly* **275**
incidence **278**
incident **151, 643**
incidental *extrinsic* **6**
  circumstance **8**
  irrelative **10**
  occurring **151**
  casual **156**
  liable **177**
incipience **66**
incise **44, 259**
incision *cut* **44**

furrow **259**
incisive **171, 821**
incite *exasperate* **173**
  urge **615**
incitement [*see* incite]
incivility **895**
inclement *cold* **383**
  severe **739**
  pitiless **914a**
inclination [*see* incline]
  tendency **176**
  will **600, 602**
  desire **865**
incline *tend* **176**
  slope **217**
  be willing **602**
inclined *oblique* **217**
  disposed **820**
inclose **221, 227, 229**
INCLOSURE **229, 232,
  370**
include
  comprehend **54, 76**
INCLUSION **76**
inclusive **56, 76**
incognito **528**
INCOHERENCE
  physical **47**
  mental **503**
incombustible **385**
income **623, 775**
incomer **294**
incoming **294**
incommode **706**
incomparable **33**
incompassionate **914a**
incompatibility **15**
incompatible **24**
incompetence *inability* **158**
  unskillfulness **699**
incomplete *fractional* **51**
  not complete **53, 730**
INCOMPLETENESS **53,
  304**
incomprehensible **519**
incomprehension **491**
inconceivable
  impossible **471**
  improbable **473**
  incredible **485**
inconclusive **477**
incongruous **15, 24**
inconsequence **10**
inconsiderable *small* **32**
  unimportant **643**
inconsiderate
  thoughtless **452**
  inattentive **458**
inconsistent *contrary* **14**
  disagreeing **24**
  illogical **477**
  absurd **497**
  capricious **608**
inconsolable **859**
inconspicuous **447**
inconstant **149**

INEXPEDIENCE 647, 699
inexpedient 647
inexpensive 815
inexperience
  ignorance 491
  unskillfulness 699
inexpert 699
inexplicable 519
inexpressible *great* 31
  unintelligible 519
inexpressive 517
infallibility 474
infallible 474
infamous 940
infamy *shame* 874
  dishonor 940
infancy *beginning* 66
  youth 127
INFANT 129
infantile 129
infantine 129
infantry 726
infatuation *credulity* 486
  love 897
infect 659
infection 270, 655
infectious 270, 657
infelicitous 24, 828
infelicity *misery* 828
infer *presume* 472
  deduce 480
inference 476, 480
inferior 34, 207, 651
INFERIORITY
  in degree 28, 34
  in size 195
  imperfection 651
infernal *malevolent* 907
  wicked 945
infertility 169
infest 830
infidel 487, 989
infidelity *dishonor* 940
  irreligion 989
infiltrate *mix* 41
  interpenetrate 294
  ooze 295
infiltration 41, 302
infinite 105, 180
infinite, the - 976
infinitely *great* 31
infinitesimal 32
INFINITY 105
infirm *weak* 160
infirmary 662
infirmity 160, 655
inflame *give energy* 171
  render violent 173
  burn 384
  excite 824
inflamed *red* 434
inflammatory *heated* 384
  [*see* inflame]
inflate *increase* 35

expand 194
  blow 349
inflated *vain* 482, 880
inflation [*see* inflate]
inflect 245
inflexible *straight* 246
  hard 323
  resolved 604
  obstinate 606
  stern 739
inflict 680, 739
infliction *adversity* 735
  mental pain 828, 830
  punishment 972
influence *cause* 153
  physical - 175
  tendency 176
  inducement 615
  instrumentality 631
  importance 642
  authority 737
  absence of - 175a
influential 175
influx 294
inform 527
- *against accuse* 938
informal *irregular* 83
informality 83
informant 527, 938
INFORMATION
  knowledge 490
  communication 527
infraction
  infringement 303
  disobedience 742
INFREQUENCY 103, 137
infrequent 137
infringe *transgress* 303
  disobey 742
  not observe 773
  violate 925
infuriate *inflame* 173
  excite 824
  anger 900
infuse *mix* 41
  insert 300
  teach 537
infused 6
infusion [*see* infuse]
ingathering 72
ingenious *original* 515
  skillful 698
ingenuity 698
ingenuous *artless* 703
inglorious 374
ingot 800
ingraft *join* 43
  insert 300
ingrafted 6
ingrain 329
ingrained *intrinsic* 5
  inborn 820
ingratiate 897
INGRATITUDE 917
ingredient 56
INGRESS 294

inhabit 186, 188
INHABITANT 188
inhale *receive* 296
  breathe 349
inharmonious 15, 24
inhere in 56
inherence 5
inherent 56, 221, 820
inherit *acquire* 775
  possess 777
inheritance 777, 780
inherited 5
inheritor 779
inhibit *hinder* 706
  restrain 751
  prohibit 761
inhospitable 893
inhuman 907
inimical 14, 708
inimitable 20, 28, 650
iniquity 923, 945
initial 66
initiate *begin* 66
  receive 296
  teach 537
initiatory 296
inject 300, 337
injudicious 499, 863
injunction *command* 741
  prohibition 761
injure *harm* 619
  damage 659
  spite 907
injurious 619, 923
injury *evil* 619
  badness 649
  damage 659
injustice 923
inkling 514, 527
inland 221
inlay 300
inlet 66, 294
  -of the sea 343
inmate 188, 221
inmost 221
inn 189
innate 5, 221
inner 221
- *reality* 1
innkeeper 188, 637
INNOCENCE 946
innocent, *n. child* 167
  fool 501
innocent, *adj. good* 648
  artless 703
  guiltless 946
innocuous *healthy* 656
  innocent 946
innovation 20a, 123, 140
innuendo *hint* 527
innumerable 105
inobservance 773
inoculate *insert* 300
  influence 615
inodorous 399
INODOROUSNESS 399

inoffensive *innocent* 946
inofficious 907
inoperative *powerless* 158
  useless 645
inopportune 135
inordinate 31, 641
inorganic 358
INORGANIZATION 358
inquest 461, 967
inquietude 828, 832
inquire 461
inquirer **461**
inquiring **461**
INQUIRY 461
inquisition *inquiry* 461
  severity 739
inquisitive 455
inroad *ingress* 294
  trespass 303
  invasion 716
insane 503
INSANITY 61, **503**
insatiable 865
inscribe *write* 590
inscription 590
inscrutable 519
insect 193, **366**
insecure 665
insensate *foolish* 499
  insane 503
INSENSIBILITY
  physical **376**
  moral 823
insensible 376, **381**
INSENSITIVENESS 823
inseparable *junction* 43
  coherence 46
insert *interpose* 228
  enter 294
  put in 300
  record 551
INSERTION 37, 228, **300**
inside 221
  -out 218
insidious *deceitful* 545
  cunning 702
insight 490
insignia 550
insignificance 32
insignificant 517, 643
insincere 544, 855
insinuate *intervene* 228
  insert 300
  hint 527
  blame 932
insipid *tasteless* **391**
INSIPIDITY 391
insist *argue* 476
  command 741
  -upon *affirm* 535
  be determined 604
insistence [*see* insist]
insaner 545
INSOLENCE 885
insolent *defiant* 715
  arrogant **885**

disrespectful 929
insoluble *dense* 321
  unintelligible 519
insolvable 519
insolvency 808
insolvent 804, 806, 808
insomnia 682
inspect *look* 441
  attend to 457
inspector 694
inspiration *breathing* 349
  wisdom 498
  imagination 515
  motive 615
  revelation 985
inspire *breathe* 349
  prompt 615
  animate 824
  cheer 836
inspired 615
  -writers **985**
inspirit *incite* 615
  animate 824
  cheer 834
instability 149, **605**
install 184, 883
installment *portion* 51
  payment 809
instance *example* 82
instant 113, 152
instantaneity 113
instantaneous 113
instanter 113
instate 883
instead *147*
  -of 755
instigate 615
instigator 615
instill *introduce* 296
  insert 300
  teach 537
instinct *intuition* 477
  impulse 601
instinctive 5, 477
institute, n. 542, 712
institute, v. *begin* 66
  cause 153
  produce 161
institution 542, 712
instruct *teach* 537
  advise 695
  order 741
instruction 537, **695**
instructive 537
instructor 540
INSTRUMENT
  implement **633**
  security 771
  musical - 417
  optical - 445
instrumental 631, **632**
  -music 415
INSTRUMENTALITY
  170, 631
insubordinate 742
insufferable 830, 867

INSUFFICIENCY 53, **640**
insufficient **640**
insufficiently 32
insular *apart* 44, **346**
  narrow 481
  bigoted 988
insulate 44, 87, **346**
  dull 843
insult *insolence* 885
  rudeness 895
  disrespect 929
insuperable 471
insupportable 830
insurance 768
insure *make sure* 474
  obtain security 771
insurgent 146, **742**
insurmountable 471
insurrection 719, 742
insurrectionary 146
insusceptible 823
intact 52, 141
intaglio 22, 252
intangible 381
integer 50
integral 50
integrity *whole* 50, 52
  probity 939
integument 223
INTELLECT 450
  absence of - 405a
intellectual 450
INTELLIGENCE
  mind 450
  capacity 498
  news 532
intelligent 498
INTELLIGIBILITY 518
intelligible 518
INTEMPERANCE 954
  drunkenness 959
intemperate **954**
intend 620
intense *great* 31
  energetic 171
intensify 35, 835
intensity *degree* 26
  greatness 31
  energy 171
intensive 35
intent, *adj.* 457
intent, *n. design* 620
INTENTION 620
intentional 620
inter 363
interact 12
interaction 170
intercalate 228
intercede *mediate* 724, 976
intercept *hinder* 706
  take 789
intercession 724, 976
  [*see* intercede]
intercessor 714
INTERCHANGE 12, **148**
  barter 794

interchangeable 148
intercollegiate 148
intercourse 888, 892
interdependence 12
interdict 971
interest, *n. influence* 175
  curiosity 455
  advantage 618
  importance 642
  property 780
  debt 806
interest, *v.* 824, 829, 840
interested *selfish* 943
interfere *disagree* 24
  counteract 179
  intervene 228
  thwart 706
interim 106, 111
interior 221
INTERIORITY 221
interjacence 228
interject 228
interlace 43, 219
interlard *mix* 41
  interpolate 228
interlineation 228
INTERLOCATION 228
interloper 57
interlude 106
intermediary 228, 534
intermediate *mean* 29
  middle 68
  intervening 228
  -time 106
intermediation 170
INTERMENT 363
interminable
  infinite 105, 112
  long 200
intermingle 41
intermission 106, 142
intermit *interrupt* 70
  recur 138
  discontinue 142
intermittent 138
intermix 41, 48
intern 221
internal *intrinsic* 5
  interior 221
international 148
interpenetration 228
interpolation 228
interpose *intervene* 228
  hinder 706
interpret 522, 595
INTERPRETATION 522
INTERPRETER 524
interregnum 111, 187, 198
interrogate 461
interrogation 461
interrupt *suspend* 70, 142
  hinder 706
interruption
  [see interrupt]
  interval 187, 198
intersect 219

intersection 219
intersperse *diffuse* **73**
interstice 198
intertwine *unite* 41, 43
  cross 219
INTERVAL *degree* 26
  -of time 106
  absence 187
  -of space 198
  at intervals 70
intervene *interrupt* 70
  -in space 228
  be instrumental 631
  mediate 724
intervention 228
interview 588
interviewer 553
interweave *join* 41, 43
  cross 219
inthrall *subject* 749
intimacy 888
intimate, *n.* 890
intimate, *adj. close* 197
  friendly 888
intimate, *v. tell* 527
intimation 527
intimidate 860, 909
intimidation 860
intolerable 830
intolerance *prejudice* 481
  obstinacy 606
  impatience 825
intolerant 481, 489
intomb 363
intonation *sound* 402
  voice 580
intone *sing* 416
intoxicated 959
intoxication 959
intrap 545
intrench 664, 717
intrepid 861
intricacy 533
intricate 59, 248
intrigue *plot* 626
  finesse 702
intrinsic 5, 121
introduce *add* 37
  lead 62
  interpose 228
  precede 280
  admit 296
  insert 300
introduction
  [see introduce]
  preface 64
  reception 296
introductory *precursor* **64**
  beginning 66
  receptive 296
introspective 451
intrude
  be inopportune 135
  intervene 228
  trespass 303
intruder 57

intrusion 135, 228
intrusive 228, 706
intrust *commit* 755
  lend 787
  credit 805
INTUITION 477, 490
intwine 43, 248
inundate 348
inure 613, 823
INUTILITY 645
invade 294, 716
invalid, *n.* 655
invalid, *adj. illogical* **477**
invalidate *disable* 158
  confute 479
invaluable 644, 648
invariable 16
invasion 294, 716
invective 908, 932
inveigh 932
inveigle *deceive* 545
  seduce 615
invent *imagine* 515
  lie 544
  devise 626
invention 515
inventive *skillful* 698
inventor 164
inventory 86
inverse 14, 218
INVERSION
  contrariety **14**
  change 140
  reversion 145
  of position **218**
invert 14, 218
  [see inversion]
invertebrate *weak* 945
invest *impower* 157
  clothe 225
  surround 227
  besiege 716
  give 784
  lend 787
  -in purchase 795
investigate 461
investment [see invest]
investor 784
inveterate *old* 124
  established 150
invidious 898, 921
invigorate 159, 171
invincible 159
inviolate *permanent* 141
  secret 528
  stainless 939
INVISIBILITY 447
invisible 193, 447, 526
invitation [see invite]
invite *induce* 615
  offer 763
  ask 765
invocation [see invoke]
invoice 86
invoke *address* 586
  implore 765

J

K

L

statute 697, **741**
legality 963
law-abiding 743
lawful *permitted* 760
legal 924, 963
lawless *irregular* 83
mutinous **742**
vicious 945
arbitrary 964
lawlessness 964
lawn 344
LAWSUIT 969
LAWYER 968
lax *incoherent* 47
soft 324
remiss 738
weak 945
laxative 652
LAXITY 47, **738**
laxness 738, 773
lay, *n. ballad* 415
lay, *adj. secular* 997
lay, *v. place* 184
level 213
-aside *reject* 610
disuse 678
give up 782
-by *store* 636
disuse 678
-down the law 535
-to *attribute* 155
-up *store* 636
disuse 678
-waste 162
LAYER 204, **223**
lay *figure* 4
layman 997
lazy *inactive* 683
lea 344
lead, *n. supremacy* 33
lead, *v. forerun* 62, 280
influence 175
tend 176
induce 615
direct 693
leaden *dim* 422
gray 432
leader *precursor* 64
dissertation 595
leadership 737
leading 280
leaf *part* 51
layer 204
plant 367
leafage 367
league, *n.* 712
league, *v. combine* 48
leak 295, 638
-out *disclose* 529
leakage [*see* leak]
leaky 295
lean *thin* 203
oblique 217
leaning *tendency* 176
willingness 602
desire 865

LEAP *jump* 309
leaping 309
learn 490, 539
learned 490, 539
LEARNER 492, **541**
LEARNING 539
knowledge 490
lease, *n.* 780
lease, *v.* 787
leash *tie* 43
least 34
leave, *n. permission* 760
leave, *v. part company* 44
relinquish 624
bequeath 784
leaven, *n.* 153
leaven, *v. lighten* 320
leave-taking 293
leavings 40
lecture, *n.* 595
lecture, *v. teach* 537
speak 582
censure 932
lecturer *teacher* 540
speaker 582
ledge *shelf* 215
ledger 86
lee *side* 236
leer *stare* 441
lees 321
leeway 180
LEFT *residuary* 40
sinistral 239
left-handed 239
leg *support* 215
legacy 270, 784
legal *permitted* 760
legitimate 924
relating to law 963
LEGALITY 963
legalize 963
legation 755
legend 551, 594
legendary 515, 979
legerdemain 545
leggings 225
legible 518
legion *multitude* 102
legislation 963
legislator 694
legislature 72, **696**
legitimate *permitted* 760
right 922
legal 924, 963
LEISURE *spare time* **685**
opportunity 134
at one's - *late* 133
leisurely 133, 275
lend 787
lender 787
LENDING 787
LENGTH 200
lengthen *increase* 35
make long 200
lengthwise 200
lengthy *long* 200

diffuse 573
lenient *mild* **740**
lenity 740
lens 445
Lent 956
lenten 956
leper *outcast* 892
less 34, 38
lessee 779
lessen - *in quantity or degree* 36, 174
-*in size* 195
lesson *teaching* 537
warning 668
lessor 805
let *permit* 760
lend 787
-alone *avoid* 623
disuse 678
not do 681
-be *not do* 681
-fall *drop* 308
inform 527
speak 582
-go *neglect* 460
liberate 750
relinquish 782
-off *explode* 173
-out *lengthen* 200
disclose 529
liberate 750
lethal *deadly* 361
lethargy 683, **823**
LETTER *character* **561**
epistle 592
letter carrier 271, **534**
letterpress 591
letters *knowledge* 490
language 560
levee *assemblage* 72
sociality 892
level, *adj. uniform* 16
equal 27
low 207
horizontal 213
flat 251
smooth 255
level, *v. destroy* 162
smooth 255
overturn 308
level-headed 826
lever 307, 633
leverage 175
LEVITY *lightness* 320
triviality 643
jocularity 836
levy *muster* 72
military **726**
distrain 789
demand 812
lexicon 562
LIABILITY 177
debt 806
duty 926
liable 177
liar 548

libel *detraction* 934
   accusation 938
libelant 938
libeler 936
liberal *ample* 639
   expending 809
   generous 816
LIBERALITY 784, 816
liberate *disjoin* 44
   deliver 672
   free 748, 750
LIBERATION 750
LIBERTINE 962
liberty *freedom* 748
   permission 760
   right 924
library 593
lice 366
license *laxity* 738
   permission 760
   right 924
lid 223
lie, *n. untruth* 546
lie, *v. be situated* 183
   be present 186
   recline 213
   fib 544
  -in *be* 1
lien *security* 771
   credit 805
lieutenant *officer* 745
   deputy 759
LIFE *essence* 5
   events 151
   vitality **359**
   biography 594
   activity 682
  -to come 152
lifeboat 273
life-giving 168
lifeless *inert* 172
   dead 360
lifelike 17, 21
lifelong 110
lifetime 108
lift *raise* 307
ligament 45
ligature 45
LIGHT, *n. window* 260
   luminosity 420
   luminary 423
   aspect 448
   knowledge 490
light, *adj. not heavy* **320**
   luminous 420
   trivial 643
   unburdened 705
   gay 836
light, *v. arrive* 292
   descend 306
   kindle 384
   illumine 420
light-colored 429
lighten *illume* 420
   facilitate 705
light-fingered 791

light-footed *fleet* 274
   active 682
lightheaded 503
lighthearted 836
lighthouse 550
lightning 420
like, *adj. similar* 17
like, *v. relish* 394
   enjoy 827
   wish 865
   love 897
likely 472
likeness *similarity* 17, 21
   portrait 554
likewise 37
lilac *color* 437
Liliputian 193
limb *member* 51
limber *pliable* 324
LIMIT, *n. end* 67
   boundary 233
limit, *v. circumscribe* 195,
   229
   qualify 469
   restrain 751
limitation [see limit]
limited 32
limitless 105
limp, *adj. weak* 160
   supple 324
limp, *v.* 275
limpid 425, 570
line, *n. fastening* 45
   row 69
   lineage 69, 167
   length 200
   direction 278
   mark 550
   vocation 625
   armed force 726
line, *v.* 224
lineage *kindred* 11
   series 69
   ancestry 122, 166
   posterity 167
lineament *outline* 230
   appearance **448**
linear 200
linen 225
liner 273
linger *delay* 133
   loiter 275, 281, 291
  -on *time* 106
lingo 563
lingua franca 563
lingual 560
linguistic 560
liniment *ointment* 356
LINING 224
link, *n. tie* 9
   vinculum 45
link, *v. connect* 43
lion *animal* 366
   celebrity 873
lion-hearted 861
lionize 873

lip 231
LIQUEFACTION 335
liquefy 335
liquid *fluid* **333**
liquidate 807
liquidity 333
liquor 298
lisp 583
LIST, *n. catalogue* **86**
   leaning 217
   schedule 611
   arena 728
list, *v. classify* 69
   hear 418
   record 551
listen 418
listless *inactive* 683
   indifferent 866
literal *exact* 516
literally 19
literary 560
literature 490, **560**
lithe 324
litigant 938, 969
litigate 969
litigation 969
litigious 713
litter, *n. disorder* 59
litter, *v. derange* 61
   bed cattle 370
little *-in degree* 32
  -in size 193
   bigoted 988
LITTLENESS 32, 193
liturgy 998
live *exist* 1, 359
   continue 141
   dwell 186
livelihood 803
liveliness 836 [see lively]
livelong 110
lively *frisky* 309
   keen 375
   active 682
   acute 821
   sensitive 822
   sprightly 836
livery 225
livid 431, 437
living *alive* 359
   benefice 995
lizard 366
load, *n. quantity* 31
   cargo 190
   hindrance 706
   anxiety 828
load, *v. fill* 52
   lade 184, 190
loadstar [see lodestar]
loadstone *attraction* 288
loaf *dawdle* 683
loafer 268, 927
loan 787
loath 603, 867
loathe *dislike* 867
   hate 898

relinquish 624
lure *charm* 288
  deceive 545
  entice 615
lurid *dark* 421
  dim 422
lurk 526, 528
luscious *savory* 394
luster 420, **873**

lustily *loud* 404
lustrous *shining* 420
lusty *strong* 159
  big 192
luxuriant *fertile* 168
  rank 365
luxurious *pleasant* 377
  intemperate **954**
luxury

enjoyment 377, 827
  sensuality 954
lying 544
lymphatic *slow* 275
lynch 972
  -*law* 964
lyncher 975
lyric 597
lyrist 597

M

mace *weapon* 727
  scepter 747
machination 626, 702
machine *automobile* 272
  instrument 633
  party 712
machinery 633
machinist 690
mackintosh 225
mad *violent* 173
  insane 503
  excited 824
madam 374, 877
madden 824
MADMAN 504
madness 503
Madonna 977
maelstrom *whirl* 312
magazine *book* 593
  store 636
magenta 434, 437
magic 992
magician 548, 994
magisterial 878, 885
magistrate 967
magnanimity 942
magnanimous 942
magnate 875
magnet *attraction* 288
  desire 865
magnetic 157, 829
magnetism *power* 157
  influence 175
  attraction 288
magnetize 157, 288
magnificent *fine* 845
  grand 882
magnify *increase* 31, 35
  enlarge 194
  overrate 549
magnitude 25, 31, 192
maharajah 875
mahogany *color* 433
maid *girl* 129
  servant 746
  spinster 904
maiden *first* 66
  girl 129
maidenly 374
mail *post* 270, **534**
  armor 717
maim *injure* 659

main, *n. ocean* 341
  land 342
  conduit 350
  in the - *principally* **642**
main, *adj. principal* 642
  -*force strength* 159
  violence 173
  compulsion 744
mainland 342
mainspring *cause* 153
mainstay *support* 215
  refuge 666
  hope 858
maintain *keep* 141
  continue 143
  sustain 170
  assert 535
  preserve 670
maintenance
  [see maintain]
majestic *grand* 31
  glorious 873
  stately 882
majesty 745, 873
major, *adj. greater* 33
major, *n. officer* 745
majority *superiority* 33
  plurality 100
  age 131
make *constitute* 54, 56
  render 144
  produce 161
  form 240
  complete 729
  compel 744
  create 976
  -*believe* **545**
  -*good*
  demonstrate 478
  -*out discover* 480*a*
  know 490
  interpret 522
  -*up complete* 52
maker *artificer* 690
Maker, the - 976
makeshift *substitute* 147
  excuse 617
make-up *composition* 54
makeweight 30
malady 655
malcontent 710, **832**
male *man* 373

MALEDICTION **908**
malefaction 947
malefactor 975
maleficent 907
MALEVOLENCE **907**
malevolent 907
malformation 243
malformed 241
malice *hate* 898
  spite 907
  bear - 907
malign, *adj. malevolent* 907
malign, *v. detract* 934
malignant 907
malignity 907
malinger 544
malison 908
malleable *soft* 324
maltreat *injure* 649
  aggrieve 830
  molest 907
mamma 166
mammal 366
Mammon 803
mammoth 192
MAN, *n. mankind* **372**
  male 373
  workman 690
  servant 746
  -of action **682**
man, *v. prepare* **673**
  defend 717
manacle *fetter* 752
manage 175, 693
manageable *easy* **705**
management 692, 693
manage *director* 694
mandate *requirement* 630
  command 741
mane 256
manege 370
maneuver *operation* **680**
  stratagem 702
manful *strong* 159
  resolute 604
  brave 861
manger 191
mangle *smooth* 255
  injure 659
manhood 131, 861
mania *insanity* 503
  desire 865

summit 210
mayor 745
maze *convolution* 248
  enigma 533
  difficulty 704
mazy 248
mead 344
meadow 344, 371
meager *small* 32
  thin 203
  scanty 640
meal *repast* 298
MEAN, *n. average* **29**
  middle 68
mean, *adj. middle* 68
  contemptible 643
  stingy 819
  shabby 874
  ignoble 876
  selfish 943
mean, *v. signify* 516
  intend 620
meander *wind* 248
  stroll 266
  deviate 279
MEANING 516
meaningless 517
meanness *inferiority* 34
  [see mean]
MEANS *appliances* **632**
  wealth 803
meantime 106
meanwhile 106
measurable 466
measure, *n. extent* 25
  degree 26
  proceeding 626
measure, *v.* 466
measureless 105
MEASUREMENT 25,
  466
meat 298
mechanic 690
mechanical 601
  -powers 633
mechanics 276
mechanism 633
medal *record* 551
  palm 733
meddle 682
meddlesome 682, 706
medial 68
mediate *intervene* 631
  intercede 724, 976
MEDIATION
  instrumentality 631
  intercession 724
  Christ 976
Mediator *Saviour* 976
mediator 724
medical 662
medicine 662
  -man 548, 994
medieval 124
mediocre *mean* 29
  ordinary 736

MEDIOCRITY
  average 29
  smallness 32
  -of fortune 736
meditate *think* 450, 451
meditation 451
medium, *n. mean* 29
  middle 68
  instrument 631
  seer 992a
medium, *adj.* 736
medley *mixture* 41
  disorder 59
meed *reward* 973
meek *gentle* 826
  humble 879
meet, *v agree* 23
  assemble 72
  converge 290
  fulfill 772
  -with *experience* 151
meeting [see meet]
  junction 43
  convergence 290
  arrival 292
  assembly 696
melancholy 830, **837**
mellow, *adj. old* 128
  soft 324, **428**
  ripe 673
mellow, *v.* 673
melodious 413
melodrama 599, 824
melody 413
melt *vanish* 111
  convert 144
  liquefy 335
  heat 382
  fuse 384
  pity 914
  -away *cease to exist* 2
  vanish 4
melting pot 691
member *part* 51
  component 56
  councilor 696
membrane 204
membranous 204
memento 505
memoir 594, 595
memorable 151
memorandum 551
memorial *record* 551
memorialize 505
memorize 505
MEMORY 505
  fame 873
menace 909
ménage 692
menagerie 370
mend *improve* 658
  repair 660
mendacity 544
mendicancy 804
mendicant 800
menial *servant* 746

mensuration 466
mental 450
  -reservation 528
mentality 450
mention 527
menu 86, 298
mercantile 794
mercenary, *n. soldier* 726
  servant 746
mercenary, *adj.* 943
MERCHANDISE 798
MERCHANT 797
merciful 914
merciless 914a
mercurial *mobile* 264
  excitable 825
mercy *lenity* 740
  pity 914
mere *simple* 32
  trifling 643
meretricious 851
merge *combine* 48
  insert 300
  -into *become* 144
merit *goodness* 648
  due 924
  virtue 944
merited 924
meritorious 931
mermaid 979
merriment 836, 840
merry *cheerful* 836
mesh 219
mesmerism 992
mesmerist 992a
mess *mixture* 41
  disorder 59
  derangement 61
  difficulty 704
message *dispatch* 527
  intelligence 532
  command 741
MESSENGER
  traveler 268
  envoy 534
Messiah 976
messmate 890
metallic *harsh* 410
metaphor *figure* 521
metaphorical 521
metaphysics 450
mete *measure* 466
  distribute 786
metempsychosis 140
meteoric *transient* 111
meteorology 338
meter *length* 200
  versification 597
METHOD *order* 58
  agency 170
  way 627
methodical *orderly* 58
  regular 80, 138
  businesslike 692
methodize 60
meticulous *exact* 494

fastidious 868
metrical *measured* 466
metropolis 189, 222
mettle *energy* 171
   spirit 820
   courage 861
mew *cry* 412
microbe 193
microscopic 32
mid 68
MID-COURSE 628
midday 125
MIDDLE *-in degree* 29
   -in order 68
   -in space 222
   -age 131
middle-aged 131
middle-class 29
middleman 228
middling 736
midmost 68
midnight 126
midriff 228
midshipman 269
midst 68
midsummer 125
midway 68
mien 448
might 31, 157
mighty *much* 31
   strong 157, 159
migrate 266
mild *moderate* 174
   warm 382
   lenient 740
   calm 826
MILDNESS 740
mile 200
militant 722
military 722
   soldiers 726
   -authorities 745
militia 726
milksop *coward* 862
milky 430
mill, *n.* 691
mill, *v. indent* 257
   pulverize 330
millennium *period* 108
   hope 858
millinery *ornament* 847
million 98, 876
millionaire 803
mimic *imitate* 19
mince *step short* 275
   lisp 583
   affect 855
mind, *n. intellect* 450
   will 600
   purpose 620
   desire 865
   bear in - 505
mind, *v. attend to* 457
   dislike 867
mindful 457, 505
mine, *n.* 545, 636

mine, *v. sap* 162, 252, **717**
miner 252
   sapper and - 726
mineral 358
mineralize 358
mingle 41
miniature *small* 32
minimize 36
minimum 32, 34
minister *deputy* 759
   clergy 996
   -to help 707, 746
ministerial 995
ministration *aid* 707
ministry *direction* 693
   aid 707
   church 995
   clergy 996
minor *inferior* 34
   infant 129
minority *few* 103
   youth 127
minster 1000
minstrel 416, 597
mint 22
minuend 38
minus *subtracted* 38
   absent 187
minute, *n. period* 108
   record 551
minute, *adj. -in degree* 32
   -in size 193
minutemen 726
minuteness 457, 459
minutiae 32, **643**
miracle *exceptional* 83
   prodigy 872
miraculous *wonderful* 870
mirage 443
mire 653
mirror, *n. reflector* 445
mirror, *v. imitate* 19
mirth 836
misadventure 735
misanthrope 911
MISANTHROPY 911
misapply *misinterpret* 523
   misuse 679
   mismanage 699
misapprehend *mistake* 495
   misinterpret 523
misappropriate 679
misbehave 851, 945
misbehavior
   discourtesy 851, 895
   guilt 947
misbelief 485
misbeliever 984
miscalculate 481, 495
miscall 565
miscarry 732
miscellany 41, 72, 78
mischance *misfortune* 735
mischief 619
mischief-maker 913
mischievous 649

misconceive *mistake* 481,
   495
   misinterpret 523
misconception 481, **495**
misconduct *guilt* 947
misconstrue 523
miscreant 949
misdate 115
misdeed 947
misdemeanor 947
misdoubt 485
misemploy 679
miser 819
miserable *unhappy* 828
miserably 32
miserly 819
misery 828
misfire 732
misfortune *adversity* **735**
misgiving 485, 860
misguide 495, 538
misguided 699
mishap *failure* 732
   misfortune 735
misinform 495, 538
misinstruct 538
MISINTERPRETATION
   523
MISJUDGMENT 481, **495**
mislay *derange* 61
   lose 776
mislead 495
mismanage 699
mismatch 15
misname 565
MISNOMER 565
misplace *derange* 61
   displace 185
misprint 495
mispronounce 583
misproportioned *ugly* 846
misreckon 481
misrepresent
   misinterpret 523
   misteach 538
   lie 544
   distort 555
MISREPRESENTATION
   523, 555
misrule 699, 738
miss, *n. girl* 129
   error 495
miss, *v. neglect* 460
   fail 732
   lose 776
   want 865
misshapen *shapeless* 241
   distorted 243
   ugly 846
missile 284, **727**
missing 2, 187
mission 625, 755
missionary 540
missive 592
misspell 523
misspend 818

misstate 495
misstatement *error* 495
  untruth 546
  misrepresentation 555
mist *cloud* 353
  semitransparency 427
mistake 495, 699
mistaken 495
MISTEACHING 538
mister 373
mistime 135
mistress *lady* **374**
mistrust 485
misty [*see* mist]
misunderstand 495, 523
misunderstanding
  disagreement 24
  error 495
MISUSE 679
mite *bit* 32
  infant 129
  small **193**
mitigate *decrease* 36
  abate 174
  relieve 834
mitigation
  [*see* mitigate]
mitten 225
mix 41
mixed **41**
mixture 41, **335**
mizzen 235
mnemonics **505**
moan *cry* 411
  lament 839
moat *inclosure* 232
  canal 350
mob 72, 102, 876
  -*law* 738
mobile *inconstant* 149
  movable 264
  sensitive 822
mobilization 264, **722**
mobilize 264
moccasin 225
mock, *v. imitate* 17, 19
mock, *adj. derisive* 856
  -*modesty* 855
mockery 19, 856
mode *state* 7
  habit 613
  method 627
  fashion 852
model *copy* 21
  prototype 22
  form 240
  sculpture 557
  perfection 650
  good man 948
moderate, *adj. small* 32
  slow 275
  lenient 740
  cheap 815
  temperate 953
moderate, *v. allay* **174**
MODERATION 174

  patience 831
  [*see* moderate]
moderator *lenitive* **174**
  judge 967
modern 123
modernism **123**
modernization 123
modest *small* 32
  humble 879
  diffident **881**
MODESTY 879, 881
modicum *little* **32**
modification *difference* **15**
  variation 20a
  change 140
  qualification 469
modify 469
modish **852**
modulation 140
Mohammedanism 976
moiety 51
moil 682
moist **339**
moisten **339**
MOISTURE 339
mold, *n. matrix* 22
  form 240, 554
  structure 329
  earth 342
mold, *v. convert* 144
  carve 557
  decay 653
  create 976
moldy *fetid* 401
molecular 32
molecule 32, **193**
molest 907
mollify *allay* **174**
  soften 324
mollycoddle **158**
molten *liquefied* 384
moment 113
momentous 151, 642
momentum 276
monarch 745
monarchy 737
monastery 1000
monasticism **995**
monetary 800
MONEY 800
money-changer 797
moneylender **797**
monger 797
mongrel 41, 83
monitor *oracle* 513
  director 694
  adviser 695
  warship 726
monitory *prediction* **511**
  dissuasion 616
  warning 668
monk 996
monkey *imitator* 19
  ape 366
  butt 857
monocycle 272

monograph 594
monologue 589
monoplane 273
monoplanist 269a
monopolist 751, 943
monopolize 777
monopoly *restraint* 751
  possession 777
monotone 104
monotonous *uniform* 16
  equal 27
  repetition **104**
  weary 841
monotony 13
  [*see* monotonous]
monsoon 348, 349
monster *exception* 83
  giant 192
  prodigy 872
  evildoer **913**
  ruffian 949
monstrosity
  [*see* monster]
  distortion 243
monstrous *excessive* **31**
  exceptional 83
  huge 192
  wonderful 870
month 108
monument *tomb* 363
  record 551
moo 412
mood *nature* 5
  state 7
  tendency 176
  humor 602
moody *sad* 837
  sullen 901a
moon 108, **318**
  -*shaped* 245
moonbeam *light* 420
moonlight 422
moonshine *absurdity* 497
moonstruck *insane* 503
moor, *n. open space* 180
  plain 344
moor, *v. fasten* 43
  locate 184
moorings 184
moot -*point topic* 454
  question 461
mop 256, 652
mope 837
moraine 270
moral, *n. maxim* 496
moral, *adj. right* 922, **926**
  virtuous 944
  -*courage* 604
  -*obligation* 926
morality 926, 944
moralize 476
morals *duty* 926
  virtue 944
morass 345
moratorium 133
morbid 655

mordant *keen* 171
  pungent 392
  rigorous 574
more *superior* 33
  extra 37
moreover 37
moribund *dying* 360
MORNING 125
morose 901a, 911
morris chair 215
morrow 121
morsel 32, 51
mortal, *n. man* 372
mortal, *adj. transient* 111
  fatal 361
mortality *evanescence* 111
  death 360
mortar *cement* 45
  pulverizer 330
  crucible 691
  cannon 727
mortgage *security* 771
  lend 787
  sale 796
  credit 805
mortification
  vexation 830
  humiliation 879
mortify 879
mortise *intersect* 219
mosaic 41, 440
mosque 1000
moss 367
most 31
mote 32
mother *parent* 166
  -tongue 560
motherhood 166
motherland 181, 189
motherly 897, 906
MOTION
  change of place **264**
  topic 454
  proposal 763
  request 765
motionless 265
MOTIVE 264, **615**
  absence of **-615a**
  -power 264
motley 41, 81
motor, *n. vehicle* 272
motor, *adj. motion* 264
motor, *v. journey* 266
motor car 272
motorcycle 266, **272**
motorist 268
motorize **266**
motorman 268
mottled 440
motto *maxim* 496
  device 550
mould [see mold]
mound *hill* 206
mount, *n.* 206, 250
mount, *v. increase* 35
  ascend 305

raise 307
mountain 206
mountainous 206
mountebank *quack* 548
  buffoon 844
mourn *grieve* 828
  lament 839
mourner 363, **839**
mournful *sad* 837
mourning **839**
mouth *entrance* 66
  opening 260, 294
  jaws **298**
  estuary 343
mouthful *quantity* 25
  food **298**
movable 264, 270
move *begin* 66
  go **264**
  propose 514
  induce 615
  offer 763
  excite 824
  -slowly **275**
movement 264, 680
movies *theater* 599
moving 185, **264**
  -pictures 448, 599
mow *shorten* 201
  -down *destroy* 162
  level 213
much 31
mud 345, 352, **653**
muddle *disorder* 59
  derange 61
  blunder 497, 732
muddle-headed 499
muddy *moist* 339
  opaque 426
muff
  dress 225
  bungler 701
muffle *wrap* 225
  silence **403**
  deaden 405, **408a**
  gag 581
muffler *dress* 225
  silencer 408a
mufti *undress* 225
mug *cup* 191
muggy *moist* 339
mulatto 41
mulct 974
mule 41, 271
mulish 606
multifarious
  diverse 16a
multifold 81
MULTIFORMITY 81
multiplex 81
multiplication
  productiveness 168
multiplicity 102
multiply 163, 168
MULTITUDE 31, **102**
mum *mute* 581

mumble *mutter* **583**
mummy 362
munch 298
mundane *worldly* 318
  irreligious 989
municipal 965
munificent 816
munition 717
murder 361
murderer 361
murderous 361
murky *dark* 421
murmur 405
muscle 159
muscular 159
muse, *v.* 451
Muse *poetry* 597
Muses, the - 416
mushroom *upstart* 734
MUSIC 415
musical 413, **415, 416**
  -instruments **417**
  -terms 413
musicale 415
music hall 840
MUSICIAN 416
musing *thought* 451
musket 727
musketeer 726
musketry 727
muss 61
mussy 653
mustache 256
mustang 271
muster 72, **85**
muster roll *list* 86
mutable *changeable* 149
mutation 20a 140
mute, *adj. silent* 403
  letter 561
  speechless 581
  sordine 408a
mutescence 408a
mutilate *retrench* **38**
  deform 241
mutilated **53**
mutilation 38, 619
mutineer 742
mutiny 146, 742
mutter 583
mutual 12, 148
muzzle *silence* 403, 581
  restrain 751
  gag 752
myriad 102
myrmidon 726
mysterious *uncertain* 475
  obscure 519
  concealed 528
mystery
  [see *mysterious*]
  latency 526
  secret 533
mystic 528, 992a
mysticism 992a
mystify *perplex* 519

hide 528
deceive 545

myth fancy 515
MYTHIC DEITIES 979

mythical 515, **979**
mythology **979**

N

nadir 211
nag, *n. horse* 271
nag, *v. quarrel* 713
nail *fasten* 43
naked 226
namby-pamby
  affected 855
name *indication* 550
  appellation 564
nameless 565
namely 79
namesake 564
nap *texture* 256, 329
  sleep 683
narcotic 662
narration 594
narrative 594
narrator 529, 532, **594**
narrow *thin* 203
  bigoted 481, 988
narrow-minded
  bigoted 481
  foolish 499
  selfish 943
NARROWNESS 203
nasty *foul* 653
  offensive 830
nation 372
national 372
  -guard 726
nationality 372, 910
nationwide 78
native, *n.* 188
native, *adj.* 5, **367**
  -land 342
nativity *birth* 66
natural *intrinsic* 5
  true 494
  artless 703
  simple 849
  -history 357
  -philosophy 316
naturalist 357
naturalization 184
naturalized 188
nature *essence* 5
  tendency 176
  world 318
naught 4, 101
naughty 945
nausea 841, 867
nauseate *sicken* 395, 867
  give pain 830
nauseous *unsavory* 395
  unpleasant 830
  disgusting 867
nautical 267, 273
naval 267, 273
  -authorities **745**

NAVIGATION 267
navigator 269
navvy *laborer* 690
navy 273, **726**
nay 536
neap *low* 207
  -tide 36
near *like* 17
  -in space **197**
  -in time 121
  soon 132
  impending 152
  approach 286
  stingy 819
nearly 32
NEARNESS 9, 197
nearsighted 443
neat *orderly* 58
  trim 240, 845
  clean 652
nebula 353
nebulous *misty* 353
  obscure 519
necessarily 154
necessary 601, **630**
necessitate 630
NECESSITY *fate* 601
  predetermination 611
  compulsion 744
  indigence 804
  need 865
necromancy 511
necropolis 363
nectar 394, 396
need *necessity* 601
  requirement 630
  want 640
  indigence 804
  desire 865
needful 601, 630
needle 262
needless 641
needlework 847
nefarious 945
NEGATION 536, 764
negative, *n.* 22
negative, *adj. inexisting* 2
  denying 536
negative, *v. confute* 479
  deny 536
NEGLECT 460
  leave undone 730
  omit 773
  evade 927
negligence 460
negligent 460
negotiable 270
negotiate *mediate* **724**
  bargain **769**

negotiator 724, **758**
Negro *black* **431**
neigh 412
neighbor *near* 197
  friend 890
neighborhood 197, 227
neighborly *aiding* **707**
  friendly 888
  social 892
nemesis 972
neologist 563
NEOLOGY 563
Nereid 979
nerve *strength* 159
  courage 861
nerveless *impotent* 158
  imperturbable 871
nervous *excitable* 825
  timid 860
nest 102, **153**
nestle 186, 902
net, *adj.* 40
net, *n.* 219, 232
nether 207
netlike 219
netting 219
nettle 830
network 59, **219**
neutral *mean* 29
  no choice 609a
  mid-course 628
  indifferent 866
neutrality
  indifference 609a, 866
  [see neutral]
neutralize 179
never 107
  -more 107
new *different* 18
  novel 123
newcomer 294
newfangled 851
NEWNESS 123
NEWS 532
newsmonger *gossip* 532
newspaper 531, 551
next 63, 121
nib *end* 67
nibble *eat* 298
nice *discriminative* **465**
  exact 494
  pleasing 829
  fastidious 868
niceness [see nice]
nicety 494
niche 191, 244
nick *notch* 257
nickel 800
nickname 565

nicotine 392
niggard 819
night 421
nightgown 225
nightmare 515
nightshirt 225
nihilism 2, 738
nihilist 165, 913
nihility 4
nil 4
nimble *swift* 274
   active 682
nine 98
   team 759
nip *cut* 44
   shorten 201
Nirvana 2
no *negation* **536**
NOBILITY 875
noble, *n. peer* 875
noble, *adj. great* 31
   upright 930
   virtuous 944
nobody 876
nocturnal 126
nod *wag* 314
   signal 550
   sleep 683
   bow 894
noise 402, 404
noiseless 403
noisy 404
nol-pros 756
nomad 268
nomadic 266
NOMENCLATURE 564
nominal 564
nomination
   appointment 755
nominee 758
nonadhesive 47
NONASSEMBLAGE 73
nonattendance 187
NON-BIBLICAL
   -writings 986
nonchalance 866
noncohesive 47
noncommittal 864
NONCOMPLETION 730
nonconformity
   exception 83
   dissent **489**
   sectarianism 984
nonconformist 984
nonco-operation 927
nondescript 83
none 101
nonentity 2, 4, 643
nonessential 6, 643
NONEXISTENCE 2
nonexpectant 508
NONEXPECTATION
   508

nonidentical 18
NONIMITATION 20
NONINCREASE 36
NONOBSERVANCE
   infraction 773
NONPAYMENT 808
NONPREPARATION
   674
nonresidence 187
nonresistance 725, 743
NONRESONANCE 408a
nonsense 497, 517
noodle 501
nook 244
noon *midday* **125**
noose 45, 247
normal *average* 29
   orderly 58
   regular 80, 82
   sane 502
normalcy 80
normality
   [*see* normal]
Morse deities **979**
north 237
northern **237**
nose 250
nose dive 267
nostrum *contrivance* 626
   remedy 662
not *negation* 536
notable *great* 31
   distinguished 873
notary 553, 968
NOTCH *gully* 198
   nick 257
   mark 550
note, *n. music* 413
   explanation 522
   record 551
   epistle 592
   money 800
   fame 873
note, *v. notice* 450
   remark 457
notebook 551
noted *famous* 873
noteworthy *great* 31
   exceptional 83
nothing *nihility* 4
   zero 101
   trifle 643
nothingness 2
notice, *n.* 480, 527, 668
notice, *v.*
   observe 450, 457
noticeable 31
notification 527
notion *idea* 453
notoriety 531
notorious *public* 531
   infamous 874
notwithstanding 30, 179

nought 4, 101
nourish 707
nourishment *food* **298, 359**
   aid 707
novel, *n.* 594
novel, *adj.*
   dissimilar 18
   new 123
novelist 594
novice *ignoramus* **493**
   learner 541
   religious 996
now 118
   -and then 136
noway 32
nowhere 187
nowise 32
noxious *bad* 649
   unhealthy 657
nozzle 260
nucleus *cause* 153
   center 222
nude 226
nudge 550
nudity 226
nugatory 158
nugget 800
nuisance *evil* 619
   annoyance 830
null *inexistent* 2
nullify 1, 162, 756
nullity 2, 4
numb 376, **381, 823**
NUMBER, *n.*
   part 51
   abstract – **84**
number, *v. count* **85**
numberless 105
numbers *many* 102
   verse 597
NUMBNESS **381**
numeral 84, 95
NUMERATION **85**
numerical 85
numerous 102
numskull 493, 501
nun 996
nunnery 1000
nuptial 903
nuptials 903
nurse, *n* 746, **753**
nurse, *v.* 707
nursery 127
nursling 129
nurture, *n.* 298
nurture, *v.*
   prepare 673
   aid 707
nutriment 298
nutrition 707
nutritious 298, **656**
nuzzle 902
nymph 979

O

oaf *fool* 501
oar *paddle* 267
  oarsman 269
oarsman 269
oasis 342
oath *assertion* 535
  bad language 908
obdurate *obstinate* 606
  impenitent 951
OBEDIENCE 743
obeisance *bow* 308
  submission 725
obelisk 206, 551
obesity 192
obey 743, 749
object, *n. thing* 3
  matter 316
  intention 620
object, *v. disapprove* 932
  -to *dislike* 867
objection 706, 932
objectionable
  inexpedient 647
  wrong 923
objective 6, 316
OBJECTIVENESS 6
oblation 784, 990
obligation *necessity* 601
  promise 768
  debt 806
  duty 926
obligatory 926
oblige *benefit* 707
  compel 744
obliging *helping* 707
  courteous 894
  kind 906
oblique 217
OBLIQUITY 217, 243
obliterate 2, 162, 552
OBLITERATION 552
OBLIVION 506
oblivious 506
obnoxious 898
obscure, *adj. dark* 421
  unseen 447
  unintelligible 519
  ignoble 876
obscure, *v.* 874
OBSCURITY 421, 571
  [*see obscure*]
obsequies 363
obsequious 746, 886
OBSERVANCE *rule* 82
  habit 613
  fulfillment 772
  duty 926
observant 772
observation *attention* 457
  assertion 535
observe 457, 772
observer *aviator* 269a

spectator 444
obsess *haunt* 860
obsession 481, 503, 992a
obsolete 122, 124, 851
obstacle 706
OBSTINACY 141, 606
obstinate 606
obstreperous 173
obstruct *close* 261
  hinder 706
obstructionist 710
obstructive 710
obtain 775
obtainable 470
obtrude *interfere* 228
  insert 300
obtrusion 228, 706
obtrusive *interfering* 228
  rude 895
obtuse 254, 499
obverse 234
obviate 706
obvious *visible* 446
  manifest 525
occasion *juncture* 8
  opportunity 134
  cause 153
occasional 134
occasionally 136
occult 526
occultism 526, 992a
occupancy 186, 777
occupant 188, 779
occupation *business* 625
occupier *dweller* 188
  possessor 779
occupy 186, 777
  -oneself with 625
occur *exist* 1
  happen 151
  -to the mind 451
occurrence 151
OCEAN 341
oceanic 341
octave *eight* 98
  period 108
  poetry 597
octopus *mollusk* 366
  monster 913
ocular 441
odd *remaining* 40
  exceptional 83
  single 87
  insane 503
  ridiculous 853
oddity 83, 503
odds *inequality* 28
  chance 156
  discord 713
ode 597
odious *disagreeable* 830
  hateful 898

odium *disgrace* 874
  hatred 898
ODOR 398
of course 478
offend *pain* 830
  anger 900
offense *attack* 716
  anger 900
  guilt 947
offensive *fetid* 401
  foul 653
  displeasing 830
  distasteful 867
  obnoxious 898
OFFER *volunteer* 602
  proposal 763
  give 784
offering *gift* 990
offertory 990
offhand *careless* 460
  spontaneous 612
office 170, 625, 799
officer *director* 694
  soldier 726
  commander 745
official, *n.* 694, 745
official, *adj. true* 494
  authoritative 737
officiate 625, 680
officious 682
offing *distance* 196
offset 30, 179
offshoot 39, 154
offspring *posterity* 167
often *repeated* 104
  frequent 136
ogle 441, 865
ogre 913, 980
OIL *grease* 355, 356
oily *smooth* 255
  greasy 355
ointment 356, 662
old 124, 128
  -age 128
  -maid *spinster* 904
older 128
old-fashioned 851
oldness 124
oleaginous 355
oligarchy 737
olive *color* 435
olive branch
  pacification 723
olive green 435
OMEN 512
ominous *predicting* 511
  hopeless 859
omission 53, 55, 773
omit [*see omission*]
omitted *absent* 287
omnibus 272
omnipotence *power* 157

God 976
omnipresence 1, 186
omniscience 976
omnivorous 957
on *forward* 282
once 119
one 13, 87
onerous *difficult* 704
 burdensome 706
oneself 13
one-sided 481, 923
onlooker 444
only 32
onset *beginning* 66
 attack 716
onslaught 716
ontology 1
onus *burden* 706
 duty 926
onward 282
oodles 102
ooze *emerge* 295
 flow 348
OPACITY 426
opaque 426
open, *n. begin* 66
 unclose 260
 reveal 529
open, *adj. frank* 543
 artless 703
opener 260
OPENING *beginning* 66
 opportunity 134
 aperture 260
opera *music* 415
operate *produce* 161
 act 170
 work 680
operation [*see* operate]
operative, *adj. acting* 170
operative, *n. workman* 690
operator *doer* 690
opiate 174
opine 484
opinion 484
opinionated 474, 606
OPPONENT
 antagonist 710
 enemy 891
opportune *well timed* 134
 expedient 646
opportunism 646
opportunist 605
opportunity 134, 646
oppose *be contrary* 14
 counteract 179
 front 234
 refute 468
 clash 708, 719
OPPOSITE 14, 237
OPPOSITION 708
 [*see* oppose]
oppositionist 710
oppress *molest* 649
 domineer 739
 harry 907

oppressive *hot* 382
 painful 649, 830
oppressor 739, 913
opprobrium 874
optic 420
OPTICAL 441
 -instruments 445
optics *light* 420
 optical instruments 445
optimism 858
optimist 858, 935
option 609
optional 609
opulence 803
ORACLE *prediction* 511
 prophet 513
oracular *ambiguous* 475
 wise 500
 predicting 511
oral 467, 582
ORANGE *color* 439
oration 582
orator 582
oratorical 582
oratory *speaking* 582
orb *circle* 247
orbit *circle* 247
 path 627
orchestra *musicians* 416
 instruments 417
orchestration 413
ordain *command* 741
 install 755, 995
ordained 996
ordeal 463, 828
ORDER *regularity* 58
 requirement 630
 command 741
orderly, *adj. regular* 58,
 60, 80
ordinance *command* 741
 law 963
ordinary *usual* 82
 imperfect 651
 mediocre 736
ordination *commission* 755
 church 995
ordnance 727
organ *instrument* 633
organic *structural* 329
 organized 357
organism 367
ORGANIZATION
 arrangement 60, 626
 production 161
 animated nature 357
organize *arrange* 60
 produce 161
 form 357
 plan 626
organizer 626
orgy 954
Orient *East* 236
orifice *opening* 260
origin *beginning* 66
 cause 153

original *dissimilar* 18
 not imitated 20
 model 22
 individual 79
 exceptional 83
 causal 153
 invented 515
originality [*see* original]
 will 600
originate *begin* 66
 cause 153
 invent 515
 -in 154
originative 153
originator 164
orison *request* 765
 worship 990
ORNAMENT
 in writing 577
 adornment 847
 glory 873
ornamentation 847
ornate *in writing* 577
 ornamental 847
orthodox 82, 983a
ORTHODOXY 983a
orthography 561
oscillate 314
OSCILLATION *perio-
dicity* 138
 change 149
 motion 314
osseous 323
ossify 323
ostensible *probable* 472
 manifest 525
 alleged 617
OSTENTATION 880, 882
ostentatious 880, 882
ostracism [*see* ostracize]
ostracize *exclude* 55
 banish 893
 censure 932
other *different* 15
 extra 37
otherwise 18
ottoman 215
ouija board 992a
Our Lady 977
oust *eject* 297
 dismiss 756
 deprive 789
out *exterior* 220
 -of the way
 distant 196
outbalance 33
outbound 295
outbreak *beginning* 66
 violence 173
 egress 295
 revolt 742
outburst *violence* 173
 egress 295
 rage 825
outcast 83, 876, 893
outcome *effect* 154

outcry *noise* **411**
  censure 932
outdo 33, 303
outdoor 220
outdoors 338
outer 220
outfit *clothes* **225**
outflank 236
outflow 295
outgeneral 731
outgrowth 65, 154
outhouse 191
outing 266
outlandish *foreign* 10
  barbarous 851
  ridiculous 853
outlast 110
outlaw, *n. outcast* 83
outlaw, *v. seclude* 893
outlet *opening* 260
  egress 295
OUTLINE *contour* **230**
  form 240
  features 448
  plan 626
outlines *rudiments* 66
  principles 596
outlive *survive* 110
  continue 141
outlook *view* 448
outlying *exterior* 220
outnumber 102
outpost 196, 234
output *produce* 775
outrage *violence* 173
  evil 619
  injury 659, 907
outrageous *violent* 173
  scandalous 874
outrank 33, 62
outrival 33, 303
outrun 303
outset *beginning* 66
  departure 293
outshine *glory* 873
outside 220
outsider 57, 893
outskirts *environs* 227
outspan 292
outspoken 703
outspread 202
outstanding *outside* 220
  unpaid 806
outstretched 202
outstrip 33, 280, **303**
outward 220
outweigh *exceed* 33

outwit *deceive* **545**
  defeat 731
outwork *defense* **717**
oval 247
ovation *continuity* 69
  triumph 883
oven 386
over *more* 33
  remainder 40
  ended 67
  past 122
  opposite **237**
  too much 641
  -and above
  redundance **641**
overact 855
overawe *sway* 737
  intimidate 860
overbalance 33
overbear *influence* 175
overbearing 885
overburden *fatigue* 688
overcast 421, 422
overcharge *extort* **814**
overcloud 353
overcoat 225
overcome, *v. counteract*
  179
  conquer 731
overcome, *adj. sad* **837**
overconfident *rash* 863
overdo 855
overdose 641
overdraw *exaggerate* 549
  misrepresent 555
overdue 115, 133
overeat 957
OVERESTIMATION 482
overfed 869, 957
overfeed 641
overflow 348, 641
overgrown *large* 192
  expanded 194
overhang 206, 214
overhanging 152, 306
overhaul *count* 85
  inquire 461
  censure 932
overhead 206
overhear 418
overjoyed 827
overlay *cover* 223
overload 641, 706
overlook *slight* 458
  neglect 460
  superintend 693
  forgive 918
overlord 745

overman 33
overmatch 33
overpersuade 615
overpower 179, 731
overpowering *strong* 159
overpraise *overrate* 482
  flatter 933
overrate 482
overreach 545
override *influence* 175
  pass 303
  abrogate 756
overrule *control* 737
  cancel 756
overrun *move beyond* 303
  damage 659
OVERRUNNING 303
oversee 693
overseer 694
oversensitive 822
overshadow
  darken 353, 421
  eclipse 873
overshoe 225
oversight *inattention* 458
  error 495
  superintendence 693
overstate 549, 555
overstep 303
overstock 641
overtake 292
overtask *misuse* **679**
  fatigue 688
overtax 679, 688
overthrow, *n.*
  revolution 146
overthrow, *v. destroy* 162
  level 308
  vanquish 751
overtop *surpass* 33
overture 64
overturn *revolt* 146
  invert 218
  level 308
overwhelm *ruin* 162
  thwart 706
overwork *misuse* **679**
  fatigue 688
overwrought 549
owe 806
owl *bird* 366
own *divulge* 529
  possess 777
owner *possessor* 779
ownership 777
ox *animal* 366
oxygen 359

P

pace *walk* 264
  gait 274, 275
  journey 266

  measure 466
pacific 721
PACIFICATION 174, 723

pacifism 721
pacify *allay* 723
pack, *n. assemblage* 72

burden 706
pack, v. locate 184
package 72
packet 72
pact 769
pad thicken 194
  line 224
padding lining 224
  diffuseness 573
paddle, n. oar 267
paddle, v. walk 266
paean rejoicing 838
PAGAN 984
  -deities 979
paganism 984
page 746
pageant 448, 882
pagoda 206, 1000
pail 191
PAIN physical - 378
  moral - 828
  hurt 830
painful 378, 830
PAINFULNESS 830
painless 827
painstaking active 682
  laborious 686
paint coat 223
  color 428
  delineate 556
  ornament 847
painter rope 45
  artist 559
PAINTING 556
pair, n. similar 17
  couple 89
  horses 272
pair, v. combine 48
pajamas 225
pal ally 711
  chum 890
palace 189
palanquin 272
palatable savory 394
palate 390
palatial 882
palaver colloquy 588
  council 696
pale, n. inclosure 232
  limit 233
pale, adj. dim 422
  colorless 429
palfrey 271
paling fence 232
palisade 717
palisades cliff 212
pall, v. weary 841
  satiate 869
palliate moderate 174
  relieve 834
  extenuate 937
palliative 174
pallid 429
pallor 429
palm tree 367
  trophy 733

laurel 877
  -off on 545
palmy prosperous 734
  joyous 836
palpable material 316
  obvious 446
  manifest 525
palpitate 315, 821
palter 605
paltry small 32
  unimportant 643
  mean 940
pampas 344
pamper 954
pan 191
panacea 662
pandemonium 404, 414
pander to 933
panegyric 931
panel list 86
  partition 228
  jury 967
pang 378, 828
panic 860
panorama view 448
panoramic 78
pant be hot 382
  fatigue 688
  be excited 821
  pantomimist 599
pantheism 984
Pantheon gods 979
  temple 1000
pantomime 550
pantry 191
pap pulp 354
papa father 166
papacy 995
papal 995
paper 590
  -money 800
par 27
parable 521, 537
parabola curve 245
parade procession 69
  journey 266
  ostentation 882
Paradise 981
paradox absurdity 497
  difficulty 704
paradoxical uncertain 475
  absurd 497
paragon perfect 650
  glory 873
parallel, n. 17
parallel, adj. 17, 242
parallel, v. imitate 19
  agree 23
  equal 216
PARALLELISM 17, 216,
  242
paralysis 158, 376, 823
paralyze 158, 376, 823
paramount supreme 33
parapet 717
paraphernalia 780

paraphrase imitation 19
  copy 21
  synonym 522
parasite follower 65
  puppet 711
  flatterer 935
parasol 223
parboil 384
parcel divide 44
  group 72
parch 340, 382
parched 340
parchment 590
pardon 918
pardonable 937
pare cut 38
  reduce 195
  peel 204
  divest 226
parent 166
parentage 11, 166
parental 166
parenthesis 198, 228
parenthetical 10, 228
pariah 876, 893
parish 181
parishioner 997
parity 27
park, n. 367, 840
park, v. 184
parlance 582
parley talk 588
  mediation 724
parliament 696
parliamentary 696
parlor 191
parochial regional 181
  narrow 481
parody imitation 19
  copy 21
  misrepresentation 555
  travesty 856
parole 768
  on - restraint 751
paroxysm violence 173
  agitation 315
  emotion 825
parquetry 440
parrot imitation 19
parrotism 19
parry confute 479
  avert 623
  defend 717
parsimonious 819
PARSIMONY 819
parson 996
parsonage 1000
PART, n. portion 51, 100a
  role 599
  function 625
  duty 926
part, v. divide 44
partake 778
partial unequal 28
  part 51
  fractional 100a

misjudging 481
unjust 923
partiality desire 865
  love 897
  favor 923
partially 32, 51
participate co-operate 709
  share 778
PARTICIPATION 778
participator 690
particle 32, 50, 193
particular, n. item 51
  event 151
particular, adj. special 79
  careful 494
  exact 494
  fastidious 868
particularize 79, 594
particularly 31, 33
particulars 79
parting 44
partisan follower 65
  auxiliary 711
  friend 890
partisanship 481, 709
partition divide 44
  wall 228
partly 51
partner companion 88
  auxiliary 711
partnership 88, 709
PARTY assemblage 72
  person 372
  association 712
  sociality 892
  -spirit warped judgment 481
  co-operation 709
party-colored 428, 440
parvenu 123, 734, 876
paschal 998
pass, n. predicament 7
  conjuncture 8
  interval 198
  defile 203
  way 627
  difficulty 704
  thrust 716
pass, v. be superior 33
  elapse 109, 122
  happen 151
  transfer 270
  move through 302
  vanish 449
  an examination 648
  away
  cease 2, 142
  -time 106
passable unimportant 643
  imperfect 651
  pretty 845
PASSAGE 302
  conversion 144
  corridor 191
  opening 260
  motion 264

navigation 267
transit 270
[see pass]
passenger 268
passing 31, 111
passion emotion 820
  excitability 825
  desire 865
  love 897
  anger 900
passionate impetuous 825
  irascible 901
passionless 823
passive inert 172
  obedient 743
passport 760
password 550
PAST 122
paste 352
pastime 840
pastor 996
pastoral 371
pastorate 995
pastry 396
pasture 232, 344
pat, adj. pertinent 23
pat, v. strike 276
patch change 140
  blemish 848
  -up restore 660
  compromise 774
patchwork mixture 41
  variegation 440
patent, n. 760
patent, adj. open 260
  manifest 525
pater father 166
paternal father 166
  benevolent 906
PATERNITY 166
paternoster 990
path direction 278
  way 627
pathetic 830
pathless 180
pathos 821
patience
  perseverance 604a
  endurance 826
  moderation 831
patient, n. 655
patriarch veteran 130
patriarchal 124, 166
patrician 875
patriot 910
patriotism 910
patrol safeguard 664
patrolman 664
patron auxiliary 711
  customer 795
  friend 890
patronage influence 175
  aid 707
patronize aid 707
patter, n.
  unmeaningness 517

talk 584
patter, v. strike 276
  sound 407
pattern model 22
  perfection 650
paucity 32, 103
Paul Pry 455
paunch 191, 250
pauper 640, 804
pause cessation 142
  quiescence 265
pavement 211
pavilion 189
paving 211
paw handle 379
pawn 788
pawnbroker 787
pay, n. compensation 30
  income 810
pay, v. defray 807
  remunerate 973
PAYMENT 30, 807
  remuneration 973
PEACE rest 265
  silence 403
  amity 721
peaceable 721
peaceful 174, 265, 721
peacemaker 714
peace offering 723
peace pipe 550
pea-coat 225
peak height 206
  summit 33, 210
  sharpness 253
peal 404, 407
pearly semitransparent 427
  white 430
  gray 432
peasant 876
peck, n. 31, 102
peculate 791
peculator 792
peculiar special 79
  exceptional 83
peculiarity 5
peculiarly greatly 31
  more 33
pecuniary 800
pedagogic 540
pedagogue scholar 492
  teacher 450
pedal 633
pedant 492
pedantic 855
pedantry 491, 855
peddler 797
pedestal 215
pedestrain 268
pedigree 69, 166
pedlar [see peddler]
peek 441
peel pare 204
  skin 223
  uncover 226
peep chirp 412

look 441
peer, *n. equal* 27
  lord 875
peer, *v. pry* 441
  inquire 461
peerage 875
peerless *unequaled* 28
  supreme 33
peevish *cross* 895
  irascible 901
peg 250
pelf *gain* 775
  money 803
pellet 249
pellmell 825
pellucid 425, 570
pelt, *n. skin* 223
pelt, *v. throw* 284
pen, *n. inclosure* 232
pen, *v. write* 590
  restrain 751
penal 972
penalize 974
PENALTY 974
penance 998
pendant 214
PENDENCY 214
pendulous 214
penetrate *enter* 294
  pass 302
  see through 498
  pierce 824
penetrating *sagacious* 498
  feeling 821
penetration 294
peninsula 342
PENITENCE 950
penitent 950
penitentiary 752
penknife 253
penman 590
penmanship 590
pen name 565
pennant 550
penniless 804
penny 800
pension *income* 810
pensioner 785
pensive *thoughtful* 451
  sad 837
penurious 819
penury *poverty* 804
PEOPLE, *n*
  kindred 11
  mankind 372
  commonalty 876
people, *v. inhabit* 186
peopled 186
pep 171
pepper, *n.* 392
pepper, *v. attack* 716
peppery *irascible* 901
perambulate 266
perceive
  be sensible of 375
  see 441

know 490
percentage 84, 813
perceptible 446
perception *idea* 453
  knowledge 490
perceptive 375
perchance 470
percolate *ooze out* 295
  stream 348
percussion 276
perdition *destruction* 162
  ruin 732
peremptory
  authoritative 737
  rigorous 739
  compulsory 744
perennial 69, 110
perfect, *adj. entire* 52
  excellent 650
  beautiful 845
perfect, *v.* 729
PERFECTION 650
perfidy 940
perforate 252, 260
perforation 260
PERFORATOR 262
perforce 744
perform *produce* 161
  do 170
  –*music* 415, 416
  act 599, 680
  achieve 729
performance *effect* 154
  achievement 161
  music 416
  action 599
  [*see* perform]
performer *musician* 416
  actor 599
  agent 690
perfume 400
perfumery 400
perfunctory 53
perhaps *possible* 470
peril 665
perimeter 230
PERIOD *end* 67, 142
  –*of time* 106, 108
periodical, *n* 593
periodical, *adj.* **138**
PERIODICITY 138
peripatetic 266, 268
periphery 230
perish *cease to exist* 2
  be destroyed 162
  die 360
perishable 111
periwig 225
perjurer 548
perjury 544
PERMANENCE
  uniformity 16
  durability 110
  unchangeableness **141**, 150
permanent 110, **141**, 150

permeate *pervade* 186
  pass through 302
permissible 760
PERMISSION 760
permit 760
pernicious 649
peroration 65
perpendicular 212
perpetrate 680
perpetrator 690
perpetual 112, 136, 143
perpetually 16, **112**, **136**
perpetuate 112
  continue 143
  establish 150
PERPETUITY 112
perplex *distract* 458
  puzzle **475**
perplexity *uncertainty* 475
  difficulty 704
perquisite 973
persecute *annoy* 830
  oppress 907
PERSEVERANCE
  continuance 143
  persistence **604a**
persevere 143, **604a**
persiflage 842, 856
persist *endure* 106
  remain 141
  continue 143
  persevere 604a
persistence 110, 141, 143
persistent 110, 141, 604a
person *substantiality* 3
  man 372
personal [*see* person]
  special 79
  subjective 317
  –*property* 780
personality
  [*see* personal]
  person 317
  censure 932
personality 780
personate *represent* **554**
personify *represent* 554
personnel 56, 690
perspective *view* 448
perspicacity
  intelligence 498
  fastidiousness 868
PERSPICUITY 570
perspiration 299
persuade *convince* **484**
  induce 615
persuasion *opinion* 484
  inducement 615
persuasive 615
pert *vain* 880
  insolent 885
  discourteous 895
pertain to *relate to* 9
  included under 76
  belong to 777
pertinacity 604a

pertinent *relative* 9
  congruous 23
perturbation *agitation* 315
  excitation 824, 825
  fear 860
peruse 539
pervade *influence* 175
  extend 186
perverse *reactionary* 283
  obstinate 606
  sulky 901a
perversion *sophistry* 477
  misinterpretation 523
  misteaching 538
  falsehood 544
perversity [see perverse]
pervert *quibble* 477
  distort 523
pervious 260
pessimism *dejection* 837,
  859
pessimist 482, 862, 859
pest *bane* 663
pester 830
pestilence 655
pestle 330
pet, *n. favorite* 899
  anger 900
pet, *v. love* 897
  fondle 902
petal 367
petition *ask* 765
  pray 990
PETITIONER 767
pet name 565
petrify *thicken* 321
  harden 323
  organization 357
  thrill 824
  astonish 870
petroleum 356
petticoat 225
pettifogger 968
pettifogging 477
pettish 901
petty 643
  -cash 800
petulance 901
petulant 901
pew 191
pewter 41
phalanx 712, 726
phantasm 443
phantom *unreality* 4
  specter 980a
pharisaical 544, 988
Pharisee 988
pharmacy 662
phase *aspect* 8
  apperance 448
phenomenon *event* 151
  prodigy 872
phial 191
philander 902
philanderer 902
philanthropic 906, 910

philanthropist 906, 910
PHILANTHROPY 906,
  910
Philistine 82
philosopher 500
philosophical
  thoughtful 451
  calm 826
philosophy *intellect* 450
  calmness 826
phlegmatic 823
phonetic *sonant* 402
  tonic 561
  voice 580
  vocal 582
phonograph 418
phonography 402
phosphorescence *light* 420
  luminary 423
phosphorus 423
photograph 554
photographer 554
photography 554, 556
PHRASE 566
phraseology 569
physic *remedy* 662
physical 316
  -pain 378
  -pleasure 377
physician 662, 695
physics 316
physiognomy 234
physiology 357, 359
physique 159, 364
piazza 189
picayune 643
pick, *n. best* 648
pick, *v. select* 609
  -a quarrel 713
  -up *learn* 539
  get better 658
  gain 775
pickaninny 129
picket, *n. fence* 229
  guard 668
picket, *v. join* 43
  locate 184
  restrain 751
pickings *gain* 775
  booty 793
pickle 670
pickpocket 792
picnic 298, 840
pictorial 556
picture *appearance* 448
  representation 554
  painting 556
picture gallery 556
picturesque 556, 845
pie 396
piebald 440
piece, *n. bit* 51
piece, *v.* 140
  cannon 727
  -together 43
piecemeal 51

pied 440
pierce *perforate* 260
  chill 385
  wound 659
  affect 824
piercer 262
piercing *cold* 383
  shrill 410
  acute 821
PIETY 987
pig *animal* 366
  glutton 954a
pigeonhole, *n.* 191
pigeonhole, *v. shelve* 460
piggish 954
pigment 428
pigmy [see pygmy]
pike 727
pikestaff 206
pilaster 215
pile *heap* 72
  edifice 161
pilfer *steal* 791
pilferer 792
pilgrim 268, 996
pilgrimage *journey* 266
  undertaking 676
pill 249
pillage *theft* 791
pillar 206, 215
pillory 975
pillow 215
pilot 269, 269a
pimple 250
pin 43
pinch, *n. emergency* 8
  need 630
  difficulty 704
pinch, *v. contract* 195
  chill 385
pinched [see pinch]
  thin 203
pine *mope* 837
  -for 865
pinion *restrain* 751
  fetter 752
pink, *adj.* 434
pink, *v. pierce* 260
pinnace 273
pinnacle 210
pioneer *precursor* 64
pious 987
pipe, *n. tube* 260
pipe, *v. sound* 410
piper 416
piquant *pungent* 392
  impressive 821
pique *excite* 824
  pain 830
  hate 898
piracy 773
pirate, *n.* 792
pirate, *v. plagiarize* 788
pirouette 312
pistol 727
piston 263

pit 208, 252
pitch *degree* 26
 obliquity 217
 descent 306
 musical - 413
pitch, *v. erect* 212
 throw 284
 plunge 310
 reel 314
pitchfork *throw* 284
piteous *painful* 830
PITFALL 667
pith *gist* 5
 meaning 516
pithy *concise* 572
 vigorous 574
pitiable *bad* 649
 painful 830
 contemptible 930
pitiful *bad* 649
 mean 874
 pitying 914
pitiless 914a
PITILESSNESS 914a
pittance *quantity* 25
 dole 640
PITY 914
pivot *junction* 43
 cause 153
pivotal 222
placard 531
placate *pacify* 723
 conciliate 918
PLACE, *n.*
 situation 182, 183
 abode 189
 office 625
place, *v. arrange* 60
 locate 184
 invest 787
placid 826
plagiarism 19, 791
plagiarist 792
plagiarize 788, 791
plague, *n.* 655
plague, *v. worry* 830
plaid 440
PLAIN, *n.* 251, 344
plain, *adj. clear* 446
 manifest 525
 lucid 576
 homely 846
 simple 849
 -speaking
 candor 525
plainly 525
PLAINNESS 576, 849
plaint *cry* 411
 lament 839
plaintiff 938
plaintive 839
plait 219, 258
PLAN *map* 183
 scheme 626
planchette 992a
plane 251, 255

planet 318
plank *platform* 626
PLANT, *n, shrub* 367
 property 780
 management of - 371
plant, *v.* 184, 300
plantation *location* 184
 estate 780
planter 188
plash 348, 408
plaster 45, 223
plastic 240
plate, *n. dish* 191
 coating 204
plate, *v. cover* 223
plateau 251, 344
platform *support* 215
 stage 542
 scheme 626
platitude 843
platoon 726
platter *receptacle* 191
plaudit 931
plausible *probable* 472
 vindicative 937
play, *n. scope* 180
 drama 599
 freedom 748
 amusement 840
play, *v. operate* 170
 music 416
 sport 840
 -truant 623
player *musician* 416
 actor 599
playfellow 890
playful 836
playground 728
playing field 728
playmate 890
plaything *trifle* 643
 toy 840
playwright 599
PLEA *answer* 462
 argument 476
 excuse 617
 vindication 937
plead *answer* 462
 argue 467, 968
 allege 617
 beg 765
pleader *lawyer* 968
pleadings 969
pleasant *agreeable* 829
 amusing 840
pleasantry 842
please 377, 829
 if you - 765
 -oneself 943
pleased 827
pleasing 394, 829
PLEASURABLENESS
 829
PLEASURE *physical -* 377
 moral - 827
pleat 258

plebeian 876
plebiscite 480, 609
pledge, *n. promise* 768
 security 771
pledge, *v. borrow* 788
plenipotentiary 758
plenitude 639
plenteous 639
plenty *sufficient* 639
plethora 641
pliable 324
pliant *soft* 324
 irresolute 605
 servile 886
plight *state* 7
 circumstance 8
 promise 768
plinth 211
plod *journey* 266
 be slow 275
 work 682
plodder *worker* 686
plodding 682
plot *-of ground* 181
 scheme 626
plough [*see* plow]
plow 259
pluck, *n. resolution* 604
 grit 604a
 courage 861
pluck, *v. take* 789
plucky 604, 861
plug, *n.* 263
plug, *v. close* 261, 348
plumage 256
plumb, *adj. vertical* 212
 straight 246
plumb, *v. measure* 466
plume *feather* 256
plummet 208
plump *fat* 192
plumpness 192
plunder, *n. gain* 35
 booty 793
plunder, *v.* 791
PLUNGE *depth* 208
 dive 310
PLURALITY 33, 100
plutocrat 639
pluvial 348
ply *use* 677
 exert 686
pneumatics 334, 338
poach *steal* 791
poacher 792
pocket, *n.* 191
pocket, *v. receive* 785
 take 789
pocketbook 802
pocket money 800
poem 597
poet 597
poetic 597
poetize 597
POETRY 597
poignant 378

point *small* 32
  end 67
  place 182
  sharpness **253**
  topic 454
  mark 550
  intention 620
  wit 842
  -at *direct attention* 457
  disparage 929
  -of view 441
  -out *indicate* 79
  -to *direct* 278
  predict 511
point-blank *direct* 278
  plain 576
pointed *sharp* 253
  marked 550
  concise 572
pointedly 620
pointer 550
pointless 254
poise *balance* 27
  weight 319
  inexcitability 826
poison 659, 663
  -gas 727
poisonous 657
poke 191
polar 210
  -lights **423**
polarity 89, 237
pole *pikestaff* **206**
  axis 222
  oar 267
polemic 713
polestar *attraction* 288
  luminary 423
  indication 550
police 965
policeman 664
policy 626, 692
polish, *n. smooth* 255
  gloss 332
  taste 850
  politeness 894
polish, *v. rub* 331
  furbish 658
polished *fashionable* 852
  polite 894
polite 894
politeness 894
politic *wise* 498
  cautious 864
politician 694, 700
politics 702
polity 926
poll *count* 85
  list 86
  vote 609
pollute *soil* 653
  corrupt 659
pollution *disease* 655
poltroon 862
pommel, *n.* 215

pommel, *v. beat* 972
pomp 882
pompom 727
pomposity 878, 882
pompous *inflated* 577
  proud 878
  ostentatious 882
pond 343
ponder 451
ponderous *heavy* 319
poniard 727
pontiff 996
pontificate 995
pony 271
  translation 522
poodle 366
pool, *n. lake* 343
pool, *v. co-operate* 709
poor *feeble* 477
  insufficient 640
  indigent 804
  -man **640, 804**
poorness [*see poor*]
  inferiority 34
pop *noise* 406
pope 996
popinjay 854
populace 876
popular *choosing* 609
  desirable 865
  celebrated 873
  approved 931
popularize 518
population 188, 372
populous 72, 102, 186
porch 66, 191, 260
pore, *n.* 260
pore over
  apply the mind 457
  learn 539
porous 252, 295, 322
port *harbor* 189, 666
  left 239
  gait 448
portable 270
portage 270
portal 66, 260
portend 511
portent 512
portentous *prophetic* 511
  fearful 860
porter 263, 271
portfolio *case* 191
  authority 747
  jurisdiction 965
portico 191
portion *part* 51
  allotment 786
portly 192
portmanteau 191
  -word **572**
portrait 554, **556**
portraiture 554
portray 554
pose, *n. situation* 183
  form 240

pose, *v. inquire* 461
  puzzle 475
  affect 855
poser 855
position *circumstances* 8
  situation 183
  post 625
  status 873
positive *real* 1
  great 31
  certain 474
  narrow-minded 481
  assertive 535
posse 72
possess 777, 780
  bedevil 978, 992
POSSESSION **777, 780**
POSSESSOR 779
POSSIBILITY *chance* 156
  liability 177
  likelihood 470
possible 177, 470
post, *n. situation* 183
  support 215
  mail 534
  employment 625
post, *v. list* 86
  send 270
  publish 531
  enter accounts 811
postal 592
post card 592
postdate 115
poster 531
posterior *in time* 117
  in space 235
POSTERIORITY 117
POSTERITY 121, 167
posthaste *swiftly* 274
  rash 863
posthumous 117, 133
postilion *rider* 268
postman 271, 534
post-mortem 363
post office 534
postpone 133, 460
postscript 37, 65
posture *situation* 183
  form 240
posy *bouquet* 400
pot *mug* 191
potency 157
potent 157, 159
potentate 745
potential 2, 157
potentiality *power* 157
  possibility 470
potion *beverage* 298
potpourri *mixture* 41
pouch 191
poultry 366
pounce upon *attack* 716
  seize 789
pound *bruise* 330
  -the piano 416
pour *emerge* 295

rain 348
pout 250, 901a
POVERTY
  insufficiency 640
  indigence 804
powder 330
  gunpowder 727
POWDERINESS 330
powdery 330
POWER number 84
  efficacy 157
  influence 175
  authority 737
powerful 157, 159
powerless 158, 160
practicable possible 470
  practical 646
practical acting 170
  practicable 646
practically 5
practice, n. training 537
  exertion 686
  conduct 692
practice, v. train 537
  use 677
  act 680
practiced skilled 698
practitioner general - 662
  doer 690
pragmatic practical 646
pragmatism 646
prairie space 180
  plain 344
praise 931, 990
praiseworthy 931
prance leap 309
  dance 315
prank caprice 608
prate 584
prattle talk 582
  chatter 584
pray beg 765
  worship 990
prayer request 765
  worship 990
preach 537
preacher teacher 540
  priest 996
preamble 62, 64
precarious transient 111
  dangerous 665
precaution care 459
  safety 664
  preparation 673
precede be superior 33
  forerun 62, 280
PRECEDENCE 62, 280
  rank 873
precedent prototype 22
  habit 613
  legal decision 969
PRECEDING 280
PRECEPT
  requirement 630
  maxim 697
preceptor 540

precinct 181, 227
precious great 31
  valuable 814
  beloved 897
  -metals 800
precipice 212
precipitancy haste 684
  rashness 863
precipitate, adj. early 132
  rash 863
precipitate, v. sink 308
precipitous 217
precise 494
precisely 19
preclude 706
preclusive 55
precocious 132, 674
preconception 481
PRECURSOR 64
predatory 789
predecessor 64
predesigned 611
predestinate 976
predestination 611, 976
predestine 976
PREDETERMINATION
  611
predicament 7, 8, 43
predicate 514
predict 507, 511
PREDICTION 511
predilection bias 481
  affection 820
predispose 615
predominance 157
predominant 157
predominate 33, 175
pre-eminent superior 33
  celebrated 873
pre-exist 116
preface 62, 64
prefer choose 609
preference 62
prefix 62
pregnant 642
prehistoric 124
prejudge 481
prejudice 481
prejudicial 649
prelacy 995
prelate 996
preliminary, n. 64, 296
preliminary adj. 673
prelude 62, 64
premature early 132
  unripe 674
premeditate 611
premier 759
premise 62
premises ground 182
  evidence 467
  logic 476
premium 810, 973
premonish 668
premonition 668, 992a
premonitory 511, 668

preoccupation 458
PREPARATION 60, **673**
  instruction 537
preparatory 673
prepare 537, 673
preparedness 673
preponderance
  superiority 33
  influence 175
prepossessing 829
prepossession
  prejudice 481
preposterous absurd 497
  imaginative 515
  ridiculous 853
  improper 925
prerogative 924
prescribe advise 695
  order 741
  entitle 924
prescription decree 741
  remedy 662
prescriptive 924
PRESENCE 1, **186**
  -of mind 864
present, n. gift 784
present, v. offer 763
  give 784
PRESENT, adj.
  -in time 118
  -in space **186**
  -events 151
  -time 118
presentable 845
presentiment 481, **510**
presently 132, 507
PRESERVATION
  continuance 141
  conservation 670
preserve continue 143
  keep 670, 976
preserver 670
preside 693
presidency 737
president, 694, 745
press, n. newspapers **531**
press, v. crowd 72
  smooth 255
  weigh 319
  offer 763
  solicit 765
pressing urgent 642
pressure
  influence 175
  weight 319
  urgency 642
  adversity 735
presto instantly 113
presumable 472
presume 472, 514
presumption probability
  472
  rashness 863
  arrogance 885
presumptive 924
presumptuous 885

improving 658
prohibit 761
PROHIBITION 761
 exclusion 55
prohibitionist 958
prohibitive 55, 761
project *bulge* 250
 impel 284
 intend 620
 plan 626
projectile 284, 727
projecting 214, 250
projection 250, 283
projector *promoter* 626
proletariat 876
prolific 168
prolix 573
prolixity 573
prologue 64, 599
prolong *protract* 110
 delay 133
 continue 143
 lengthen 200
prolongation 117
 [see prolong]
prolonged 110
promenade *walk* 266
prominence
 [see prominent]
prominent *convex* 250
 important 642
 eminent 873
promiscuous *mixed* 41
 indiscriminate 465a
PROMISE 768
promissory 768
 -note *security* 771
promontory 206
promote *improve* 658
promoter *planner* 626
promotion 541, 658
prompt, adj. *early* 132
 active 682
prompt, v. *remind* 505
 tell 527
promulgate 531
prone *horizontal* 213
 disposed 820
proneness *tendency* 176
 disposition 820
prong 91
pronounce *judge* 480
 assert 535
 voice 580
 speak 582
pronounced 525
pronouncement 531
pronunciation 580
proof *test* 463
 demonstration 478
 printing 591
 -against 664
prop *support* 215
propaganda 673
propagate 161
propel 284

propensity *tendency* 176
 inclination 820
proper *individual* 79
 due 924
PROPERTY 342, 780
prophecy 511
prophet *seer* 513
prophetic 511
prophylactic *healthful* 656
 preventive 706
propinquity 197
propitiate *pacify* 723
 mediate 724
 atone 952, 976
propitiator 724
propitiatory 952
propitious *timely* 134
 prosperous 734
 auspicious 858
proportion *relation* 9
 symmetry 242
proportions *space* 180
 size 192
proposal 763, 765
propose *suggest* 514
 offer 763
 offer marriage 902
proposition *supposition* 454
 reasoning 476
 project 626
 offer 763
propound *suggest* 514
proprietor 779
propriety *agreement* 23
 elegance 578
 fashion 852
 duty 926
PROPULSION 284
propulsive 284
prorogue 133
prosaic *sober* 576
 dull 843
proscribe *interdict* 761
 curse 908
 condemn 971
PROSE, n. 598
prose, v. 584
prosecute *pursue* 622
 arraign 969
prosecutor 938
proselyte 144, 607
prospect *destiny* 152
 futurity 121
 view 448
 expectation 507
prospector 463
prospective 120, 507
prospectus *list* 86
 scheme 626
prosper 618, 734
PROSPERITY 734
prostrate, adj. *powerless* 158
 low 207
 horizontal 213, 251

submissive 725
 dejected 837
prostrate, v. *depress* 308
prostration
 [see prostrate]
 sickness 655
prosy *weary* 841
 dull 843
protect 664
protection *influence* 175
 defense 717
protectionist 751
protective 717
protector 664, 717, 912
protectorate 737
protest *dissent* 489
 deprecate 766
 not pay 808
protestant
 dissenting 489
protoplasm 357
PROTOTYPE 22
protract *prolong* 110
 delay 133
 lengthen 200
protrude 250
protrusive 250
protuberance 250
proud *dignified* 873
 lofty 878
prove *arithmetic* 85
 demonstrate 478
 indicate 550
proverb 496
proverbial 490
provide *furnish* 637
provided 8, 469
providence 976
provident *careful* 459
 prepared 673
providential
 opportune 134
 fortunate 734
province *department* 75
 region 181
 office 625
provincial *rural* 189
 narrow 481
provincialism 563
PROVISION *food* 298
 supply 637
 preparation 673
provisional
 conditional 8, 770
 temporary 111
 contingent 134
proviso 469, 770
provocation 900
provoke *cause* 153
 excite 824
 vex 830
 anger 900
prow 234
prowess 861
prowl *walk* 266
 lurk 528

Q

revolt *revolution* 146
 rebellion 742
 shock 830
REVOLUTION
 periodicity 138
 change **146**
 rotation 312
 rebellion 742
revolutionary 146, 742
revolutionize 140, **146**
revolve 138, 312
revolver 727
revulsion *reversion* 145
 recoil 277
REWARD 30, **973**
rhapsody 515
rhetoric *speech* 582
rhetorical 577
rhyme 597
rhythm 104, 138
 verse 597
rhythmic 413, 578
rib 250
ribald 851
ribaldry 908
ribbon 205
rich *abundant* **639**
 wealthy 803
 -man **639**, **803**
riches 803
richly *much* 31
rickety *weak* 160
ricochet 277
RIDDANCE 672, 776, **782**
riddle, n. *sieve* 260
 secret 533
 enigma 519
ride 266
 -a horse 370
rider *appendix* 39
 equestrian 268
ridge 206, 250
ridicule 856
ridiculous *absurd* 497
 foolish 499
 grotesque 853
RIDICULOUSNESS 853
riding
 journey 266
rife 78, 175
riffraff 876, **949**
rifle, n. 727
rifle, v. *plunder* 791
rift *fissure* 44, 198
rig *dress* 225
 prepare 673
rigging *ropes* 45
right, n. *justness* **922**
 privilege **924**
right, adj. *dextral* 238
 straight 246
 true 494
 proper **924**
 fitting **926**
 virtuous 944
righteous *virtuous* 944

rightful 922
right-handed 238
rigid *regular* 82
 hard 328
 exact 494
rigor 739
rigorous *exact* 494
 severe 739
rile 830
rill 348
rim 231
rind *covering* 223
ring, n. *circle* 247
 clique 712
 arena 728
ring, v. *resound* 408
ringleader 694
ringlet 256
rinse 652
riot *confusion* 59
 violence 173
 mutiny 742
rioter 742
riotous 173
rip *open* 260
ripe 673
ripen *perfect* 650
 prepare 673
ripple 315
 murmur 405
rise *ascend* 35, 305
 begin 66
 revolt 146, 742
 slope 217
rising 305 [*see* rise]
risk, 621, 665
RITE 998
ritual *ceremony* 882
 worship 990
 rite 998
ritualism 998
rival, n. 710
rival, v. *emulate* 648
 oppose 708
 compete 720
 outshine **873**
rivalry 708
rive 44
RIVER 348
rivet *fasten* 43
rivulet 348
road 278, 627
roadstead 666
roadster 272
roadway 627
roam 266
roan *color* 433
roar *be violent* **173**
 sound 404
 bellow 411, 412
 laugh 838
roast 384
rob *plunder* 791
robber 792
robbery 791
robe *dress* **225**

robust *strong* 159
 healthy 654
rock, n. 342, 667
rock, v. *oscillate* 314
rocket *signal* 550
rocky 323
rod *support* 315
 scourge **975**
rogue 941
roguery 940
roguish *playful* 840
roisterer 887
role *drama* 599
 conduct 692
ROLL, n. *list* **86**
 sound 407
 convolution 248
 rotundity 249
 rotate 312
 flow 348
roll, v. *make smooth* 255
 move 264
 wallow 311
roll call 85
roller 255
rollers *billows* 348
rollick 836
romance, n.
 imagination 515
 fiction 546, 594
romance, v. 497
romantic *imaginative* 515
 descriptive 594
 sentimental 822
romanticism 515
romp 309, 840
Röntgen ray 420
roof *house* 189
 summit 210
 cover 223
rookie 726
rookery *nests* 189
room *space* 180
 chamber 191
roommate 890
roomy 180
roost 189, 215
rooster 366
root *algebraic* - **84**
 cause 153
 place 184
 base 211
 -out *eject* 297
 -up *extract* 301
rooted *old* 124
 firm 150
 located 184
rope *cord* 205
ropy 352
rosary 998
rose *fragrance* 400
 red 434
roseate *red* 434
 hopeful 858
rosin *resin* 356a
roster

S

set out 293
sailor 269
saint 987
saintly *virtuous* 944
   pious 987
salable 796
salary 775, 973
SALE 796
salesman 758
salesmanship 796
salient *projecting* 250
   sharp 253
   manifest 525
sallow *yellow* 436
sally, *n. attack* 716
   wit 842
sally, *v. issue* 293
salmon-colored 434
salon 191
saloon 191
salt, *adj. pungent* 392
salt, *v. preserve* 670
salubrity 656
salutary *healthful* 656
salutation [*see* salute]
salute *accost* 586
   greet 894
salvation 976, 987
salve *remedy* 662
salver 191
salvo 406
same 13
sameness 13, 16
samovar 191
sample 82
sanatorium 189, 662
sanctification 976
sanctify 976, 987
sanctimony 988
sanction 924
sanctitude 987
sanctity 987
sanctuary 666
sanctum *chamber* 191
sand *powder* 330
   resolution 604
sandal 225
sandy *red* 434
sane 502
sang-froid 871
sangraal 998
sanguinary 361
sanguine *red* 434
   hopeful 858
sanitarium 189, 662
sanitary 656
SANITY 502
sap, *n.* 333
sap, *v. weaken* 160
   excavate 252
sapper *excavator* 252
   soldier 726
sapphire 438
sarcasm 932, 934
sarcastic 856, 932
sash 247

SATAN 978
satanic *diabolic* 978
satchel 191
sate 869
satellite *companion* 88
   heavenly body 318
satiate 869, 957
SATIETY 869
satire *metaphor* 521
   ridicule 856
satirical 521, 856, 932
satirize 856, 932
satisfaction [*see* satisfy]
satisfactory 831
   [*see* satisfy]
   good 648
satisfy *convince* 484
   suffice 639
   gratify 829
   satiate 869
saturate *fill* 52
   moisten 339
   satiate 869
sauce 393
saucepan 191
saucer 191
saucy *insolent* 885
   flippant 895
saunter *ramble* 266
   dawdle 275
savage, *n.* 913
savage, *adj. violent* 173
   brave 861
   angry 900
   malevolent 907
savagery 907
savanna 344
savant *learned man* 492
   sage 500
save, *adv. except* 38
save, *v. preserve* 670
   deliver 672
   economize 817
savings *economy* 817
savior *benefactor* 912
Saviour 976
savor 390
SAVORINESS 394
savory 390, 394
saw, *n. notch* 257
   adage 496
saw, *v. cut* 44
say *assert* 535
   express 560
   speak 582
saying *maxim* 496
   assertion 535
scabbard 191
scaffold *support* 215
   execution 975
scald *burn* 382
scale, *n. series* 69
   slice 204
   skin 223
   weight 319
   gamut 413

   measure 466
scale, *v. mount* 305
scallop *notch* 257
scalp 226
scaly 223
scamp, *n. rascal* 949
scamp, *v. neglect* 460
scamper *speed* 274
scan *see* 441
   attend to 457
   inquire 461
scandal *news* 532
   obloquy 934
scandalize 932
scandalmonger 532
scandalous 874
scant *small* 32
   few 103, 137
   narrow 203
scanty [*see* scant]
scapegoat 147
scapegrace 949
scar *blemish* 848
scarce *few* 103
   infrequent 137
   insufficient 640
scarcely 32, 137
scarcity 103, 640
scare 860
scarecrow 846
scarf 225
scarlet 434
scathe 649
scatheless *perfect* 650
scatter *derange* 61
   disperse 73
   diverge 291
scatterbrained 458
scavenger 652
scene *appearance* 448
   drama 599
   excitement 825
scenery 448, 599
scenic 599, 882
scent *smell* 398, 400
   trail 551
scentless 399
SCEPTER 747
sceptic [*see* skeptic]
scepticism
   [*see* skepticism]
schedule 86, 611
scheme *plan* 626
schemer 702
schism *dissent* 489
   heterodoxy 984
SCHOLAR
   learned man 492, 873
   learner 541
scholarly 539
scholarship 539
scholastic 490, 537, 542
SCHOOL *herd* 72
   academy 542
schoolbook 542
schoolboy *lad* 129

learner 541
schoolfellow 541
schoolgirl 129, 541
schoolmaster 540
schoolmate 541, 890
schoolmistress 540
schoolroom 191, 542
schooner 273
science *knowledge* 490
  skill 698
scientific *exact* 494
scientist 492
scimitar 727
scintilla *particle* 193
  spark 420, 423
scintillate
  [see scintillation]
  be brilliant 498
scintillation *heat* 382
  light 420
  wit 842
scion *part* 51
scissors 253
scoff *deride* 929, 988
  -at 932
scold, *n. shrew* 901
scold, *v. denounce* 908
  censure 932
scollop *notch* 257
scoop *hollow out* 252
scope *degree* 26
  extent 180
  freedom 748
scorch 382
scorching *violent* 178
score *list* 86
  twenty 98
  furrow 259
  music 415
scorn 930
scoundrel 949
scour *rub* 331
  clean 652
SCOURGE 975
scout, *n. vanguard* 234
  aviator 269a
  spectator 444
  patrol 664
scout, *v. reject* 610
  disregard 930
scowl *complain* 839
  frown 895
  sulk 901a
scraggy 241
scramble *climb* 305
  contend 720
scrap *small* 32
  piece 51
scrape, *n. difficulty* 704
  mischance 732
scrape, *v. pare* 38
  reduce 195
  pulverize 330
  abrade 331
  clean 652
scratch, *n.* 619

scratch, *v. abrade* 331
  write 590
  wound 649
scrawl 517
scream *blow* 349
  cry 411
  wail 839
screech 411
screen, *n. sieve* 260
  shade 424
  hider 530
  defense 717
screen, *v. hide* 528
  shelter 666
screw, *n. distortion* 243
  propeller 267
screw, *v. fasten* 43
  distort 243
scribble 517, 590
scribe 590
scrimmage 713
script 590
scriptural 983a, 985
Scripture 985
scroll *list* 86
scrub, *adj. short* 201
scrub, *v. rub* 331
  clean 652
scruple *doubt* 485
  reluctance 603
scrupulous *careful* 459
  exact 494
  reluctant 603
  fastidious 868
  punctilious 939
scrutiny *attention* 457
  inquiry 461
scud *sail* 267
  speed 274
scuffle 720
scull *row* 267
sculptor 559
SCULPTURE *form* 240
  carving 557
scum *foam* 353
scurrilous 929
scurry *haste* 274
scuttle *destroy* 162
  speed 274
scythe 253
sea *ocean* 341
  at - *uncertain* 475
seacoast 342
seafarer 269
seafaring 267, 273
seagirt 346
seagoing 267
seal, *n. matrix* 22
  mark 550
seal, *v. close* 261
  complete 729
seam 43
seaman 269
séance 525, 992a
sear *dry* 340
  burn 384

deaden 823
search 461
searching 739
searchlight 423, 550
seashore 342
season, *n.* 106
season, *v. mix* 41
  spice 392
  accustom 613
seasonable *early* 132
  opportune 134
seasoning *condiment* 393
seat *place* 183
  support 215
seaweed 367
secede *dissent* 489
  disobey 742
seceder 984
Secessionist 742
seclude 893
SECLUSION 893
second, *n. instant* 113
second, *adj.* 90
second, *v. abet* 707
secondary *inferior* 34
seconder 711
second-rate 34, 651
secrecy 528
SECRET, *n.* 533
secret, *adj. latent* 526
secretary *desk* 191
  recorder 553
  writer 590
  servant 746
secrete *conceal* 528
secretion 299
secretive 528
sect 75
  religious - 984
sectarian 489, 984
sectarianism 984
sectary 489, 984
section *division* 44
  class 75
  troops 726
sector *part* 51
secular 997
secure, *adj.* 664
secure, *v. fasten* 43
  bespeak 132
  restrain 751
  gain 775
securities 802
SECURITY *safety* 664
  pledge 771
sedan 272
sedan chair 272
sedate *thoughtful* 451
  calm 826
  grave 837
sedative 174
sedentary 265
sediment 321, 653
sedition 742
seditionist 891
seduction 829

seductive 288, 829
sedulous *active* 682
  desirous 865
see, *n. bishopric* 995
see, *v. view* 441
  look 457
  know 490
seed *cause* 153
  grain 330
seedy *weak* 160
  exhausted 688
  needy 804
seeing 441
  -that 476
seek *inquire* 461
  pursue 622
seem 448
seemly *expedient* 646
  due 924
seep 295, 337
seer *oracle* 513
seesaw 12
seethe *moisten* 339
  simmer 382
  boil 384
  fume 824
segment 51
segregate 44
segregated 47
seine *net* 232
seize *take* 789
  -an opportunity 134
seizure 315, 925
seldom 137
select *specify* 79
  choose 609
selection 75
self *identity* 13
  -assertion 885
  -command
    resolution 604
  -conscious 855
  -control 604, 826
  -convicted 950
  -deceit *error* 495
  -deception 495
  -defense 717
  -delusion 486, 347
  -denial 604, 942
  -determination 737, 748
  -educated 490
  -esteem 878
  -government 737
  -importance 878
  -indulgence
    intemperance 954
  -interest 943
  -luminous 423
  -moving 266
  -possessed 852
  -possession
    inexcitability 826
    caution 864
  -preservation 717
  -reliance
    resolution 604

  courage 861
  -reproach 950
  -respect 878
  -restraint 826
  -sacrifice 942
  -satisfied 880
  -seeker 943
  -seeking 943
  -sufficiency 880
  -sufficient 880
selfish 943
SELFISHNESS 911, 943
selfsame 13
sell *vend* 796
seller 796
selvage 231
semblance *similarity* 17
  imitation 19
  copy 21
semester 108
semicircle 247
semifluid 352
SEMILIQUIDITY 352
seminar 542
seminary 542
SEMITRANSPARENCY 427
senate 72, 696
senator 696
send *transfer* 270
  propel 284
senile 128, 158
senior 128
seniority 128
sensation 375
sensational 824
SENSATIONS OF TOUCH 380
sense *wisdom* 498
  meaning 516
senseless *insensible* 376
  absurd 497
  foolish 499
  unmeaning 517
senses *sanity* 502
SENSIBILITY
  physical - 375
  moral - 822
sensible *wise* 498
sensitive 375, 822
SENSITIVENESS 822
sensual 954
SENSUALIST 954a
sensuous 821
sentence *decision* 480
  phrase 566
  judgment 969
  condemnation 971
sententious *concise* 572
  taciturn 585
sentient - *physically* 375
  -*morally* 821
sentiment *idea* 453
sentimental *sensitive* 822
  affected 855
sentinel 263, 668

sentry 668
separable 44
separate *disjoin* 44
  bisect 91
  diverge 291
  divorce 782
separation 54, 55, 905
septic 655, 657, 662
sepulcher 363
sepulchral 408
SEQUEL *adjunct* 39
  following 65
  -*in time* 117
  sequence 281
SEQUENCE
  -*in order* 63
  -*in time* 117
  motion 281
sequester *take* 789
  confiscate 974
seraph 977
Seraphim 977
serenade 415
serene *calm* 826
serf *slave* 746
serfdom 749
sergeant 745
serial *continuous* 69
  periodic 138
series *continuity* 69
serious *important* 642
  sedate 837
sermon 537, 998
serpent *snake* 366
serpentine 248
serrated *notched* 257
serried *dense* 321
serum *lymph* 333
SERVANT *minister* 631
  help 711
  retainer 746
serve *benefit* 618
  officiate 625
  avail 644
  aid 707
  help 746
service *good* 618
  utility 644
  use 677
  warfare 722
  servitude 749
  worship 990
serviceable
  instrumental 631
  useful 644, 746
servile *serving* 746
  obsequious 879, 886
SERVILITY 886
  [*see* servile]
servitude 749
session 696
sessions *law* 966
set, *n. group* 72
  class 75
  tendency 176
  direction 278

shoals *rocks* 667
shock, *n. cluster* 72
  concussion 276
  seizure 655
  excitement 82
  ordeal 828
shock, *v. startle* 508
  agitate 824
  repel 830, 867
  scandalize 932
shocking *bad* 649
  painful 830
  fearful 860
  disreputable 874
  hateful 898
shoe 225
shoot, *n. tendril* 367
shoot, *v. expand* 194
  dart 274
  propel 284
  kill 361
  pain 378
shop 799
shopkeeper 797
shoplifter 792
shoplifting 791
shore 231, 342
shore up 215
shorn 51
short *incomplete* 53
  not long 201
  brittle 328
  concise 572
  uncivil 895
  -commons
  fasting 956
  -cut straight 246
  -of lacking 38
shortage 53
SHORTCOMING
  inequality 28
  inferiority 34
  incompletness 53
  motion short of 304
shorten 36, 38, 201
shorthand 590
short-lived 111
SHORTNESS 201
shortsighted *myopic* 443
  misjudging 481
shot, *n.* 727
shotgun 727
shoulder, *v.* 215
shout *cry* 406, 411
  cheer 838
shove 276
shovel 191
show, *n. opportunity* 134
  drama 599
  ornament 847
  parade 882
show, *v. appear* 446, 448
  draw attention 457
  evince 467
  demonstrate 478
  manifest 525

-off *display* 882
  boast 884
-up *censure* 932
  accuse 928
shower *assemblage* 72
  rain 348
showy *ugly* 846
  ornamental 847
  tawdry 851
  ostentatious 882
shrapnel 727
shred 32, 205
shrew 901
shrewd *knowing* 490
  wise 498
  cunning 702
shriek 410, 411
shrift 952
shrill 404, 410
shrine 1000
shrink *decrease* 36
  shrivel 195
  avoid 623
  blench 822
  fear 860
shrive 952
shrivel 195, 258
shroud, *n.* 223, 363
shroud, *v. invest* 225
  hide 528
shrub *plant* 367
shrug *sign* 550
shrunk 195
shudder *shiver* 383
  fear 860
  -at hate 898
shuffle *change* 140, 149
  move slowly 275
  prevaricate 544
  palter 605
shun *avoid* 623
  dislike 867
shut 261
  -out exclude 55
  prohibit 761
  -up 751
shutter 424
shuttle *alternate* 314
shy, *adj.* 862, 881
shy, *v. deviate* 279
  draw back 283
  propel 284
  avoid 623, 860
Shylock 787
SIBILATION *hiss* 409
sibyl *oracle* 513
sick *ill* 655
  -of averse 867
  satiated 869
sicken *nauseate* 395
  pain 830
  weary 841
  disgust 867
sickle 253
sickly *weak* 160
sickness 655

SIDE *edge* 231
  laterality 236
  party 712
  -by side 712
  -issue 39
  -with *aid* 707
  co-operate 709
side arms 727
sidelong 236
sidereal 318
sidetrack 279
sidewalk 627
sidewise 217, 236
sidle 217, 236, 279
siege 716
siesta 683
sieve 219, 260
sift *simplify* 42
  inquire 461
  clean 652
sigh 839
sight *vision* 441
  appearance 448
  prodigy 872
sightless *blind* 442
sight-seeing 441
sight-seer 444
sign, *n. omen* 512
  indication 550
  prodigy 872
sign, *v. attest* 467, 550
signal, *n. light* 423
  sign 550
signal, *adj. great* 31
  eventful 151
signalize *indicate* 550
  celebrate 883
signature 467
signet 550, 747
significant 642
  [*see* signify]
signify *forebode* 511
  mean 516
  indicate 550
SILENCE, *n.* 403, 585
silence, *v. confute* 479
  gag 581
  quell 731
silencer 408a
silent 403, 585
silhouette *outline* 230
silken 255
sill 215
silly *credulous* 846
  imbecile 499
silo 636
silt *dirt* 653
silver, *n. money* 800
silver, *adj. white* 430
  gray 432
SIMILARITY 9, 17, 27
simile *similarity* 17
  comparison 464
  metaphor 521
similitude *copy* 21
simmer *boil* 382, 384

seethe 824
simoom 349
simper *smile* 838
  affect 855
simple *mere* 32
  unmixed 42
  credulous 486
  ignorant 493
  silly 499
  artless 703
  unadorned 849
simple-minded 849
SIMPLENESS 42
simpleton 501
SIMPLICITY 849
  ignorance 499
  [see simple]
simplify 849 [see simple]
simply *little* 32
simulate *resemble* 17
  imitate 19
  cheat 544
simulation 19
simultaneous 120
SIMULTANEOUSNESS
  120
sin, *n. guilt* 947
sin, *v. transgress* 945
since *under the circum-*
  stances 8
  after 117
  because 155, 476
sincere *veracious* 543
  ingenuous 703
  earnest 821
sinecure 681
sinew 159
sinewy 159
sinful 945
sing *chant* 416
  rejoice 838
singe 382
singer *musician* 416
single *unmixed* 42
  sole 87
  unmarried 904
single-handed 87
single-minded 703
singleness [see single]
singsong 16
singular *exceptional* 83
  one 87
sinister *left* 239
  bad 649
  adverse 735
sink *disappear* 4
  destroy 162
  lower 308
  submerge 310
  fail 732
sinless 946
sinner 949, 988
Sinn Feiner 712, 742
sinuous 248
sip *drink* 298
sir *man* 373

title 877
sire 166
siren *sea nymph* 341
  tempter 615
  alarm 669
  evil spirit 980
sirocco *wind* 349
sirup 396
sissy *milksop* 158
sister *likeness* 17
  nurse 662
sisterhood 11, 712, 888
sisterly 888
sit 308
site 182, 183
sitting [see sit]
  assembly 696
sitting room 191
situate 183, 184
SITUATION
  circumstances 8
  place 183
  location 184
  business 625
six 98
SIZE *magnitude* 31
  glue 45
  dimensions 192
sizzle 409
skate, *n.* 272
skate, *v.* 266
skeleton, *remains* 40
  essential part 50
  outline 626
skeptic *agnostic* 485, 989
skeptical 989
skepticism *doubt* 485
  irreligion 989
sketch *form* 240
  represent 554
  paint 556
  outline 626
sketchy *incomplete* 53
  unfinished 730
ski 225, 272
skid, *v.* 217, 306
skiff 273
SKILL 698
skillful 698
skim *move* 266
  neglect 460
  summarize 596
skin *tegument* 223
  peel 226
skin-deep 220
skinny *thin* 203
skip *jump* 309
  rejoice 838
skipper *sea captain* 269
  captain 745
skirmish 720
skirt, *n. dress* 225
  edge 231
skirt, *v. environ* 227
  flank 236
skit *ridicule* 856

detraction 934
skittish *excitable* 825
skulk *hide* 528
  sneak 862
skull 450
sky 318
skylight 260
skyscraper 210
slab 251
slack *loose* 47
  inert 172
  slow 275
  unwilling 603
  insufficient 640
  shiftless 674
  lax 738
  nonobservant 773
slacken *loosen* 47
  moderate 174
  retard 275
slacker 623, 927
slake *quench* 174
  satiate 869
slam *shut* 261
slander 934
slanderer 936
slang 563
slant 217
slap 276
slapdash 684
slash 44
slate, *n. schedule* 611
  plan 626
slate, *v. list* 86
slatternly 653
slaughter 361
slave 746
slavery *toil* 686
  subjection 749
slavish *servile* 746, 886
  subject 749
slay 361
slayer 361
sled 272
sledge 272
sleek *smooth* 255
sleep 376, 683
sleepy 683
sleet 383
sleigh 272
sleight *skill* 698
  -of hand *deception* 545
slender 203
sleuth 527
slice, *n.* 51
slice, *v. cut* 44
  shave 204
slide *elapse* 109
  pass 264
  glide 266
  descend 306
slight, *n.* 929, 930
slight, *adj. shallow* 209
  rare 322
  feeble 575
slight, *v. neglect* 460

disparage 483
violate 927
depreciate 929
despise 930
slightly 32
slim 203
slime 352, 653
sling, *n. weapon* 727
sling, *v. hang* 214
project 284
slink *hide* 528
slip, *n. stripling* 129
strip 205
error 495, 568
guilt 947
slip, *n. elapse* 109
descend 306
fail 732
slipper 225
slippery *smooth* 255
greasy 355
vacillating 607
elusive 773
slipshod 575
slit 44, 198
slogan 722
sloop 273
slope 217
sloping 306
sloppy *sodden* 339
slot 260
sloth 172, 683
slouch 217, 275
slough, *n. quagmire* 345
difficulty 704
slough, *v. divest* 226
sloven 701
slovenly *untidy* 59
dirty 653
slow *tardy* 133, 275
inert 172
inactive 683
dull 843
slow goer 275
SLOWNESS 275
slowpoke 275
slug *bullet* 727
sluggard 275, 683
sluggish *inert* 172
slow 275
lazy 683
sluice 295
slum 653
slumber 683
slump 304, 306
slur *scamp* 460
defame 874
reproach 938
slush 345, 352, 653
slut *slattern* 701
sly *stealthy* 528
cunning 702
smack *tinge* 41
boat 273
blow 276
taste 390

kiss 902
small - *in degree* 32
-*in size* 193
-arms 727
-coin 800
-talk 588
smaller 34
SMALLNESS 32
smart, *adj. active* 682
clever 698
witty 842
pretty 845
ornamental 847
-set 852
smart, *v. pain* 378
smarten 847
smartness 682
smash *destruction* 162
smatterer 493
smattering 491
smear *cover* 223
grease 355
soil 653
smell 398
-a rat 845
smelt *heat* 384
smile *rejoice* 838
smirch *blacken* 431
smirk 838
smite *maltreat* 649
afflict 830
punish 972
smock *clothing* 225
smoke *vapor* 336
heat 382
tobacco 392
smolder 172, 382
smooth, *adj. uniform* 16
calm 174, 714
flat 251
not rough 255
smooth, *v. soothe* 174
level 213
smoother, *n.* 255
smoothly [*see* smooth]
smoothness 255
smother *repress* 174
kill 361
restrain 751
smudge 653, 848
smug *affected* 855
smuggle *steal* 791
smuggler 792
smut *dirt* 653
snaffle *curb* 706
snag *danger* 667
snail *slow coach* 275
snake *serpent* 366
snaky 248
SNAP, *n. time* 106
noise 406
activity 682
snap, *v. break* 44
shut 261
snarl 895
snare *deception* 545

snarl *growl* 412, 895
threaten 909
snatch *seize* 789
sneak, *n.* 862
sneak, *v.* 528
sneakers *shoes* 225
sneer *disparage* 929
sneeze 349
snicker *rejoicing* 838
ridicule 856
sniff *smell* 398
sniffle 349
snigger *laugh* 838
ridicule 856
snip *cut* 44
snob 851
snooze 683
snore 441
snort 411
snout 250
snow 383
snowshoes 225
snowstorm 383
snub 719, 879
snuff *blow* 349
sniff 398
snuffle *blow* 349
snug *closed* 261
comfortable 377
snuggle 902
snugness 827
so *therefore* 476
soak 337
soar *rise* 31, 305
tower 206
fly 267, 338
sob 839
sober *moderate* 174
wise 498
sane 502
temperate 953
abstinent 958
soberness 953
SOBRIETY 958, 963
sobriquet 565
sociable 892
social *sociable* 892
-gathering 892
socialism 737, 778
SOCIALITY 892
society *mankind* 372
party 712
fashion 852
sock *hose* 225
socket *receptacle* 191
sod 344
sodality 712
sodden *moist* 339
sofa 215
soft *weak* 160
not hard 324
moist 339
marshy 345
silence 403
not loud 405
soften [*see* soft]

moderate 174
mollify **324**
pity 914
palliate 937
softening 324
softhearted 914
softness 324
soggy 339
soil, *n. land* **342**
soil, *v. dirty* 653
soiree 892
sojourn *dwell* 186
solace *relief* 834
solar 318
solder, *n.* 45
solder, *v.* 43, 46
soldier 726
sole, *n. base* 211
sole, *adj. alone* 87
SOLECISM 568
solemn *soft* 403
grave 837
solemnization 883
solicit *request* 765
solicitor *lawyer* 758, 968
petitioner 767
solicitude *care* 459
pain 828
anxiety 860
solid *stable* 140
dense 321
exact 494
-body **321**
solidarity 52
solidify 46, 321
solidity [*see* solid]
solvency 800
SOLILOQUY 589
solitary *alone* 87
solitude 893
solo 415
soluble 335
solution *fluid* 333
answer 462
explanation 522
solve *discover* 480a
unriddle 522
solvency 800 [*see* solvent]
solvent, *n. liquefier* 335
solvent, *adj. sound* 800
somber *dark* **421**
dull 428
sad 837
some 25
somebody 372
somehow 631
somersault 218
something 3
sometimes 136
somewhat *a little* 32
somewhere 182
son 167
Son, God the 976
sonant 402
sonata 415
song *music* 415

songbird 416
songster 416
sonnet 597
sonorous 402, 404
soon *future* **121**
early 132
expected **507**
soot 653
soothe *allay* 174
relieve 834
soothing 834
soothsayer 513
sop, *n. inducement* 615
sop, *v.* 339
sophism **477**
sophisticated 498, 698
SOPHISTRY **477**
soporific *sleepy* 683
soprano 410
SORCERER 548, **994**
sorceress 994
SORCERY 511, **992**
sordid *stingy* 819
covetous 865
sore, *n* 378
sore, *adj. acute* 830
discontented 832
angry 900
sorely *very* 31
sorority 712
sorrow 735, 828
sorry *trifling* 643
grieved 828
mean 876
sort, *n. kind* 75
sort, *v. arrange* 60
sortie 716
sot *drunkard* 959
sough *faint sound* 405
soul *essence* 5
person 372
intellect 450
affections 820
SOUND, *n. strait* 343
noise **402**
sound, *adj. strong* 159
true 494
sane 502
perfect 650
healthy 654
solvent 800
orthodox 983a
sound, *v. fathom* **208**
resound 408
investigate 461
measure 466
sounding 402
soundings 208
sour, *adj. acid* **397**
uncivil 895
sour, *v. embitter* 825
source *beginning* 66
cause 153
soured *glum* 832
SOURNESS **397**
souse *plunge* 310

south 278
southern 237
souvenir 505
sovereign, *n. ruler* 745
sovereign, *adj.* 737
sovereignty 737
sow, *n. pig* 366
sow, *v. scatter* 73
cultivate 371
SPACE, *n. music* 26
time 106
extension 180
space, *v. arrange* 60
spacious 180
spade 272
span, *n. pair* 89
time 106
distance 196
length 200
team 272
span, *v. join* 43
link 45
measure 466
spangle *ornament* 847
spank *flog* 992
spar *quarrel* 713
contend 720
spare, *adj. additional* **37**
meager 203, 640
redundant 641
economical 817
spare, *v. not do* 681
relinquish 782
give 784
exempt 927a
sparing [*see* spare]
small 32
economical 817
parsimonious 819
spark 120, 423
sparkle *glisten* **420**
sparkling *spirited* 574
cheerful 836
witty 842
sparse 73, 103
sparseness 32, 73, 103
spasm
sudden change **146**
violence 173
agitation 315
pain 378
spasmodic *irregular* 139
violent 173
spatter *dirt* 653
spawn 168
speak 580, **582**
speaker 524, **581**
chairman 694
spear, *n. weapon* **727**
spear, *v. pierce* 260
special *particular* **79**
speciality 79
specialize 79
SPECIALTY **79**
specie 800
species *kind* 75

specific, *n. remedy* 662
specific, *adj. special* 79
specification *class* 75
specify *particularize* 79
  tell 527
  name 564
specimen 82
specious *probable* 472
  sophistical 477
  showy 846
speck 32, 193
speckle *variegate* 440
spectacle *show* 599, 882
  appearance 448
  prodigy 872
spectacles 445
spectacular 599, 882
SPECTATOR 197, 444
SPECTER 4, 361, 980a
spectral 980a
spectrum 428
speculate *think* 451
  suppose 514
  chance 621
speculation *chance* 156
  experiment 463
  venture 621
speculative
  thoughtful 451
  experimental 463
speculator 463
SPEECH 582
speechless 581
speed *journey* 266
  velocity 274
speedily *soon* 132
SPELL, *n. period* 106
  influence 175
  exertion 686
  charm 993
spell, *v.* 561
spellbind 586
spellbound 870
spelling 561
spend *waste* 638
  give 784
  expend 809
spendthrift 818
spent *weak* 160
  tired 688
sphere *rank* 26
  class 75
  space 180
  region 181
  ball 249
  function 625
sphinx 513, 520
spice *n.* 41, 393
spice, *v. season* 392
spicy *fragrant* 400
  exciting 824
spike, *n.* 253, 263
spike, *v. pierce* 260
spill *shed* 297
  waste 638
spin, *n. journey* 266

aviation 267
spin, *v. rotate* 312
  -out *protract* 110
  prolong 200
spindle-shanked 203
spine 253
spineless *weak* 945
spinster 374, 904
spiny 253
spiral 248, 311
spire *height* 206
  peak 253
SPIRIT *essence* 5
  immateriality 317
  intellect 450
  vigorous language 574
  activity 682
  courage 861
  ghost 980a
  evil - 980a
spirited *vigorous* 574
  active 682
  brave 861
spiritism 317, 992a
spiritist 317
spiritual *immaterial* 317
  psychical 450
  divine 976
  pious 987
spiritualism
  immateriality 317
  psychical research 992a
spiritualist 317
spiritualize 317
spit, *n. saliva* 299
spit, *v. pierce* 260
spite 907
spiteful 907
spitfire *shrew* 901
splash 348, 653
splendid 873
splendor *luster* 420
  beauty 845
  glory 873
  display 882
splice *join* 43, 228
  cross 219
splinter, *n.* 205
splinter, *v.* 44, 328
split, *n. quarrel* 713
split, *v. divide* 44
  bisect 91
  break 328
  -hairs 477
spoil, *n. booty* 793
spoil, *v. botch* 699
  hinder 706
spokesman 524, 582
sponge, *n. stopper* 263
  pulpiness 354
  drunkard 959
sponge, *v. moisten* 339
  dry 340
  clean 652
  cringe 886
sponger 886

sponsor *witness* 467
  security 771
spontaneous
  voluntary 600
  willing 602
  impulsive 612
spoon, *n.* 191
spoon, *v. court* 902
spoonerism 495
spoonful 25
spoor 550
sporadic *infrequent* 137
  infectious 657
spore 330
sport *killing* 361
  amusement 840
sportive *gay* 836
  frolicsome 840
sportsman 361, 840
spot, *n. place* 182
  mark 550
  blemish 848
spot, *v. discover* 480a
  soil 653
spotless *perfect* 650
  clean 652
  innocent 946
spotted *variegated* 440
spouse 88, 903
spout, *n.* 295
spout, *v. declaim* 582
sprain 160
sprawl 200, 308
spray, *n. sprig* 51
  foam 353
  flowers 400
spray, *v. atomize* 336
spread, *n. expanse* 180
  meal 298
spread, *v. disperse* 73
  universalize 78
  expand 194
  diverge 291
  publish 531
spree 840
sprig *branch* 51
sprightly *cheerful* 836
  witty 842
spring, *n. early* 125
  source 153
  strength 159
  elasticity 325
  rivulet 348
spring, *v. leap* 309
springy 325
sprinkle *scatter* 73
  wet 337
sprinkler 337
sprint 274
sprout *grow* 365
  expand 194
spruce *neat* 652
  beautiful 845
spur, *n. projection* 250
  prick 253
spur, *v. incite* 370, 615

spurious *deceptive* 545
  illegitimate 925
spurn *reject* 610
  disdain 866, **930**
spurt *sprint* 274
  gush 348
spy, *n.* 444, 664
spy, *v.* 441
squabble 713
squad 72, 726
squadron 726
squalid *dirty* 653
  unsightly 846
squall, *n.* 349
squall, *v. cry* 411
squalor 653
squander 776, **818**
square, *n. four* 95
  place 182
  rectangle 244
  measure 466
square, *adj. just* 922, 924
square, *v. compensate* 30
squash *quell* 162
  pulp 354
squat, *v.* 184, 308
squat, *adj. short* 201
  thick 202
  low 207
squatter 188
squaw 374
squeak *cry* 411
squeal 411
squeamish *sick* 655
  fastidious 868
squeeze *contract* 195
  condense 321
  -out extract 301
squib *lampoon* 856
squint, *n.* **443**
squint, *v. look* 441
squire *attendant* 746
  gentry 875
squirm 315
squirt *eject* 297
stab *pierce* 260
  kill 361
  pain 649
STABILITY 16, 141, **150**
stabilize 150
stable, *n.* 189, 370
stable, *adj.*
  permanent 141, 150
  quiescent 265
stack 72
staff *support* 215
  music 413
  council 696
  cast 712
  weapon 727
  retinue 746
stag *deer* 366
  male 373
  sociality 892
stage *degree* 26
  term 71

time 106
  position 183
  platform 215
  drama 599
stagecoach 272
stagger, *n. be slow* 275
  reel 314, 821
  shake belief 485
  startle 508
  astonish 870
stagnant *inert* 172
  quiescent 265
  unprogressive 659
stagnate 265
stagnation *inertness* 172
  quiescence 265
staid *grave* 837
stain *color* 223, 428
  blemish 848
  disgrace 874
stainless *clean* 652
  honorable **939**
  innocent 946
staircase 305
stairs 305
stairway 305
stake *wager* 621
  security 771
  execution 975
stale *old* 124
  insipid 391
stalk, *n.* 215
stalk, *v. walk* 266
  chase 622
stall *cot* 189
  booth 799
stalwart *strong* 159
stamina *strength* 159
STAMMERING 583
stamp *character* 7
  prototype 22
  kind 75
  form 240
  mark 550
  security 771
  -out *extinguish* 385
stampede 860
stanch, *adj.* **939**
stanch, *v.* 348
stand, *n. time* 106
  support 215
  quiescence 265
stand, *v. resist* 719
  brook 821
  endure 826
  -by *near* 197
  aid 707
  -fast 141
  -for *indicate* 550
standard *model* 22
  degree 26
  average 29
  rule 80
  measure 466
  flag 550
  perfection 650

standardize 58
standing *footing* 8
  degree 26
  permanence 141
  situation 183
  rank 873
standpatter 150
standpoint 441
stanza 597
staple, *n. whole* 50
  material 635
staple, *adj.* 794
star *luminary* 318, **423**
  actor 599
  glory 873
  -s and stripes 550
starched *proud* 878
stare *look* 441
  gape 455
  wonder 870
stark *very* 31
  sheer 32
starry 318
start *begin* 66
  arise 151
  move **284**
  depart 293
  leap 309
  offer 763
  fear 860
  wonder 870
startle *doubt* 485
  stagger 508
  fear 860
  amaze 870
starvation [*see* starve]
  insufficiency 640
  fasting 956
starve *be poor* 804
  stint 819
  fast 956
STATE, *n. condition* 7
  position 71
  realm 372, 780
  government **737**
state, *v.* 535
statehouse 966
stately *grand* 873
  pompous 882
statement 535
stateroom 191
statesman 694
statesmanship **693**
static 319
statics 159, 319
station, *n. degree* 26
  term 71
  situation 183
  journey 266
  prison 752
  rank 873
station, *v. locate* 184
stationary 265
statistical 85
statistics 85, 86
statue 554

stature 206
status *position* 8
  terms 71
  situation 183
  repute 873
statute *act* 697
  law 963
statutory 963
staunch [see stanch]
stave *music* 413
  -in *concave* 252
  -off *defer* 133
  hinder 706
stay *continue* 106, 141
  wait 133
  stop 142
  dwell 186
  support 215
  not move 265
  prevent 706
steadfast 150, 604a
steady *regular* 80
  periodic 138
  stable 150
  persevering 604a
  imperturbable 871
steal 791
  -away *avoid* 623
STEALING 791
stealth *concealment* 528
stealthy 528
steam 267, 353
steamboat 273
steamer *ship* 273
steed 271
steel, *n. sharpener* 253
  sword 727
steel, *v. harden* 823
  -the heart 951
steep, *n. cliff* 212
steep, *adj.* 217, 306
steep, *v. soak* 337
steeple, 206, 253
steer *direct* 693
  -for 278
steersman 269
stem, *n. origin* 153
  ancestor 166
  front 234
  stalk 367
stem, *v. oppose* 708
stench 401
stenographer 590
stenography 590
stent 233
stentorian *loud* 404
step *degree* 26
  term 71
  motion 264
  expedient 626
steppe 180, 344, 367
steppingstone *link* 45
stereotyped 150, 613
sterile *unproductive* 169
  abortive 732
sterling *true* 494

  monetary 800
  virtuous 944
stern, *n. rear* 235
stern, *adj. resolute* 604
  severe 739
stew, *n. difficulty* 704
stew, *v. heat* 382
  cook 384
steward *caterer* 637
  agent 690
  director 694
stewardship 692, 693
stick, *n.* 215, 975
stick, *v. adhere* 46
  continue 106, 143
  cease 142
  stab 260
  -at *demur* 603
  -to *continue* 143
  persevere 604a
  -up for *aid* 707
  applaud 931
stickler *viscid* 352
stiff *rigid* 323
  severe 739
  prudish 751
  affected 855
  haughty 878
stiffen 321, 323
stiff-necked 606
stiffness [see stiff]
stifle *kill* 361
  silence 403
stifling *hot* 382
stigma *disgrace* 874
stigmatize 874
stiletto 262, 727
still, *n. retort* 336
still, *adj. moderate* 174
  not moving 265
  silent 403, 585
still, *adv.* 30
stilted 577, 855
stimulant 662
stimulate *energize* 171
  incite 615
  excite 824
stimulating
  [see stimulate]
  suggestive 514
stimulus 615
sting, *n.* 663
sting, *v. pain* 378
  tingle 380
  irritate 824, 830
stingy 819
stink 401
stint, *n. limit* 233
stint, *v. begrudge* 819
stipend *salary* 973
stipulate *bargain* 769
  condition 770
stir, *n. energy* 171
  agitation 315
  activity 682
stir, *v. move* 264

  be active 682
  excite 824
  -up *excite* 173, 824
stirring 151
stitch 43
stock, *n. kinship* 11
  quantity 25, 31
  stew 166
  store 636
  merchandise 798
  -in trade *means* 632
  merchandise 636, 798
stock, *adj. habitual* 613
stockade 232, 717
stock exchange 799
stocking 225
stocks *funds* 802
stock-still 265
stocky 201
stoic 823
stoicism 823
stoke 388
stolid *stupid* 499
  dull 843
stomach, *n.* 191
stomach, *v. endure* 826
stone, *n.* 321
stone, *v.* 972
stony 323
stool 315
stoop *crouch* 308
  submit 725
  condescend 879
stop, *n. end* 67
  delay 133
  station 266
stop, *v. cease* 142
  close 261
  rest 265
  hinder 706
stopgap *substitute* 147
  stopper 263
stoppage *end* 67
  cessation 142
  hindrance 706
STOPPER 263
STORE, *n. quantity* 31
  stock 636
  shop 799
store, *v. keep* 637
storehouse 636
storm *crowd* 72
  agitation 315
  wind 349
  passion 825
storm, *v. rage* 173, 900
  attack 716
stormy 349
story *rooms* 204
  tale 594
storyteller 594
stout *strong* 159
  fat 192
stove *fireplace* 386
stow *locate* 184
  store 636

affect 823, 824
astonish 870
stunt *shorten* 201
stunted 32, 195
stupefy *stun* 376
 affect 823
 astonish 870
stupendous 31, 192
stupid *unintelligent* 499
 dull 843
stupor *insensibility* 376,
 823
 wonder 870
sturdy *strong* 159
stutter 583
sty *inclosure* 232
 dirt 653
STYLE *state* 7
 name 564
 diction 569
 fashion 852
stylish 852
suave 894
suavity 894
subaltern 745
subconscious 450, 992a
 -self 450, 992a
subdivide 44
subdivision 44, 51
subdue *calm* 174
 succeed 731
subject, *n. topic* 454
 meaning 516
 servant 746
subject, *adj. liable* 177
 enthrall 749
subject, *v. dominate* 175
SUBJECTION 749
subjective *intrinsic* 5
 immaterial 317
SUBJECTIVENESS 5
subjoin 37, 63
subjugate 731, 749
sublet 787
sublease 787
sublime
 great 31
 high 206
 eminent 873
 magnanimous 942
subliminal 450
 -consciousness 450, 992a
 -self 317, 992a
sublimity [*see* sublime]
submarine, *adj.* 208
submarine, *n. boat* 726
submerge, 310, 337
submergible 310
submersible 310
submersion 310
SUBMISSION 725
 obedience 743
 humility 879
submissive 725, 879
submit *propound* 514
 yield 725

subordinate 34
subpoena *writ* 960
subscribe *agree to* 769
 give 784
subscriber [*see* subscribe]
subscription *gift* 784
subsequent
 -in order 63
 -in time 117
subserviency 886
subservient
 instrumental 631
 aiding 707
 servile 746
subside *decrease* 36
 sink 306
subsidence 36
subsidiary 707
subsidy *aid* 707
 gift 784
subsist *exist* 1
 continue 141
subsistence *food* 298
substance *thing* 3
 gist 5
 quantity 25
 matter 316
 meaning 516
 wealth 803
substantial *existing* 1, 3
 material 316
 dense 321
 true 494
SUBSTANTIALITY 3,
 316
substantially 5, 50
substantiate
 materialize 316
 verify 467
SUBSTITUTE, *n.* 634,
 759
substitute, *v.* 147
SUBSTITUTION 147
substratum 204
subterfuge *sophistry* 477
 quirk 481
 cunning 702
subterranean 208
subtle *light* 320
 rare 322
 cunning 702
subtlety *rarity* 322
 sophistry 477
 wisdom 498
subtraction 36, 38
subtrahend 38
suburb 197, 227
suburban 227
subversion 14
subvert *destroy* 162
 invert 218
succeed *follow* 63, 117
 triumph 731
 acquire 783
SUCCESS 731
successful 731

succession *sequence* 63,
 117
 continuity 69
 repetition 104
successor 65, 117
succinct 572
succor 707
succulent *nutritive* 298
 juicy 333
succumb *yield* 725
suckle 707
suckling *infant* 129
suction 296
sudden *transient* 111
 instantaneous 113
 soon 132
suds *froth* 353
sue 969
suffer *endure* 151, 826
 ail 378, 655
 allow 760
 feel 821
 ache 828
sufferance 826
suffering 639
SUFFICIENCY 31, 639
sufficient *enough* 639
 satisfactory 831
suffix *adjunct* 39
suffocate *kill* 361
suffocation 361
suffrage 535, 609
sugar 396
sugary 396
suggest *suppose* 514
 inform 527
 advise 695
 -itself 451
suggestion *hint* 527
 plan 626
 advice 695
suggestive 505, 514
suicidal *destructive* 162
suicide 361
suit, *n. clothes* 225
 petition 765
 courtship 902
 lawsuit 969
suit, *v. accord* 23
 befit 646
 -the occasion 134, 646
suitable 23, 134, 646
suite *sequel* 65
 series 69
 retinue 88, 746
suitor *petitioner* 767
 lover 897
sulk 901a
sulkiness [*see* sulky]
sulky *obstinate* 606
 discontented 832
 dejected 837
 sullen 901a
sulks 895
sullen *obstinate* 606
 gloomy 837

discourteous 895
sulky 901a
SULLENNESS 901a
sully dirty 653
dishonor 874
sultan 745
sultry 382
sum total 50
number 84
money 800
-up reckon 37, 85
discriminate 465
review 596
summarize 201, 596
summary, n. 596
summary, adj. transient
111
short 201
concise 572
summer 125, 382
SUMMIT 33, 210
summon command 741
indict 969
summons 741, 969
sumptuous 882
sun 318, 423
-god 423
sunbeam 420
sunburnt 433
Sunday 687
sunder 44
sundial 114
sundry 102
sunny warm 382
cheerful 836
sunrise 125
sunset 126
sunshade 223
sunshine 420
sup feed 298
superabound 641
superannuated 128, 158
superb 845
supercilious proud 878
insolent 885
scornful 930
superficial shallow 209
extrinsic 220
ignorant 491
superficies 220
superfluity 40, 641
superfluous 641
superhuman godlike 976
superintend 693
superintendent 694
superior, n. head 694
superior, adj. greater 33
high 206
SUPERIORITY 33
superlative 33
superman 33
supernatural 976, 980a
supersede substitute 147
relinquish 782
superstition 486
superstitious 486, 984

supervene succeed 117
supervise 693
supervision 693
supervisor 694
supervisory 693
supine flat 213, 251
sluggish 462
supplant 147
supple soft 324
supplement 37, 39
suppliant 767
supplicate beg 765
supplies 707
supply store 636
provide 637
give 784
-deficiencies 52
SUPPORT, n. footing 175
foundation 215
support, v. perform 170
evidence 467
escort 664
aid 707
feel 821
endure 826
supporter 215
suppose 472, 514
SUPPOSITION 514
suppress destroy 162
conceal 528
restrain 751
suppression [see suppress]
supremacy 33
supreme superior 33
highest 210
ruling 737
Supreme Being 976
sure certain 474
safe 664
sure-footed careful 459
skillful 698
cautious 864
sureness [see sure]
surety certainty 474
safety 664
sponsor 771
surf 348, 353
surface 220
surfeit redundance 641
satiety 869
surge swarm 72
swell 305
wave 348
surgeon 662
surgery 662
surly gruff 895
sullen 901a
surmise 514
surmount tower 206
overtop 210
ascend 305
surname 564
surpass be superior 33
go beyond 303
outshine 873
surplus remainder 40

redundance 33, 641
surprise, n. 508
surprise, v.
take unawares 674
wonder 870
surrender submit 725
relinquish 782
surreptitious
furtive 528
deceptive 545
surround 227
surrounding 227
surroundings 227
surveillance care 459
direction 693
survey view 441
measure 466
surveyor 466
survive remain 40, 141
outlast 110
susceptibility
tendency 176
sensibility 375
impressibility 822
suspect doubt 485, 920
suppose 514
suspend defer 133
discontinue 142
hang 214
suspense cessation 142
uncertainty 475
irresolution 605
suspension lateness 133
cessation 142
hanging 214
suspicion doubt 485
supposition 514
fear 860
jealousy 920
suspicious 485
sustain continue 143
strengthen 159
support 215
aid 707
endure 821
sustenance 298, 707
sustentation [see sustain]
swab dry 340
clean 652
swag booty 793
swagger, n. pride 878
swagger, v. boast 884
bluster 885
swain man 373
rustic 876
lover 897
swallow, n. 366
swallow, v. gulp 296
be credulous 486
brook 826
swamp, n. marsh 345
swamp, v. 162
swampy 345
swan 366
swap exchange 148
barter 794

swarm, n. crowd 72
  multitude 102
swarm, v. climb 305
swarthy 431
swath 72
swathe clothe 225
sway, n. power 157
  influence 175
  agitation 315
  authority 737
sway, v. influence 175, 615
  lean 217
  oscillate 314
swear affirm 535
  promise 768
sweat, n. excretion 299
  fatigue 688
sweat, v. 295, 382, 686
sweater 225
sweep, n. space 180
  curve 245
sweep, v. curve 245
  speed 274
  clean 652
sweeping whole 50
  complete 52
  inclusive 76
  general 78
sweepings 645
sweet saccharine 396
  melodious 413
  clean 652
  lovely 897
sweeten 396
sweetheart 897
SWEETNESS 396
sweets 396
swell, n. bulge 250
  wave 348
  blare 404
  fop 854

swell, v. increase 31
  expand 194
swelter 382
swerve change 140
  deviate 279
swift 274
swim 267, 320
swindle cheat 545
  peculate 791
swindler cheat 548
  thief 792
swine 366
swing, n. operation 170
  space 180
  freedom 748
swing, v. hang 214
  oscillate 314
swirl 348
swish 409
switch, n. rod 975
switch, v. deviate 279
  flog 972
swollen 194, 250
swoon 158, 688
swoop descend 274
  seize 789
sword 727
swordsman 726
Sybarite 954a
sycophant 65, 886
syllable 561
syllabus list 86
  compendium 596
sylvan 367
symbol sign 550
symbolic latent 526
  indicative 550
symbolize involve 526
  indicate 550
  represent 554
symmetrical 27, 242

SYMMETRY
  equality 27
  regular form 242
  beauty 845
sympathetic
  [see sympathy]
sympathizer 914
sympathize with 906
sympathy
  feeling 821
  love 897
  kindness 906
  pity 914
  condolence 915
symphony music 415
symposium 72, 596
symptom 550
synagogue 1000
synchronism 120
syndicate council 696
  league 712
synod 696
synodic (al) 696
synonym 522
synonymous 27, 516
synopsis 86, 596
syntax 567
synthesis
  combination 48
  reasoning 476
synthetic 476
syringe, v. 337
syrup [see sirup]
system order 58
  rule 80
  plan 626
systematic 60, 80
systematize order 58
  arrange 60
  organize 357
  plan 626

T

tabernacle 189, 1000
table, n. arrangement 60
  list 86
  support 215, 251
  repast 298
table, v. defer 133, 460
tableau 448, 599
tableland 344
tablet 251, 551
taboo prohibited 761
tabular 60
tabulate 60, 69, 86
tabulation 551
tacit implied 516
  latent 526
TACITURNITY 585
tack, n. direction 278
tack, v. change course 140
  turn 279
tackle, n. fastening 45
  gear 633

tackle, v. undertake 676
  manage 693
tact discrimination 465
  wisdom 498
  skill 698
tactful [see tact]
  affable 894
tactics conduct 692
  warfare 722
tactlessness 895
tactual 379
tag, n. addition 37
  sequel 65
  end 67
tag, v. follow 63, 235
tail 65, 67, 235
taint, n. imperfection 651
  disease 659
  disgrace 874
taint, v. 659
take receive 785

  appropriate 788, 789
-after 17
-away subtract 38
  remove 185
  seize 789
-from subtract 38
  seize 789
-in shorten 201
  admit 296
  understand 518
  deceive 545
-place 1, 151
-to like 827
  desire 865
  love 897
-up pursue 622
  undertake 676
  use 677
taker 789
TAKING 789
tale counting 85

torpid *inert* 172
　inactive 683
　insensible 823
torpor 823
torrent 348
torrid 382
tortuous *twisted* 248
torture, *n. physical* 378
　moral 828
　cruelty 907
torture, *v.* 972
torturer 975
toss *throw* 284
　oscillate 314
　-up 156
tot *child* 129
total, *n. whole* 50
　number 84, 85
total, *adj.* 50
　-abstinence, 953, 955
total, *v. add* 37, 800
totality 52
totally 52
totter 160
　limp 275
TOUCH, *n. mixture* 41
　sensation 379, 380
　act 680
touch, *v. relate to* 9
　adjoin 199
　feel 379
　excite 824
　excite pity 914
touched *crazy* 503
　tainted 653
　penitent 950
touching 830
touchy 901
tough, *ruffian* 876, 887, 913
tough, *adj. adhesive* 46
　tenacious 327
　difficult 704
tour 266
touring *car* 272
tourist 268
tournament 720
tourniquet 263
tousle 61
tow 285
toward 278
tower, *n.* 150, 191, 206
tower, *v. loom* 31
　soar 305
towering *great* 31
　high 206
town 189
township 181
toy, *n.* 643, 840
toy, *v. fondle* 902
trace, *n.* 550, 551
trace, *v. follow* 63
　inquire 461
　discover 480a
　delineate 554
tracing 21

track *trace* 461
　spoor 550
tract *region* 181
　book 593
　dissertation 595
tractable *malleable* 324
　willing 602
　easy 705
tractile 285
TRACTION 285
trade *business* 625
　traffic 794
trader 797
trademark 550
tradesman 797
trade-union 712
trade wind 349
tradition 124
traduce 934
traducer 936
traffic 794
tragedian 599
tragedy *drama* 599
　evil 619
tragic *dramatic* 599
tragical 830
trail, *n. sequel* 65
　odor 398
　track 550
　record 551
trail, *v. dawdle* 275
　tow 285
　inquire 461
train, *n. in sequence* 63
　sequel 65
　suite 88, 235, 281
　vehicle 272
train, *v. teach* 537
trainer 370
training *education* 537
trait 79, 550
traitor 891, 941
trajectory 627
tram 272
trammel *hinder* 706
　restrain 751
tramp, *n. stroller* 268
　vagabond 876
tramp, *v.* 266
trample upon 649
trance 992a
tranquil *calm* 174
　quiet 265
　peaceful 721
tranquilize *moderate* 174
　quell 265
　pacify 723
　soothe 826
transact 680, 692
transaction 151, 680
transcend 33, 303
transcendency 33
transcendent *superior* 33
　glorious 873
transcendental 450
transcribe 19, 525

transcript *copy* 21
TRANSFER *copy* 21
　-of *things* 270
　-of *property* 783
transferable 270, 783
TRANSFERENCE 140, 270
transfiguration *change* 140
　divine - 908
transfix 260
transform 140
transformation 140
transfuse *mix* 41
　transfer 270
transgress *go beyond* 303
　infringe 773
　sin 945
transgression 303, 947
transgressor 949
TRANSIENCE 111
transient 111
transit 144, 270
transition 144, 270
transitional 140, 264
transitory 111
translate *interpret* 522
translation
　transference 270
　interpretation 522
transmigration 144
transmission 270, 302
transmit 270, 302
transmutation 140
TRANSPARENCY 425
transparent
　transmitting light 425
　obvious 518
transpire *appear* 525
　be disclosed 529
transplant 270
transport, *n. ship* 273
　war vessel 726
　delight 827
transport, *v. transfer* 270
　enrapture 829
transportation 270
transposal 270
transpose *invert* 14, 218
　exchange 148
　transfer 270
transubstantiation
　change 140
　sacrament 998
transverse *oblique* 217
　crossing 219
trap *snare* 545
　pitfall 667
trappings *clothes* 225
　equipment 633
trash *trifle* 643
　rubbish 645
　riffraff 876
trashy 517
travel 266
traveler 268
　bagman 758

traveling 266
traverse 302
travesty *imitate* 19
  copy 21
  misinterpret 523
  burlesque 555
trawl 285
trawler 273
tray 191
treacherous 907, 940
treachery *deception* 545
  dishonesty 940
tread 266
treason *revolt* 742
  treachery 940
treasure 636, 800
TREASURER 801
TREASURY 802
treat
  physical pleasure 377
  bargain 769
  delight 827, 829
  -of 595
treatise 593, 595
treatment
  conduct 692
  medical - 662
treaty 769
treble *three* 93
  shrill 410
tree *pedigree* 166
  plant 367
trellis 219
tremble *totter* 160
  shake 315
  fear 860
tremendous *painful* 830
  fearful 860
tremor *agitation* 315
  emotion 821
  fear 860
tremulous *changeable* 149
  agitated 315
  fearful 860
trench *dike* 232
  furrow 259
  defense 717
trenchant *energetic* 171
  concise 572
  vigorous 574
  keen 821
trend *tendency* 176
  bend 278
trepidation *agitation* 315
  excitement 825
  fear 860
trespass *go beyond* 303
  sin 945
tress 256
triad 92
trial *inquiry* 461
  experiment 463
  essay 675
  adversity 735
  suffering 828
  lawsuit 969

TRIALITY 92
triangle 92
tribe *race* 11
  assemblage 72
  clan 166
tribulation 828
TRIBUNAL 966
tributary, *n. river* 348
tributary, *adj. giving* 784
tribute *donation* 784
  money paid 809
  reward 973
trick *deception* 545
  habit 613
  contrivance 626
  skill 698
  artifice 702
trickery *deceit* 545
trickiness [*see* tricky]
trickle 295, 348
trickster *deceiver* 548
  schemer 702
tricky *deceiving* 545
  cunning 702
tricycle 272
trident 92
trifle, *n.* 32, 643
trifle, *v. neglect* 460
  fool 499
  -with *deceive* 545
trifler 460
trifling 643
trig 845
trill *sound* 407
  sing 416
trim, *n. state* 7
trim, *adj. neat* 652, **845**
trim, *v. adjust* 27
  form 240
  lie 544
  waver 605
  change sides 607
  adorn 847
trimmer
  timeserver 607, 943
trimming *border* 231
  ornament 847
trinity 92
Trinity, Holy - 976
trinket 643, 847
trio 92
trip, *n. jaunt* 266
  fall 306
trip, *v. run* 274
  leap 309
  mistake 495
triple 93
triplet 92
TRIPLICATION 93
triplicity 92
TRISECTION 94
trite *known* 490
  conventional 613
triumph *succeed* 731
  exult 838
trivial *unmeaning* 517

trifling 643
triviality 643
troglodyte 893
troll, *n.* 980
troll, *v.* 416
trolley 272
  -car 272
troop *assemblage* **72**
  soldiers 726
trooper 726
troopship 726
trope 521
TROPHY 733
tropical 382
trot *run* 266, 274
  translation 522
troth 768
troubadour 597
trouble, *n. turmoil* 59
  exertion 686
  adversity 735
  care 828
trouble, *v. derange* 61
troublesome
  inexpedient 647
  difficult 704
  painful 830
troublous 59
trough 259
trounce *censure* 932
  punish 972
trousers 225
trousseau 225
trow 484
truant 187, 623
truce 133, 142, **723**
truck *vehicle* 272
  barter 794
truckman 268
truculent 907
trudge *walk* 266
  more slowly 175
true *real* 1
  straight 246
  accurate **494**
  veracious 543
  faithful 772
trueness [*see* true]
truism *axiom* 496
truly *really* **494**
trumpery 517, **643**
truncheon 727
trundle 284
trunk *stem* 166
  box 191
truss *bundle* 72
  support 215
trust, *n. belief* 484
  firm 712
  property 780
  credit 805
  hope 858
trust, *v.* 484, 858
trustee 758, 801
trustful 484, 486
trustworthy *certain* **474**

vogue *custom* 613
  fashion 852
VOICE, *n.*
  sound 402
  judgment 480
  vote 535
  human – 580
  choice 609
voice, *v.* 566
voiceless 581
void, *n. waste* 180
  abyss 667
void, *adj.*
  unsubstantial 4
  absent 187
volatile *transient* 111
  light 320
  gaseous 334, 336
volcanic *violent* 173
  excitable 825
volcano 173
volley *violence* 173
  report 406

  attack 716
volplane 267
volplaning 267
Volstead Act 761
voluble 584
volume
  bulk 25, 31, 192
  book 593
voluminous *great* 31
  bulky 192
voluntary, *n. prelude* 62, 64
voluntary, *adj.* 600, 602
volunteer, *n.* 602, 726
volunteer, *v. will* 600
  offer 602, 763
  endeavor 676
vomit 297
voodoo 621, 992, 994
voracious 957
vortex 312
votary *devotee* 865
vote *choice* 480, 609
  affirmation 535

voter 609
votive 768
vouch *assert* 535
  –for 467
voucher *evidence* 467
  indication 550
  security 771
vouchsafe *permit* 760
  consent 762
  condescend 879
vow *affirm* 535
  promise 768
  worship 990
voyage 267
voyager 268
vulgar 579, 851
vulgarian 851
VULGARITY
  inelegance 579
  want of refinement 851
vulnerable 665
vulture *bird* 366
  evildoer 913

W

wad, *n. money* 800
wad, *v. line* 224
wadding, *lining* 224
  stopper 263
waddle 275
wade 267
wafer 204
waft *blow* 349
wag, *n. joker* 844
wag, *v. oscillate* 314, 315
wager 621
wages 775, 973
waggle 314, 315
wagon 268
wagoner 268
waif *derelict* 782
wail 412, 839
wainscot *base* 211
waist 225
waistcoat 225
wait *tarry* 133
  –for 133, 507
  –upon *serve* 746
waiter *servant* 746
waive *not use* 678
wake, *n. sequel* 65
  rear 235
  funeral 363
wake, *v. excite* 824
wakeful *careful* 459
walk, *n. excursion* 266
  slowness 275
  business 625
  career 692
walk, *v.* 266
walker 268
wall *cliff* 212
  inclosure 232

  defense 717
wallet 191, 800
wallow *grovel* 207
  plunge 310
  welter 311
waltz 840
wampum 800
wan *pale* 429
  sad 837
wand 747, 993
wander *move* 264
  journey 266
  deviate 279
  rave 503
wanderer 268
wane *decrease* 36
  contract 195
  decay 659
want, *n. incompleteness* 53
  insufficiency 640
  poverty 804
  desire 865
want, *v. fall short* 304
  require 630
  need 640
  desire 865
  –of uniformity 16a
wanting *incomplete* 53
  absent 187
wanton 608
war 361, 722
warble 416
warbler 366
ward *parish* 181
  dependent 746
  custody 751
  –off 706, 717
warden *guardian* 664

  master 745
warder *guardian* 664
  keeper 753
warehouse 636
WARFARE 361, 722
warlike 720, 722, 861
warm, *adj. hot* 382
  orange 439
  ardent 821
  irascible 901
warm, *v.* 834
war medal 722
warmhearted 888, 906
warmth 382
  vigorous language 574
warn *dissuade* 616
  caution 668
WARNING *omen* 512
  caution 668
warp, *n. tendency* 176
  deviation 279
  bias 481
warp, *v. change* 140
  tend 176
  distort 243
  prejudice 481
  injure 659
warrant, *n. evidence* 467
  decree 741
  permit 760
  security 771
warrant, *v. certify* 535
  promise 768
  justify 937
warranty 768
warrior 726
warship 726
wary *cautious* 864

wash *color* 428
  cleanse 652
  -out *discolor* 429
  obliterate 552
washerman 652
washerwoman 652
washhouse 652
washing 337
washout 348
WASTE, *n. decrement* 40a
  desert 169
  space 180
  consumption 638
  rubbish 645
  loss 776
  prodigality 818
waste, *v. decrease* 36
  destroy 162
  contract 195
  consume 638
  injure 659
  -time 135
wasted *weak* 160
  deteriorated 659
wasteful 638, 818
watch, *n. company* 72
  timepiece 114
  sentinel 668
watch, *v. observe* 441
  attend to 457, 459
  guard 664
  -for 507
watchdog 263, 668
watcher 459
watchful 459
  -waiting *inaction* 681
  caution 864
watchman *guardian* 664
  sentinel 668
watchtower 550, 668
watchword *sign* 550
WATER 337
watercourse 350
water drinker 958
waterfall 348
waterman 269
waterproof, *n. dress* 225
waterproof, *adj.* 340, 664
waterspout 348
watertight 340, 664
watery *wet* 337
  moist 339
wave, *n.* 248, 348
wave, *v. oscillate* 314
waver *change* 149
  doubt 485
  vacillate 605
waverer 605
wavy 248
wax, *n.* 356
wax, *v. increase* 31
  become 144
  expand 194
way *opening* 260
  habit 613
  road 627

wayfarer 268
wayfaring 266
waylay 545
ways 692
wayward *changeable* 149
  obstinate 606
  capricious 608
wayworn 266
weak *feeble* 160
  insipid 391
  illogical 477
  irresolute 605
  lax 738
  vicious 945
weaken *decrease* 36
  diminish 38
  enfeeble 160
  refute 468
weakly *feeble* 160
  unhealthy 655
weak-minded 499
WEAKNESS 160, 945
WEALTH *riches* 803
wean 614
weapon *arms* 727
wear, *n. use* 677
  -and tear *waste* 638
  injury 659
wear, *v. decrease* 36
  dress 225
  deflect 279
  -away *cease* 142
  -off 614
WEARINESS *ennui* 841
wearisome *slow* 275
  laborious 686
  painful 830
weary *fatigue* 688, 841
  sad 837
weather 338
  -prophet 513
  -vane 550
weathercock
  changeableness 149
  vane 349, 550
weatherproof 664
weather vane 338
weave *compose* 54
  interlace 219
web 219
wed 903
wedded 903
wedding 903
wedge 633
wedlock 43, 903
weed, *n. plant* 367
  cigar 392
weed, *v. cultivate* 371
  clean 652
  -out *eliminate* 55
  thin 103
  eject 297
  extract 301
ween *believe* 484
  know 490
weep *lament* 839

weeping 839
weft 329
weigh *influence* 175
  load 319
  ponder 451
weight *influence* 175
  gravity 319
  vigor 574
  importance 642
  have - evidence 467
weighty 319, 642
  significant 467
weir 232, 350
weird *spectral* 980a
welcome, *n.* 892
welcome, *adj.*
  grateful 829
  friendly 888
welcome, *v.* 894
weld *join* 43
welfare 734
well, *n. origin* 153
  depth 208
  pool 343
well, *adj. good* 618
  healthy 654
well, *v. flow* 348
well behaved
  courteous 894
well being 734, 827
well beloved 897
well bred 852, 894
well founded *existent* 1
  certain 474
  true 494
well grounded
  existent 1
  informed 490
well known 490
well laid 611
well nigh *almost* 32
well off *prosperous* 734
  rich 803
well timed 134
well-wisher 890, 906, 914
welter 310, 311
wench *girl* 129
wend 266
west 236
western 236
wet, *adj.* 339, 348
wet, *v.* 337
whack 276
whale 366
wharf 189, 231
wheedle *coax* 615
  caress 902
  flatter 933
wheedler 615
wheel, *n. circle* 247
  bicycle 272
wheel, *v. deviate* 279
  turn back 283
  turn 311
  rotate 312
wheelbarrow 272

X

Y

yarn *filament* 205
   untruth 546
   exaggeration 549
yaw 279
yawl *ship* 273
yawn *gape* 198, 260
   be tired 688
yawning *deep* 208
year 106
yearn 828, 837
yearning *love* 897
years *age* 128
yeast *leaven* 320
yell *cry* 406, 410, 411
   cheer 838
YELLOW 436

sensational 824
   -journalism 824
yellowness 436
yelp *cry* 406, 412
   whine 839
yeoman 371, 373
yeomanry 726
yes 488
yesterday 122
yet 30, 106
yield *soften* 324
   submit 725
   consent 762
   resign 782
   gain 810
   fetch 812

yielding *soft* 324
   facile 705
yogi *ascetic* 955
yoke, *n. vinculum* 45, **752**
   couple 89
   servitude 749
yoke, *v. join* 43
   harness 370
yokel *rustic* 876
yonder 196
young 127
youngster 129
youth *juvenility* **127**
   lad 129
youthful 127
yuletide 138

Z

zeal *willingness* 602
   activity 682
   feeling 821
   ardor 865
zealot *bigot* 474, 606
zealous 602, 821
zenith *height* 206
   summit 210
zephyr 349
zeppelin 273, **726**

ZERO *nothing* 4
   nought 101
zest *relish* 394
   enjoyment 827
Zeus 979
zigzag *oblique* 217
   angle 244
   deviating 279
zip 409
zodiac 230

zone *region* 181
   belt 230
   circle 247
zoo 370
zoological 366
   -garden 370
zoologist 368
ZOOLOGY 368
Zoroastrianism 976
zouave 726

FOREIGN WORDS AND PHRASES

à bas. [F.] Down, down with.

ab initio. [L.] From the beginning.

à bon marché. [F.] Cheap; a good bargain.

ab origine. [L.] From the origin.

ab ovo. [L.] From the egg; from the beginning.

à cheval. [F.] On horseback.

addenda. [L.] Things to be added; list of additions.

ad finem. [L.] To the end.

ad hoc. [L.] To or with respect to this (object); said of a body elected or appointed for a definite work (as a school board for education).

ad infinitum. [L.] To infinity.

ad libitum. [L.] At pleasure; as much as one pleases.

ad nauseam. [L.] To the point of disgust or satiety.

ad rem. [L.] To the purpose; to the point.

adsum. [L.] I am present; here!

ad valorem. [L.] According to the value.

advocatus diaboli. [L.] Devil's advocate; a person chosen to dispute before the papal court the claims of a candidate for canonization.

æquo animo. [L.] With an equable mind; with equanimity.

ære perennius. [L.] More lasting than brass (or bronze).

affaire d'amour. [F.] A love affair.

affaire de cœur. [F.] An affair of the heart.

affaire d'honneur. [F.] An affair of honor; a duel.

a fortiori. [L.] With stronger reason.

Agnus Dei. [L.] Lamb of God.

à haute voix. [F.] Aloud.

à la belle étoile. [F.] Under the stars; in the open air.

à la bonne heure. [F.] In good time; very well.

à la carte. [F.] According to the bill of fare.

à la mode. [F.] According to the custom (or fashion).

al fresco. [It.] In the open air.

alter ego. [L.] Another self.

amende honorable. [F.] Satisfactory apology; reparation.

à merveille. [F.] Admirably; marvelously.

amour propre. [F.] Self-love; vanity.

ancien régime. [F.] The former order of things.

anglice. [NL.] In the English language or fashion.

anguis in herba. [L.] A snake in the grass; an unsuspected danger.

anno urbis conditæ. [L.] In the year (or from the time) of the founded city (Rome).

à outrance. [F.] To the utmost.

aperçu. [F.] A general sketch or survey.

à perte de vue. [F.] Till beyond one's view.

441

à peu près. [F.] Nearly.

à pied. [F.] On foot.

a posteriori. [L.] From effect to cause; empirical.

a priori. [L.] From cause to effect; presumptive.

arbiter elegantiarum. [L.] A judge or supreme authority in matters of taste.

arcana imperii. [L.] State secrets.

argumentum ad hominem. [L.] An argument to the individual man; *i.e.*, to his interests and prejudices.

arrière-pensée. [F.] Mental reservation.

ars est celare artem. [L.] It is true art to conceal art.

ars longa, vita brevis. [L.] Art is long, life is short.

au contraire. [F.] On the contrary.

au courant. [F.] Fully acquainted with matters.

au désespoir. [F.] In despair.

au fait. [F.] Well acquainted with; expert.

au fond. [F.] At bottom.

au reste. [F.] As for the rest; besides.

au revoir. [F.] Until we meet again.

autant d'hommes, autant d'avis. [F.] So many men, so many minds.

avant-propos. [F.] Preliminary matter; preface.

à votre santé! [F.] To your health!

ballon d'essai. [F.] A trial balloon; a device to test opinion.

bas bleu. [F.] A bluestocking; a literary woman.

beau idéal. [F.] The ideal of perfection.

beau monde. [F.] The world of fashion.

beaux esprits. [F.] Men of wit.

beaux yeux. [F.] Fine eyes; good looks.

bel esprit. [F.] A person of wit or genius; a brilliant mind.

ben trovato. [It.] Well found.

bête noire. [F.] A bugbear; a special aversion; *lit.*, black beast.

bis dat qui cito dat. [L.] He gives twice who gives quickly.

bona fides (bona fide). [L.] Good faith (in good faith).

bon ami. [F.] Good friend.

bon gré, mal gré. [F.] With good or ill grace; willing or unwilling.

bon jour. [F.] Good day; good morning.

bon mot. [F.] A witty saying.

bonne foi. [F.] Good faith.

bon naturel. [F.] Good nature.

bon soir. [F.] Good evening.

bon ton. [F.] Fashionable society; good style.

bon vivant. [F.] A lover of good living; a gourmet.

bon voyage! [F.] A good voyage or journey to you!

campo santo. [It.] A burying-ground; *lit.*, a holy field.

canaille. [F.] Rabble.

carpe diem. [L.] Enjoy the present day; improve the time.

casus belli. [L.] That which causes or justifies war.

catalogue raisonné. [F.] A catalogue arranged according to subjects.

cause célèbre. [F.] A celebrated or notorious case (in law).

caveat emptor. [L.] Let the purchaser beware (*i.e.*, he buys at his own risk).

cave canem. [L.] Beware of the dog.

cela va sans dire. [F.] That goes without saying; that is a matter of course.

c'est-à-dire. [F.] That is to say.

c'est égal. [F.] It's all one.

c'est magnifique, mais ce n'est pas la guerre. [F.] It is magnificent, but it is not war.

c'est autre chose. [F.] That's quite another thing.

ceteris paribus. [L.] Other things being equal.

chacun à son goût. [F.] Every one to his taste.

chef-d'œuvre. [F.] Masterpiece.

cherchez la femme. [F.] Look for the woman (who is at the bottom of the affair).

chère amie. [F.] A dear (female) friend.

chevalier d'industrie. [F.] One who lives by his wits; a swindler.

ci-gît. [F.] Here lies.

circa. [L.] About.

cogito, ergo sum. [L.] I think, therefore I exist.

comme il faut. [F.] As it should be; in good form.

compte rendu. [F.] An account rendered; a report.

con amore. [It.] With love; very earnestly.

confrère. [F.] Colleague.

contretemps. [F.] An unexpected or untoward event; a hitch.

coram populo. [L.] Publicly; in public.

corpus delicti. [L.] The body of the crime.

corrigenda. [L.] Things to be corrected; a list of errors.

coup. [F.] A stroke.—**coup d'essai**, a first attempt.—**coup d'état**, a sudden decisive blow in politics; a stroke of policy.—**coup de grâce**, a finishing stroke.—**coup de main**, a sudden attack or enterprise.—**coup de maître**, a master stroke.—**coup d'œil**, a rapid glance of the eye.—**coup de pied**, a kick.—**coup de soleil**, sunstroke.—**coup de théâtre**, a theatrical effect.

coûte que coûte. [F.] Cost what it may.

credat Judæus Apella. [L.] Let Apella, the superstitious Jew, believe it; I won't.

credo quia absurdum. [L.] I believe because it is absurd, or contrary to reason.

cui bono? [L.] For whose advantage?

cul-de-sac. [F.] A blind alley (often used figuratively).

cum grano salis. [L.] With a grain of salt; with some allowance.

d'accord. [F.] In agreement.

débâcle. [F.] The break-up of ice in a river; *hence*, a general, confused rout.

de bonne grâce. [F.] With good grace; willingly.

de facto. [L.] In point of fact; actual or actually.

dégagé. [F.] Free; easy; unconstrained.

de gustibus non est disputandum. [L.] There is no disputing about tastes.

Dei gratia. [L.] By the grace of God.

de jure. [L.] From the law; by right.

delenda est Carthago. [L.] Carthage must be destroyed.

de mortuis nil nisi bonum. [L.] (Say) nothing but good of the dead.

dénoûement. [F.] The issue; the end of a plot.

de novo. [L.] Anew.

Deo gratias. [L.] Thanks to God.

de profundis. [L.] Out of the depths.

de rigueur. [F.] Indispensable; obligatory.

dernier ressort. [F.] A last resort.

de trop. [F.] Too much; more than is wanted; out of place.

deus ex machina. [L.] A god from a machine; used in reference to forced or unlikely events introduced in a drama, novel, etc., to resolve a difficult or awkward situation; derived from the use of deities in the ancient drama.

dies iræ. [L.] Day of wrath.

Dieu et mon droit. [F.] God and my right (British royal motto).

distingué. [F.] Distinguished; of elegant appearance.

dolce far niente. [It.] Sweet doing-nothing; sweet idleness.

Dominus vobiscum. [L.] The Lord be with you.

double entente (or, esp. in English, **entendre**). [F.] A double meaning; a play upon words.

dramatis personæ. [L.] Characters of the drama or play.

dulce et decorum est pro patria mori. [L.] It is sweet and glorious to die for one's country.

dum spiro, spero. [L.] While I breathe, I hope.

dum vivimus, vivamus. [L.] While we live, let us live.

ecce homo. [L.] Behold the man!

édition de luxe. [F.] A splendid and expensive edition of a book.

editio princeps. [L.] The first printed edition of a book.

ego et rex meus. [L.] I and my king.

élite. [F.] The best part; the pick.

emeritus. [L.] Retired or superannuated after long service.

en avant. [F.] Forward.

en déshabillé. [F.] In undress.

en effet. [F.] In effect; substantially; really.

en famille. [F.] With one's family; in a domestic state.

enfant gâté. [F.] A spoiled child.

enfants perdus. [F.] Lost children; a forlorn hope.

enfant terrible. [F.] A terrible child, *that is*, one who makes disconcerting remarks.

enfant trouvé. [F.] A foundling.

enfin. [F.] In short; at last; finally.

en masse. [F.] In a mass (or body).

en rapport. [F.] In harmony; in agreement.

en route. [F.] On the way.

en suite. [F.] In company; in a set.

entente cordiale. [F.] Cordial understanding, especially between two states.

entourage. [F.] Surroundings; friends, confidants, etc., closely associated with a person.

entre nous. [F.] Between ourselves.

en vérité. [F.] In truth; verily.

e pluribus unum. [L.] One out of many; one composed of many (motto of the United States).

errata. [L.] Errors; list of errors.

esprit de corps. [F.] The animating spirit of a collective body, as a regiment.

est modus in rebus. [L.] There is a medium in all things.

et cætera (or **et cetera.**) [L.] And the rest.

et id genus omne. [L.] And everything of the sort.

et tu, Brute! [L.] And thou also, Brutus!

eureka! [Gr.] I have found (it)!

Ewigkeit. [G.] Eternity.

ex cathedra. [L.] From the chair; with high authority.

excelsior. [L.] Higher, that is, taller, loftier.

exeunt omnes. [L.] All go out (or retire).

exit. [L.] He goes out.

ex nihilo nihil fit. [L.] Out of nothing, nothing comes.

ex officio. [L.] In virtue of (his) office.

ex parte. [L.] From one party or side.

ex pede Herculem. [L.] From the foot we recognize a Hercules; we judge of the whole from the specimen.

experto crede. [L.] Trust one who has had experience.

exposé. [F.] A statement; a recital.

ex post facto. [L.] After the deed is done; retrospective.

extra muros. [L.] Beyond the walls.

ex uno disce omnes. [L.] From one judge of the rest.

facile princeps. [L.] Easily pre-eminent; indisputably the first.

facilis est descensus Averni. [L.] The descent to Avernus (or hell) is easy.

façon de parler. [F.] Way of speaking.

fait accompli. [F.] A thing already done.

faux pas. [F.] A false step; a slip in behavior.

femme de chambre. [F.] A chambermaid; lady's maid.

festina lente. [L.] Hasten slowly.

feu de joie. [F.] A discharge of firearms as a sign of rejoicing.

fiat justitia, ruat cœlum. [L.] Let justice be done though the heavens should fall.

fiat lux. [L.] Let there be light.

fides Punica. [L.] Punic (or

Carthaginian) faith; treachery.

fidus Achates. [L.] Faithful Achates; a true friend.

fin de siècle. [F.] End of the (nineteenth) century.

finis coronat opus. [L.] The end crowns the work.

flagrante delicto. [L.] In the commission of the crime; redhanded.

fons et origo. [L.] The source and origin.

force majeure. [F.] Greater force or strength; overwhelming force; compulsion.

fortiter in re. [L.] With firmness in acting.

fortuna favet fortibus. [L.] Fortune favors the bold.

furor loquendi. [L.] A rage for speaking.

furor scribendi. [L.] A rage for writing.

gaucherie. [F.] Awkwardness.

gaudeamus igitur. [L.] So let us be joyful.

genius loci. [L.] The genius (or guardian spirit) of a place.

gens d'armes. [F.] Men at arms.

gloria in excelsis (Deo). [L.] Glory (to God) in the highest.

gloria Patri. [L.] Glory be to the Father.

goût. [F.] Taste; relish.

grâce à Dieu. [F.] Thanks to God.

habitué. [F.] One in the habit of frequenting a place.

hic et ubique. [L.] Here and everywhere.

hic jacet. [L.] Here lies.

hinc illæ lacrimæ. [L.] Hence these tears.

hodie mihi, cras tibi. [L.] Mine today; yours tomorrow.

hoi polloi. [Gr.] The many; the vulgar; the rabble.

homme d'esprit. [F.] A man of wit or genius.

homo sum; humani nihil a me alienum puto. [L.] I am a man; I count nothing human indifferent to me.

honi soit qui mal y pense. [O. F.] Shamed be he who thinks evil of it (motto of the Order of the Garter).

horribile dictu. [L.] Horrible to relate.

hors de combat. [F.] Out of the combat; disabled.

hors d'œuvre. [F.] A relish.

hôtel de ville. [F.] A town hall.

hôtel-Dieu. [F.] A hospital.

humanum est errare. [L.] To err is human.

ibidem. [L.] At the same place (in a book).

ich dien. [G.] I serve (motto of the Prince of Wales).

ici on parle français. [F.] French is spoken here.

ignotum per ignotius. [L.] The unknown (explained) by the still more unknown.

il n'y a pas de quoi. [F.] Don't mention it; it's not worth speaking of.

il n'y a que le premier pas qui coûte. [F.] It is only the first step that costs.

il penseroso. [It.] The pensive man.

impasse. [F.] A deadlock; an insurmountable difficulty.

impedimenta. [L.] Encumbrances; luggage; baggage.

in æternum. [L.] Forever.

in articulo mortis. [L.] At the point of death; in the last struggle.

index expurgatorius. [L.] A list of prohibited works.

in esse. [L.] In being; in actuality.

in extenso. [L.] At full length.

in extremis. [L.] At the point of death.

infra dignitatem. [L.] Below one's dignity.

in loco. [L.] In the place; in the natural (*or* proper) place.

in loco parentis. [L.] In the place of a parent.

in medias res. [L.] Into the midst of things.

in memoriam. [L.] To the memory of; in memory.

in nomine. [L.] In the name of.

in omnia paratus. [L.] Prepared for all things.

in perpetuum. [L.] Forever.

in posse. [L.] In possible existence; in possibility.

in præsenti. [L.] At the present moment.

in propria persona. [L.] In one's own person.

in puris naturalibus. [L.] Quite naked.

in re. [L.] In the matter of.

in rerum natura. [L.] In the nature of things.

in sæcula sæculorum. [L.] For ages on ages.

in situ. [L.] In its original position.

in statu quo. [L.] In the former state.

inter alia. [L.] Among other things.

inter nos. [L.] Between ourselves.

in terrorem. [L.] As a warning.

in toto. [L.] In the whole; entirely.

intra muros. [L.] Within the walls.

in transitu. [L.] In course of transit.

in vacuo. [L.] In empty space; in a vacuum.

in vino veritas. [L.] There is truth in wine; truth is told under the influence of liquor.

invita Minerva. [L.] Against the will of Minerva; without genius or natural abilities.

ipse dixit. [L.] He himself said it; a dogmatic saying or assertion.

ipsissima verba. [L.] The very words.

ipso facto. [L.] By that very fact.

ipso jure. [L.] By the law itself.

jacquerie. [F.] French peasantry; a revolt of peasants.

je ne sais quoi. [F.] I know not what; a something or other.

jeu de mots. [F.] A play on words; a pun.

jeu d'esprit. [F.] A display of wit; a witticism.

jeunesse dorée. [F.] Gilded youth; rich and fashionable young men.

jubilate Deo. [L.] Rejoice in God; be joyful in the Lord.

jure divino. [L.] By divine law.

jure humano. [L.] By human law.

juste milieu. [F.] The golden mean.

laborare est orare. [L.] To labor is to pray; work is worship.

labor omnia vincit. [L.] Labor conquers everything.

laissez-faire. [F.] Let alone; noninterference.

l'allegro. [It.] The merry man.

lapsus calami. [L.] A slip of the pen.

lapsus linguæ. [L.] A slip of the tongue.

lapsus memoriæ. [L.] A slip of the memory.

lares et penates. [L.] Household gods.

lasciate ogni speranza voi ch'entrate. [It.] All hope abandon ye who enter here (inscription on the entrance to the hell of Dante's Inferno).

laudator temporis acti. [L.] A praiser of past times.

laus Deo. [L.] Praise to God.

l'avenir. [F.] The future.

le beau monde. [F.] The fashionable world.

lebe wohl. [G.] Farewell.

la grand monarque. [F.] The great monarch; Louis XIV of France.

le pas. [F.] Precedence in place or rank.

le roi est mort, vive le roi! [F.] The king is dead, long live the king (his successor)!

le roy le veult. [Norm. F.] The king wills it; the formula used by the sovereign in assenting to a bill.

le roy s'avisera. [Norm. F.] The king will consider; the formula formerly used by the sovereign in rejecting a bill.

lèse-majesté. [F.] High treason.

l'état c'est moi. [F.] It is I who am the state.

le tout ensemble. [F.] The whole (taken) together.

lettre de cachet. [F.] A sealed letter containing private orders; a royal warrant.

lex non scripta. [L.] Unwritten law; common law.

lex scripta. [L.] Statute law.

l'homme propose, et Dieu dispose. [F.] Man proposes, and God disposes.

l'inconnu. [F.] The unknown.

littera scripta manet. [L.] The written word remains.

locum tenens. [L.] One occupying the place of another; a substitute.

longo intervallo. [L.] By *or* at a long interval.

lucus a non lucendo. [L.] Used as typical of an absurd derivation—*lucus*, a grove, having been derived by an old grammarian from *luceo*, to shine—"from not shining."

lusus naturæ. [L.] A sport or freak of nature.

ma chère. [F.] My dear (fem.).

ma foi. [F.] Upon my faith.

magna est veritas, et prevalebit. [L.] Truth is mighty, and will prevail.

magnum opus. [L.] A great work.

maison de santé. [F.] A private asylum *or* hospital.

maître d'hôtel. [F.] A house steward.

mala fide. [L.] With bad faith; treacherously.

mal-à-propos. [F.] Ill-timed; out of place.

mal de mer. [F.] Seasickness.

malgré nous. [F.] In spite of us.

mañana. [Sp.] Tomorrow.

mardi gras. [F.] Shrove Tuesday.

mare clausum. [L.] A closed sea; a sea belonging to a single nation.

mariage de convenance. [F.] Marriage from motives of interest rather than of love.

materfamilias. [L.] Mother of a family.

matériel. [F.] Baggage and munitions of an army; material equipment as opposed to men.

mauvaise honte. [F.] Bashfulness; shamefacedness.

mauvais goût. [F.] Bad taste.

mauvais sujet. [F.] A bad subject; a worthless scamp.

mea culpa. [L.] My fault; by my fault.

me judice. [L.] I being judge; in my opinion.

mêlée. [F.] A confused conflict.

memento mori. [L.] Remember that you must die; a reminder of death.

mens sana in corpore sano. [L.] A sound mind in a sound body.

mens sibi conscia recti. [L.] A mind conscious of rectitude.

meo periculo. [L.] At my own risk.

mésalliance. [F.] A bad match; marriage with one of a lower rank.

meum et tuum. [L.] Mine and thine.

mirabile dictu. [L.] Wonderful to relate.

mirabile visu. [L.] Wonderful to see.

mise en scène. [F.] Stage setting.

modus operandi. [L.] Manner of working.

modus vivendi. [L.] Manner of living; used of a temporary working agreement or compromise.

mon ami. [F.] My friend (masc.).

mon cher. [F.] My dear (masc.).

mont-de-piété. [F.] A public or municipal pawnshop.

monumentum ære perennius. [L.] A monument more lasting than brass.

more majorum. [L.] After the manner of our ancestors.

morituri te salutamus. [L.] We, about to die, salute thee:— said by the Roman gladiators to the emperor.

mot d'ordre. [F.] Watchword.

motu proprio. [L.] Of his own accord.

moyen âge. [F.] Middle Ages.

multum in parvo. [L.] Much in little.

mutatis mutandis. [L.] With the necessary changes.

natura non facit saltum. [L.] Nature does not make a leap.

née. [F.] Born; used in giving

the maiden name of a married woman.

négligé. [F.] Morning dress; an easy loose dress.

nemine contradicente. [L.] No one speaking in opposition; without opposition.

nemine dissentiente. [L.] No one dissenting; with a dissenting voice.

nemo me impune lacessit. [L.] No one assails me with impunity (motto of Scotland).

ne plus ultra. [L.] Nothing further; the uttermost point; perfection.

ne quid nimis. [L.] Avoid excess.

n'est-ce pas? [F.] Isn't that so?

nicht wahr? [G.] Isn't that so?

nil admirari. [L.] To be astonished at nothing.

nil desperandum. [L.] There is no reason for despair.

n'importe. [F.] It matters not.

nisi Dominus, frustra. [L.] Except the Lord (build the house, they labor) in vain (that build it). Ps. cxxvii. (motto of Edinburgh).

noblesse oblige. [F.] Rank imposes obligations.

Noël. [F.] Christmas.

nolens volens. [L.] Unwilling or willing.

noli me tangere. [L.] Touch me not.

nom de guerre. [F.] A war name; a pseudonym; a pen name.

nom de plume. [F.] A pen name. (Incorrect for *Nom de guerre*.)

non Angli sed angeli. [L.] Not Angles but angels.

non compos mentis. [L.] Not of sound mind.

non est. [L.] He (*or* it) is not.

non est inventus. [L.] He has not been found.

non libet. [L.] It does not please (me).

non liquet. [L.] The case is not clear.

non multa, sed multum. [L.] Not many things, but much.

non nobis solum. [L.] Not for ourselves alone.

non omnis moriar. [L.] I shall not wholly die.

non sequitur. [L.] It does not follow.

nosce te ipsum. [L.] Know thyself.

nota bene. [L.] Note well; take notice.

Notre Dame. [F.] Our Lady.

nous avons changé tout cela. [F.] We have changed all that.

nous verrons. [F.] We shall see.

novus homo. [L.] A new man; one who has raised himself from obscurity.

nuance. [F.] Shade; tint.

nulla dies sine linea. [L.] Not a day without a line; no day without something done.

nunc aut nunquam. [L.] Now or never.

obiit. [L.] He (*or* she) died.

obiter dictum. [L.] A thing said by the way.

odi profanum vulgus. [L.] I loathe the profane rabble.

odium theologicum. [L.] The hatred of theologians.

œuvres. [F.] Works.

ohne Hast, ohne Rast. [G.] Without haste, without rest: —motto of Goethe.

omnia vincit amor. [L.] Love conquers all things.

on dit. [F.] They say.

onus probandi. [L.] The burden of proof.

operæ pretium est. [L.] It is worth while.

ora et labora. [L.] Pray and work.

ora pro nobis. [L.] Pray for us.

ore rotundo. [L.] With round full voice; well-turned speech.

O! si sic omnia. [L.] Oh, if all things (were) so: Oh, if he had always so spoken or acted.

O tempora! O mores! [L.] Alas for the times! Alas for the manners (or morals)!

otium cum dignitate. [L.] Ease with dignity.

ouï-dire. [F.] Hearsay.

ouvrage de longue haleine. [F.] A work of long breath; a long work or one which lasts.

pace. [L.] By leave of; not to give offence to.

palmam qui meruit ferat. [L.] Let him who has won the palm wear it.

pardonnez-moi. [F.] Pardon me; I beg your pardon.

par excellence. [F.] Pre-eminently.

par exemple. [F.] For example.

par hasard. [F.] By chance.

pari passu. [L.] With equal pace; side by side.

par nobile fratrum. [L.] A noble pair of brothers; two just alike.

parole d'honneur. [F.] Word of honor.

particeps criminis. [L.] An accomplice in a crime.

parti pris. [F.] Preconceived opinion.

parvenu. [L.] A person of low origin who has risen suddenly to wealth or position; an upstart.

pas. [F.] A step; precedence.

passim. [L.] Everywhere; throughout; in all parts of the book, chapter, etc.

pâté de foie gras. [F.] Goose-liver pie.

paterfamilias. [L.] Father of a family; head of a household.

pater patriæ. [L.] Father of his country.

pax vobiscum. [L.] Peace be with you.

peccavi. [L.] I have sinned (or been to blame).

peine forte et dure. [F.] Strong and severe punishment; a kind of judicial torture.

penchant. [F.] A strong liking.

pensée. [F.] A thought.

per. [L.] For; through; by.—per contra. On the contrary. —per annum. By the year; annually.—per capita. By heads; for each individual.—per centum. By the hundred. —per diem. By the day; daily.—per fas et nefas. Through right and wrong.—per se. By itself.

persona non grata. [L.] An unacceptable person.

peu à peu. [F.] Little by little.

peu de chose. [F.] A trifle.

pièce de résistance. [F.] A resistance piece; the main dish of a meal.

pied-à-terre. [F.] A resting-place; a temporary lodging.

pis aller. [F.] The worst or last shift.

place aux dames. [F.] Make room for the ladies.

plebs. [L.] The common people.

poco a poco. [It.] Little by little.

point d'appui. [F.] Point of support; basis.

pons asinorum. [L.] The asses' bridge; a name for the fifth proposition of the first book in Euclid.

poste restante. [F.] To remain in the post office till called for.

post hoc ergo propter hoc. [L.] After this, therefore, on account of this; subsequent to, therefore due to this—an illogical way of reasoning.

pour faire rire. [F.] To excite laughter.

pour le mèrite. [F.] For merit.

pour passer le temps. [F.] To pass the time.

preux chevalier. [F.] A brave knight.

prima donna. [It.] First lady; the chief female singer in an opera, etc.

prima facie. [L.] At first view (or consideration).

primo. [L.] In the first place.

primum mobile. [L.] The source of motion; the mainspring.

principia, non homines. [L.] Principles, not men.

pro bono publico. [L.] For the good of the public.

procès-verbal. [F.] An authenticated minute or statement.

pro et contra. [L.] For and against.

profanum vulgus. [L.] The profane herd.

pro forma. [L.] For the sake of form.

pro patria. [L.] For our country.

pro rata. [L.] According to rate or proportion.

pro tanto. [L.] For so much; as far as it goes.

protégé. [F.] One under the protection of another.

Punica fides. [L.] Punic (or Carthaginian) faith; treachery.

qualis rex, talis grex. [L.] Like king, like people.

quand même. [F.] Even if; whatever may happen.

quantum libet. [L.] As much as you please.

quantum sufficit. [L.] As much as suffices.

quelque chose. [F.] Something; a trifle.

quid pro quo. [L.] Something in return; an equivalent.

quién sabe? [Sp.] Who knows?

quis custodiet ipsos custodes? [L.] Who shall guard the guards themselves?

qui s'excuse s'accuse. [F.] He who excuses himself accuses himself.

qui va là? [F.] Who goes there?

qui vive? [F.] Who lives? Who goes there? To be on the qui vive means to be alert or watchful.

quoad hoc. [L.] To this extent.

quoad sacra. [L.] As far as sacred things are concerned; for ecclesiastical purposes only.

quem Deus vult perdere, prius dementat. [L.] Those whom God wishes to destroy, he first makes mad.

quod erat demonstrandum. [L.] Which was to be proved or demonstrated.

quod vide. [L.] Which see.

quorum pars magna fui. [L.] Of which things, I was an important part.

quot homines, tot sententiæ. [L.] Many men, many minds.

raconteur. [F.] A teller of stories.

raison d'être. [F.] The reason for a thing's existence.

rapprochement. [F.] The act of bringing (or coming) together.

rara avis. [L.] A rare bird; a paragon.

réchauffé. [F.] *Lit.*, something warmed up; *hence*, old literary material worked up into a new form.

reductio ad absurdum. [L.] A reducing to the absurd; a method of proof in which a proposition is shown to be true by demonstrating the absurdity of its contradictions.

rencontre. [F.] An encounter; a hostile meeting.

répondez, s'il vous plaît. [F.] Please reply. *R. S. V. P.*

requiescat in pace. [L.] May he rest in peace.

res angusta domi. [L.] Narrow circumstances at home; poverty.

res gestæ. [L.] Things done; exploits; history.

respice finem. [L.] Look to the end.

résumé. [F.] A summary or abstract.

resurgam. [L.] I shall rise again.

revenons à nos moutons. [F.] Let us return to our sheep; let us return to our subject.

rôle. [F.] A character represented on the stage; also other similar meanings.

rouge et noir. [F.] Red and black; a game of chance.

rus in urbe. [L.] The country in town.

salle à manger. [F.] Dining room

sanctum sanctorum. [L.] Holy of holies.

sang froid. [F.] Coolness; indifference.

sans façon. [F.] Without ceremony.

sans peur et sans reproche. [F.] Without fear and without reproach.

sans souci. [F.] Without care.

sartor resartus. [L.] The patcher repatched; the tailor patched (or mended).

satis superque. [L.] Enough, and more than enough.

satis verborum. [L.] Enough of words; no more need be said.

sauve qui peut. [F.] Let him save himself who can.

savoir-faire. [F.] The knowing how to act; tact.

savoir-vivre. [F.] Good breeding; refined manners.

scripsit. [L.] Wrote (it).

sculpsit. [L.] Engraved (it).

secundum artem. [L.] According to art (*or* rule).

semper idem. [L.] Always the same.

semplice. [It.] Simple; plain.

seriatim. [L.] In a series; one by one.

sic itur ad astra. [L.] Such is the way to the stars, or to immortality.

sic passim. [L.] So here and there throughout; so everywhere.

sic transit gloria mundi. [L.] Thus passes away the glory of this world.

sicut ante. [L.] As before.

similia similibus curantur. [L.] Like things are cured by like.

simplex munditiis. [L.] Elegant in simplicity.

sine cura. [L.] Without charge or care.

sine die. [L.] Without a day being appointed.

sine qua non. [L.] Without which, not; something indispensable.

siste, viator. [L.] Stop, traveler.

sit tibi terra levis. [L.] Light lie the earth upon thee.

soi-disant. [F.] Self-styled.

sotto voce. [It.] In an undertone.

spero meliora. [L.] I hope for better things.

splendide mendax. [L.] Nobly untruthful; untrue for a good object.

sponte sua. [L.] Of one's (*or* its) own accord.

status quo. [L.] The state in which; the existing condition.

stet. [L.] Let it stand; do not delete.

suaviter in modo, fortiter in re. [L.] Gentle in manner, resolute in execution.

sub judice. [L.] Under consideration.

sub rosa. [L.] Under the rose; confidentially.

succès d'estime. [F.] A partial success, or one based on certain merits.

sui generis. [L.] Of its own peculiar kind; in a class by itself.

summum bonum. [L.] The chief good.

sunt lacrimæ rerum. [L.] There are tears for things; misfortunes call for tears.

suppressio veri. [L.] A suppression of the truth.

sursum corda. [L.] Lift up your hearts.

suum cuique. [L.] Let every one have his own.

tableau vivant. [F.] A living picture; the representation of some scene by a group of persons.

table d'hôte. [F.] A public dinner at an inn or hotel.

tabula rasa. [L.] A smooth or blank tablet.

tant mieux. [F.] So much the better.

tant pis. [F.] So much the worse.

te Deum laudamus. [L.] We praise Thee, O God (*or rather*, as God).

te judice. [L.] You being the judge.

tempus fugit. [L.] Time flies.

terminus ad quem. [L.] The term (*or* limit) to which.

terminus a quo. [L.] The term (*or* limit) from which.

terra firma. [L.] Solid earth; a secure foothold.

terra incognita. [L.] An unknown country.

tertium quid. [L.] A third something; a nondescript.

tiers état. [F.] The third estate; the commons.

timeo Danaos et dona ferentes. [L.] I fear the Greeks, even when they bring gifts.

tot homines, quot sententiæ. [L.] So many men, so many minds.

toto cælo. [L.] By the whole heavens; diametrically opposite.

tour de force. [F.] A notable feat of strength or skill.

tout à fait. [F.] Wholly; entirely.

tout à l'heure. [F.] Instantly.

tout au contraire. [F.] On the contrary.

tout de suite. [F.] Immediately.

tout ensemble. [F.] The whole taken together.

tu quoque. [L.] You also.

ubi supra. [L.] Where above mentioned.

ultima Thule. [L.] Most distant Thule; utmost limit.

una voce. [L.] With one voice; unanimously.

und so weiter. [G.] And so forth.

urbi et orbi. [L.] To the city and to the world.

utile dulci. [L.] The useful with the agreeable.

ut infra. [L.] As below.

ut supra. As above.

væ victis. [L.] Woe to the vanquished.

vale. [L.] Farewell.

valet de chambre. [F.] A personal attendant; a body servant.

varium et mutabile semper femina. [L.] Woman is ever a changeful and capricious thing.

veni, vidi, vici. [L.] I came, I saw, I conquered. (Cæsar's message to the senate when he conquered Pharnaces, king of Pontus.)

verbatim et literatim. [L.] Word for word and letter for letter.

verbum sat sapienti. [L.] A word is enough for a wise man.

via, veritas, vita. [L.] The way, the truth, the life.

vice versa. [L.] The terms of the case being interchanged or reversed; conversely.

videlicet. [L.] Namely (*lit.*, one may see).

vide ut supra. [L.] See what is stated above.

vi et armis. [L.] By force and arms; by main force.

vincit qui se vincit. [L.] He conquers who conquers himself.

virginibus puerisque. [L.] For maidens and boys.

vis a tergo. [L.] A force from behind.

vis-à-vis. [F.] Opposite; face to face.

vis inertiæ. [L.] The power of

inertia; resistance to force applied.

vis medicatrix naturæ. [L.] The healing power of nature.

vis vitæ. [L.] Living force; energy.

vivat regina (rex)! [L.] Long live the queen (king)!

viva voce. [L.] By the living voice; orally.

vive la bagatelle! [F.] Long live trifles (*or* frivolity)!

vive le roi! [F.] Long live the king!

vogue la galère! [F.] Row the galley; come what may!

voilà. [F.] Behold; there is; there are.

voilà tout. [F.] That's all.

vox et præterea nihil. [L.] A voice and nothing more; sound but no sense.

vox populi, vox Dei. [L.] The voice of the people is the voice of God.

vraisemblance. [F.] Probability; apparent truth.

vulgo. [L.] Commonly.

Wanderjahr. [G.] Year of wandering.

Wanderlust. [G.] Passion for traveling (*or* wandering).

Weltanschauung. [G.] World view; theory or conception of life or of the world in all its aspects.

Weltschmerz. [G.] World sorrow; sentimental pessimism.

Zeitgeist. [G.] Time-spirit; spirit of the age.

zum Beispiel. [G.] For example.

ABBREVIATIONS USED
IN WRITING AND PRINTING

A

a. About; acre; adjective; afternoon; answer; are (metric system); at.

A. Academician; Academy; America; American; artillery.

A. A. A. Amateur Athletic Association.

A. A. A. S. American Association for the Advancement of Science.

A. A. of A. Automobile Association of America.

A. A. U. Amateur Athletic Union.

ab. About.

A. B. Artium Baccalaureus (L., Bachelor of Arts); (also l. c.) able-bodied (seaman).

abbr., *or* **abbrev.** Abbreviated; abbreviation.

abd. Abdicated.

A. B. F. M. American Board of Foreign Missions.

abl. Ablative.

Abp. Archbishop.

abr. Abridged; abridgment.

abs. Absolutely; abstract.

A. B. S. American Bible Society.

A. C. Alpine Club; ambulance corps; ante Christum (L., before Christ); Army Corps.

Acad. Academy.

acc. Acceptance; account; accusative.

acct. Account.

ad. (*pl.* **ads.**) Advertisement.

a. d. After date; ante diem (L., before the day).

A. D. Anno Domini (L., in the year of our Lord).

A. D. C. Aid-de-camp; aide-de-camp.

ad fin. Ad finem (L., at the end).

ad inf. Ad infinitum (L., to infinity).

ad int. Ad interim (L., in the meantime).

adj. Adjective.

Adj., *or* **Adjt.** Adjutant.

Adj. Gen. Adjutant General.

ad. lib. Ad libitum (L., at pleasure).

Adm. Admiral; Admiralty.

admix. Administratrix.

admr. Administrator.

admx. Administratrix.

adv. Ad valorem; adverb; advocate.

Adv. Advent.

Adv. Gd. Advance guard.

advt. Advertisement.

æ., æt., ætat. Ætatis (L., of age, aged).

A. E. F. American Expeditionary Forces.

AF. *or* **A.-F.** Anglo-French.

457

aff. Affectionate; affirmative; affirming.

afft. Affidavit.

Afr. Africa; African.

A. G. Adjutant General; Advance guard; Attorney-general.

agr., or **agric.** Agriculture; agricultural.

agt. Agent.

A. H. Anno Hegiræ (L., in the year of the Hegira).

A. H. C. Army Hospital Corps.

A. I. American Institute.

Ala. Alabama.

A. L. A. American Library Association; Automobile Legal Association.

ald., or **aldm.** Alderman.

Alex. Alexander.

alg. Algebra.

alt. Alternate; altitude; alto.

Alta. Alberta (Canada).

Am. America; American; ammunition.

a. m. Ante meridiem (L., before noon).

A. M. Anno mundi (L., in the year of the world); Annus Mirabilis (L., the Wonderful Year, i.e., 1666); Artium Magister (L., Master of Arts).

A. M. D. Army Medical Department.

Amer. America; American.

A. M. S. Army Medical Staff.

amt. Amount.

anal. Analogous; analogy; analysis; analytic.

anat. Anatomy.

anc. Ancient; anciently.

anon. Anonymous.

ans. Answer.

ant. Antonym; antiquarian.

Ant. Anthony; Antigua.

anthrop. Anthropology; anthropological.

antiq. Antiquities; antiquarian.

A. N. Z. A. C., or **Anzac.** Australian and New Zealand Army Corps.

A. O. Army order.

A. O. C. Army Ordnance Corps.

A. O. D. Army Ordnance Department.

A. O. F. Ancient Order of Foresters.

A. O. H. Ancient Order of Hibernians.

aor. Aorist.

A. P. C. Army Pay Corps.

A. P. D. Army Pay Department.

Apoc. Apocalypse; Apocrypha; Apocryphal.

app. Appendix; appointed.

App. Apostles.

approx. Approximately.

Apr. April.

aq., Aq. Aqua (L., water).

Ar. Arabian; Arabic.

A. R. Anno regni (L., in the year of the reign); Army Regulations.

A. R. A. Associate of the Royal Academy (of Arts, London).

Arab. Arabian; Arabic.

arch. Archaic; archaism; archery; archipelago; architect; architecture.

Arch. Archibald.

archaeol. Archæology.

Archd. Archdeacon; Archduke.

arith. Arithmetic.

Ariz. Arizona.

Ark. Arkansas.

Arm. Armenian.

arr. Arranged; arrived; arrivals.

art. Article; artificial; artillery; artist.

Art. *or* **A.** Artillery.

AS., *or* **A.-S.** Anglo-Saxon.

A. S. C. Army Service Corps; Army Staff Corps (British Army).

A. S. C. E. American Society of Civil Engineers.

A. S. M. E. American Society of Mechanical Engineers.

assd. Assigned.

assn. Association.

assoc. Associate; association.

asst. Assistant.

A. S. S. U. American Sunday School Union.

astr., astron. Astronomer; astronomy.

astrol. Astrologer; astrology.

Atl. Atlantic.

att., atty. Attorney.

at. wt. Atomic weight.

A. U. C. Ab urbe condita (L., from the founding of the city; i.e., Rome, about 753 B. C.).

Aug. August.

Aus., Aust. Austria; Austrian.

Austral. Australasia; Australia.

Auth. Ver. Authorized Version.

auxil. Auxiliary.

av. Avenue; average.

A. V. Artillery Volunteers; Authorized Version.

A. V. C. Army Veterinary Corps.

A. V. D. Army Veterinary Department.

ave. Avenue.

A. W. L. Absent with Leave.

A. W. O. L. Absent without Leave.

ax. Axiom.

az. Azure.

B

b. Base; bass; battery; bay; book; born; brother.

B. A. Bachelor of Arts; British Academy; British America.

B. Agr. Bachelor of Agriculture.

bal. Balance.

bap. Baptized.

Bapt. Baptist.

bar. Barometer; barometric; barrel.

Barb. Barbados.

barr. Barrister.

Bart. Baronet.

bat., batt., *or* **bn.** Battalion.

batt. *or* **b.** Battery.

bbl. (*pl.* bbls.) Barrel.

B. C. Before Christ; British Columbia.

B. C. L. Bachelor of Civil Law.

bd. Board; bond; bound.

B. D. Bachelor of Divinity.

bdl. (*pl* bdls.) Bundle.

b. e. Bill of exchange.

B. E. F. British Expeditionary Forces.

Belg. Belgian; Belgium.

Benj. Benjamin.

B. ès L. Bachelier ès Lettres (F. Bachelor of Letters).

bg. (*pl.* bgs.) Bag.

b. h. p. Brake horse power.

B. I. British India.

Bib. Bible; Biblical.

biog. Biographer; biography.

biol. Biologist; biology.

bk. Bank; book.

bkg. Banking.

bkt. (*pl.* bkts.) Basket.

b. l. Bill of lading; breech-loading.

B. L. Bachelor of Laws.

bldg. (*pl.* bldgs.) Building.

B. Litt. Bachelor of Literature, *or* of Letters.

B. L. R. Breech-loading rifle.

b. m. Board measure.

B. M. Bachelor of Medicine; Brigade Major.

B. Mus. Bachelor of Music.

b. o. Branch office; buyer's option.

Boh. Bohemia; Bohemian.

Bol. Bolivia.

bor. Borough.

bot. Botanical; botanist; botany.

Bp. Bishop.

b. p. Below proof; bill of parcels; bills payable.

B. P. O. E. Benevolent and Protective Order of Elks.

br. Brig; brother; brown.

Br. British.

Br. Am. British America.

b. rec. Bills receivable.

brig. Brigade; brigadier.

Brit. Britain; British.

bro. (*pl.* bros.) Brother.

b. s. Balance sheet; bill of sale.

B. S. Bachelor of Surgery.

B. Sc. Bachelor of Science.

bu., bus. Bushel; bushels.

bul. Bulletin.

Bulg. Bulgaria; Bulgarian.

B. V. M. Beata Virgo Maria (L., Blessed Virgin Mary).

Bvt. Brevet; breveted.

Brig. Gen. Brigadier General.

C

c. Carton; cathode; cent; centime; centimeter; century; chapter, child; circa (L., about); cost; cubic; current.

C. Cape; Catholic; centigrade (thermometer); Chancellor; Congress; Conservative; Consul; Corps; Court.

C. A. Chartered Accountant; Chief Accountant; Confederate Army; Controller of Accounts; Court of Appeal.

cal. Calendar; calends; calorie.

Calif. California.

Cam., Camb. Cambridge.

Can. Canada; Canadian.

Cant. Canterbury, Canticles.

Cantab. Cantabrigiensis (L., of Cambridge).

Cantuar. Cantuaria (LL., Canterbury); Cantuariensis (LL., of Canterbury).

cap. Capital; capitalize; capitulum (L., chapter); captain.

Capt. Captain.

car. Carat; carpentry.

Card. Cardinal.

cash. Cashier.

cat. Catalogue; catechism.

cath. Cathedral.

Cath. Catherine; Catholic.

cav. Cavalry.

C. B. Cape Breton; Cavalry Brigade; Chief Baron; Common Bench; Companion of the Bath; Confined to Barracks.

cc. Cubic centimeter, *or* centimeters.

c. c. Compte courant (F., account current); cubic centimeter, *or* centimeters.

C. C. Caius College (Cambridge, Eng.); Circuit Court; Civil Court; County Clerk.

C. C. D. Commander of Coast Defenses.

C. C. P. Court of Common Pleas.

c. d. v. Carte de visite.

C. E. Church of England; Civil Engineer; Corps of Engineers.

cel. Celebrated.

Celt. Celtic.

cen. Central; century.

cent. Centigrade; central; century; centum.

cert. Certificate; certify.

certif. Certificate; certificated.

cf. Confer (i.e., compare).

C. F. A. Chief of Field Artillery.

c. f. & i. *or* **c. f. i.** Cost, freight, and insurance.

cg. Centigram.

C. G. Captain General; Captain of the Guard; Coast Guard; Commanding General; Consul General.

C. G. H. Cape of Good Hope.

C. G. S. *or* **c. g. s.** Centimeter-gram-second (system of units); Chief of General Staff in the field.

ch. Chapter; chief; child, church.

Ch. Chancery; Charles; China; Church.

C. H. Captain of the Horse; Courthouse; Customhouse.

chanc. Chancellor; chancery.

chap. Chaplain; chapter.

Chas. Charles.

chem. Chemical; chemist; chemistry.

Chin. China; Chinese.

Ch. J. Chief Justice.

Chr. Christ; Christian; Christopher.

chron. Chronological; chronology.

Chron. Chronicles.

chs. Chapters.

c. i. f. Cost, insurance, and freight.

circ. Circa. circiter, circum (L., about).

cit. Citation, cited; citizen.

civ. Civil; civilian.

C. J. Chief Justice.

cl. Centiliter; class; clause; clergyman; cloth.

class. Classic; classical; classification.

cld. Cleared; colored.

clk. Clerk.

cm. Centimeter.

cml. Commercial.

C. M. Certificated Master; common meter; Corresponding Member; court-martial.

C. M. G. Companion of St. Michael and St. George.

cml. Commercial.

Co. Company; county.

c. o. Care of; carried over.

C. O. Colonial Office; Commanding Officer; Crown Office.

coad. Coadjutor.

C. O. D. Cash, or collect, on delivery.

C. of S. Chief of Staff.

cog. Cognate.

col. College; collegiate; colonial; colony; colored; column.

Col. Colonel; Colossians.

coll. Colleague; collection; collector; college.

collat. Collateral; collaterally.

colloq. Colloquial; colloquially.

Colo. Colorado.

Col. Sergt. Color Sergeant.

com. Comedy; commentary; commerce; common; commonly; communication.

Com. Commander; Commission; Commissioner; Committee; Commodore.

comdg. Commanding.
Comdr. Commander.
Comdt. Commandant.
comp. Compare; comparative; composer; compositor; compound; comprising.
Com. Ver. Common Version.
con. Contra (L., against).
Cong. Congregational; Congress; Congressional.
conj. Conjunction.
Conn. Connecticut.
const. Constable; constitution.
cont. Containing; contents; continent; continue; continued.
contemp. Contemporary.
contr. Contracted; contraction; contrary.
cor. Corner; cornet; corrected; correction; correlative; correspondent; corresponding.
Cor. Corinthians.
Corp. Corporal.
cos. Cosine.
cosec. Cosecant.
cot. Cotangent.
cp. Compare.
c. p. Candle power; chemically pure.
C. P. Common Pleas; Common Prayer; Court of Probate.
C. P. A. Certified public accountant.
cps. Coupons.
C. P. S. Clerk of Petty Sessions.
cr. Created; credit; creditor; crown.
cresc. Crescendo.
C. S. Christian Science; Civil Service.
C. S. A. Confederate States

Army; Confederate States of America.
C. S. C. Conspicuous Service Cross.
C. S. I. Companion of the Star of India (Brit. order).
C. S. N. Confederate States Navy.
C. S. O. Chief Signal Officer.
ct. Cent; county
cts. Cents; centimes.
cu., cub. Cubic.
cur. Currency; current.
C. V. Common Version.
c. w. o. Cash with order.
cwt. Hundredweight or hundredweights.
cyc., or cyclo. Cyclopedia; cyclopedic.
C. in C. Commander in Chief.

D

d. Date; daughter; day; dead; degree; denarius, or denarii (L., penny or pence); deputy; died; dime; dollar; dose.
D. Democrat; department; Deus (L., God); Duke; Dutch.
Dan. Danish, Daniel.
D. A. R. Daughters of the American Revolution.
dat. Dative.
dau. Daughter.
D. C. Da capo (It., from the beginning); Dental Corps; District Court; District of Columbia.
D. C. L. Doctor of Civil Law.
d. d. Days after date.
D. D. Divinitatis Doctor (L., Doctor of Divinity).
D. D. S. Doctor of Dental Surgery.

Dea. Deacon.

deb. Debenture.

dec. Declension; declination; decorative.

Dec. December.

def. Defendant; definition.

deft. Defendant.

deg. Degree.

del. Delegate; delineavit (L., he, *or* she, drew it).

Del. Delaware.

Dem. Democrat; Democratic.

Den. Denmark.

dep. Department; departs; deponent; deputy.

dept. Department; deponent.

der., *or* **deriv.** Derivation; derivative; derived.

Deut. Deuteronomy.

D. F. Dean of the Faculty; Defensor Fidei (L., Defender of the Faith).

dft. Defendant; draft.

dg. Decigram.

D. G. Dei gratia (L., by the grace of God); Deo gratias (L., thanks to God); Director General; Dragoon Guards.

diam. Diameter.

dict. Dictator; dictionary.

dim., *or* **dimin.** Diminuendo; diminutive.

dis. Discipline; discount.

disc. Discount; discovered.

disct. Discount.

disp. Dispensatory.

dist. Distant; distinguished; district.

div. Divide; divided; dividend; divine; division; divisor.

dl. Deciliter.

D. Lit. Doctor of Literature.

D. L. O. Dead Letter Office.

dm. Decimeter.

do. Ditto.

dol. (*pl.* dols.) Dollar; dollars.

dom. Domestic; dominion.

D. O. M. Deo Optimo Maximo (L., to God, the Best, the Greatest).

D. O. R. C. Dental Officers' Reserve Corps.

dow. Dowager.

doz. Dozen; dozens.

dpt. Department; deponent.

dr. Dram; drawer.

Dr. Debtor; doctor.

dram. pers. Dramatis personæ.

d. s. Dal segno (It., from the sign; — *musical direction*); day's sight; days after sight.

D. S. Director of Supplies.

D. Sc. Doctor of Science.

D. S. C. Distinquished Service Cross.

D. S. O. Distinquished Service Order (British, Army and Navy).

D T Double Time; "rush." (Signal).

D. T.'s. Delirium tremens. *Colloq.*

Du. Dutch.

D. V. Deo volente (L., God willing).

D. V. M. Doctor of Veterinary Medicine.

D. V. S. Director of Veterinary Services.

dwt. Pennyweight *or* pennyweights.

E

E. Earl; Earth; East; Eastern; Engineer; English.

ea. Each.

Ebor. Eboracum (L., York); Eboracensis (L., of York).

E. C. Eastern Central (Postal District, London); Established Church.

eccl., *or* **eccles.** Ecclesiastical.

Eccl., *or* **Eccles.** Ecclesiastes.

Ecclus. Ecclesiasticus.

Ecua. Ecuador.

ed. Edition; editor.

E. D. Eastern Department; Extra Duty.

Edin. Edinburgh.

edit. Edition.

Edw. Edward.

E. E. Early English; Electrical Engineer; errors expected.

E. E. & M. P. Envoy Extraordinary and Minister Plenipotentiary.

Eg. Egypt; Egyptian.

e. g. Exempli gratia (L., for example).

E. I. East India; East Indies.

elec. Electrical; electrician; electricity.

Eliz. Elizabeth; Elizabethan.

Em. Emmanuel; Emily; Emma.

E. M. F. Electromotive force.

Emp. Emperor; Empress.

ency., *or* **encyc.** Encyclopedia.

ENE. East-northeast.

eng. Engineer; engraving.

Eng. England; English.

engin. Engineer; engineering.

entom. Entomology.

E. O. Engineer Officer.

E. O. R. C. Engineer Officers' Reserve Corps.

Eph. Ephesians, Ephraim.

Epiph. Epiphany.

Epis., *or* **Episc.** Episcopal.

eq. Equal; equivalent.

ESE. East-southeast.

esp., *or* **espec.** Especially.

Esq. Esquire.

est., *or* **estab.** Established.

Esth. Esther.

et al. Et alibi (L., and elsewhere); et alii (L., and others).

etc. Et cetera (L., and others, and so forth).

et seq. Et sequens (L., and the following).

et sqq. Et sequentes (L., and the following), *masc. & fem. pl.*, or sequentia, *neut. pl.*

etym., *or* **etymol.** Etymology.

ex. Examined; example; excursion; executed; executive; export; extract.

ex div. Without dividend.

Exod. Exodus.

exp. Export; express.

Expl. Explosives.

exr. Executor.

exrx. Executrix.

ext. External; extinct; extra; extract.

Ezek. Ezekiel.

F

f. Farthing; fathom; feminine; fine; flower; folio; foot; forte; franc.

F. Fahrenheit; French.

F. A. Field Artillery.

fac. Facsimile.

Fahr. Fahrenheit.

F. A. I. A. Fellow of the American Institute of Architects.

fam. Familiar; family.

F. A. M. Free and Accepted Masons.

far. Farriery; farthing.

F. A. R. C. Field Artillery Reserve Corps.

F. B. A. Fellow of the British Academy (scientific society).

F. C. Free Church (of Scotland).

fcap. Foolscap.

fcp. Foolscap.

F. D. Fidei Defensor (L., Defender of the Faith).

Feb. February.

fem. Feminine.

ff. Folios; following (pages); fortissimo.

F. F. V. First Families of Virginia.

f. i. For instance.

fict. Fiction.

fig. Figurative; figuratively; figure.

Fin. Finland; Finnish.

fir. Firkin; firkins.

fl. Florin; flourished; fluid.

Fl. Flanders; Flemish.

Fla. Florida.

Flem. Flemish.

fm. Fathom.

F. M. Field Marshal; Foreign Mission.

fo. Folio.

F. O. Field Officer; Field Order.

f. o. b. Free on board.

fol. Folio; following.

for. Foreign.

fort. Fortification.

fr. Fragment; franc; from.

Fr. Father; France; Frau; French; Friar.

Fred. Frederick.

freq. Frequent; frequentative.

F. R. G. S. Fellow of the Royal Geographical Society (London).

Fri. Friday.

F. R. S. Fellow of the Royal Society (London).

frs. Francs.

F. S. Field Service.

ft. Feet; foot; fort; fortified.

fur. Furlong; further.

fut. Future.

G

g. Gauge; genitive; gram; guide; guinea or guineas; gulf.

G. German.

Ga. Georgia.

G. A. General Assembly.

gal. (*pl.* gals.) Gallon.

Gal. Galatians.

G. A. R. Grand Army of the Republic.

gaz. Gazette; gazetteer.

G. B. Great Britain.

G. B. & I. Great Britain and Ireland.

G. C. Grand Chancellor (*or* Chaplain, Chapter, Council, Conclave, etc.).

g. c. d. Greatest common divisor.

g. c. m. Greatest common measure.

G. C. M. General Court Martial.

Gd. Guard.

gen. Gender; general; generic; genitive; genus.

Gen. General; Genesis.

gent. Gentleman.

Geo. George.

geog. Geographer; geographic; geographical; geography.

geol. Geologic; geological; geologist; geology.

geom. Geometry.

ger. Gerund.

Ger. German; Germany.

G. H. Q. General Headquarters.

gi. Gill; gills.

G. L. Grand Lodge.

gm. Gram.
G. M. Grand Master.
G. O. General order.
G. O. C. General Officer Commanding.
gov. Government; governor.
Gov. Gen. Governor General.
govt. Government.
G. P. Gloria Patri (L., Glory to the Father); Graduate in Pharmacy.
G. P. O. General Post Office.
gr. Grain; grand; great; gross.
Gr. Greece; Greek; Grecian.
gram. Grammar.
Gr. Br., Gr. Brit. Great Britain.
G. S. General Secretary; General Service; General Staff; Grand Scribe; Grand Secretary.
gt. Gilt; great; gutta (L., drop).
gtt. Guttæ (L., drops).
gun. Gunnery.

H

h. Harbor; hard; hardness; height; high; hour; husband.
H., HQ., or Hqrs. Headquarters.
ha. Hectare.
H. A. Horse Artillery.
Hab. Habakkuk.
Hag. Haggai.
H. B. C. Hudson's Bay Company.
H. B. M. His (or Her) Britannic Majesty.
H. C. Heralds' College, House of Commons.
h. c. f. Highest common factor.
H. E. High explosive; His Eminence; His Excellency.
Heb. Hebrew; Hebrews.

hectol. Hectoliter.
hectom. Hectometer.
H. E. I. C. Honorable East India Company.
her. Heraldry.
hg. Hectogram; heliogram.
H. G. His (or Her) Grace; Horse Guards, High German.
H. H. His (or Her) Highness; His Holiness (the Pope).
hhd. Hogshead; hogsheads.
H. I. H. His (or Her) Imperial Highness.
H. I. M. His (or Her) Imperial Majesty.
Hind. Hindustan; Hindustani.
hist. Historian; historical; history.
H. J. Hic jacet (L., here lies).
hl. Hectoliter.
H. L. House of Lords.
hm. Hectometer.
H. M. His (or Her) Majesty.
H. M. S. His (or Her) Majesty's Service; or Ship.
ho. House.
Hon. Honorable; honorary.
hort. Horticulture.
Hos. Hosea.
Hosp. Hospital.
H. P., or h. p. Half pay; high pressure; horse power.
hr. (pl. hrs.) Hour.
H. R. House of Representatives.
H. R. E. Holy Roman Emperor, or Empire.
H. R. H. His (or Her) Royal Highness.
H. S. H. His (or Her) Serene Highness.
ht. Height.
Hun., Hung. Hungarian; Hungary.

H. W. M. High-water mark.
Hy. Henry.
hyd. Hydrostatics.
hyp. Hypothesis; hypothetical.

I

I. Imperator (L., Emperor); island.
I. A. Indian Army.
ib., *or* **ibid.** Ibidem (L., in the same place).
Ice., Icel. Iceland; Icelandic.
id. Idem (L., the same).
I. D. R. Infantry Drill Regulations.
i. e. Id est. (L., that is).
i. h. p. Indicated horse power.
IHS. A symbol representing Greek IH (ΣΟΥ) Σ Jesus.
ill., illus., illust. Illustrated; illustration.
Ill. Illinois.
imp. Imparted; imperative; imperfect; imperial; impersonal; imported; importer.
in. (*pl.* ins.) Inch.
inc. Including; inclusive; incorporated; increase.
incl. Including; inclusive.
incog. Incognito.
incor. Incorporated.
ind. Independent; indicative; indigo.
Ind. India; Indian; Indiana.
inf. Infantry; infinitive.
I. N. R. I. Iesus Nazarenus, Rex Iudæorum (L., Jesus of Nazareth, King of the Jews).
ins. Inches; inscribed; inspector; insurance.
insp. Inspector.
inst. Instant; institute; institution.

int. Interest; interior; interjection; internal; international; interpreter; intransitive.
interj. Interjection.
intrans. Intransitive.
in trans. In transitu (L., on the way).
introd. Introduction; introductory.
I. O. O. F. Independent Order of Odd Fellows.
I. O. U. I owe you.
I. R. Inland Revenue; Internal Revenue.
I. R. C. Infantry Reserve Corps.
Ire. Ireland.
is. Island; isle.
Isa. Isaiah.
isl. Island; isle.
It. Italian; Italy.
ital. Italic, italics.
Ital. Italian; Italy.
I. W. Isle of Wight.

J

J. Judge; Justice.
J. A. Judge Advocate.
Jam. Jamaica.
Jan. January.
Jap. Japan; Japanese.
Jas. James.
Jav. Javanese.
J. C. Jesus Christ; Julius Cæsar; jurisconsult.
J. C. D. Juris Civilis Doctor (L., Doctor of Civil Law).
Jer. Jeremiah.
JJ. Justices.
Jno. John.
Jon., Jona. Jonathan.
Jos. Joseph.
Josh. Joshua.
Jour. Journal; journeyman

J. P. Justice of the Peace.
Jr. Junior.
Judg. Judges.
Jun., *or* **jun.** Junior.
Junc. Junction.
jus., just. Justice.

K

K. King; Kings; Knight.
Kans. Kansas.
K. B. King's Bench.
K. C. Knights of Columbus.
K. C. B. Knight Commander of the Bath (Brit. order).
kg. Kilogram.
K. G. Knight of the Garter.
Ki. Kings.
kilom. Kilometer.
K. K. K. Ku-Klux Klan.
kl. Kiloliter.
km. Kilometer; kingdom.
K. M. Knight of Malta (European religious order).
knt. Knight.
K. O. Commanding Officer.
K. P. Kitchen Police; Knight *or* Knights of Pythias.
K. T. Knight Templar.
Ky. Kentucky.

L

l. Lake; land; latitude; leaf; league; left; length; libra (L., a pound); line; link; liter.
L. Lady; Latin; Law; Liber (L., book); Liberal; Low.
La. Louisana.
Lab. Labrador.
Lam. Lamentations.
lat. Latitude.
Lat. Latin.
lb. (*pl.* lbs.) Libra *or* libræ (L., pound *or* pounds).

l.c. Loco citato (L., in the place cited); lower case.
L. C. Lord Chamberlain; Lord Chancellor.
L/C Letter of Credit.
L. C. J. Lord Chief Justice.
l. c. m. Least common multiple.
Ld., ld. Lord.
L. D. Lady Day; (*or* LD.) Low Dutch.
Ldp. Lordship.
lea. League.
leg. Legal; legate; legato; legislative; legislature.
Lev. Leviticus.
LG., *or* **L. G.** Low German.
LGr., *or* **L. Gr.** Low Greek.
l. h. Left hand.
L. H. A. Lord High Admiral.
L. I. Light Infantry; Long Island.
lib. Liber (L., book); librarian; library.
Lieut. *or* **Lt.** Lieutenant.
lin. Lineal; linear.
liq. Liquid; liquor.
lit. Liter; literal; literally; literary; literature.
Lit. D. Literarum Doctor (L., Doctor of Letters).
Lith. Lithuanian.
Litt. D. Litterarum Doctor (L., Doctor of Letters).
LL., *or* **L. L.** Late Latin; Low Latin.
L. L. Lord Lieutenant.
LL. B. Legum Baccalaureus (L., Bachelor of Laws).
LL. D. Legum Doctor (L., Doctor of Laws).
log. Logarithm.
lon., *or* **long.** Longitude.
L. S. Licentiate in Surgery.
L. S. D., *or* **£. s. d.,** *or* **l. s. d.**

Libræ, solidi, denarii (L., pounds, shillings, pence).

Lt. *or* Lieut. Lieutenant.

l. t. Long ton.

M

m. Male; manual; married; masculine; measure; medicine; medium; meridian; meter; middle; mile; mill; minute; month; moon; morning; mountain.

M. Majesty; Manitoba; Marshal; Marquis; Monsieur.

M. A. Magister Artium (L., Master of Arts); Military Academy.

Mac., Macc. Maccabees.

mach. Machinery.

Mad. Madam.

mag. Magazine; magnitude.

Maj. Major.

Mal. Malachi.

man. Manège; manual.

Manit. Manitoba.

manuf. Manufactory; manufacture.

mar. Maritime.

Mar. March.

March. Marchioness.

Marq. Marquis.

mas., *or* masc. Masculine.

Mass. Massachusetts.

math. Mathematician; mathematics.

Matt. Matthew.

max. Maximum.

M. C. Medical Corps; Member of Congress.

Md. Maryland.

M. D. Medicinæ Doctor (L., Doctor of Medicine).

mdse. Merchandise.

Me. Maine.

ME., *or* M. E. Middle English.

M. E. Mechanical, Military, *or* Mining Engineer; Methodist Episcopal; Most Excellent.

meas. Measure.

mech. Mechanics; mechanical.

med. Medical; medicine; medieval; medium.

Medit. Mediterranean.

mem. Memento; memoir; memorandum; memorial.

mer. Meridian; meridional.

Messrs. Messieurs.

metal. Metallurgy.

meteor. Meteorology.

Meth. Methodist.

Mex. Mexican; Mexico.

Mf., *or* mf. Mezzo forte (It., moderately loud).

mfg. Manufacturing.

mfr. (*pl.* mfrs.) Manufacturer.

mg. Milligram.

Mgr. Monseigneur; Monsignore.

M. H. G., *or* MHG. Middle High German.

M. H. R. Member of the House of Representatives.

M. I. Mounted Infantry.

Mic. Micah.

Mich. Michaelmas; Michigan.

mid. Middle; midshipman.

mil. Military; militia.

min. Minim; minimum; mining; minister; minor; minute.

Minn. Minnesota.

Min. Plen. Minister Plenipotentiary.

misc. Miscellaneous.

Miss. Mississippi.

ml. Mail; milliliter.

M. L. A. Modern Language Association.

M. L. G., *or* **MLG.** Middle Low German.

Mlle. Mademoiselle.

mm. Millimeter.

MM. Their Majesties; Messieurs.

Mme. (*pl.* **Mmes.**) Madame (*pl.* Mesdames).

mo. (*pl.* **mos.**) Month.

Mo. Missouri.

M. O. Medical officer; money order.

mod. Moderate; moderato (It., moderately); modern.

Moham. Mohammedan.

mol. wt. Molecular weight.

Mon. Monastery; Monday.

Monsig. Monseigneur; Monsignor.

Mont. Montana.

Mor. Morocco.

M. O. R. C. Medical Officers' Reserve Corps.

M. P. Member of Parliament.

M. P. C. Member of Parliament, Canada.

m. p. h. Miles per hour.

Mr. Mister.

M. R. C. Medical Reserve Corps.

Mrs. Mistress.

MS., *or* **ms.** Manuscript.

M. S. Master of Science; Master of Surgery.

m. s. l. Mean sea level.

MSS. *or* **mss.** Manuscripts.

mt. (*pl.* **mts.**) Mount; mountain.

mun. Municipal.

mus. Museum; music; musician.

Mus. B. Musicæ Baccalaureus (L., Bachelor of Music).

Mus. D. *or* **Musc. Doc.** Musicæ Doctor(L., Doctor of Music).

M. W. Most Worshipful; Most Worthy.

myg. Myriagram.

myl. Myrialiter.

mym. Myriameter.

myth. Mythology.

N

n. Natus (L., born); nephew; neuter; new; nominative; note; noun; number.

N. Navy; Noon; Norse; North; Northern.

N. A. National Academy; National Army; North America; North American.

N. A. A. National Automobile Association.

Nah. Nahum.

nat. National; native; natural.

Nath. Nathanael; Nathaniel.

naut. Nautical.

nav. Naval; navigable; navigation.

N. B. New Brunswick; North Britain; North British; nota bene (L., note well, *or* take notice).

N. C. New Church; Nurses' Corps; North Carolina.

N. C. O. Noncommissioned Officer.

n. d. No date.

N. Dak. North Dakota.

N. E. New England.

N. E. A. National Education Association.

Nebr. Nebraska.

N. E. D. New English Dictionary;—better, O. E. D. (which see).

neg. Negative.

Neh. Nehemiah.

Neth. Netherlands.

neut. Neuter.

Nev. Nevada.

N. F. Newfoundland; (or NF.) Norman French.

Ng. Norwegian.

N. G. National Guard; New Granada; (Slang) no good.

N. Gr., or NGr. New Greek.

N. H. New Hampshire.

Nicar. Nicaragua.

N. J. New Jersey.

N. L., or NL. New Latin.

N. Lat. North latitude.

N. Mex. New Mexico.

NNE. North-northeast.

NNW. North-northwest.

N. O. Natural order (Bot.); New Orleans.

No., or no. (pl. Nos., nos.) Numero (L., [by] number).

nol. pros. Nolle prosequi (L., to be unwilling to prosecute).

nom. Nominative.

non seq. Non sequitur (L., it does not follow).

Nor. Norman; North.

Norw., or Nor. Norway; Norwegian.

Nov. November.

N. P. New Providence; Notary Public.

nr. Near.

N. R. North Riding; North River.

N. S. National Society; New Series; New Style (since 1752); Novia Scotia.

N. S. W. New South Wales.

N. T. New Testament; Northern Territory.

Num. Numbers.

NW. Northwest; Northwestern.

N. W. T. Northwest Territories.

N. Y. New York.

N. Z. New Zealand.

O

O. Old; Ontario; Order.

o/a. On account (of).

ob. Obiit (L., he, or she, died).

Obad. Obadiah.

obdt. Obedient.

obj. Object; objection; objective.

obl. Oblique; oblong.

obs. Observation; observatory; obsolete.

obt. Obedient.

oc. Ocean.

Oct. October.

O. D., or OD. Old Dutch.

O. E., or OE. Old English.

O. E. Omissions excepted.

O. E. D. Oxford English Dictionary.

O. F., or OF. Old French.

off. Offered; officer; official; officinal.

O. H. G., or OHG. Old High German.

O. H. M. S. On His (or Her) Majesty's Service.

O. K., or OK. Correct; all right. Cant.

Okla. Oklahoma.

ol. Oleum (L., oil).

O. M. Old measurement; Order of Merit.

Ont. Ontario.

O. O. R. C. Ordnance Officer ? Reserve Corps.

op. Opera; opposite; opus.

opp. Opposed; opposite.

opt. Optative; optics.

Or. Oriental.

O. R. C. Order of the Red Cross; Officers' Reserve Corps.

ord. Ordained; order; ordinance; ordinary; ordnance.

Oreg. Oregon.

orig. Original; originally.

O. S. Old School; Old Series; Old Style; ordinary seaman.

O. T. Old Testament.

O. T. C. Officers' Training Camp.

Oxon. Oxonia (L., Oxford); Oxoniensis (L., Oxonian).

oz. Ounce; ounces.

P

p. Page; part; participle; past; penny; piano (It., softly); pint; pipe; pole; population; professional.

P. Pastor; pater (L., father); père (F., father); post; president; priest; prince.

Pa. Pennsylvania.

p. a. Participial adjective; per annum (L., by the year).

P/A. Power of attorney; private account.

Pac. Pacific.

pam. Pamphlet.

Pan. Panama.

par. Paragraph; parallel; parenthesis; parish.

Para. Paraguay.

parl. Parliament; parliamentary.

part. Participle.

pass. Passive.

P. B. Prayer Book.

p. c. Per cent; postal card; post card.

pd. Paid.

P. E. Presiding Elder; Protestant Episcopal.

P. E. I. Prince Edward Island.

pen. Peninsula.

Pent. Pentecost.

per an. Per annum (L., by the year).

per ct. Per cent.

perf. Perfect.

perh. Perhaps.

pers. Person; personal.

Pers. Persia; Persian.

pert. Pertaining.

Pet. Peter.

pf. Preferred.

Pg. Portugal; Portuguese.

P. G. M. Past Grand Master.

Phar. Pharmacy; Pharmacopœia.

Ph. B. Philosophiæ Baccalaureus (L., Bachelor of Philosophy).

Ph. D. Philosophiæ Doctor (L., Doctor of Philosophy).

Ph. G. Graduate in Pharmacy.

Phil. Philemon; Philip; Philippians; Philippine.

Phila. Philadelphia.

philol. Philology; philologist.

philos. Philosopher; philosophical; philosophy.

physiol. Physiologist; physiology.

P. I. Philippine Islands.

pinx. Pinxit (L., he, *or* she, painted it).

pk. (*pl.* pks.) Peck.

pkg. (*pl.* pkgs.) Package.

pl. Place; plural.

plf., *or* **plff.** Plaintiff.

plup., *or* **plupf.** Pluperfect.

plur. Plural.

pm. Premium.

P. M., *or* **p. m.** Post meridiem.

(L., afternoon); post mortem.

P. M. G. Postmaster-General.

P. O. Post office; Province of Ontario.

P. O. B. Post-office box.

P. O. D. Pay on delivery; Post Office Department.

Pol. Poland; Polish.

pol., polit. Political.

pol. econ. Political economy.

pop. Popular; population.

Port. Portugal; Portuguese.

pos. Positive; possessive.

poss. Possession; possessive.

pp. Pages; past participle; pianissimo.

p. p. Past participle; postpaid.

P. P. C. *or* **p. p. c.** Pour prendre congé (F., to take leave).

pph. Pamphlet.

p. pr. Present participle.

P. Q. Previous question; Province of Quebec.

pr. Pair; present; price; priest; prince.

Pr. Preferred stock.

P. R. Puerto Rico.

prep. Preparatory; preposition.

pres. President; presidency.

Presb. Presbyterian.

pret. Preterit.

prin. Principal.

priv. Privative.

prob. Probably; problem.

Prof. Professor.

pron. Pronominal; pronoun; pronounced; pronunciation.

propr. Proprietor.

pros. Prosody.

Prot. Protestant.

pro tem. Pro tempore (L., temporarily).

prov. Provident; province; provisional.

Prov. Provençal; Proverbs; Provost.

prox. Proximo (L., next, of the next month).

prs. Pairs.

Prus. Prussia; Prussian.

Ps. Psalm; Psalms.

P. S. Postscriptum (L., postscript); Privy Seal.

pseud. Pseudonym.

psychol. Psychologist; psychology.

pt. (*pl.* pts.) Part; payment; pint; point; port.

P. T., *or* **p. t.** Post town.

p. v. Post village.

pwt. Pennyweight; pennyweights.

pxt. See *pinx.*

Q

q. Quart; queen; query; question; quintal; quire.

Q. Quebec (province)

Q. E. D. Quod erat demonstrandum (L., which was to be demonstrated).

Q. F. Quick-Fire, *or* quick-firing.

ql. Quintal.

Q. M. Quartermaster.

Q. M. G. Quartermaster-General.

Q. M. O. R. C. Quartermaster Officers' Reserve Corps.

Q. M. S. Quartermaster-Sergeant.

qr. (*pl.* qrs.) Quadrans (L., a farthing); quarter; quire.

qt. Quantity; (*pl.* qts.) quart.

qu. Quart; quarterly; queen; query; question.

ques. Question.

qy. Query.

R

r. Railroad; railway; rare; received; rector; resides; retired; right; river; rises; road; rod; rood; royal.

R. Rabbi; Radical; Réaumur; Republican; response.

R. A. Rear Admiral; Regular Army; Royal Academy; Royal Artillery.

rad. Radical; radix.

R. C. Red Cross; Roman Catholic.

R. C. A. Reformed Church in America.

Re. Rupee.

R. E. Reformed Episcopal; Right Excellent; Royal Engineers.

Réaum. Réaumur.

rec. Receipt; recipe; record; recorded; recorder.

recd. Received.

rec. sec. Recording secretary.

rect. Receipt; rector; rectory.

ref. Referee; reference; referred; reformation; reformed.

Ref. Ch. Reformed Church.

reg. Regent; region; register; registered; registry; regular.

Reg. Regina (L., queen).

regt. Regiment.

rel. Relating; relative (-ly); religion; religious.

rep. Repeat; report; reporter; representative; republic.

Rep. Republican.

Repub. Republic; Republican.

retd. Returned.

rev. Revenue; reverse; review; revise; revised; revision; revolution.

Rev. Revelation; Reverend.

Rev. Ver. Revised Version.

R. F., or r. f. Rapid-fire.

R. F. D. Rural Free Delivery.

R. G. S. Royal Geographical Society (London).

r. h. Right hand.

R. H. Royal Highness.

rhet. Rhetoric; rhetorical.

R. I. Rhode Island.

R. I. P. Requiescat in pace (L., may he, or she, rest in peace).

riv. River.

rm. Ream.

R. M. Resident Magistrate; Royal Marines.

R. M. S. Royal Mail Steamer.

R. N. Royal Navy.

R. N. R. Royal Naval Reserve.

ro. Rood.

Robt. Robert.

Rom. Roman; Romance; Romans.

Rom. Cath. Roman Catholic.

R. O. T. C. Reserve Officers' Training Corps (or Camp).

R. P. O. Railroad Post Office.

rpt. Report.

R. R. Railroad.

Rs. Rupees.

R. S. Recording Secretary; Revised Statutes.

R. S. V. P. Répondez, s'il vous plaît (F., reply, if you please).

Rt. Hon. Right Honorable.

Rt. Rev. Right Reverend.

Rum. Rumania; Rumanian.

Rus., or Russ. Russia; Russian.

R. V. Revised Version; Rifle Volunteers.

R. W. Right Worshipful; Right Worthy.

Ry. Railway.

R. Y. S. Royal Yacht Squadron.

S

s., *or* **S.** Section; see; series; shilling; signed; singular; son; stem; sun; surplus.

S. Sabbath; Saint; Saxon; school; senate; Socialist; Society; Socius (L., Fellow); soprano; South; Southern.

S. A. Salvation Army; Small-arms; South Africa; South America; South Australia.

sa. Sable.

Sab. Sabbath.

S. Afr. South Africa; South African.

Salv. Salvador.

Sam. Samaritan; Samuel.

S. Amer., *or* **S. Am.** South America; South American.

S. & T. Supply and Transport.

Sans. Sanskrit.

S. A. R. South African Republic.

Sar. Sardinia; Sardinian.

Sask. Saskatchewan.

Sat. Saturday.

Sax. Saxon; Saxony.

sb. Substantive.

S. B. Bachelor of Science; South Britain.

sc. Scene; and see sci., scil., scr., sculp.

Sc. Scotch; Scottish.

s. c. Small capitals.

S. C. Signal Corps; South Carolina; Staff Corps; Supreme Court.

Scand. Scandinavia; Scandinavian.

S. caps. Small capitals.

sch. Scholium; schooner.

sci. Science; scientific.

scil. Scilicet (L., namely).

Scot. Scotch; Scotland; Scottish.

scr. Scruple.

Script. Scripture.

sculp. Sculpsit (L., he, *or* she, carved it).

s. d. Sine die (L., without [appointing] a day).

S. Dak. South Dakota.

SE. Southeast.

sec. Secant; second; secretary; section; secundum (L., according to).

Sec. Leg. Secretary of Legation.

sect. Section.

Sem. Seminary; Semitic.

Sen. Senate; Senator; Senior.

Sep., *or* **Sept.** September; Septuagint.

ser. Series; sermon.

serg., sergt., *or* **Sgt.** Sergeant.

Serv. Servian.

s. g. Specific gravity.

S. G. Solicitor-general; Surgeon-General.

Sgt. Maj. Sergeant-Major.

Sh., *or* **sh.** Share; shilling; shillings.

Shak. Shakespeare.

S. I. Sandwich Islands; Staten Island.

Sib. Siberia; Siberian.

Sic. Sicilian; Sicily.

sing. Singular.

S. J. Society of Jesus.

S. J. C. Supreme Judicial Court.

Skr., *or* **Skt.** Sanskrit.

S. L. Solicitor at Law.

S. Lat. South latitude.

Slav. Slavic; Slavonic.

sld. Sailed.

S. M. Sa Majesté (F., His, *or* Her, Majesty); Sergeant-Major; Society of Mary

sm. c., *or* **sm. caps.** Small capitals.

S. O., *or* **s. o.** Seller's option.

S. O. Staff Officer; Signal Officer; Special Order.

soc. Society.

S. of Sol. Song of Solomon.

sol. Solution.

sop. Soprano.

S. O. R. C. Signal Officers' Reserve Corps.

sov. Sovereign.

sp. Species; specimen; spelling; spirit.

Sp. Spain; Spaniard; Spanish.

s. p. Sine prole (L., without issue).

S. P. C. A. Society for Prevention of Cruelty to Animals.

S. P. C. C. Society for Prevention of Cruelty to Children.

specif. Specifically.

sp. gr. Specific gravity.

S. P. Q. R. Senatus Populusque Romanus (L., the Senate and People of Rome); small profits, quick returns.

spt. Seaport.

sq. Squadron.

sq. Sequens (L., the following [one]); square.

sqq. Sequentes (L., the following [ones]).

Sr. Sir; Senior.

S. R. S. Fellow (L., Socius) of the Royal Society.

ss. Scilicet (L., namely); semis (L., half).

S. S. Steamship; Supply Sergeant.

SSE. South-southeast.

SSW. South-southwest.

st. Stanza; stone; stet (L., let it stand).

St. Saint; Strait; Street.

stat. Statuary; statue; statutes.

S. T. D. Sacræ Theologiæ Doctor (L., Doctor of Sacred Theology).

str. Steamer.

Sub. Subaltern.

subj. Subject; subjunctive.

subst. Substantive; substitute.

suff. Suffix.

Sun. Sunday.

sup. Superior; superlative; supine; supplement; supra (L., above).

Sup. C. Superior Court; Supreme Court.

superl. Superlative.

Sup. O. Supply Officer.

supp. Supplement.

Supt. Superintendant.

surg. Surgeon; surgery.

surv. Surveying; surveyor.

s. v. Sub verbo (L., under the word); sub voce (L., under the title).

S. V. Sancta Virgo (L., Holy Virgin); Sanctitas Vestra (L., Your Holiness).

SW. Southwest.

Sw., *or* **Swed.** Sweden; Swedish.

Switz. Switzerland.

syn. Synonym; synonymous.

Syr. Syria; Syriac.

T

t. Temperature; tenor; time; tome; ton; town; township; transitive.

T. Territory; Testament; trains; Turkish.

tan. Tangent.

tel. Telegram; telegraph; telephone.

Tenn. Tennessee.
ter. Terrace; territory.
Test. Testament.
Teut. Teuton; Teutonic.
Tex. Texas.
Th. Thomas.
Theo. Theodore; Theodosia.
Theoph. Theophilus.
Thess. Thessalonians.
Tho., or **Thos.** Thomas.
Thurs. Thursday.
Tim. Timothy.
T. M. True mean.
T. N. T. Trinitrotoluene or Trinitrotoluol.
t. o. Telegraph office; turn over.
topog. Topographical; topography.
tp. Township.
tr. Translated; translation; translator; transpose; treasurer; trustee.
trav. Travel; traveler.
treas. Treasurer; treasury.
trig. Trigonometric; trigonometrical; trigonometry.
Trin. Trinity.
trop. Tropic; tropical.
T. S. Transport and Supply.
T. T. Telegraphic transfer; Trinity term.
T. U. Trade Union.
Tues. Tuesday.
Turk. Turkey; Turkish.
typ. Typographer; typographic (-ical); typography.

U

U. Uncle; Unionist; upper.
U. K. United Kingdom.
ult. Ultimately; ultimo.
Unit. Unitarian.
univ. Universally; university.

Univ. Universalist.
U. of S. Afr. Union of South Africa.
U. P. C. United Presbyterian Church.
Uru. Uruguay.
U. S. Uncle Sam; United States.
U. S. A. United States Army; United States of America.
U. S. C. United States of Colombia.
U. S. M. United States Mail; United States Marine.
U. S. M. A. United States Military Academy.
U. S. N. United States Navy.
U. S. N. A. United States Naval Academy.
U. S. N. G. United States National Guard.
U. S. S. United States Senate; United States Ship or Steamer.
usu. Usual; usually.
u. s. w. Und so weiter (G., and so forth).

V

v. Verb; verse; version; versus; very; vicar; vice-; vide (L., see); village; vocative; volume; von (G., of).
V. Venerable; Victoria; Viscount, Volunteers.
Va. Virginia.
v. a. Verb active.
V. A. Vicar Apostolic; Vice Admiral.
var. Variant; variation; variety; various.
Vat. Vatican.
vb. n. Verbal noun.
V. C. Veterinary Corps; Vice Chancellor; Victoria Cross.

Ven. Venerable; Venice.

Venez. Venezuela.

ver. Verse; verses.

Vet. Veterinary.

V. G. Vicar-general.

v. i. Verb intransitive.

Vic. Victoria.

vid. Vide (L., see).

vil. Village.

Vis., or **Visc.** Viscount.

viz. Videlicet (L., namely).

V. M. D. Veterinariæ Medicinæ Doctor (L., Doctor of Veterinary Medicine).

v. n. Verb neuter.

voc. Vocative.

vocab. Vocabulary.

vol. (*pl.* vols.) Volume; volunteer.

vol. Volcano; volcanic.

V. P. Vice-President.

v. r. Verb reflexive.

V. R. Victoria Regina (L., Queen Victoria).

V. Rev. Very Reverend.

vs. Versus.

v. s. Vide supra (L., see above).

V. S. Veterinary Surgeon.

Vt. Vermont.

v. t. Verb transitive.

Vul. Vulgate.

vv. Verses; violins.

W

w. Wanting; week; wide; wife; with.

W. Wales; Washington; Welsh; West; Western.

W. A. West Africa; Western Australia.

Wash. Washington.

W. C. Wesleyan Chapel; Western Central (Postal District, London).

W. C. T. U. Woman's Christian Temperance Union.

W. D., or **War D.** War Department.

Wed. Wednesday.

w. f. Wrong font.

w. g. Wire gauge.

W. G. C. Worthy Grand Chaplain.

W. G. M. Worthy Grand Master.

whf. Wharf.

W. I., or **W. Ind.** West Indies; West Indian.

Wis. Wisconsin.

Wisd. of Sol. Wisdom of Solomon.

wk. Week.

W. long. West longitude.

Wm. William.

W. M. Worshipful Master.

WNW. West-northwest.

W. O. War Office.

wp. Worship.

W. R. Water reserve; West Riding.

WSW. West-southwest.

wt. Weight.

W. Va. West Virginia.

Wyo. Wyoming.

X

X. Χριστος (Gr., Christ).

X-c., or **X-cp.** Ex coupon.

Xmas [no period] Christmas.

Xn. Christian.

Xnty., or **Xty.** Christianity.

Xper., or **Xr.** Christopher.

Xt. Christ.

Y

y. Yard; year.

yd. (*pl.* yds.) Yard.

Y. M. C. A. Young Men's Christian Association.

Y. M. Cath. A. Young Men's Catholic Association.

Y. M. C. U. Young Men's Christian Union.

Y. P. S. C. E. Young People's Society of Christian Endeavor.

yr. (*pl.* yrs.) Year; younger; your.

Y. W. C. A. Young Women's Christian Association.

Z

Zach. Zacharias; Zachary.

Zeb. Zebadiah; Zebedee.

zoogeog. Zoogeography.

zool. Zoological; zoologist; zoology.

Z. S. Zoological Society.

Zech. Zechariah.

Zeph. Zephaniah.

About

ROGET'S INTERNATIONAL THESAURUS

from which

ROGET'S POCKET THESAURUS

is derived

In 1852, Peter Mark Roget, an English doctor, published the first thesaurus. It filled an important need and became an immediate success. That little book with the long title—*Thesaurus of English Words and Phrases Classified and Arranged so as to Facilitate the Expression of Ideas and Assist in Literary Composition*—was the father of all thesauruses. Fortunately, perhaps, his title has been shortened; but that is the only thing about it which has shrunk. Today *Roget's Pocket Thesaurus* and the bigger volume from which it is derived, *Roget's INTERNATIONAL Thesaurus*, are lineal descendants of *Roget's Thesaurus of English Words*. In these two volumes reside not only the genius of Roget himself, but the work of many subsequent compilers and editors who have expanded the original book into one of the largest and certainly one of the most useful word books in the English language.

Peter Roget was surely inspired when he devised his *Thesaurus*. Known as a brilliant physician, a Fellow of the Royal Society, and a founder of the Society for the Diffusion of Knowledge, this amazing and versatile man invented a slide rule, did pioneer work on a calculating machine, and wrote volumes on phrenology, electricity, physiology, and other scientific problems of his time. But today he is best known for his *Thesaurus*, a book which, ironically enough, he always considered a mere side line.

The basic principle of Roget's *Thesaurus*, which has been scrupulously observed in *Roget's Pocket Thesaurus* and in *Roget's INTERNATIONAL Thesaurus*, is the *grouping of words according to their ideas* rather than the listing of words, as the dictionaries do, according to the alphabet. This is the secret of a genuine thesaurus and is the basis for its remarkable usefulness.

Good writing depends on using the exact word; but how often do you have to grope—usually without success—for the exact word to fit the idea you have in mind? A thesaurus solves just that problem. With a thesaurus you start with an idea and find the word or phrase that suits it. A dictionary, on the other hand, is just the reverse: you start with a word and find its definition. It is impossible, because of the very nature of these two basic reference books, to compile a thesaurus in dictionary form, and it was the genius of Roget which saw this first and the wisdom of subsequent editors which has warned them not to tamper with a proved success.

Roget's Pocket Thesaurus and the more complete *Roget's INTERNATIONAL Thesaurus* are arranged in two basic sections. The first, or main text, consists of hundreds of lists of related words and phrases. These lists cover all areas of knowledge. Originally devised by Peter Roget, they represent a famous breakdown of knowledge which, in its own right, was a feat of human intelligence. Within these lists are placed words and phrases of related meanings; the words themselves are clustered into tiny groups of almost synonymous meanings. But these groups grow and spread like animal cells into a network of related meanings so that if, for example, you want to find a word similar in meaning, though not completely synonymous, to "gay," a thesaurus can help you where a dictionary of synonyms cannot. No dictionary of synonyms has been so useful or enjoyed such success as Roget's *Thesaurus*.

The second section is the all-important index. Here are listed in alphabetical order all the words of the first section and the exact places where they appear. "Gay," for example, appears several places in the text: it is listed in its senses of bright, cheerful, and showy. The index tells you this, and shows you where to turn to find the lists of related words and phrases for every one of these basic meanings of "gay." Without this index a thesaurus is useless. It is the quick and efficient key that unlocks the hundreds of lists of related words and phrases—it is the essential key that is lacking in so-called "dictionary thesauruses."

The extraordinary usefulness of *Roget's Pocket Thesaurus* and *Roget's INTERNATIONAL Thesaurus* is attested to by many famous writers. Kenneth Roberts has written: "I can't possibly remember how many copies of this book I've owned and worn to tatters; but ever since the days when I was writing verse for the old *Life*, I have regarded it as the most valuable reference book that an author could have." Mary Roberts Rinehart said that she has "used at least four of these books since I first commenced to write, and even the fourth one is now in poor shape." And Philip Van Doren Stern wrote that "with the exception of the dictionary, it is the reference book I most often use and find indispensable for that elusive word that slips the mind when you want it most. To the professional writer whose everyday job has to do with words the book is an absolute necessity."

Roget's Pocket Thesaurus, then, and *Roget's INTERNATIONAL Thesaurus* derive their extraordinary usefulness from the fidelity with which they adhere to Peter Mark Roget's original concept. Naturally both volumes have been expanded. For example, many new listings have had to be added to Roget's original divisions of knowledge to provide room for the advances in science and technology which even this amazing doctor did not dream of. Altogether, in the larger edition, there are more than 200,000 words and phrases, and in both editions appear contemporary American colloquialisms and slang.

Pocket Books and the Thomas Y. Crowell Company have taken exceptional pride in bringing this famous reference book to a peak of usefulness for the modern American; it is pre-eminently suitable for the student, teacher, housewife, business and professional man, writer —in short, for everyone who ever has need of writing anything from a letter to a play, from a business report to a scientific treatise.